DEEPER, STRATEGIC COLLABORATION IN THE SECURITIES SECTOR

INDIA AND AUSTRALIA

DEEPER, STRATEGIC COLLABORATION IN THE SECURITIES SECTOR

INDIA AND AUSTRALIA

SONIA KHOSA

Australian
National
University

ANU PRESS

अयं बन्धुरयं नेति गणना लघुचेतसां उदारचरितानां तु वसुधैव कुटुम्बकं
ayam bandhurayam neti ganana laghuchetasam
udaracharitanam tu vasudhaiva kutumbakam

Only small men discriminate saying:
One is a relative; the other is a stranger.
For those who live magnanimously the entire
world constitutes a family.

—Sanskrit Vedic scripture,
Maha Upanishad (Chapter 6, Verse 72)

This book is a humble tribute, dedicated to the two nations, India and Australia, and to their wonderful people.

Australian
National
University

ANU PRESS

Published by ANU Press
The Australian National University
Canberra ACT 2600, Australia
Email: anupress@anu.edu.au

Available to download for free at press.anu.edu.au

ISBN (print): 9781760467036
ISBN (online): 9781760467043

WorldCat (print): 1528997581
WorldCat (online): 1529001540

DOI: 10.22459/DSCSS.2025

Cover design and layout by ANU Press

This book is published under the aegis of the Law editorial board of ANU Press.

Contents

Foreword

Australia and India are united by shared values and commonalities. Both countries are democracies, members of the Commonwealth of Nations and follow the common law legal system. India's economy is growing rapidly, while Australia's is more mature and advanced.

In an era marked by unprecedented global connectivity and economic interdependence, the collaboration between financial and securities markets regulators across borders has emerged as a pivotal factor in promoting financial stability, enhancing investor confidence and facilitating economic growth. The proposal for strengthening bilateral financial and securities sector partnership between India and Australia exemplifies a proactive approach towards addressing the challenges and seizing the opportunities presented by an interconnected global economy.

Australia, home to the world's fifth-largest pension market worth more than $3.5 trillion, is actively seeking markets for investments from these funds. Potential investments in India from such pension funds would play a role in India's growth trajectory and forge deeper ties between the two countries.

This academic volume on India–Australia securities sector collaboration is the first comparative account of the securities legal and regulatory frameworks of the two nations. It represents a comprehensive examination of how these two diverse, yet economically robust, nations can synergise their regulatory efforts to foster a conducive environment for capital flow, innovation and sustainable market development that contributes to the economic growth of both countries and of the wider Indo-Pacific region. At its core, this book explores the advantages and profound implications of regulatory convergence on market efficiency and development, regulatory approach, investor protection and the broader economic integration of India and Australia into the global financial system.

The importance of the financial and securities sectors cannot be overstated. They serve as the lifeblood of modern economies, enabling the efficient allocation of capital, facilitating economic growth, and supporting entrepreneurship and innovation. Effective regulation of these sectors is not merely about creating a robust framework of appropriate rules and regulation; it is about creating an environment where markets can flourish while safeguarding the interests of investors and maintaining systemic resilience.

India and Australia, with their distinct economic landscapes and regulatory frameworks, share common imperatives in enhancing market transparency, integrity, reducing regulatory burdens, and promoting free capital flow. The chapters in this volume delve into the historical evolution of the financial and securities markets and regulation in both countries, tracing important milestones, legal and regulatory frameworks and their implementation within each country's domestic setting, and pivotal regulatory reforms that have shaped their respective market structures. This work highlights the tremendous opportunity that exists before India and Australia to share perspectives and learn from each other's experiences.

The current needs of India and Australia in their financial and securities markets are multifaceted and evolving. Both nations are navigating the disruptive forces of technological innovation, including advancements in fintech, digital assets and algorithmic trading. These innovations bring immense opportunities for efficiency gains and market expansion but also pose challenges related to cybersecurity, investor protection and regulatory oversight.

Immediate priorities for common areas of focus may include sustainable finance, financial, cyber and operational resilience, digitisation and crypto assets, cross-border payments and harnessing the benefits of digital innovation. Alongside these, both nations also need to cooperate towards containing its risks, and addressing financial risks from climate change, resolution reforms, the impact of market outages, assurance standards for sustainability information, social stock exchange and the G20 financial reforms.

Moreover, the imperative of reducing regulatory fragmentation and harmonising standards across jurisdictions has never been more pronounced. As global capital flows continue to transcend national boundaries, and the India–Australia relationship strengthens under the Australia–India

Economic Cooperation and Trade Agreement and forthcoming Australia–India Comprehensive Economic Cooperation Agreement, the alignment of regulatory frameworks between the two nations would not only enhance market efficiency but also mitigate regulatory arbitrage, fostering a level playing field for market participants.

Until now, several collaborative efforts between securities jurisdictions under the aegis of the International Organization of Securities Commissions have yielded tangible benefits. Through the deeper and strategic bilateral collaboration proposed in this book, key stakeholders in the financial and securities markets across both countries can deepen engagement through strategic bilateral dialogues and information sharing, with the aim to achieve greater outcomes, such as mutual recognition agreements. Regulators from both countries can lay the foundation for deeper market integration and enhanced regulatory cooperation. This book critically examines the areas of interest for such collaboration, offering insights into their effectiveness, identifying best practices and exploring avenues for further collaboration.

Investor protection remains a cornerstone of effective financial and securities regulation. Ensuring that investors in both India and Australia are adequately protected requires robust regulatory frameworks that safeguard against market abuse, promote transparency, and uphold ethical standards. The comparative analysis presented in this volume sheds light on how regulatory enforcement and collaboration in this area can contribute to enhancing investor confidence and safeguarding the integrity of financial markets.

Looking forward, the regulatory landscape for financial and securities markets in India and Australia will continue to evolve in response to global trends, technological advancements and geopolitical shifts. The chapters in this book not only analyse the current state of regulatory affairs but also anticipate future challenges and opportunities. From fostering innovation in financial services to addressing systemic risks and promoting sustainable finance, the regulatory agenda for both India and Australia is vast and multifaceted.

In conclusion, this academic volume represents a seminal contribution to the study of international securities regulation and regulatory collaboration. The proposed bilateral cooperation between India and Australia serves as a blueprint for other bilateral and multilateral partnerships seeking to harmonise regulatory approaches across borders. It underscores the importance of dialogue, cooperation and shared objectives in achieving regulatory harmonisation that supports economic growth and resilience. I commend the author for her scholarly rigor and dedication in illuminating the complexities and possibilities inherent in the India–Australia securities sector collaboration.

Ananta Barua

- former member of the SEBI Board (2018–23) and executive director (2010–18)
- member of the Fund Management Advisory Committee of International Financial Service Centre Authority in GIFT City (2023)
- chairman of Expert Committee on REITs and InvITs in IFSCA in GIFT City (2024)
- adviser, Indian REITs Association
- member of Confederation of Indian Industries (CII WR) Taskforce on Banking and Finance (2024–25)

Abstract

The rapid transnationalisation and globalisation of finance in recent decades has caused securities and financial systems across the world to be intricately, and inextricably, interwoven into a single financial ecosystem. This heightened cross-border financial activity has accelerated the trend towards cooperation across the globe. In the securities sector, while such cooperation has been successful in enhancing standards for the monitoring, supervision and regulation of these markets, it begets the question: is it possible to leverage cross-border collaboration as a strategic tool to catalyse and achieve transformative results in three fundamental areas of securities markets—market development, integration and regulation? If so, are India and Australia well suited for such cooperation?

To answer this question, this book carries out a comparative analysis of the two securities jurisdictions, India and Australia, and proposes a deeper, strategic bilateral collaboration between the two securities regimes. The book delves into a high-level analysis of the securities regulatory regimes of the Securities and Exchange Board of India and the Australian Securities and Investments Commission, set against the International Organization of Securities Commission's widely endorsed *Objectives and Principles of Securities Regulation*, with a particular focus on the supervisory and enforcement powers of these regulators and the effectiveness of their compliance regimes. Based on this assessment, this book determines the level of alignment for both securities regimes with the international securities standards, the IOSCO Principles, which then informs its conclusions on the degree of comparability between the two securities regimes and the possible areas of collaboration.

This book addresses a fundamental gap in the international and legal scholarship on the comparative study of the securities regimes of India and Australia. The academic assessment of the two securities regimes provides the foundation for a useful and practical roadmap for strategic collaboration proposed between the two jurisdictions. The uniqueness of the proposed collaboration lies in the fact that its possibility and success are not contingent upon the absolute comparability of regulatory standards in the two jurisdictions but on the overarching compatibility of the political, legal and governance structures underpinning the regulatory regimes, along with other geopolitical realities. The proposed collaboration model is scalable and may be replicated in other sectors of the financial sector or economy. Most significantly, the proposal is capable of being effectively transformed into a broader, multilateral strategic cooperation initiative in the future.

Acknowledgements

Foremost, I am deeply grateful to my principal supervisor, Professor Gail Pearson, University of Sydney (USyd). Without her incredible guidance, patience and belief in me, it would have been impossible for me to undertake and persist through the researching and writing of my PhD thesis, which has culminated in this book. I am fortunate to still have her as my mentor and guide, years after completing my degree.

I also want to profusely thank my associate supervisor, Associate Professor David Chaikin, USyd, for his unwavering support and encouragement through the research stage of my PhD, and his continuing mentorship and kindness.

I am grateful to professors Joanne Wright, Richard Miles and Felicity Blackstock, as well as Dr Elisabeth Valiente-Riedl and others from the Office of the Deputy Vice-Chancellor (Education), USyd, for their continuing inspiration and encouragement at work.

I would like to extend my sincere thanks to Associate Professor Akshaya Kamalnath and Dr Jason Chin, both from The Australian National University's Law School, for their helpful guidance and feedback on my manuscript. I was fortunate to be awarded the ANU Press ECR Prize in Legal Scholarship and am grateful for the opportunity to work with ANU Press in publishing this book. I acknowledge the excellent assistance of Dr Rani Kerin, who copyedited the book.

I am deeply grateful to the Securities and Exchange Board of India (SEBI) for giving me the opportunity to pursue my PhD. I am particularly grateful to SEBI's Human Resources Department for its cooperation throughout my thesis journey. I am thankful to all my seniors and ex-colleagues and other well-wishers at SEBI who encouraged and supported me during my research. I wish to particularly thank Mr Amarjeet Singh, whole time member (WTM) of the SEBI Board, and Mr Ananta Barua, ex-WTM of the SEBI Board, for guiding and mentoring me through both the good and difficult times of my research journey. I also want to thank my seniors for their guidance through the formative years of my career at SEBI: Mr Aliasgar Mithwani, executive director, SEBI; Mr Santosh Kumar Shukla, executive director, Insolvency & Bankruptcy Board of India; and Mr J Ranganayakulu, ex-executive director, SEBI. Finally, I must thank my colleagues Mr Robin J Baby, Mr Vikas SS, Mr Sanjay Singh Bhati and Mr Pradeep Ramakrishnan for their unflinching support and encouragement through my thesis journey.

I would like to thank Emeritus Professor Terry Carney, Professor Steven Greaves and other faculty members and colleagues at the USyd Business School, who have supported me, in one way or the other, during this long and challenging journey.

My deepest gratitude to my pillars of support, my parents, Geeta and Krishen, for making me the person I am today. A special mention of my dear grandparents, whose blessings gave me the confidence to proceed with this book. I sincerely thank my parents-in-law, siblings, family and friends for giving me encouragement and believing in my ability to complete this book.

Finally, to my dear husband, Shivam, and beloved sons, Viraj and Vyom, who I hope someday will be drawn by the curiosity of research—a big thank you for being by my side through all the highs and lows!

List of key abbreviations

AASB	Australian Accounting Standards Board
ACCC	Australian Competition and Consumer Commission
ADI	authorised deposit-taking institutions
AFP	Australian Federal Police
AFS	Australian financial services
AFSL	Australian financial service licence
AIF	alternative investment funds
ALRC	Australian Law Reform Commission
AMC	Asset Management Company
AML	Australian market licence
APRA	Australian Prudential Regulatory Authority
APS	Australian Public Service
ASIC	Australian Securities and Investments Commission
ASX	Australian Securities Exchange
AUASB	Auditing and Assurance Standards Board
BSE	Bombay Stock Exchange
CADB	Companies Auditors Disciplinary Board
CALDB	Companies Auditors and Liquidators Disciplinary Board
CBA	Commonwealth Bank of Australia
CCP	central counterparties
CDPP	Commonwealth Director of Public Prosecutions
CFD	corporate finance department
CFI	Consolidated Fund of India
CFPL	Commonwealth Financial Planning Ltd

CFR	Council of Financial Regulators
CFTC	Commodity Futures Trading Commission
CIS	collective investment schemes
CLERP	Corporate Law Economic Reform Program
CPSS	Committee on Payment and Settlement Systems
CRA	credit rating agencies
CS	clearing and settlement
CSFL	Clearing and Settlement Facility Licence
DWBIS	Data Warehouse and Business Intelligence System
EMH	efficient market hypothesis
EMMoU	enhanced multilateral memorandum of understanding
ERC	Emerging Risk Committee
ESMA	European Securities and Markets Authority
EU	European Union
FAR	Financial Accountability Regime
FASEA	Financial Adviser Standards and Ethics Authority
FCA	Federal Court of Australia
FMC	Forwards Market Commission
FMI	financial market infrastructures
FOFA	Future of Financial Advice
FRAA	Financial Regulator Assessment Authority
FRC	Financial Reporting Council
FSAP	Financial Sector Assessment Program
FSB	Financial Stability Board
FSDC	Financial Stability and Development Council
FSI	Financial System Inquiry
FSLRC	Financial Sector Legislative Reforms Commission
FSR	financial sector regime
FVCF	foreign venture capital funds
GFC	global financial crisis
GFIN	Global Financial Innovation Network
ICAI	Institute of Chartered Accountants of India

IEPF	Investor Education and Protection Fund
IFC	Indian Financial Code
IFRS	International Financial Reporting Standards
IMF	International Monetary Fund
IMSS	Integrated Market Surveillance System
IOSCO	International Organization of Securities Commissions
IRDAI	Insurance Regulatory and Development Authority of India
IT	information technology
KYC	know your customer
MABRA	*Mutual Assistance in Business Regulations Act 1992* (Cth)
MACMA	*Mutual Assistance in Criminal Matters Act 1987* (Cth)
MCA	Ministry of Corporate Affairs
MDP	Markets Disciplinary Panel
MEA	Ministry of Economic Affairs
MF	mutual funds
MII	market infrastructure institutions
MIS	managed investment schemes
MMoU	multilateral memorandum of understanding
MoF	Ministry of Finance
MoU	memoranda of understanding
MRA	mutual recognition agreement
MSEI	Metropolitan Stock Exchange of India Ltd
NAB	National Australia Bank
NBFC	non-banking financial companies
NBFE	non-bank financial entities
NBI	non-banking institutions
NFRA	National Financial Reporting Authority
NISM	National Institute of Securities Markets
NSE	National Stock Exchange
OASIS	old age, social and income security
OECD	Organisation for Economic Co-operation and Development
OTC	over-the-counter

PAIRS	Profitability and Impact Rating System
PFRDA	Pension Fund Regulatory and Development Authority
RBA	Reserve Bank of Australia
RBI	Reserve Bank of India
RE	responsible entity
RIA	regulatory impact assessment
RIS	regulation impact statements
RSE	recognised stock exchanges
SAP	strategic action plan
SAT	Securities Appellate Tribunal
SEBI	Securities and Exchange Board of India
SCRR	*Securities Contracts (Regulation) (Stock Exchanges and Clearing Corporations) Regulations 2018*
SOARS	Supervisory Oversight and Response System
SRO	self-regulatory organisations
SSS	securities settlement systems
TRN	transnational regulatory networks
US SEC	United States Securities and Exchange Commission
VCF	venture capital funds
WTM	whole time member

1

Introduction

Introduction

'Today's markets are international with a vengeance'—this assertion is far more relevant today than when it was made three decades ago by Grundfest who was commenting on the 'internationalization' of world securities markets.[1] The phenomenon of internationalisation has fuelled the rise of transnational regulatory networks (TRNs) that operate internationally and have been instrumental in fostering cross-border cooperation among national securities authorities.[2] The prime TRN in the securities sector is the International Organization of Securities Commissions (IOSCO).[3] The strength of cross-border securities cooperation varies. This book addresses the potential to enhance cooperation between India and Australia in the securities sector.

---

1   Joseph A Grundfest, 'Internationalization of the world's securities markets: economic causes and regulatory consequences' in *International Competitiveness in Financial Services* (Springer, 1990) 349, 373, doi.org/10.1007/978-94-011-3876-5_8. See also Robert P Austin, 'Regulatory principles and the internationalization of securities markets' (1987) 50(3) *Law and Contemporary Problems* 221–250, doi.org/10.2307/1191672.
2   See generally Pierre-Hugues Verdier, 'Transnational regulatory networks and their limits' (2009) 34 *Yale Journal of International Law* 113. See also Geoffrey RD Underhill, 'Keeping governments out of politics: transnational securities markets, regulatory cooperation, and political legitimacy' (1995) 21(3) *Review of International Studies* 251–278, doi.org/10.1017/S0260210500117681.
3   IOSCO is the premier standards-setting organisation in the securities sector with over 115 signatories and its role and importance is discussed in Chapter 3 of this book. On IOSCO's significance, see Robert Baxt, Ashley Black and Pamela F Hanrahan, *Securities and Financial Services Law* (LexisNexis Butterworths, 2016) 11.

The global financial crisis (GFC) of 2007–08 and, more recently, the Covid-19 pandemic, exemplified the extent of the interconnectedness of markets and evoked a number of responses.[4] The GFC, in particular, caused a reimagination of some of the basic tenets and principles of securities regulation.[5] It also presented a need for more effective and coordinated regulation,[6] including the raising of international regulatory standards through international cooperation.[7] In recent years, the global financial landscape has witnessed revitalised international cooperation,[8] exacerbated through the Covid-19 crises, against a widespread acknowledgement that 'the growing interactions between national financial systems require international cooperation by authorities'.[9]

Cross-border cooperation in securities markets is not new.[10] However, the 9/11 attacks in the United States underscored weaknesses in existing cross-border networks and supported calls for better information-sharing platforms and efforts, including in securities.[11] This renewed realisation of

---

4   See generally Roberta S Karmel, 'IOSCO's response to the financial crisis' (2012) 37 Brooklyn Law School, Legal Studies Paper No 268, doi.org/10.2139/ssrn.2025115; Cally Jordan, 'The new internationalism? IOSCO, international standards and capital markets regulation' (2018), doi.org/10.2139/ssrn.3257800.

5   One of the key responses to the GFC was the incorporation of eight new IOSCO Principles: see for example Karmel (n 4). See also Greg Tanzer, *Building a Better Financial System: IOSCO's Role*, Intergovernmental Working Group of Experts on International Standards of Accounting and Reporting (12 October 2011), iosco.org/library/speeches/pdf/IOSCOSP05-11.pdf.

6   See generally The Joint Forum, 'Review of the differentiated nature and scope of financial regulation: key issues and recommendations' (2010).

7   Barbara Black, 'Introduction: the globalization of securities regulation—competition and coordination.' (2011) 79(2) *University of Cincinnati Law Review* 462–463.

8   Ibid 463. The process of revitalisation of international cooperation is evident from a number of events, including reorganisation of the key international organisations, such as the Financial Stability Forum that was re-established as the Financial Stability Board with an expanded membership, enhanced mandate and strengthened institutional foundations: see Robert B Ahdieh, 'Imperfect alternatives: networks, salience, and institutional design in financial crises' (2010) 79 *University of Cincinnati Law Review* 527.

9   Financial Stability Forum, 'FSF Principles for Cross-Border Cooperation on Crisis Management' (2009) 2. The strengthening of the process of international cooperation is obvious against the augmentation in the information sharing mechanisms among authorities, development of similar tools or mechanisms for support and due to globally coordinated solutions for managing a financial crisis: see Barbara Black (n 7) 463.

10   See for example Harold M Williams and Lee B Spencer Jr, 'Regulation of international securities markets: towards a greater cooperation' (1982) 4 *Journal of Comparative Corporate Law and Securities Regulation* 55. They state that cooperation among regulators can 'present a united, powerful front against fraud and can eliminate unnecessary regulatory differences and inconsistencies and other obstacles to an efficient system of international market finance'.

11   See generally David Kempthorne, 'Governing international securities markets: IOSCO and the politics of international securities market standards' (2013). See also the Preamble to the IOSCO MMoU that makes specific reference to events of 11 September 2001: IOSCO, 'Multilateral Memorandum of Understanding Concerning Consultation and Cooperation and the Exchange of Information (MMoU)', iosco.org/about/?subsection=mmou.

the significance of cross-border cooperation has expanded mechanisms for cooperation available to the global securities authorities.[12] One example in the Indo-Pacific region is the Asia Region Funds Passport, 'a multilateral framework intended to support the development of an Asia region funds management industry through market access and regulatory harmonisation'.[13] Similarly, cooperation has received greater serious academic attention,[14] with recent empirical analysis showing how securities cooperation has been successfully applied to reduce 'cross-border barriers' and increase 'the feasibility in cost and logistics of cross-border enforcement'.[15]

Notwithstanding these developments, knowledge of the utility of cross-border cooperation in securities markets remains embryonic, and there is only a limited body of academic literature. The full expanse of cooperation as a collaborative tool in securities markets is not well understood in the literature. This tool is underutilised in practice and the existing cooperation networks are limited in delivering the fast-paced, transformative results that are needed in the securities sector, particularly in the Indo-Pacific region. Despite their potential, several Indo-Pacific markets exhibit weaknesses in the three fundamental areas of market development, integration and regulation, which are, arguably, key determinants for classifying securities markets as 'developed' or 'emerging'.

---

12   See IOSCO, *IOSCO Task Force on Cross-Border Regulation* (Final Report No FR23/2015, September 2015), iosco.org/library/pubdocs/pdf/IOSCOPD507.pdf. IOSCO discusses new regulatory tools for cooperation that expand the options available with regulators for cooperating with one another.
13   Asia-Pacific Economic Cooperation, *Asia Region Funds Passport* (28 April 2016). See also Andrew Godwin and Ian Ramsay, 'The Asia Region Funds Passport initiative—challenges for regulatory coordination' (2015) 26(7) *International Company and Commercial Law Review* 236–243.
14   For literature highlighting the importance of cooperation, see for example Janet Austin, 'IOSCO's Multilateral Memorandum of Understanding Concerning Consultation, Cooperation and the Exchange of Information: a model for international regulatory convergence' (2012) 23(4) *Criminal Law Forum*, doi.org/10.1007/s10609-012-9180-6.
15   See Roger Silvers, 'Cross-border cooperation between securities regulators' (2020) 69(2–3) *Journal of Accounting and Economics* 101301, doi.org/10.1016/j.jacceco.2020.101301. This empirical analysis demonstrates how the jurisdictions have successfully cooperated under the IOSCO Multilateral Memorandum of Understanding.

Markets are characterised as 'developed' or 'emerging' based on a wide range of factors[16] and the exhibition of distinct characteristics.[17] For example, emerging securities markets when compared with G-7 markets show higher returns on average, lower correlations with the world economy, higher predictability of returns and volatility.[18]

Commentators assert that the level of development of a securities market is a significant parameter for assessing the lure of an economy as an investment destination. As a natural corollary, market development often forms part of a major area of focus for regulators, in addition to their other mandates. Demirguc-Kunt and Levine determine 'stock market development' by a 'multifaceted' approach based on factors such as 'market size, market liquidity and integration with world capital markets', as well as 'volatility, concentration, and institutional development'.[19] Bekaert, Harvey and Lundblad consider 'three variables'—namely, equity market size, number of listed, domestic companies and equity market turnover— as proxies of the 'general development of the equity market'.[20] However, despite the significance of 'strong public securities markets', Black argues that creating them is difficult,[21] because there is a requirement of additional

---

16   See generally Tiziana Di Matteo, Tomaso Aste and Michel M Dacorogna, 'Long-term memories of developed and emerging markets: using the scaling analysis to characterize their stage of development' (2005) 29(4) *Journal of Banking & Finance* 827–851, doi.org/10.1016/j.jbankfin.2004.08.004.

17   In times of financial crisis, 'developed' stock markets are seen to be affected less, both in terms of the extent of price decline and the duration of the crises, while for 'emerging' markets, prices are seen to fall 'rapidly and steeply' and the recovery period is longer, averaging around three years: see Sandeep A Patel and Asani Sarkar, 'Crises in developed and emerging stock markets' (1998) 54(6) *Financial Analysts Journal* 261, doi.org/10.2469/faj.v54.n6.2225.
Stock market returns are seen to be more 'synchronous' in emerging economies than in developed markets, and this is 'more correlated with measures of institutional development'. Developed markets show 'stronger legal protection' for public shareholders against company insiders, more regard for 'private property rights protection' and process information better than emerging markets. See Randall Morck, Bernard Yeung and Wayne Yu, 'The information content of stock markets: why do emerging markets have synchronous stock price movements?' (2000) 58(1–2) *Journal of Financial Economics* 215–260, doi.org/10.1016/S0304-405X(00)00071-4.

18   See Fabian Lipinsky and Li Lian Ong, 'Asia's stock markets: are there crouching tigers and hidden dragons?' (International Monetary Fund, 2014, WP/14/37), doi.org/10.5089/9781484320143.001.

19   See Asli Demirgüç-Kunt and Ross Levine, 'Stock markets, corporate finance, and economic growth: an overview' (1996) 10(2) *The World Bank Economic Review* 223–239, 231, doi.org/10.1093/wber/10.2.223. Long-run economic growth is dependent on multiple factors, including the effectiveness of the legal system: see Ross Levine, 'The legal environment, banks, and long-run economic growth' (1998) *Journal of Money, Credit and Banking* 596–613, doi.org/10.2307/2601259.

20   Geert Bekaert, Campbell R Harvey and Christian Lundblad, 'Emerging equity markets and economic development' (2001) 66(2) *Journal of Development Economics* 465–504, doi.org/10.1016/S0304-3878(01)00171-7.

21   See Bernard Black, 'The core institutions that support strong securities markets' (1999) 55 *Business Lawyer* 1565, doi.org/10.2139/ssrn.231120. Black emphasises two essential prerequisites for strong public securities markets: 1) 'good information about the value of a company's business', 2) 'confidence that the company's insiders won't cheat investors' out of the 'value of their investment'.

prerequisites, including legal and institutional preconditions that address critical factors such as information asymmetry, controlling self-dealing, weaknesses in domestic laws and institutions, and ensuring an effective mechanism for investor protection.[22] Ahdieh considers whether such strong 'markets emerge, or are they made?', and concludes that more often than not, markets are 'created' and that a variety of factors, such as law, play a critical and structural role in the securities markets transition.[23] Black further contends that the 'complex institutions that support securities markets' are not a product of haste and are developed over years.[24] Collectively, these views show that strong markets need to be nurtured and developed with a proactive, measured and long-term strategic approach.

In addition to market development, the extent to which a securities market is liberalised and integrated with global markets is also critical for its characterisation as emerging and developed.[25] Liberalisation[26] and integration[27] impact a market's standing as an investment destination,

---

22 Bernard S Black, 'The legal and institutional preconditions for strong securities markets' (2001) 48 *UCLA Law Review* 781, doi.org/10.2139/ssrn.182169.

23 See Robert B Ahdieh, 'Making markets: network effects and the role of law in the creation of strong securities markets' (2002) 76 *Southern California Law Review* 277, 279. See also J Harold Mulherin, Jeffry M Netter and James A Overdahl, 'Prices are property: the organization of financial exchanges from a transaction cost perspective' (1991) 34(2) *The Journal of Law and Economics* 591–644, doi.org/10.1086/467237. These authors state that 'markets are not a fixture of the economy, but are the results of decisions made by private economic agents and government agencies' and that 'we should not expect exchanges to be loosely run organizations that arise as if by magic'.

24 Bernard Black (n 22). Black emphasises this by citing Lou Lowenstein who, analysing US accounting practices, states that the disclosure regime for accounting, and all its components such as the accounting rules, legal professionals, oversight mechanisms, analysts and the media, has been built steadily and diligently over a lengthy time period.

25 On the significance of liberalisation and privatisation for stock markets and their development, see Enrico C Perotti and Pieter Van Oijen, 'Privatization, political risk and stock market development in emerging economies' (2001) 20(1) *Journal of International Money and Finance* 43–69, doi.org/10.1016/S0261-5606(00)00032-2.

26 Stock market liberalisation has been a fascinating field of inquiry among scholars in the last three or four decades, and refers to a government's decision to allow foreigners to purchase shares in the domestic stock market: see Peter Blair Henry, 'Stock market liberalization, economic reform, and emerging market equity prices' (2000) 55(2) *The Journal of Finance* 529–564, 529, doi.org/10.1111/0022-1082.00219.

27 There is a significant volume of literature on the evolution of markets: see for example Geert Bekaert and Campbell R Harvey, 'Research in emerging markets finance: looking to the future' (2002) 3(4) *Emerging Markets Review* 429–448, doi.org/10.1016/S1566-0141(02)00045-6. Bekhaert and Harvey argue that this evolution from segmented to integrated consists of economic integration that is evidenced by decreased barriers to trading in goods and services, and financial integration through free access of foreigners to local capital markets and vice versa (ie access by local customers to foreign capital markets). Illustrating the significance of 'market integration', Stulz states that only when markets are fully integrated can they be considered optimal to diversify internationally: see René M Stulz, 'A model of international asset pricing' (1981) 9(4) *Journal of Financial Economics* 383–406, doi.org/10.1016/0304-405X(81)90005-2.

particularly in the context of foreign participants and investment.[28] Liberalisation has generally been regarded as a positive step for an economy.[29] Similarly, studies analysing the effect of market integration on securities prices show that segmented markets demonstrate high volatility and high expected returns, while in an integrated market the expected return is determined in view of the 'world market portfolio' and the 'risk premium', making it lower but the price of securities higher.[30]

The academic literature supports integration as it 'induces a structural change', particularly in the context of emerging economies.[31] Once the process of market integration begins in an economy, it usually progresses

On other literature examining the issue of pricing in emerging markets and exploring the effect of segmentation and integration of markets, see generally Vihang Errunza, Lemma W Senbet and Ked Hogan, 'The pricing of country funds from emerging markets: theory and evidence' (1998) 1(01) *International Journal of Theoretical and Applied Finance* 111–143, doi.org/10.1142/S0219024998000060; Vihang Errunza and Etienne Losq, 'International asset pricing under mild segmentation: theory and test' (1985) 40(1) *The Journal of Finance* 105–124, doi.org/10.1111/j.1540-6261.1985.tb04939.x; Cheol S Eun and Sundaram Janakiramanan, 'A model of international asset pricing with a constraint on the foreign equity ownership' (1986) 41(4) *The Journal of Finance* 897–914, doi.org/10.1111/j.1540-6261.1986.tb04555.x. Bekaeret and Harvey argue that 'markets are completely integrated if assets with the same risk have identical expected returns irrespective of the market'. In such markets, there are 'common rewards to risk associated with risk exposures': see Geert Bekaert and Campbell R Harvey, 'Time-varying world market integration' (1995) 50(2) *Journal of Finance* 403–444, doi.org/10.1111/j.1540-6261.1995.tb04790.x.

28   See Henry (n 26). Scholarly discussions in this area also make a clear distinction between 'liberalisation' and 'market integration'. While the former refers to the dropping of 'barriers' to foreign investment into a local market, such liberalisation may or may not lead to an actual and 'effective' market integration. See Bekaert and Harvey, 'Research in emerging markets finance' (n 27) 3.

29   Many scholars have argued that liberalisation reduces market segmentation and thus leads to risk sharing between domestic and foreign participants: see for example Henry (n 26). See also Errunza and Losq (n 27). See generally Michael Brennan, Richard C Stapleton and Marti G Subrahmanyam, 'Market imperfections, capital market equilibrium and corporation finance' (1977) 32(2) *The Journal of Finance* 307–319, doi.org/10.1111/j.1540-6261.1977.tb03271.x. Liberalisation has a positive effect on bringing the 'cost to capital' down for a country that liberalises its markets: René M Stulz, 'Globalization, corporate finance, and the cost of capital' (1999) 12(3) *Journal of Applied Corporate Finance* 8–25, doi.org/10.1111/j.1745-6622.1999.tb00027.x.

30   See Bekaert and Harvey, 'Research in emerging markets finance' (n 27).

31   Such change may be measured in four different ways: 'event association', financial, economic and market infrastructure: see ibid 3–4. On the use of finance strategies to assess change in the 'behaviour of asset returns' associated with market integration, such as through a 'permanent' increase in price, see generally Geert Bekaert, Campbell R Harvey and Robin L Lumsdaine, 'The dynamics of emerging market equity flows' (2002) 21(3) *Journal of International Money and Finance* 295–350, doi.org/10.1016/S0261-5606(02)00001-3; P Basu, H Kawakatsu and M Morey, 'Liberalization and stock prices in emerging markets' (2000) 4(3) *Emerging Markets Quarterly* 7–17.

The use of economic strategies refers to the analysis of economic aggregates, such as a sharp increase in the equity capital flows by foreigners. See generally National Bureau of Economic Research, *Capital Flows and the Behavior of Emerging Market Equity Returns* (1998); Geert Bekaert, Campbell R Harvey and Robin L Lumsdaine, 'Dating the integration of world equity markets' (2002) 65(2) *Journal of*

gradually to lower the barriers to investment.[32] Although the scholarship appears divided on whether market integration has an impact on market volatility, on balance the views appear to favour the position that the impact is largely negative, while such integration 'on average' leads to 'higher correlations with the world'.[33] Further, integration is argued to have a converse relationship with expected returns in the market, which is why the higher the integration of markets, the lesser the returns that may accrue to the investor.[34] Moreover, a telling effect of a higher degree of correlations is that, usually, the benefits from having a diversified portfolio decreases, except in the case of emerging markets, where the correlations are still much lower despite liberalisation, and this in turn creates more opportunities for a significant portfolio diversification.[35] Notably, among the fall-out of market

Financial Economics 203–247, doi.org/10.1016/S0304-405X(02)00139-3; Hyuk Choe, Bong-Chan Kho and René M Stulz, 'Do foreign investors destabilize stock markets? The Korean experience in 1997' (1999) 54(2) *Journal of Financial Economics* 227–264, doi.org/10.1016/S0304-405X(99)00037-9. Finally, the use of market infrastructure strategy to gauge the degree of integration involves analysing 'investor protection' and the 'quality of accounting' practises and standards, such as by assessing 'insider trading prosecutions'. See generally Geert Bekaert and Campbell R Harvey, 'Foreign speculators and emerging equity markets' (2000) 55(2) *The Journal of Finance* 565–613, doi.org/10.1111/0022-1082.00220; Utpal Bhattacharya and Hazem Daouk, 'The world price of insider trading' (2002) 57(1) *The Journal of Finance* 75–108, doi.org/10.1111/1540-6261.00416.

32   See Geert Bekaert, 'Market integration and investment barriers in emerging equity markets' (1995) 9(1) *The World Bank Economic Review* 75–107, doi.org/10.1093/wber/9.1.75. Bekaert argues that barriers to emerging markets investment fall into several categories, such as legal barriers, risks and other indirect barriers arising from information asymmetry that collectively impact foreign investment negatively.

33   Bekaert and Harvey, 'Research in emerging markets finance' (n 27) 6. See also Geert Bekaert and Campbell R Harvey, 'Emerging equity market volatility' (1997) 43(1) *Journal of Financial Economics* 29–77, doi.org/10.1016/S0304-405X(96)00889-6; E Han Kim and Vijay Singal, 'Opening up of stock markets: lessons from and for emerging economies' (1994); Giorgio De Santis and Selahattin imrohoroğlu, 'Stock returns and volatility in emerging financial markets' (1997) 16(4) *Journal of International Money and Finance* 561–579, doi.org/10.1016/S0261-5606(97)00020-X; Reena Aggarwal, Carla Inclan and Ricardo Leal, 'Volatility in emerging stock markets' (1999) 34(1) *Journal of Financial and Quantitative Analysis* 33–55, doi.org/10.2307/2676245; Anthony J Richards, 'Volatility and predictability in national stock markets: how do emerging and mature markets differ?' (1996) 43(3) *Staff Papers* 461–501; S Narayan, S Srinanthakumar and SZ Islam, 'Stock market integration of emerging Asian economies: patterns and causes' (2014) 39 *Economic Modelling* 19–31, doi.org/10.1016/j.econmod.2014.02.012.

34   Bekaert and Harvey show this by contrasting the average annual geometric returns for 20 emerging markets, 'pre' and 'post' 1990: see Bekaert and Harvey, 'Research in emerging markets finance' (n 27). For literature on 'expected returns' decreasing post integration, see Bekaert and Harvey, 'Foreign speculators and emerging equity markets' (n 31); Henry (n 26); Kim and Singal (n 33); Frank De Jong and Frans A De Roon, 'Time-varying market integration and expected returns in emerging markets' (2005) 78(3) *Journal of Financial Economics* 583–613, doi.org/10.1016/j.jfineco.2004.10.010.

35   On portfolio diversification benefits, see generally De Santis (n 33); CR Harvey, 'Predictable risk and returns in emerging markets' (1995)(8) *Review of Financial Studies* 773–816, doi.org/10.1093/rfs/8.3.773. See also Vicente J Bermejo et al., 'Do foreign stocks substitute for international diversification?' (ESADE Business School Research Paper No 267, 2017), doi.org/10.2139/ssrn.2973060; Larry R Gorman and Bjorn Jorgensen, 'Domestic versus international portfolio selection: a statistical examination of the home bias' (2015).

integration stands the 'contagion effect', which refers to an 'abnormally high correlation between markets during a crisis period', seen especially during the Asian crisis and also during the GFC.[36]

On balance, the literature shows that liberalisation can lead to an effective integration of a domestic economy's securities markets with global markets and is, therefore, seen as a positive development. Similarly, the Organisation for Economic Co-operation and Development (OECD) refers to integration as 'a powerful driver of increased economic efficiency and improved living standards around the world', but also as raising concerns for emerging economies relating to 'external shocks' and policy 'spillovers'.[37] However, if supported by the right policy and regulatory changes, such integration can cause fundamental impacts for both the financial and real sectors of developing countries.[38] Thus, economies that are looking to advance will eventually need to embrace liberalisation and integration among other effective policy and structural changes.

Along with development and integration, the vital role of regulation in financial and securities markets is widely acknowledged.[39] Even though the objectives and mandates of national securities regulators across the world are theoretically similar or considerably well aligned,[40] there are compelling

---

36   Bekaert, 'Market integration and investment' (n 32). On aspects of financial liberalisation and contagion, see also Ettore Panetti, 'Financial liberalization and contagion with unobservable savings' (2014) 36 *International Review of Financial Analysis* 20–35, doi.org/10.1016/j.irfa.2014.05.005; Abdullahil Mamun, 'An investigation into the factors causing financial crisis: lessons from recent overwhelming episodes' (2017) 9(1) *Journal of Academic Research in Economics*.

37   *Policy Challenges from Closer International Trade and Financial Integration: Dealing with Economic Shocks and Spillovers* (2018) 50. Increased inter-connectedness leads to significant cross-border issues that have primarily risen in the period from 1995 to the GFC when cross-border financial transactions tripled as a share of the world GDP. The OECD states that this 'wave of financial globalisation' was largely due to the progressive removal of capital and exchange controls, betterment in the payment and settlement systems, 'financial deregulation and falling communication costs'.

38   G Bekaert, CR Harvey and CT Lundblad, 'Equity market liberalization in emerging markets' (2003) 26(3) *Journal of Financial Research* 275–299, doi.org/10.1111/1475-6803.00059.

39   In common parlance, 'regulation' refers to the act of enforcement of a law, rule or regulation by a regulatory agency, formed by law and mandated to carry out the purpose or of a legislation: see *Business Dictionary*, 'Regulation'. In the context of securities markets, regulation broadly translates into a mandate by law on a regulatory authority to essentially pursue the following tasks: first, monitoring individual institutions for their impact on system stability, and second, ensuring the investor and consumer protection regulation: see Tobias Adrian and Hyun Song Shin, *The Shadow Banking System: Implications for Financial Regulation* (FRB of New York Staff Report No 382, 2009) 15, doi.org/10.2139/ssrn.1441324.

40   The US Securities and Exchange Commission has a three-part mission to protect investors; maintain fair, orderly and efficient markets; and facilitate capital formation: see US Securities and Exchange Commission, 'The role of the SEC', investor.gov/introduction-investing/basics/role-sec. SEBI has a mandate to protect investors, regulate the markets and develop the markets: see Securities and Exchange Board of India, 'Powers and functions of the board', www.sebi.gov.in/powers-and-functions.html.

practical differences in the standard and overall quality of securities regulation, corporate governance standards, and other norms related to financial products, services and market infrastructure.[41] This variance in the standards or quality of regulation leads to several effects. First, it impacts risk perceptions of a jurisdiction, in turn affecting the long-term cost of financing.[42] Second, weak regulation is often associated with more volatility in markets.[43] Third, when an economy looks for deeper integration with global markets, or specifically when garnering foreign investment, the underlying quality of regulation plays an important role in its determination as a safe and sound investment destination.[44]

Even prior to the revitalised interest in regulation post-GFC, considerable academic attention had been devoted to this field of inquiry. Ayres and Braithwaite's inspirational work on responsive regulation as an approach is essentially about efficient and effective regulation.[45] Responsive regulation as an approach has been adopted by an array of regulatory bodies, across different fields.[46] Since its first conception, this approach has been

---

IOSCO highlights the importance of three core objectives: protecting the interests of investors; ensuring that markets are fair, efficient and transparent; and reducing systemic risk: see IOSCO, *Objectives and Principles of Securities Regulation* (2010).

41   As an example, Lipinsky and Ong argue that stock markets of the Asia-Pacific region, excluding Japan, have a weaker implementation of regulations as compared with the G-7 counterparts: see Lipinsky and Ong (n 18) 17.

42   Ibid 17–18.

43   Ibid 17.

44   Lipinsky and Ong test for and demonstrate 'a relationship between the overall strength of regulation and the extent of idiosyncratic influences on stock pricing' and find that countries with 'better implementation of securities regulations are associated with stock markets that are less subject to idiosyncratic influences': see ibid 17.

45   Responsive regulation principally states that regulators must be responsive to culture, conduct and context when they are regulating to effectively decide if they should adopt a more or less interventionist response to a situation: see Charlotte Wood et al, 'Applications of responsive regulatory theory in Australia and overseas' (2010) 15 *Occasional Paper* 3. The 'responsive regulation' term and approach was first coined in 1992: see Ian Ayres and John Braithwaite, *Responsive Regulation: Transcending the Deregulation Debate* (Oxford University Press, 1995). For more literature on 'responsive regulation', see John Braithwaite, *Restorative Justice and Responsive Regulation* (Oxford University Press, 2002), doi. org/10.1093/oso/9780195136395.001.0001; John Braithwaite, 'The essence of responsive regulation' (2011) 44 *UBC Law Review* 475.

The concept of 'responsive regulation' has found appreciation in a large number of fields, including financial and medical: see for example Judith Healy and John Braithwaite, 'Designing safer health care through responsive regulation' (2006) 184(10) *Medical Journal of Australia* S56, doi. org/10.5694/j.1326-5377.2006.tb00364.x.

46   Responsive regulation has been adopted by a number of regulators that transcend a singular or specific field of study: see generally John Braithwaite, Toni Makkai and Valerie A Braithwaite, *Regulating Aged Care: Ritualism and the New Pyramid* (Edward Elgar Publishing, 2007), doi.org/10.4337/ 9781847206855; Vibeke Lehmann Nielsen and Christine Parker, 'Testing responsive regulation in regulatory enforcement' (2009) 3(4) *Regulation & Governance* 376–399, doi.org/10.1111/j.1748-

significantly developed, critiqued, applied and tweaked by the contributions of other authors,[47] although, Ayres and Braithwaite's version is regarded as the most influential.[48] Similarly, due to its wide appeal, some scholars prefer to apply the term regulation to governance or 'new-governance'.[49] Others have broadened the approach to a 'regulatory diamond' that incorporates the two regulatory activities of 'compliance' and 'aspirational regulation',

5991.2009.01064.x; Braithwaite (n 45) 31; Neil Gunningham, *Mine Safety: Law Regulation Policy* (Federation Press, 2007) 129; Sagit Leviner, 'An overview: a new era of tax enforcement—from "big stick" to responsive regulation' (2008) 2(3) *Regulation & Governance* 360–380, doi.org/10.1111/j.1748-5991.2008.00039.x; Peter Mascini and Eelco Van Wijk, 'Responsive regulation at the Dutch Food and Consumer Product Safety Authority: an empirical assessment of assumptions underlying the theory' (2009) 3(1) *Regulation & Governance* 27–47, doi.org/10.1111/j.1748-5991.2009.01047.x.

47 Kolieb asserts that the 'responsive' approach to regulation has been enhanced and continually developed since its inception through versatile ideas and concepts: J Kolieb, 'When to punish, when to persuade and when to reward: strengthening responsive regulation with the regulatory diamond' (2015) 41 *Monash University Law Review* 136, 137. Kolieb discusses developments in this area as 'polycentric regulation': see Julia Black, 'Constructing and contesting legitimacy and accountability in polycentric regulatory regimes' (2008) 2(2) *Regulation & Governance* 137–164, 140, doi.org/10.1111/j.1748-5991.2008.00034.x. For the open corporation approach to regulation, see Christine Parker, *The Open Corporation: Effective Self-regulation and Democracy* (Cambridge University Press, 2002) ix, doi.org/10.1017/CBO9780511550034. For the decentred regulation approach see Julia Black, 'Critical reflections on regulation' (2002) 27 *Australian Journal of Legal Philosophy* 1, 4. For literature on regulatory capitalism, see David Levi-Faur, 'The global diffusion of regulatory capitalism' (2005) 598(1) *The Annals of the American Academy of Political and Social Science* 12–32, 14, doi.org/10.1177/0002716204272371.

48 See Nielsen and Parker (n 46); Robert Baldwin and Julia Black, 'Really responsive regulation' (2008) 71(1) *Modern Law Review* 59–94, doi.org/10.1111/j.1468-2230.2008.00681.x; Julia Black, 'Decentring regulation: understanding the role of regulation and self-regulation in a "post-regulatory" world' (2001) 54(1) *Current Legal Problems* 103–146, doi.org/10.1093/clp/54.1.103; Neil Gunningham, Peter N Grabosky and Darren Sinclair, *Smart Regulation: Designing Environmental Policy* (Oxford Socio-legal Studies, 1998), doi.org/10.1093/oso/9780198268574.001.0001; Neil Gunningham and Richard Johnstone, *Regulating Workplace Safety: Systems and Sanctions* (Oxford University Press, 1999), doi.org/10.1093/oso/9780198268246.001.0001.

For other references on responsive regulation in corporate regulation, see Fiona Haines, *Corporate Regulation: Beyond 'Punish or Persuade'* (Clarendon Press, 1997); Parker (n 47); Sally S Simpson, *Corporate Crime, Law, and Social Control* (Cambridge University Press, 2002), doi.org/10.1017/CBO9780511606281.

Some scholars have argued their own version of 'responsive regulation' such as 'flexible enforcement': see Robert A Kagan, 'Regulatory enforcement' (1994) 383 *Handbook of Regulation and Administrative Law* 383–385.

For literature on another version of 'responsive regulation', 'tit-for-tat' regulation, see generally John T Scholz, 'Cooperation, deterrence, and the ecology of regulatory enforcement' (1984) *Law & Society Review* 179–224, doi.org/10.2307/3053402; John T Scholz, 'Voluntary compliance and regulatory enforcement' (1984) 6(4) *Law & Policy* 385–404, doi.org/10.1111/j.1467-9930.1984.tb00334.x; John T Scholz, 'Cooperative regulatory enforcement and the politics of administrative effectiveness' (1991) 85(1) *American Political Science Review* 115–136, doi.org/10.2307/1962881; Raymond J Burby and Robert G Paterson, 'Improving compliance with state environmental regulations' (1993) 12(4) *Journal of Policy Analysis and Management* 753–772, doi.org/10.2307/3325349; Kathryn Harrison, 'Is cooperation the answer? Canadian environmental enforcement in comparative context' (1995) 14(2) *Journal of Policy Analysis and Management* 221–244, doi.org/10.2307/3325151.

49 Kolieb (n 47) 137; Christine Parker, 'Twenty years of responsive regulation: an appreciation and appraisal' (2013) 7(1) *Regulation & Governance* 2–13, doi.org/10.1111/rego.12006.

in which regulatory mechanisms, on the one hand, require adherence to certain behavioural standards and, on the other, encourage regulatees to go beyond the requisite minimum standards.[50] In particular, Baldwin and Black's 'really responsive regulation', which builds on the original responsive regulation theory, expands the conventional regulator–regulatee relationship and requires regulators to be responsive in even more ways, such as through the 'broader institutional environment of the regulatory regime' and 'own performance' of such a regime.[51] Fundamentally, both 'responsive regulation' and 'really responsive regulation' employ a 'performance sensitive, dynamic and systematic' approach that is key to developing a superior quality of regulation in a jurisdiction; this can otherwise suffer greatly due to regulators who may get 'locked into a static conception of the regulatory challenges', failing to respond to challenges in a 'systematic' as opposed to 'sporadic' manner.[52] This shows that regulators and jurisdictions need to adopt a proactive, systematic, performance-based and responsive approach to regulation that demonstrates the effectiveness and efficiency of securities market regulation in that jurisdiction. A regulatory regime founded on such an understanding will manifest in many added opportunities for the overall development and integration of, and investments into, a securities market and the greater economy of that jurisdiction.

In conclusion, the presence of strong, deep and efficient securities markets necessitates strengthening the core fundamentals of market development, integration and regulation within a jurisdiction. This understanding leads to two fundamental questions:

1. Is it possible to strategically leverage cross-border cooperation to deliver specific, speedy and transformative results for securities markets for mutually beneficial results in these three critical areas?
2. Can the securities regimes of India and Australia align for a deeper collaboration? If yes, in what areas and how?

---

50   'The regulatory diamond is an evolutionary, not revolutionary proposal': see Kolieb (n 47) 150.
51   Baldwin and Julia Black (n 48). In really responsive regulation, Baldwin and Black argue that regulators need to be responsive in five further ways, in addition to the 'compliance performance of the regulatee': responsive to the 'firm's own operating and cognitive frameworks (the attitudinal settings)'; to the 'broader institutional environment of the regulatory regime'; 'to the different logics of regulatory tools and strategies'; 'to the regime's own performance'; and 'to the changes in each of these elements'.
52   Ibid 46–47.

To demonstrate that cross-border cooperation can be strategically leveraged as a tool, this book proposes collaboration between the securities regimes of India and Australia, and proposes a model for such collaboration. To build this case, the book undertakes a comparative analysis of the securities regimes of India and Australia applying the IOSCO *Objectives and Principles of Securities Regulation* (IOSCO Principles) as a base to ascertain each jurisdiction's degree of alignment with each of the principles, and determine the degree of comparability and potential relevance for cooperation between the two regimes.

Hypothesis and argument

The report *An India Economic Strategy to 2035*[53] and the *Australia Economic Strategy Report*[54] highlight the alignment of India and Australia's strategic economic interests in the Indo-Pacific region and provide the support for deeper cross-border cooperation between the two countries in the securities sector argued for in this book.

Demirguc-Kunt, Erik Feyen and Ross Levine assert that securities markets 'exert robust, independent, and positive effects on economic activity'.[55] The Indo-Pacific region is slated as a high-growth region against several predictions, including the OECD's *Economic Outlook for Southeast Asia, China and India 2020*.[56] To fulfil the positive economic and long-term growth projections in the Indo-Pacific region, it is imperative to optimise the region's securities markets,[57] which will in turn boost both national and regional economic output.

---

53   See generally Peter Varghese, *An India Economic Strategy to 2035* (2018).

54   See generally Confederation of Indian Industry, *Australia Economic Strategy Report* (2020).

55   Asli Demirgüç-Kunt, Erik Feyen and Ross Levine, 'The evolving importance of banks and securities markets' (2013) (27)(3) *The World Bank Economic Review* 477, doi.org/10.1093/wber/lhs022.

56   OECD, 'Executive summary: economic outlook to 2024' in *Economic Outlook for Southeast Asia, China and India 2020: Rethinking Education for the Digital Era* (2020) 15, doi.org/10.1787/a3906a11-en. The OECD predicted a gross domestic growth of 5.7 per cent in the region for the period 2020–24, with India's expected growth to be 6.6 per cent and China's 5.6 per cent. Despite the COVID-19 pandemic–induced recession, World Bank projections show that the East Asia and Pacific region's economies are expected to contract by only 1.2 per cent in 2020 before rebounding to 5.4 per cent in 2021, South Asia region to contract by 2.7 per cent in 2020 against the European and Central Asian economies that are forecast to contract by 4.7 per cent, and Latin America and the Caribbean to contract by 7.2 per cent in 2020.

57   See generally Lipinsky and Ong (n 18).

This book first presents a case for a deeper, strategic collaboration between India and Australia in the securities sector to enable the countries to work towards the common objectives of market development, integration and regulation, to be achieved through cross-border initiatives between both jurisdictions' securities regulators and authorities, markets and participants, and academia. Second, it argues—and demonstrates—that a comparative analysis of the two regimes against the IOSCO Principles provides a basis for such collaboration. Third, it establishes a clear need for an enhanced cross-border securities cooperation framework, as the existing cooperation mechanisms and networks are fraught with limitations. Many existing bilateral cooperation arrangements in the Indo-Pacific region in the securities sector are either ad hoc or restricted to a narrow range of issues and typically lack a clear vision and strategy. Fourth, the book argues that a deeper, strategic collaboration between an advanced jurisdiction (Australia) and a fast-growing one (India) has the potential to deliver specific, transformative and speedy outcomes for both, including laying a foundation for more ambitious cross-border initiatives within the securities markets, such as a mutual recognition agreement (MRA),[58] or in other sectors of the financial system[59] or economy.

Research gap/objectives

The main gap that this book addresses is the lack of any comprehensive comparative analysis of the securities regimes of India and Australia. One of its objectives is to analyse the core legal and regulatory framework of these two jurisdictions against the IOSCO Principles, which have been endorsed by more than 90 per cent of the world's securities markets.[60] To this end, the book examines the two countries major regulatory institutions—the Securities and Exchange Board of India (SEBI) and the Australian Securities and Investments Commission (ASIC)—to understand how issues of comparability, compliance and cooperation may work in practice.

---

58   To understand the benefit of an MRA, see IOSCO, *IOSCO Task Force* (n 12). An MRA is a very significant tool of collaboration in the securities markets, with myriad benefits that range from reducing the costs of regulation, to easing cross-border business transactions, to integrating two well-regulated securities markets.
59   The idea of an MRA is to maximise the flow of capital across the two cooperating jurisdictions, the home and the host countries, while minimising regulatory costs, processes and other burdens. For instance, an MRA can allow financial market intermediaries to operate in either jurisdiction without having the need to re-register or seek a licence from the host country.
60   Baxt, Ashley Black and Hanrahan (n 3) 11.

Contribution to the literature

This book contributes to knowledge on cross-border collaboration, international securities regulation, and corporate and securities law. At a broader level, it contributes to academic literature in the field of international financial and securities law, and, more particularly, to evolving deliberations in the field of securities regulation as well as cross-border cooperation. The book expands knowledge on cross-border cooperation by using a case study to show how fast-growing and advanced securities jurisdictions, that have sufficient underlying commonalities in objectives, values and principles, can collaborate more effectively through deeper, bilateral and strategic partnerships for transformative and speedy outcomes. It thus makes a substantial contribution to literature in the areas of financial and securities markets and regulation by proposing a novel collaboration technique.[61]

This book is the first comparison of the securities regimes of India and Australia. It conducts an independent and objective evaluation of the degree of alignment of the Indian and Australian securities regimes with each of the 38 IOSCO Principles. Based on this assessment, it offers conclusions on the degree of comparability and relevance for cooperation in respect of each principle. Such comparative analysis of the Indian and Australian regimes has never previously been undertaken. Each regime has been separately benchmarked against the IOSCO Principles under country reviews and assessment by other organisations such as the World Bank, the International Monetary Fund (IMF) and IOSCO itself. The basis for the analysis undertaken in this book is considerably different, as it also takes into account the academic literature while benchmarking both jurisdictions. While it takes into consideration the approaches of the IOSCO/IMF/ World Bank reviews, this book adds to knowledge by integrating academic literature with regulatory documents. Significantly, the tables and graphs in Chapter 5 on SEBI's and ASIC's enforcement outcomes make an important contribution towards comparisons of India and Australia.[62]

---

61   The proposal for bilateral collaboration in Chapter 9 of this book contains the enhanced strategic cross-border collaboration framework between an advanced and a fast-growing jurisdiction. See also Sonia Khosa, 'A game-changer or a routine drill? Cooperation in the Indo-Pacific Securities Markets' (2019) 47 *Australian Business Law Review* 182–199.

62   These tables consolidate the enforcement data released by SEBI and ASIC for the five-year period between approximately FY2014–15 and FY2018–19.

The book makes an original, substantial contribution to the existing academic literature on India–Australia securities markets, as detailed above. It aims to lay the foundation and provide a blueprint for an enhanced bilateral cross-border cooperation initiative between the securities regulators of India and Australia, with the hope that this may be translated into actual policy measures in the years to come.

Methodology

Rationale for the research approach and method

This book proposes a deeper, strategic collaboration between the securities sectors of India and Australia and, to that end, conducts a high-level comparative analysis to ascertain the comparability of the two securities regimes and suggest areas for cooperation for mutually beneficial outcomes.

Securities regulation is a dynamic field of research within which cooperation is a less explored niche area. Comparative analysis with the objective of furthering strategic cooperation can be approached through the perspectives of several individual disciplines[63] or an interdisciplinary approach,[64] synthesising overlapping areas of knowledge.[65] Both India and Australia are common law countries.[66] To compare their securities regimes, this book compares the regulatory, legal and implementation frameworks of each

---

63 Such disciplines include business, economics, finance or law. A discipline refers to a certain range of structural, specific, patterned activity that serves as a base for underlying assumptions, key features and behaviours and values: see Christopher Tomlins, 'Framing the field of law's disciplinary encounters: a historical narrative' (2000) *Law and Society Review* 911–972, 912, doi.org/10.2307/3115128.

64 While applying an interdisciplinary approach, it is worth noting that the object is not to erase the disciplinary identity altogether, but, in fact, to frame one's research within the fundamental tenets of a defined discipline, simultaneously enriching it with insights from another field of research so as to enhance the overall scholarship and value in such a manner that would not have been possible to do by relying on any one single discipline: see Douglas W Vick, 'Interdisciplinarity and the discipline of law' (2004) 31(2) *Journal of Law and Society* 163–193, 165, doi.org/10.1111/j.1467-6478.2004.00286.x. See generally Joseph LC Cheng et al, 'From the editors: advancing interdisciplinary research in the field of international business: prospects, issues and challenges' (2009) 40 *Journal of International Business Studies* 1070–1074, doi.org/10.1057/jibs.2009.41.

65 Vick (n 64); Moti Nissani, 'Fruits, salads, and smoothies: a working definition of interdisciplinarity' (1995) 29(2) *Journal of Educational Thought (JET)/Revue de la Pensée Educative* 121–128, 125, doi.org/ 10.55016/ojs/jet.v29i2.52385; Garry D Brewer, 'The challenges of interdisciplinarity' (1999) 32(4) *Policy Sciences* 327–337, 328, doi.org/10.1023/A:1004706019826.

66 Both Australia and India are common law jurisdictions: see Philip R Wood, 'How to compare regulatory regimes' (2007) 2(4) *Capital Markets Law Journal* 332–344, 333, doi.org/10.1093/cmlj/ kmm032.

jurisdiction.[67] Such analysis, when rooted in the discipline of law, can either be undertaken through a traditional, well-established doctrinal research method,[68] discussed in influential reports in Australia,[69] or through the comparative law method,[70] or via an interdisciplinary path, with law as the main discipline.[71] Given this study's unique objectives—to propose areas of comparability and cooperation between India and Australia to facilitate strategic cooperation—this book takes an analytical yet flexible approach, drawing on and amalgamating useful elements of both comparative law and doctrinal methods for a qualitative analysis of the two securities systems. This analysis also incorporates an interdisciplinary approach, to the extent that the main legal academic sources are supplemented with useful securities studies and literature emanating from other disciplines, including business and finance.

---

67   Ibid 335.

68   Terry Hutchinson and Nigel Duncan, 'Defining and describing what we do: doctrinal legal research' (2012) 17(1) *Deakin Law Review* 83, doi.org/10.21153/dlr2012vol17no1art70. The legal analysis conducted using this method relies on a sequence of linear steps that include gathering relevant legal material for investigation and understanding the facts, stating the issues, examining the issues in view of the legal framework, going over the relevant secondary materials, and, finally, synthesising issues under examination, before concluding appropriately. This methodology is the dominant legal research method as far as the common-law countries are concerned: see Terry Hutchinson, 'The doctrinal method: incorporating interdisciplinary methods in reforming the law' (2015) 3 *Erasmus Law Review* 130, doi.org/10.5553/ELR.000055.

69   For example, in its report in 1987, the Australian Pearce Committee emphasised the doctrinal method as the primary method in its research taxonomy, describing it as research that enables a systematic elaboration of provisions governing a legal classification, and that evaluates the relationship between rules and explains issues and difficulties and even predicts future developments: see D Pearce, E Campbell and D Harding, *Australian Law Schools: A Discipline Assessment for the Commonwealth Tertiary Education Commission* (1987).
The Council of Australian Law Deans extended the doctrinal research definition, stating that the research method, at its best, provides a rigorous analysis and synthesis, makes connections between varying doctrinal strands and extracts general principles from a collection of primary materials: see Christopher Roper, 'Australian law schools: a discipline assessment for the Commonwealth Tertiary Education Commission' (1987) 5 *Journal of Professional Legal Education* 201.

70   See Mark Van Hoecke, 'Methodology of comparative legal research' (2015) *Law and Method* 1–35, doi.org/10.5553/REM/.000010. Scholars have attempted to describe the comparative law method as a mechanism for knowledge by understanding information on the law in a specific jurisdiction, a tool of evolutionary and taxonomic science, a mechanism that contributes to the better understanding of one's own legal system or leads to harmonisation of law.

71   In the context of legal and other disciplinary research, interdisciplinary research aims at creating a space of encounter between the discipline of law and other disciplines that the research was based upon: see Laura Kalman, *The Strange Career of Legal Liberalism* (Yale University Press, 1998) 239–40. Where the research demands application of the legal discipline with another, it implies interaction at levels beyond the traditional boundaries of training offered at law schools or in the field of legal practice to the extent that it transcends the specific professional cultural understanding: see Janet Weinstein, 'Coming of age: recognizing the importance of interdisciplinary education in law practice' (1999) 74 *Washington Law Review* 319, 353.

Considering the extensive field of securities regulation and the distinctiveness of the two regimes (with no previous comprehensive comparison undertaken), it is necessary and useful to achieve some practical standardisation. To this end, the book adopts the IOSCO Principles to provide a comprehensive base for the comparison.[72] Given that both SEBI and ASIC are members of IOSCO, standardisation against the IOSCO Principles[73] will facilitate a better understanding of the unique elements and complexities of the two regimes for the regulators, experts and readers of this comparative assessment in both jurisdictions, and globally. However, even though IOSCO has published a detailed methodology to assess compliance of a securities regime with the IOSCO Principles,[74] IOSCO's methodology is not suitable for the comparative analysis undertaken in this book for two main reasons. First, IOSCO's methodology is mainly used for intensive country reviews and assessments conducted by IOSCO, and also by organisations such as the World Bank and IMF, which undertake detailed and penetrating country assessments under the Financial Sector Assessment Programme (FSAP).[75] These reviews and assessments assess the precise levels of compliance of a regime with the 38 IOSCO Principles,[76] and reveal lacunae or shortcomings with the expectation that the jurisdiction will address or remedy such limitations before the next country review.[77] By contrast, while the comparative analysis undertaken in this book may reveal shortcomings within a securities regime (and thus be of interest to academics, practitioners, regulators and market stakeholders), the thrust of the assessment of the two regimes is towards devising a novel approach towards a more invigorated, meaningful and strategic collaboration in the securities sector. Thus, compared to the lengthy and rigorous analysis

---

72   IOSCO, *Objectives and Principles of Securities Regulation* (n 40). The IOSCO Principles for securities regulation are widely accepted as the leading securities standards, and both SEBI and ASIC are members of IOSCO. Chapter 3 of this book discusses the rationale for adopting these principles.

73   Both SEBI and ASIC are active members of IOSCO: see IOSCO, 'Ordinary Members of IOSCO', iosco.org/about/?subsection=membership&memid=1.

74   IOSCO, *Methodology for Assessing Implementation of the IOSCO Objectives and Principles of Securities Regulation* (2017).

75   FSAP assessment is one of the most rigorous reviews of financial markets and securities regulatory regimes conducted jointly by the World Bank and the IMF: see for example IMF, *India: Financial Sector Assessment Program—Detailed Assessments Report on IOSCO Objectives and Principles of Securities Regulation* (2013) (*India FSAP Report*).

76   IOSCO's methodology uses very specific criteria for rating a securities regime in respect of each IOSCO Principle in the following categories: fully implemented, broadly implemented, partly implemented and not implemented: see IOSCO, *Methodology for Assessing Implementation* (n 74).

77   To an extent, these assessments also inform investors and relevant market stakeholders about a country's level of compliance with international standards to help them make suitable investment or market-related decisions.

undertaken in the country-specific assessments employing IOSCO's methodology, the assessment undertaken in this book focuses on a high-level analysis to present key characteristics of each regime's securities framework relating to the IOSCO Principles, and assesses implementation in a succinct yet sufficiently nuanced manner to satisfy the objective of this book. Second, assessments conducted by IOSCO, the World Bank, IMF and similar authorities, based on IOSCO's methodology, use a wide set of information and data-gathering tools, such as surveys and interviews with government officials, regulatory institutions, stock exchanges and other market stakeholders. By contrast, this book conducts a qualitative analysis of the two securities regimes through an examination of publicly available legal and regulatory materials and the academic literature.

Thus, having considered extant relevant methodologies and strategies,[78] I chose to devise a new methodology more suited to the objectives of this book. This methodology builds on the peer review methodology to assess the comprehensiveness of the securities regimes and draw conclusions on the areas of comparability and cooperation between India and Australia in the securities sector. The next section elaborates on this rational, simple and flexible methodology.

The methodology of this book

The book, in Chapters 3–8, presents a layered, flexible and qualitative analysis of SEBI's and ASIC's regimes based on the 38 IOSCO Principles. At first, the analysis in each of these chapters sets out the core requirements for an IOSCO Principle or set of principles and provides a brief academic overview relating to the subject matter of the principle(s). Each regime is then separately assessed for its alignment with the IOSCO Principle(s) through:

1. an exposition of the key features of the broader legal and regulatory securities framework relating to the core requirements of the IOSCO Principle(s)

---

78   Other methodologies explored included the European Securities and Markets Authority's peer review methodology: see ESMA, *ESMA Peer Review Methodology* (2020). See also Financial Stability Board, *Key Attributes of Effective Resolution Regimes for Financial Institutions* (2014). On the approach for assessing really responsive regulation, see Robert Baldwin and Julia Black, 'Really responsive regulation' (2008) 71(1) *Modern Law Review* 59–94, doi.org/10.1111/j.1468-2230.2008.00681.x. See also Australian Government, The Treasury, *Fit for the Future: A Capability Review of the Australian Securities and Investments Commission* (2015).

2. an analysis of the adequacy of such a framework and its actual implementation.

Based on this examination, the degree of alignment of the regime with the core requirements of the IOSCO Principle(s) is assessed as 'high', 'moderate' or 'low'. Analysis of each IOSCO Principle further determines the extent of reform undertaken by each jurisdiction in the last decade, assessed as either 'substantial' or 'minor'; the overall standing or stage of development of the regime relating to the specific IOSCO Principle(s) is assessed as either 'evolving' or 'mature'. This assessment of each regime informs the final conclusions on the degree of comparability and the relevance for cooperation between the two regimes across different areas of the securities landscape: these are also classified as 'high', 'moderate' or 'low'.

The criteria and method for the assessments undertaken in the book is described below. While these criteria establish the general rules for the assessment, in exceptional situations, the assessment for an IOSCO Principle may digress from these general rules, for the reasons explained in the analysis.

Degree of alignment

The degree of alignment of each regime with the core requirements of the international standards (ie each IOSCO Principle) is determined through a high-level examination of the legal and regulatory frameworks and implementation of the two regimes. Such alignment is assessed as follows:

- Low:[79]
  - if the legal and regulatory framework does not reflect or support the core requirements of the IOSCO Principle(s), or does so in an extremely cursory or rudimentary manner,[80] and the implementation of the framework is non-existent or below average.[81]

---

79   For the degree of alignment to be assessed as low, both the framework relating to the core requirements of an IOSCO Principle and the implementation of such framework must be non-existent or evidently below average.

80   For instance, if the IOSCO Principle requires a regulator to have a specific power (eg the power to supervise intermediaries and enforce securities laws) or be given a specific mandate (eg investor protection) and the regulator has no such power or mandate under the legal and regulatory framework, this would contribute to the degree of alignment being assessed as low.

81   Where the regulator is given the power under the legal or regulatory framework (eg the power to enforce law through criminal action) but there is no evidence in the regulator's enforcement data to show that such power or provision is being used, or if the regulator has implemented it in an entirely inadequate manner (ie below average), it contributes to the alignment assessed as low.

- Moderate:
  - if the legal and regulatory framework reflects and supports the core elements of the relevant IOSCO Principle comprehensively, and the implementation of this framework is average, or even below average
  - if the legal and regulatory framework is detailed though not comprehensive, and implementation of the framework is above average evidenced through significant regulatory attention and action.
- High:
  - if the framework reflects and supports the core elements of the relevant IOSCO Principle as comprehensive, and the implementation of such framework is determined as above average.

Stage of development, sophistication of regulatory tools, longevity of experience

As well as assessing degree of alignment with the IOSCO Principle(s), the analysis considers the stage of development of the regime for the principle(s) as 'mature' or 'evolving'. This assessment takes into account the level of sophistication and reliability of regulatory mechanisms and tools within a jurisdiction as well as the longevity of experience.

The stage of development or overall landscape of a regime is assessed as mature if it has achieved a significant level of consistency, stability and reliability relating to the core requirements of the IOSCO Principle(s), as evident from the assessment of its framework and implementation.[82] Importantly, in a mature landscape, any divergences from the observance of the core requirements of an IOSCO Principle would be aberrations from the generally sophisticated environment rather than systemic issues or repeated failures. Finally, given the dynamic character of securities markets, a mature assessment does not indicate perfection, nor is it an absolute condition, as the regime may continue further refinements or fine-tuning of the domestic framework and its implementation.

The stage of development or overall landscape of a regime is assessed as 'evolving' if the analysis identifies substantial room for improvement for achieving better consistency, stability and reliability of the regime

---

82 A regime can be assessed as 'mature' if the degree of alignment with the IOSCO Principle is either assessed as 'high' or 'moderate' but not if the regime is assessed as 'low', as that would suggest the absence of a framework, or only rudimentary one, and below-average implementation.

in fulfilling the core requirements of the IOSCO Principle(s). In most circumstances, where a regime is assessed as evolving, there is copious scope for improvement.[83] However, in select circumstances, the analysis may justify an evolving assessment even though only minor refinements of a subtler character are required.[84]

Extent of change or reform

Next, the analysis assesses the extent of change or reform introduced in the last decade to the legal and regulatory framework and approach, particularly taking into account changes since the most recent, comprehensive country review for each regime[85] conducted under the FSAP Review by the IMF and World Bank. The extent of reform is assessed as either 'substantial' or 'minor' depending on the magnitude and nature of reform or change undertaken. This extent of change or reform is useful to understanding which securities areas are being reorganised and reformed in a domestic jurisdiction, and which areas are dormant or undergoing minor changes. This assessment signals the areas of regulatory interest, attention and improvement within a jurisdiction.

Degree of comparability and relevance for cooperation

Upon achieving some standardisation and comparative understanding through analysis of the degree of alignment, stage of development and extent of reform for each regime, the final synthesis and assessment of the IOSCO Principle(s), included at the end of each of Chapters 3–8 of this book, draws conclusions on the degree of comparability and relevance for cooperation between the two regimes. For uniformity and simplicity, comparability and relevance for cooperation are expressed as 'high', 'moderate' and 'low'.

---

83   For instance, if the degree of alignment of a regime with an IOSCO Principle is assessed as 'moderate' or 'low', it would generally imply that there is copious scope for improvement and thus attract an 'evolving' assessment—except in certain cases in which, due to very specific reasons, the degree of alignment is assessed as 'moderate', even though the overall landscape, regulatory mechanisms and practices operate with reliability and consistency indicating a 'mature' stage of development.

84   For example, if the degree of alignment is assessed as 'high' for a principle, the overall landscape may still be characterised as 'evolving' considering substantial reorganisation within the regime and further significant reform underway or needed: this does not detract from the assessment of the regime for that principle as 'high'.

85   The comprehensive World Bank–IMF FSAP securities regime assessment for India was in 2013 and Australia in 2012: see IMF, *India FSAP Report* (n 75); IMF, *Australia: IOSCO Objectives and Principles of Securities Regulation—Detailed Assessment of Implementation* (Country Report No 12/314, 2012), doi.org/10.5089/9781475563412.002.

The degree of comparability between the two regimes for each IOSCO Principle is generally determined as:

- Low when the degree of alignment and the stage of development relating to the IOSCO Principle(s) for both regimes is radically far apart, such as one regime's alignment is assessed as high and the other as low, or if one regime has a mature landscape while the other has an evolving one.
- Moderate when the degree of alignment and the stage of development is dissimilar but not drastically apart, such as one regime is high and the other regime is moderate, and if one regime has a mature landscape while the other has an evolving one.
- High when the degree of alignment and the stage of development relating to the IOSCO Principle(s) is highly similar, such as both regimes being individually assessed as high or moderate or even low, and the overall landscape being similar.

The relevance for cooperation between the two regimes for each IOSCO Principle is generally determined as:

- Low or moderate if the analysis shows that this is not a priority area for either of the two jurisdictions, or beyond the mandates of the regulatory authorities.[86]
- High if—notwithstanding assessment of the degree of alignment, stage of development or degree of comparability between the two jurisdictions—there is a high interest demonstrated through the extent of reform in recent years for either jurisdiction, or if cooperation on subject matter relating to the IOSCO Principle is likely to bring benefits to both regimes, as determined by the analysis.

Suitability for undertaking this research

My interest in this research stemmed from my direct involvement with the proposal to develop of a recognition agreement between the National Stock Exchange of India (NSE) and the US Commodity Futures Trading Commission (CFTC) in 2015. The recognition agreement sought to exempt NSE brokers/members from compliance with CFTC regulations

---

86 For instance, cooperation on enhancing independence and accountability mechanisms and practices of the two regulators will generally be a matter of concern for the central or federal governments within the jurisdiction and beyond the ambit of the regulatory authorities themselves.

based on 'substituted compliance' with SEBI regulations and NSE rules. My interest in the topic also stems from my direct handling of some of the important cooperation agreements signed by SEBI, including with EU member jurisdictions in pursuance of the Alternative Investment Fund Managers Directive requirement.

Further, in my capacity as assistant general manager (law) within SEBI's Office of International Affairs (2012–17), I handled cross-border cooperation requests raised under IOSCO's multilateral memorandum of understanding (MMoU) and drafted legal clauses for SEBI's bilateral MoUs with other jurisdictions. This role gave me a profound understanding of the scope, advantages, limitations and practical application of these arrangements.

Finally, my academic background in law, particularly business law, work experience of 10 years in policy-oriented, regulatory fields, and close association with TRNs like IOSCO, the European Securities and Markets Authority (ESMA) and Joint Forum gave me the confidence and background needed to undertake this research.

Chapter overview

This book comprises nine chapters. Chapter 2 provides a high-level overview of the financial sector architecture in India and Australia for the purposes of the main comparative analysis of the securities regimes of the two jurisdictions. To enhance comparative understanding, the chapter also provides a historical overview of the foundation, evolution and design of the financial and securities markets in both jurisdictions, and critiques the current financial sector regimes.

Chapter 3 commences the examination of the 38 IOSCO Principles and the detailed comparative analysis and benchmarking. It provides a rationale for choosing the 38 IOSCO Principles as a basis for the comparative analysis, and specifically examines the role and responsibilities of the two securities regulators, SEBI and ASIC, applying IOSCO Principles 1–7. It further explores the adequacy of their cooperation regimes relating to IOSCO Principles 13–15 to fulfil their regulatory objectives.

Chapters 4 and 5 analyse in detail the supervisory and enforcement powers of SEBI and ASIC, and their compliance regimes relating to the requirements of IOSCO Principles 10–12. Chapter 4 describes the main features of the supervisory and enforcement measures available at SEBI and ASIC and assesses their adequacy for achieving the regulatory mandates of each regulator. Chapter 5 conducts an empirical analysis of the enforcement outcomes for each regulator to draw significant trends, extrapolate findings from these trends and analyse effectiveness of their compliance regimes in achieving regulatory objectives such as deterring and punishing wrongdoing, maintaining integrity in the markets and protecting the interests of investors.

Chapter 6 analyses SEBI's and ASIC's regimes relating to IOSCO Principles 9 and 19–23 on self-regulation and select gatekeepers. Principle 9 on self-regulation in securities markets focuses on the use of self-regulatory organisations within a securities regime, while Principles 19–23 relate to the role, responsibilities and requirements for securities markets gatekeepers, namely the auditors, credit agencies, and evaluative and analytical research service providers.

Chapter 7 analyses the regimes for issuers, collective investment schemes (CISs) and hedge funds relating to the requirements of Principles 16–18 and 24–28. Principles on issuers focus on disclosure of information, fair and equitable treatment of holders of securities and the use of high-quality accounting standards for preparation of financial documents. Principles 24–28 provide the conditions for effective functioning and governance of CISs and hedge funds.

Chapter 8 relates to the regime for secondary markets, market intermediaries and settlement systems within the securities markets. It analyses key features of SEBI's and ASIC's regimes relating to IOSCO Principles 8 and 29–38. Principles 33–37 relate to the framework and implementation of secondary markets, Principles 29–32 relate to the requirements for market intermediaries and Principle 8 assesses how the regimes address conflicts of interest in the securities markets. Finally, Principle 38 discusses the clearing and settlement regimes for securities transactions.

Chapter 9 concludes the argument of the book. It consolidates the main findings of the comparative analysis conducted in Chapters 3–8 relating to the degree of alignment of each regime with the core requirements of the IOSCO Principles, the degree of comparability between the two securities regimes and the relevance for cooperation for each principle. Chapter 9 proposes a model for deeper, strategic collaboration between the securities regimes of India and Australia to work towards the common objectives of market development, integration and regulation through cross-border collaboration between the two jurisdictions' securities regulators and authorities, markets and participants, and academia. To this end, Chapter 9 proposes a model vision and strategic action plan based on the key findings of this book.

2

The financial systems of India and Australia: Structure and regulation

Introduction

The report *An India Economic Strategy to 2035*[1] (Varghese Report) and the *Australia Economic Strategy Report*,[2] released in 2020 by the Confederation of Indian Industry, highlight several reasons for increasing cooperation between India and Australia. Given several commonalities between the political and legal systems of India and Australia,[3] and the complementarities

---

1   The Varghese Report has made a detailed case for strengthening and deepening of India and Australia's economic ties, citing scale and complementary economies among other reasons for creating better ties: see Peter Varghese, *An India Economic Strategy to 2035* (2018).
India is among the fastest growing major economies in the world, growing at a growth rate of over 7 per cent. Australia is the fifth largest export market valued at approximately A\$19.2 billion in 2016–2017. The bilateral trade between India and Australia, comprising merchandise and services, is valued at A\$25.7 billion: see Australian Trade and Investment Commission, 'Doing business in India', austrade. gov.au/Australian/Export/Export-markets/Countries/India/Market-profile.
2   Confederation of Indian Industry, *Australia Economic Strategy Report* (2020). This report was prepared in response to the Varghese Report. It was put together by the Confederation of Indian Industry team alongside contributions from KPMG, India. It contains seven chapters, highlights the potential areas for strengthening the India–Australia relationship and specifically recognises Australia's strengths in governance that have resulted in a stable and transparent work environment, strong research and development capacity across sectors that support innovation, automation and dependence on labour.
3   The Republic of India is a constitutional democracy that follows a parliamentary system of government that is largely founded on the UK model of governance. The titular head of the state is the president who is obliged to act on the advice of the Council of Ministers, chosen by the prime minister. India is the world's largest democracy and its parliament is bicameral, comprising upper and the lower houses known as the 'Lok Sabha' and 'Rajya Sabha'; see generally Australian Government, Department of Foreign Affairs and Trade, 'India country brief: overview', dfat.gov.au/geo/india/Pages/india-country-

between the two markets,[4] this book proposes a meaningful partnership in the securities sectors of the two countries through a deeper, strategic collaboration program. India and Australia possess deep and vibrant securities markets with the potential for cross-border bilateral cooperation to benefit both economies.[5]

This book conducts a high-level evaluation of the securities regimes of the Indian securities regulator, the Securities and Exchange Board of India (SEBI), and the Australian financial conduct regulator, the Australian Securities and Investments Commission (ASIC), as they apply broadly to market entities (market operators, select gatekeepers, intermediaries and others). The particular focus is on the legal and regulatory securities frameworks and implementation relating to traditional listed investment instruments commonly referred to as 'securities'.[6] The analysis also encompasses some hybrid instruments,[7] collective or managed investments,[8] and risk management instruments such as derivatives if these are regulated

---

brief.aspx; V Bhaskara Rao and B Venkateswarlu, *Parliamentary Democracy in India* (Mittal Publications, 1987); BL Shankar and Valerian Rodrigues, *The Indian Parliament: A Democracy at Work* (Oxford University Press, 2014).

Australia also follows a democratic parliamentary system of governance modelled on the UK political system, sometimes referred to as the Westminster system of government: see Australia Government, 'Our country: legal system', australia.gov.au/about-australia/our-country (page discontinued). For more literature on the Australian federal democracy, see Graham Maddox and Frances Evans, *Australian Democracy in Theory and Practice* (Longman/Pearson Education Australia, 2000).

India has a legal system that derives, to a large extent, from common law, and personal and customary law systems: see generally University of Melbourne, 'Indian Law Research Guide: introduction to the Indian legal system and Indian legal research', unimelb.libguides.com/indian_law/intro#s-lg-box-wrapper-14726254 (site discontinued). Australia, too, follows 'a common law' legal system that has been adopted and influenced by the British colonial rule: see The Australian National University Library, 'The Australian legal system', libguides.anu.edu.au/c.php?g=634887&p=4547083.

4   Complementarities between the markets include India's economic needs and government priorities that align with Australia's competitive advantages. For a detailed account see Varghese Report (n 1), 'Introduction'.

5   'Securities markets' is defined as a 'financial market where bonds, shares, etc. are made available and traded': see *Cambridge Dictionary*, 'Definition: securities markets'.

The International Organization of Securities Commissions (IOSCO) has recently noted that both the Australian and Indian securities markets regulators have robust measures in place for the proper functioning of the secondary markets; see generally IOSCO, *IOSCO Standards Implementation Monitoring (ISIM) on Secondary and Other Market Principles* (February 2019) (FR04/19). See generally Varghese (n 1).

6   Robert Baxt, Ashley Black and Pamela Hanrahan, 'Regulating securities and markets' in *Securities and Financial Services Law* (LexisNexis Butterworths, 9th ed, 2017) 4. Securities are those 'financial instruments created and issued by commercial or financial sector entities … customarily traded through established exchanges'.

7   Hybrid instruments may contain some features of a securities instrument combined with other features of another asset class such as insurance.

8   These also include mutual funds in the case of India.

by either SEBI or ASIC. The purpose of the examination is to facilitate a more nuanced academic understanding of the two securities regimes and propose a deeper collaboration program between the two jurisdictions.

As 'securities markets are an important subset of … broader financial markets',[9] it is useful to reflect on the financial sector structures and overarching regulatory approach in both jurisdictions. This is more so since the global financial crisis (GFC) of 2007–08 demonstrated that 'institutional design', among other features, was critical for 'combating financial crises'.[10] This chapter provides an overview of the financial structure, regulatory architecture and key features of the financial sector regulation in India and Australia relevant for the securities regimes of each country. The first section covers Indian financial regulation, particularly the sector-specific method and institution-based and rules-based approach to financial regulation, while reflecting on key historical developments leading to the current financial regime. The second section outlines Australia's securities and financial sector regime with a focus on the 'twin-peaks' regulatory model, Australia's functional or objective-based approach and principles-based regulation method. The final section provides a brief synthesis of the analysis and a conclusion.

---

9   Baxt, Black and Hanrahan (n 6) 3.
10   See Andrew Godwin, Steve Kourabas and Ian Ramsay, 'Twin peaks and financial regulation: the challenges of increasing regulatory overlap and expanding responsibilities' (2016) 49(3) *The International Lawyer* 275.
For more literature on the integral part played by institutional design in preserving the financial see Suzanne J Konzelmann and Marc Fovargue-Davies, 'Australia: economic liberalization and financialization—an introduction' (2012), noting positively the performance of Australian financial system in the aftermath of the global crisis. See also Kim Hawtrey, 'The global credit crisis: why have Australian banks been so remarkably resilient?' (2009) *Agenda: A Journal of Policy Analysis and Reform* 95–114, doi.org/10.22459/AG.16.03.2009.08; Donato Masciandaro, Rosaria Vega Pansini and Marc Quintyn, *The economic crisis: did financial supervision matter?* (IMF Working Paper No 11/261, 2011) 1–47, doi.org/10.2139/ssrn.1961908; Elizabeth F Brown, 'A comparison of the handling of the financial crisis in the United States, the United Kingdom, and Australia' (2010) 55 *Villanova Law Review* 509.

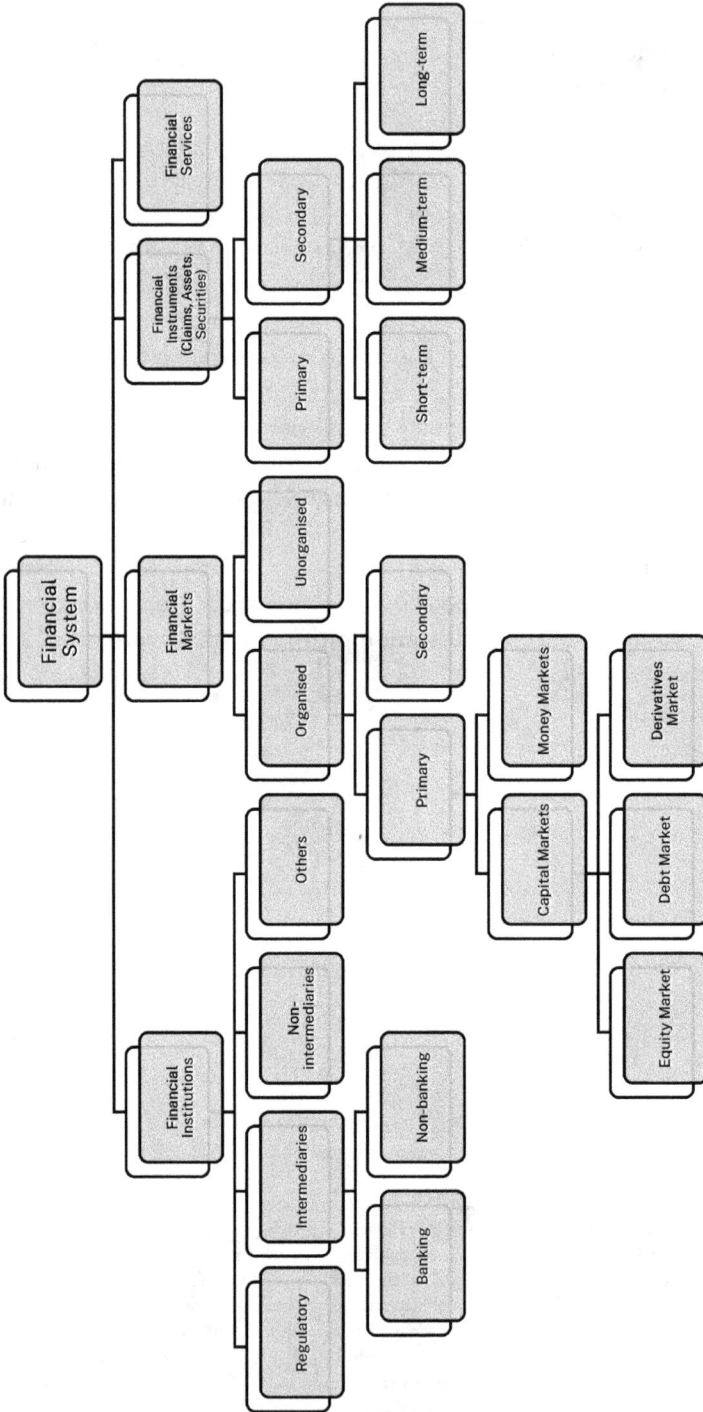

Figure 2.1: Components of the Indian financial system

Source: Adapted from LM Bhole, *Financial Institutions and Markets Structure, Growth and Innovations* (Tata McGraw-Hill Publishing Company Ltd, 2004).

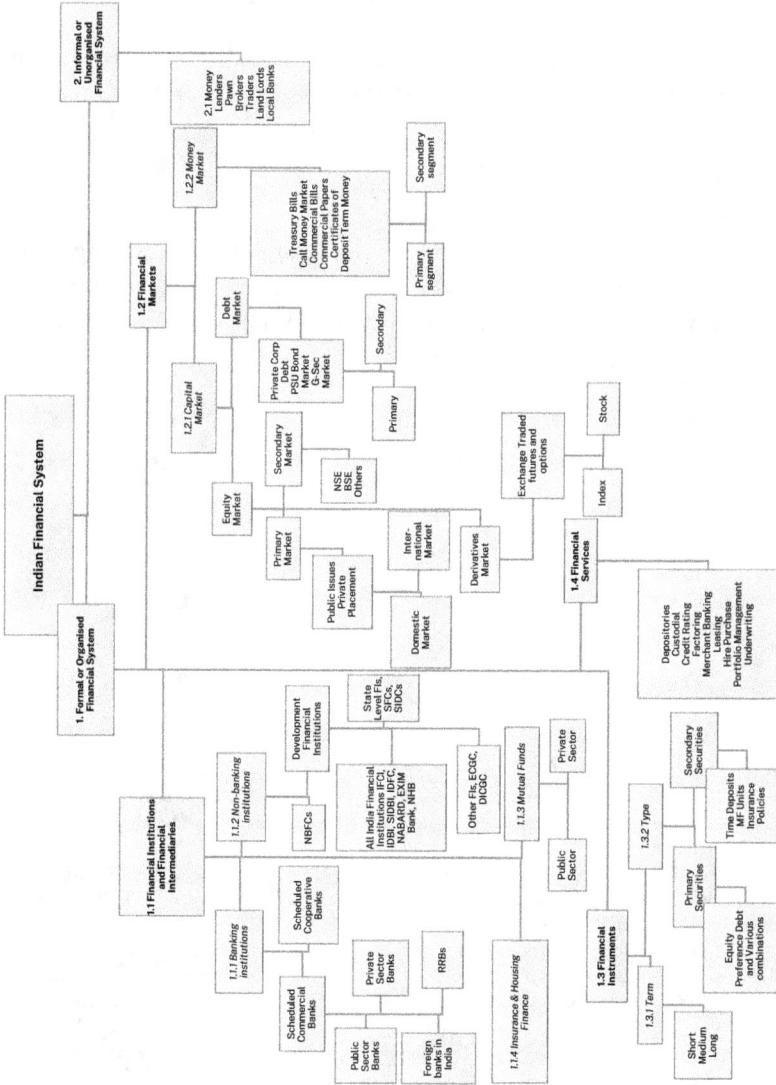

Figure 2.2: A detailed representation of the components of the Indian financial system

Source: Adapted from BV Pathak, *The Indian Financial System* (Pearson Education India, 2009), 4.

An overview of the Indian financial system

Structure

The Indian financial system comprises a complex network of financial institutions, instruments, markets[11] and 'financial services'.[12] Bhole asserts that these components of the financial sector are not 'mutually exclusive' but closely connected to each other.[13] He depicts the financial system as shown in Figure 2.1.

The next section briefly describes these financial institutions, instruments and services and markets and their specific role in the Indian financial system.

Financial institutions

Financial institutions act like intermediaries that 'mobilise savings and facilitate the allocation of funds in an efficient manner'.[14] Mohan and Ray, as well as Bhole, classify Indian financial institutions along the lines of 'banking' and 'non-banking' institutions.[15]

---

11 See Reserve Bank of India (RBI), 'Financial market evolution and globalisation' in *Reports* (2006) [6.12]. For another overview of the Indian financial system, see Abinash Panda, Rajen K Gupta and Satish K Kalra, 'Gurgaon Branch' (2006) 10(1) *Asian Case Research Journal* 103–142, doi.org/10.1142/S0218927506000764.

12 See LM Bhole, *Financial Institutions and Markets Structure, Growth and Innovations* (Tata McGraw-Hill Publishing Company Ltd, 2004). See also M Balasubramanian and S Umamageswari, 'Indian financial system—an overview' (2020) 68(17) *Our Heritage* 349–354.

13 Bhole (n 12). For instance, financial institutions are part of the financial markets and the two are not exclusive of each other. Bhole's description of financial system structure continues to be relevant.

14 See generally MY Khan, *Indian Financial System* (McGraw Hill Education (India) Private Ltd, 8th ed, 2019) 93.

15 Bhole (n 12); Rakesh Mohan and Partha Ray, *Indian Financial Sector: Structure, Trends, and Turns* (Working Paper No 580, 2016), doi.org/10.2139/ssrn.2924370.

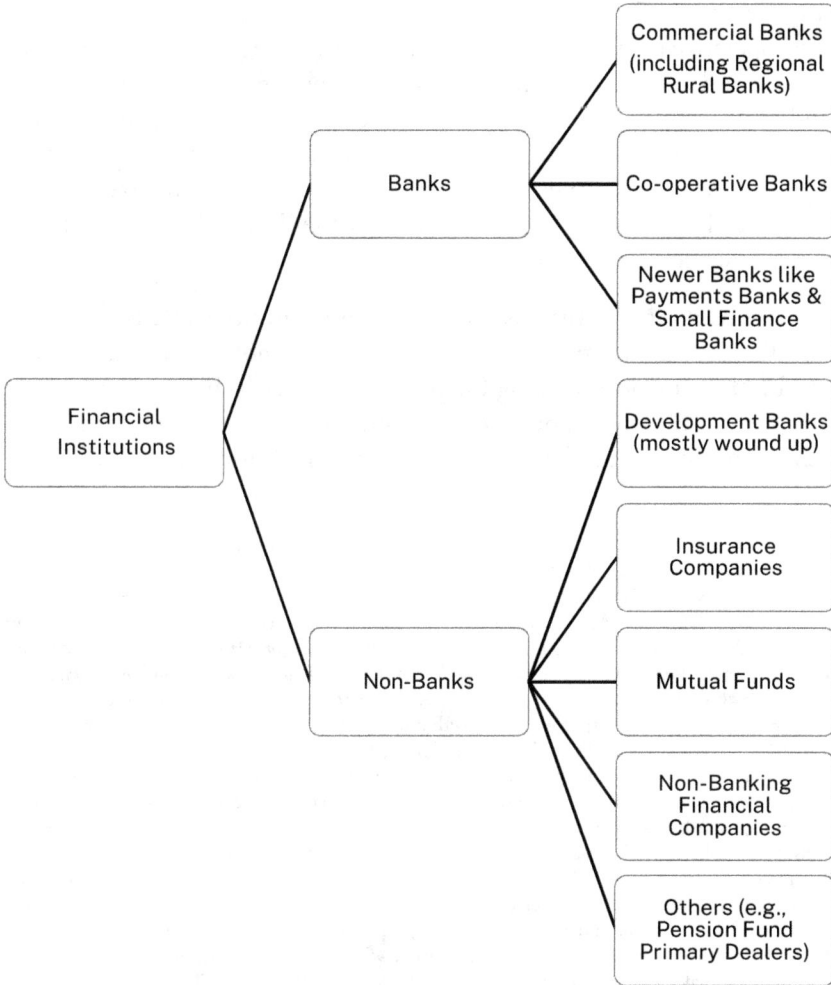

Figure 2.3: Financial institutions in India
Source: Adapted from Rakesh Mohan and Partha Ray, *Indian Financial Sector: Structure, Trends, and Turns* (Working Paper No 580, 2016).

According to Khan, the distinction between banking and non-banking institutions is that the former are the 'creators' and 'purveyors of credit' while the latter are only 'purveyors' of credit and do not create it.[16] An efficient banking and financial system is required for the overall growth

---

16   Khan (n 14).

of an economy.[17] The banking sector is 'classified into commercial banks and co-operative credit institutions'—the former category comprising non-scheduled and scheduled commercial banks.[18] Cooperative credit institutions include various cooperative banks.[19] As in other jurisdictions, the banking system is regarded as the backbone of the Indian economy.[20] Due to its unique evolutionary journey to its current form, some commentators assert that it is difficult to draw a parallel between the 'Indian banking industry and any other country in the world'.[21]

Much like banking institutions, non-banking institutions (NBIs) also raise financial resources from surplus areas of the economy.[22] An important subset of NBIs are non-banking financial companies (NBFCs) that include 'investment companies, housing companies and leasing companies, hire purchase companies [and] specialized financial institutions'.[23]

17   See for example Rakesh Mohan, 'Financial sector reforms in India' (2015) 40(12) *Economic and Political Weekly* 1106; Madan Lal Bhasin, 'Menace of frauds in the Indian banking industry: an empirical study' (2015) 4(12) *Australian Journal of Business and Management Research* 1–13, doi.org/10.52283/NSWRCA.AJBMR.20150412A02; KV Kamath et al, 'Indian banking sector: challenges and opportunities' (2003) 28(4) *Vikalpa: The Journal for Decision Makers* 84, doi.org/10.1177/0256090920030308; Nachiket Mor Committee, *Committee on Comprehensive Financial Services for Small Businesses and Low Income Households Report* 25; Panicos O Demetriades and Kul B Luintel, 'Financial development, economic growth and banking sector controls: evidence from India' (1996) 106(435) *The Economic Journal* 359–374, doi.org/10.2307/2235252.
18   Reshu Sharma and Swati Sharma, 'Banking sector in India: an overview' (2014) 3(3) *Global Journal of Commerce and Management Perspective* 37. Scheduled commercial banks are further classified into public sector banks, private banks, foreign banks and regional rural banks. In statistical terms, the banking sector comprises 12 public sector banks, 22 private sector banks, 46 foreign banks, 56 regional rural banks, 1,485 urban cooperative banks and 96,000 rural cooperative banks in addition to the cooperative credit institutions: see Department of Commerce India Brand Equity Foundation, Ministry of Commerce and Industry, 'Banking sector in India', ibef.org/industry/banking-india.aspx. See generally International Monetary Fund (IMF), *Detailed Assessment of Observance of the Basel Core Principles for Effective Banking Supervision* (IMF Staff Country Report 18/4, January 2018), doi.org/10.5089/9781484337080.002.
19   Sharma and Sharma (n 18) 32.
20   'Think out-of-box: Jaitley asks banks which seeks higher capital', *Deccan Chronicle* (21 December 2016), deccanchronicle.com/business/in-other-news/201216/think-out-of-boxjaitley-asks-banks-which-seeks-higher-capital.html.
21   See for example Lal Bhasin (n 17). It is difficult to compare the Indian financial system with any other, mainly because of complex features of the country, such as its population and market size, incomparable urban and rural demographic structure that influences the financial sector growth and development, and the unique pace and style of financial sector evolution that the sector has witnessed since the 1950s.
22   See generally Khan (n 14). Companies like the Life Insurance Corporation, General Insurance Corporation, Development Financial Institutions and other pension organisations and provident funds classify as NBIs.
23   Ibid 98 [2]. Khan, while writing on NBIs, states that these companies proliferated in the 1980s and the early 1990s. Thereafter, as they were brought under the purview of RBI, their numbers reduced from 13,815 in 2001 to 12,409 in 2012, and the public deposits decreased from Rs18,085 in 2001 to Rs1,964 in 2011. However, the total assets of these companies surged from Rs53,878 crores during 2001 to Rs116,897 crores during 2011 and over the years has continued to grow.

2. THE FINANCIAL SYSTEMS OF INDIA AND AUSTRALIA

Financial instruments and services

Financial instruments[24] and services within a financial system are indicators of the depth and stage of development of the financial system.[25] Bhole discusses instruments in India along the lines of a) financial assets[26] and b) financial securities.[27] Financial services assist a financial sector with 'borrowing and funding, lending and investing, buying and selling securities, making and enabling payments and settlements, and managing risk exposures in financial markets'.[28] Khan lists financial services under several categories, including 'funds intermediation, payments mechanism, provision of liquidity, risk management, and financial engineering'.[29] Together, financial instruments and services are essential in the management and transfer of risk as well as for channelling funds from 'lenders to borrowers' in a financial system.[30]

Financial markets

Academics categorise Indian financial markets as a) organised or formal, and b) unorganised or informal.[31] They also categorise them as a) money markets and b) capital markets: the former deals in short-term claims[32] and the latter is concerned with medium- or long-term claims (ie instruments that have a period of maturity usually of more than one year).[33] Another useful classification of financial markets is given by Mohan and Ray in Figure 2.4.

Financial markets have several components including money, credit, government securities, foreign exchange, capital and insurance.[34]

---

24   Bhole (n 12) 104. Financial instruments can include both marketable and non-marketable instruments, and different kinds of instruments can be designed according to the risk and return preferences of different classes of investors. See also Khan (n 14). A financial instrument is understood as 'a claim against or an institution for payment, at a future date, of a sum of money and/or a periodic payment in the form of interest or dividend'. Financial instruments are classified according to the marketability, liquidity, reversibility, type of options, return, risk and transaction costs'.
25   Bhole (n 12).
26   Bhole discusses a financial asset to be a claim to payment of a sum of money at a future time coupled with/or a periodic payment in the manner of interest or dividend: see ibid.
27   Financial securities may be primary or secondary securities: see ibid.
28   Khan (n 14) 106 [1].
29   Ibid 106 [1].
30   Ibid.
31   Balasubramanian and Umamageswari (n 12). The formal or organised financial system comes under the governance of the Ministry of Finance, RBI, the Securities and Exchange Board of India (SEBI) and other regulators.
32   Money market claims refer to instruments when the period of maturity of an instrument is one year or less. Instruments include Treasury Bills, Commercial Papers and Repurchase Agreements.
33   Bhole (n 12) [1.5]. Financial markets are also sometimes classified along other lines—for example, 'organized' and 'unorganised', 'formal' and 'informal', 'official' and parallel and 'domestic' and 'foreign'. A significant amount of overlap exists between all these categories.
34   See generally Reserve Bank of India (RBI), 'IV—financial market structure' in *Handbook of Statistics on Indian Economy* (2000) [4.1].

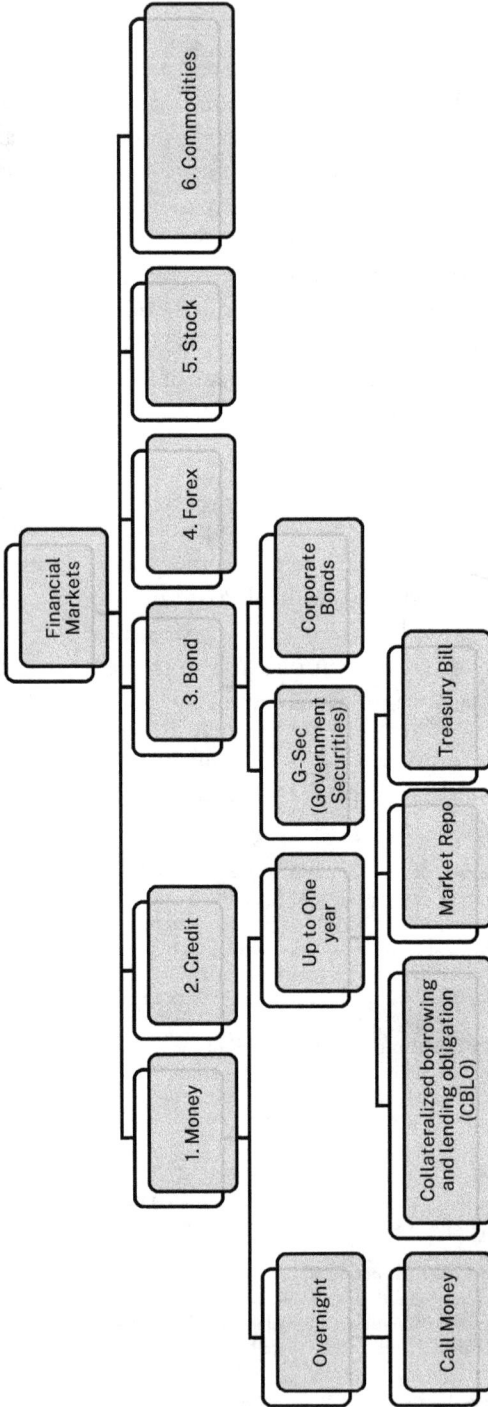

Figure 2.4: Financial markets in India

Source: Adapted from Rakesh Mohan and Partha Ray, *Indian Financial Sector: Structure, Trends, and Turns* (Working Paper No 580, 2016).

Legal and regulatory framework

The legal and regulatory framework of the Indian financial system is carved along relatively strict, sector-specific lines, with several regulatory authorities tasked with the role of regulating different parts of the financial sector. Tables 2.1–2.6 highlight the legal and regulatory landscape of these sectors.

Table 2.1: Banking

Reserve Bank of India (RBI)	
Legislation	**Details**
Banking Regulation Act 1949	RBI governs money markets and the government securities and foreign exchange markets.[35] Alongside RBI, the Ministry of Finance, Department of Financial Services, also regulates some issues relating to banks and financial institutions.[36] Apart from the banking sector, RBI regulates the non-banking financial corporations (NBFCs) and monitors the operations of development financial institutions as well as cooperative banks, jointly regulating these with state governments.[37] RBI also oversees currency-related transactions and bond markets that include government securities.[38]
Reserve Bank of India Act 1934	

Table 2.2: Securities

Securities and Exchange Board of India (SEBI)	
Legislation	**Details**
SEBI Act 1992	SEBI governs the Indian capital and securities markets.[39]
SCRA 1956	The Ministry of Corporate Affairs (MCA) registers and regulates all companies other than 'listed companies in respect of issue, transfer and non-payment of dividend',[40] and is the primary authority in charge of reviewing the annual financial reports (including financial statements) that all companies, including listed issuers, are required to submit pursuant to the *Companies Act 1956*.[41]
Depositories Act 1996	
Companies Act 1956	
	RBI governs contracts on government securities, gold-related securities and money market securities and securities derived from those securities and repo contracts in debt securities.[42] However, the execution of the contracts on the stock exchanges is within SEBI's regulatory ambit.

---

35   RBI, [Homepage], rbi.org.in/.
36   Bahram N Vakil et al, 'Banking regulation in India: overview' (2017) *Thomson Reuters Practical Law*.
37   Bhole (n 12) [4.28].
38   Rajesh Chakrabarti, 'The financial sector in India: an overview' (2012) 10 [3], doi.org/10.2139/ssrn.2078448.
39   SEBI, [Homepage], sebi.gov.in/.
40   IMF, *India: Financial Sector Assessment Program—Detailed Assessments Report on IOSCO Objectives and Principles of Securities Regulation* (2013) 7 [2].
41   Ibid.
42   Ibid.

Table 2.3: Insurance

Insurance Regulatory and Development Authority of India (IRDAI)	
Legislation	**Details**
Insurance Act 1938	IRDAI regulates the insurance market.[43] Its key objects include 'promotion of competition so as to enhance customer satisfaction through increased consumer choice and fair premiums, while ensuring the financial security of the Insurance market'.[44]
Insurance Regulatory and Development Authority Act (IRDA Act) 1999	
General Insurance Business (Nationalisation) Act 1972	Several rules, regulations and notifications complement the legal framework of the insurance sector.[45] The power to frame regulations by notification is bestowed upon IRDAI by s 26(1) of the *IRDA Act 1999* and s 114A of the *Insurance Act 1938*.[46]
Actuaries Act 2006	

Table 2.4: Pension

Pension Fund Regulatory and Development Authority (PFRDA)	
Legislation	**Details**
Pension Fund Regulatory and Development Authority Act (Pension Fund Act) 2013	The *Pension Fund Act* was passed on 19 September 2013 and notified on 1 February 2014.[47] The PFRDA governs the pension sector.[48] The pension architecture in India was revamped by the central government in the 2000s with the establishment of an interim authority, the PFRDA.[49] The Preamble to the *Pension Fund Act* lays down the fundamental functions of the PFRDA as 'to promote old age income security by establishing, developing and regulating pension funds, to protect the interests of subscribers to schemes of pension funds and for matters connected therewith or incidental thereto'.[50]

---

43   See Insurance Regulatory and Development Authority of India, [Homepage], irdai.gov.in/.

44   Government of India, Ministry of Finance, Department of Financial Services, 'Insurance overview', financialservices.gov.in/beta/en/page/insurance-overview.

45   Ibid. This legal framework for the sector governs the functioning of several entities including life insurance companies and general insurance companies, both in the public and private sector. Other entities are re-insurance companies, agency channel and several intermediaries including corporate agents, brokers, third party administrators, surveyors and loss assessors.

46   See *Insurance Regulatory and Development Authority Act 1999* (India). See also *Insurance Act 1938* (India).

47   Pension Fund Regulatory and Development Authority, [Homepage], pfrda.org.in/index.cshtml.

48   Ibid.

49   Ibid. The Government of India passed a resolution on 23 August 2003 establishing the PFRDA and aiming at promoting, developing and regulating the pension sector in India.

50   *Pension Fund Regulatory and Development Authority Act 2013* (India).

Table 2.5: Financial Stability and Development Council

Financial Stability and Development Council (FSDC)
The FSDC was created in 2013 to institutionalise and strengthen the mechanism for maintaining financial stability, financial sector development and inter-regulatory coordination. The FSDC is supported by other working groups, including the FSDC Sub-Committee, the Inter-Regulatory Technical Group and the Early Warning Group.

Table 2.6: Ministry

Ministry of Finance (MoF), Ministry of Economic Affairs (MEA) and Ministry of Corporate Affairs (MCA)
Several central government authorities play a role in overseeing matters related to the corporate and financial sector, including the MoF, MEA and MCA.

Financial sector regulation: Design and approach

After the GFC, a review of financial regulatory architecture[51] by several countries[52] reaffirmed the 'continued importance of institutional design' and approach for financial stability.[53] Generally, there are four widely accepted methods of financial system regulation:[54] functional,[55] institutional or silo-based,[56] integrated,[57] and the objectives-based or twin-peaks method.[58]

---

51   See generally Eilís Ferran, 'The significance of institutional design' in *The Oxford Handbook of Financial Regulation* (Oxford University Press, 2015) 98.

52   See for example Eilís Ferran, 'The break-up of the Financial Services Authority' (2011) 31(3) *Oxford Journal of Legal Studies* 455–480, doi.org/10.1093/ojls/gqr006.

53   Godwin, Kourabas and Ramsay (n 10) 275.

54   See Darshana Rajendaran, 'Approaches to financial regulation and the case of South Africa' (2012) 6 *IFMR Finance Foundation*. For a detailed analysis of the various models of regulation, see Eddy Wymeersch, 'The structure of financial supervision in Europe: about single financial supervisors, Twin Peaks and multiple financial supervisors' (2007) 8(2) *European Business Organization Law Review (EBOR)* 237–306, doi.org/10.1017/S1566752907002376. See also Ferran, 'The break-up of the Financial Services Authority' (n 52).

55   The functional approach is followed by Italy and France: see AD Schmulow, 'The four methods of financial system regulation: an international comparative survey' (2015) 26 *Journal of Banking and Finance Law and Practice* 151–172, doi.org/10.2139/ssrn.2556545.

56   The institutional, traditional or silos approach is followed by nations such as China and Mexico: see ibid.

57   An integrated or unified approach to regulation is followed by Japan: ibid. For literature considering arguments for and against the creation of a unified regulatory agency, see Richard K Abrams and Michael W Taylor, *Issues in the Unification of Financial Sector Supervision* (IMF Working Paper, 2000), doi.org/10.2139/ssrn.1445742.

58   The objectives-based approach to regulation is followed by Australia: see Wymeersch (n 54); Andy Schmulow, 'Financial regulation: is Australia's "twin peaks" model a successful export?' (2016) *The Interpreter*; Andy Schmulow, 'Doing it the Australian way: twin peaks and the pitfalls in between', *The CLS Blue Sky Blog* (31 March 2016), clsbluesky.law.columbia.edu/2016/03/31/doing-it-the-australian-way-twin-peaks-and-the-pitfalls-in-between-2/. Australia's twin-peaks method of regulation is discussed later in this chapter.

Stemming from the regulatory design, the financial system may either adopt an institution-based or neutrality approach towards the regulated entities. Finally, the regulatory approach of a financial system is classified along the lines of a 'rules-based' or 'principles-based' system.[59]

Key features of financial regulation in India

The regulatory design and approach of India's financial sector are relevant to the main analysis of the securities regimes in this book. To provide a more nuanced understanding of India's current financial regulatory architecture, this section discusses the key characteristics of financial sector regulation in India and traces the major historical developments that contributed to these foundational facets of India's financial regulation.

Sector-specific regulation

The first key feature is 'sector-specific' regulation, which segregates responsibility for financial sector regulation among various authorities based on the nature of the product.[60] India's sector-specific approach to financial sector regulation is evident through the existing division of responsibilities at the government and regulatory level. For instance, Chakrabarti notes that six different federal ministries, including the Ministry of Finance and the Ministry of Corporate Affairs, are involved in the regulation of the financial system; he describes the financial regulatory environment as 'heavily fragmented'.[61]

Apart from federal ministries, the financial sector is regulated by at least four sector-specific regulators. This sector-specific governance is widely acknowledged as prone to problems of 'regulatory gaps and overlaps' as well as 'regulatory capture and arbitrage'.[62] In India, these problems were

---

59   Regulations can be drafted from a 'principles-based' or 'rules-based' approach. The former is characterised by specific and detailed legal provisions and the latter 'involves formulating rules which are broad, general and purposive and which may or may not be elaborated in further rules or guidance', for example, 'you shall act with integrity' or 'firms shall act in the best interests of their clients'; see Julia Black, 'Paradoxes and failures: "new governance" techniques and the financial crisis' (2012) 75(6) *The Modern Law Review* 1043, doi.org/10.1111/j.1468-2230.2012.00936.x. On the various aspects of principles-based regulation, including the advantages and risks, see Julia Black, 'Principles-based regulation: risks, challenges and opportunities' (2007), eprints.lse.ac.uk/62814/. For more literature on rules-based versus principles-based regulatory compliance, see Brigitte Burgemeestre, Joris Hulstijn and Yao-Hua Tan, 'Rule-based versus principle-based regulatory compliance' (2009) *JURIX* 37–46.

60   The Indian financial system has different regulators for securities, insurance, banks and pension.

61   Chakrabarti (n 38). The other four ministries include the Ministry of Consumer Affairs (oversees the commodities markets), Ministry of Labour (oversees the Employees' Provident Fund Organization) and the Ministry of Urban Development (oversees the National Housing Bank).

62   An example of a regulatory overlap that led to a turf war between SEBI and IRDA was the matter of the Unit-Linked Insurance Plans that SEBI argued was a form of mutual fund and thus under its jurisdiction; see ibid 10 [4].

2. THE FINANCIAL SYSTEMS OF INDIA AND AUSTRALIA

extensively discussed in the 2008 *Report of the Committee on Financial Sector Reforms* chaired by Raghunath Rajan.[63] The Financial Sector Legislative Reforms Commission (FSLRC) of 2013, set up to report on streamlining the financial regulation architecture in India, also reflected on measures necessary to remove gaps and inconsistencies within the system.[64] (The details are discussed later in this chapter.) Despite these efforts, the current financial sector regulatory architecture continues along sectoral lines, even though gradual reforms have begun.[65]

Institution-based approach

As a natural corollary of sector-specific regulation, India's financial sector entities are regulated through an institution-based approach, referred to as the traditional or silos approach. This approach focuses on the form of legal entity under regulation,[66] and is in stark contrast to Australia's functional or objective-based approach to regulation driven by competitive neutrality discussed later in the chapter.[67]

The challenges associated with the sector-specific method in India also extend to the institution-based approach to regulation. Thus, the financial sector's institution-based characteristics represent a 'fragmented, silo-based' regulatory system that, Chakrabarti notes, is unable to effectively govern financial conglomerates, such as the State Bank of India, operating across the banking, insurance and securities sectors.[68]

Several measures have been adopted to minimise the shortcomings associated with this form of regulation by significant coordination measures adopted by the central government and financial regulators.[69] The best example of

---

63   See generally Government of India Planning Commission, 'A hundred small steps' in *Report of the Committee on Financial Sector Reforms* (2008).
64   Jaimini Bhagwati, M Shuheb Khan and Ramakrishna Reddy Bogathi, 'Financial Sector Legislative Reforms Commission (FSLRC) and financial sector regulation in India' (Indian Council for Research on International Economic Relations, 2016).
65   For a detailed discussion, see the analysis in the later part of this chapter.
66   Schmulow, 'The four methods of financial system regulation' (n 55) 152.
67   See Caner Bakir, 'Who needs a review of the financial system in Australia? The case of the Wallis Inquiry' (2003) 38(3) *Australian Journal of Political Science* 518, doi.org/10.1080/10361140320001340 29. In the 1990s, as Australia was assessing the need to reform its existing financial regulation approach, the Treasury stressed the functional approach to regulation instead of the institution-based approach, as the former ensured 'competitive neutrality', the main feature of which is that products, intermediaries or markets that provide financial services must be subject to similar regulation as otherwise it could lead to regulatory arbitrage and a waste of time and resources towards exploitation of regulatory loopholes.
68   Chakrabarti (n 38).
69   These coordination measures include bilateral channels such as between SEBI and MCA, and SEBI and RBI, as well as separate multilateral channels such as among SEBI, IRDA and RBI specifically directed towards financial conglomerates.

41

such measures is the Financial Stability and Development Council (FSDC), chaired by the finance minister, which acts like a coordination agency among apex financial sector regulators.[70]

Rules-based regulation

A third feature attributed to financial sector regulation in India is an 'exceedingly' rules-based approach towards financial regulation[71] that is evident across the main financial sector statutes and regulations.[72] This approach, which is prevalent in several emerging markets, places emphasis on 'getting the regulated to obey the letter of the regulation' and 'typically involves more direct control by the regulatory authority'.[73] This approach is criticised as being narrow and cumbersome with a tilt 'towards avoiding crises' rather than 'boosting market growth'.[74] As a consequence of this approach in India, the regulatory response time to financial innovations has been arguably extended, at times taking more than five years.[75] A principles-based approach is suggested as more suited, both for advanced and emerging economies, as it better promotes adherence to the 'spirit of the regulation' while also encouraging 'innovation and risk taking'.[76] Given this, several recommendations have been made in India for adopting a 'lighter, principle-based approach' towards financial regulation.[77]

The rules-based approach to financial regulation in India points to the more cautious and largely risk-averse approach adopted by the authorities. Even though this may be problematic in the long run for the reasons enumerated above, conservatives have highlighted its advantages, attributing India's faring reasonably well through the GFC precisely to this approach of putting 'caution before innovation'.[78]

---

70   Chakrabarti (n 38). The FSDC was created in 2010. Another measure towards a holistic approach of the financial sector entities is the publication of an annual financial stability report by the RBI to keep a check on the monitoring of financial institutions.

71   Ibid 10 [3].

72   The banking or securities markets Acts and regulations framed thereunder reflect a rules-based approach rather than a principles-based approach: see for example *Securities and Contracts (Regulation) Act 1956*; *Securities Contracts (Regulation) (Stock Exchanges and Clearing Corporations) Regulations 2012*.

73   Eswar S Prasad, 'Financial sector regulation and reforms in emerging markets: an overview' (National Bureau of Economic Research Working Paper No 16428, 2010) 4, doi.org/10.3386/w16428.

74   The rules aim at 'keeping the worst performers in line rather than facilitating innovations in more capable players': see Chakrabarti (n 38).

75   Such as the case of the introduction of gold-ETFs and the USD–INR futures: see ibid.

76   Prasad (n 73) 4. Both approaches are focused on micro prudential regulation of individual firms and financial institutions, and thus, in themselves, will not be sufficient to deal with systemic risk.

77   See Government of India Planning Commission (n 63).

78   Chakrabarti (n 38).

In analysing the importance of such a sector-specific, institution- and rules-based approach to regulation, and its effectiveness for the financial regulatory architecture in India, the next section reflects on the historical developments that have shaped, or at least contributed to, the current architecture.

Historical evolution

India's current financial sector structure and regulatory framework can only be fully appreciated by understanding the key financial sector developments of the past. India's economic liberalisation of 1991 was an historic event for the entire economy, including the financial sector. However, developments and the state of India's financial sector prior to these reforms are also relevant for explaining the current state and form of India's financial sector regulation. From this standpoint, it is necessary to reflect on three fundamental questions:

1. What was the nature of India's liberalisation reforms?
2. What was the reason for the liberalisation reforms?
3. What was the state of India's financial sector prior to the liberalisation reforms?

Liberalisation reforms of 1991: Financial and securities market

India's economic liberalisation of 1991 directly impacted all segments of its financial markets.[79] The main theme of the reforms was 'scaling back capital controls' and 'fostering' a 'domestic financial system' as India embarked on a new economic journey 'embracing globalization' and adopting 'market-based mechanisms for resource allocation'.[80]

---

79   The liberalisation phase is attributed to the recommendations of three key committees, namely: the Committee to Review the Working of the Monetary System in India, 1985, headed by Chairman, Sukhmoy Chakravarty; the Committee on the Financial System, 1991; and the Committee on the Banking System Reforms, 1998—both chaired by M Narasimham: see N Nagarajan, 'Regulation as an augmentor of competition: the Indian experience with the banking sector' (2003) 4(2) *South Asia Economic Journal* 206, doi.org/10.1177/139156140300400203; B Joseph et al, 'Productivity, performance and technical efficiency in banking: the foreign bank's saga in the context of financial reforms in India' 4(1) *Kelaniya Journal of Management* 50–64, doi.org/10.4038/kjm.v4i1.7488. See also Mohan and Ray (n 15) 5.
80   Ila Patnaik and Ajay Shah, *Reforming India's Financial System* (JSTOR, 2014) 4.

As a result of such liberalisation, money markets, a critical segment of the financial system that governs short-term demand for and supply of funds, and influences monetary policy,[81] burgeoned in terms of new instruments, depth and liquidity.[82] Similarly, credit markets evolved from being tightly governed under a complex web of 'credit controls, directed lending and administered interest rates'[83] to a more flexible regime that allowed banks to price their products based on their risk assessment, slowly removing restrictions on lending for project finance activity and for personal loans.[84] Credit norms in India have continued to evolve and are currently well aligned with international standards and best practices, and more linked with other segments of the financial sector. Thus, credit norms today feature 'norms on capital adequacy, income recognition, asset classification and provisioning' with stronger linkages between 'credit' and 'equity' markets since the participation of banks in equity markets for raising capital.[85]

In addition to money and credit markets, sweeping reforms were initiated in the government securities markets as well as in the foreign exchange markets.[86] Foreign exchange (forex) markets comprising 'authorised dealers' that are mainly 'banks, exporters and importers, individuals and the Reserve Bank' itself[87] rapidly transformed in the post-liberalisation era, moving from

---

81   RBI, 'Financial market evolution and globalisation' (n 11). One of the primary objectives of the RBI is to ensure the short-term interest rates and liquidity in the money markets are at a level that is consistent with the overall monetary policy of the nation (ie the maintaining of price stability), making sure that there is an ample flow of credit to the productive sectors of the economy and keeping the markets stable.

82   In the 1990s, the money market instruments mainly comprised: a) call/notice money, b) term money, c) certificates of deposit, d) commercial paper, e) treasury bills, f) repurchase agreements (repos), g) interest rate swaps/forward rate agreements and h) rediscounting of commercial bills schemes. Since the reforms, the introduction of new money market instruments, such as the rupee derivatives like the interest rate swaps/forward rate agreements, has enabled market players to hedge risks more effectively. See ibid.

83   Deepak Mohanty, 'Evidence of interest rate channel of monetary policy transmission in India' (Second International Research Conference at the Reserve Bank of India) 13.

84   Ibid. Further, several other banking reforms were initiated such as 'reductions in reserve and liquidity ratios, entry deregulation', and introduction of an 'inter-bank money market': see P Gupta, K Kochhar and S Panth, 'Bank ownership and the effects of financial liberalization: evidence from India' (2015) 8(1) *Indian Growth and Development Review* 7, doi.org/10.1108/IGDR-08-2014-0028. Gradual reduction was made to the cash reserve ratio from 15 per cent to 4 per cent and also in the statutory reserve ratio from 40 per cent to 21.5 per cent: see Mohan and Ray (n 15) 5.

85   Mohanty (n 83).

86   Gupta, Kochhar and Panth (n 84). Government securities markets reforms included measures such as the introduction of primary dealers, floating rate bonds and interest rate derivatives. Government securities markets form a major segment of the overall debt markets and are significant for the reason that interest rates in this segment of the market act as a benchmark for other financial market segments: see RBI, 'Financial market evolution and globalisation' (n 11). Foreign exchange market reforms included steps towards convertibility for current account transactions, gradual opening of capital account, currency swap market, foreign currency accounts, etc.

87   RBI, 'Financial market evolution and globalisation' (n 11).

a controlled and fixed exchange rate to a flexible/floating rate regime,[88] in the process experiencing a nine-fold increase between 2004 and 2011.[89] Gradually, currency futures were permitted (in 2008) followed by currency options that also began trading on stock exchanges,[90] as linkages between the Indian forex market and the global financial system continually improved, mainly due to corporates and banks being permitted to borrow abroad and use derivative products.[91]

Similarly, the liberalisation reforms of the 1990s induced a reset of India's pension sector that began in 1999 with the Indian government commissioning the national project OASIS (old age, social and income security) to examine policy for post-retirement and old age income security in India.[92] Based on policy recommendations, the Defined Benefit Pension System was replaced with the Defined Contribution Pension System for new entrants to the national/state public service, other than the armed forces.[93]

In tandem with other financial segments, reforms were successfully introduced in the securities and insurance sectors, and also in the functioning of non-banking financial institutions.[94] For instance, the insurance sector[95] 'exhibited unprecedented growth in the period that followed' the economic reforms, expanding at 'an annual rate exceeding 30% for the life sector and close to 16% for the non-life sector between 2000 and 2010'.[96]

In the securities sector, economic liberalisation had a telling effect and capital markets witnessed a structural transformation.[97] Several fast-paced and multifaceted reforms were introduced that focused on creating 'growth-

---

88   Ibid [6.83–6.84].
89   Chakrabarti (n 38). The recommendations for deepening and liberalisation of the forex markets came from several committee reports such as the Rangarajan Committee (1992), the Sodhani Committee (1995) and the Tarapore Committee (1997).
90   Ibid 9.
91   Mohanty (n 83).
92   Pension Fund Regulatory and Development Authority (n 47).
93   Ibid. The contributory pension system was notified officially on 22 December 2004 and renamed the National Pension System (NPS) from 1 January 2004. With effect from 1 May 2009, the NPS was extended to all Indian citizens, including 'self-employed professionals and others in the unorganized sector on a voluntary basis'.
94   The major reforms introduced in the securities sector during the liberalisation era are discussed in this chapter; for other measures across other financial sector segments, see Mohan and Ray (n 15) 16, 29, 22.
95   The main products in the insurance industry comprise life insurance, general insurance and health insurance: see Insurance Regulatory and Development Authority of India (n 43).
96   Chakrabarti (n 38) 9.
97   Capital markets are classified along the lines of 'primary' and 'secondary' markets, or as equity, debt and derivatives markets. Bhole describes primary markets as those that deal in new financial claims or new securities and, thus, are sometimes called 'new issue markets', while secondary markets 'deal in securities already issued or existing or outstanding': see Bhole (n 12) [1.5].

enabling institutions', appropriate regulatory frameworks and enhanced competition through improved price discovery mechanisms, reducing transaction costs and information asymmetry and consequently boosting investor trust and confidence.[98]

The most significant of the securities-related reforms was arguably the repeal of the *Capital Issues (Control) Act 1947*, resulting in the liberalisation of the process to raise capital.[99] Following this, norms for public issues were tightened in 1996 and disclosure requirements enhanced.[100] Issuers of capital were provided an option to raise resources through a 'fixed-price mechanism' or the 'book-building process'.[101] Other notable reforms included upgrading the 'trading infrastructure' of the stock exchange by replacing the 'open outcry system' with 'on-line screen based electronic trading'.[102] Trading and settlement cycles were shortened from 14 to 7 days and, subsequently, 'rolling settlement' was introduced on a T+5 basis, with securities transactions completing five business days after the date of trading.[103] In 2002, the settlement cycle was reduced to T+3 and in 2003 to T+2,[104] which has been further reduced in 2024 by SEBI to T+1 and for select stocks to T+0.

In sum, the liberalisation process ushered in changes to prudential regulations, caused a deregulation of interest rates, and, importantly, with the easing out of the 'statutory pre-emption of resources', led to a spurt in 'private sector players' and an overall strengthening of the system.[105]

---

98   RBI, 'Equity and corporate debt market' in *Report on Currency and Finance* (2007).

99   This paved the way for market determination of pricing of issues and allocation of resources for competing uses, and for the first time, the issuers of securities were allowed to raise capital from the market without requiring any consent from any authority for making or pricing the issue: see ibid.

100 Mohan and Ray (n 15) 22.

101 Book building refers to the mechanism by which the 'demand' for securities that are proposed to be issued is 'built-up' and the 'price' for securities is 'assessed for determination of the quantum of such securities to be issued': see RBI, 'Equity and corporate debt market' (n 98) 260. This method of price discovery was introduced to bring in more transparency in pricing of the scrips and to determine proper market price for securities.

102 Ibid 260.

103 Ibid. Improvements in clearing and settlement systems aided in reducing transaction costs.

104 SEBI, 'Chapter 3—Settlement' (2018) *Master Circular* 3. Similarly, measures were introduced to improve the safety and integrity of securities markets, including 'capital requirements, trading and exposure limits, daily margins comprising mark-to-market margins and VaR based margins'. Trade and settlement guarantee funds were also established for smooth settlement in the instance of default by any member.

105 S Pan, 'An overview of the Indian banking industry' (2015) 4(5) *International Journal of Management and Social Science Research* 67–71. The period of liberalisation saw a greater spurt from 2004 onwards when the foreign direct investment ceiling limits were increased from 49 per cent to 74 per cent, a plan for inclusion of foreign banks was put in place and a 'more liberal branch licencing policy followed'.

Economic liberalisation is seen as a watershed moment in India's financial sector journey and, thus, it is necessary to reflect briefly on the reasons provoking such a major overhaul.

The need for economic liberalisation

India embarked on an economic liberalisation path not as a result of a preferred policy measure but because it was the only recourse available to bring the country out of its economic morass. Corbridge and Harriss argue that the Indian economy was overheated in the late 1980s. Observing a gap between the 'real economy' and the 'financial economy', they point to several indicators supporting this argument.[106] For instance, increases in rural wage rates in the 1980s were not fully financed by increases in productivity. Further, the government had been spending more on subsidies, loan waivers and even defence without an adequate increase in taxes.[107] To finance its deficits, the Indian government in the 1980s borrowed heavily from both domestic financial institutions and commercial banks abroad.[108] This fiscal deficit had an adverse impact on India's balance of payments in the late 1980s; India found itself under mounting debt and dwindling foreign currency reserves.[109]

At the time, India's foreign exchange market was very underdeveloped and also tightly regulated under the *Foreign Exchange Regulation Act 1973*.[110] The secondary market of government securities was 'dormant',[111] while the financial markets were 'highly segmented', 'arguably inefficient'[112] and 'underdeveloped' in most respects—until the process of gradual reform commenced.[113]

---

106 Stuart Corbridge and John Harriss, 'The dialectics of reform: the state and economic liberalization' in *Reinventing India: Liberalization, Hindu Nationalism and Popular Democracy* (John Wiley & Sons, 2013) [7.2].

107 Ibid. For more literature on the economic reforms of India, see Isher Judge Ahluwalia and Ian Malcolm David Little, *India's Economic Reforms and Development: Essays for Manmohan Singh* (Oxford University Press, 2012).

108 Corbridge and Harriss (n 106).

109 Ibid. In 1991, India's reserves were so low that it had enough to pay only two weeks' worth of imports, while credit rating agencies such as Moody's and Standard and Poor downgraded India.

110 See Pradyot Ranjan Jena, 'Integration of financial markets in India: an empirical analysis' (2012). See also V Ananthakrishnan, 'Foreign exchange market of India' (1994) 7 *Journal of Foreign Exchange and International Finance* 394–99.

111 Jena (n 110).

112 Ibid.

113 RBI, 'Financial market evolution and globalisation' (n 11) 6.13.

Even though liberalisation brought economic benefits to India through an increase in competition and efficiency,[114] as liberalisation is known to have done in other parts of the world,[115] it is worth re-emphasising that India only turned to liberalisation because there was little other choice. This factor underscores India's general hesitation/reluctance or more cautious and gradual approach towards a liberalised economy. Another noteworthy aspect of this liberalisation is that all the reforms that were introduced along sector-specific, institution-based and rules-based lines reinforced the fragmented or segmented approach to financial regulation that continues to this day. Importantly, India's sectoral or fragmented approach to regulation predates its liberalisation reforms, making it necessary to reflect on early historical developments within the economic and financial sector.

Pre-liberalisation environment

The financial and economic environment prevailing in India before 1991 is significant for understanding why the country's financial sector is fragmented and segmented, as well as the rationale for its current approach for financial sector regulation. The pre-liberalisation era also highlights the underlying theme of welfare economy that continues to drive India and, to some extent, impairs the chances of more drastic and wider-ranging reforms.

The economic environment in early independent India

India's independence from the British in 1947 marked the beginning of its modern socio-economic era.[116] Prior to this, the primary economic activity in India was agriculture, in which large plots of land were owned by 'feudal lords' and smaller plots by other members of the population.[117] In Kaushik's words, India at the time of its independence from the British Raj was characterised by low productivity and output, abject poverty and illiteracy.[118]

---

114 See for example Petya Koeva Brooks, *The Performance of Indian Banks During Financial Liberalization* (IMF Working Paper 03/150, 2003), doi.org/10.5089/9781451856989.001.

115 On the benefits of liberalisation, see Sonia Khosa, 'A game-changer or a routine drill? Cooperation in the Indo-pacific securities markets' (2019) 47 *Australian Business Law Review* 182–199.

116 One of the first economic measures taken in this era was 'assessing the economic resources and productive capacity in existence': see SK Kaushik, 'India's evolving economic model: a perspective on economic and financial reforms' (1997) 56(1) *American Journal of Economics and Sociology* 70, doi.org/10.1111/j.1536-7150.1997.tb03452.x. India received independence from the British on 15 August 1947.

117 Ibid.

118 Ibid.

Against this backdrop, the economic model adopted post-independence was of 'self-reliance',[119] which placed barriers on foreign trade and investment.[120] During this time, even though the small-scale industries sector, among others, was given a boost, the move achieved limited success.[121] To intensify economic progress, India, under its first prime minister, Jawaharlal Nehru, adopted the concept of 'economic planning' to develop a 'two-sector model'—the first sector being 'agriculture' and the second industry.[122] In some sense, this sowed the seeds of the sectoral model that prevails in India's current approach to economic and financial growth and development.

The policies of this post-independence period yielded mixed results. On the one hand, they promoted self-sufficiency, diverted scarce resources into investments and actively discouraged and banned consumption of certain products through licensing[123] measures that proved beneficial for political stability.[124] On the other hand, modern industries of that era, such as the automobile sector, suffered, with academics asserting they were delayed for 40 years.[125] In this environment, India also witnessed a strict control on foreign exchange.[126] In hindsight, the policies adopted in this era made India suffer economic damage and miss many opportunities.[127]

---

119 See Shreekant Vattiikuti, 'Accelerating towards globalization: Indian securities regulation since 1992' (1997) 23 *North Carolina Journal of International Law and Commercial Regulation* 105. For a description of the socialist measures in India after its independence, see also D D'Monte, 'Market manipulation comes to India' (1992) 75(15) *The New Leader* 13.

120 Vattiikuti (n 119). For a description of India's foreign trade policy prior to 1991 reforms, see Raj G Javalagi and Vijay S Talluri, 'The emerging role of India in international business' (1996) 39(5) *Business Horizons* 79, 81–82, doi.org/10.1016/S0007-6813(96)90071-3.

121 See Kaushik (n 116). See also Ajit Dasgupta, 'India's cultural values and economic development: a comment' (1964) 13(1[Part1]) *Economic Development and Cultural Change* 100–102, doi.org/10.1086/450091; John Goheen et al, 'India's cultural values and economic development: a discussion' (1958) 7(1) *Economic Development and Cultural Change* 1–12, doi.org/10.1086/449776.

122 See Kaushik (n 116) 72. See also NA Khan, 'Resource mobilization from agriculture and economic development in India' (1963) 12(1) *Economic Development and Cultural Change* 42–54, doi. org/10.1086/450037.

123 Kaushik (n 116) 72. For more literature on India's early economic development model, see NA Sarma, 'Economic development in India: the first and second five year plans' (1958) 6(2) *International Monetary Fund Staff Papers* 180–238, doi.org/10.2307/3866051. On post-independence regulatory and licensing structures that guided private investment, see Jerome B Cohen, 'Problems of economic development in India' (1952) 1(3) *Economic Development and Cultural Change* 196–208, doi.org/10.1086/449619.

124 Kaushik (n 116).

125 Ibid. See Kangayappan Kumar, 'Some policy issues on mitigating poverty in India' (1973) 49(1) *Land Economics* 76–81, doi.org/10.2307/3145331.

126 Kaushik (n 116) 73. Incidentally, India was among the first signatories to the Bretton Woods agreement that established the IMF, which encouraged the principles of 'convertibility' and 'free movement of currencies'. See M Millikan, 'Economic thought and its application and methodology in India' (1956) 46(2) *American Economic Review* 399–407; W Malenbaum, 'Comparative costs and economic development: the experience of India' (1964) 54(3) *American Economic Review* 390–399.

127 Kaushik (n 116).

In conclusion, the sectoral approach adopted for economic development in post-independence India helped galvanise the country's limited resources to the sectors that were determined to be most significant. The downside was the creation of a siloed or segmented approach towards development that has come to be the norm in India, including for the financial sector.

The financial sector environment during 1947–91

The tightly regulated economic environment of newly independent India was also reflected in the financial sector. Mohan and Ray describe India's post-independence financial sector developments as falling within three distinct phases: the first phase, the 1950s and 1960s, was marked by 'underdeveloped banking'; the second phase, extending from the 1970s to the 1980s, comprised measures towards financial development that were 'accompanied by a degree of financial repression'; the third phase, beginning in the 1990s, has been characterised by 'gradual and calibrated financial deepening and liberalization'.[128] The following discussion traces significant developments in these stages across the financial sector.

In the banking sector,[129] during the first phase starting in 1947, there were just 97 scheduled[130] private banks, 557 'non-scheduled' small private banks that were 'organized as joint stock companies' and 395 'cooperative banks'.[131] This phase of development was marked by several events, such as the growth in joint stock banking companies and the introduction of deposit banking.[132] Concurrently, the productive sector had 'limited access

---

128 Mohan and Ray (n 15).

129 The post-independence banking era is discussed from the viewpoint of two significant events: a) the Bank 'nationalisation' drives of 1969 and 1980 in which banks were nationalised by the government to be used as instruments of social and welfare policies, and b) the Bank 'liberalisation' measures initiated by the RBI following the economic liberalisation policies adopted by the government post 1991. For the first category, see Joseph et al (n 79); Mohan (n 17); A Pandey, GL Sharma and VK Mehta, *Financial System and Its Regulation in India* (McGraw-Hill Education, 2015); Demetriades and Luintel (n 17) 21. For the second category, see Anand Pawar and M Pandya Nayak, 'Financial performance of public sector banks in India' (2013) 3(10) *International Journal of Management Research and Review* 3668.

130 'Scheduled' banks were banks 'which were included in the Second Schedule to the *RBI Act* and those banks in British India that subsequently became eligible for inclusion in this Schedule by virtue of their paid-up capital and reserves being more than Rs. 500,000 in the aggregate ... the power to include or exclude banks in or from the Schedule was vested with the Governor General in Council': see RBI, *Report on Currency and Finance, 2006–08* (2008) 1 & 2.

131 Mohan and Ray (n 15) 2. At this time of post-independence, the organised banking sector had three main participants: the Imperial Bank of India, joint-stock banks (this included both English and Indian joint stock banks) and foreign owned exchange banks.

132 Pan (n 105).

to finance' during this phase and there were several banking failures.[133] Overall, this phase, marked by low levels of government control, had elements of instability associated with a laissez faire market.

The limitations of this phase paved the way for the major financial developments of the second phase that started during the 1970s when several banks were nationalised.[134] According to Pan, this phase saw the 'introduction of social banking'.[135] Mohan and Ray argue that this phase exhibited 'classical symptoms of financial repression', including measures such as a 'high pre-emption of banks' investible resources' that led to the 'crowding out of credit to the private sector' and measures like quantitative ceilings on sectoral credit.[136] At the same time, some more successful initiatives, such as 'nationalisation and social control' of financial intermediaries, are attributed to this period.[137] There was a sharp rise in the number of banks in rural areas, contributing to an increase in deposited savings across the country.[138] Agriculture and many small-scale industries got a boost from the increased credit flow to rural sectors.[139] Finally, and importantly, there were no major financial collapses or failures in this period.[140] Eventually, this phase of stringent regulation and nationalisation paved the way for the 1991 reforms and a more open financial sector.

For the securities sector, it is important to mention that, until the 1991 liberalisation reforms, the securities markets in India were tightly regulated through a complex regulatory structure and 'extensive restrictions'.[141] Though the Bombay Stock Exchange had been in existence since 1875,[142] the securities markets, particularly the equity market, remained underdeveloped and ineffective.[143] The governance structure for the sector was 'archaic' and came under the purview of the Controller of Capital Issues under the Finance

---

133 In 1951, there were 566 commercial banks in operation but, by 1969, only 89 banks survived while others were amalgamated or liquidated in the period 1951–69: see RBI, *Report on Currency and Finance, 2006–08* (n 130).
134 Mohan and Ray (n 15).
135 Pan (n 105).
136 Mohan and Ray (n 15).
137 Rakesh Mohan, 'Financial sector reforms in India: policies and performance analysis' (2004) *Reserve Bank of India Bulletin* 852.
138 Ibid 852.
139 Ibid.
140 Ibid.
141 Ibid 851.
142 Other stock exchanges in India prior to its independence from the British in 1947 included the Madras Stock Exchange (now defunct), Ahmedabad Stock Exchange and the Calcutta Stock Exchange.
143 Mohan and Ray (n 15) 3.

Ministry.[144] The level of transparency and depth of the markets was low.[145] In the segment of fixed-income securities, government securities held a predominant share, the interest rates of which were fixed on the basis of an 'administered fiat'.[146] Mohan described the market for such government securities as a 'captive' one that required financial intermediaries to compulsorily invest in government securities to fulfil 'high statutory reserve requirements'.[147]

Overall, the broader economic and financial sector conditions and policies adopted during the pre-liberalisation era in India reflected a welfare-oriented, highly controlled, segmented and sectoral approach towards economic and financial growth and regulation. Some elements of this era continued to carry forward even after the 1991 liberalisation reforms, and to some extent prevail in India's current financial sector and regulation even today.

A critique, and the way ahead

India's economic liberalisation of 1991 marked a decisive shift from a 'bank-based' to a 'market-based' economy.[148] Liberalisation was prompted by the threat of severe economic collapse and resulted in a spate of radical and structural changes for the entire economy. In the financial sector, these reforms established a new regulatory system,[149] setting up new financial regulators such as SEBI,[150] IRDAI and PFRDA and the enactment of several major financial statutes.[151]

Notwithstanding the progressive outlook of the liberalisation measures, the reforms retained ties with the pre-liberalisation period, with several reforms constructed on the foundations of the former era. Thus, for

---

144 Ibid 3.

145 LC Gupta, 'Challenges before the Securities and Exchange Board of India' (1996) *Economic and Political Weekly* 751–757. See also LC Gupta, 'What ails the Indian capital market?' (1998) *Economic and Political Weekly* 1961–1966.

146 Mohan (n 137). Government bonds were catering to and financing the deficit of the government: see Mohan and Ray (n 15) 3.

147 Mohan (n 137).

148 Mohan and Ray (n 15) 18.

149 SK Samim Ferdows and Abhijit Roy, 'A study on the international diversification in the emerging equity market and its effect on the Indian capital market' (2012) *Contemporary Business Studies*.

150 SEBI was constituted on 12 April 1988 as a non-statutory body through an administrative resolution of the government with the objectives of dealing with development and regulation of the securities markets and investor protection; on 30 January 1992, SEBI acquired the status of a statutory body through an ordinance passed by the government that was replaced by the *Securities and Exchange Board of India Act 1992* on 4 April 1992. See *Trade Execution Cost of Equity Shares in India* (Working Paper No 6, January 2002).

151 See Ila Patnaik and Ajay Shah, 'Fundamental redesign of financial law: the Indian approach' (2015) 14(1) *India Review* 92, doi.org/10.1080/14736489.2015.1004257.

example, liberalisation measures were rolled out within rigid constructs of a segmented and sectoral frame that in turn affirmed the institution-based approach to regulation. Further, several elements of the 'command and control economy' that involved 'containing and controlling financial markets and banning activity' continued to survive in the post-liberalisation financial sector framework, instead of achieving 'sophisticated interventions' to address 'market failures'.[152] Similarly, many older financial laws—enacted during the pre-independence era and deeply out of touch with current realities—also survived.[153] Finally, the restrained and conservative approach to regulation that favours stability over innovation continues to be reflected in a heavily rules-based and risk-averse approach to financial regulation.[154]

Further, although liberalisation reforms progressed in the right direction, they were arguably inadequate,[155] thus prompting repeated calls[156] and some efforts[157] towards a rigorous financial sector reorganisation and reform. The most prominent effort to redraw financial law in India in the recent decade unfolded in 2011 with the establishment of the FSLRC under the chairmanship of a former judge of the Supreme Court of India, Justice BN Srikrishna. The commission submitted a report[158] containing a thorough analysis of the financial regulatory architecture along with a draft Indian Financial Code (IFC) to 'replace the bulk of the existing financial laws'.[159] The report aimed to revamp the fragmented financial regulatory approach that was fraught with 'regulatory gaps, overlaps, inconsistencies and regulatory arbitrage',[160] and to that end proposed a draft IFC comprising a non-sectoral, principles-based framework for financial regulation with

---

152 Patnaik and Shah, *Reforming India's Financial System* (n 80) 7.

153 Patnaik and Shah, 'Fundamental redesign of financial law' (n 151). Both the *RBI Act 1934* and *Insurance Act 1938* are examples of near century-old laws.

154 See generally YV Reddy, 'Financial sector regulation in India' (2010) 45(14) *Economic and Political Weekly*.

155 See generally Patnaik and Shah, 'Fundamental redesign of financial law' (n 151).

156 See for example Richard Herd et al, 'Financial sector reform in India: time for a second wave?' (2011). See also Saugata Bhattacharya and Urjit R Patel, 'Reform strategies in the Indian financial sector' in *India's and China's Recent Experience with Reform and Growth* (Springer, 2005) 91–131. See also Prasad (n 73).

157 For example, see Government of India Planning Commission (n 63); Government of India, *Report of the Financial Sector Legislative Reforms Commission* (22 March 2013).

158 The FSLRC report comprises two volumes. Volume I contains the analysis and recommendations: see Government of India, 'Volume I: analysis and recommendations', *Report of the Financial Sector Legislative Reforms Commission* (2013). Volume II contains the proposed draft law, the Indian Financial Code: see Government of India, 'Volume II: draft law', *Report of the Financial Sector Legislative Reforms Commission* (2013).

159 Vishnu Padmanabhan, 'Financial Sector Legislative Reforms Commission' (Blog Post), prsindia. org/policy/report-summaries/financial-sector-legislative-reforms-commission.

160 See 'Executive Summary' in Government of India, 'Volume I: analysis and recommendations' (n 158) xiii.

nine distinct components.[161] The main elements of the draft IFC included adopting ownership neutrality;[162] making the Reserve Bank of India (RBI) the banking and payments system regulator; establishing a unified financial agency to subsume regulators like SEBI, IRDAI, PFRDA and the Forwards Market Commission (FMC);[163] establishing the FSDC as the statutory agency for systemic risk and development;[164] establishing a unified Financial Sector Appellate Tribunal to replace the existing Securities Appellate Tribunal for all finance appeals;[165] and setting up two new entities, the Debt Management Agency and the Financial Redressal Agency, to manage debt independently and hear all consumer complaints.[166]

The FSLRC's report was 'the first comprehensive effort after the 2008 crisis to introspect and improve institutional structures' and recommend fresh, legal and regulatory architecture for the financial sector, constituting a massive overhaul.[167] Apart from limited criticism,[168] the report has generally been well received with positive reviews.[169] In spite of this, the IFC, as recommended by the FSLRC, has not been implemented.[170]

While there are no clear or officially stated reasons to explain the delay in the adoption of the IFC, several factors point to a general reluctance towards initiating an extensive revamp of the financial sector. First, and

161 These nine components address the following aspects of financial sector regulation: consumer protection, micro-prudential regulation, resolution, capital controls, systemic risk, development and redistribution, monetary policy, public debt management and contract, trading and market abuse: see Padmanabhan (n 159). See also Sunitha Natti, 'Financial sector reforms: a status check', *The Indian Express* (online, 29 May 2019), newindianexpress.com/business/2019/may/29/financial-sector-reforms-a-status-check-1983063.html.

162 The draft IFC proposed a framework in which governance standards for regulated entities do not depend on the form of organisation of financial firm or its ownership structure, and, resultantly, regulatory treatment of public and private entities would be identical: see Government of India, 'Volume I: analysis and recommendations' (n 158) 17.

163 Ibid 134.

164 Government of India, Ministry of Finance, 'Financial Stability and Development Council (FSDC)' (3 May 2013), pib.gov.in/newsite/PrintRelease.aspx?relid=95543.

165 Securities Appellate Tribunal, 'Introduction', satweb.sat.gov.in/.

166 See Padmanabhan (n 159).

167 Bhagwati, Khan and Bogathi (n 64) 56.

168 See for example K Kanagasabapathy, 'The Indian Financial Code: the good, the bad and the ugly' (2015) *Economic and Political Weekly* 12–15. See also Raghuram Rajan, 'Financial Sector Legislative Reforms Committee Report (FSLRC): what to do and when?', *RBI Monthly Bulletin*; Ashoak Upadhyay, 'One regulator too many?' *Business Line* (online, 13 March 2018), thehindubusinessline.com/opinion/columns/ashoak-upadhyay/one-regulator-too-many/article20804816.ece1.

169 See for example Patnaik and Shah, 'Fundamental redesign of financial law' (n 151); Patnaik and Shah, *Reforming India's Financial System* (n 80); Rajan (n 168).

170 Sneha Alexander, 'How to reform India's financial sector', *Mint* (online, 20 May 2019). It is not entirely clear as to why the IFC was not implemented, but several amendments were proposed to the IFC draft leading to a second draft proposed by the government. See generally Kanagasabapathy (n 168).

at the risk of oversimplification, India's past economic journey reveals a general disinclination for drastic reform, unless there is simply no other choice.[171] The liberalisation overhaul of the 1990s was carried out in the face of acute necessity; it was not a matter of choice or preferred policy. Since the India of today is neither bankrupt nor in dire straits, as it was in the early 1990s, there is little urgency or incentive for a massive overhaul. Hence, a piecemeal approach is preferred to reorganise the financial sector architecture. Second, even though the liberalisation reforms were radical and fast-paced in the initial years, subsequent reforms followed a more gradual approach, a feature that is almost institutionalised in the Indian growth story. Moreover, since continuous, gradual reforms over the past decades have yielded positive results,[172] there is a sense that even with a piecemeal approach, financial sector reforms will continue to yield positive outcomes, albeit slowly. Third, a revolutionary overhaul, as recommended by the FSLRC report, would consolidate the role and powers of some authorities and negatively impact the domain of other authorities,[173] which is unlikely to be equally palatable to all governmental, regulatory and other stakeholders.[174]

While these challenges render it difficult to introduce radical reforms and a fast-tracked implementation of the IFC through a singular measure, the FSLRC report and the draft IFC are still relevant and present a desirable and far more conducive framework for the financial sector. Reforms initiated in recent years[175] appear to have been implemented slowly, through a 'piecemeal approach', even though it is not entirely clear if the country will see a full implementation of the FSLRC recommendations.[176]

---

171 However, it is interesting to note that, time and again, when pushed to the corner, India has opted for drastic policies, including the GST revamp for the country.

172 For example, as a consequence of the reforms, the Bombay Stock Exchange and the National Stock Exchange are today among the top 10 capital markets of the world from the viewpoint of market capitalisation and although they lag behind the other significant world stock exchanges on the count of 'liquidity', they are impressive on several other counts: see Chakrabarti (n 38).

173 See generally Rajan (n 168) 4. For instance, the FSLRC recommended government managing its own debt instead of giving it to RBI to manage.

174 In the context of revolutionary banking reform, 'there are strong interests against change' and the 'greatest stumbling block has been the government, the bureaucracy and the interests within it': see Viral V Acharya and Raghuram G Rajan, *Indian Banks: A Time to Reform?* (University of Chicago Booth School of Business Working Paper No 7, 2020).

175 Several measures in the financial sector indicate that the process of reform in the financial sector is well begun. First, the merger of SEBI and FMC indicates a step to consolidate the functions of two regulators. Second, the role and responsibilities of the judicial appellate body for securities, the Securities Appellate Tribunal, have been extended to take up appeals of the entire financial sector.

176 For examples of the recommendations accepted and put into practice, see Bhagwati, Khan and Bogathi (n 64).

In sum, India's current financial sector architecture is complex and recent developments suggest that it is on the cusp of introducing a further set of structural reforms. Given this, what can realistically be expected in the short to medium term?

First, although a radical overhaul of financial regulatory architecture may be overdue, given the complexity of issues and multiplicity of stakeholders, a radical transformation looks improbable, unless driven by a major crisis.[177] What is exceedingly likely is that reform will continue to be ushered in at the fringes, in a measured and gradual manner, and there are strong indications to suggest that such reform is already underway.[178] While this gradual approach would result in significant delays and, arguably, missed opportunities, the silver lining is that such reforms are continuing in the right direction, allowing all stakeholders to build capacity, prepare and adjust to the changes.

Second, in the absence of a massive financial sector overhaul, the adoption of several sophisticated measures for regulating the fast-changing financial environment, particularly emerging from the rise of fintech firms, hybrid financial products and systemically important institutions, is very probable. Hence, an attempt to consolidate the segmented approach to regulation, including through strengthened, formal and more refined coordination mechanisms and channels, is likely to be prioritised and continue at a faster pace.[179]

---

177 The NSEL payment crisis of 2014 that led to the collapse of India's biggest spot exchange is said to have contributed to the FMC–SEBI merger in 2015: see Santanu Chakraborty, Abhishek Shanker and Siddhartha Singh, 'Govt planning Sebi–FMC merger after NSEL collapse: report', *Mint* (online, 20 January 2014), livemint.com/Politics/JnshZdKzzceE3g9OnlyvKN/Govt-planning-SebiFMC-merger-after-NSEL-collapse-sources.html.

178 For instance, the first instance of consolidation in the financial sector occurred in 2015 with the repeal of the *Forward Contracts Regulation Act 1952* and the regulation of commodities derivatives market shifting to SEBI with effect from 28 September 2015, thus marking the merger of the Forwards Market Commission (FMC) with SEBI: see 'FMC to be merged with Sebi from September 28', *Business Today* (online, 2 September 2015), businesstoday.in/markets/stocks/story/fmc-sebi-merger-from-sept-28-arun-jaitley-52190-2015-09-02. See also Ashish Rukhaiyar, 'Budget 2015: FMC to be merged with Sebi', *Mint* (online, 28 February 2015), livemint.com/Politics/ui91waHGuyV5fSlmmspyRM/FMC-to-be-merged-with-Sebi-Jaitley.html.

Another example of consolidation of the financial sector architecture is the increase in the mandate given to the Securities Appellate Tribunal that now hears appeals from not just SEBI, but PFRDA and IRDA too: see Securities Appellate Tribunal (n 165).

179 See generally YV Reddy, 'Regulation of financial sector in developing countries: lessons from the 2008 financial crisis' (2009). Given the uniqueness of the Indian experience, establishing standing mechanisms including technical committees, for close and constant coordination among regulatory authorities, is considered more desirable.

Third, it is doubtful that a principles-based approach to regulation will fully replace the existing rules-based approach, owing mainly to the current maturity level of the financial market, institutions and participants. However, it is likely that a principles-based approach will be ushered in gradually and selectively by regulators after 'reasonable assurance of sound practices of governance'.[180]

Fourth, India's risk-averse and conservative approach to regulation is unlikely to whither, presenting a constant challenge to innovation. This risk-averse approach is not entirely undesirable, considering that the Indian financial sector's relative resilience and stability during the GFC has been attributed to its continuing conservative outlook to regulation. However, a balance between innovation and stability is far more desirable.

India's economic and financial sector journey of the post-independence era reveals the rationale for its current approach to financial sector regulation. The general approach and characteristics of financial regulation in India as discussed in this chapter are relevant and directly applicable to the securities sector and its regulation. Due to the vast size and complexities of the financial sector, and challenges outlined in this chapter, it is difficult to assess the next set of reforms that will be implemented, or the pace of these reforms. However, what is undoubtedly clear is that India's financial sector reform journey is currently underway, and headed in the right direction, strengthening the case for a deeper collaboration with other jurisdictions.

An overview of the Australian financial system

The financial sector dominates Australia's economy and is 'a key driver of economic growth' that is connected globally with increasing 'cross border financial flows'.[181] Despite high global financial linkages,[182] the system proved

---

180 Ibid.
181 Australian Government, The Treasury, 'The strength of Australia's financial sector' (2016), treasury. gov.au/publication/backing-australian-fintech/the-strength-of-australias-financial-sector. Australia's four main banks rank as the world's largest banks by market capitalisation and for safety and profitability. See also Jennifer G Hill, 'Why did Australia fare so well in the global financial crisis?' (2012). On international capital flows and challenges, see K Henry, 'Mutual recognition of financial services regulation: opportunities and challenges for Australia' (Address to the ASIC Summer School, Our Financial Markets: The Big Issues, Melbourne, Australia, 20 February 2008), treasury.gov.au/speech/mutual-recognition-of-financial-services-regulation-opportunities-and-challenges-for-australia.
182 See generally Ferran, 'The break-up of the Financial Services Authority' (n 52).

stable during the GFC,[183] with the Organisation for Economic Co-operation and Development (OECD) noting that it was 'one of the most resilient in the OECD during the global economic and financial crisis'.[184]

Structure

Several institutions make up the Australian financial system. Authorised deposit-taking institutions (ADIs), comprising mainly banks, credit unions and building societies, account for more than half the share of total financial system assets.[185] Insurance and superannuation funds also contribute in a major way to total financial system assets,[186] as do registered financial corporations, securitisation vehicles and managed funds.[187] The following discussion details some of the main financial institutions under two headings: ADIs and non-bank financial entities (NBFEs).

ADIs

ADIs[188] hold around 55 per cent of the total assets of Australian financial institutions, constituting the largest part of the financial system.[189] ADIs comprise institutions such as banks, building societies, credit unions and other deposit-taking institutions authorised by the regulator, the Australian Prudential Regulatory Authority (APRA).[190]

---

183 See Hill (n 181) 10 (unlike in the UK and the US). Australia, much like Canada, did not bail out any major financial institutions during the GFC: see W Swan, 'Emerging from the Crisis: The G20 and the Asia-Pacific' (Address to Canada 2020 and the Canadian Australian Chamber of Commerce, Toronto, Canada, 27 June 2010).

184 OECD, 'OECD Economic Surveys: Australia 2010—overview' (2010) 2.

185 Bernadette Donovan and Adam Gorajek, 'Developments in the structure of the Australian financial system' (June 2011) *RBA Bulletin* 29. ADIs contributed approximately $5,355 billion at the end of 30 June 2021: see APRA, *APRA Annual Report 2020–21* (2021) 12.

186 Australia's total superannuation assets were $3,303.2 billion at the end of June 2021: see APRA, 'APRA releases superannuation statistics for June 2021' (24 August 2021), apra.gov.au/news-and-publications/apra-releases-superannuation-statistics-for-june-2021. The life and general insurance market in Australia recorded assets of approximately $129 and $135 billion, respectively, at the end of June 2021: see APRA, *APRA Annual Report 2020–21* (n 185) 12. See also Donovan and Gorajek (n 185). Insurance and superannuation funds hold almost a quarter of the financial system assets.

187 Donovan and Gorajek (n 185). These contribute to a much lesser degree as compared with the ADIs, insurance and superannuation funds.

188 Section 9 of the *Corporations Act 2001* (Cth) (*Corporations Act*) defines an ADI as: a) an ADI (authorised deposit-taking institution) within the meaning of the *Banking Act 1959* Cth) (*Banking Act*); and b) a person who carries on state banking within the meaning of para 51(xiii) of the Constitution. Section 5 of the *Banking Act* defines an ADI as 'a body corporate in relation to which an authority under s 9(3) [of the *Banking Act*] is in force'.

189 Royal Commission into Misconduct in the Banking, Superannuation and Financial Services Industry, *Background Paper 1: Some Features of the Australian Banking Industry* (2018) 3. As of 30 June 2021, there were 143 ADIs registered with APRA: see APRA, *APRA Annual Report 2020–21* (n 185) 12.

190 An ADI is a financial organisation, or a body corporate, authorised by APRA to conduct banking business: see King & Wood Mallesons (Mallesons), 'Regulation of the Australian financial system' in John Stumbles (ed), *Australian Finance Law* (Thomson Reuters, 7th ed, 2016) 19.

Among ADIs, banks play a pivotal role for the financial system, serving all sectors of the economy.[191] Through their banking subsidiaries, banks also provide funds management and insurance services.[192] Building societies raise funds mainly in the form of deposits from households, and provide loan amounts (such as mortgage finance for owner-occupied housing) and payment services.[193] Credit unions are mutually owned bodies that provide deposit, personal and housing loans payment services to their members.[194] Both building societies and credit unions are governed by APRA and also hold significant assets under management.[195]

NBFEs

NBFEs also contribute to the financial system.[196] NBFEs are not authorised to take deposits and are generally not subject to prudential regulation.[197] The main NBFEs are discussed under two headings: non-ADI financial intermediaries and managed funds.

Non-ADIs

Non-ADIs intermediate between lenders and borrowers but are not authorised to accept deposits.[198] Sometimes referred to as 'registered financial corporations', they are not supervised by APRA but instead are monitored

---

191 Banks account for nearly 97 per cent of the total ADI assets in Australia: see Donovan and Gorajek (n 185). As of 30 June 2021, there were 97 banks regulated by APRA with $5,290 billion assets under management: see APRA, *APRA Annual Report 2020–21* (n 185) 12. In Australia, the banking sector includes wealth management firms.

192 RBA, 'The structure of the Australian financial system: Appendix' in *Financial Stability Review* (2006). Foreign banks that are authorised by APRA to operate within Australia are required to keep their deposit-taking activities restricted to wholesale markets.

193 Ibid. Although these societies were mostly mutually owned, they are now increasingly issuing share capital and becoming public. As of 2019, there were only two registered societies with APRA: see APRA, *Annual Report 2018–19* (2019) 25.

194 RBA (n 192).

195 APRA, *Annual Report 2018–19* (n 193) 15. As of 30 June 2021, there were 37 registered credit unions and building societies with $58 billion assets under management.

196 NBFEs are also referred to as non-bank financial institutions or as shadow banking: see David G Millhouse, 'From Campbell to Hayne: w[h]ither Australia? Australian financial regulation and supervision at a cross-roads' (2019) 13(2–3) *Law and Financial Markets Review* 81, 95, doi.org/10.1080/17521440.2019.1602696. NBFEs provide benefits from broader access to financial services, promote competition and diversification of the financial sector and include financial advice and wealth management, bank controlled wealth management entities, non-bank financial products providers, collective investment schemes, investment managers, trustees, custodians, research houses, asset allocation consultants, securities brokers, securities platforms, hedge funds, insurance entities, finance companies, workers entitlement funds, and superannuation entities (public, industry corporate and self-managed super funds).

197 Millhouse (n 196) (other than some superannuation entities).

198 RBA, 'The structure of the Australian financial system: registered financial corporations' in *Financial Stability Review* (2006).

by ASIC through conduct and disclosure regulations specified for the non-financial corporate sector. The main non-ADI intermediaries include money market corporations,[199] finance companies[200] and securitisation vehicles.[201]

Managed funds

Managed funds, also known as pooled or collective investments or managed investment schemes, refer to a pooled contribution of 'money or money's worth' by multiple investors to get an interest in the scheme.[202] A 'responsible entity' or 'fund manager' operates the scheme without investors having any day-to-day control.[203] Australia's managed funds sector is mainly supervised by ASIC.[204] Legislative changes in retirement savings arrangements and investors seeking higher returns than what has been traditionally available under ADIs have contributed to this growth.[205]

Within the managed funds sector, superannuation funds hold the biggest percentage of funds under management, followed by insurance companies.[206] Superannuation funds accept and manage compulsory contributions from employers and/or employees with the aim of providing retirement income benefits.[207] Such funds are controlled by trustees who use professional funds managers and advisers.[208] At the end of June 2021, there were 27 life insurance companies in Australia with A$133 billion in assets under

---

199 Money market corporations holding over A$50 million assets under management operate mainly in the wholesale markets. They borrow from and lend to large corporations and government agencies, and engage in other services such as advisory, relating to corporate finance, capital markets, foreign exchange and investment management. See RBA (n 192).

200 Finance companies give loans to households and to small- and medium-sized businesses. These companies 'raise funds from wholesale markets and, using debentures and unsecured notes, from retail investors': see ibid.

201 Finally, securitisation involves the use of special purpose vehicles that issue securities backed by a pool of assets such as mortgage-based housing loans. Most securities are credit enhanced through use of guarantees from third parties. See RBA, 'The structure of the Australian financial system: securitisation vehicles' in *Financial Stability Review* (2006). See also RBA (n 192).

202 Australian Securities and Investments Commission (ASIC), 'Managed funds', asic.gov.au/regulatory-resources/funds-management/.

203 Ibid.

204 Mallesons (n 190).

205 RBA, 'The structure of the Australian financial system: managed funds' in *Financial Stability Review* (2006).

206 See APRA, *APRA Annual Report 2020–21* (n 185) 12.

207 RBA, 'The structure of the Australian financial system' (n 205).

208 Ibid. Within the superannuation funds is another category, approved deposit funds (ADFs), which are managed by professional fund managers. Similar to superannuation funds, ADFs accept superannuation lump sums and eligible redundancy payments when a person resigns, retires or is made redundant by their workplace. Both superannuation funds and ADFs invest in an array of assets such as equity, property, debt securities and deposits.

management.[209] Primarily supervised by APRA, their assets are managed in statutory funds on a fiduciary basis, and are mostly invested in equities and debt securities.[210] Similarly, general insurance companies are also regulated by APRA and provide insurance, such as property, motor vehicles and employers' liability.[211] APRA also governs friendly societies[212]—mutually owned cooperative financial institutions offering benefits to their members through a trust-like structure.[213]

Finally, other regulated institutions, including public unit trusts,[214] cash management trusts[215] and trust companies,[216] also operate within the Australian financial system and contribute to varying degrees.

Legal and regulatory framework

Australia has a sophisticated regulatory system for the financial sector,[217] commonly referred to as the twin peaks.[218] It is a function or objectives-based regulatory system,[219] with distinct 'prudential' and 'conduct' regulators. Together, APRA and ASIC form the twin peaks, with the Reserve Bank of

209 APRA, *APRA Annual Report 2020–21* (n 185) 12.
210 RBA 'The structure of the Australian financial system' (n 205).
211 APRA, *APRA Annual Report 2020–21* (n 185) 12. At the end of June 2021, there were 93 general insurers with $150 billion assets under management.
212 At the end of June 2021, there were 11 friendly societies registered with APRA with $9 billion assets: see APRA, *APRA Annual Report 2020–21* (n 185) 12.
213 Friendly societies provide investment products through insurance or education bonds, and also insurance relating to funeral, accident or sicknesses: see RBA 'The structure of the Australian financial system' (n 205).
214 These are pooled investors' funds, drawn from a particular category of assets, such as cash equities, property, money market investments, mortgages and overseas securities; such trusts are mainly managed by bank's subsidiaries, insurance companies or money market corporations: ibid.
215 Regulated by ASIC, cash management trusts are another type of unit trust; they usually have investments in financial securities in the short-term money market, are governed by a trust deed and are open to the public: see ibid.
216 Trust companies, also referred to as common funds, are under the regulatory purview of state authorities: see ibid. They collect money from the public, or hold money on behalf of estates, or under powers of attorney and pool it into common funds. Funds are then invested into various assets such as money market instruments, equities and mortgages.
217 The Treasury, 'The strength of Australia's financial sector' (n 181).
218 See generally Andrew Godwin and Andrew Schmulow, 'Introduction: the genealogy and topography of twin peaks' in Andrew Godwin and Andrew Schmulow (eds), *The Cambridge Handbook of Twin Peaks Financial Regulation* (Cambridge University Press, 2021), doi.org/10.1017/9781316890592. See also Pamela Hanrahan, 'Twin peaks after Hayne: tensions and trade-offs in regulatory architecture' (2019) 13(2–3) *Law and Financial Markets Review*, doi.org/10.1080/17521440.2019.1622849.
219 See generally Schmulow, 'The four methods of financial system regulation' (n 55).

Australia (RBA) sometimes referred to as the third peak. The twin-peaks model of regulation, illustrated in Figure 2.5,[220] is discussed at length in the next section.

Reserve Bank of Australia	Australian Prudential Regulatory Authority	Australian Securities and Investments Commission

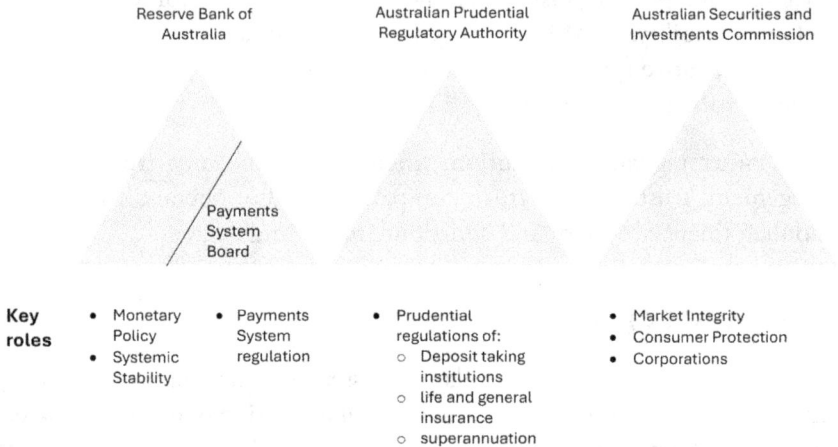

Payments System Board

Key roles	• Monetary Policy • Systemic Stability	• Payments System regulation	• Prudential regulations of: ○ Deposit taking institutions ○ life and general insurance ○ superannuation	• Market Integrity • Consumer Protection • Corporations

Figure 2.5: Main regulatory agencies in the Australian financial sector

Source: Adapted from Australian Government, The Treasury, 'Globalization and the role of institution building in the financial sector — the policy response' (*G-20 Case Study: An Australian Perspective*, 2003).

The following tables outline the role and functions of Australia's financial authorities and the main legislation that guides their functioning.[221] They also outline the roles of other financial authorities, including the Treasury and the competition and consumer regulator, the Australian Competition and Consumer Commission (ACCC).[222]

---

220 Australian Government, The Treasury, 'Globalization and the role of institution building in the financial sector—the policy response' (*G-20 Case Study: An Australian Perspective,* 2003).

221 Prudence Weaver, 'Can too many regulators be too much of a good thing?' (2011) 22 *Journal of Banking and Finance Law and Practice* 201.

222 The ACCC is an independent Commonwealth statutory authority whose mandate is to enforce the *Competition and Consumer Act 2010* (Cth) along with other legislation, promote competition and fair trading, and regulate the national infrastructure for Australia: see Australian Competition and Consumer Commission, 'About the ACCC', www.accc.gov.au/about-us/accc-role-and-structure/about-the-accc.

Table 2.7: Market and conduct

Australian Securities and Investments Commission (ASIC)	
Legislation	Details
Australian Securities and Investments Commission Act 2001 (Cth) (ASIC Act) Corporations Act 2001 (Cth) (Corporations Act)	ASIC, Australia's corporate markets, financial services and consumer credit regulator, is established under the ASIC Act.[223] ASIC's corporate mandate and regulatory activities include regulation of companies, financial markets and services, entities and professionals dealing in, or advising consumers in, 'investments, superannuation, insurance, deposit taking and credit'.[224] ASIC regulates managed investment schemes and consumer protection issues pertaining to all financial service providers, including the institutions that are regulated by APRA, such as banking institutions.[225]
	The ASIC Act sets out detailed objectives for ASIC that include maintaining, facilitating and improving the performance of the financial system and the entities functioning within the system.[226] The Act requires ASIC to achieve these in the 'interests of commercial certainty, reducing business costs, and the efficiency and development of the economy'.[227]
	Issues relating to consumer protection in respect of financial services are dealt with under the ASIC Act (which mirrors provisions in the Competition and Consumer Act 2010 [Cth] discussed below) and the Corporations Act provisions for 'retail clients'. ASIC also has powers under other sector-specific legislation that apply to financial products and services.[228] (Chapters 3–8 of this book discuss ASIC's role and responsibilities in the securities sector.)

223 ASIC is an independent Australian government body established as a body corporate with continued existence under the *Australian Securities and Investments Commission Act 2001* (Cth) (*ASIC Act*): see s 8 of the *ASIC Act*. In its earlier avatar, ASIC existed as the securities regulator, Australian Securities Commission (ASC), and became ASIC on 1 July 1998: see Mallesons (n 190) 10 [1.30]. See also Gail Pearson, *Financial Services Law and Compliance in Australia* (Cambridge University Press, 2009) 41 [2.3.3], doi.org/10.1017/CBO9781139113816.

ASIC's enforcement activities centre around violations of the *Corporations Act*, the *ASIC Act* and other Acts that regulate financial matters, such as insurance, superannuation and managed funds: see Helen Louise Bird et al, 'ASIC enforcement patterns' (2004)(71) *Public Law Research Paper*; Australian Securities and Investments Commission, 'Our role', asic.gov.au/about-asic/what-we-do/our-role/#what. See also Sharon Horgan, *Finance Law of Australia* (Butterworths, 2001) 8.

224 IMF, *Australia: IOSCO Objectives and Principles of Securities Regulation—Detailed Assessment of Implementation* (IMF Staff Country Report No 12/314, 2012) (*Australia Country Report*) 7, doi.org/10.5089/9781475563412.002. ASIC regulates market integrity and consumer protection by maintaining high investor confidence in markets and their protection against misconduct, unfair and fraudulent trade practises: see Horgan (n 223, 7).

225 Mallesons (n 190) 9.

226 *ASIC Act* s 1(2). See also Mallesons (n 190) 9.

227 See *ASIC Act* s 1(2). ASIC's other objectives include promoting confident and informed investors and consumers, administering laws effectively with minimum procedural requirements, receiving and storing information, ensuring availability of such information to the public, and taking whatever action is possible and necessary to enforce and give effect to Commonwealth laws.

228 For example, other statutes bestow ASIC with consumer protection responsibilities, such as the *Insurance Contracts Act 1984* (Cth), *Superannuation Act 1993* (Cth), *Superannuation Industry (Supervision) Act 1993* (Cth), *Retirement Savings Accounts Act 1997* (Cth), *Life Insurance Act 1995* (Cth), *Medical Indemnity (Prudential Supervision and Product Standards) Act 2003* (Cth).

Table 2.8: Prudential

Australian Prudential Regulatory Authority (APRA)	
Main Legislation	**Details**
Australian Prudential Regulation Authority Act 1998 (Cth) (*'APRA Act 1998'*)	APRA, the prudential regulator for banking, superannuation and insurance, is set up under the *APRA Act 1998*.[229] APRA is an independent authority with two main responsibilities: supervise institutions across banking, insurance and superannuation, and promote financial system stability in Australia. APRA oversees how financial institutions manage their risks and meet financial obligations so that the financial system remains strong and robust.[230] It balances differing objectives such as financial safety and efficiency, competition, contestability and competitive neutrality,[231] and derives its mandate from sector-specific legislations.[232]
	APRA follows a risk-based approach to regulation and aims at consistency and uniformity in its approach.[233] Such Australian financial services licence[234] holders that are regulated by APRA are exempt from requirements of the *Corporations Act 2001* relating to financial, technological and human resources and risk management as APRA's provisions on these aspects are regarded as sufficient.[235] APRA's Annual Report FY 2020–21 states the number of APRA-regulated institutions as 2,109 and the total worth of its assets as $7,927 billion (Table A1.1).[236]

---

229 See Pearson, *Financial Services Law* (n 223) 28 [2.3.2]; Steve Kourabas, 'Improving Australia's regulatory framework for systemic financial stability' (2018) 195. APRA regulates the prudential aspects of banks, life insurers, general insurers, building societies, credit unions, friendly societies and superannuation: see Australian Prudential Regulatory Authority, 'About APRA', apra.gov.au/about-apra.
230 On how APRA maintains prudential regulation, see APRA, 'About APRA' (n 229). APRA's responsibilities include creating and enforcing standards in the financial sector, advising the Australian government regarding regulatory policy and ensuring stability of the entire system from extremely risky, ill-advised behaviour or fraud and negligence by financial services companies: see Mallesons (n 190) 4 [1.15].
231 See *Australian Prudential Regulation Authority Act 1998* (Cth) s 8(2). See also APRA, *Annual Report 2014–15* 94, apra.gov.au/news-and-publications/apra-annual-reports.
232 These include the *Banking Act 1959, Insurance Act 1973, Private Health Insurance (Prudential Supervision) Act 2015* and the *Superannuation Industry (Supervision) Act 1993*. For the complete list of enabling legislation that applies to APRA, see APRA, 'Enabling legislation', apra.gov.au/enabling-legislation. An example of APRA's powers is an ADI that fails to discharge its obligations can be acted against by the APRA, for which APRA has investigative powers, and powers to 'assume control and carry on the business of the ADI': see Mallesons (n 190) 6 [1.15].
233 See APRA, 'About APRA' (n 229). The main areas that APRA looks into are capital adequacy, liquidity, large exposures, associations with related entities, credit quality, outsourcing, securitisation, covered bonds, and audit and related matters: see Mallesons (n 190) 5 [1.15]. For literature exploring APRA's risk-based regulation, see Julia Black, 'Managing regulatory risks and defining the parameters of blame: a focus on the Australian Prudential Regulation Authority' (2006) 28(1) *Law & Policy* 1–30, doi. org/10.1111/j.1467-9930.2005.00215.x. See also Pearson, *Financial Services Law* (n 223) 45 [2.3.3.2].
234 AFSL holders come within the regulatory purview of ASIC. The AFSL regime is discussed in detail in Chapter 8 of this book.
235 See *Corporations Act* s 912A. ASIC oversees the functioning of the other AFSL holders that are not subjected to APRA's regulation, including ensuring compliance with their prudential requirements.
236 APRA, *APRA Annual Report 2020–21* (n 185) 12.

Table 2.9: Monetary policy, systemic stability and payments

Reserve Bank of Australia (RBA)	
Legislation	**Details**
Reserve Bank Act 1959 (Cth) (*Reserve Bank Act*)	Australia's central bank, the RBA,[237] derives its powers and responsibilities under the Reserve Bank Act.[238] The RBA's responsibilities include contributing to the stability of the financial system and the maintenance of liquidity.[239] To achieve these objectives, the RBA is empowered but not obligated to provide a 'lender of last resort' facility to commercial banks.[240]
	The RBA provides specialised banking services to the Australian government and its agencies, other central banks and overseas official institutions, and also provides registry services to a number of foreign institutions that include the Asian Development Bank and the International Bank for Reconstruction and Developments.[241] In relation to the securities markets, the RBA provides services such as issuance of securities, transfer and registration of securities and distribution of interest payments and redemption proceeds at maturity.[242]

Table 2.10: Government

Australian Treasury
The Australian Treasury plays an important role in maintaining financial stability by advising the Australian government on relevant issues and events as well as on any matters relating to the legislative and regulatory framework that supports the financial system.[243]

---

237 The governance structure for the RBA is organised under two boards: the Reserve Bank Board, which bears responsibility for monetary policy and financial stability; and the Payments System Board, which 'has the responsibility for matters relating to payments system policy': see Reserve Bank of Australia, 'Governance', rba.gov.au/about-rba/governance.html.

238 *Reserve Bank Act 1959* (Cth).

239 Horgan (n 223) 5. In terms of s 10(2) of the *Reserve Bank Act 1959* (Cth), the RBA is required to contribute to the stability of the Australian currency, the maintenance of full employment in Australia, and the economic prosperity and welfare of Australians: see RBA, 'Our role', rba.gov.au/about-rba/our-role. html. The RBA pursues these goals by 'setting the cash rate to meet an agreed medium-term inflation target', maintaining a 'strong financial system and efficient payments systems', and issuing bank notes for Australia.

240 See Mallesons (n 190) 12. The RBA, in maintaining a stable financial system, does not guarantee each and every financial institution facing difficulties if they do not impact the overall stability of the financial system.

241 RBA, 'Banking services', rba.gov.au/fin-services/banking.html. In recent years, the RBA's focus has been around issues related to monetary policy for Australia while striving to keep the inflation between 2–3 per cent each year: Mallesons (n 190) 13.

242 RBA, 'Registry services', rba.gov.au/fin-services/registry.html.

243 See RBA, 'Financial system regulation in Australia', rba.gov.au/education/resources/in-a-nutshell/ pdf/financial-system-regulation.pdf. See also Australian Government, The Treasury, 'About Treasury', treasury.gov.au/the-department/about-treasury.

Table 2.11: Australian Competition and Consumer Commission

Australian Competition and Consumer Commission (ACCC)	
Legislation	**Details**
Competition and Consumer Act 2010 (Cth)	The ACCC[244] is responsible for enforcing provisions of the *Competition and Consumer Act 2010* (Cth) along with other legislation.[245]
	The ACCC does not regulate conduct or consumer protection for financial services, as this is the province of ASIC. Its chief role for securities is competition regulation particularly with respect to mergers and acquisitions. Consumer protection provisions relating to financial services and credit are excluded from the general jurisdiction of the ACCC and placed within the purview of ASIC.[246]
	In respect of securities, the ACCC plays a central role in permitting or prohibiting mergers and acquisitions between corporations[247] but, regarding certain aspects, such as the disclosure of information and conduct in the markets by financial services companies, the application of consumer law provisions is excluded[248] and placed under the regulatory ambit of the ASIC.[249]

---

244 See ACCC (n 222). See also Mallesons (n 190) 13–14. The ACCC's role is to encourage competition by educating, investigating and enforcing through the powers bestowed upon it. It has four priorities: 'Maintaining and promoting competition and remedying market failure; Protecting the interests and safety of consumers and supporting fair trading in markets; Promoting the economically efficient operation of, use of and investment in monopoly infrastructure; and Increasing engagement with business and consumer groups'.

245 ACCC (n 222). The ACCC has a vast remit and looks after many different market relationships such as those between suppliers, wholesalers, retailers, competitors and customers and addresses concerns stemming from anti-competitive behaviour, unconscionable conduct, unfair trade practices and product safety: see Mallesons (n 190) 14–15.

246 IMF, *Australia Country Report* (n 224) 11.

247 For example, the *Competition and Consumer Act 2010* (Cth) prohibits mergers that have an adverse effect on the competition within the economy: see ACCC (n 222).

248 See *Competition and Consumer Act 2010* (Cth) s 131A.

249 See Mallesons (n 190) 15.

Table 2.12: Coordination and oversight

The Council of Financial Regulators (CFR)	
Legislation	**Details**
	The CFR is a non-statutory body established to ensure effective cooperation and coordination of the three main financial regulators, RBA, APRA and ASIC, as well as the Treasury.[250] The governor of the RBA chairs the CFR.[251]
	The objectives of the CFR are laid down in the charter and include the promotion of stability of the Australian financial system and supporting effective and efficient regulation of the financial system.[252] CFR's focus on effective cooperation among financial regulators is achieved through a number of bilateral arrangements and multilateral memoranda of understanding (MoUs) among regulators.[253] These MoUs cover a vast number of areas for cooperation, including sharing of information and immediate notification of regulatory actions that impact other regulators.[254] Measures for cooperation are complemented by 'overlapping representation' on the regulators' governance committees, such as through the APRA chairman representing APRA on the Payment System Board of the RBA and the RBA Board member acting as secretary to the Treasury.[255] Further, given the close financial linkages between Australia and New Zealand, the CFR maintains effective coordination networks with New Zealand through the Trans-Tasman Council on Banking Supervision.[256]
Financial Regulator Assessment Authority Act 2021 (Cth)	A Financial Regulator Assessment Authority (FRAA) has been recently established to assess the effectiveness and capability of ASIC and APRA.[257]
	The FRAA will consist of three independent statutory appointees and will submit biennial reports on the regulators' effectiveness and capability to be tabled in parliament complementing existing accountability mechanisms.

---

250 The CFR is not set up under any specific legislation and thus, only acts as a means for collaboration among the regulators: see CFR, 'About', cfr.gov.au/about.html.
251 RBA, 'Financial system' (n 234).
252 Council of Financial Regulators, 'Charter', cfr.gov.au/about/charter.html.
253 See for example the MoU between APRA and ASIC: *Memorandum of Understanding between the Australian Prudential Regulatory Authority and the Australian Securities and Investments Commission* (signed 28 November 2019), download.asic.gov.au/media/5362689/apra-asic-memorandum-of-understanding-2019.pdf. For the MoU between APRA and the Treasury, see *Memorandum of Understanding between the Treasury (Treasury) and the Australian Prudential Regulation Authority (APRA)*, apra.gov.au/sites/default/files/MoU-Treasury.pdf. For the MoU between the RBA and APRA, see *Memorandum of Understanding, The Reserve Bank of Australia and The Australian Prudential Regulation Authority* (signed 12 October 1998), apra.gov.au/sites/default/files/MoU-RBA-Reserve-Bank-of-Australia.PDF. For the MoU between the RBA and ASIC, see *Memorandum of Understanding between the Australian Securities and Investments Commission and the Reserve Bank of Australia*. Finally, an MoU on Financial Distress Management has been signed by the regulators: see *Memorandum of Understanding on Financial Distress Management between the Members of the Council of Financial Regulators* (signed 18 September 2008), cfr.gov.au/financial-institutions/crisis-management-arrangements/pdf/mou-financial-distress-management.pdf.
254 CFR, 'About' (n 250).
255 Ibid.
256 See CFR, 'Trans-Tasman Council on Banking Supervision', cfr.gov.au/about/trans-tasman-council-on-banking-supervision.html.
257 Australian Government, The Treasury, 'Financial Regulator Assessment Authority' (2021).

Financial sector regulation: Design and approach

Key features of financial regulation in Australia

The objectives-based model of financial regulation, popularly referred to as twin peaks,[258] is the cornerstone of Australia's financial regulatory architecture.[259] As a result of this model, Australia has adopted competitive neutrality in its financial regulation of entities. Further, the Australian financial regulatory framework relies on a principles-based form of regulation.[260] These features of Australia's financial sector regime are discussed in greater detail below.

The twin peaks

The Wallis Inquiry in 1997 recommended a shift from the traditional 'sectoral' approach of financial regulation to the twin-peaks model,[261] leading to the division of the financial sector responsibilities between two regulators, ASIC and APRA,[262] and the RBA as an additional pillar within the financial system, sometimes referred to as the third peak.[263] The Netherlands,[264]

---

258 The twin-peaks model was introduced in 1998 by the Howard government after the submission of the Financial System Inquiry Final Report (Wallis Report) and following the Ministerial Statement to Parliament by Treasurer Peter Costello on 2 September 1997: see generally Parliament of Australia, 'Background—Australian Prudential Regulation Authority (APRA)' (2003) *Australian Prudential Regulation Authority Amendment Bill 2003*. This form of financial regulation was first recommended by Michael Taylor: see Michael Taylor, *'Twin Peaks: A Regulatory Structure for the New Century* (Centre for the Study of Financial Innovation, London, 1995). For a review of the positives of the twin-peaks model as compared with the integrated model, see Michael W Taylor, 'The road from Twin Peaks—and the way back' (2009) 16 *Connecticut Insurance Law Journal* 61. See also Alex Holevas, 'Twin Peaks: the envy of the world' (22 February 2012) *Wealth Professional*. See also Godwin and Schmulow (n 218). But see Minter Ellison, 'Submission to the Financial System Inquiry' (2014).
259 See generally Holevas (n 258). See also Andrew Godwin and Ian Ramsay, *Twin peaks—the legal and regulatory anatomy of Australia's system of financial regulation* (CIFR Paper No 074/2015, University of Melbourne Legal Studies Research Paper No 725, 2015), doi.org/10.2139/ssrn.2657355.
260 See generally IMF, *Australia Country Report* (n 224).
261 See Godwin and Ramsay (n 259). See also Bakir (n 67).
262 Apart from ASIC and APRA, the RBA is responsible for overseeing monetary policy and ensuring financial stability and a stable payments system: see Godwin and Ramsay (n 259). For more on the twin peaks, see Taylor (n 258).
263 The RBA is 'the lender of the last resort', responsible for 'system stability', the 'payments system' and, at times, is referred to as the 'third, unofficial "pillar" of the Australian financial regulatory framework'. It is also 'Australia's central bank': see Godwin, Kourabas and Ramsay (n 10) 280; Commonwealth of Australia Financial System Inquiry, *Final Report* (1997) (Wallis Report) 313–17. The Wallis Report considered the aspect of keeping the prudential regulation with the RBA and the reasons for ultimately placing the prudential regulation with a separate entity, APRA.
264 See generally Rajendaran (n 54). The Kingdom of the Netherlands was second to adopt the twin-peaks model in 2002 as it retained the prudential supervision with the De Nederlandsche Bank NV: see IMF, *Kingdom of the Netherlands—Netherlands: Publication of Financial Sector Assessment Program*

Switzerland,[265] Qatar,[266] South Africa,[267] the United Kingdom[268] and Spain[269] have also adopted the twin-peaks model of regulation, and other countries have shown interest in this form of governance.[270]

After the GFC, and due to Australia's weathering of the 'crisis relatively well', the twin-peaks model of regulation garnered global attention,[271] with Australia's financial architecture described as a 'policy exemplar'.[272] International financial agencies gave positive reviews, with the International Monetary Fund (IMF) noting in its post-GFC review:

Documentation—Technical Note on Financial Sector Supervision: The Twin Peaks Model (IMF Country Report No 11/208, Monetary and Capital Markets Department, Financial Sector Assessment Program Update, July 2011) Tables 1, 6.
265 See Schmulow, 'The four methods of financial system regulation' (n 55) 166–167. In the case of Switzerland, the Swiss National Bank (SNB) is the primary authority for ensuring financial stability, while the oversight of systemically important institutions is assigned to SNB: see Swiss National Bank, 'Financial stability', snb.ch/en/the-snb/mandates-goals/financial-stability. Supervision of the banking sector, and protection of creditors, investors and policyholders, as well as the smooth functioning of the financial markets, resides with the Swiss Financial Market Supervisory Authority: see Swiss Financial Market Supervisory Authority, *Annual Report 2013* (March 2014) i.
266 The Qatar Financial Markets Authority (QFMA) is an independent regulator that supervises financial markets and securities institutions, while the Qatar Financial Centre Regulatory Authority is another regulator with the responsibility for regulating firms and individuals engaged in financial services and maintaining financial stability and reducing systemic risk along with development of financial awareness and the protection for customers and investors; see Schmulow, 'The four methods of financial system regulation' (n 55) 67.
267 A Godwin and A Schmulow, *The Financial Sector Regulation Bill in South Africa: Lessons from Australia* (CIFR Paper No 52/2015, 2015), doi.org/10.2139/ssrn.2556544.
268 Prior to the GFC, the model of governance in the UK was that of an integrated regulator—the then Financial Services Authority (FSA)—which was responsible for prudential regulation, enforcement and market conduct: Schmulow, 'The four methods of financial system regulation' (n 55) 158. Post-crisis, the FSA was deemed to be 'thoroughly inadequate' in its oversight of notable banks and financial institutions, including the Royal Bank of Scotland and Halifax Bank of Scotland (HBOS): see House of Lords Parliament of the United Kingdom, House of Commons (Parliamentary Commission on Banking Standards Fourth Report, *An Accident Waiting to Happen: The Failure of HBOS* (HL Paper 144 HC 705) 28 [83].
269 The Spanish regime includes three financial authorities: the Bank of Spain, the National Securities Market Commission and the Directorate General of Insurance and Pension Funds. To understand the responsibilities and remit of the three bodies, see Schmulow, 'The four methods of financial system regulation' (n 55) 167–168.
270 Countries that have elicited an interest include Italy, France and the United States: ibid 165 [3]. On a country-based comparison of the twin-peaks model of financial regulation, see generally Andrew Godwin, Timothy Howse and Ian Ramsay, 'A jurisdictional comparison of the twin peaks model of financial regulation' (2017) 18(2) *Journal of Banking Regulation* 103–131, doi.org/10.1057/s41261-016-0005-0. See also Andrew Godwin and Andrew Schmulow, *The Cambridge Handbook of Twin Peaks Financial Regulation* (Cambridge University Press, 2021), doi.org/10.1017/9781316890592.
271 Godwin and Ramsay (n 259) 1. The IMF remarked on the soundness of Australia's regulatory and supervisory structure: see IMF, *Australia: Basel Core Principles for Effective Banking Supervision—Detailed Assessment of Observance* (IMF Country Report No 12/313, 2012). To read more on why Australia fared relatively well in the GFC, see Hill (n 181). See also Eilís Ferran et al, *The Regulatory Aftermath of the Global Financial Crisis* (Cambridge University Press, 2012), doi.org/10.1017/CBO9781139175821.
272 Schmulow, 'Financial regulation' (n 58). Schmulow argues that the twin-peaks model of Australia performed well in the GFC due to several reasons other than Australia's financial architecture, whereas

The Australian banking system was more sheltered than a number of other countries and weathered the global financial crisis relatively well. This was in part due to relative concentration of the system on a well-performing domestic economy, but also due to a material contribution from a well-developed regulatory and supervisory structure.[273]

Within Australia, twin-peaks regulation is viewed as effective in providing a strong foundation that significantly contributed to Australia's positive performance in the GFC.[274] The twin-peaks model, as Schmulow argues, has many advantages:

The model's strengths are significant. It invests regulators with a clear remit, and greater certainty as to their jurisdiction than does a heavily bifurcated model with multiple regulators, one for each type of product, or one for each type of financial firm. As a result turf wars are less frequent and less corrosive. Among regulatees there is more certainty as to which regulator has authority over them in a given situation or in respect of a given product, and hence, less confusion. The same holds true for consumers who, instead of being confronted by an 'alphabet soup' of regulators, have certainty of where to seek assistance. Two mega-regulators are far less likely to emit conflicting and contradictory regulatory signals, whereas multiple regulators would. Similarly, opportunities for regulatory arbitrage are diminished, and regulators have the opportunity to build capacity and specialisation in their field, while pooling the resources and the human capital that would otherwise be spread over multiple agencies. Finally, two mega-regulators are able to present a united front to government and industry, alike.[275]

---

some other countries, for example the Netherlands, that adopted the twin-peaks model did not: see Schmulow, 'Doing it the Australian way' (n 58). Schmulow argues that the GFC was disastrous for the Dutch banking sector due to the sector's heavy exposure to international markets, a fact significantly different from Australia's banking sector that stood exposed mainly to the domestic markets.

273 IMF, *Australia: Basel Core Principles* (n 271, 4). It is significant to note that there were other reasons why Australia fared well in the crisis: see for example Hill (n 181). The OECD has similarly endorsed the twin-peaks model of financial regulation and has held up Australia as an example of how this model provides a sound basis for supervision: see OECD, *The Financial Crisis: Reform and Exit Strategies* (2009).

274 Godwin, Kourabas and Ramsay (n 10) 281. The most recent Financial System Inquiry conducted in Australia recognised areas where the financial system's resilience, efficiency and fairness could be improved, but it did not recommend any changes to the twin-peaks model: see GFC Financial System Inquiry, *Financial System Inquiry: Final Report* (2014). The committee opined that 'although Australia was not immune to the effects of the GFC, the financial system and institutional framework held up well compared with many financial systems elsewhere in the world. In particular, Australia's regulatory frameworks proved robust during this period'.

275 See Schmulow, 'Doing it the Australian way' (n 58).

Despite the advantages and opportunities associated with the twin-peaks model, Jackson notes the existence of 'some basic trade-offs' when compared with a unified single integrated regulator.[276] Further, despite its relative success during the GFC, and despite being 're-endorsed' as the 'preferred supervisory architecture' by the Hayne Royal Commission into Misconduct in the Australian Banking, Superannuation and Financial Services Industry in 2019,[277] the twin-peaks model has received criticism. For example, Hanrahan criticised the model for its failure to safeguard consumers rights in the financial services industry, called for a 'separate consumer protection agency' and recommending recasting the current regulatory model to 'Three Peaks'.[278] Godwin and Ramsay highlighted two factors critical in ensuring the success and effectiveness of the twin-peaks model: a clear demarcation of roles and responsibilities of each regulator so as to minimise regulatory overlap, and a well-developed framework of cooperation and coordination that encourages proactive sharing of information and cooperation by regulators in performance of their supervisory and enforcement functions.[279] Apart from this, the successful application of the twin-peaks model also requires effective arrangements for ensuring 'accountability' of the regulators.[280]

Notwithstanding the limitations and conditions for a successful application of the twin-peaks model,[281] Australia's financial regulation model is holistic in its approach. It served the economy well during the GFC and continues to be relevant in this age of financial conglomerates and financial innovation. The roles of the regulators, delineated along the lines of their functions or objectives, provide more clarity on their regulatory mandates and minimise the chance of turf wars, gaps and overlaps. The MoUs between regulators and the CFR (discussed earlier in the chapter) facilitate effective cooperation

---

276 Howell E Jackson, *Learning from Eddy: A Meditation upon Organizational Reform of Financial Supervision in Europe* (Harvard Public Law Working Paper No 09-17, 2009), doi.org/10.2139/ssrn. 1325510. Single-sector agencies are associated with greater efficiency as there are better chances of enjoying economies of scale, lowering costs of financial supervision and reducing duplication in processes. Integrated regulatory supervisor is cited as more equipped to oversee conglomerates and manage risks associated with them.

277 See *Royal Commission into Misconduct in the Banking, Superannuation and Financial Services Industry* (Final Report, September 2018) (Hayne Report) vol 1, recommendation 6.1.

278 Hanrahan (n 218).

279 Godwin and Ramsay (n 259) 267. In the case of the Australian twin-peaks system, a culture of mutual trust between regulators and an effective coordination between them that is 'primarily informal, voluntary and cooperative in nature, relying more on soft law than prescriptive legislation' has been a point of distinction from other countries who also follow a similar model of regulation.

280 GFC Financial System Inquiry (n 274) (recommendations at 103–112). The FRAA, discussed at Table 2.12 of this chapter, responds to this need and has enhanced existing accountability mechanisms.

281 Hanrahan (n 218).

across regulators.[282] At the same time, the relative success of Australia's financial sector over the past two decades, particularly through the GFC, is not premised on the twin peaks alone, and other positive attributes peculiar to an economically sophisticated and advanced country like Australia continue to contribute to the success of its financial system.[283] The twin-peaks model is thus definitely not a panacea for all financial system ills, but, as Schmulow eloquently states, it is 'one quiver in a bow'.[284]

Neutrality

The principle or feature underlying the twin-peaks approach is 'competitive neutrality', whereby transactions performing the same economic functions are subject to the same regulatory burden.[285] The doctrine of neutrality is essentially 'functional regulation',[286] which contrasts with an institutional approach to regulation.[287] The rationale for a functional approach that fosters competitive neutrality was explained by the Treasury as follows:

> Ideally, products, intermediaries, or markets providing similar financial services should be subject to similar regulation. This could be defined as a 'functional' approach to regulation. Different regulatory treatment of similar institutions, products [or] markets can result in 'regulatory arbitrage', with wasteful time and effort directed at exploiting regulatory loopholes.[288]

This means that state-owned and private businesses are treated alike.[289] Additionally, the Financial System Inquiry (FSI) Report of 1996 noted other facets of the neutrality principle, including minimising 'barriers to entry

---

282 See generally Weaver (n 221).

283 See Schmulow, 'Doing it the Australian way' (n 58).

284 Ibid.

285 Warren Hogan and Ian G Sharpe, 'Financial system reform: regulatory structure, financial safety, systemic stability and competition policy' (1997) 8(2) *The Economic and Labour Relations Review* 321, doi.org/10.1177/103530469700800209.

286 The functional approach to regulation pays no heed to the kind of legal entity under consideration, but instead focuses on the kind of transaction or product under regulation, and thus each entity is subject to multiple regulators depending on the kind of transaction such an entity is engaging in. See Schmulow 'Doing it the Australian way' (n 58) 154. It is often problematic to identify or demarcate the type of functional activities that require regulation, but six main functions have been identified: clearing and settlement payments, pooling resources and subdividing shares, providing information related to price and volume of transactions, transferring resources across time and space, risk management and reducing incentive problems: see Robert C Merton and Zvi Bodie, 'A conceptual framework for analyzing the financial system' (1995) *The Global Financial System: A Functional Perspective* 3–31.

287 See Pearson, *Financial Services Law* (n 223) 28 [2.3.2]; Steve Kourabas, 'Improving Australia's regulatory framework for systemic financial stability' (2018) 195. APRA regulates the prudential aspects of banks, life insurers, general insurers, building societies, credit unions, friendly societies and superannuation: see Australian Prudential Regulatory Authority, 'About APRA', apra.gov.au/about-apra.

288 The Treasury submission before the Financial System Inquiry in 1996, as cited in Bakir (n 67) 518.

289 APRA, 'APRA's objectives: competitive neutrality', apra.gov.au/apras-objectives#competitive-neutrality.

and exit from markets and products', and applying neutrality at both global and domestic levels to ensure that rules for domestic participants are not unduly costly or restrictive as compared to rules for overseas participants.[290]

Competitive neutrality was among the foundational principles recommended by the Wallis Report,[291] but it can arguably be seen as a longstanding ambition or objective of Australian financial regulation. Almost two decades prior to the Wallis Inquiry, the Campbell Committee of Inquiry (1981) (discussed later in this chapter) also aimed to achieve 'greater competitive neutrality in the regulation of the financial system' to enable financial intermediaries to operate on a 'more equal footing'.[292] However, the institutional approach to regulation, 'considered satisfactory when the financial system was less complex' but inadequate in the face of financial innovation and technological developments, posed a significant challenge.[293] With the restructure of the Australian financial system after the Wallis Inquiry—from an institution- to a function-based approach to regulation—the Campbell Committee's aim of competitive neutrality was 'finally realised'.[294]

Competitive neutrality is embedded within all levels of government functioning in Australia through the *Competition Principles Agreement*,[295] and it is listed as a key objective under the *Australian Prudential Regulation Authority Act 1998 (APRA Act)*.[296] In recent years, the FSI of 2014 not only reinforced and recommended improvements on the principle of competitive neutrality across all spheres of the financial system,[297] but also recommended adoption of technology neutrality to support innovation.[298]

---

290 See 'Chapter 4: Approaches to financial regulation' in Wallis Report (n 263) 103 [4.53].
291 See generally Wallis Report (n 263).
292 Di Thomson and Malcolm Abbott, 'Australian financial prudential supervision: an historical view' (2000) 59(2) *Australian Journal of Public Administration* 75, doi.org/10.1111/1467-8500.00153.
293 Ibid 77.
294 Ibid 86.
295 The Competition Principles Agreement is a part of Australia's National Competition Policy Statement: see Australian Government, The Treasury, 'Commonwealth Competitive Neutrality Policy Statement' (1996), treasury.gov.au/sites/default/files/2019-03/cnps.pdf.
296 *Australian Prudential Regulation Authority Act 1998* (Cth). APRA's other objectives include efficiency, competition and contestability within the financial system.
297 *Financial System Inquiry: Final Report* (2014) (Murray Committee Report) 146. The report recommended graduation of regulations to enable smaller and newer players to enter the market while applying risk-based regulation to areas where it is most relevant.
298 See ibid 145, recommendation 39. Technology-neutral regulations are generally preferable because technology-specific regulations can hinder innovation by deterring the adoption of the most suited and required technology or innovative approaches.

Principles-based approach

Another feature of Australia's financial regulation is the principles-based character of regulation. There is no dearth of academic literature on rules-based and principles-based approaches to financial regulation.[299] Schauer uses the term 'standards' in place of 'principles' and asserts that 'it is a commonplace that there is a distinction between rules and standards'.[300] In simple parlance, 'rules' can be explained to mean 'directives' formulated by the 'crafter', which are, relatively speaking, more definitive and precise. The crafter of a rule is making 'substantive choices', while the 'interpreters, enforcers and subjects of the directive' are required to largely make only 'mechanical decisions by applying easily ascertainable facts to crisply formulated directives'.[301] 'Principles' or 'standards' reflect requirements that are more open-ended and involve the 'subject', the 'enforcer' or the 'interpreter' to make the most important decision 'at the moment of application'.[302]

In the context of the financial sector, the regulatory systems of some jurisdictions, such as the United States, have been classified as rules-based,[303] while Canada is more principles-based.[304] This classification aside, the literature is also rife with essays on the more ideal form of regulation: rules-based or principles-based.[305] While deliberating on the rules and principles debate in the context of corporate and securities laws,

---

299 See Dan Awrey, 'Regulating financial innovation: a more principles-based proposal?' (2011) 5(2) *Brooklyn Journal of Corporate, Financial and Commercial Law* 274; Pierre Schlag, 'Rules and standards' (1985) 33 *UCLA Law Review* 379. See also James J Park, 'Rules, principles, and the competition to enforce the securities law' (2012) 100 *California Law Review* 115, 130. For a recent succinct account of different regulatory approaches, see *Australian Law Reform Commission: Interim Report A Financial Services Legislation* (2021).

300 Frederick Schauer, 'The tyranny of choice and the rulification of standards' (2004) 14 *Journal of Contemporary Legal Issues* 803.

301 Ibid 803.

302 Ibid 804. See also Lawrence A Cunningham, 'A prescription to retire the rhetoric of principles-based systems in corporate law, securities regulation, and accounting' (2007) 60 *Vanderbilt Law Review* (on attempts by legal scholars to differentiate rules from principles on several parameters including inter alia the 'generality' and 'specificity' of the norms). See also Awrey (n 299) 275.

303 Cunningham (n 302).

304 Ruth O Kuras, 'Harmonization of securities regulation standards between Canada and the United States' (2003) 81 *University of Detroit Mercy Law Review* 465, 472.

305 See for example Cristie L Ford, 'New governance, compliance, and principles-based securities regulation' (2008) 45(1) *American Business Law Journal* 1, doi.org/10.1111/j.1744-1714.2008.00050.x. See also Julia Black, 'Forms and paradoxes of principles-based regulation' (2008) 3(4) *Capital Markets Law Journal* 425–457, doi.org/10.1093/cmlj/kmn026. As nations develop and their corporate laws evolve, discussions tend to centre around whether the regimes should be rules-based or principles-based: see Cunningham (n 302) 1414.

Cunningham asserts that, 'overwhelmingly, rhetoric vaunts "principle-based systems" and denigrates "rules-based systems"',[306] with some scholars such as Awrey going a step further and championing an even 'more principles-based' proposal for regulation in financial innovation.[307] The truth about Cunningham's statement is reflected clearly at least in the pre-GFC era when there were many instances of the principles-based approach being lauded. For example, an instance of when a shift to the principles-based approach to regulation was received favourably by the financial stakeholders was when the United Kingdom moved to a principles-based regulatory regime in 2003.[308] There were clamours for the United States to shift to the United Kingdom's principles-based approach to regulating capital markets,[309] and the recommendations were 'formalized in the US Treasury's *Blueprint for a Modernized Financial Regulatory Structure*'.[310] As Black writes, for firms, a principles-based approach provides flexibility, facilitates innovation and enhances competitiveness, and simultaneously benefits regulators and other stakeholders as well.[311] By contrast, a rules-based regime, such as the United States, was viewed as saddled by the burden of 'overregulation',[312] with a high focus on 'procedural' rather than 'substantive' compliance with the law.[313]

---

306 Cunningham (n 302) 1415. The US federal securities regulation is 'criticised' as rules-based and the Canadian system is 'heralded' as principles-based.

307 Awrey (n 299).

308 The transformation in the UK from a rules-based to principles-based regime was welcomed in 2005 when the largest international initial public offerings occurred in London instead of New York: see Gary Parkinson, 'Record amount raised in London this year as foreigners rush to float', *Independent* (9 August 2006) 40. The European Union Commission extolled the benefits of a principles-based regime also: see Black, 'Forms and paradoxes' (n 305) 2.

309 See Black's view on US Treasury Secretary Hank Paulson's remarks in *Accounting Today* on 16 April 2007: Black, 'Forms and paradoxes' (n 305) 2.

310 Department of The Treasury, 'Blueprint for a modernized financial regulatory structure' (2008).

311 Black, 'Forms and paradoxes' (n 305) 3. Regulators benefit also as principles-based regulation provides them with flexibility, aids in regulatory innovation, enables the regulatory regime to be durable in a fast-changing environment and enhances regulatory competitiveness. Other market players and stakeholders benefit because firms perform better as they try to improve substantive compliance and achieve outcomes and are not consumed by 'following procedures, box-ticking or on working out how to avoid the rule in substance whilst complying with its form: creative compliance'.

312 Jenny Anderson, 'US financial sector is losing its edge, Report says', *New York Times* (22 January 2007) 3. A study conducted by McKinsey stated that the United States put the blame on US overregulation for New York City's financial sector problems. Prior to the crisis, there were calls for the US to move towards a more flexible, UK-style approach for regulation of the capital markets: see Jeremy Grant and Krishna Guha, 'Paulson seeks British-style flexibility in capital markets', *Financial Times* (21 November 2006) 1.

313 See Black, 'Forms and paradoxes' (n 305) 3.

However, in the aftermath of the GFC, the principles-based approach was criticised, especially in the United Kingdom.[314] Commentators stated that this approach failed 'to provide certainty and predictability',[315] was lax and allowed firms to 'backslide' and perform a minimum level of obligations that essentially reduced the bar for protection of consumers.[316] Despite this, and according to Black, principles-based regulation—'a highly complex form of regulation, belying its rhetoric of simplicity'—can operate effectively and provide a 'durable, resilient and goal-based regulatory regime', as long as the regime is 'founded on trust'.[317]

Debate on the merits of rules- and principles-based forms of regulation has been ongoing for decades. Some commentators, asserting the need to 'retire the rhetoric', argue that the debate itself is misplaced.[318] Korobkin contends that, in the case of complex norms, it is not always easy to segregate rules from principles, and that there may be an overlap between rules and principles, or a tendency to blur one into another.[319]

Much like the twin-peaks regulatory model, Australia's principles-based approach has been a subject of much discussion in both academic and policy circles,[320] and has also been lauded (in the past) by international agencies. The IMF, in its review of Australia, found ASIC 'a highly regarded enforcer of market regulation' and stated that:

> the principles-based and outcome-oriented supervisory approach of APRA is effective, with notable strengths in risk analyses embedded in the PAIRS (Profitability and Impact Rating System) and SOARS

---

314 The Treasury Select Committee's report criticised the FSA's model of regulation, terming it a 'substantial failure of regulation': see Treasury Committee, *The Run on the Rock* (2008) [42].

315 An example of this was when, in the US, the National Association of Insurance Commissioners put the blame for the Savings and Loans crisis on the shift to principles-based regulation and contended that when the principles were applied in the courts, consumers stood to lose out and would be at a disadvantage because of the ambiguities of such principles. See Black, 'Forms and paradoxes' (n 305).

316 See Black, 'Forms and paradoxes' (n 305) 3.

317 Ibid.

318 Cunningham (n 302) 1417. Cunningham holds that it is time to retire the 'misleading use of the labels rules-based and principles-based to describe legal or accounting systems'.

319 See Russell B Korobkin, 'Behavioral analysis and legal form: rules vs standards revisited' (2000) 79 *Oregon Law Review* 23, 26, 27; Awrey (n 299) 275–276.

320 See Kevin Davis, 'Financial regulation: costs, benefits and the process of regulatory change' (2008) 27(S1) *Economic Papers—Economic Society of Australia* 1, doi.org/10.1111/j.1759-3441.2008. tb00437.x. For arguments favouring a principles-based approach to regulation in the superannuation industry, see Gerry Gallery and Natalie Gallery, 'Inadequacies and inconsistencies in superannuation fund financial disclosure: the need for a principles-based approach' (2003) 36(1) *The Australian Economic Review* 89–97, doi.org/10.1111/1467-8462.00269.

(Supervisory Oversight and Response System) system, industry-wide risk assessments, and a focus on bank boards' responsibility for risk management.[321]

While this approach has served Australia well, corporate scandals such as the HIH failure[322] reignited debate on the virtues and vices of this approach in comparison with rules-based regulation.[323] Finally, the GFC and several corporate collapses in Australia[324] have resulted in a trend to blend both rules-based and principles-based regulation in the governance of the financial system.

Historical context

How did the features outlined above come to form the core characteristics of Australia's financial regulatory architecture? This section traces the key developments within the Australian financial system that have shaped the current regulatory framework.

Wallis Inquiry, CLERP and FSR

Key features of Australia's financial regulatory system, particularly the twin peaks, were the outcome of a lengthy and intensive reform process emanating from the recommendations of the Wallis Inquiry,[325] the Corporate Law

---

321 See *Australia: Financial System Stability Assessment* (No 12/308, 26 October 2012). While giving positive feedback on Australia's approach to regulation, the IMF also noted that there was more room for improving the regulatory regime, especially around enhancing APRA's and ASIC's supervisory roles.
322 For more commentary on the HIH corporate collapse, see Soheila Mirshekary, Ali M Yaftian and Damien Cross, 'Australian corporate collapse: the case of HIH Insurance' (2005) 9(3) *Journal of Financial Services Marketing* 249–258, doi.org/10.1057/palgrave.fsm.4770157; Garry D Carnegie and Brendan T O'Connell, 'A longitudinal study of the interplay of corporate collapse, accounting failure and governance change in Australia: early 1890s to early 2000s' (2014) 25(6) *Critical Perspectives on Accounting* 446–468, doi.org/10.1016/j.cpa.2013.04.001. After the release of the HIH Royal Commission Report in 2003, questions were raised about a number of issues, such as auditor independence, accounting standards and auditor liability; alongside these, questions were also raised about Australia's legislative response, which was thought to be 'lighter' than that of the US. This was attributed to Australia's 'principles-based' instead of 'black-letter-law-based' approach: see Frank Clarke et al, *Corporate Collapse: Accounting, Regulatory and Ethical Failure* (Cambridge University Press, 2003) 218.
323 See Ford (n 305) 13. On championing a principles-based approach in Australia, see generally Gallery and Gallery (n 320) (arguing that a principles-based approach must be adopted in place of a rules-based approach in the superannuation industry). Contrastingly, see J Farrar, 'Toothless Tiger: all roar and no bite' (2005) 72 *Management* 73 (for a criticism of New Zealand's principles-based approach to corporate law, which the author contends is overly lax).
324 On Australia's most well-known corporate collapses, see Clarke et al (n 322).
325 The Wallis Inquiry, appointed in 1996 to recommend reforms for the financial sector, submitted its final report in March 1997: see generally Wallis Report (n 263). For commentary on the main recommendations, see generally Ian R Harper, 'The Wallis Report: an overview' (1997) 3 *Accountability and Performance* 7.

Economic Reform Program (CLERP) and subsequent financial services reform,[326] collectively referred to by academics as the second wave of reform.[327] Developing an understanding of these, as well as Australia's financial environment prior to these reforms, is useful for the appreciation of the current financial sector regime.

Wallis Inquiry

In 1996, an FSI[328] chaired by Stan Wallis (Wallis Inquiry) was tasked with evaluating the adequacy of Australia's financial regulatory framework.[329] The Wallis Inquiry was given a wide mandate,[330] and its recommendations resulted in a massive regulatory and financial system overhaul.[331] The main recommendation relating to the financial and securities regulatory architecture was to transition from Australia's sectoral financial regulatory framework to an objectives-based framework: the twin peaks.[332] Consequently, the Wallis Inquiry recommended ASIC as the regulator of companies, market conduct and consumer protection within the financial system,[333] and a separate agency, APRA, to undertake prudential regulation for the financial sector.[334] The Wallis Inquiry also recommended other

---

326 Reform for financial services and market regulation, proposed by CLERP, were not made a part of the *CLERP Act* reforms in 1999 but were in fact enacted under the *Financial Services Reform Act 2001*: see Baxt, Black and Hanrahan (n 6) 37 [1.48].

327 Ibid 34 [1.44]. The evolution of the current financial legal and regulatory framework is described by leading academics in three stages: the early developments in substantive regulation; second wave of reform emanating from the Wallis Inquiry, CLERP and FSR; and the third wave of reform adopted after the GFC.

328 From time to time, the Australian government orders a financial system inquiry with the aim of assessing the working of the financial system and how it can be strengthened to meet Australia's evolving needs and support the country's economy.

329 Baxt, Black and Hanrahan (n 6) 35 [1.45].

330 For more literature on the Wallis Inquiry, see Bakir (n 67). See also Harper (n 325); Vic Edwards and T Valentine, 'From Napier to Wallis: six decades of financial inquiries' (1998) 74(226) *Economic Record* 297, doi.org/10.1111/j.1475-4932.1998.tb01926.x. For more recent literature on the Wallis Inquiry, see Mathew Peckham, 'From the Wallis Report to the Murray Report: a critical analysis of the financial services regime between two financial system inquiries' (2015) 33 *Company and Securities Law Journal* 478. See also Godwin and Ramsay (n 259).

331 Australian Government, The Treasury, 'Globalisation: the role of institution building in the financial sector—historical review' (*G-20 Case Study: An Australian Perspective*, 2003).

332 Wallis Report (n 263) 25. The reforms that introduced the new regulatory structure, popularly referred to as the twin peaks, were the consequence of the Wallis Report: see Godwin and Ramsay (n 259) 4 [1]. Departing from the earlier practice and model, the Wallis Inquiry recommended a model of regulation based on functional objectives, with three 'peaks'—a single prudential regulator, a regulator for conduct and disclosure and an institution responsible for systemic stability and payments: see The Treasury, 'Globalization' (n 220).

333 Wallis Report (n 263) recommendation 1. ASIC was given the authority to watch for market misconduct and consumer protection for the financial sector.

334 Ibid, recommendation 31. This recommendation also meant that the prudential regulations that were being carried out by the state jurisdiction were also to be transferred to the Commonwealth. This

significant reforms relating to the financial regulatory architecture.[335] Figures 2.6 and 2.7 illustrate the regulatory framework in Australia, prior to and post the Wallis Inquiry.

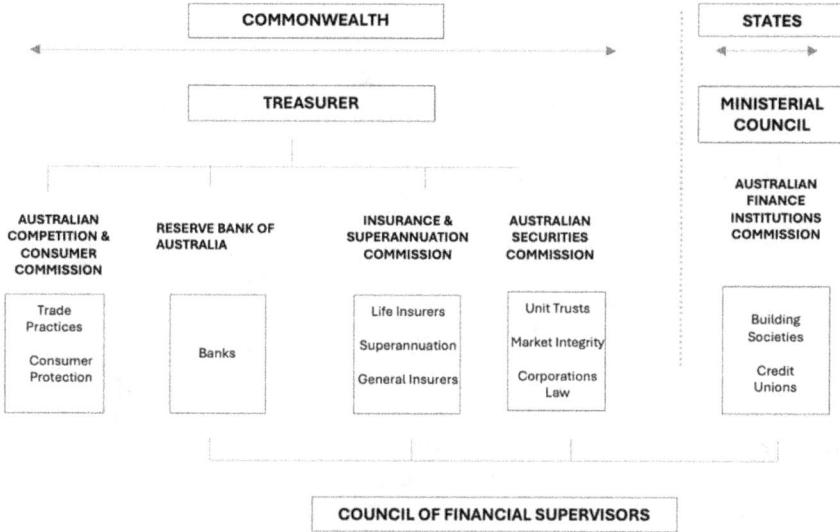

Figure 2.6: Regulatory landscape prior to the Wallis Report[336]
Source: Adapted from Brenton Goldsworthy, David Lewis and Geoffrey Shuetrim, *APRA and the Financial System Inquiry* (Working Paper 3, 2000).

---

was deemed necessary as a single regulator, at the level of the Commonwealth was considered more equipped to govern the financial conglomerates and bring more flexibility in the regulatory approach: see Godwin and Ramsay (n 259) 4.

Prudential oversight and supervision was a great focus area of the Wallis committee and, on this front, the Wallis Inquiry recommended: 'Prudential regulation should be proportional to the degree of market failure which it addresses, but should not involve a government guarantee over any part of the financial system … Prudential regulation and supervision should seek only to add an additional discipline by promoting sound risk-management practices by firms and providing for early detection and resolution of financial difficulties'. See Don Lyell, *Financial Institutions and Markets* (4th ed, 1997) 44.

335 See for example Wallis Report (n 263) recommendation 32. This recommendation called for the separation of prudential regulation from the RBA, with sufficient coordination and cooperation mechanisms between the two regulators. The Wallis Inquiry also recommended that the ACCC retain its responsibility for 'thwarting any anti-competitive behaviour' and for competition policy and consumer protection across all sectors of the economy: see Brenton Goldsworthy, David Lewis and Geoffrey Shuetrim, *APRA and the Financial System Inquiry* (Working Paper 3, 2000), muggaccinos.com/ CreditCards/APRA/APRA-and-the-Financial-System-Inquiry-Jan-2000.pdf.

336 Goldsworthy, Lewis and Shuetrim (n 335) 2.

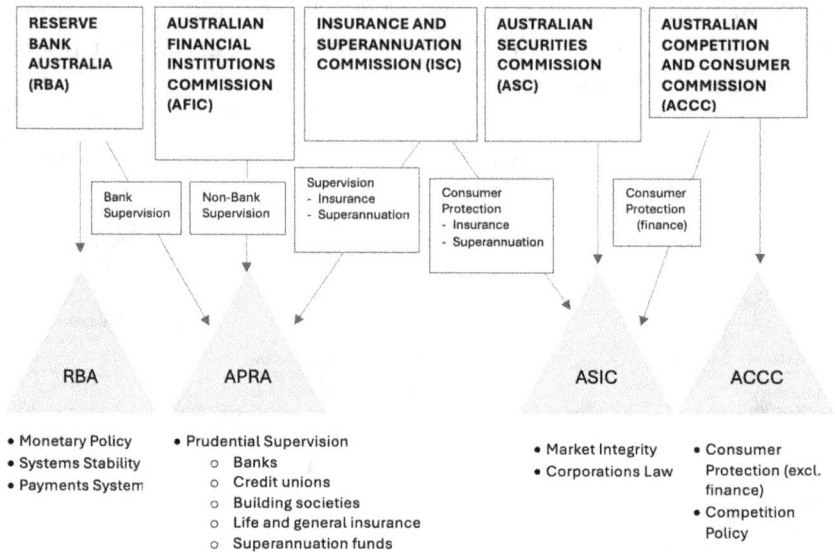

| RESERVE BANK AUSTRALIA (RBA) | AUSTRALIAN FINANCIAL INSTITUTIONS COMMISSION (AFIC) | INSURANCE AND SUPERANNUATION COMMISSION (ISC) | AUSTRALIAN SECURITIES COMMISSION (ASC) | AUSTRALIAN COMPETITION AND CONSUMER COMMISSION (ACCC) |

Bank Supervision | Non-Bank Supervision | Supervision - Insurance - Superannuation | Consumer Protection - Insurance - Superannuation | Consumer Protection (finance)

RBA | APRA | ASIC | ACCC

- Monetary Policy
- Systems Stability
- Payments System

- Prudential Supervision
  o Banks
  o Credit unions
  o Building societies
  o Life and general insurance
  o Superannuation funds

- Market Integrity
- Corporations Law

- Consumer Protection (excl. finance)
- Competition Policy

Figure 2.7: Post–Wallis Inquiry regulatory framework[337]

Source: Adapted from Brenton Goldsworthy, David Lewis and Geoffrey Shuetrim, *APRA and the Financial System Inquiry* (Working Paper 3, 2000).

In addition to the regulatory architecture rearrangements, the Wallis Inquiry recommended other changes, including a single licensing regime for the entire gamut of financial services organisations,[338] a consistent and compulsory disclosure regime for financial products,[339] and improvements to the payments systems by creating a single authorisation procedure for financial exchanges and clearing and settlement facilities.[340] A significant measure emerging from the Wallis Inquiry was to allow retail investors to invest in complex products that were previously restricted to wholesale investors.[341] Essentially, the Wallis Inquiry recommendations did not alter the range of institutions being regulated, but the organisational structure of the regulatory architecture of the Australian financial system—away 'from institutional to functional supervision' or objective supervision.[342]

---

337 Ibid 5.
338 See *Australian Financial Services Licensee-Authorised Representative Licensing Model: Current Practice, Issues and Empirical Analysis* (6th Annual Personal Finance and Investment Symposium) 3. See also Lyell (n 334) 54.
339 See Paul Wiebusch and Chris Weaver, 'Wallis Report: an overview for company secretaries' (1997) 49(6) *Australian Company Secretary* 239. See also Lyell (n 334).
340 David Kidwell et al, *Financial Markets, Institutions and Money* (John Wiley & Sons Inc, 2013) 486.
341 Lyell (n 334) 54. The Wallis Report recommended more detailed disclosures and consumer protection obligations for financial products when issued to retail customers.
342 Goldsworthy, Lewis and Shuetrim (n 335) 7.

CLERP and FSR

The Wallis Inquiry's report coincided with the Australian government's wider corporate reform initiative known as CLERP,[343] which resulted in the adoption of a flurry of financial legislative reforms.[344] This included the *Corporate Law Economic Reform Programme Act 1999* (Cth) (*CLERP Act*).[345]

The CLERP exercise highlighted significant issues within the financial system.[346] For example, it revealed that the existence of multiple regulatory authorities was deterring a convergence in relation to many financial products.[347] Similarly, it revealed that varying levels of disclosure were hindering consumers from comparing products that were functionally equivalent.[348] It thus stressed the need for a more streamlined approach. Consequently, key recommendations under CLERP were incorporated in the Australian government's proposal for the future regulation of financial markets and investment products, popularly known as CLERP 6.[349] Significantly, CLERP 6 noted the importance of retail participation in financial services, stating that:

> retail investment is growing as a result of the heightened awareness of the need to provide for retirement and the attractiveness of large privatisations as investment vehicles. This highlights the

343 First announced in the year 1997, CLERP was created as a comprehensive initiative to enhance Australia's business and corporate regulation and promote business, economic development and employment: see Commonwealth of Australia, 'Policy reforms' (1998) *Corporate Law Economic Reform Program*. See also Baxt, Black and Hanrahan (n 6) [1.46]. To boost the microeconomic reform agenda of the Australian government, CLERP proposed several reforms to companies and securities regulation to promote business and financial market activity and enhance efficiency, integrity and confidence in the market: see generally Peckham (n 330) 479.

344 The Wallis Inquiry's proposals for consistent conduct and disclosure norms across the financial sector were taken up under the CLERP project: see Baxt, Black and Hanrahan (n 6) 36 [1.46] The key legislation included the *Managed Investments Act 1998* (Cth) dealing with managed investments in a holistic manner and the *Company Law Review Act 1998* (Cth) dealing with formation of companies, share capital, financial statements and audit, filing of annual returns, deregistering and reinstating defunct companies and other such matters: see Horgan (n 223). The *Cheques and Payment Orders Amendment Act 1998* (Cth), which extended the issuing rights for cheques to building societies, credit unions and their industry Special Service Providers, and the *Cheques and Payment Orders Amendment (Turnback of Cheques) Act 1998* (Cth), were also adopted post the Wallis Inquiry.

345 Horgan (n 223) 24. The *CLERP Act* was based on a collection of research papers in the areas of director's duties, corporate governance, fundraising, accounting standards and takeovers.

346 For a critical appreciation of the proposals, see Angus Corbett, 'Self-regulation, CLERP and financial markets: a missed opportunity for innovative regulatory reform' (1999) 22(2) *University of New South Wales Law Journal* 506–534.

347 Paul Redmond, *Companies and Securities Law: Commentary and Materials* (Lawbook, 5th ed, 2009) 721.

348 Ibid.

349 Peckham (n 330) 479. See Commonwealth of Australia, *Financial Markets and Investment Products: Promoting Competition, Financial Innovation and Investment* (Corporate Law Economic Reform Program Proposals for Reform, Paper No 6, 1997) (CLERP 6) Proposals 1, 2, 5, 6, 7.

need to ensure that regulation provides appropriate protection for retail investors which will encourage participation by first time investors.[350]

Key recommendations of CLERP 6 and the Wallis Report were enacted in the *Financial Services Reform Act 2001* (Cth),[351] whereby ch 7 of the *Corporations Act 2001* (Cth) harmonised financial services regulation through a single system for financial products and services defined in functional terms rather than by reference to industry-specific characteristics.[352]

Factors necessitating FSR reforms

The Wallis Inquiry and subsequent financial sector reforms represent a critical juncture in Australia's financial regulatory restructure. This regulatory overhaul was not prompted by any specific crisis or market failure but instead was due to changing consumer needs, fast-paced technological innovations and the evolving institutional and organisational structures that created a need for more appropriate regulatory measures and reforms.[353] The terms of the Wallis Inquiry required it to evaluate the effects of earlier deregulation,[354] resulting from the Campbell Committee Report of 1981,[355] and also to propose a new structure to improve the Australian financial regulatory framework.

---

350 CLERP 6 (n 349) 7, 27, 28. Interestingly, CLERP 6 contended that consumers were, by and large, 'assumed to be the best judges of their own interests', and emphasised 'disclosure' and free flow of information to enable informed decision-making.

351 Explanatory Memorandum, Financial Services Reform Bill 2001 (Cth). The FSR Bill was a culmination of the comprehensive reform initiative of the Australian government.

352 Redmond (n 347) 721. See also Kidwell et al (n 340) 486. The *Financial Services Reform Act 2001* (Cth) was enacted on 27 September 2001 and became operational on 11 March 2002: see Shyam S Bhati, 'An analysis of the financial services regulations of Australia' (2008). The FSR regime is mainly consolidated under the *Corporations Act*, the *ASIC Act* and other general and sector specific laws and regulations; see Baxt, Black and Hanrahan (n 6) 30 [1.39]. The *Corporations Act* contains both Australia's company law, which provides for the formation, governance and termination of companies and the law relating to managed investment schemes, and law related to financial markets, which includes takeovers, provisions on listed entities, disclosure, fundraising and financial services and markets.

353 Goldsworthy, Lewis and Shuetrim (n 335). Changing consumer wants were reflected through demographic changes in Australia with respect to its ageing population and necessitated a compulsory superannuation.

354 See also Lyell (n 334) 140. Essentially, the terms of reference included assessing the consequences of deregulation and the existing regulatory structures, measures to encourage 'competition' and attract more foreign investments and international financial institutions; identifying 'forces of change' and commenting upon the 'impact of technological changes' and 'globalisation' on the Australian financial markets; recommending a framework to usher consistency when regulating financial products that are similar but regulated by different financial institutions; analysing and commenting upon any regulatory change that may be required; and making recommendations bearing in mind the monetary policy, superannuation, taxation and corporate law.

355 Goldsworthy, Lewis and Shuetrim (n 335). The deregulation caused the financial system to evolve rapidly, not only gaining institutional depth but also witnessing significant complexities in the organisational structures and financial products. Consequently, the financial system changed

Pre-Wallis era

The Wallis Inquiry and reforms after 1997 were not a spin-off or derivative of an immediate crisis, but a consequence of an evolving financial sector. This factor necessitates knowledge of key historic developments that set the context for the massive financial reforms after 1997.

General economic conditions through the twentieth century

For most of the twentieth century, the Australian economy was 'protected' and 'inward-looking' compared with its current form.[356] The foreign exchange market was 'tightly controlled', with the Australian dollar pegged to the British pound; the flow of capital into and outside the country was restricted; and foreign banks were barred from operating in Australia, while domestic banks and aspects of lending and interest rates were strictly regulated.[357]

Australia's economy transformed to its current form[358] through changes that occurred in three stages: the first stage, the 1970s to the early 1980s, comprised 'reactive reforms aimed at improving macroeconomic stability'; the second stage, the 1980s to the 1990s, witnessed more 'premeditated' measures towards improving the 'efficiency' of the domestic market; and

---

substantially due to the pressures arising from technological innovation, globalisation of financial markets and customers' demands for new and varied financial products and services. All these factors contributed to the financial sector reforms initiated after the 1997.

356 L Berger-Thomson, J Breusch and L Lilley, *Australia's Experience with Economic Reform* (Treasury Working Paper, October 2018) 2 [1]. Australia's economic development for the period between 1860 and 1940 is divided into two phases: 1) the 'golden age' of economic development from 1860 to 1890, a period in which Australia had the highest real GDP per capita income in the entire world; and 2) a period of low economic growth interspersed with negative events such as the 'deep depression' starting from the 1890s, followed by a period of drought, the outbreak of World War I and the period of low economic activity that persisted until the end of World War II: see Christine de Souza and Stephen Nicholas, 'Height, health, and economic growth in Australia, 1860–1940', *Health and Welfare during Industrialization* (University of Chicago Press, 1997) 379–422. For comparative economic development statistics, see generally Angus Maddison, 'Phases of capitalist development' (1977) 30(121) *PSL Quarterly Review*.

357 Treasury Working Paper (n 356). High international tariffs guarded the interests of domestic industry. Iron ore exports were banned until the 1960s, wages were set by a centralised authority, and government dictated business operations in an array of industries such as transport, retail and dairy. The dictates included directions on pricing, opening hours and output of a variety of businesses. In addition, Australia's biggest bank at the time came under government ownership and control, and several state-based banks, along with the monopoly telecommunications provider, the biggest airline, power, water and gas utilities were also government controlled.

358 Ibid 2 [2]. Australia's economic conditions today contrast dramatically with conditions in the first half of the twentieth century in the following ways: i) Australia now has very low tariffs, ii) most workers' wages are fixed at the enterprise level, iii) Australia has a floating exchange rate and an open capital account, iv) public ownership is very limited in trading companies or in the utility sector but the government retains public services such as universal school and medical facilities, and v) commercial banks are free to make their own decisions on how to allocate credit.

the third stage, which began in the latter half of 1990s, focused on the regulatory and government sector, including revised 'tax and spending policies'.[359] With this general economic overview, the following section highlights specific historical developments within the Australian financial and securities sector.

Modern Australian financial markets: Regulation (1945–79) and deregulation (1980s–90s)

Australian financial markets evolved in five stages.[360] While the first two phases contributed immensely to shaping Australia's financial markets, this section outlines the key regulatory developments through the last three stages: the periods of regulation and deregulation,[361] as well as the financial sector reforms of the 1990s leading to the Wallis Inquiry.[362]

Australia's modern era of financial regulation begins with the passing of banking legislation in 1945 and the subsequent creation of the RBA.[363] According to Edey and Gray, until the 1950s, banking was the main form

---

359 Ibid 2 [3]. For more on Australia's economic reform, see Fred Argy, 'The liberal economic reforms of the last two decades: a review' (2001) 60(3) *Australian Journal of Public Administration* 66–77, doi. org/10.1111/1467-8500.00225. See also Anoop Singh et al, *Australia: Benefiting from Economic Reforms* (IMF, 1998).

360 For a detailed description of the stages, see The Treasury, 'Globalisation' (n 331) [1]. The first phase began with the British setting up financial institutions in the nineteenth century, thus the monetary and banking system is regarded to have evolved in the early part of the nineteenth century. See generally Lance E Davis and Robert E Gallman, *Evolving Financial Markets and International Capital Flows: Britain, the Americas, and Australia, 1865–1914* (Cambridge University Press, 2001). The second phase involved the 1890s depression and subsequent rationalisation. In aggregate, between mid-1891 and mid-1893, only 10 out of 64 banks were not forced to close or refuse payment for longer or shorter periods: see Robin Gollan, *The Commonwealth Bank of Australia: Origins and Early History* (Australian National University Press, 1968) 28 [2]. For more capital markets and capital formation in Australia, see David T Merrett, 'Capital markets and capital formation in Australia, 1890–1945' (1997) 37(3) *Australian Economic History Review* 181–201, doi.org/10.1111/aehr.373002. The third phase set in with the evolution of the modern Australian financial system after the postwar banking legislation of 1945: see The Treasury, 'Globalisation' (n 331).

361 Mallesons (n 190) 6.

362 Wallis Report (n 263). The regime established after the Wallis Inquiry introduced uniform regulation of various financial services: see generally Peckham (n 330).

363 The Treasury, 'Globalisation' (n 331) [1]. Two pieces of legislation, the *Commonwealth Bank Act* and the *Banking Act*, were passed in 1945, giving legislative authority to the central banking roles and functions that the Commonwealth Bank had assumed over previous decades. Central banking functions were transferred from the Commonwealth Banking Corporation (CBC) to the RBA, and commercial bank operations were left with the CBC: see RBA, 'Origins of the Reserve Bank of Australia: timeline', rba.gov.au/education/resources/explainers/origins-of-the-reserve-bank-of-australia. html; *Commonwealth Banks Act 1959* (Cth) s 5 and the *Reserve Bank Act*. See generally MK Lewis and RH Wallace, *The Australian Financial System: Evolution, Policy and Practice* (Addison Wesley Longman, 1997).

of 'financial intermediation'.[364] This period was characterised by tight regulation of the banking sector,[365] 'violent liquidity swings', a fixed exchange rate, soaring interest rates and a reduction in the supply of money in the financial system, with government bonds and other debt instruments being sold at pegged prices.[366] The prevailing conditions generated an intellectual demand for a review of monetary policies and regulation, eventually paving the way for the Campbell Committee of Inquiry.[367] The years following the Campbell Report saw a string of deregulatory measures and removal of direct controls.[368] The deregulation and other recommendations of the committee, which were endorsed in 1984 by the Martin Review,[369] arguably fit well with the general ethos and history of the Australian financial markets, which, prior to 1945, had never been tightly regulated.[370]

---

364 Malcolm Edey and Brian Gray, *The Evolving Structure of the Australian Financial System* (RBA, 1996). For example, in 1953, banks held 88 per cent of the total assets of the financial sector and the next biggest group, the 'pastoral financiers' held only 4 per cent. The early years of this modern financial period witnessed the rise of 'savings banks' as the predominant financial institutions and saw an increase in the government-owned banks: see Bijit Bora and Mervyn K Lewis, 'The Australian financial system: evolution, regulation, and globalization' (1996) 28 *Law and Policy in International Business*. The government-owned banks, such as the Commonwealth Savings Bank and other state savings banks, dominated the personal finance sector. In this stage of evolution, the states were allowed to regulate their own savings banks as well as other state-owned financial enterprises, such as building societies, credit unions and friendly societies: see ibid 788.

365 See generally Bora and Lewis (n 364) 790. The institutions that developed at this stage included finance companies, building societies, merchant banks and credit unions that acted as substitute banks. By this time, a high cost had been paid by the economy for the stringent regulatory norms, which was clear in light of a sharp decline in the market share as well as the trading assets of banks: see Lewis and Wallace (n 363).

366 Kidwell et al (n 340) 483. In addition to this, government also used the variable cash reserve requirement to neutralise external sector disturbances and stabilise internal monetary conditions: see Lewis and Wallace (n 363).

367 *Australian Financial System: Final Report of the Committee of Inquiry* (September 1981) (Campbell Committee Report). The announcement of the Campbell Committee was made in 1979 and its final report was submitted in 1981. The Campbell Committee held the view 'that the best results for the community will be achieved if the financial sector is subject to as little government interference as possible'. The Wallis Inquiry of 1997 (discussed later) noted that banking regulation was not achieving its objectives in the 1960s and 1970s and that direct control was thwarting rather than serving the efficient operation of monetary policy: see Wallis Report (n 263) 582.

368 In November 1981, the Campbell Committee tabled its final report before parliament for a competitive financial system using minimum government intervention and regulation: see Lyell (n 334). In its interim report, tabled in parliament in August 1980, the Campbell Committee examined the structure and operation of the financial system and the levels of government intervention.

369 Ibid. The Martin Report of February 1984 largely favoured the recommendations of the Campbell Committee and agreed with the recommendation for deregulation. In May 1983, the treasurer announced the establishment of a Review Group, chaired by Mr V Martin, to review the findings of the Campbell Committee, with due regard to the government's social and economic agenda.

370 Ibid. For a detailed perspective on reasons contributing to the deregulation, see generally Amanda Fitzgibbons, 'The financial sector and deregulation in Australia: drivers of reform or reluctant followers?' (2006) 16(3) *Accounting, Business & Financial History* 371–387, doi.org/10.1080/09585200600969455.

The deregulation of the 1980s resulted in transformative changes for banking[371] and the financial markets.[372] Alongside major structural developments in the banking sector, which led to the growth of new banking institutions and consolidation or rationalisation of existing ones,[373] deregulation caused a substantial spurt in capital flows as well as credit,[374] and, within a decade, nearly doubled the size of the financial sector relative to GDP.[375] The lowering of barriers to entry into financial markets boosted competition that in turn facilitated technological innovation and enhanced consumer choice.[376] The Parliamentary Inquiry into the Australian Banking Industry stated that:

---

371 The RBA switched from direct controls over financial institutions to open market operations as the sole instrument of monetary policy: see The Treasury, 'Globalisation' (n 331) [2]. See also Crane Lyell and Fraser Crowley, *Financial Institutions and Markets* (The Law Book Co, 4th ed, 1997) 123. As a consequence of deregulation, Lyell and Crowley note the following fundamental overhauls: a) tight regulation of the financial markets was replaced by supervision, particularly prudential supervision, that continues to be a cornerstone in the governance of Australian financial markets; b) introduction of a floating exchange rate; c) prudential supervision replaced direct controls as the stated objective of the RBA; d) the RBA adopted an informal but extensive consultative approach while dealing with bank management; e) as deregulation gathered momentum, the RBA moved to a more formal and comprehensive approach to supervision that was on par with international developments. Further, 1989 saw amendments to the *Banking Act* that increased the supervisory power of the RBA over banks by allowing it to specify its prudential supervision requirements by regulation, conduct investigations of banks, procure prudential information from banks and remove the distinction between savings and trading banks.

372 The sweeping changes that occurred through reduced controls over the Australian financial system in the 1980s transformed it from a controlled banking system to one of the least controlled in the world: see JON Perkins, *The Deregulation of the Australian Financial System: The Experience of the 1980s* (Melbourne University Press, 1989). Academics attributed this deregulation to a variety of measures ranging from institutional developments—both within the country and globally—to other technological developments, economic factors and, finally, the official reports of both the Campbell Committee and the Martin Review Group: see Lyell (n 334) 113.

373 An example of this was the merger of the Bank of New South Wales and Commercial Bank of Australia Ltd (Westpac), while the National Bank of Australasia and Commercial Banking Corporation of Sydney consolidated into a single institution mainly due to size, efficiency and spread of branch networks designed to meet expected competition: see Lyell (n 334) 128. To some extent, the entry of foreign banks to the Australian market spurred mergers among the domestic banks. Since these mergers, the Australian banking industry has been dominated by four large interstate banks, the Australian and New Zealand Bank, the Westpac Banking Corporation, the Commonwealth Bank of Australia and the National Australia Bank: see Jan-Egbert Sturm and Barry Williams, 'Foreign bank entry, deregulation and bank efficiency: lessons from the Australian experience' (2004) 28(7) *Journal of Banking and Finance* 1779, doi.org/10.1016/j.jbankfin.2003.06.005.

374 In the period between 1983 and 1988, the amount of capital in the financial sector grew from A$4.5 billion to A$20 billion. At the same time, there was a spike in the number of banking groups within Australia, their number rising from 15 to 34, while the merchant banks grew from 48 to 111: see The Treasury, 'Globalisation' (n 331) [1]. There was an expansion in the credit sector, with a jump of 147 per cent between 1983 and 1988.

375 Edey and Gray (n 364) 7 [2]. The continuous rise in the credit sector also led to the expansion of asset prices that in turn led to credit growth, while rising real asset prices contributed to high real interest rates that led to the 'exceptionally high rates of return in the 1980s'.

376 The Treasury, 'Globalisation' (n 331) [2]. Deregulation improved efficiency in the sector, as it enabled the concentration of efforts and activity towards innovation and minimised unproductive

It is evident that deregulation has led to a significantly more competitive environment within the banking industry and financial system as a whole. There is [a] far greater number of institutions competing for market share than was the case prior to deregulation. Also, the substantial erosion of traditional lines of demarcation has allowed bank and non-bank financial intermediaries to compete across a wider range of activities for a more varied spread of business.[377]

Finally, deregulation led to an increase in product innovation and development.[378]

Although a step in the right direction, deregulation also unleashed considerable challenges and problems, particularly associated with its rapid pace.[379] The easy access to credit post deregulation through lowered credit standards resulted in problems within the property sector,[380]creating bubbles and over-leveraging,[381] and contributing to the period of recession in the early 1990s.[382] Deregulation also created challenges for regulators who were still regulating products largely along institutional lines, while product innovation was causing erstwhile boundaries between financial

acts, such as circumventing outdated regulations. Technological enhancements lowered the costs of cross-border transactions, while deregulation effectively reduced the obstacles to such transactions and consequently accelerated the forces of globalisation within Australia: ibid [3]. Deregulation also transformed Australia's forex markets: see Lyell (n 334) 36.

377 *A Pocket Full of Change: Banking and Regulation* (Report of the House of Representatives Standing Committee on Finance and Public Administration, November 1991) 126. Deregulation in the mid-1980s increased competition within the banking sector: see Bryan Fitz-Gibbon and Marianne C Gizycki, *A History of Last-Resort Lending and Other Support for Troubled Financial Institutions in Australia* (RBA, 2001).

378 Edey and Gray (n 364) 30 [3].

379 See for example Gordon de Brouwer, 'Deregulation and open capital markets: the Australian experience before Wallis' (1999) 6(1) *Agenda: A Journal of Policy Analysis and Reform* 51–68, doi.org/10.22459/AG.06.01.1999.07. The adjustment to financial deregulation was associated with asset price bubbles and a deterioration in the quality of bank assets. See also Brian Head and Elaine McCoy, *Deregulation or Better Regulation?: Issues for the Public Sector* (Macmillan Education Australia, 1991). See also Peter J Drake, 'Financial deregulation in Australia' in *Experiences with Financial Liberalization* (Springer, 1997) 45–68, doi.org/10.1007/978-94-011-5370-6_3.

380 Funds post deregulation increased competition within the banking sector to attract new business, which led to expansion of credit for investment specifically in the commercial property sector: see de Brouwer (n 379) 60 [3]. This sudden demand for credit was strengthened by rising asset values that boosted collateral and encouraged further expansion of bank loans. The expansion of credit was so rapid that it grew by 147 per cent in just five years, 1983–88, and brought several problems with it: see The Treasury, 'Globalisation' (n 331).

381 Credit standards were significantly lowered so when Australia's economy slowed down, and the bubble burst, the banks were left with several non-performing loans and several firms were left over-leveraged: see de Brouwer (n 379). See also The Treasury, 'Globalisation' (n 331).

382 Edey and Gray (n 364) 36. The lowering of credit standards, extreme credit expansion, and subsequent loan losses and balance sheet contractions contributed to the period of recession of the early 1990s.

instruments and institutions to blur significantly.[383] Thus, ensuring 'competitive neutrality' in the regulation of similar financial products offered by different institutions became an important goal for regulation, which was accomplished through the rearrangement of financial system regulation along functional lines following the Wallis Committee Report.[384]

Notwithstanding the problems that ensued from the process of deregulation, financial deregulation in Australia is regarded as a success[385] and a process that accelerated the 'forces of globalisation' in the Australian financial markets.[386]

Key developments in the securities sector (pre-Wallis)

Alongside significant developments within the broader financial system, it is necessary to briefly highlight specific reforms within the securities landscape for two main reasons: first, because it relates directly to the main theme of securities analysis in this book; second, because it underscores the complexities of a federation and the manner in which Australia overcame its longstanding challenge regarding the division of constitutional powers between the states/territories and the Australian government.

Eighteenth-century British corporate history played an influential role in shaping Australia's early corporate legislation.[387] A uniform corporate code for Australia only emerged in the 1950s,[388] with specific securities markets

---

383 The Treasury, 'Globalisation' (n 331). The financial providers were able to take advantage of the existing institutional approach to regulation and exploit regulatory gaps. As a result, there was a spurt in non-bank financial institutions and in their offering of savings products that had a competitive edge over other savings products by banks that were subject to more strict regulations.
384 Ibid.
385 See generally Drake (n 379).
386 The Treasury, 'Globalisation' (n 331). Deregulation, where successful, had led to economic freedom, opened up new markets, enhanced competition and flexibility of the Australian economy: see Justin Douglas, 'Deregulation in Australia' (2014)(2) *The Treasury Economic Roundup*. See also Drake (n 379) 45.
387 For an overview of corporations law in Britain since the eighteenth century, see Roman Tomasic, Stephen Bottomley and Rob McQueen, *Corporations Law in Australia* (Federation Press, 2002) 15. For more on the history of company law in Australia, see Philip Lipton, 'A history of company law in colonial Australia: legal evolution and economic development' (2007) 31 *Melbourne University Law Review* 805, doi.org/10.2139/ssrn.1030196; Niall Coburn and Kristine Goodin, 'Understanding and researching company law' (1998) 6 *Australian Law Librarian* 14; Bernard Mees and Ian Ramsay, *Corporate Regulators in Australia (1961–2000): From Companies' Registrars to the Australian Securities and Investments Commission* (University of Melbourne Legal Studies Research Paper No 335, 2008), doi.org/10.2139/ssrn.1123830.
388 Uniform Companies Acts were adopted by the states and territories with their own modifications: see Tomasic, Bottomley and McQueen (n 387). Uniform Companies Acts were adopted by Australia's various states and territories in 1961–62 and were broadly based on the *Companies Act 1958* (Vic). For the passing of this Act, many sources (other than UK ones) were consulted—for example, the United States *Model Business Corporation Act*.

statutes emerging even later in the 1970s.[389] To move from the state-specific securities regime to a more centralised regime of securities regulation, a Senate Select Committee chaired by Senator Peter Rae was set up in 1974.[390] The Rae Report recommended the introduction of national securities legislation and a national regulator to oversee the securities markets similar to the United States Securities and Exchange Commission.[391] Considerable effort towards such consolidation yielded results in the 1980s with the Australian government enacting several national statutes that were adopted by individual states.[392] The Australian government and the states and territories collaborated in overseeing the functioning of these legislative enactments.[393] However, these cooperative arrangements caused other problems,[394]

---

389 In 1970, New South Wales, Victoria, Queensland and Western Australia enacted legislation for the regulation of the security industry, which, though it aspired to be uniform, had significant variations. The legislation had provisions for the licensing of investment advisers and stock brokers and also prohibited many 'improper practices in the share market': see Tomasic, Bottomley and McQueen (n 387) 21.

390 The committee was set up to respond to the proposal of a securities and exchange commission at the Commonwealth level: see Senate Select Committee on Securities and Exchange, *Australian Securities Markets and Their Regulation* (1974) v.

391 Tomasic, Bottomley and McQueen (n 387) 20 [3]. In consonance with the recommendations of the Rae Committee, and drawing on the existing state securities legislations as well as the securities legislations of other jurisdictions, the federal Labor government prepared the Corporations and Securities Industry Bill 1974, a measure that eventually lapsed due to the dismissal of the Labor government in November 1975.

392 Ibid 23 [5]. The *Companies Act 1981* (Cth) mainly dealt with matters relating to incorporation of a company, company affairs and the process of winding up; the *Companies (Acquisition of Shares) Act 1980* (Cth) dealt with takeovers; the *Securities Industry Act 1980* (Cth) dealt with matters of the securities industry and the stock markets; and the *Futures Industry Act 1986* (Cth) was passed to regulate the newly developed trading in futures contracts. Futures were later introduced within corporate legislation, and for all the years leading up to the Wallis Report, other financial products such as superannuation, life and general insurance, foreign exchange and banking products were all regulated by legislation specific to the particular industry: see Redmond (n 347).

393 The Commonwealth and the states cooperated in establishing regulatory mechanisms spanning three levels of administration: the Ministerial Council for Companies and Securities, the National Companies and Securities Commission (NCSC) and State and Territory Corporate Affairs Commissions or Offices. The NCSC was established under the *National Companies and Securities Commission Act 1979* (Cth). The state bodies were the third limb of the administrative set up and were responsible for the everyday administration of the legislation as well as the cooperative scheme between the Commonwealth and the states/territories: see Tomasic, Bottomley and McQueen (n 387) 23–24.

394 On the various issues flagged by the Senate Standing Committee, see Senate Standing Committee of Constitutional and Legal Affairs, 'The role of parliament in relation to the National Companies Scheme' (1987). Several problems were identified with the 'co-operative arrangement' between the Commonwealth and the states/territories, such as: a) a lack of 'direct ministerial responsibility and accountability to the Federal Parliament'; b) administrative duplication and inefficiency due to having too many bodies and bureaucracies involved in the administration of the scheme; and c) 'lowest common denominator' decision-making impacting the overall standards of the arrangement: see Tomasic, Bottomley and McQueen (n 387) 24–25.

eventually paving the way for further consolidation of the companies and securities landscape through the enactment of the *Corporations Act 1989* (Cth),[395] as well as the *Australian Securities Commission Act 1989* (Cth).[396]

Despite this achievement, the traditional tussle between the Australian government and the states/territories continued in the area of corporate and securities law,[397] reaching its peak in 1990[398] when a new agreement was adopted.[399] The constitutional crisis was finally resolved in 2001 when the states referred their constitutional powers in respect of corporations law to the Australian government, and the existing *Corporations Act 2001* and the *ASIC Act 2001* were passed.[400]

A brief critique of the FSR and recent developments

Australia's current financial sector regime (FSR) derives from the recommendations of the Wallis Report of 1997 and the *Financial Services Reform Act 2001* (Cth) (*FSR Act*).[401] Even so, as the historical account above shows, the extant FSR regime in many ways is a result of systematic reform

---

395 The *Corporations Act 1989* (Cth) dealt with all aspects of the erstwhile legislation, namely the *Companies Act 1981* (Cth), *Companies (Acquisition of Shares) Act 1980* (Cth), *Securities Industry Code 1980* and the *Futures Industry Act 1986* (Cth): see Tomasic, Bottomley and McQueen (n 387) 25 [4].
396 *Australian Securities Commission Act 1989* (Cth). The ASC replaced the NCSC.
397 The states and territories resisted the Commonwealth's attempts to take over the regulation of corporations law. Traditionally, the regulation of corporate law has been regarded as a matter of state legislation and the 1989 legislation was seen by the states as the Commonwealth's attempt to take over their regulatory domain: see Abe Herzberg, Philip Lipton and Michelle Welsh, 'Pathways—legislative framework' in *Understanding Company Law* (2019).
398 In 1990, the High Court of New South Wales, in the landmark judgment of *NSW v Commonwealth* (1990), ruled that the Australian Constitution did not grant the power to the Commonwealth to make laws in respect of companies, especially in respect of the formation of companies: see ibid. This judgement, resulting in a state of constitutional and legislative pandemonium, propelled the two sides to once again renegotiate their stance. An agreement was reached in Alice Springs in June 1990 between the Commonwealth and the states and the Northern Territory for the adoption of a new national scheme of legislation and administration based on the *Corporations Act 1989* and the *Australian Securities Commission Act 1989*, in which the states/territories continued to play an active role for the rest of the decade. As a consequence of this negotiation, the Australian Securities Commission was given the responsibility to administer the legislation and became accountable to the Commonwealth attorney-general: see Tomasic, Bottomley and McQueen (n 387) 27 [4].
399 For a detailed account of the constitutional arrangements that gave the Commonwealth the exclusive legislative and administrative responsibility of securities and financial law in Australia, see generally Baxt, Black and Hanrahan (n 6) ch 2.
400 See Herzberg, Lipton and Welsh (n 397). See also Explanatory Memorandum, Corporations Bill 2001 (Cth).
401 See generally Baxt, Black and Hanrahan (n 6).

spanning several decades,[402] including extensive legislative exercises,[403] both prior to and after the Wallis Inquiry.[404] This evident attention on the financial system and related matters stems from the widely accepted notion that 'free and competitive markets can produce an efficient allocation of resources and provide a strong foundation for economic growth and development'.[405] Alongside such acknowledgement, the Wallis Inquiry also recognised the need for regulation—especially specialist regulation[406]— of financial markets, mainly to address various kinds of 'market failure'[407] and to accomplish separate yet interconnected objectives of 'stability, prudence, integrity and fairness' within the financial markets.[408] Collectively, these conditions and purposes led the Wallis Inquiry to recommend the adoption of defining tenets that form the foundations of financial regulation in Australia, including 'competitive neutrality, cost effectiveness, transparency, flexibility and accountability'.[409] Successive legislative overhauls under CLERP (discussed earlier in this chapter), particularly CLERP 6,[410] also 'reiterated the Wallis objectives of market integrity, investor protection, enhanced competition and minimisation of systemic risk'.[411]

---

402 Mallesons (n 190) 3 [1.05]. See also Thomson and Abbott (n 292). Thomson and Abbott assert that the institutional design of the financial regulation prior to Wallis was mainly an historical accident.
403 Baxt, Black and Hanrahan (n 6). There were two prominent strands of development of the financial laws in Australia: the first pertains to the development of substantive regulation across decades of restructuring, and the second relates to the shift from a wholly state-based regulatory framework to a national framework.
404 Pearson, *Financial Services Law* (n 223) 70. Pearson describes the process of FSR across four key phases: first, the formation of a companies and market regulator; second, comprehensive product-neutral licensing, disclosure and conduct regime within the corporations legislation; third, extensive amendments to product specific legislation to synthesise with the overarching regime and remove anomalies; and, fourth, ongoing refinements to corporations legislation to balance regulatory obligations and protection of the consumer, the financial citizen.
405 Wallis Report (n 263) 177. See also the then treasurer's statements on creating a world-class regulatory structure to support growth and development of the entire Australian economy, cited in Pearson, *Financial Services Law* (n 223) 69.
406 The Wallis Inquiry concluded that there were two main justifications for specialist regulation of the financial system: to maintain market integrity and retail consumer protection: see Baxt, Black and Hanrahan (n 6) 8 [1.6]. The need for specialist regulation was also recognised by the Murray Inquiry, which concluded that the financial system was capable of creating or amplifying economic shocks due to use of leverage, its complexity and interconnectedness with the entire economy. Further, consumers required specialist regulations to promote fairness and protect them from dishonest or predatory practices within a complex financial system.
407 Mallesons (n 190) 3 [1.05].
408 Wallis Report (n 263) vii.
409 Ibid 176. See also Pearson, *Financial Services Law* (n 223) 20.
410 CLERP 6 (n 349).
411 Pearson, *Financial Services Law* (n 223) 70.

These foundations of the FSR regime laid by Wallis and CLERP were revisited under the 2014 FSI chaired by David Murray (Murray Inquiry).[412] Tasked with examining how to position Australia's financial system to best meet the country's evolving needs and economic development, the 2014 FSI concentrated on two themes—funding the Australian economy and boosting competition—resulting in 44 recommendations.[413]

In relation to the overarching architecture of the FSR regime, the FSI canvassed the possibility of change to the financial services institutional framework, but rejected it.[414] Thus, the Murray Inquiry did not recommend changes to the core features of the FSR regime—that is, the twin peaks and neutrality.[415] Yet, it cautiously diverged from some principles and approaches underlying the FSR regime since the Wallis and CLERP initiatives. For instance, it cautioned against the general confidence placed on the principles of 'inherent efficiency' and 'stability' of financial markets, highlighting the understanding of the financial system as a 'complex, adaptive network'.[416] The Murray Committee Report considered developments since the Wallis Inquiry relating to behavioural biases that limited the efficacy of disclosure as a regulatory tool, technological innovations that were producing new risks and challenges, and the rising significance of the role of government in protecting the real economy,[417] and concluded with a strong emphasis on ensuring the financial system was efficient, resilient and fair.[418]

More recently, the Hayne Royal Commission recommended retaining the twin-peaks architecture,[419] albeit with several improvements and refinements.[420] As a direct consequence of this, the Australian Law Reform Commission was set up to inquire into the potential simplification of

---

412 See Murray Committee Report (n 297).
413 Ibid xxi. See also Mallesons (n 190) 30 [1.140].
414 Gail Pearson, 'A credit lens: implementing twin peaks' (2017) 11(4) *Law and Financial Markets Review* 179, doi.org/10.1080/17521440.2017.1419621. The Murray Committee Report did not recommend any changes to the financial stability mechanisms in place nor to ASIC's or CFR's responsibilities.
415 Murray Committee Report (n 297) 235.
416 Ibid 8. The Murray Inquiry mentioned how the GFC had demonstrated that financial systems were prone to instability and, thus, Australia would be susceptible to financial crises.
417 Ibid 9.
418 Baxt, Black and Hanrahan (n 6) 10 [1.7]. Efficiency means the ability of the financial system to allocate scarce financial and other resources for the greatest benefit of the economy and includes operational efficiency, allocative efficiency and dynamic efficiency. Resilience means the ability of the financial system to adapt to normal business cycles and severe economic shocks. Fair treatment refers to participants acting with integrity, honesty, transparency and non-discrimination.
419 Hayne Report (n 277) vol 1, recommendation 6.1.
420 Ibid. The Hayne Report made 76 recommendations in total, including the need to strengthen cooperation between APRA and ASIC, and the need to strengthen enforcement practices especially relating to ASIC.

financial services laws in Australia 'to facilitate a more adaptive, efficient, and navigable framework of legislation' and achieve 'meaningful compliance with the substance and intent of the law'.[421] Thus, further adjustments to the FSR are currently underway.

This brief account of recent developments in the FSR exemplify the continuous and rigorous attention accorded to regulatory and governance matters in Australia. The FSR's intrinsic strength lies in the holistic approach it takes towards financial sector regulation rather than a narrow, segmented and fragmented one. This holistic approach, manifest in the FSR's fundamental features of twin peaks and neutrality, has several advantages. First, it promotes a sharper focus on the financial system as a whole and on the use of the system as a means to achieve goals of financial independence, employment, economic growth and development.[422] The holistic approach directly relates to the foundational principle of efficiency and, by drawing on the core fundamentals of a 'financial product',[423] avoids 'unnecessary distinctions between financial products'[424] and services based on their nomenclature. By treating financial products as alike—that is, by focusing on their similarities rather than their differences—the FSR regime has achieved significant feats, such as adopting 'a single licensing regime for financial sales, advice and dealings in relation to financial products', as well as a more consistent and comparable regime for financial product disclosures, among other outcomes.[425]

The implementation of the FSR regime has contributed to Australia's sophisticated, efficient and resilient financial sector, generating significant outcomes for the financial sector[426] and the larger economy,[427] and also

---

421 Australian Law Reform Commission, 'Terms of Reference' (2020) *Review of the Legislative Framework for Corporations and Financial Services Regulation*.

422 See generally Pearson, 'A credit lens' (n 414) 70. See also CLERP 6 (n 349).

423 Financial product is defined in broad terms under the *Corporations Act*: see s 763A.

424 CLERP 6 (n 349) 11.

425 Baxt, Black and Hanrahan (n) 6 [1.2]. The single regulatory regime reduced administration costs and costs imposed on intermediaries with different regulatory regimes: see CLERP 6 (n 349) 11.

426 The Australian financial services sector is the largest contributor to the national economy, with contributions of beyond $140 billion in 2015; it employs over 450,000 people and is likely to continue being the core sector of Australia's economy into the future: see The Treasury, 'The strength of Australia's financial sector' (n 181).

427 Australian GDP in USD billions has steadily risen to $1,330.90 billion in 2020 from $415.22 billion in 2000: see World Bank Group, 'Country profile: Australia', databank.worldbank.org/views/reports/reportwidget.aspx?Report_Name=CountryProfile&Id=b450fd57&tbar=y&dd=y&inf=n&zm=n&country=AUS. Further, according to the OECD, Australia's economic sector, in spite of the COVID-19 pandemic, is projected to grow by 4 per cent in 2021 and 3.3 per cent in 2022: see OECD, 'Australia Executive Summary', *OECD Economic Surveys* (September 2021) 4.

creating economic prosperity[428] for financial consumers, investors and the Australian population in general.[429] Recent achievements of the FSR regime include the World Economic Forum's *Global Competitiveness Report 2018* ranking Australia number six on its 'financial markets development' out of a total of 137 countries (Figure A1.1),[430] and Australia's four major banks—the Commonwealth Bank of Australia, Westpac, ANZ and National Australia Bank—being ranked among the top 25 banks globally.[431] The FSR regime is 'widely acknowledged as a key reason for the relatively strong performance of the Australian financial system' through the GFC of 2007–08.[432]

While the FSR regime is conceptually sound, it has not been free from critique.[433] The regime has witnessed significant financial failures[434] and has attracted criticism for its over-reliance on disclosure and efficient

---

428 Australia's economic prosperity is attributed to many factors—from 'Australia's natural-resource base—especially farmland and minerals' to the 'quality of the institutional arrangements within which the economy [operates]': see Ian W McLean, *Why Australia Prospered: The Shifting Sources of Economic Growth* (Princeton University Press, 2012) 5–6, doi.org/10.23943/princeton/9780691154671.001.0001. McLean argues that a country's ability to exploit its natural resources to promote growth largely depends on the quality of its key institutional arrangements: how they are formed, how they function and how 'responsively they [evolve] in the light of experience or changed circumstances'.

429 For over a century, Australia, along with the US and UK, has remained among the richest countries in the world, with its people enjoying not just high incomes but also maintaining a standard of living that most other countries are still aspiring to reach: see ibid 2 [1]. Also see Ian W McLean, 'Australian economic growth in historical perspective' (2004) 80(250) *Economic Record* 330–345, doi.org/10.1111/j.1475-4932.2004.00192.x.

430 Klaus Schwab (ed), *The Global Competitiveness Report 2017–2018* (World Economic Forum, 2018), www3.weforum.org/docs/GCR2017-2018/05FullReport/TheGlobalCompetitivenessReport2017%E2%80%932018.pdf. The Global Competitiveness Index (GCI) tracks the performance of almost 140 nations and ranks them on the following '12 pillars of competitiveness': 1) institutions, 2) infrastructure, 3) macroeconomic environment, 4) health and primary education, 5) higher education and training, 6) goods market efficiency, 7) labour market efficiency, 8) financial market development, 9) technological readiness, 10) market size, 11) business sophistication and 12) innovation. Within the global financial sector, Australia ranks fourth on 'soundness of banks'; however, it lags behind several countries on 'affordability of financial services', ranking thirty-eighth, and fortieth on 'venture capital availability'.

431 The Treasury, 'The strength of Australia's financial sector' (n 181) [3]. Australian banks are among the largest from a viewpoint of market capitalisation.

432 Kidwell et al (n 340).

433 Cindy Davies, Samuel Walpole and Gail Pearson, 'Australia's licensing regimes for financial services, credit and superannuation: three tracks toward the twin peaks' (2021) 38(5) *Company and Securities Law Journal* 332–354, doi.org/10.2139/ssrn.3895447. See also Hanrahan (n 218); Godwin, Kourabas and Ramsay (n 10).

434 After the implementation of the FSR regime, there were critical financial and corporate collapses, such as the Trio Capital fraud that exposed some shortcomings within the system: see Parliament of Australia Joint Committee on Corporations and Financial Services, *Inquiry into the Collapse of Trio Capital* (2012) (Trio Report). The Trio Capital collapse of 2010 is regarded among Australia's largest superannuation frauds. The Trio scandal involved a series of nefarious and complex transactions by which the superannuation funds under Trio's management were illegally channelled into managed investment schemes of which Trio was a responsible entity and subsequently invested into associated offshore hedge funds. Such a complex path was deliberately designed to hide and obfuscate the financial

market hypothesis.[435] Such issues have provoked a series of adjustments[436] and reforms[437] that are likely to strengthen the FSR regime and address widespread problems in some areas of financial mis-selling and advice (examined in detail in Chapter 5 of this book).[438]

Notwithstanding recent issues and criticism of the financial system and its regulation,[439] from a global perspective it is safe to state that Australia's FSR, constructed on the strong foundations of efficiency, resilience and fairness, is well designed, sophisticated and of high quality.[440]

In conclusion, Australia's modern financial sector journey of tight regulation,[441] deregulation,[442] re-regulation[443] and ongoing adjustments demonstrates its commitment to building a strong governance regime and continuously enhancing it. Moreover, commentators assert that Australia's financial system and economic success are particularly creditable considering how it has responded to 'shocks—positive and negative—that have punctuated its history'.[444] The manner in which Australian financial institutions and society have coped with stress and adversity, and the policies adopted in the face of deteriorating economic conditions to ensure

---

trail so that the underlying assets or the ownership could be untraceable. The Trio Report estimated the loss of around $176 million to investors. The Trio fraud was notable because it highlighted both the significance of the superannuation funds industry as well as the high-risk of financial frauds in this sector. Other collapses, such as Westpoint and Storm Financial, are discussed in Chapter 5 of this book.

435 See Peckham (n 330) 499. However, this approach is now changing.

436 See Pearson, 'A credit lens' (n 414) 332. See also Hayne Report (n 277).

437 Hayne Report (n 277). See also the changes recommended to the supervisory duties of APRA and ASIC through the *Financial Sector Reform (Hayne Royal Commission Response) Act 2020* (Cth) sch 9. See also the increase in powers of the regulators through the *Financial Sector Reform (Hayne Royal Commission Response—Stronger Regulators (2019 Measures)) Act 2020* (Cth).

438 See for example Peckham (n 330). Issues related to financial mis-selling and advice in Australia are examined in detail in Chapter 4 of this book.

439 For a more detailed account of some issues relating to ASIC, refer to the discussion in Chapters 4 and 5 of this book.

440 See for example IMF, *Australia: Basel Core Principles* (n 271) 4. See also The Treasury, 'The strength of Australia's financial sector' (n 181).

441 The era before the Campbell Report, discussed earlier in this chapter, comprised tight regulations and control.

442 The process of deregulation commenced as a result of the Campbell Report of 1981: see generally *Australian Financial System: Final Report of the Committee of Inquiry* (1981) (Campbell Report). The main guiding principle behind the Campbell Committee's recommendations was that, for 'best results for the community', the government sector must be subject to as little 'government interference' as possible.

443 The process of re-regulation began after the Wallis Inquiry, which recommended a neutral approach to the regulation of financial services and products: see generally Wallis Report (n 263).

444 McLean, *Why Australia Prospered* (n 428). Sometimes these shocks arose in the resource sector. A positive shock was the discovery of gold, which was managed appropriately due to the existence of well-functioning institutions. Negative shocks included events such as World War I and the oil price spike in the 1970s.

the country has remained resilient to shocks and on track to sustaining prosperity, are also noteworthy. The FSR's evolution thus reflects bold and open innovative-thinking and calculated risk-taking followed by decisive action and continuing refinements, in many ways personifying the functioning and approach of Australia's economy and generally the entire country.

Synthesis and conclusion

This chapter has presented a high-level overview of the financial sector structures and regulation in India and Australia, along with their historical context. A notable similarity between the two countries is that, despite having well-diversified financial sectors,[445] the banking sector in both countries dominates the financial sector with most assets.[446] Similarly, although India's current financial and securities sector architecture and approach are vastly different to Australia's, the historical and current developments in both countries suggest that India is also headed on a path to financial deregulation and reform, although the process is more gradual as compared with Australia's rapid pace of financial sector reform.

Australia's financial regulation, through the twin peaks, neutrality and a principles-based approach, is notably better equipped to handle the challenges of a dynamic financial and securities environment, particularly in the face of burgeoning hybrid products, fintech companies and systemic risks. Further, although commentators have highlighted some challenges with the current financial sector framework in Australia,[447] they are not as complex as issues in growing markets such as India. At the same time, India's sectoral, institution- and rules-based financial regulation, though arguably outdated and problematic for India, is still stable, resilient and on a definite path of reform.

---

445 In India, there is a strong presence of financial services (ie commercial banks, insurance, mutual and pension funds, and new entities such as payment banks) entering the market. See Department of Commerce, India Brand Equity Foundation, 'Financial services in India' (Blog Post), ibef.org/industry/financial-services-india.aspx.

446 In India, commercial banks account for more than 64 per cent of the total assets of the financial system: see ibid. Likewise in Australia, ADIs held 55 per cent of the total assets in 2018: see Hayne Report (n 277).

447 Despite the twin peaks, Australian financial regulation also suffers from some amount of ambiguity, complexity and fragmentation, among other problems: see Millhouse (n 196) 82–83.

Notwithstanding the different financial regulation architecture and approaches, it is significant that both India and Australia, for different reasons, performed relatively well during the GFC and were less adversely affected compared with several other countries. Australia's impressive performance during that crisis, despite its high global linkages, principles-based approach and less controlled financial environment, was attributed to the effectiveness of its financial architecture, regulatory framework and the strength of its financial institutions. In India's case, despite its somewhat outmoded financial architecture and inadequate institutional strength, the crisis was overcome with remarkable resilience mainly due to India's fewer global linkages, patented low-risk financial sector approach and high level of government involvement.

This fact leads to at least one critical conclusion, namely, that it is more appropriate to consider organisational structure relating to financial supervision as a 'second-order problem rather than a fundamental concern'.[448] In this regard, Ferran argues that structures matter only to a limited extent towards 'supervisory efficiency, effectiveness, accountability, and transparency'. Ferran states that:

> A good institutional model will not neutralize weak supervisory policies and practices but, on the other hand, dedicated high-quality supervisory personnel and sensible working practices and arrangements for cooperation can compensate for limitations in the formal institutional arrangements. 'What works'—that is, whether a financial supervisor has been equipped with appropriate powers and with adequate resources to deploy them effectively in the pursuit of sound policies that will promote economic well-being and protect society from harm—is a concern that goes far beyond questions pertaining to the supervisor's institutional set-up.[449]

Thus, even though Australia's well-designed financial framework is a creditable feature, there are other strengths that contribute to the success of its financial system, most importantly, its unrelenting focus on attaining the goals of efficiency, resilience and fairness within the financial system, making it attractive to both local and foreign investors.

---

448 Ferran, 'The break-up of the Financial Services Authority' (n 52).
449 Ibid 98.

In conclusion, the financial sector overview presented in this chapter shows that India's current financial sector architecture resembles, in some ways, Australia's pre-Wallis framework that was drawn along sectoral lines. As a growing economy, India's financial and securities sectors encounter complex challenges of a more rudimentary nature. However, as an advanced economy with far fewer complexities and fundamental challenges,[450] Australia's current financial sector architecture has clearly acquired a more sophisticated iteration and is on a continuous path to further adjustments. To state it simply, Australia's financial sector architecture is well ahead on the curve that India is aspiring to climb, or, rather, should be considering. Hence, a greater understanding of Australia's financial sector architecture and approach is potentially both relevant and useful for India, while the proposal for deeper collaboration between the two jurisdictions is full of opportunities for both.

---

450 This does not suggest that Australia did not face any challenges in the adoption of the FSR regime, as evident in the struggle between the Commonwealth and the states to adopt a pan-Australia securities regime.

3

The role and responsibilities of the regulator and its cooperation regime: IOSCO Principles 1–7 and 13–15

Introduction

The financial system architecture and evolutionary journey of the Securities and Exchange Board of India (SEBI) and the Australian Securities and Investments Commission (ASIC) was presented in Chapter 2. With this necessary background in mind, this and following chapters conduct a comparative analysis of the two regulators through the lens of the leading principles for securities regulation and cooperation. The *Objectives and Principles of Securities Regulation* (IOSCO Principles),[1] a set of 38 principles, is issued by the world's leading standard-setting securities body,

---

1   IOSCO is the leading global standard-setting body for securities markets with a membership of 118 nations: see IOSCO, 'Ordinary members of IOSCO', iosco.org/about/?subsection=membership &memid=1. Both SEBI and ASIC, as ordinary members of IOSCO, have endeavoured to abide by the standards set by IOSCO, and their respective regulatory frameworks have been periodically adjudged by the International Monetary Fund's (IMFs) Financial Sector Assessment Program: see IMF, *India: Financial Sector Assessment Program—Detailed Assessments Report on IOSCO Objectives and Principles of Securities Regulation* (2013) (*India FSAP Report*). On Australia's assessment by the IMF, see IMF, *Australia: IOSCO Objectives and Principles of Securities Regulation—Detailed Assessment of Implementation* (Country Report No 12/314, 2012) (*Australia Country Report*), imf.org/en/Publications/CR/Issues/2016/12/31/ Australia-IOSCO-Objectives-and-Principles-of-Securities-Regulation-Detailed-Assessment-of-40116. IOSCO prescribes 38 principles that national regulators are expected to incorporate within their legal and policy frameworks: see IOSCO, *Objectives and Principles of Securities Regulation* (2010), iosco.org/ library/pubdocs/pdf/IOSCOPD323.pdf.

the International Organization of Securities Commissions (IOSCO).[2] The analysis in Chapters 3–8 independently describes and evaluates key features of each regime pertaining to each IOSCO Principle, and ascertains the degree of alignment of SEBI and ASIC with these. This analysis informs the overall analysis and conclusions drawn at the end of each chapter on the degree of comparability and relevance for cooperation between the two securities regimes in respect of each IOSCO Principle.

This chapter focuses on the roles and responsibilities of the securities markets regulators of India and Australia and the cooperation regimes. Essentially, it covers and assesses each regime against the requirements under IOSCO Principles 1–7 and 13–15. The first part extends on the approach adopted for the comparative analysis in this book. The second part describes and critically analyses the key features of SEBI's and ASIC's securities landscapes and how well they align with IOSCO Principles 1–7 and 13–15. The final part provides a brief synthesis and conclusion.

The comparative analysis: The approach

The following discussion extends on the approach set out in Chapter 1 for the comparative analysis of the Indian and Australian securities regimes in this book. It specifically looks at IOSCO's objectives and background, the relevance of the IOSCO Principles and the rationale for choosing them as the basis of the comparative analysis in this book.

IOSCO and the objectives of securities regulation

IOSCO is the premier standard-setting international organisation for securities markets.[3] Established in 1983, IOSCO derives its strength as an institution from its wide membership of more than 95 per cent of the world's

---

2   See IOSCO, *Objectives and Principles of Securities Regulation* (n 1).

3   IOSCO, 'About IOSCO', iosco.org/about/?subsection=about_iosco. IOSCO is the leading international organisation of securities commissions that provides 'high quality technical training assistance, education and training, and research to its members and other regulators' with the objective of building sound markets and encouraging the existence of a robust regulatory framework: ibid.
For more on the role and importance of IOSCO, see Hector Danny D Uy, 'ASEAN's legal framework on financial integration' (2015) 89 *Philadelphia Law Journal* 231, 245; Janet Austin, 'The power and influence of IOSCO in formulating and enforcing securities regulations' (2015) 15 *Asper Review of International Business and Trade Law* 1; Hannah L Buxbaum, 'Transnational legal ordering and regulatory conflict: lessons from the regulation of cross-border derivatives' (2016) 1 *UC Irvine Journal*

securities markets that operate in over 115 jurisdictions.[4] IOSCO's operations and work are guided by three fundamental objectives for regulatory standards on markets, investor protection and global information sharing:

- developing and implementing internationally recognised and consistent standards of regulation, oversight and enforcement for protecting investors, maintaining fair and transparent markets, and addressing systemic risks
- enhancing investor protection and investor confidence
- encouraging exchange of information at both global and regional levels.[5]

To achieve its objectives, IOSCO and its members adopted the IOSCO Principles.[6] Although soft law,[7] these are highly significant in the global securities arena as they are endorsed by more than 90 per cent of global securities authorities.[8] The next section elaborates on these principles.

---

of International, Transnational and Comparative Law 91. IOSCO is even more critical than regulatory dialogues in promoting cross-border regulatory standards: see Chris Brummer, 'Post-American securities regulation' (2010) 98 California Law Review 327, 338. See also Anne-Marie Slaughter, A New World Order (Princeton University Press, 2004).

'IOSCO is the primary institution through which international standards, memoranda, and guidelines concerning the securities markets are promulgated': see Antonio Marcacci, 'IOSCO: the world standard setter for globalized financial markets' (2012) 12 Richmond Journal of Global Law and Business 23. See also David E Van Zandt, 'The regulatory and institutional conditions for an international securities market' (1991) 32 Vanderbilt Journal of International Law 47; David Kempthorne, 'Governing international securities markets: IOSCO and the politics of international securities market standards' (PhD book, University of Waterloo, Canada, 2013).

4   See IOSCO, 'About IOSCO' (n 3) 6. IOSCO's membership is divided into three categories: ordinary, associate and affiliate. At present, there are 128 ordinary members, 32 associate members and 65 affiliate members. Ordinary members comprise the national securities markets regulators or governmental agencies that have significant authority over securities or derivatives markets in their home jurisdictions. Associate members are supranational governmental regulators, subnational governmental regulators, intergovernmental international organisations and other standard setting bodies, as well as other governmental bodies that work around securities regulation. Affiliate members are self-regulatory organisations, securities markets exchanges and such other bodies that have an interest in securities regulations. For more on IOSCO's historical origins and structure, see Marcacci, 'IOSCO: the world standard' (n 3).

5   See IOSCO, Objectives and Principles of Securities Regulation (n 1).

6   It is pertinent to note that IOSCO's reference to 'securities markets' and their regulation includes reference to the 'derivatives' markets, which is in steep contrast to some jurisdictions, such as the US, where securities and financial futures regulation is separate: see Roberta S Karmel, 'IOSCO's response to the financial crisis' (2011) 37 Journal of Corporation Law 849, 851.

7   Refer to Chapter 1, this book, for the difference between 'soft' and 'hard' law. Also see Roberta S Karmel and Claire R Kelly, 'The hardening of soft law in securities regulation' (2008) 34 Brooklyn Journal of International Law 883.

8   On the significance of the IOSCO Principles, see Brummer (n 3). On the significance of IOSCO, see Robert Baxt, Ashley Black and Pamela F Hanrahan, Securities and Financial Services Law (LexisNexis Butterworths, 9th ed, 2017). See also AA Sommer, 'IOSCO: its mission and achievement' (1996) 17 Northwestern Journal of International Law and Business 15; Janet Austin, 'IOSCO's Multilateral Memorandum of Understanding Concerning Consultation, Cooperation and the Exchange of Information: a model for international regulatory convergence' (2012) 23(4) Criminal Law Forum 393–423, doi.org/10.1007/s10609-012-9180-6.

IOSCO Principles: Importance and rationale for using them as the basis of the comparative analysis

The national regulators of all major securities markets, including those of India and Australia, have endorsed the IOSCO Principles.[9] These were first published in 1998 as a set of 30 principles of securities regulations and were revised in 2010, post the global financial crisis (GFC), to a set of 38 principles.[10]

The preamble to IOSCO's by-laws amplifies the three objectives of securities regulation[11] and, together with other documents (including the foreword and executive summary to the IOSCO Principles), emphasises the practical implementation of the principles by national regulators to achieve these objectives.[12] The 38 IOSCO Principles are organised under 10 separate headings,[13] collectively covering all fundamental aspects of a

---

9   The IOSCO Principles are a comprehensive set of standards that securities regulators across the globe refer to and adopt into their domestic policymaking and regulation: see IOSCO, *Objectives and Principles of Securities Regulation* (n 1). Both the securities regulators of India and Australia, SEBI and ASIC, are ordinary members of IOSCO, and are signatories to the IOSCO MMoU for Cooperation: see IOSCO, *Multilateral Memorandum of Understanding Concerning Consultation and Cooperation and the Exchange of Information* (2002) (MMoU). In both India and Australia, the regulators are authorised by the respective governments (Treasury in Australia and the Ministry of Finance in India).

10   IOSCO, *Objectives and Principles of Securities Regulation* (n 1). For more on the revision of IOSCO's Principles post GFC, see Karmel (n 6) 9. Several IOSCO Principles, such as the requirement for credit rating agencies to be registered, were introduced in the aftermath of the GFC: see Susan K Schroeder, 'Regulatory capture', in *Public Credit Rating Agencies* (Springer, 2015) 105–124, doi.org/10.1057/9781137359117_5. See also Phuong Duong, Jinghui Liu and Ian Eddie, 'Development of the regulatory framework of securities market supervision post-GFC' in Hasan Dincer and Ümit Hacioglu (eds) *Globalization of Financial Institutions* (Springer, 2014) 185–199, doi.org/10.1007/978-3-319-01125-7_14. For literature proposing a more streamlined framework for securities regulation post-GFC, see generally Alex Erskine, 'Framework for securities regulation post-GFC' (2010)(4) *JASSA* 37.

11   IOSCO, 'Preamble: by-laws of IOSCO' (1996), iosco.org/library/by_laws/pdf/IOSCO-By-Laws-Section-1-English.pdf. Considering the fundamental role played by securities markets and the increase in globalisation and integration, securities authorities from around the world resolved in 1996 to cooperate in developing and promoting consistent standards of regulation to enhance investor protection and exchange information at both global and regional levels.

12   IOSCO, 'Foreword' and 'Executive Summary', *Objectives and Principles of Securities Regulation* (n 1).

13   See IOSCO, *Objectives and Principles of Securities Regulation* (n 1). The 10 separate heads deal with the following themes: standards relating to the role and functioning of the regulator; standards on self-regulation; standards on supervision and enforcement of securities regulation; regulator's cooperation regime; standards for issuers; standards for auditors, credit rating agencies and other information providers; standards for collective investment schemes; standards for intermediaries; principles for secondary markets; and standards for clearing and settlement systems.

securities market regime, and have been endorsed as the relevant standards for securities markets by the premier international organisations in the international financial sector.[14]

The principles are used to evaluate the performance of securities jurisdictions across the world, the most prominent example being the Financial Sector Assessment Program (FSAP) conducted by the International Monetary Fund (IMF) and the World Bank.[15] Although the IOSCO Principles have attracted criticism,[16] they are the leading comprehensive international standards in this area.[17] Therefore, this book benchmarks the securities regimes of India and Australia utilising these principles.

The role and responsibilities of the regulator and its cooperation regime: An evaluation of the Indian and Australian securities regimes relating to IOSCO Principles 1–7 and 13–15

This section commences the comparative analysis of SEBI's and ASIC's securities regimes in relation to IOSCO Principles 1–7 and 13–15. Principles 1–7 lay down the roles and responsibilities of the regulator that are fundamental for enabling the regulator to perform its duties and

---

14 Both the Group of 20 and the Financial Stability Board (FSB) have endorsed the IOSCO Principles. The FSB is an international organisation that 'monitors and makes recommendations about the global financial system': see Financial Stability Board, 'Mandate of the FSB', fsb.org/about/. Where relevant, these organisations work with IOSCO for global systemic stability: see for example FSB and IOSCO, 'Summary and main takeaways' (FSB–IOSCO Roundtable on Compensation Practices in the Securities Sector, Basel, 13 December 2016), iosco.org/library/pubdocs/pdf/IOSCOPD559.pdf. For more on IOSCO's significance as a securities markets standard setter, see Sommer (n 8). IOSCO's importance is enhanced through its enforcement cooperation mechanisms: see Austin, 'IOSCO'S Multilateral Memorandum of Understanding' (n 8).

15 The IMF and the World Bank have been using the IOSCO Objectives and Principles for assessments for almost two decades: see IMF and World Bank, *Experience with the Assessments of the IOSCO Objectives and Principles of Securities Regulation under the Financial Sector Assessment Program* (18 April 2002).

16 The IOSCO Principles have been criticised as 'duplicative, overlapping and even contradictory': see Cally Jordan, 'The new internationalism? IOSCO, international standards and capital markets regulation' (CIGI Paper No 189, 2018), doi.org/10.2139/ssrn.3257800. This piece is pessimistic about IOSCO's aim of regulatory regulation convergence.

17 Thomas Papadopoulos, 'International Organization of Securities Commissions (IOSCO)' (2015) *Max Planck Encyclopedia of Public International Law* (Oxford University Press, 2014). IOSCO is seen to be based on a US-like regulatory philosophy of fair and efficient markets: see Antonio Marcacci, 'IOSCO and the spreading of a US-like regulatory philosophy around the world' (2014) 25(6) *European Business Law Review* 759, doi.org/10.54648/EULR2014034.

functions effectively. Principles 13–15 relate to the cooperation regime—both domestic and foreign—of the regulator, which also plays an integral role in ensuring that the regulator carries out its mandate efficiently.

The comparative analysis for each IOSCO Principle examined in this chapter is presented along the following lines:

- overview of the key features of each jurisdiction's framework relating to the requirements of the specific principle
- analysis of the strengths and weaknesses of the framework and implementation
- consideration of degree of alignment with the core requirements of the IOSCO Principle(s), overall stage of development of the cooperation regime and extent of change or reform introduced in recent years in the specific area.[18]

Based on this analysis, the final part of the chapter draws conclusions on the degree of comparability and the relevance for cooperation in respect of the principles analysed.

Table 3.1: Snapshot of the analysis in this chapter of the role and responsibilities of the regulator and its cooperation regime (IOSCO Principles 1–7, 13–15)

IOSCO Principles of Securities Regulation	SEBI's degree of alignment, stage of development and extent of reform in recent years	ASIC's degree of alignment, stage of development and extent of reform in recent years	Degree of comparability	Relevance for cooperation
Principles relating to the regulator				
Principle 1: Regulator's responsibilities should be clearly stated	**High** Evolving Substantial	**High** Mature Substantial	**Moderate**	**High**
SEBI's FSAP 2013* rating: 'broadly implemented' ASIC's FSAP 2012** ratings: 'fully implemented'				
Principle 2: Regulator should be independent and accountable	**Moderate** Evolving Minor	**Moderate** Evolving Substantial	**High**	**Low**

---

18 For a detailed understanding of the methodology, see Chapter 1 of this book.

IOSCO Principles of Securities Regulation	SEBI's degree of alignment, stage of development and extent of reform in recent years	ASIC's degree of alignment, stage of development and extent of reform in recent years	Degree of comparability	Relevance for cooperation
SEBI's FSAP 2013 rating: 'partly implemented' ASIC's FSAP 2012 ratings: 'partly implemented'				
Principle 3: Regulator should have adequate power, resources and capacity to perform its duties	**Moderate** Evolving Minor	**Moderate** Mature Substantial	**Moderate**	**High**
SEBI's FSAP 2013 rating: 'broadly implemented' ASIC's FSAP 2012 ratings: 'partly implemented'				
Principle 4: Regulator should adopt clear and consistent processes	**Moderate** Evolving Minor	**High** Mature Minor	**Moderate**	**High**
SEBI's FSAP 2013 rating: 'fully implemented' ASIC's FSAP 2012 ratings: 'fully implemented'				
Principle 5: Regulator's staff should observe the highest professional standards	**High** Evolving Minor	**High** Mature Minor	**Moderate**	**Low**
SEBI's FSAP 2013 rating: 'fully implemented' ASIC's FSAP 2012 ratings: 'fully implemented'				
Principle 6: Regulator should have, or contribute to, a process to monitor, mitigate and manage systemic risk	**High** Evolving Substantial	**High** Mature Substantial	**Moderate**	**High**
SEBI's FSAP 2013 rating: 'not assessed' (P6 was a new principle adopted post-GFC) ASIC's FSAP 2012 ratings: 'fully implemented'				
Principle 7: Regulator should have or contribute to a process to review the perimeter of regulation	**High** Mature Substantial	**High** Mature Minor	**High**	**High**

IOSCO Principles of Securities Regulation	SEBI's degree of alignment, stage of development and extent of reform in recent years	ASIC's degree of alignment, stage of development and extent of reform in recent years	Degree of comparability	Relevance for cooperation
SEBI's FSAP 2013 rating: 'not assessed' (P7 was a new principle adopted post-GFC) ASIC's FSAP 2012 ratings: 'fully implemented'				
Principles for cooperation in regulation				
Principle 13: Regulator should have power to share public and non-public information with domestic and foreign counterparts	**High** Mature Substantial	**High** Mature Minor	**High**	**High**
SEBI's FSAP 2013 rating: 'fully implemented' ASIC's FSAP 2012 ratings: 'fully implemented'				
Principle 14: Regulator should establish information-sharing mechanisms that state when and how information will be shared with domestic and foreign counterparts	**High** Mature Substantial	**High** Mature Minor	**High**	**High**
SEBI's FSAP 2013 rating: 'fully implemented' ASIC's FSAP 2012 ratings: 'fully implemented'				
Principle 15: Regulatory system should allow for assistance to foreign regulators in their discharge of regulatory responsibilities	**High** Mature Substantial	**High** Mature Minor	**High**	**Moderate**
SEBI's FSAP 2013 rating: 'fully implemented' ASIC's FSAP 2012 ratings: 'fully implemented'				

Note: * FSAP 2013 refers to IMF, *India: Financial Sector Assessment Program — Detailed Assessments Report on IOSCO Objectives and Principles of Securities Regulation* (Country Report No 13/266, 2013). ** FSAP 2012 refers to IMF, *Australia: IOSCO Objectives and Principles of Securities Regulation — Detailed Assessment of Implementation* (Country Report No 12/314, 2012).

Principles relating to the regulator

Principle 1: The responsibilities of the regulator should be clear and objectively stated.

Principle 2: The regulator should be operationally independent and accountable in the exercise of its functions and powers.

Principle 3: The regulator should have adequate powers, proper resources and the capacity to perform its functions and exercise its powers.

Principle 4: The regulator should adopt clear and consistent regulatory processes.

Principle 5: The staff of the regulator should observe the highest professional standards including appropriate standards of confidentiality.

Principle 6: The regulator should have or contribute to a process to identify, monitor, mitigate and manage systemic risk, appropriate to its mandate.

Principle 7: The regulator should have or contribute to a process to review the perimeter of regulation regularly.

Black argues that the presence of a strong regulatory authority is imperative for the effective oversight, supervision and regulation of a securities market.[19] The importance of clear provisions and sufficient powers that enable a market regulator to undertake its regulatory mandate is underscored through IOSCO Principles 1–7, shown above. The academic literature, drawn on in the discussion below, supports these principles in relation to the role of the regulator.[20]

---

19 See Bernard Black, 'The core institutions that support strong securities markets' (1999) 55 *Business Lawyer* 1565, 1577, doi.org/10.2139/ssrn.231120. See also Bernard S Black, 'The legal and institutional preconditions for strong securities markets' (2000) 48 *UCLA Law Review* 781, 807, doi. org/10.2139/ssrn.182169. Scholars have underscored the importance of strong regulators, noting that FSAP assessments of regulatory regimes have revealed that many regulators lack the ability to effectively enforce compliance with rules and regulations: see Ana Carvajal and Jennifer A Elliott, *Strengths and Weaknesses in Securities Market Regulation: A Global Analysis* (IMF Working Paper 07/259, 2007), doi.org/ 10.2139/ssrn.1030688.

20 See for example John Braithwaite, 'Accountability and governance under the new regulatory state' (1999) 58(1) *Australian Journal of Public Administration* 90–94, doi.org/10.1111/1467-8500.00077. On the importance of 'independence' and adopting 'transparency' in decision-making to the degree permitted while 'preserving commercial confidentiality', see Marc Quintyn and Michael W Taylor, 'Regulatory and supervisory independence and financial stability' (2003) 49(2) *CESifo Economic Studies* 259, doi.org/10.1093/cesifo/49.2.259.

Principle 1: The responsibilities of the regulator should be clear and objectively stated

IOSCO's Principle 1 requires a securities markets authority to have clearly defined duties and objectives that enable it to perform its statutory mandate. A clear mandate is a prerequisite for a 'competent' and 'effective' regulatory authority.[21] Wilson argues that successful regulators generally have well-defined objectives and missions,[22] while Quintyn and Taylor suggest that regulators with clear mandates are likely to be more effective and accountable.[23]

This principle's core requirements can be summarised as:

1. A clear and objective statement of the regulator's role and responsibilities to assure investors and participants about the regulator's capability to protect and safeguard market integrity through 'fair and effective oversight'.[24]

2. The legislative framework demonstrates that the regulator is authorised and empowered to perform its mandate.[25]

3. There are sufficient regulatory arrangements to demonstrate the framework's capacity to create and implement a system that protects investors' interests, ensures 'fair, efficient and transparent markets', and minimises 'systemic risk'.[26]

In the case of two or more domestic regulators, sufficient arrangements ought to be put in place to ensure problems of 'gaps and inequities' within the sector are minimised, similar products and conduct is met with similar regulatory standards, and effective channels of cooperation and communication are available among regulators.[27]

---

21 Generally, the work of a regulator is 'always grounded in first principles' that are usually set out in the 'governing legislation': see Timothy Baikie et al, 'A framework for responsive market regulation' in *Global Algorithmic Capital Markets: High Frequency Trading, Dark Pools, and Regulatory Challenges* (Oxford University Press, 2018) 340. Often, these first principles relate to duties towards investor protection, regulation and development of securities markets.

22 James Q Wilson, *Bureaucracy: What Government Agencies Do and Why They Do It* (Basic Books, 2019).

23 Quintyn and Taylor (n 20).

24 IOSCO, *Methodology for Assessing Implementation of the IOSCO Objectives and Principles of Securities Regulation* (2017) 22.

25 Ibid.

26 Ibid. Such 'arrangements' are especially applicable to instances where the regulatory responsibilities are divided among two or more regulators.

27 See ibid. The methodology for this principle requires the framework of domestic legislation to be designed in a way that minimises gaps and inequities.

As set out in Chapter 2, ASIC's mandate and role as a market conduct regulator relates to the entire financial system and is much wider than SEBI's role as the securities market regulator. Keeping this distinction in mind, SEBI's and ASIC's mandates and roles relating to the securities sector are described and analysed below.

SEBI
Key features of SEBI's framework supporting clarity of regulatory mandate

As Chapter 2 discusses, the securities markets regulator, SEBI, is established under the *Securities and Exchange Board of India Act 1992* (*SEBI Act*). Additionally, the Reserve Bank of India (RBI) and Ministry of Corporate Affairs (MCA) under the central government play a limited role in the governance of securities markets.[28] SEBI is entrusted with the responsibilities of protecting investors' interests and regulating and promoting the development of the Indian securities markets.[29] SEBI derives its powers from several statutes: *SEBI Act, Securities Contract (Regulation) Act 1956* (*SCR Act*), *Depositories Act 1996* and *Companies Act 2013*.[30] SEBI has wide statutory powers to take any measure it deems fit to meet its responsibilities as the securities market regulator.[31] Other provisions confer specific powers such as licensing, conducting investigations and initiating enforcement proceedings.[32] To fulfil its mandate under the *SEBI Act*, SEBI has the authority to draft regulations for securities markets to complement the relevant statutes.[33] Further, SEBI is empowered to issue circulars and guidelines to clarify or elaborate on any provision of the Acts,

---

28 See IMF, *India FSAP Report* (n 1). The MCA is the primary authority to register and regulate all companies other than those whose share is listed on the exchange (such companies fall within SEBI's purview); RBI regulates 'contracts in government securities, gold related securities and money market securities and securities derived from those securities and repo contracts in debt securities'.

29 *Securities and Exchange Board of India Act 1992* (*SEBI Act*) s 11(1). SEBI's mandate is restricted to securities markets while ASIC is the conduct regulator for the entire Australian financial system.

30 See SEBI, 'List of all SEBI Acts (Updated)', sebi.gov.in/sebiweb/home/HomeAction.do?doListing= yes&sid=1&ssid=1&smid=1. See *Securities and Contracts (Regulation) Act 1956*; *Depositories Act 1996* (*Depositories Act*); *SEBI Act*. In relation to the *Companies Act 2013*, SEBI's mandate extends to 'listed companies and companies proposed to be listed on the Recognized Stock Exchanges (RSEs)'.

31 See *SEBI Act* s 11(1). SEBI's powers are widespread in relation to the securities market and include the power to license/register intermediaries, specify regulations for the markets, enforce such provisions and take action for any contravention of the securities laws. SEBI's powers are described and compared with those of ASIC's in the later part of the book.

32 Ibid s 11(2).

33 Section 30. All regulations drafted by SEBI must be tabled before parliament: see ibid s 31.

rules or regulations that apply to securities markets.[34] Finally, SEBI issues regulatory guidance known as 'Informal Guidance' for interpreting the Acts/regulations affecting securities markets.[35]

Analysis

Generally, the legal framework for regulation of securities markets is broad, prescriptive and granular,[36] and as the above enumerated provisions show, SEBI's regulatory mandate and powers are enunciated clearly in the governing statutes and other applicable legal provisions.

Further, SEBI is granted wide powers to frame regulations for securities markets, issue circulars and guidelines and, in fact, take 'any measure that it deems fit' and necessary to achieve the regulatory objectives defined in the *SEBI Act*.[37] Thus, the framework empowers SEBI with a rich quiver of regulatory powers that SEBI uses extensively in practice.[38] This suggests that a significant core of Principle 1 is satisfied to a large degree through clear legal enunciation of SEBI's roles and responsibilities, and sufficient powers. A vision and mission statement for SEBI, as adopted by leading securities jurisdictions,[39] could further clarify and effectively communicate the legislative intent of Principle 1.

As regards the more subtle but fundamental requirement of sufficient arrangements that support a regulator to achieve its mandate, there exist certain challenges associated with the sectoral nature of financial regulation, which often leads to problems of gaps and inequities, and a 'fragmented'

---

34   Section 11(1) of the *SEBI Act* calls for circulars to be issued in a wide range of areas: see SEBI, 'Circulars', sebi.gov.in/sebiweb/home/HomeAction.do?doListing=yes&sid=1&ssid=7&smid=0.

35   SEBI has the power to issue informal guidance for interpreting a provision of the Act, rules, regulations, guidelines or circulars to clarify how such a provision may be applied in the case of a specific transaction and not a hypothetical one: see *Securities and Exchange Board of India (Informal Guidance) Scheme* (2003), sebi.gov.in/legal/guidelines/jun-2003/sebi-informal-guidance-scheme-2003_16004.html.

36   In addition to the statutory Acts, SEBI's regulatory framework for securities markets comprises over 50 regulations for various securities activities and participants: see SEBI, 'List of all SEBI regulations', sebi.gov.in/sebiweb/home/HomeAction.do?doListing=yes&sid=1&ssid=3&smid=0. Most regulations are extensive and detailed in all respects connected with the subject matter: for instance, the *SEBI (Issue of Capital and Disclosure Requirements) Regulations 2018* provides a comprehensive understanding of the requirements for issue of capital and disclosure for companies listed or intending to be listed on the stock exchanges.

37   See *SEBI Act* s 11.

38   Chapter 8 of this book discusses SEBI's use of its powers.

39   See for example Financial Conduct Authority (UK), 'How we work', fca.org.uk/publications/corporate-documents/our-mission. See also ASIC, 'Our vision and strategic priorities', asic.gov.au/about-asic/what-we-do/our-role/asic-vision-and-mission/.

approach to regulation.[40] Significantly, there have been several attempts to address this problem, including a proposal to create a 'more streamlined regulatory architecture that reduces regulatory costs, overlaps, silos and gaps'.[41]

In recent years this problem of lack of coordination has been addressed to some extent by the Financial Stability and Development Council (FSDC), set up to coordinate efforts between the central government and various financial regulators including SEBI, the RBI and the MCA.[42] The FSDC aside, until recently, the financial regime in India relied upon more informal rather than formal mechanisms to share information between agencies, though several formal memoranda of understanding (MoUs) have been signed by SEBI with several domestic agencies.[43] The detailed FSAP in 2013 rated SEBI's regime for Principle 1 as 'broadly implemented'.[44]

Conclusion

The conclusions for each regime's alignment with the requirements of a specific IOSCO Principle are expressed in the following terms: the degree of alignment of each regime is assessed as high, moderate or low in respect of the principle, considering both the framework and implementation; the extent of reform or change undertaken in the past decade, and particularly after the last detailed FSAP Review for securities markets (2012 for ASIC and 2013 for SEBI), is assessed as substantial or minor; and the overall landscape relating to the specific principle is assessed as mature or evolving.

For Principle 1, given SEBI's clear and concise mandate and comprehensive legal framework that gives it wide powers, I assess the degree of alignment of SEBI's regime with Principle 1 as high. That said, the landscape for 'domestic arrangements' highlighted above is still evolving and a clear vision and mission statement by SEBI is still missing. These show that there is little room for complacency as further refinements are needed, suggesting

---

40 See Government of India Planning Commission, *A Hundred Small Steps* (Report of the Committee on Financial Sector Reforms, 2008) 14. This report is also referred to as the Raghuram Rajan Report.
41 See the recommendation of the Raghuram Rajan Report proposing to create better coordination between regulators so that systemic risks are recognised early and tackled in a coordinated way.
42 See Government of India, Ministry of Finance, 'Financial Stability and Development Council (FSDC)' (3 May 2013), pib.gov.in/newsite/PrintRelease.aspx?relid=95543. See also the description in Chapter 2 of this book.
43 See the description and analysis of SEBI's framework for cooperation relating to Principles 13, 14 and 15 in Chapter 5 of this book.
44 See IMF, *India FSAP Report* (n 1) 14. One chief reason for this assessment is the lack of formal arrangements among agencies and shortcomings in the coordination.

that the overall landscape for Principle 1 is evolving. Considering ongoing reform and enhancement of domestic, interagency arrangements in recent years, the extent of reform is characterised as substantial.

ASIC

Key features of ASIC's framework supporting clarity of regulatory mandate

As Chapter 2 sets out, ASIC is the main regulator for the Australian securities markets even though the Australian Prudential Regulatory Authority (APRA), the Reserve Bank of Australia (RBA), the Australian Competition and Consumer Commission (ACCC) and the Australian Securities Exchange (ASX) contribute towards governing by undertaking activities mandated by law.[45] The Australian securities markets are governed by the *Corporations Act 2001* (Cth) (*Corporations Act*) and the *Australian Securities and Investments Commission Act 2001* (*ASIC Act*). Section 760A of the *Corporations Act* states the key objectives of Australia's financial laws. Sections 1(1) and (2) of the *ASIC Act* set out the objects of the Act,[46] as well as the mandate for ASIC.[47] Significantly, s 1(2)(g) empowers ASIC with the ability to 'take whatever action it can take, and is necessary, in order to enforce and give effect to the laws of the Commonwealth'.[48] In addition, ASIC has powers to issue regulatory guides to interpret the law.[49] In administering financial laws, ASIC issues other regulatory documents, such as consultation papers, information sheets and reports.[50]

---

45   IMF, *Australia Country Report* (n 1). For a basic understanding of Australia's corporate regulators, see Richard Grant, *Australia's Corporate Regulators: The ACCC, ASIC and APRA* (2005).

46   The main objectives of the *Australian Securities and Investments Commission Act 2001* (Cth) (*ASIC Act*) are to provide for ASIC's functions and powers to administer the laws of the Commonwealth, state or territory governments, and establish other statutory bodies and panels, including the Takeovers Panel and Accounting and Auditing Boards.

47   *ASIC Act*. The Act sets out ASIC's main functions and exercise of powers, which include maintaining, facilitating and improving performance of the financial system, reducing business costs, efficiency and development of the economy, and investor participation.

48   See *ASIC Act* s 1(2)(g).

49   Regulatory guides help regulated entities, either by 'explaining when and how ASIC will exercise specific powers under legislation', or by 'explaining how ASIC interprets the law', or by 'describing the principles underlying ASIC's approach', or by 'giving practical guidance' in specific cases: see ASIC, 'Regulatory guides', asic.gov.au/regulatory-resources/find-a-document/regulatory-guides/.

50   Consultation papers are published to obtain feedback from stakeholders on matters that are under consideration with ASIC; information sheets are issued to give succinct guidance on a 'specific process or compliance issue or an overview of detailed guidance': see for example ASIC, *Product Intervention Power* (Regulatory Guide 272, 2020) 2.

ASIC's website and annual reports unambiguously express ASIC's vision and mission as a regulator.[51] To realise ASIC's vision for a 'fair, strong and efficient financial system',[52] ASIC's mission is to use its regulatory mechanisms to:

a. 'change behaviour to drive good customer and investor outcomes'

b. 'act against misconduct to maintain trust and integrity in the financial system'

c. 'promote strong and innovative development of the financial system'

d. 'help Australians to be in control of their financial lives'.[53]

ASIC has formal arrangements or memoranda of understanding with other regulators, institutions and authorities operating in the Australian financial sector, such as APRA,[54] the ACCC,[55] the RBA[56] and the Australian Taxation Office.[57]

Analysis

As seen from the short description above, ASIC's responsibilities and functions are clearly enunciated through the governing Acts.[58] A perusal of these statutes, along with ASIC's regulatory guides, information sheets and other similar documents, suggests that the legislative and regulatory framework is clear and suitably empowers ASIC to pursue its regulatory mandate. Chapters 4 and 5 of this book describe the manner and extent to which ASIC makes use of these powers.[59] Further, in terms of ASIC's

---

51 See generally ASIC, 'Section 1—ASIC's role' in *Annual Report 2019–20* (2020).

52 ASIC, 'Our vision' (n 39).

53 Ibid.

54 *Memorandum of Understanding between the Australian Prudential Regulatory Authority and the Australian Securities and Investments Commission* (signed 28 November 2019). This MoU replaced an earlier MoU between the two authorities signed in 2010.

55 *Memorandum of Understanding between the Australian Securities and Investments Commission and the Australian Competition and Consumer Commission* (2004).

56 *Memorandum of Understanding between the Australian Securities and Investments Commission and the Reserve Bank of Australia* (2002).

57 *Memorandum of Understanding between the Australian Taxation Office and the Australian Securities and Investments Commission* (2017).

58 ASIC exercises a wide array of powers conferred by the *Corporations Act 2001* (Cth) (*Corporations Act*). Additionally, ss 11(2) and 12A of the *ASIC Act* define ASIC's functions. For more on ASIC's powers, see Parliament of Australia, Senate Standing Committees on Economics, 'Chapter 3: overview of ASIC' in *The Performance of the Australian Securities and Investments Commission* (2014). ASIC's powers are discussed in more detail in the later chapters of this book.

59 Chapters 4 and 5 of this book analyse ASIC's main supervisory and enforcement powers. On the effectiveness of ASIC, see generally Zehra G Kavame Eroglu and KE Powell, 'Role and effectiveness of ASIC compared with the SEC: shedding light on regulation and enforcement in the United States and Australia' (2020) 31 *Journal of Banking and Finance Law and Practice* 71, doi.org/10.2139/ssrn.3612987.

arrangements with domestic institutions, as noted above, ASIC cooperates with other domestic agencies through formal arrangements. While these arrangements encourage a smooth interagency interface, the implementation of this coordination framework has seen several shortcomings in the past, and has even been held responsible to an extent for overlaps and financial collapses in Australia.[60] Similarly, while the detailed FSAP Review of 2012 for ASIC's securities regime rated ASIC's compliance with Principle 1 as 'fully implemented',[61] it also highlighted the need for smoother coordination between ASIC, APRA, the ASX and the RBA,[62] and recommended further simplification of the complex supervisory structure that could potentially lead to overlaps—for example, in respect of supervision of certain market participants such as Australian financial service licence holders.[63]

More recently, the Hayne Royal Commission criticised the coordination arrangements and recommended closer collaboration and information sharing between ASIC and APRA.[64] Following this, the coordination mechanisms for financial agencies were further upgraded to ensure smoother collaboration, as evident from the joint statement by ASIC and APRA in 2020[65] and the other financial sector legislative reforms.[66]

Conclusion

ASIC's regulatory mandate is clear and supported by an extensive legislative framework, as well as a clear vision and mission, that allows it to discharge its regulatory duties. Formal arrangements and a framework for interagency cooperation are in place and the weaknesses pointed out by the Hayne Royal Commission are being addressed. This suggests that the interagency coordination regime, specifically among the two key regulators, APRA and ASIC, is well on its way to second-generation refinement and efficacy.

---

60   Andrew Godwin, Steve Kourabas and Ian Ramsay, 'Twin Peaks and financial regulation: the challenges of increasing regulatory overlap and expanding responsibilities' (2016) 49(3) *The International Lawyer* 278.
61   IMF, *Australia Country Report* (n 1), 21.
62   Ibid 42. The report highlighted the need for improved coordination among regulatory bodies, even though the Council of Financial Regulators oversees such collaboration.
63   Ibid 40. Both ASIC and APRA have supervisory roles over AFSL holders, and the *Corporations Act* deals with the overlap by making some provisions of the Act not applicable to AFSL holders that are supervised by APRA. Chapter 8 of this book provides a detailed examination of the AFSL regime.
64   *Royal Commission into Misconduct in the Banking, Superannuation and Financial Services Industry* (Final Report, September 2018) (Hayne Report) vol 1, recommendation 6.10.
65   ASIC and APRA published their first update on engagement between the two bodies on 22 December 2020: see APRA, 'APRA and ASIC publish annual update on joint engagement' (22 December, 2020), apra.gov.au/news-and-publications/apra-and-asic-publish-annual-update-on-joint-engagement.
66   Hayne Report (n 64).

For these reasons, the degree of alignment of ASIC's regime with IOSCO Principle 1 is determined as 'high'. Overall, ASIC's regime is assessed to operate in a sufficiently 'mature' manner, with 'substantial' improvements being carried out in the recent years towards making interagency arrangements more effective.

Principle 2: The regulator should be operationally independent and accountable in the exercise of its functions and powers

For effectiveness of market regulators, Levine argues that a high degree of independence is vitally important.[67] IOSCO's Principle 2 requires regulators to hold adequate independence, both operational and financial, to carry forth their regulatory objectives and responsibilities while remaining 'accountable' through a system of checks and balances that ensures responsible behaviour.[68]

In a sense, 'independence' and 'accountability' of regulators can be regarded as two sides of a scale that requires delicate balancing. Such 'independence' needs to be determined against two chief parameters: 1) interference from outside—both external political interference and interference from commercial or sectoral interests; and 2) availability of stable and continuous funding to the regulator for its regulatory tasks.[69] In circumstances where regulatory policy requires regulators to consult with or seek approval of a government or minister or any other legislative authority, the precise circumstances for such consultation or approval should be 'clear' and 'transparent' and 'subject to review'.[70]

---

67   The independence of regulatory authorities, both from political and market influence, is significant, as it ensures that 'regulators [act] in the best interests of public': see Ross Levine, 'The governance of financial regulation: reform lessons from the recent crisis' (2012) 12(1) *International Review of Finance* 39–56, 11, 12, doi.org/10.1111/j.1468-2443.2011.01133.x. For a contrary view, Gadinis contends that there has been 'a shift away from the ideals of regulatory independence towards a model of greater political intervention in financial regulation', a trend that has found more force post-GFC: see Stavros Gadinis, 'The Financial Stability Board: the new politics of international financial regulation' (2012) 48 *Texas International Law Journal* 157.

68   Kerwer argues that non-majoritarian institutions, such as ministries, regulatory agencies, central banks and the like, need to be made accountable to the democratic process: see generally Dieter Kerwer, 'Holding global regulators accountable: the case of credit rating agencies' (2005) 18(3) *Governance* 453–475, doi.org/10.1111/j.1468-0491.2005.00284.x.

69   IOSCO, *Methodology for Assessing* (n 24) 25.

70   Ibid 25.

The requirement of accountability under this principle translates into the regulator being subject to varying levels of review and scrutiny, including periodic public reporting of its performance, transparency in process and conduct, and judicial review of its decisions.[71]

SEBI

Key features of SEBI's independence and accountability framework

SEBI is statutorily empowered under the *SEBI Act 1992, Depositories Act 1996* and *Companies Act 2013* to perform licensing/registration, surveillance, investigation and enforcement functions without having to consult with central government authorities.[72] Under the *SEBI Act 1992, Depositories Act 1996* and *SCR Act 1956*, SEBI is endowed with powers to frame regulations for securities markets.[73] Further, SEBI enjoys financial independence and non-reliance on funding from the government;[74] and legal protection from suits, prosecution or any legal proceedings for SEBI's employees for bona fide acts performed in the course of their official duties.[75]

As regards accountability, first, SEBI is accountable to the central government, primarily through the Ministry of Finance (MoF) that oversees its functioning.[76] Second, s 18 of the *SEBI Act* requires SEBI to submit to the central government annual reports on its activities and programs within 90 days after the end of each financial year.[77] A copy of this report is also submitted to each house of parliament[78] and published on SEBI's website.[79]

---

71 Ibid.
72 IMF, *India FSAP Report* (n 1) 29.
73 See *SEBI Act* s 30. It is pertinent to note, however, that the regulations issued by SEBI are required to be tabled in parliament for 30 days and may be subject to modifications; this serves as an important check and balance measure on SEBI's power: ibid s 31.
74 Section 14(1) of the *SEBI Act* provides for the constitution of a fund by the name of Securities and Exchange Board of India General Fund to which 'all grants, fees and charges received by the Board under this Act' are required to be credited: see ibid. It is worth noting that the amendment to the Act in 2002 omitted a clause that allowed SEBI to credit 'all sums realized by way of Penalties under this Act', which had been inserted into the Act by amendment in 1995.
75 Section 23 of the *SEBI Act* states that no suit, prosecution or other legal proceeding shall be filed against any officer or other employee of SEBI for anything that is done in good faith or any action taken under this Act: see ibid s 23.
76 See Government of India, Ministry of Finance, 'Department of Economic Affairs', finmin.nic.in/ (page discontinued).
77 Section 18 of the *SEBI Act* requires SEBI to furnish to the central government returns and statements and particulars of any existing or proposed developments of the securities market. In addition, SEBI is required to submit a report that gives an account of the accurate position of its 'activities, policy and programmes' during the previous financial year: see *SEBI Act* s 18(1) and (2).
78 See ibid s 18(3).
79 See for example SEBI, *Annual Report 2018–19* (2019).

As another facet of accountability, SEBI is also subject to transparency norms ensured through the application of the *Right to Information Act 2005* (*RTI Act*) to SEBI. Further, the *SEBI Act* ensures transparency in enforcement actions initiated by SEBI by requiring reasons to be given in its orders.[80]

Finally, SEBI's power to suspend or revoke a license/certificate of registration or levy a monetary penalty is subject to the procedure laid out in the *SEBI (Intermediaries) Regulations 2008* and the *Adjudication Rules 1995* or *Adjudication Rules 2005* that require 'due process of law' to be observed, which includes adherence to natural justice rules, such as according an opportunity of being heard to the parties against whom action is considered to be taken. SEBI's orders are subject to judicial review and can be appealed against before the Securities Appellate Tribunal.[81]

Analysis

The above provisions reflect regulatory independence in SEBI's ability to license and register intermediaries; frame norms for the securities markets through regulations, as well as issue other circulars and guidelines; and raise funds independently for its regulatory functions and requirements.[82] Further, SEBI's staff enjoy sufficient immunity from legal suits for actions performed in the course of their duties, which ensures independence in their functioning.[83]

Notwithstanding these positives, it is clear that the central government, through MoF, plays a significant role by overseeing SEBI's functioning. Due to such government control, the detailed FSAP Review of 2013 granted SEBI a 'partly implemented' rating for Principle 2, primarily as the assessors regarded government control as a restraint on SEBI's autonomy.[84] Nevertheless, it is worth noting that, on a day-to-day basis, SEBI enjoys considerable freedom to operate without any significant political interference in a majority of its operational duties, as the FSAP Review also recognised.[85]

---

80   See generally Shubho Roy et al, 'Building state capacity for regulation' in Devesh Kapur and Madhav Khosla (eds), *Regulation in India: Design, Capacity, Performance* (2019) 379.

81   See *SEBI Act* s 15T. The provision requires for appeals to be filed within 45 days from the day the order was received by the aggrieved person. Moreover, under s 15Z the decisions of the Securities Appellate Tribunal can be further appealed before the Supreme Court, but on matters of law and not facts.

82   SEBI is empowered under the *SEBI Act* to generate its own funding.

83   See *SEBI Act* s 24B.

84   IMF, *India FSAP Report* (n 1) 14.

85   For instance, SEBI is not required to seek comments or consult with the central government for any matter pertaining to licensing or registering intermediaries in the securities markets: see *SEBI Act* s 12.

Besides the observation of political control over SEBI, certain concerns have surfaced in respect of SEBI's financial independence in recent years, particularly with the central government requiring a transfer of SEBI's surplus funds to the Consolidated Fund of India (CFI),[86] a move that has been resisted by SEBI as amounting to an 'infringement' of its regulatory independence.[87]

To sum up, accountability and transparency in SEBI's case are well reflected from the examples discussed above,[88] although there are a number of areas where such accountability and transparency standards may be enhanced.[89] The FSAP Review of SEBI in 2013 regarded the provisions of accountability, on the whole, as adequate for SEBI.[90]

Conclusion

The above position suggests that SEBI's regime demonstrates a significant level of sufficiency in observance of Principle 2, with many provisions in existence to ensure accountability and transparency of the regulator. However, the central government's control over SEBI—though not affecting its day-to-day functioning—and attempt to require it to transfer its surplus funds to the CFI and make further improvements in transparency structures, suggest that the degree of alignment with the core requirements of Principle 2 is 'moderate', with plenty of areas needing further refinement, both in respect of regulatory independence and accountability.

Further, given that SEBI's regime has tremendous potential to transition to higher levels of transparency and accountability, the 'overall landscape' relating to this principle is assessed as rapidly 'evolving'. At the same time, while there

---

86   Recently, the central government has required SEBI to move its surplus funds to the CFI: see Reena Zachariah, 'Moving SEBI surplus to government will hit fin autonomy: Tyagi', *The Economic Times* (18 July 2019), economictimes.indiatimes.com/markets/stocks/news/moving-sebi-surplus-to-government-will-hit-fin-autonomy-tyagi/articleshow/70269758.cms?from=mdr. See also JP Upadhyay, 'SEBI fights to retain Rs.1672 crore in surplus funds', *The Mint* (5 January 2018).

87   Shrimi Choudhary, 'Govt, Sebi spar over transfer of surplus funds as Budget 2020 nears', *Business Standard* (28 December 2019), business-standard.com/budget/article/budget-2020-centre-sebi-spar-over-transfer-of-surplus-funds-to-exchequer-119122800029_1.html. See also Rajeev Jayaswal, 'Centre pushes for transfer of Sebi's surplus into its accounts', *Hindustan Times* (26 December 2019), hindustan times.com/india-news/centre-pushes-for-transfer-of-sebi-s-surplus-into-its-accounts/story-LWQCz2L SWr7GhvhgTYbxyL.html.

88   For example, the accountability to the central government, the applicability of the *Right to Information Act 2005 (RTI Act)* and of judicial review over SEBI demonstrate accountability to a large degree: see notes 57–62 above.

89   SEBI's transparency is discussed at length later in this chapter under Principle 4. SEBI's public consultation process has been criticised as being opaque, with SEBI neither publishing comments received by it nor its response: see B Zaveri, 'Participatory governance in regulation making: how to make it work?' *The Leap Blog* (17 January 2016), blog.theleapjournal.org/2016/01/participatory-governance-in-regulation.html.

90   IMF, *India FSAP Report* (n 1) 14.

have been continuing attempts to improve transparency and accountability, such as through public consultations and prior publication of reports, the quality of improvements to such consultations and reports in the recent years is assessed as 'minor'. Human resource constraints, as discussed later under Principle 3, are argued to have contributed to this limitation.

ASIC
Key features of ASIC's independence and accountability framework

The financial and securities framework safeguards ASIC's independence and accountability in several ways. In terms of the mechanisms ensuring independence, ASIC adopts open consultations before introducing new policies, which ensures its independence from commercial or sectoral interests.[91] Further, the framework provides for internal policy mechanisms, for instance, the Regulatory Policy Committee deliberates on submissions on new or reformed policies and considers applications seeking exemptions from provisions administered by ASIC,[92] protecting ASIC's staff from legal liability in relation to bona fide acts performed in the course of their duties.[93] Collectively, these measures contribute to maintaining ASIC's operational independence.

As regards ASIC's financial independence, until recently ASIC relied solely on government for its funding, with parliament approving its budget and providing an appropriation revenue to ASIC each year from the Commonwealth's Consolidated Revenue Fund.[94] A key change stemming from the recommendations of the 2014 Financial System Inquiry in respect of ASIC's financial resources was the introduction of the industry-funding model.[95] ASIC's Annual Report 2020–21 notes that ASIC

---

91   IMF, *Australia Country Report* (n 1) 43.
92   The Regulatory Policy Committee was earlier the Regulatory Policy Group: see ASIC, *Regulatory Policy Group: Purpose, Governance and Practices Summary* (March 2012), download.asic.gov.au/media/1346306/RPG--Purpose-governance-and-practices--March-2012.pdf. This group comprises senior executives; its purpose is to make decisions on regulatory policy and law reform and to provide guidance on relief applications.
93   *ASIC Act* s 246.
94   In 2017–18, ASIC received approximately $348 million as appropriation revenue, reflecting an increase of $6 million as compared with 2016–17. This was mainly on account of the royal commission's appointment: see ASIC, *Annual Report 2017–18* (2018) 4. Interestingly, there has been an increase in this budget over the past years and ASIC's 2020–21 *Annual Report* notes that it received $437 million in appropriation revenue: see ASIC, 'Financial summary—ASIC's role' in *Annual Report 2020–21* (2021).
95   ASIC, 'ASIC industry funding: background information about industry funding', asic.gov.au/about-asic/what-we-do/how-we-operate/asic-industry-funding/. The government's industry-funding model for ASIC became law in 2017.

raised $1,513 million as revenue through fees levied on financial market participants and charges (including industry funding), all of which was transferred to the Australian government.[96] ASIC received consolidated revenue of approximately $437 million from the Australian government and generated approximately $41 million of own-source revenue that includes revenue generated and retained by ASIC.[97] As ASIC's total expenses for the same year were approximately $492 million, it incurred a deficit of approximately $14 million. This suggests that ASIC is still on a tightrope walk towards financial independence and self-sufficiency, although, as Chapters 4 and 5 discuss, financial constraints are not the only restraint on ASIC's performance as a regulator.

For accountability and transparency, ASIC is subject to an extensive and robust governance and accountability framework detailed on its website, with many updates to the framework introduced in December 2019 (Figure A1.2 shows ASIC's current accountability and governance structure). The Financial Accountability Regime Bill 2021 (Cth) is likely to enhance the accountability of ASIC's staff.[98] The governance framework creates a hierarchical structure within the securities regime that ensures that the treasurer, the minister for financial services and superannuation, and the parliamentary secretary to the treasurer are all made responsible for overseeing ASIC's functioning.[99] Further, the framework establishes broad-ranging and comprehensive parliamentary oversight mechanisms over ASIC,[100] ensures accountability of the management and senior staff,[101] and ultimately makes ASIC accountable to the Australian public through a

---

96   See ASIC, 'Financial summary' (n 94) 28. For a detailed discussion of ASIC's funding sources, prior to the introduction of the industry funding model, see IMF, *Australia Country Report* (n 1) 44.

97   Own-source revenue includes court costs recovered, royalties and other sundry income: see ASIC, 'Financial summary' (n 94) 27.

98   See ASIC, 'ASIC's governance and accountability framework', asic.gov.au/about-asic/what-we-do/how-we-operate/asic-s-governance-and-accountability/#framework. See also *Financial Accountability Regime Bill 2021* (Cth). It is significant to note that, even though ASIC as a statutory authority is not subject to a legislative accountability regime, the commission has to apply key features of the existing Banking Executive Accountability Regime to its senior staff: see *Banking Act 1959* (Cth) pt IIAA.

99   See *ASIC Act* s 12. The minister for financial services and superannuation looks after superannuation, financial services, credit and financial markets; the parliamentary secretary to the treasurer oversees corporate governance, audit, insolvency, financial literacy and the functioning of ASIC.

100 ASIC is accountable to parliament through 1) the Parliamentary Joint Committee on Corporations and Financial Services, 2) the Senate Standing Committee on Economics and 3) the House of Representatives Economics Committee: see ASIC, '8.1 Appendices relating to ASIC's governance and operations' in *Annual Report 2019–20* (2020).

101 ASIC's Management Accountability Regime clearly identifies the accountabilities of ASIC's chair, commission members and executive directors: see ASIC, 'ASIC's governance and accountability framework' (n 98).

range of high-quality publications, such as ASIC's annual reports, corporate plans, annual portfolio budget statements and self-assessments.[102] ASIC conducts its self-assessments against the six outcomes-based performance indicators in the federal government's *Regulator Performance Framework* (published in October 2014) while the *Public, Governance, Performance and Accountability Act 2013* (Cth) that applies to Commonwealth staff imposes high standards for governance and accountability for public resources, and focuses on planning, performance and reporting.[103]

In addition to this framework, the relevant minister is empowered to send written directions to ASIC on policies to pursue and priorities to follow in exercising its powers under the *Corporations Act* and the *ASIC Act*.[104] Accountability is further enhanced through a mechanism allowing ministers to issue a 'Statement of Expectations' to clarify the expectations they set for statutory bodies.[105] ASIC is required to follow the natural justice principles of procedural fairness, which include according an opportunity to a person who may be 'adversely affected' by its decisions, thereby further ensuring accountability.[106] Moreover, ASIC's orders are subject to judicial review under the *Administrative Decisions Judicial Review Act 1977* on aspects

---

102 ASIC, 'ASIC's governance and accountability framework' (n 98). ASIC's corporate plan covers its purpose, performance, capability and management, while the annual portfolio budget statements inform the Senate and parliament of ASIC's proposed resource allocation. Its annual reports are tabled in parliament.

103 The Regulator Performance Framework was introduced in 2014 to assess operations and performance of Regulators. It mandates outcome-based key performance indicators that cover reducing regulatory burden, communication, risk-based and proportionate approaches to regulation, efficient and coordinated monitoring, transparency and continuous improvement of regulatory frameworks: see ASIC, 'Regulator Performance Framework', asic.gov.au/about-asic/what-we-do/how-we-operate/performance-and-review/regulator-performance-framework/. The *Public Governance, Performance and Accountability Act 2013* (Cth) imposes personal statutory obligations on commissioners and executive duties on ASIC's chair: see ASIC, 'ASIC's governance and accountability framework' (n 98).

104 The minister can 'express his expectations' of ASIC, give directions and 'decide on matters relating to AML and CSFL holders': see IMF, *Australia Country Report* (n 1) 21. The minister is not authorised to issue a direction under s 12 if such direction is in respect of a specific case: see *ASIC Act* s 12(3). However, the minister can direct ASIC to investigate in a matter that is of public interest: see *ASIC Act* s 14. It is also significant to note that this power is rarely used: for example, it was used in 1992 when the minister 'directed ASIC under s 12 of the *ASIC Act* to develop and implement policy for the discharge of its powers vis-à-vis those of the Commonwealth Director of Public Prosecutions': see IMF, *Australia Country Report* (n 1).

105 The federal government expects ASIC to contribute to the government's changing economic objectives especially in the post-pandemic world: see Treasurer of the Commonwealth of Australia, 'New Statement of Expectation for the Australian Securities and Investments Commission' (Media Release, 26 August 2021). Until 2019, there had been three such statements of expectations—2007, 2014 and 2018: see ASIC, 'Statements of expectations and intent', asic.gov.au/about-asic/what-we-do/how-we-operate/accountability-and-reporting/statements-of-expectations-and-intent/.

106 IMF, *Australia Country Report* (n 1) 46.

that relate to questions of legality, such as lack of jurisdiction or errors of law.[107] Decisions of a 'regulatory nature' can be appealed against before the Administrative Appeals Tribunal set up under the *Administrative Appeals Tribunal Act 1975* (Cth).[108] Further, ASIC has the power to makes rules for markets and for their integrity, and such rules are subject to the approval of the relevant minister as detailed in s 798G of the *Corporations Act*.

Analysis

A perusal of the above features of ASIC's governance and accountability framework, along with significant literature examining or relating to ASIC's independence[109] and accountability,[110] leads to the following conclusions. First, ASIC's monetary dependence on government funding,[111] which has often led to funding cuts in the past for ASIC,[112] has been the subject of repeated discussion[113] and has been linked to ASIC's below par performance

---

107 See *Administrative Decisions (Judicial Review) Act 1977* (Cth). ASIC's decisions may also be subject to 'merits review' by the Administrative Appeals Tribunal. The tribunal's decisions may be appealed before the Federal Court, the Supreme Court and the High Court of Australia: see also IMF, *Australia Country Report* (n 1).

108 Administrative Appeals Tribunal, 'About the AAT: overview', aat.gov.au/about-the-aat [site discontinued]. See also *Administrative Appeals Tribunal Act 1975* (Cth).

109 For literature that discusses ASIC's financial resources, see Julia Stannard, 'ASIC update: armoury and funding, supervisory approach and reforms' (2018)(438) *Superfunds Magazine* 14; Andrew Main, 'Beefing up ASIC makes sense' (2018)(153) *Investment Magazine* 13; Ashley Matthews, 'The financial services industry: whistleblowing and calls for a royal commission' (2016) 136 *Precedent* 35; John Price, 'Regulator: funding changes ahead' (2017) 33(10) *Company Director* 38. See generally Ian Ramsay and Miranda Webster, 'ASIC enforcement outcomes: trends and analysis' (2017) 35(5) *Company and Securities Law Journal* 289–321.

110 For a critical assessment of ASIC's accountability framework, see Diana Nestorovska, 'Assessing the effectiveness of ASIC's accountability framework' (2016) 34(3) *Company and Securities Law Journal*; Margaret Hyland, 'Who is watching the watchdog? A critical appraisal of ASIC's administrative powers' (2009) *JALTA: Journal of the Australasian Law Teachers Association* 29–46. See also Joanna Bird, 'Regulating the regulators: accountability of Australian regulators' (2011) 35 *Melbourne University Law Review* 739. See Pamela Hanrahan, 'Directors' counsel: who will watch the watchmen?' (2019) 35(3) *Company Director* 28. See Adrian Brown, 'ASIC: the Senate inquiry into the performance of ASIC' (2014) 26(1) *Australian Insolvency Journal* 44. For literature supporting the need for greater accountability and transparency in the use of ASIC's discretionary powers, see Margaret Hyland, 'Is ASIC sufficiently accountable for its administrative decisions? A question of review' (2010) *Company and Securities Law Journal* 32–53.

111 *Financial System Inquiry: Final Report* (2014) (Murray Report) 250. According to the Murray Report, government only covered a small proportion of 'ASIC's costs directly from industry participants, through the Financial Institutions Supervisory Levies, application fees and fees for market supervision'.

112 Pat McGrath and Michael Janda, 'Senate inquiry demands royal commission into Commonwealth Bank, ASIC', *ABC News* (26 June 2014); Parliament of Australia, *Report on the Performance of Australian Securities and Investments Commission* (Senate Economic References Committee, 26 June 2014) [1.7].

113 See for example Price, 'Regulator: funding' (n 109); George Gilligan et al, 'Penalties regimes to counter corporate and financial wrongdoing in Australia–views of governance professionals' (2017) 11(1) *Law and Financial Markets Review* 4–12, doi.org/10.1080/17521440.2017.1309162.

as a regulator, particularly in the realm of surveillance and enforcement.[114] The industry-funding model to address the issue of shortage of financial resources by enabling ASIC to 'recover most of its regulatory costs from regulated industries',[115] though a step in the right direction, is unlikely to resolve all of ASIC's financial woes, for the reasons set out in the previous section.

Second, ASIC enjoys significant operational and functional independence particularly as regards its day-to-day regulatory activity,[116] though the existing framework allows for a considerable level of federal government and ministerial-level control over ASIC.[117] While such a close link with the government may not, axiomatically, lead to concerns about ASIC's independence, it is certainly a relationship that needs cautious observation.

Third, to an extent, governmental control over ASIC is useful for ensuring its accountability, with the body subject to frequent assessments that are designed to enhance its accountability and effectiveness.[118] The appointment of royal commissions is a strong example of ensuring a level accountability that goes beyond traditional mechanisms of parliamentary and executive oversight.[119] Notwithstanding such measures, there have been decisive calls in recent times to further increase ASIC's accountability.[120] These lead to the Hayne Royal Commission recommending a new and independent 'oversight authority' to assess ASIC's effectiveness in discharging its statutory obligations, and significantly, to the proposed

---

114 Parliament of Australia, *Report on the Performance* (n 112) 250. On how ASIC's underfunding has affected its effectiveness as a regulator, see Kavame Eroglu and Powell (n 59).

115 ASIC, 'ASIC industry funding' (n 95).

116 IMF, *Australia Country Report* (n 1) 21. The detailed review of the Australian financial system revealed no particular evidence of interference from the minister with the everyday activities and decision-making at ASIC.

117 See for example (n 104) above.

118 'Australian regulators are subject to a comprehensive array of accountability mechanisms' and despite 'frequent calls for increased accountability, the case for change is not overwhelming': see Bird (n 110) 739.

119 Royal commissions are the apex form of public inquiry in Australia, which makes them unique and significant: see John Price, 'Emerging lessons from the Financial Services Royal Commission for the regulation of health practitioners' (AHPRA—National Registration and Accreditation Scheme Combined Meeting, Melbourne, Australia, 28 February 2019), asic.gov.au/about-asic/news-centre/speeches/emerging-lessons-from-the-financial-services-royal-commission-for-the-regulation-of-health-practitioners/.

120 The Murray Report recommended the setting up of a financial regulator assessment board to take 'annual ex post reviews of overall regulator performance against their mandates': see Murray Report (n 111) 235.

Financial Accountability Regime (FAR), which aims to further enhance the accountability mechanisms within the financial system, including ASIC's own accountability as a regulator.[121]

In respect of Principle 2, the detailed FSAP Review of ASIC's regime in 2012 assessed the regime as 'partly implemented', primarily due to ASIC's apparent dependencies on government for its funding, and due to the ministerial control exercised over ASIC, though the accountability provisions, on the whole, were considered adequate.[122]

Conclusion

The above discussion shows that regulatory independence and accountability are not static but dynamic fields, and, therefore, that they are subject to constant improvements, adjustments and developments. This is demonstrated in ASIC's case through continuous shifts in the past decade towards attaining an optimum level of independence and accountability. Considering both the legislative framework and its implementation, ASIC's degree of alignment with the core requirements of Principle 2 is assessed as 'moderate' at present, but on track to further refinement and effectiveness. On accountability, ASIC's answerability to royal commissions, robust parliamentary oversight and the range of other mechanisms that keep a check on its operations and performance, such as the Regulator Performance Framework and FRAA, are a genuine feat that most securities jurisdictions across the world currently lack. While accountability is very high, the overall landscape is assessed as 'evolving' given developments to strengthen ASIC's financial independence through adoption of new initiatives such as the industry-funding model. The extent of change in recent years is assessed as 'substantial'.

---

121 See Hayne Report (n 64) recommendation 6.14. Such authority is proposed to be independent of the government and will assess ASIC's effectiveness in discharging its statutory obligations. See also Australian Government, The Treasury, *Financial Accountability Regime—List of Prescribed Responsibilities and Positions* (Policy Proposal Paper, 2021) 2. FAR aims to extend the Banking Executive Accountability Regime to directors and other senior executives of APRA-regulated entities to further strengthen responsibility and accountability of the financial entities. FAR also proposes both prudential and conduct requirements and therefore will be jointly administered by ASIC and APRA.

122 IMF, *Australia Country Report* (n 1) 21.

Principle 3: The regulator should have adequate powers, proper resources and the capacity to perform its functions and exercise its powers

IOSCO Principle 3 directly relates to the adequacy of powers, resources (human, financial and technological) and the capacity of a regulator to undertake the responsibilities entrusted to it by the governing statutes.

The adequacy of powers generally refers to a whole gamut of supervisory, rule-making, licensing, enforcement and other powers. Quintyn and Taylor assert that regulators should be given 'broad powers to issue rules and regulations'.[123] Carvajal and Elliott state that various IOSCO assessments expose the 'lack of broad sanctioning powers' among regulators, 'a common weakness across jurisdictions'.[124] According to them, many regulators continue to lack sufficient powers, including adequate 'licensing powers', which curtails their abilities to 'verify the fitness and propriety of market participants'; they also lack sufficient investigative and enforcement powers, which interferes with their ability to perform their responsibilities of enforcement and compliance within the securities markets.[125]

In relation to the resources of a securities regulator, Black, in his inspirational work *The Legal and Institutional Preconditions for Strong Securities Markets*, mentions certain 'core institutions' that are pivotal, generally, to the existence of strong securities markets and, more specifically, to 'counter information asymmetry'.[126] The first of the core institutions that Black emphasises is 'a securities regulator that (a) is honest; and (b) has the staff, skill and budget to pursue complex securities disclosure cases'.[127] In a similar vein, Jackson and Roe assert the significance of regulators' budgetary resources and staffing levels and show how a:

---

123 Quintyn and Taylor (n 20).

124 See Ana Carvajal and Jennifer Elliott, *The Challenge of Enforcement in Securities Markets: Mission Impossible?* (IMF Working Paper 09/168, 2009) 20, doi.org/10.2139/ssrn.1457591.

125 Ibid [59].

126 See Black (n 19) 789.

127 Ibid 790. Black points out that this 'pre-condition' is almost always taken for granted in developed countries and often partly or wholly absent in developing countries. Further, the funding issue is often a 'hidden problem' with market regulators often operating on a 'minimal budget' or pressed by 'salary rules that prevent it from paying salaries sufficient to retain qualified people or to keep them honest'.

higher budget and greater staffing allow the regulator to examine allegations of wrongdoing, to write its rules carefully, to conduct market surveillance and review filings, to act more often to remedy, prevent, and punish wrongdoing.[128]

Ford, too, posits that the most significant lesson for 'effective regulatory capacity' learnt from the GFC is to have an adequate number of staff.[129] Viñals et al stress the significance of owning, as well as applying, resources in a manner that would mitigate the highest risk in a financial market.[130]

Finally, a key requirement of Principle 3 relates to the *capacity* of the regulator to carry forth its mandate, with 'an active role in promoting the education of investors and other market participants'.[131] The following sections delve into the requirements of this principle insofar as they relate to SEBI's and ASIC's regimes.

SEBI

Key features of the framework indicating sufficiency of powers, proper resources and capacity

SEBI enjoys a separate legal personality and considerable autonomy.[132] The *SEBI Act* and the other securities legislation confer a variety of powers on SEBI for the effective supervision and regulation of the securities markets.[133] Among many such statutory powers, SEBI enjoys the power to

---

128 Howell E Jackson and Mark J Roe, 'Public and private enforcement of securities laws: resource-based evidence' (2009) 93(2) *Journal of Financial Economics* 207–238, doi.org/10.1016/j.jfineco.2008.08.006. They assert that the central issue is not about the regulatory body possessing 'formal powers to sanction offending parties' but 'whether that power has actually been exercised'.

129 Cristie Ford, 'Principles-based securities regulation in the wake of the global financial crisis' (2010) 55(2) *McGill Law Journal/Revue de droit de McGill* 288, doi.org/10.7202/045086ar. For a more detailed examination of issues related to financial regulation, Cristie Ford, *Innovation and the State* (Cambridge University Press, 2017).

130 José Viñals et al, 'The making of good supervision: learning to say "no"' in *Building a More Resilient Financial Sector: Reforms in the Wake of the Global Crisis* (IMF, 2012) 83, 84. 'Countries that put more resources into securities regulation and have a better track record of implementation and enforcing regulations' are in a better position to implement new directives, such as the EU Directives: see Hans B Christensen, Luzi Hail and Christian Leuz, *Capital-Market Effects of Securities Regulation: The Role of Implementation, and Enforcement* (NBER Working Paper 16737, 2011) 35, doi.org/10.3386/w16737.

131 IOSCO, *Methodology for Assessing* (n 24) 31.

132 S Agrawal and RJ Baby, *Agrawal & Baby on SEBI Act* (Taxmann, 2011) 9–10.

133 SEBI's powers range from licensing of intermediaries and surveillance of activities to investigations into any breach of securities laws, and enforcement powers. SEBI's primary source of powers is the *SEBI Act*. In addition, SEBI has certain powers under the *Securities and Contracts Regulations Act 1956*, *Depositories Act 1996* and *Companies Act 2013*. The latter part of the book discusses the powers of SEBI at length. On the supervisory and enforcement powers available to SEBI, as specifically required under IOSCO Principles 10–12, Chapters 4 and 5 discuss these in detail.

draft regulations for securities markets.[134] Chapter 4 of this book describes and discusses the full expanse of SEBI's supervisory and enforcement powers, and their use.

As regards SEBI's human resources, the data from SEBI's annual reports show that, despite efforts to increase numbers, the SEBI officers count remains stable and on the low side.[135] In the area of technology, SEBI has made investments at multiple levels and within a range of departments. For example, it maintains a highly sophisticated surveillance system at its head office in Mumbai.[136] In recent years, SEBI upgraded to an automated system of filing complaints, the SEBI Complaints Redress System, to enable effective redress of complaints received against market intermediaries and listed companies.[137]

Finally, determining the financial resources available to SEBI, it is clear that the body 'enjoys financial autonomy as it can meet its expenditure from fees and charges it levies without relying on the Government'.[138] Given the size and high volume of transactions in the Indian securities markets, SEBI has accumulated a vast surplus that it utilises for meeting its growing financial regulatory needs, and through which it carries forth various objectives delineated by the *SEBI Act*. However, since 2011 the Indian government has directed SEBI to transfer SEBI's surplus funds, which were as high as Rs1,672 crores (approximately $297 million) in 2017, into 'a public account controlled by the Government'.[139] This move was resisted by SEBI

---

134 *SEBI Act* s 30.

135 SEBI has approximately 700 officers. The strength of SEBI's officers in FY 2014–15 was 746, of which 652 were officers and 94 were secretaries and other staff: see SEBI, *Annual Report 2014–15* (2015) 182. By 2017–18, SEBI's strength had increased to 794 employees, of which 698 were officers and 96 were secretaries and other office staff: see SEBI, *Annual Report 2017–18* (2018) 196. By FY 2018–19, the number of staff members reduced as compared with the previous year: from 794 to 785 (including employees on deputation and contract), of which 699 were officers and 86 comprised secretaries and other staff: see SEBI, *Annual Report 2018–19* (n 79) 227.

136 The Integrated Market Surveillance System (IMSS) was put in place in 2013 to 'collect transaction and master data from exchanges (NSE, BSE, MSEI, NCDEX, MCX) and depositories (NSDL, CDSL) on a daily basis to generate alerts for predefined market manipulation scenarios'; it 'provides powerful data analysis and benchmarking tools': see 'Request for proposal for supply, installation, configuration, operationalization and maintenance for upgrade of IT infrastructure for IMSS project' (4 October 2018), sebi.gov.in/sebi_data/tenderfiles/sep-2018/1536032748260.pdf.

137 SEBI, 'SEBI complaints redress system', scores.sebi.gov.in/.

138 See Umakanth Varottil, 'Securities markets' in Devesh Kapur and Madhav Khosla (eds), *Regulation in India: Design, Capacity, Performance* (Hart Publishing, 2019) 5; doi.org/10.5040/9781509927753. ch-005; SEBI Act s 14.

139 See Varottil (n 138) 6. See also Upadhyay (n 86).

for several years on the basis that such an act by the government would 'undermine the autonomy' of the market regulator as envisaged by the *SEBI Act*.[140]

In terms of capacity, SEBI's annual reports include information on the staff-oriented measures taken by SEBI including job rotations and transfers to ensure an overall training of officers,[141] yet questions have been raised about the adequacy of skill development and expertise at SEBI.[142] SEBI also invests in the training and welfare of its officers through both domestic and foreign training programs and provides salaries and benefits that are at par with other governmental bodies, although not equivalent to market remuneration, especially in the senior roles.[143] The National Institute of Securities Markets, an educative organisation set up by SEBI, is also focused on providing training to SEBI staff, as well as meeting other objectives.[144]

Analysis

The short description above of SEBI's resources (human, technological and financial) and capacity is now followed by a detailed analysis, while SEBI's compliance powers are analysed separately in Chapters 4 and 5 of this book. In terms of SEBI's human resources, the figures on SEBI's staff provide a sharp contrast to other notable regulators, such as the United States Securities and Exchange Commission (US SEC), which, in the *Agency Financial Report 2019*, is reported to have 4,350 full-time employees.[145] The comparative difference between SEBI's 785 employees and US SEC's 4,350 employees is very stark in relation to the number of listed companies governed by each regulator, as was highlighted by the SEBI-appointed governance committee, chaired by Uday Kotak in 2017.[146] As noted by this committee: 'SEBI has one employee for six listed companies', the 'SEC has almost one employee for each listed company'; US SEC's corporate finance department (CFD)

---

140 '14 regulatory bodies, including SEBI, IRDA, AICTE and UGC, kept public money of Rs 6,064 crore outside govt account: CAG' (27 December 2017) *MoneyLife*, moneylife.in/article/14-regulatory-bodies-including-sebi-irda-aicte-and-ugc-kept-public-money-of-rs6064-crore-outside-govt-account-cag/52596.html.

141 SEBI, *Annual Report 2018–19* (n 79).

142 See generally Varottil (n 138).

143 IMF, *India FSAP Report* (n 1) 92.

144 National Institute of Securities Markets (NISM), 'About NISM', nism.ac.in/.

145 US Securities and Exchange Commission, *Agency Financial Report: Fiscal Year 2019* (2017).

146 See SEBI, 'Report of the Committee on Corporate Governance' (2017) *Committee Reports* 100. The mandate of the committee was to usher improvements into corporate governance areas.

has 477 staff members while SEBI's CFD has 31 staff employees and, most importantly, US SEC's enforcement department has 1,380 employees while SEBI's has just 214 members.[147]

In addition to these statistics, Varottil asserts that 'the growth in SEBI's human resources has failed to keep pace with market developments',[148] and supports this assertion on the basis of the following statistics: from 2007 to 2017, the Indian equity markets grew over six times, from a 'total turnover of Rs18,463,603 crores to Rs115,696,292 crores', with the market capitalisation increasing 'exponentially' as well.[149] In comparison, SEBI's staff increased from 408 officers in 2008 to 692 in April 2017, 'a little over 1.5 times'.[150]

The above statistics need to be considered in light of other aspects of SEBI's recruitment and handling of its human resources. First, SEBI recruits most employees at entry level and then provides them with training to fulfil their regulatory assignments; there are almost negligible staff members recruited from markets with the exception of certain members recruited at the senior level, such as some executive directors.[151] Second, keeping aside the issue of the significant shortage of staff, the quality, skills, expertise and capacity of SEBI's staff has also been examined and commented upon as a separate issue by academics including Varma and Varottil.[152] Commenting on the skills and expertise of employees, Varma argues that:

> enforcement … is not about a handful of people at the top; it is about a large army of competent (but not necessarily outstanding) foot soldiers. The constraints of public sector compensation structure are far more stifling at this level … The regulator's low pay scale therefore makes it uncompetitive at this level as a long-term career.[153]

---

147 Ibid.
148 Varottil (n 138).
149 Ibid.
150 Ibid.
151 See generally the chapter on human resources in SEBI, *Annual Report 2018–19* (n 79) 227. See also IMF, *India FSAP Report* (n 1) 92.
152 JR Varma, 'Indian financial market development and regulation: what worked and why?' in Masahiro Kawai and Eswar Prasad (ed), *Asian Perspectives on Financial Sector Reforms and Regulation* (Brookings Institution Press, 2011). See also Varottil (n 138) 21.
153 Varma (n 152) 253, 264.

Varottil, while referencing the *Report of the Financial Sector Legislative Reforms Commission*,[154] argues that 'regulatory expertise is in short supply' and the 'method of transplanting civil servants and the regulatory structures of the civil service to authorities such as SEBI' has not been a successful strategy.[155]

The above analysis can be summed up as follows. First, the number of staff members engaged in regulation (aside from secretarial and other staff) at SEBI is low compared with the size of the market and the number of participants. Second, there are clear hurdles in the recruitment of quality staff at different levels of the organisation. Third, the salaries and incentives, though high or at least on par when compared with other public sector authorities in India, still fall short in terms of attracting the richest talent pool in the market and may also contribute to the high attrition rate at SEBI. Fourth, while SEBI continues to invest keenly in boosting the strength, calibre and quality of its staff and employees (as noted in several annual reports published by SEBI), it still has a wide gap to cover when compared with the talent, quality and remuneration scales available in the private sector, both at the lower officer levels and at the executive levels.

Notwithstanding the above, that a low number of SEBI officers handles the regulation of a large, diverse and complex securities market such as India's, and persists with prosecuting several high-pressure and complicated enforcement cases within India and abroad (as detailed in Chapter 5 of this book), speaks volumes about SEBI's many proficient, capable and driven employees. It is in this area that there lies a large window of opportunity to hone further that skillset of SEBI's motivated and inspired staff, to the highest level, by partnering with other leading markets and regulators, through mutually beneficial cross-border collaborations as this book proposes. In such long-term, strategic collaborations, while it is important to have cross-border regulatory exchanges, training and brainstorming among the top and executive levels of the leadership from both jurisdictions, it is absolutely critical to include officers from the middle-level management and even from the most fundamental level to drive a bottom-up approach.

In relation to technological resources, SEBI clearly draws on India's IT prowess as evident from instances such as the governance and surveillance mechanisms adopted by SEBI, as well as the investor protection portal.

---

154 *Report of the Financial Sector Legislative Reforms Commission* (22 March 2013).
155 Varottil (n 138) 21.

At the same time, there is not enough literature examining SEBI's full use of technology in its day-to-day operation to be able to comment on whether SEBI has fully adopted and explored the maximum potential of technology in driving its internal processes.

In relation to SEBI's financial independence, the independent generation of funding and the flexibility of use of such resources are among SEBI's greatest strengths, although the ramifications, if any, of the recent central government requirement for the transfer of SEBI's surplus funds to the CFI are yet to be witnessed.

The FSAP Review of 2013 granted SEBI a 'broadly implemented' grade for conformity with IOSCO Principle 3, recognising that SEBI had wide powers but serious staff limitations, particularly 'salary limitations'.[156]

Conclusion

From an overview of SEBI's governing statutes, it is clear that SEBI is endowed with wide statutory powers, makes use of its powers[157] and has been successful in seeking an expansion of its powers through legislative amendments when such need arises.[158] As regards its resources, particularly financial resources, SEBI is self-sufficient and, therefore, does not have the same budgetary constraints as other regulators, although the recent move by the central government in relation to SEBI's surplus funds has raised concerns over SEBI's financial independence.[159] SEBI is also seen to rely upon and harness new technology for achieving its regulatory objective. Finally, as regards SEBI's human resources, it is clear that SEBI strives to recruit and hone talent; however, this is an area that requires more attention—possibly a transformation—and an area that can gain a massive advantage through strategic collaborations, as proposed in the final chapter of this book.

---

156 IMF, *India FSAP Report* (n 1) 14. The number of SEBI employees as compared with the size and number of entities in the securities markets was seen to be significantly less, among other limitations noted in the IMF's report.

157 Chapters 4 and 5 of this book elaborate on these powers and their use by SEBI.

158 See for instance the *Securities Laws (Amendment) Act 2014*. SEBI secured wide powers, such as the power to seek information from 'any' person when investigating a securities matter, from a legislative amendment.

159 'Centre pushes for transfer of SEBI's surplus funds into its accounts', *LatestLaws.com* (26 December 2019), latestlaws.com/latest-news/centre-pushes-for-transfer-of-sebi-s-surplus-funds-into-its-accounts/.

Even though SEBI focused on recruitment in the years between 2013 and 2020, as explained above, overall staff numbers rose only marginally, given the high attrition rate. In conclusion, SEBI has adequate powers and significant funding independence but severe constraints around human resources that place a strain on its capacity to perform its regulatory functions optimally. Thus, the degree of alignment with Principle 3 is assessed as 'moderate'. The extent of reform in recent years is assessed as 'minor' and the overall landscape is assessed as 'evolving'.

ASIC

Key features of the framework indicating sufficiency of powers, proper resources and capacity

The *ASIC Act* and the *Corporations Act* confer a variety of powers on ASIC, including registration of companies, granting financial services licences, registering auditors and liquidators, making rules that ensure the integrity of financial markets, investigating and taking action when breaches of law are suspected, and enforcing the disclosure requirements for the efficient functioning of markets.[160] To fulfil its role, ASIC can use a wide array of tools: for example, issuing infringement notices for persons who stand in breach of the law; banning people from providing financial services or credit-related services; initiating prosecutions; obtaining civil penalties from courts; monitoring and regulating corporate activity, such as financial reporting, prospectus fundraising and takeover activity; supervising market participants on a real-time basis; and initiating financial education and literacy programs.[161] The *ASIC Act* grants ASIC wide powers to 'take whatever action it can take, and is necessary, to enforce and give effect to' the responsibilities given to ASIC.[162]

---

160 IMF, *Australia Country Report* (n 1). For disclosure requirements, see *Corporations Act* ch 7.

161 IMF, *Australia Country Report* (n 1). Infringement notices are administered by ASIC or the Markets Disciplinary Panel with the authority of ASIC: see ASIC, 'Infringement notices', asic.gov.au/about-asic/asic-investigations-and-enforcement/infringement-notices/. See Chapter 8 of this book for more on ASIC's enforcement and compliance regime.

162 ASIC, 'Royal Commission into Misconduct in the Banking, Superannuation and Financial Services Industry Submissions of the Australian Securities and Investments Commission Response to Interim Report' (2018) 2. See also *ASIC Act*.

In terms of rule-making powers, ASIC makes market integrity rules under the *Corporations Act*.[163] ASIC also issues interpretative instruments such as regulatory guides for giving interpretations on an existing law,[164] as well as legislative instruments (earlier referred to as class orders) in a range of circumstances.[165]

In terms of human resource capabilities, ASIC's staff strength for FY 2017–18 was reported as 1,656 (full-time employees).[166] ASIC recruits its staff at a variety of levels from the market, offers attractive remuneration packages and performance-based bonuses, and provides regular training, study and other professional development programs.[167]

ASIC's financial dependence on the federal government and limitations were discussed earlier in this chapter under Principle 2, with reference to the changes that are underway with the industry-funding model. Earlier, ASIC's funding from the government was split into 'core' and 'non-core', with the former providing for the carrying out of ASIC's regulatory objectives and the latter for other 'specific purposes'.[168]

Finally, even though after the 2020–21 federal budget the Australian Treasury was given the responsibility of financial capability policy and coordination,[169] ASIC also contributes towards increasing financial capability through investor education, literacy and other consumer-centric initiatives aimed at creating financially aware and informed consumers through programs such as the National Financial Literacy Strategy.[170]

---

163 ASIC issues market integrity rules under the *Corporations Act 2001*: see s 798G (1). For a recent compilation of the securities markets rules, see *ASIC Market Integrity Rules (Securities Markets) 2017* (2017).

164 See IMF, *Australia Country Report* (n 1). To understand how regulatory guides are employed by ASIC, see ASIC, 'Regulatory guides' (n 49).

165 ASIC, 'Legislative instruments', asic.gov.au/regulatory-resources/find-a-document/legislative-instruments/. Legislative instruments are issued to exempt a person from certain provisions of the statutes or to alter or clarify the operations of some provisions and also make certain declarations about a person or a set of persons.

166 See ASIC, 'Our people', asic.gov.au/about-asic/what-we-do/our-people/. Since ASIC is the financial markets regulator, and not just for securities markets, many of its employees look after aspects of superannuation, insurance, consumer credit, deposit-taking, etc.

167 IMF, *Australia Country Report* (n 1).

168 IMF, *Australia Country Report* (n 1). Non-core funding is funding for specific projects taken up by ASIC, such as new policy proposals or initiatives in any area of need, such as credit reform or market supervision.

169 Australian Government, *Budget 2021–21*, archive.budget.gov.au/2021-22.

170 See ASIC, 'Consumer education', asic.gov.au/for-consumers/financial-capability/. See also *ASIC Act* s 1(2). For more on the Strategy, see Greg Medcraft, 'ASIC's National Financial Literacy Strategy' (Financial Capability Breakfast Briefing, Canberra, Australia, 16 February 2017), download.asic.gov.au/media/4153965/greg-medcraft-speech-financial-capability-breakfast-16-february-2017.pdf.

Analysis

At a general level, ASIC enjoys a wide set of powers that allow it to achieve its regulatory tasks under the larger combined framework of the *Corporations Act* and *ASIC Act*.[171] However, key inquiries have acknowledged the need for further strengthening of ASIC's powers for more effective consumer protection given the public expectation for ASIC to be a 'pro-active watchdog'.[172] Such periodic reviews are among the key strengths of the Australian financial system, in which continuous assessments of all fundamental regulatory and governance aspects, including the adequacy of ASIC's powers and resources, are examined in detail and then suitably expanded.[173] A recent example of such expansion is the inclusion of a new set of product intervention powers for ASIC.[174]

In terms of adequacy of resources, given ASIC's very wide remit,[175] it is neither easy nor straightforward to assess the resources allocated to securities sector–related regulatory activities, though a general impression emerges that ASIC needs more resources—not only for enforcement but also, and particularly, for its supervision activities.[176] ASIC recruits talent at various levels of the organisation, pays them at market level, including through performance bonuses, and offers them training. Generally, ASIC strives to 'motivate, develop and retain' talent.[177] But, despite recent changes to ASIC's funding model, ASIC still remains significantly dependent on government for funding of its regulatory duties, human resource capabilities and spending on consumer education and awareness. Such financial constraints and other dependencies interfere with ASIC's ability to provide better regulatory services, and, arguably, are its Achilles heel.

---

171 See for example *ASIC Act* s 1(2).

172 See Murray Report (n 111) 236. See generally Hayne Report (n 64).

173 ASIC's AFSL licensing powers were significantly strengthened in 2012 as part of the Future of Financial Advice law reforms: see Murray Report (n 111) 251. See also submissions made by ASIC to the royal commission for further expansion of its powers: ASIC, 'Royal Commission' (n 162).

174 See *Treasury Laws Amendment (Design and Distribution Obligations and Product Intervention Powers) Act 2019* (Cth). ASIC agrees that such design and distribution powers and increased penalties have further strengthened its powers: see 'Additional powers (and funding) for ASIC rather than a narrower remit and/or a separate regulator?', *MinterEllison* (11 November 2018), www.minterellison.com/articles/asic-submission-on-royal-commission-interim-report.

175 Murray Report (n 111) 236.

176 IMF, *Australia Country Report* (n 1) 51.

177 See for example ASIC, 'Priorities' in *ASIC Accessibility Action Plan 2020–22* (2020).

For some of these reasons, the detailed FSAP Review of 2012 granted ASIC a 'partly implemented' grade for IOSCO Principle 3, recognising its wide powers but highlighting the shortage of funds that hamper provision of an adequate standard of proactive supervision activities.

Conclusion

It is clear that ASIC is guided by a robust legal framework. However, despite recent changes to funding, ASIC cannot be said to be financially comfortable (as explained under Principle 2 in the discussion of the key features of ASIC's financial framework); this is especially so given that ASIC's remit as a market conduct regulator is much wider than just the securities sector. ASIC's financial constraints are likely to affect its future performance and create needless barriers for its necessary growth, both in terms of its staff numbers and the proactive nature of its regulatory activities.[178] However, as the analysis shows, ASIC continues to make full use of its resources,[179] incentivise its staff and offer competitive remuneration. Given the requirement for further improvement, the degree of alignment for Principle 3 is assessed as 'moderate' at present. Since 2012, this area has been subject to several domestic reviews and academic discussions within Australia,[180] leading to many changes especially around enhancement of ASIC's powers and funding. Thus, the 'extent of reform' in recent years is assessed as 'substantial'. Despite the changes underway, the overall landscape relating to this principle is assessed as sufficiently 'mature'.

Principle 4: The regulator should adopt clear and consistent regulatory processes

IOSCO's Principle 4 requires regulators to have clear and consistent regulatory processes that ensure a variety of objectives such as transparency, adherence to natural justice principles, fair process in procedures, and a consultative approach to policy formulation and development.[181] Carvajal and Elliott argue that the overall 'organisational structure should also support

---

178 This conclusion is supported by the observation that, despite an increase in ASIC's total revenue for 2020–21, ASIC's total expenses exceeded its total revenue, and led to an overall deficit of $14 million. This shows that ASIC is still held back in its regulatory role due to funding issues and cannot freely increase its spending for bolder steps and legitimate proactive regulatory spending.

179 See ASIC, 'Financial summary' (n 94) 28.

180 See for example Murray Report (n 111). See also ASIC, 'ASIC capability review', asic.gov.au/about-asic/what-we-do/how-we-operate/performance-and-review/asic-capability-review/. See generally Hayne Report (n 64).

181 See generally Carvajal and Elliott (n 124) 33.

a fair and transparent process'.[182] They also state that most countries have seen significant progress in transparency and implementation of Principle 4, although there are numerous improvements that are required to be taken up in 'regulatory measures, including interpretations and explanatory notes'.[183] The regulatory impact assessment (RIA), a measure directed towards enhancing clarity and consistency in the regulatory process, has garnered attention in the last decade.[184] Much emphasis has been laid on such assessment by IOSCO through its *Impact Assessment Guidelines*.[185]

The key features of SEBI and ASIC's regime in relation to Principle 4 are discussed below, focusing on transparency, procedural fairness and other aspects of a clear and consistent approach to regulation.

SEBI

Key features of the framework supporting clarity and consistency in regulatory processes

Transparency in SEBI's operations is ensured at the highest level under the *RTI Act*, which requires SEBI and all other public authorities to publish or disclose information to the citizens of India. The *RTI Act* requires public authorities to disclose a variety of information, such as particulars of its organisation, function and duties; the powers and duties of its officers and employees; remuneration received by each of its officers and employees; and

---

182 Transparency is critical at multiple levels of securities regulation, such as in the case of settlement orders where a great level of confidence and credibility is required: see Carvajal and Elliott (n 124) 21. Transparency is also significant in the building of effective legal infrastructure upon which the operational and regulatory infrastructure of securities markets can rest. A securities regime should strive to provide speedy, consistent and transparent decisions: see Robert Pardy and Banco Mundial, *Institutional Reform in Emerging Securities Markets* (World Bank, 1992) vol 907.

183 Carvajal and Elliott (n 124). In a study conducted by them, 80 per cent of the securities markets reflected high observation of this principle.

184 The main objective of a regulatory impact assessment is the 'optimisation of policy' and ensuring that 'the benefits to society from regulatory action are maximised and costs minimised': see Rex Deighton-Smith and Scott H Jacobs, 'Regulatory impact analysis: best practices in OECD countries' in *Regulatory Impact Analysis: Best Practices in OECD Countries* (OECD, 1997). See also Scott H Jacobs, 'An overview of regulatory impact analysis in OECD countries' in *Regulatory Impact Analysis: Best Practices in OECD Countries* (OECD, 1997) 13–30.

185 IOSCO, *Impact Assessment Guidelines* (2011). On the importance of the RIA, see Colin Kirkpatrick and David Parker, 'Regulatory impact assessment—an overview' (2004) 25(5) *Public Money & Management* 267–270, doi.org/10.1111/j.1467-9302.2004.00432.x. For an academic discussion of RIAs in the context of developing countries, see Colin Kirkpatrick and David Parker, 'Regulatory impact assessment and regulatory governance in developing countries' (2004) 24(4) *Public Administration and Development* 333–344, doi.org/10.1002/pad.310. For a detailed academic view on RIAs especially in regard to Commonwealth government entities, including ASIC, see Andrew Serpell, 'Regulation impact assessment' (2008) 27(S1) *Economic Papers: A Journal of Applied Economics and Policy* 41–52, doi.org/10.1111/j.1759-3441.2008.tb00440.x.

rules, regulations, instructions, manuals and records held by it or under its control or used by employees for discharging its functions, among other information.[186]

Further, SEBI adopts a consultative rule-making process in its policy formulation,[187] and issues circulars and guidelines that clarify or elaborate the requirements of the securities Acts, rules and regulations, all available on its website.[188] SEBI also issues press releases to disclose the regulatory measures and policy initiatives that it undertakes.[189] While pursuing enforcement actions for breaches of securities laws, SEBI is bound by the statute to observe certain procedural requirements: for example, conducting an investigation, making the findings of such an investigation available to the person against whom action is sought, according them the opportunity to be heard and passing a written order with reasons.[190]

Analysis

The above description of the framework enumerates some of the measures around clarity and transparency in SEBI's regulatory practice. Varottil emphasises that 'SEBI has led the path in introducing transparency in regulation-making' in India, and that, 'comparatively', SEBI follows an elaborate consultative process before issuing regulations that affect securities markets, including obtaining feedback before finalising them.[191] While the *SEBI Act* itself does not impose the requirement of a consultation mechanism to be adopted by SEBI before it issues regulations,[192] SEBI has established a process to publish a concept note or policy paper before finalising the

---

186 *RTI Act*, s 4 (1)(b). At the same time, s 8 of the *RTI Act* exempts SEBI from the disclosure of certain information in the interests of maintaining 'confidentiality', such as when such information is provided to SEBI in the course of its fiduciary duty.

187 For example, each SEBI draft regulation is put up on its website for comments before it is finalised. SEBI's recent consultative papers are available on its website: see SEBI, 'Reports for public comments', sebi.gov.in/sebiweb/home/HomeAction.do?doListing=yes&sid=4&ssid=38&smid=35.

188 SEBI's Acts, rules, regulations, general orders, guidelines, master circulars and circulars are available on its website: see SEBI, 'Legal', sebi.gov.in/legal.html.

189 SEBI, 'Media and notifications', sebi.gov.in/sebiweb/home/HomeAction.do?doListing=yes&sid=6& ssid=23&smid=0.

190 SEBI is bound by the procedural requirements laid down in the *SEBI (Intermediaries) Regulations 2008* and Adjudication Rules of 1995 and 2005: see SEBI, 'Legal' (n 188). SEBI's adherence to natural justice principles, and observance of fairness and transparency in its procedures, are discussed in detail in Chapter 8 of this book.

191 Varottil (n 138) 12.

192 Dharmishta Raval, *Improving the Legal Process in Enforcement at SEBI* (Indira Gandhi Institute of Development Research Working Paper No 2011-008, 2011) 11.

draft of such regulations.[193] For 'significant' reforms, SEBI has followed the practice of establishing committees comprising a diverse range of members to provide recommendations or even draft regulations.[194]

Although SEBI is regarded as 'comparatively transparent in [the] regulatory process',[195] some deficiencies have been highlighted, such as non-provision of a regulatory impact assessment and the absence of a 'robust and informative' consultative mechanism,[196] features regarded as critical to most well-functioning and advanced markets as they 'allay fears of regulatory capture'.[197] Varottil has critiqued other aspects of SEBI's consultative practice, such as a lack of uniformity,[198] and suggested several improvements to bring further transparency to the same (refer to Principle 2).[199]

Despite such criticism, on balance, given SEBI's low human resources numbers (discussed earlier under Principle 3),[200] the requirement of clear and consistent regulatory practices and procedures is reflected to a significant degree in SEBI's regulatory practice. Moreover, SEBI's self-developed practices of seeking public comments and its consultative approach demonstrate a definite will to adopt a more broad-based, open and transparent process for securities markets. The FSAP Review of SEBI in 2013 granted a 'fully implemented' grade for conformity with this principle on account of clear procedures that have been put in place by SEBI for rule-

---

193 Ibid.

194 Varottil (n 138) 12. For instance, in areas of corporate governance reform, SEBI established several committees, such as the Kumar Mangalam Birla Committee, Narayana Murthy Committee and the Uday Kotak Committee, and invited them to submit reports on corporate governance reforms: see SEBI, 'Report of Shri NR Narayana Murthy Committee on Corporate Governance' (2003) *Committee Reports*; SEBI, 'Report of the Kumar Mangalam Birla Committee on Corporate Governance' (2000) *Committee Reports*; SEBI, 'Report of the Committee on Corporate Governance' (n 146).

195 Varottil (n 138) 3.

196 Such robust consultation is required to allow SEBI to procure adequate information from the markets and participants to formulate better policies: see Raval (n 192).

197 Varottil (n 138) 3.

198 Ibid 13. Varottil argues that as SEBI is not required by legislation to adopt a consultative process, its own consultative mechanisms are not uniformly adopted and are not applied when issuing circulars and guidelines. One study on SEBI revealed that 'SEBI sought public comments on 44.4% of its regulations and on 17.4% of its circulars': see Arpita Pattanaik and Anjali Sharma, 'Regulatory governance problems in the legislative function at RBI and SEBI' *The Leap Blog* (23 September 2015), blog.theleapjournal. org/2015/09/regulatory-governance-problems-in.html.

199 Varottil (n 138) 13. Suggested improvements include bringing more quality and transparency to SEBI's consultation process by publishing public comments received by SEBI. See also Zaveri (n 89) raising concerns on the non-publication of comments by SEBI that makes the process opaque rather than transparent.

200 SEBI, *Annual Report 2018–19* (n 79). SEBI's total strength of officers excluding secretaries was close to 700.

making, licensing, carrying out enforcement proceedings and several other regulatory activities. However, given the discussion above, although SEBI displays a convergence with this regulatory principle, the subjective nature of this standard leaves copious room for improvement. This is indicated by the non-inclusion of a regulatory impact assessment and the inadequate response mechanism for public comments.[201]

Conclusion

The above analysis supports the following conclusions about SEBI's regulatory processes:

1. the overall regulatory framework provides several measures to ensure transparency and clarity, such as making SEBI accountable to the *RTI Act*
2. SEBI's process for the adoption of regulations is consultative
3. further clarity and transparency are required in the publication of public comments
4. a significant need exists for the inclusion of a regulatory impact assessment.

The degree of alignment with Principle 4 is judged as 'moderate' given the scope for further improvement. The extent of reform or improvements to the process of clear and consistent regulation in recent years is assessed as 'minor' and, given the room for further improvement, the overall landscape is assessed as 'evolving' for this principle.

ASIC

Key features of the framework supporting clarity and consistency in regulatory processes

ASIC, in general, adopts an open, consultative process with industry participants, market stakeholders and consumer protection organisations.[202] After a consultation exercise, ASIC prepares and publishes a regulatory impact statement that is reviewed by a governmental body, the Office of Best Practice Regulation.[203] In addition, ASIC ensures clarity and openness

---

201 See generally Varottil (n 138).

202 In addition to seeking comments on new policy proposals, ASIC engages in roundtable consultations, formal and informal consultation procedures, funds consumer advisory panels that give feedback on policy from the viewpoint of consumers and appoints an external advisory panel to consult on issues: see IMF, *Australia Country Report* (n 1). See ASIC, 'Regulatory resources: consultations', asic.gov.au/regulatory-resources/find-a-document/consultation-papers/.

203 For a deeper understanding of the best practice regulation requirements, see Australian Government, Department of the Prime Minister and Cabinet, *Best Practice Regulation Report 2015–16* (2017).

in its processes by disclosing and explaining regulatory actions and policies through the use of media releases, regulatory guides, market integrity rules and other similar mechanisms. As mentioned earlier under Principle 2, ASIC also follows procedures that ensure adherence to principles of fairness and natural justice.

When granting or denying licences under the *Corporations Act*, ASIC follows a set of pre-defined procedures that include granting an opportunity to the licence holder to be heard.[204] ASIC is also required to take appropriate steps to ensure that it keeps confidential any information that it obtains in the course of carrying out its responsibilities.[205]

Analysis

The above brief description of ASIC's regulatory processes suggests that the core requirements of IOSCO Principle 4 are fulfilled to a large degree. In this regard, the following aspects are highlighted. First, ASIC's public consultation process comes across as par excellence. A basic search on ASIC's website reveals as many as 330 consultation papers released by ASIC on a range of issues.[206] 'Non-confidential' submissions received by ASIC in respect of a consultation paper are published with the relevant paper on ASIC's website.[207] These are followed by detailed reports published by ASIC that respond to the submissions made in relation to a particular consultation paper.[208] This process reflects a comprehensive public engagement and consultation process.

A further achievement for ASIC is its publication of comprehensive regulation impact statements (RISs).[209] Again, a search on ASIC's website reveals 764 RISs,[210] with each statement containing an in-depth analysis

---

204 See for example *Corporations Act* s 913B. In terms of this section, an AFSL can be granted upon the fulfilment of criteria laid down under the provisions.

205 See *ASIC Act* s 127(1). See also *Privacy Act 1988* (Cth) s 14.

206 ASIC, 'Past consultation papers', www.asic.gov.au/regulatory-resources/find-a-document/consult ations. However, it must be borne in mind that ASIC's remit is much wider than only being a securities market regulator.

207 See for example the submissions made by Australian Investment Council and the Law Council of Australia, among others, in respect of the following paper: ASIC, *Initial Public Offers: Relief for Voluntary Escrow Arrangements and Pre-prospectus Communications* (Consultation Paper 328, 2020).

208 See for example ASIC's response to the submissions received on CP 301 and CP 315: ASIC, *Response to Submissions on CP 301 and CP 315 on Foreign Financial Services Providers* (Report 656, 2020).

209 RIS is 'mandatory for all Cabinet submissions and applies to every government agency operating under the PGPA Act 2013': see Suzanne Taylor, Julie-Anne Tarr and Anthony Asher, 'Australia's flawed Regulatory Impact Statement (RIS) process' (2016) 44(5) *Australian Business Law Review* 361–376.

210 ASIC, 'Regulation Impact Statement', sitesearch.asic.gov.au/s/search.html?query=regulation+impact +statement&collection=asic&profile=asic.

on the subject matter under consideration.[211] The publication of RISs in Australia has been subject to some criticism,[212] and it has been suggested that the strain on regulatory resources may have affected the quality of RISs.[213] Yet the detailed RISs published by ASIC remains among its notable accomplishments.

Lastly, ASIC applies the law consistently through a set of internal manuals and guides that ensure consistency and the smooth functioning of regulatory activities.[214] The FSAP Review of ASIC in 2012 granted ASIC a 'fully implemented' grade for conformity with this principle, on account of clear procedures for rule-making, licensing, carrying out enforcement proceedings and other regulatory activities.[215]

Conclusion

Given ASIC's comprehensive public consultation practices, publication of a detailed RIS and the internal guidelines developed to ensure consistency, the degree of alignment with the core requirements of Principle 4 is assessed as 'high' in this book. The extent of change in this area of regulatory activity in recent years is assessed as 'minor', but the overall regime of ASIC is assessed as sufficiently 'mature', as ASIC exhibits a strong sense of commitment and consistency in its approach to maintain fairness and transparency in its regulatory activities.

Principle 5: The staff of the regulator should observe the highest professional standards including appropriate standards of confidentiality

The objective behind IOSCO Principle 5 is to ensure that the regulators themselves are subject to a high standard of professional conduct to ensure all market stakeholders and investors have confidence in them.[216] Principle 5 has several facets, such as the avoidance of conflicts of interest, appropriate use of information by staff of the regulator, observance of confidentiality and

---

211 See for example ASIC, *Risk Management Systems of Responsible Entities* (Regulation Impact Statement, 2017). The regulation impact statement discusses a range of parameters starting from the problem ASIC is trying to solve, the options available to the net benefit of options, as well as who ASIC will consult about these options.
212 Taylor, Tarr and Asher (n 209).
213 Interview with Werner Bijkerk, Head of Research, IOSCO, iosco.org/research/pdf/Financial-Markets-Impact-Studies-Needed-Before-Regulations-Are-Introduced.pdf.
214 IMF, *Australia Country Report* (n 1) 52.
215 Ibid 22.
216 IOSCO, *Methodology for Assessing* (n 24) 37.

maintenance of procedural fairness standards.[217] Black argues stringently for the importance of professionalism in his assessment of the preconditions for strong securities markets.[218] Thus, high professional standards are regarded as another hallmark for quality supervision of markets as they instil confidence in participants.

The key features of SEBI's and ASIC's regime relating to Principle 5 are discussed below.

SEBI

Key features of the framework on professionalism

SEBI is bound by the *SEBI (Employees' Service) Regulations 2001*, which lay down a code of conduct for its employees.[219] The regulations are detailed and relate to a wide number of areas, such as appointments, probation, termination of service, promotions and seniority, pay, allowance and other benefits.[220] In addition, the regulations make explicit the responsibility of employees to maintain secrecy, prohibit the use of information outside employees' course of duties, and restrain employees from dealing in securities or accepting gifts that are beyond the prescribed minimum value.[221] For breaches of conduct, Regulation 79 specifies penalties that may include criminal liability.[222] Over and above these measures, the Central Vigilance Commission, established by the central government, keeps a check on SEBI officers to ensure no instances of corruption have occurred.[223]

Analysis

The above provisions represent measures taken by SEBI towards ensuring that its staff adhere to professional standards and maintain confidentiality in the course of their duties. In the absence of literature relating to this area, it is not entirely feasible to analyse SEBI's adherence with this principle in great depth. However, in terms of the framework, the *SEBI (Employees' Service) Regulations 2001* are well developed and detailed.

---

217 Ibid. The term 'staff' includes the 'head' of the regulator and the other employees.

218 See *Good Training Helps—Professionalism Can Be a Bulwark against Corruption;* see also Black (n 19) 19.

219 See also IMF, *India FSAP Report* (n 1).

220 See *SEBI (Employees' Service) Regulations* regs 6, 10, 11, 15, 16, 18.

221 See ibid regs 49, 62, 64, 65.

222 Ibid reg 79.

223 The Central Vigilance Commission has been set up under the *Central Vigilance Commission Act 2003* to inquire into offences alleged to have been committed under the *Prevention of Corruption Act 1988*. The CVC oversees SEBI through the central vigilance officer who is appointed from within the organisation.

The FSAP Review of 2013 assessed SEBI's regime relating to Principle 5 as 'fully implemented' given a strong code of conduct in place for SEBI employees, and prohibition on receiving gifts or transacting in equities.[224] The review report, however, recommended that SEBI develop an even more 'comprehensive regulation on conflict of interest for staff' considering that many responsibilities of SEBI Board members are delegated to lower staff officials.[225]

Conclusion

To a great degree, SEBI's employee regulation framework reflects the core requirement of IOSCO Principle 5 for professionalism in the conduct of regulatory duties through conflict of interest provisions and vigilant checks on SEBI's staff. Accordingly, the degree of alignment for this principle is assessed as 'high'. The extent of reform in recent years in areas relating to this principle is assessed as 'minor', while the overall landscape is assessed as 'evolving', reflecting the scope for strengthening the conflict of interest requirements for both senior and lower-level SEBI officials.

ASIC

Key features of the framework on professionalism

ASIC's Management Accountability Regime identifies and applies accountability standards for ASIC's chair, commission members and senior executives. As well, the *ASIC Act* requires ASIC commissioners to observe high standards of professionalism and disclose all interests they hold that may interfere with or cause a conflict in the performance of their obligations.[226] The *Public Service Act 1999* (Cth) and ASIC's internal policies also require ASIC employees to refrain from acts that cause any conflicts of interest or involve use of information that they receive in the course of their duties.[227] Further, ASIC's staff are required to avoid a 'conflict of interest' between personal interests and their responsibilities under the *ASIC Act* or the *Corporations Act* through the Declarations of Interest Program.[228]

---

224 IMF, *India FSAP Report* (n 1) 14.

225 Ibid 36.

226 See *ASIC Act* s 124(2). See also ASIC, 'ASIC's governance and accountability framework' (n 98).

227 IMF, *Australia Country Report* (n 1) 53. See also *Public Service Act 1999* (Cth). ASIC's staff are also required to avoid a conflict of interest between personal interests and their responsibilities under the *ASIC Act* or the *Corporations Act* through the Declarations of Interest Program. ASIC prohibits the trading of securities by ASIC employees handling market sensitive information except if they have specifically sought requisite permission and exemption for such trading.

228 IMF, *Australia Country Report* (n 1) 44.

ASIC also prohibits trading of securities by such ASIC employees that handle market sensitive information except if they have specifically sought permission for such trading.[229] The *ASIC Act* also provides for protection of confidential information. Further, although, as an independent statutory authority, ASIC is not subject to legislative accountability requirements, it has chosen to apply essential features of the Banking Executive Accountability Regime to its senior staff (proposed to be replaced with the FAR).[230]

For any violation of the code of conduct, ASIC staff members may attract the provisions of the Australian Public Service (APS) values and code of conduct, and may also be subject to disciplinary action by ASIC, including imprisonment for up to two years under s 70 of the *Crimes Act 1914* (Cth) if s 13 of the *Public Service Act 1999* (Cth) has been breached.[231] Compliance with the APS code of conduct is monitored by ASIC and ASIC investigates any violation of the code in terms of s 15 of the *Public Service Act*.[232] ASIC publishes information sheets that detail the procedure for handling of complaints and how allegations of improper conduct of a staff member are to be investigated.[233] For a breach of the APS code of conduct, s 15(1) of *the Public Service Act* makes it possible for the ASIC chairman to impose a range of sanctions against the offending employee, including permanent termination from service.[234]

Analysis

The provisions described above relating to legislative provisions are self-explanatory and suggest that the observance of 'professionalism' and 'confidentiality' in the conduct of the regulator are well entrenched requirements. The detailed FSAP Review of 2012 granted a 'fully implemented' grade to ASIC's regime in relation to Principle 5, particularly in light of the detailed conflicts of interest requirements that apply to ASIC staff.[235] Obviously, this does not ipso facto lead to a conclusion that

---

229 Ibid 53.

230 *ASIC Act* s 127(1). See also ASIC, 'ASIC's governance and accountability framework' (n 98); Australian Government, The Treasury, *Financial Accountability Regime—List of Prescribed Responsibilities and Positions* (Policy Proposal Paper, 2021).

231 IMF, *Australia Country Report* (n 1).

232 Ibid.

233 ASIC, 'Information sheets', asic.gov.au/regulatory-resources/find-a-document/information-sheets/.

234 The attention paid to the code is evident in the recent inquiry into ASIC commissioners, which cleared them of wrongdoing: see The Hon Josh Frydenberg MP, 'Outcomes of review of ASIC Governance' (Media Release, 29 January 2021).

235 IMF, *Australia Country Report* (n 1).

all such conflicts are eliminated from the regulatory regime,[236] but, on balance, ASIC's standards are strongly aligned with the core requirements of this principle.

Conclusion

IOSCO Principle 5, which necessitates professionalism in the regulator's conduct, including through observing confidentiality in the course of duties, is appropriately reflected in several aspects of ASIC's regime, including the code of conduct and internal guidelines that apply to the professional conduct of all ASIC officers. Thus, the degree of alignment of ASIC's regime with this principle is assessed as 'high' in this book. The changes and improvements introduced to enhance professionalism since the detailed FSAP Review of 2012 are assessed as 'minor', but the overall regulatory regime pertaining to this principle is assessed as sufficiently 'mature'.

Principle 6: The regulator should have or contribute to a process to identify, monitor, mitigate and manage systemic risk, appropriate to its mandate

The increased emphasis on identification and monitoring of systemic risk post the GFC of 2007–08 led to the adoption of IOSCO Principle 6.[237] Schwarcz refers to systemic risk as an economic scenario in which a 'trigger event, such as an economic shock or institutional failure, causes a chain of bad economic consequences—sometimes referred to as a domino effect'.[238]

---

236 While such policy exists at ASIC, its effectiveness was recently questioned after allegations of conflict of interest were cast upon an earlier ASIC chairman and his close relationship with the senior counsel of a leading financial services company, AMP: see Australian National Audit Office, 'Request for audit: declaration of interests and conflicts of interest within the Australian Securities and Investments Commission' (24 April 2018), anao.gov.au/work/request/declaration-interests-and-conflicts-interest-within-the-australian-securities-and-investments.

237 IOSCO, *Objectives and Principles of Securities Regulation* (n 1). Even before the GFC, systemic risk had been examined for decades by academics: see for example Michael E Hewitt, 'Systemic risk in international securities markets' in Franklin R Edwards and Hugh T Patrick (eds) *Regulating International Financial Markets: Issues and Policies* (Springer, 1992) 243–255, doi.org/10.1007/978-94-011-3880-2_19. For other literature taking note of the significant dangers of systemic risks and calling for the development of a suitable regulatory framework to address these risks: see generally Duong, Liu and Eddie, 'Development of the regulatory framework' (n 10). In addition to Principle 6, other IOSCO principles seek to identify, mitigate and manage systemic risks, such as Principle 7 relating to perimeter of regulation, Principles 13–15 on cooperation and information sharing with other regulators, Principle 22 on credit rating agencies, Principle 28 on oversight of hedge funds, managers and advisers, Principle 32 on procedures for dealing with failure of market intermediary and Principle 38 on supervisory requirement of clearing and settlement: see IOSCO, *Methodology for Assessing* (n 24) 41.

238 See Steven L Schwarcz, 'Systemic risk' (2008) 97 *Georgia Law Review* 193. Schwarcz discusses, at length, the various definitions given to this term, the way systemic risk affects financial institutions and markets, and its regulation, in both domestic and international, contexts.

Systemic risk has been identified as a critical risk factor due to its 'potential widespread effects and potential to harm a large number of investors and market participants'.[239] The requirements for both regimes relating to systemic risk are examined in the following section.

SEBI
Key features of the framework on identification and management of systemic risk

SEBI's formal strategy to identify and monitor systemic risk was introduced in the aftermath of the GFC, although, in practice, SEBI's approach towards risk assessment was previously incorporated in its general supervision of the various market segments.[240] For example, even prior to a formal risk supervision strategy, SEBI required the recognised stock exchanges to have a strategy to address 'settlement risks', such as by having margins and settlement funds in place.[241] Similarly, SEBI's strategy to address market disruption included the use of 'circuit breakers'.[242]

Another requirement for ensuring 'systemic stability' is having a set of 'coordination' mechanisms in place between the major regulatory agencies, which in the case of India's financial sector are SEBI and RBI.[243] Additionally, a Financial Stability Development Council (FSDC), chaired by the MoF, was established to provide greater financial stability, and address issues relating to systemic risk.[244]

---

239 IOSCO, *Methodology for Assessing* (n 24) 39.

240 IMF, *India FSAP Report* (n 1).

241 See ibid. On the different kinds of margins required for securities trading by the National Stock Exchange of India, see National Stock Exchange, 'Margins'.

242 'A market disruption is a situation wherein markets cease to function in a regular manner, typically characterized by rapid and large market declines': see 'Market disruption', *Investopedia*, investopedia. com/terms/m/marketdisruption.asp. A market disruption can cause panic and disorder in market conditions. A circuit breaker is a mechanism put in place to halt trading in a security or index for a certain period. This is usually adopted when there is a 'runaway move in any security or the index in either direction': see 'What is "circuit breakers"', *The Economic Times,* economictimes.indiatimes.com/ definition/circuit-breakers.

243 After the collapse of the Lehman Brothers subsidiaries in India, SEBI and RBI took coordinated measures in the money market industry to address redemption pressures: see IMF, *India FSAP Report* (n 1). One of the immediate steps by RBI after the Lehman failure was to ring-fence the two Lehman subsidiaries: a primary dealer and an NBFC: see MC Govardhana Rangan, Joel Rebello and ET Bureau, 'We took both conventional and unconventional steps: Duvvuri Subbarao' (10 September 2018) *ET Markets.*

244 Government of India, Ministry of Finance (n 42).

In 2011, SEBI established a Systemic Stability Unit to access and mitigate systemic risk.[245] In recent years, SEBI has introduced a significant number of measures towards risk-based supervision, such as by 'prescribing norms for [the] Core Settlement Guarantee Fund (Core SGF), Default Waterfall and Stress Testing'.[246] At its board meeting in November 2014, through 'Agenda item (V)', SEBI formally adopted a risk-based supervision model for the securities markets and its intermediaries.[247] Following this, SEBI appointed a Risk-Based Supervision Task Force that presented its report on risk-based supervision.[248]

Analysis

The above-described features of the Indian regime show that systemic risk is monitored across the financial sector, both collectively and independently, by financial authorities. SEBI's proactiveness in this area is evident from the continuous measures it has taken to manage systemic risk and through its active engagement with other domestic regulatory bodies to coordinate efforts to address systemic risk issues.[249]

The detailed FSAP Review of 2013 for SEBI discussed this principle in the review report but did not formally rate it, as it was among the eight new principles adopted by IOSCO that were not officially assessed in the report. The academic analysis in this area is also limited. However, considering the measures adopted by SEBI towards management of systemic risk, such as its clear risk-based strategy for supervision of markets, it is reasonable to conclude that SEBI places a great amount of importance on the mitigation and management of systemic risk.

Conclusion

To sum up, many features of SEBI's regime, such as requirements of margins, settlement funds, circuit breakers and stress testing, support the fulfillment of Principle 6 to a large degree. Further, given the resilience of

---

245 SEBI has established the SSU under its Department of Economic and Policy Analysis: see SEBI, 'Systemic Stability Unit', sebi.gov.in/department/department-economic-and-policy-analysis-3/contact. html.

246 SEBI, 'SEBI issues circular on Core Settlement Guarantee Fund, default waterfall and stress testing' (PR No:102/2014, 27 August 2014), sebi.gov.in/media/press-releases/aug-2014/sebi-issues-circular-on-core-settlement-guarantee-fund-default-waterfall-and-stress-testing_27859.html.

247 SEBI, 'SEBI Board meeting' (PR No 130/2014, 19 November 2014), sebi.gov.in/sebi_data/docfiles/29593t.html.

248 *SEBI—Risk Based Supervision Task Force* (Report of the Risk Based Supervision Task Force, 2014).

249 Refer to the measures taken by SEBI for risk supervision, and its coordination with other authorities, discussed above.

institutions to systemic shocks in the past, such as during the GFC, the degree of alignment of SEBI's regime with this principle is assessed to be 'high'. The extent of change or new measures introduced by SEBI in recent years are assessed as 'substantial', and, in some ways, transformational for this area, considering the ongoing changes and consistent adoption of risk-based strategies by SEBI for its regulatory activities. Notwithstanding this, the overall regime in relation to addressing systemic risk issues is assessed as 'evolving' to a higher standard, as it is in a rapid state of transition.

ASIC

Key features of the framework on identification and management of systemic risk

Prior to the GFC, ASIC relied on the central bank and the prudential regulator, APRA, to a large extent to contain systemic risk,[250] as it did not have an explicit legislative mandate to monitor, mitigate or manage systemic risk.[251] However, in the aftermath of the crisis, ASIC adopted a more proactive role in risk identification and management for the securities markets.[252] In this exercise, ASIC in FY 2011–12 introduced several new processes to support its systemic identification and management outlook, such as through the establishment of an Emerging Risk Committee chaired by an ASIC commissioner.[253] ASIC's risk regime and mechanisms have recently been enhanced, and now include the Executive Risk Committee, the Commission Risk Committee and a Specialist Sub-Committee to assess emerging threats and harm (Figure A1.2).[254] In recent years ASIC has issued several documents on its risk management strategy and system, including its Regulatory Guide 259, *Risk Management Systems of Responsible Entities*.[255]

---

250 Greg Medcraft, 'Systemic risk: the role of securities regulators' (Systemic Risk, Basel III, Financial Stability and Regulation Conference, 28 June 2011) 7.

251 IMF, *Australia Country Report* (n 1) 54.

252 Medcraft (n 250) 5.

253 John Price, 'Challenge and change: ASIC's regulatory focuses for 2017–18 and beyond and what risk managers should be thinking about' (Risk Management Association, Chief Risk Officers Conference, 12 September 2017). Alongside the Emerging Risk Committee (ERC), ASIC appoints specialist sub-committees, including the Emerging Threats and Harm Committee, which advise on the 'management of emerging risks and strategic risks': see ASIC, 'What we do: ASIC's governance and accountability', asic.gov.au/about-asic/what-we-do/how-we-operate/asics-governance-and-accountability/#emerging. The ERC used an advanced risk assessment framework to assess emerging risks and develop appropriate responses to identified risks: see IMF, *Australia Country Report* (n 1) 54–55.

254 ASIC, 'ASIC's governance and accountability framework' (n 98).

255 ASIC, *Risk Management Systems of Responsible Entities* (Regulatory Guide 259, 2017).

To ensure a holistic approach towards systemic risks in the Australian financial system, ASIC coordinates effectively with other domestic regulators within the Council of Financial Regulators (CFR) to 'monitor, mitigate and manage risks' (see Chapter 2).[256] CFR has four members, APRA, ASIC, the Australian Treasury and the chair of RBA, and its objectives are stated in a charter.[257]

Analysis

According to Godwin, Kourabas and Ramsay, the GFC caused an elevation of 'systemic financial stability to the top of the regulatory hierarchy' along with the 'use of the once-neglected concept of macroprudential regulation' to realise this goal of stability.[258] As the description in the previous section outlines, systemic issues in Australia are monitored and managed at two levels. First, at the broader level, through a holistic and coordinated approach under the CFR structure to promote financial stability by 'identifying important issues and trends in the financial system'.[259] Second, through the 'twin-peaks' model for regulation that not only responds to systemic risks 'efficiently'[260] but also is considered instrumental in promoting financial stability.[261] Specifically with reference to securities regulation, ASIC's approach to managing systemic issues has been invigorated in the post-GFC era[262] through the introduction of internal and external mechanisms,

---

256 Council of Financial Regulators, 'Quarterly Statement by the Council of Financial Regulators—March 2019' (Media Release No 2019-01, 20 March 2019), cfr.gov.au/news/2019/mr-19-01.html.

257 Council of Financial Regulators, 'Charter' (2019), cfr.gov.au/about/charter.html.

258 Andrew Godwin, Steve Kourabas and Ian Ramsay, 'Twin peaks, microprudential regulation and systemic financial stability' in Andrew Godwin and Andrew Schmulow (eds), *The Cambridge Handbook of Twin Peaks Financial Regulation* (Cambridge University Press, 2021) 347, doi.org/10.1017/9781316890592.025.

259 Council of Financial Regulators, 'Charter' (n 257).

260 Duong, Liu and Eddie, 'Regulatory and supervisory framework' (n 10). In the twin peaks system, regulators have dedicated objectives and clear mandates towards which they are fully committed: see T David Llewellyn, 'Institutional structure of financial regulation and supervision: the basic issues' (World Bank Seminar, Aligning Supervisory Structures with Country Needs, 6–7 June 2006).

261 See Andrew Godwin and Andrew Schmulow, 'Introduction: the genealogy and topography of twin peaks' in Andrew Godwin and Andrew Schmulow (eds), *The Cambridge Handbook of Twin Peaks Financial Regulation* (Cambridge University Press, 2021) 1, doi.org/10.1017/9781316890592.002. See also Erskine (n 10). The twin peaks structure, which separates responsibilities for market conduct regulation from prudential regulation and evaluation of financial stability, is regarded as conducive to financial stability.

262 See generally Erskine (n 10). The paper elaborates on myriad issues and learnings from the GFC including the understanding that 'over-reliance on markets to self-stabilise' needs to be 'avoided' and a broader view needs to be taken on systemic risks that threaten financial stability.

including various panels[263] and committees and sub-committees on risk,[264] and through a proactive, strengthened risk-based approach to supervision of markets,[265] such as ASIC's 'close and continuous monitoring' measure.[266] Further, given that risk identification and mitigation are specialist areas that require substantial expertise, the IMF's detailed assessment of ASIC's regime in 2012 noted that ASIC was clearly moving in the right direction by developing expertise in these areas since the GFC.[267] The FSAP Review for this principle accorded a 'fully implemented' grade to ASIC, recognising the sufficiency of measures adopted by ASIC towards systemic risk issues.[268]

Conclusion

The requirements relating to Principle 6 are well reflected in ASIC's regime given the establishment of internal risks committees and other panels as well as ASIC's coordination networks with other domestic regulatory authorities. Considering the adoption of a risk-based strategy by ASIC, and other measures underway to improve supervision of market participants with the aim of reducing systemic risk, the degree of alignment with this principle is assessed as 'high'. The extent of reform introduced to ASIC's systemic risk regime since the detailed FSAP Review of 2012 is assessed as 'substantial', while the overall landscape is assessed as 'mature', though refinements are ongoing.

---

263 See for example ASIC's External Advisory Panel and Director Advisory Panel that were both established in the post-GFC years to assess systemic risk correctly: see ASIC, 'Appendices relating to how our staff achieve our vision' in *Annual Report 2017–18* (2018).

264 See (n 253).

265 Prior to the GFC, supervision of markets was primarily carried out by the ASX for Australia's licensed equity, derivatives and futures markets and the supervision of these entities was significantly strengthened when the responsibility was assumed by ASIC in 2010: see Belinda Gibson, 'Market supervision moves to ASIC—what does it mean for brokers?' (Speech, Annual Stockbrokers' Conference, 9 June 2010), download.asic.gov.au/media/1347308/speech-market-supervision-moves-to-asic-Belinda-Gibson.pdf.

266 John Price, 'An ASIC update by John Price, Commissioner' (FINSIA, The Regulators panel event, Melbourne, Australia, 15 November 2018), asic.gov.au/about-asic/news-centre/speeches/an-asic-update-by-john-price-commissioner/.

267 Expertise such as within the Office of the Chief Economist and ERC at ASIC: see IMF, *Australia Country Report* (n 1) 55.

268 Ibid 22.

Principle 7: The regulator should have or contribute to a process to review the perimeter of regulation regularly

Given the dynamic character of securities markets, it is imperative that an efficient regulator has the capability to review its regulatory ambit. Medcraft, a former chair of the IOSCO Board and ASIC, stressed the importance of continuously extending the regulatory perimeter and the need to 'be ahead of the game'.[269] In light of the learnings from the GFC, academics as well as international organisations such as the G-20 supported the call for a 'review of the scope of financial regulation'.[270]

This significant principle, which was among the eight new principles added in 2010, is examined below in the context of SEBI's and ASIC's regimes.

SEBI

Key features of the framework on review of perimeter of regulation

SEBI is empowered through ss 30(1) and 12(1) of the *SEBI Act* to frame regulations for the governance of the securities markets. In the exercise of this power, SEBI reviews its perimeter of regulation based on the risks it identifies.[271] Additionally, SEBI sets up interdepartmental regulations review committees to review its regulations, identify gaps and comply with relevant global standards and amend laws if necessary.[272] In 2012, SEBI appointed an external global management consulting firm, Oliver Wyman, to make recommendations on SEBI's functioning, organisational restructuring and risk management approach as well as its regulatory ambit.[273]

---

269 Greg Medcraft, 'Extending the regulatory perimeter: mapping the IOSCO agenda' (2014) 8(2) *Law and Financial Markets Review* 95–97, doi.org/10.5235/17521440.8.2.95.

270 Ana Carvajal et al, *The Perimeter of Financial Regulation* (IMF Staff Position Note No 09/07, 2009), doi.org/10.5089/9781455296620.004. One of the learnings in the post-GFC era has been that the regulatory perimeter in most countries has been too narrow, and ought to be expanded, but with due care to any compliance or economic efficiency–related costs that may arise from such expansion.

271 IMF, *India FSAP Report* (n 1).

272 See *Plan of Actions for Compliance to Eight New IOSCO Objectives and Principles of Securities Regulation* (signed 28 July 2011) 5, sebi.gov.in/sebi_data/meetingfiles/1313055313828-a.pdf.

273 IMF, *India FSAP Report* (n 1).

Analysis

The *SEBI Act* makes it clear in s 12(1) that SEBI has the power and ability to expand its regulatory perimeter. SEBI has demonstrated the use of this critical power many times, such as by introducing new regulations for market participants,[274] and by revamping and enlarging the scope of its existing regulations.[275] Given that Principle 7 was newly incorporated in 2010, the detailed FSAP Review of 2013 did not officially assess the compliance of SEBI's regime against this principle. However, it is clear that SEBI has the legal mandate to extend its perimeter and unhesitatingly makes use of such power.

Conclusion

In view of SEBI's powers under the *SEBI Act* to expand its regulatory perimeter according to the risk it perceives, as well as SEBI's record of revamping and introducing new regulations where required, the degree of alignment with this IOSCO standard is assessed as 'high'. In recent years, SEBI has taken 'substantial' measures to enhance its perimeter, by drafting new regulations and overhauling existing ones. Finally, the overall landscape for this principle is determined as sufficiently 'mature' because SEBI has shown agility, capability and responsiveness in extending its regulatory perimeter when necessary.

ASIC

Key features of the framework on review of perimeter of regulation

ASIC is cognisant of the need to extend its regulatory perimeter[276] to overcome challenges in securities regulation that are induced by structural changes in the global financial system caused by the increase of market-

---

274 For example, SEBI framed new regulations for investment advisers in 2013, for alternative investment funds in 2012 and for research analysts in 2014, and further codified listing obligations through SEBI: see *Listing Obligations and Disclosure Requirements Regulations 2015*; *SEBI (Research Analysts) Regulations 2014*; *SEBI (Investment Advisers) Regulations 2013*.

275 In recent years, SEBI entirely redrafted, revamped and strengthened many of its existing regulations, such as the *SEBI (Insider Trading) Regulations 2015*, *SEBI (Portfolio Managers) Regulations 2020* and *SEBI (Foreign Portfolio Investors) Regulations 2019*, as and when the perimeter needed to be extended: see *SEBI (Prohibition of Insider Trading) Regulations 2015*, *Securities and Exchange Board of India (Foreign Portfolio Investors) Regulations 2019* and *Securities and Exchange Board of India (Portfolio Managers) Regulations 2020*.

276 See 'ASIC's growing regulatory perimeter', *Money Management* (30 March 2012), money management.com.au/news/financial-planning/asics-growing-regulatory-perimeter.

based financing, innovation-driven complexity and globalisation.[277] Bearing these challenges in mind, ASIC reviews its regulatory perimeter through different mechanisms. First, ASIC's Risk Committee considers 'unregulated products and activities' and determines the need for added regulatory measures.[278] Second, ASIC's specialist sub-committees, particularly the Regulatory Policy Committee, reviews the adequacy of legal provisions such as under the *Corporations Act*, on the basis of which ASIC may approach the Treasury with a proposal to amend the law.[279] Finally, ASIC extends its regulatory perimeter to protect investors and achieve other regulatory outcomes through issuing 'class orders' or 'regulatory guidance', both of which are an effective means of amplifying the law.[280]

Analysis

The above mechanisms highlight ASIC's approach to keeping pace with the dynamic requirements of securities regulations. Broadly, these show that ASIC recognises both the need and areas for an extension of its remit, as necessary.[281] In recognition of this, the detailed FSAP Review in 2012 accorded a 'fully implemented' status to ASIC for observance of Principle 7.[282]

Conclusion

The requirements of Principle 7 are well reflected in ASIC's approach to regulation and its degree of alignment with this principle is assessed as 'high'. The extent of reform or changes related to this principle in recent years are assessed to be 'minor', while the overall landscape pertaining to this principle is assessed as 'mature' given that ASIC does show agility and adaptability in extending its regulatory domain when need arises.

---

277 Peter Kell, 'The changing perimeter of securities regulation: the perspective from Australia' (Berle V Conference, Capital Markets, the Corporation and the Asian Century: Governance, Accountability and the Future of Corporate Law, Sydney, Australia, 13 May 2013), download.asic.gov.au/media/1322965/Changing-perimeter-of-securities-regulation--The-perspective-from-Australia.pdf.

278 For example, the ERC has discussed the 'lack of transparency in structured products, risks from commodity futures markets, and monitoring of complex shadow banking groups': see IMF, *Australia Country Report* (n 1).

279 Ibid. For recent changes to ASIC's regime, see ASIC, 'ASIC's governance and accountability framework' (n 98).

280 Ibid.

281 Greg Medcraft, 'ASIC's challenges in the years ahead' (Asian and Oceanian Stock Exchanges Federation 30th AOSEF General Assembly & Working Committee Meeting, 29 March 2012), download.asic.gov.au/media/1316143/ASICs-Challenges-in-the-years-ahead-20120329.pdf.

282 IMF, *Australia Country Report* (n 1) 22.

Principles for cooperation in regulation

In their persuasive *Harvard International Law Journal* article, Tafara and Peterson proposed a new framework for cooperation among securities regulators, highlighting that interconnectedness of markets made it necessary to approach regulation, investor protection and capital formation in a more coordinated manner rather than in isolation.[283] The cross-border nature of securities transactions has necessitated regulators, more than ever before, to have authority to request and share information with domestic and foreign counterparts.[284] The significance of such cooperation for effective securities regulation is embodied in IOSCO Principles 13, 14 and 15, discussed below.

> Principle 13: The regulator should have authority to share both public and non-public information with domestic and foreign counterparts.
>
> Principle 14: Regulators should establish information-sharing mechanisms that set out when and how they will share both public and non-public information with their domestic and foreign counterparts.
>
> Principle 15: The regulatory system should allow for assistance to be provided to foreign regulators who need to make inquiries in the discharge of their functions and exercise of their powers.

Principles 13, 14 and 15

IOSCO Principles 13, 14 and 15 require a regulator to have authority to share and receive information, establish appropriate mechanisms for sharing and receiving such information, and provide assistance to foreign regulators who have requested the use of the powers and functions of the domestic regulator to progress a foreign inquiry.[285] These principles apply at the domestic as well as the cross-border level, and cover a variety of situations and information sets.[286] Similarly, mechanisms for sharing information refer

---

283 Tafara Ethiopis and Robert J Peterson, 'A blueprint for cross-border access to US investors: a new international framework' (2007) 48 *Harvard International Law Journal* 32. They proposed a framework based on substituted compliance with SEC regulations.

284 'Regulators should institute information sharing mechanisms': see Carvajal and Elliott (n 124).

285 See IOSCO, *Objectives and Principles of Securities Regulation* (n 1).

286 IOSCO, *Methodology for Assessing* (n 24) 80. The IOSCO Principles hold that the regulator must have the authority to share both public and non-public information with domestic and foreign counterparts without its domestic laws impeding such processes of international cooperation, and with the regulator obtaining such information having the authority to maintain confidentiality at all times.

to a number of key requirements[287] that include a mandate under legislation or by administrative practice for the regulator to share information with domestic and foreign counterparts; capacity of the regulator to develop information-sharing mechanisms that allow for detection and deterrence of cross-border misconduct and other regulatory duties; and, finally, status of the regulator as a signatory to IOSCO's *Multilateral Memorandum of Understanding Concerning Consultation Cooperation and the Exchange of Information* (IOSCO's MMoU).[288]

IOSCO's MMoU has been instrumental in cross-border information sharing and enforcement cooperation; its usage has steadily risen from 56 information exchanges among signatories in 2003 to 4,319 information exchanges in 2019.[289]

Despite this recent success, IOSCO's MMoU was considered to fall short of 'significant technological, societal and market developments', leading IOSCO to adopt an upgraded version, the *Enhanced Multilateral Memorandum of Understanding* (EMMoU) that requires regulators to possess five additional powers.[290] These are referred to as 'ACFIT'

---

287 See ibid 88 for the complete set of 'Key Questions'.

288 The IOSCO MMoU is a significant feat achieved by the securities markets regulators that allows the sharing of both public and non-public information between the signatories and calls for the Fullest Mutual Assistance Permissible. The IOSCO MMoU was established in 2002 for supporting IOSCO's objectives of 'protecting investors and ensuring the markets are fair, efficient and transparent' and, ever since, the 'MMoU has become the global benchmark for international cooperation in the enforcement of securities and derivatives laws and regulations': see IOSCO, *Multilateral Memorandum of Understanding Concerning Consultation and Cooperation and the Exchange of Information* (2002) (MMoU). Among other things, the IOSCO MMoU sets out the requirements for 1) the type of information that can be exchanged and the manner in which it can be exchanged, 2) the legal capacity to compel information, 3) the kind of information that can be compelled, 4) the legal capacity for sharing information and 5) the permissible use of information. For more on the IOSCO MMoU, see Austin, 'IOSCO'S Multilateral Memorandum of Understanding' (n 8). See also Rita Cunha, 'The IOSCO Multilateral Memorandum of Understanding (MMoU): an international benchmark for securities enforcement' (2010) 15(3–4) *Uniform Law Review* 677, doi.org/10.1093/ulr/15.3-4.677.

289 IOSCO, *Multilateral Memorandum of Understanding Concerning Consultation and Cooperation and the Exchange of Information (MMoU)*, iosco.org/about/?subsection=mmou.

290 IOSCO states that the EMMoU was a result of the critical and growing needs of IOSCO members and the lessons learnt from the GFC: see IOSCO, *Enhanced Multilateral Memorandum of Understanding Concerning Consultation and Cooperation and the Exchange of Information* (2016) (IOSCO EMMoU). Under the EMMoU, IOSCO signatories (ie securities market regulators) are required to have the following five powers, in addition to their earlier powers, to effectively cooperate in the enforcement of securities and derivatives regulations:

- obtain and share audit work papers, communications and other information relating to the audit or review of financial statements
- compel physical attendance for testimony (by being able to apply a sanction in the event of non-compliance)

powers.[291] Presently, while 124 authorities are signatories to the original IOSCO MMoU (Appendix A),[292] fewer authorities are signatories to the EMMoU: 12 are signatories to Appendix A.1[293] and eight jurisdictions are signatories to Appendix A.2.[294] The EMMoU and MMoU are expected to coexist until such time as IOSCO members migrate from the MMoU to the EMMoU.[295]

While both SEBI and ASIC cooperate under IOSCO's MMoU framework, the analysis below explores other relevant facets of their cooperation mechanisms.

SEBI

Key features of the cooperation framework

Section 11(2)(ia) of the *SEBI Act* empowers SEBI to call for information and records from *any* person that is relevant to any investigation or inquiry by the board in respect of a transaction in securities.[296] Section 11(2)(ib) of the Act empowers SEBI to call for information or furnish information to other

---

- freeze assets if possible, or, if not, advise and provide information on how to freeze assets, at the request of another signatory
- obtain and share existing internet service provider records (not including the content of communications) including with the assistance of a prosecutor, court or other authority, and to obtain the content of such communications from authorised entities
- obtain and share existing telephone records (not including the content of communications) including with the assistance of a court, prosecutor or other authority, and to obtain the content of such communications from authorised entities.

291 Under the ACFIT powers, 'A' stands for the powers to obtain and share audit work papers with the requesting authority, 'C' stands for the powers to compel testimony, 'F' stands for the power to freeze assets, or share information with the requesting authority on how to freeze assets, 'I' stands for the powers to obtain and share internet service provider records and 'T' stands for the power to obtain and share telephone records with the requesting authority: see ibid.

292 See IOSCO, 'IOSCO MMoU: Appendix A (current signatories) 124' in *Signatories to Appendix A and Appendix B List*. Apart from these, eight members are signatories to Appendix B of the MMoU, which is a list of those members who 'have committed to seeking the legal authority necessary to enable them to become full signatories to the IOSCO MMoU' (Appendix A).

293 Signatories to Appendix A.1 refers to those authorities that hold the entire set of ACFIT powers: see IOSCO, 'IOSCO EMMoU: Appendix A.1 Signatories—12', *Signatories to EMMoU*. The present member agencies in this category include Alberta Securities Commission, Alberta; Securities Commission of The Bahamas, Bahamas; British Columbia Securities Commission, British Columbia; Securities and Futures Commission, Hong Kong; Ontario Securities Commission, Ontario; AMF, Quebec; Monetary Authority of Singapore, Singapore; and US SEC, US.

294 Signatories to Appendix A.2 refers to those authorities that hold the powers under ACF: see IOSCO, 'IOSCO EMMoU: Appendix A.2 Signatories—8' in *Signatories to EMMoU*. The five members and jurisdictions are ASIC, Australia; Dubai Financial Services Authority, Dubai; Financial Services Commission/Financial Supervisory Service, Republic of Korea; Swiss Financial Market Supervisory Authority, Switzerland; and the Financial Conduct Authority, UK.

295 IOSCO EMMoU (n 290).

296 *SEBI Act* s 11(2)(ia).

authorities in India or abroad that have similar functions to those of SEBI in respect of securities laws.[297] The proviso to s 11(2)(ib) gives authority to SEBI to enter into an 'arrangement or agreement or understanding' with a foreign authority following approval of the central government. Although the *SEBI Act* does not necessitate signing of formal MoUs or arrangements with domestic regulators, and SEBI had been cooperating informally with such authorities, SEBI has entered into formal MoUs for cooperation with other domestic financial authorities, namely RBI, the Insurance Regulatory and Development Authority of India and the Pension Fund Regulatory Department Authority (PFRDA),[298] and, more recently, with the Central Board of Direct Taxes[299] and Financial Intelligence Unit.[300] Similarly, SEBI cooperates and shares information with oversees authorities through a number of mechanisms including bilateral MoUs[301] and the IOSCO MMoU framework under which SEBI makes, receives and responds to requests for information from foreign regulators.[302] SEBI is not yet a signatory to

---

297 Ibid s 11(2)(ib).

298 This MoU for supervisory cooperation was signed by RBI, SEBI, IRDAI and PFRDA in 2013 'to collaborate, co-operate, share information, coordinate on-site examinations, consult on matters of mutual supervisory/ regulatory interests and to undertake assessment of systemic risk arising from the activities of financial companies as a part of the financial companies monitoring framework' under the Intern-Regulatory Forum (IRF): see FSB, '2013 IMN Survey of National Progress in the Implementation of G20/FSB Recommendations' (2013) 42. The IRF has been constituted under the sub-committee of the FSDC as 'a college of domestic financial sectoral supervisors for strengthening the supervision of financial companies and assessing risks to systemic stability arising from the activities of the financial companies'.

299 SEBI, 'SEBI signs MoU with CBDT' (Press Release No 38/2020, 8 July 2020), sebi.gov.in/media/press-releases/jul-2020/sebi-signs-mou-with-cbdt_47030.html. See also FE Bureau, 'CBDT and SEBI sign MoU to share data', *Financial Express* (9 July 2020), financialexpress.com/market/cbdt-and-sebi-sign-mou-to-share-data/2017763/. The MoU envisages sharing of information between the authorities on an automatic and regular basis.

300 'SEBI signs memorandum of understanding with Financial Intelligence Unit to check money laundering acts', *The Economic Times* (5 May 2014), economictimes.indiatimes.com/sebi-signs-memorandum-of-understanding-with-financial-intelligence-unit-to-check-money-laundering-acts/articleshow/34696964.cms.

301 SEBI has signed 23 bilateral MoUs for cooperation with foreign regulatory authorities: see SEBI, *Annual Report 2018–19* (n 79) 190. See also SEBI, 'Bilateral MoUs', sebi.gov.in/sebi_data/internationalAffr/IA_BilMoU.html. These authorities include US SEC, US; Securities Commission, Malaysia; Financial Services Commission of Mauritius; Securities and Exchange Commission of Sri Lanka; Monetary Authority of Singapore; US CFTC, US; China Securities Regulatory Commission, China; Emirates Securities and Commodities Authority, UAE; Securities and Exchange Commission, Thailand; SEC, Nigeria; Financial Supervisory Commission, Taiwan; Indonesian Capital Market and Financial Institutions Supervisory Agency; Israel Securities Authority; State Securities Commission of Vietnam; Securities and Exchange Commission, Pakistan; Federal Financial Markets Service of Russian Federation; Dubai Financial Markets Authority; Non-Bank Financial Institutions Regulatory Authority, Botswana; Ministry of Finance, Republic of Belarus; Bangladesh Securities and Exchange Commission; and Abu Dhabi Global Markets.

302 For example, SEBI's Annual Report notes that for the year 2017–18, 56 requests for information/assistance were received from foreign regulatory authorities, while 23 requests were made by SEBI

the IOSCO EMMoU.[303] On the whole, SEBI is an active participant at IOSCO as a member of IOSCO's Board[304] and as a member of IOSCO's eight specialised, policy- and standard-setting committees[305]—particularly of IOSCO's Committee 4 (ie IOSCO's Committee on Enforcement and the Exchange of Information).[306] SEBI actively engages and cooperates with other international organisations also such as the Organisation for Economic Co-operation and Development through participation in its conferences and symposiums.[307]

Analysis

The above snapshot of SEBI's cooperation framework reveals that SEBI is sufficiently empowered to seek information from various entities, and to cooperate and share information with both domestic and foreign counterparts. Clearly, SEBI's cooperation regime has been strengthened in the last decade through specific amendments to the *SEBI Act*,[308] signing of formal MoUs with domestic authorities and through enhancement of other information-sharing, supervisory and cooperation mechanisms.[309] Interestingly, while the specific power to share information with foreign regulators was expressly incorporated in the *SEBI Act* in 2014, even prior to such inclusion, SEBI provided information and assistance to foreign regulators, such as by providing bank records.[310] Further, although SEBI does not have an express provision for compelling a person to provide testimony on behalf of a foreign regulator, in practice SEBI has been able to obtain such testimony when investor interest is at stake.[311]

---

to various foreign authorities: see SEBI, *Annual Report 2017–18* (n 135). The report notes SEBI's engagement with international bodies such as the FSB and IOSCO as well as its bilateral and multilateral engagements with foreign regulatory authorities.

303 See IOSCO, 'IOSCO MMoU: Appendix A (current signatories) 124' (n 292).

304 IOSCO, 'IOSCO Board', iosco.org/about/?subsection=display_committee&cmtid=11.

305 IOSCO has eight specialised committees for different areas: see IOSCO, *About IOSCO* (n 3).

306 IOSCO, 'Committee on Enforcement and the Exchange of Information (Committee 4)', iosco.org/about/?subsection=display_committee&cmtid=15.

307 SEBI, *Annual Report 2018–19* (n 79) 129. SEBI is a full-time member of the OECD's International Network on Financial Education that facilitates cooperation between policymakers worldwide and other stakeholders for financial literacy programs.

308 See for example *Securities Laws (Amendment) Ordinance 2014*.

309 FSB, '2013 IMN Survey' (n 298) 42.

310 Subsequently SEBI received an expanded set of powers: see *Securities Laws (Amendment) Ordinance 2014*.

311 In the matter of 'Profits Paradise', SEBI extended cooperation to US SEC in obtaining statements that assisted US SEC in filing charges against two individuals offering a high-yielding investment scheme called Profits Paradise: see Jayshree P Upadhay, 'How Sebi helped US SEC solve "Profits Paradise" case', *Business Standard* (24 November 2014), business-standard.com/article/markets/how-sebi-helped-us-sec-solving-profits-paradise-114112400766_1.html.

Generally, SEBI's cooperation regime and efforts have been 'proactive',[312] in line with international expectations[313] and, in certain cases, have even exceeded expectations (eg when US SEC sought SEBI's assistance in the Profits Paradise initiative).[314] Thus, not only does SEBI have clear powers to share information and to cooperate under the *SEBI Act*, but also it has demonstrated practical use of these powers several times. Noting the strength of SEBI's cooperation framework and its implementation, the detailed FSAP Review of 2013 graded SEBI's regime's compliance with Principles 13, 14 and 15 as 'fully implemented'.[315]

Notwithstanding this, and without detracting from SEBI's accomplishments in this area, this book identifies the need for further expansion of SEBI's cooperation regime through a more ambitious and long-term vision and strategy to attain well-defined objectives in areas such as market development, integration and better regulation.[316] Such a proposal is relevant because a general perusal of SEBI's annual reports gives the impression that, while SEBI is responsive towards its foreign counterparts, most of its cooperation occurs under IOSCO's MMoU framework in the context of oversight, supervision and enforcement activities, while its bilateral MoU network remains largely underutilised, exhibiting traits of short-termism and ad hoc cooperation on a narrow range of issues. Given the proactiveness, openness and maturity shown by SEBI while cooperating with its foreign counterparts in times of need and necessity, this book specifically proposes an expansion of its current cooperation regime through a deeper, strategic and long-term collaboration initiative with ASIC, on a broader range of issues, as put forth in Chapter 9.

---

312 For example SEBI's engagement with international forums such as OECD and ESMA: see SEBI, *Annual Report 2018–19* (n 79) 190.

313 See for example 'US market regulator may seek Sebi's help to dive deeper into Infosys crisis', *Business Standard* (26 October 2019), business-standard.com/article/pti-stories/us-sec-to-seek-sebi-s-cooperation-into-whistleblower-allegations-against-infosys-119102500645_1.html. See also 'US SEC to seek Sebi's cooperation into whistleblower allegations against Infosys', *The Economic Times* (25 October 2019), economictimes.indiatimes.com/markets/stocks/news/us-sec-to-seek-sebis-cooperation-into-whistle blower-allegations-against-infosys/articleshow/71756439.cms.

314 See for instance Upadhay (n 311).

315 IMF, *India FSAP Report* (n 1).

316 SEBI uses its cooperation regime extensively, as reported in its annual reports, and as evident from its IOSCO engagement; however, SEBI's long-term vision and strategy can be further refined for transformative effects.

Conclusion

As identified above, SEBI's cooperation framework is intrinsically well developed and effectively implemented. Hence, the degree of alignment of SEBI's cooperation regime with the core requirements of IOSCO Principles 13, 14 and 15 is assessed in this book as 'high'. In recent years, there have been several attempts to strengthen the existing cooperation arrangements, specifically in the domestic setting, and thus the overall extent of change or reform is assessed as 'substantial'. The stage of development or overall landscape is assessed as 'mature' for these principles given SEBI's continuous and effective use of its cooperation regime, its general reliability and its consistency.

ASIC
Key features of the cooperation framework

Domestically, ASIC cooperates formally with at least 18 regulatory and other agencies including the ACCC, the Australian Federal Police and APRA.[317] ASIC has entered into explicit MoUs with these agencies that define the scope of cooperation, including 'information' that may be requested by each of the authorities.[318] Scanned and signed copies of all MoUs that ASIC enters into with domestic and international agencies are publicly available on ASIC's website.[319]

As regards 'information exchange' with foreign counterparts, ASIC is a signatory to IOSCO's MMoU, which enables securities regulators across jurisdictions to seek information from each other in an ongoing investigation or enforcement matter.[320] ASIC has shown a keen interest and expertise in

---

317 ASIC's website lists 18 agencies with which it actively cooperates domestically: see ASIC, 'What we do: working with other agencies and organisations', asic.gov.au/about-asic/what-we-do/our-role/other-regulators-and-organisations/.

318 For instance, the APRA–ASIC MoU provides that agencies recognise the need for full collaboration and cooperation between them, rendering mutual assistance to each other in a timely manner relating to the exchange of information that is required in relation to regulation, compliance or any enforcement matters: see APRA and ASIC, *Memorandum of Understanding* (signed 18 May 2010).

319 For ASIC's international MoUs, see ASIC, 'Memoranda of understanding and other international agreements', asic.gov.au/about-asic/what-we-do/international-activities/international-regulatory-and-enforcement-cooperation/memoranda-of-understanding-and-other-international-agreements/. For domestic MoUs, see ASIC, 'Other regulators and organisations' (n 317).

320 ASIC may share the information in its possession with other foreign regulators (except 'colleges of supervisors'), but for information that it needs to collect or obtain for foreign regulators from other sources, there are limitations on ASIC's powers: see IMF, *Australia Country Report* (n 1).

the area of financial innovation, fintech (financial technology) and regtech (regulatory technology), and is a member and also a part of the coordination group of the Global Financial Innovation Network (GFIN).[321]

A request for information pertaining to an enforcement matter being investigated by a foreign regulator is handled under the *Mutual Assistance in Business Regulations Act 1992* (Cth) (*MABRA*) and is subject to the approval of the treasurer.[322] If a foreign authority requests information in relation to an ongoing criminal activity, the request is made to the attorney-general under the *Mutual Assistance in Criminal Matters Act 1987* (Cth) (*MACMA*).[323] In sum, ASIC has powers to share information with foreign regulators but such powers are subject to other approvals that ASIC must seek.

In the context of Principle 14, which requires regulators to have information-sharing mechanisms in place with both domestic and foreign counterparts, ASIC has entered into several MoUs with domestic and foreign institutions.[324] ASIC has put mechanisms in place that cater to information sharing such as its International Cooperation Requests team that manages requests from overseas relating to enforcement, policy information or other inquiries relating to the financial matters.[325]

IOSCO Principle 15 requires ASIC to provide 'assistance' to foreign regulators who are making inquiries to discharge their statutory obligations. As explained above, ASIC's ability to assist a foreign agency is subject to *MABRA* and *MACMA*.[326] At the same time, ASIC has been a frontrunner in signing the IOSCO EMMoU that enhances and extends cooperation among the signatories in the securities markets.[327]

---

321 GFIN, 'Our members', thegfin.com/members.

322 Pursuant to the *MABRA*, the treasurer may approve or decline a request made under the Act.

323 The attorney-general may refuse assistance in some cases, such as if the offence committed is a political offence: see *Mutual Assistance in Criminal Matters Act 1987* (Cth).

324 ASIC has signed MoUs with New Zealand, Hong Kong, Canada, the US and several other countries: see ASIC, 'Memoranda of understanding and other international agreements' (n 319).

325 ASIC, 'International regulatory and enforcement cooperation', asic.gov.au/about-asic/what-we-do/international-activities/international-regulatory-and-enforcement-cooperation/.

326 For a more detailed discussion, see IMF, *Australia Country Report* (n 1).

327 IOSCO, 'IOSCO EMMoU: Appendix A.2 Signatories—8' (n 294).

Analysis

At a glance, the framework for ASIC's cooperation and information sharing with domestic and international agencies is both extensive in its outreach[328] and impressive in its content.[329] ASIC's annual reports[330] detail how it utilises its cooperation framework—powers and mechanisms—extensively and proactively to advance domestic cooperation and information exchange,[331] promote regional and international cooperation,[332] and encourage collaboration with innovative businesses[333] and other agencies in fintech and regtech matters.[334] As part of GFIN, ASIC is a forerunner in cutting-edge regulatory work and cooperation in fintech, regtech and financial innovation, not just as a member but also as part of GFIN's core coordination group that 'sets the overall direction, strategy and annual work programme of the GFIN'.[335] Further, ASIC's speedy endorsement of IOSCO's EMMoU[336] indicates its lead in the cooperation arena among international agencies. In addition to these activities, ASIC's whole gamut of international initiatives, which includes the Asia Region Funds Passport,[337]

---

328 ASIC has signed over 18 formal domestic MoUs and over 50 MoUs with international authorities: see ASIC, 'Memoranda of understanding and other international agreements' (n 319). These MoUs are signed with a variety of objectives that range from supervisory to enforcement to fintech.

329 The MoU between ASIC and APRA contains clauses around the commitment to engage proactively; engagement areas are defined elaborately to include policy, monitoring, supervision, investigation and enforcement, as well as annual reporting through an annual joint report or update: see *Memorandum of Understanding between the Australian Prudential Regulatory Authority and the Australian Securities and Investments Commission* (n 54).

330 See for example ASIC, 'Section 5—ASIC cooperation' *Annual Report 2019–20* (2020).

331 For instance, in 2019–20, ASIC and APRA cooperated to establish a revised MoU in which the two agencies could use 'dedicated cross-agency working groups to progress work in a number of areas of shared interest' such as 'enhanced supervision, corporate governance and culture': see ASIC, 'Section 1—ASIC's role' (n 51).

332 For instance, ASIC made 497 international cooperation requests and received 528 requests in regard to surveillance, supervision, enforcement and policy-related activities; it also cooperated under IOSCO's Asia-Pacific Forum to strengthen regional collaboration, promote supervisory colleges and strengthen the Trans-Tasman Supervisory College: see ASIC, 'Section 5—ASIC cooperation' (n 330) 110.

333 One of ASIC's most impressive achievements in recent years has been the establishment of its Innovation Hub to assist Australian businesses to comply with regulatory requirements: see ibid 112.

334 ASIC promotes collaboration on fintech and regtech ideas and had a sizeable budget of $6 million in funding for the period 2018–20 to promote Australia as a leader in development and adoption of regtech solutions for financial services industry: see ibid 112.

335 See GFIN (n 321).

336 ASIC is a signatory to Appendix A.2 of the EMMoU that applies to regulators who have the ACF powers among the whole set of ACFIT powers.

337 For a detailed understanding of the Australia Region Funds Passport, see APEC, 'Asia Region Funds Passport', 28 April 2016), fundspassport.apec.org/about/.

the Trans-Tasman Agreement[338] and the Mutual Recognition Agreement with the United States,[339] suggests a strong underlying commitment to cooperation, transnational activity and growth in securities markets.[340]

Another creditable feature of ASIC's cooperation regime is the level of transparency and openness with which it operates. For example, the content and information on each of the MoUs to which ASIC is a signatory is made publicly available, and the vision, strategy and measures underlying its cooperative approach are communicated in a clear and comprehensible manner through ASIC's published reports or on its website.[341]

Further, in spite of certain constraints on ASIC's power to share information or provide assistance to foreign regulators,[342] ASIC's data on 'international cooperation requests' reveals that, in practice, ASIC provides significant assistance in enforcement matters, including requests where ASIC's assistance

---

338 ASIC and the New Zealand Securities Commission have jointly published guidelines for Australia and New Zealand issuers for 'offering shares, debentures or interests in managed or collective investment schemes in both countries': see ASIC, '11-51AD Guide for Trans-Tasman mutual recognition of securities offerings updated' (17 March 2011), asic.gov.au/about-asic/news-centre/find-a-media-release/2011-releases/11-51ad-guide-for-trans-tasman-mutual-recognition-of-securities-offerings-updated/. See also ASIC, *Offering Financial Products in New Zealand and Australia under Mutual Recognition* (Regulatory Guide No 190, 2017), asic.gov.au/regulatory-resources/find-a-document/regulatory-guides/rg-190-offering-financial-products-in-new-zealand-and-australia-under-mutual-recognition/.

339 In 2008, US SEC and ASIC entered into a Mutual Recognition Arrangement to facilitate cross-border investments through regulatory exemptions that would permit the US and Australian stock exchanges and their brokers to operate with ease in both jurisdictions: see ASIC, '08-193 SEC, Australian authorities sign mutual recognition agreement' (25 August 2008), asic.gov.au/about-asic/news-centre/find-a-media-release/2008-releases/08-193-sec-australian-authorities-sign-mutual-recognition-agreement/. The full text of the Mutual Recognition Arrangement can be accessed online: *Mutual Recognition Arrangement between the United States Securities and Exchange Commission and the Australian Securities and Investments Commission, Together with the Australian Minister for Superannuation and Corporate Law* (signed 25 August 2008), download.asic.gov.au/media/1346672/SEC_framework_arrangement_aug_08.pdf. The MRA envisaged the signing of two significant documents—the enhanced enforcement and supervisory MoU: see *Memorandum of Understanding Concerning Consultation, Cooperation and the Exchange of Information Related to the Enforcement of Securities Laws*, (25 August 2008), download.asic.gov.au/media/1346666/SEC_enhanced_enforcement_mou.pdf; *Memorandum of Understanding Concerning Consultation, Cooperation and the Exchange of Information Related to Market Oversight and the Supervision of Financial Services Firms* (25 August 2008), download.asic.gov.au/media/1346678/SEC_supervisory_mou_aug_08.pdf.

340 See generally Jennifer G Hill, 'Regulatory cooperation in securities market regulation: perspectives from Australia' (2020) 17(1) *European Company and Financial Law Review* 11–34, doi.org/10.1515/ecfr-2020-0003.

341 ASIC's annual reports enumerate its commitment towards global regulatory standard setting, capacity building and other such goals, while explaining the measures taken in a given year: see for example ASIC, 'Section 5—ASIC cooperation' (n 330).

342 Refer to the description in the framework that requires ASIC to seek permissions of the Treasury or relevant minsters to respond to information sharing requests from a foreign authority.

is sought to compel material from third parties under *MABRA*.[343] In sum, it is reasonable to say that ASIC cooperates with and provides information to foreign regulators within the constraints placed by the legislature.[344]

The FSAP Review of 2012 graded ASIC's compliance with Principles 13 and 15 as 'broadly implemented' and Principle 14 as 'fully implemented'.

Conclusion

Despite some obvious constraints in ASIC's ability to freely share information with, or provide assistance to, foreign authorities, its cooperation regime is characterised by several strong, unique and futuristic cooperation arrangements and initiatives that illustrate its foresight and commitment to domestic and international cooperation matters. Keeping this in mind, and notwithstanding the limitations pointed out in respect of ASIC's autonomy, the degree of alignment is collectively assessed as 'high' for each of Principles 13, 14 and 15. The overall landscape for ASIC's cooperation regime is sufficiently 'mature' in view of its consistent and reliable approach to cooperation, while the extent of reform or change in recent years is assessed as 'substantial', considering ASIC's expansion of its bilateral cooperation landscape, both domestic and international.

Synthesis and conclusion

The analysis of SEBI's and ASIC's regimes relating to their roles and responsibilities, as well as their cooperation regimes, highlights critical and fascinating aspects of each regulator and its regulatory approach and fundamental thinking. For example, the legislative mandate of both regulators clearly states their roles and meets the core expectations of IOSCO Principle 1. However, in terms of comparability between SEBI's and ASIC's mandates, there is a wide and perceptible chasm. SEBI's mandate of investor protection, development and regulation of securities markets comes across as far more basic, vague, underdeveloped and passé when juxtaposed with ASIC's sharper, ambitious, specific, detailed and second-generational mandate, which requires ASIC to strive to 'maintain, facilitate, and improve the performance of the financial system and the

---

343 For instance, in 2018–19, ASIC collaborated with international agencies on over 140 requests for assistance in enforcement matters, out of which 40 sought ASIC's assistance to compel material from third parties under *MABRA*: see ASIC, 'Section 5—ASIC cooperation' (n 330) 110.

344 ASIC, 'International regulatory and enforcement cooperation' (n 325) 166.

entities within it in the interests of commercial certainty, reducing business costs, and the efficiency and development of the economy' while promoting 'confident and informed participation of investors and consumers in the financial system'.[345] SEBI could adopt a clear and decisive vision and mission statement (along the lines of the vision and mission statements of other global regulators) to clearly specify its approach, priorities and long-term strategy and such statements and documents would mitigate the effects of the rather generic objectives set out in the *SEBI Act*. These statements and documents are yet to be adopted, and this exposes a fundamental gap between the two jurisdictions, with ramifications for the long-term vision and clarity of each regime. Further, the cooperation arrangements between the financial regulators in India to avoid gaps and inequities are in nascent stages as compared with Australia's financial regulatory arrangements. Given these indicators, the degree of comparability between the two regimes is assessed as 'moderate'. However, the relevance for cooperation is 'high', as it could lead to significant discussions around how SEBI's and Australia's current objectives fuel and steer the overall operations and functioning of both regulators. Also, there is an opportunity for future detailed research in this area.

For Principle 2 relating to independence and accountability, the analysis in this chapter reveals that both regulators have sufficient levels of independence, at least in the operational realm. SEBI has more financial independence and no resource dependencies on government, unlike ASIC, which still faces budgetary constraints. Generally, both regimes have sufficient accountability measures in place to ensure non-arbitrary use of power. However, ASIC is subject to considerably stronger, robust and active accountability mechanisms that not only keep a check on its functioning but also further sharpen its regulatory focus and approach. Perhaps driven by the necessities of an evolving market, the balance in India is tilted more towards the independence of regulators, while in Australia, it is on accountability. The degree of comparability is 'moderate' while the relevance for cooperation is 'low', mainly because enhancing independence and accountability mechanisms per se fall under the central and federal government's ambit and not within the regulator's realm.

---

345 *ASIC Act* s 1(2).

As regards Principle 3, SEBI has wide powers under the main legislation but is constrained for adequate human resources and capacity in relation to the size of the market. The analysis for ASIC reveals that, while it appears to have sufficient human resources, its mandate under the main legislation is also far wider. Issues around ASIC's lack of power and financial resources, which have affected its performance in the past, have been addressed through recent amendments. Despite this, ASIC's overall landscape relating to the core requirements of Principle 3 is more mature than SEBI's, leading to the conclusion that the degree of comparability between the two regulators is again 'moderate'. However, the relevance for cooperation is very 'high': regulatory staff exchanges, more meaningful partnerships, secondments, visits and other interactions are likely to benefit both regimes in terms of understanding the unique challenges that both markets face and how the regulators might approach these. Further, a cross-border collaboration among regulatory, industry and academic institutions can strengthen theoretical knowledge sharing between the two jurisdictions.

In relation to clear and consistent processes under Principle 4, ASIC's comprehensive consultative mechanisms, practices such as publication of all submissions and regulatory impact assessments, and development of high-quality internal manuals and guides to enable consistency and smooth functioning are among its core strengths. SEBI's landscape, while ahead of most other regulators in India, is still evolving in this respect. Hence, the degree of comparability is assessed as 'moderate'. However, the relevance of cooperation is assessed as 'high', as ASIC's approach can be very valuable for SEBI, given that the significance of this principle is likely to increase as India positions itself as an attractive investment destination globally.

As regards Principle 5, the analysis shows that both regimes are sufficiently aligned with the core requirement for the regulator to be professional in its conduct. Yet there is further room for enhancing the conflicts of interest framework for SEBI's officers, and thus the comparability is assessed as 'moderate'. On the whole, the relevance for cooperation is 'low' at this stage.

In relation to Principle 6, both regimes have taken adequate measures to manage and mitigate systemic risk. A robust regime for risk-based supervision and regulation is significant from the viewpoint of cross-border investment also. SEBI's risk-based approach to supervision and regulation is still evolving compared with ASIC's proactive risk-based identification approach that functions under the larger twin-peaks framework designed to holistically identify and mitigate systemic risk. The comparability is again assessed as 'moderate' and relevance for cooperation as 'high'.

The analysis for Principle 7 reveals that ASIC and SEBI have adequate powers to review their perimeter of regulation and that both regulators use these powers. Thus, the comparability is assessed as 'high' for this principle and the relevance for cooperation is also assessed as 'high', as substantive discussions on future areas of regulation can be valuable for both regulators.

Finally, the analysis in respect of SEBI's and ASIC's cooperation regimes reveals a high alignment with the core requirements of the IOSCO Principles and sufficient maturity, which suggests that the comparability of the two regimes for the cooperation principles is 'high'. The relevance for cooperation is also 'high', as both regimes can explore how to effectively collaborate on common areas of interest and develop mechanisms to extract full value out of a meaningful, strategic cross-border collaboration.

Notwithstanding some differences between SEBI's and ASIC's regimes, which this chapter has highlighted, the comparative analysis shows that both regimes appear to place value on, and are striving to achieve, similar objectives within their domestic realms, both in letter and spirit. This recognition of similar goals and objectives for their respective securities markets is more critical than any other difference between the two jurisdictions, and an appropriate indicator of the potential for successful and mutually beneficial collaboration in securities markets.

4

Supervision and enforcement powers of SEBI and ASIC: IOSCO Principles 10 and 11

Introduction

Rafael et al argue that securities laws and investor protection reflect a combination of the effectiveness of enforcement and corporate governance,[1] and influence the ability of a jurisdiction to attract foreign capital.[2] For an effective compliance regime, securities regulators need to possess powers to conduct comprehensive inspection, investigation, surveillance and enforcement in order to fulfil their duties and functions.[3] Building on the

---

1   Rafael La Porta et al, 'Investor protection and corporate governance' (2000) 58(1) *Journal of Financial Economics* 3–27, doi.org/10.1016/S0304-405X(00)00065-9. For literature discussing empirical evidence of the correlation between robust and resilient securities markets and investor protection, see Rafael La Porta et al, 'Legal determinants of external finance' (1997) 52(3) *The Journal of Finance* 1131–1150, doi. org/10.1111/j.1540-6261.1997.tb02727.x; Rafael La Porta et al, 'Agency problems and dividend policies around the world' (2000) 55(1) *The Journal of Finance* 1–33, doi.org/10.1111/0022-1082.00199; Franco Modigliani and Enrico Perotti, 'Security versus bank finance: the importance of a proper enforcement of legal rules' (2000), doi.org/10.2139/ssrn.200559; Jere R Francis and Dechun Wang, 'The joint effect of investor protection and Big 4 audits on earnings quality around the world' (2008) 25(1) *Contemporary Accounting Research* 157–191, doi.org/10.1506/car.25.1.6.
2   La Porta et al, 'Investor protection and corporate governance' (n 1).
3   Several authors have commented on the essentials of a good supervisory and regulatory regime: see for example José Viñals et al, *The Making of Good Supervision: Learning to Say 'No'* (IMF Staff Position Note 10/08, 2010), doi.org/10.5089/9781462310180.004; Martin Cihák and Alexander F Tieman, *Quality of Financial Sector Regulation and Supervision around the World* (IMF Working Paper No 08/190, 2008), doi.org/10.5089/9781451870480.001. On aspects of how effective securities regulation relies upon the existence of a consistent, strong and effective framework that includes 'good contract and corporate law, a fair and timely judicial process, effective protection of property rights, good accounting

analysis in Chapter 3 of the role, responsibilities and cooperation regimes of the Securities and Exchange Board of India (SEBI) and Australian Securities and Investment Commission (ASIC), this chapter examines the main supervisory and enforcement powers available to the securities regulators in India and Australia, and evaluates their adequacy for achieving regulatory objectives.

An evaluation of SEBI's and ASIC's supervisory and enforcement powers: IOSCO Principles 10 and 11

This section discusses the significance of a regulator's supervisory and enforcement powers and elucidates the core requirements of Principles 10 and 11 of the *Objectives and Principles of Securities Regulations* (IOSCO Principles), describes and analyses the comprehensiveness of SEBI's and ASIC's supervisory and enforcement powers, and determines their degree of alignment with the core requirements of the IOSCO Principles. The final section provides a brief synthesis and conclusion on comparability and relevance for cooperation.

Table 4.1: Snapshot of the main findings of Chapter 4 on SEBI's and ASIC's supervisory and enforcement powers

IOSCO Principles of Securities Regulation	SEBI's degree of alignment, stage of development and extent of reform in recent years	ASIC's degree of alignment, stage of development and extent of reform in recent years	Degree of comparability	Relevance for cooperation
Supervision and enforcement powers (IOSCO Principles 10 and 11)				
Principle 10: Regulator should have comprehensive inspection, investigation and surveillance powers	High Mature Substantial	High Mature Minor	High	Moderate

and audit standards and sound taxation rules', see Ana Carvajal and Jennifer A Elliott, *Strengths and Weaknesses in Securities Market Regulation: A Global Analysis* (IMF Working Paper No 07/259, 2007), doi.org/10.2139/ssrn.1030688.

IOSCO Principles of Securities Regulation	SEBI's degree of alignment, stage of development and extent of reform in recent years	ASIC's degree of alignment, stage of development and extent of reform in recent years	Degree of comparability	Relevance for cooperation
SEBI's FSAP 2013* rating: 'fully implemented' (Principle 10 corresponds to Principle 8 under the pre-GFC IOSCO document***) ASIC's FSAP 2012** ratings: 'fully implemented'				
Principle 11: Regulator should have comprehensive enforcement powers	High Mature Substantial	High Mature Minor	High	Moderate
SEBI's FSAP 2013 rating: 'fully implemented' (Principle 11 corresponds to Principle 9 under the pre-GFC IOSCO document) ASIC's FSAP 2012 ratings: 'fully implemented'				

Note: *FSAP 2013 refers to IMF, *India: Financial Sector Assessment Program — Detailed Assessments Report on IOSCO Objectives and Principles of Securities Regulation* (Country Report No 13/266, 2013). **FSAP 2012 refers to IMF, *Australia: IOSCO Objectives and Principles of Securities Regulation — Detailed Assessment of Implementation* (Country Report No 12/314, 2012). ***The pre-GFC IOSCO document refers to the previous iteration of IOSCO's *Principles of Securities Regulation* that included only 30 principles. Post-GFC, eight more principles were added and, hence, the numbering changed.

Principles for the enforcement of securities regulation

Prior to the global financial crisis (GFC) of 2007–08, neoliberal ideologies, chiefly the efficient market hypothesis (EMH), served as a theoretical framework for supervision and regulation of securities markets.[4] Not only did the EMH form the dominant theory of securities and investments regulation, but also it served as the practical foundation for the regulatory structures across many developed economics including the United States, United Kingdom and Australia through various concepts such as 'principles-based' and 'light-touch' regulation.[5] The GFC challenged this conventional

---

4   Phuong Duong, Jinghui Liu and Ian Eddie, 'Development of the regulatory framework of securities market supervision post-GFC' in Hasan Dincer and Ümit Hacioglu (eds), *Globalization of Financial Institutions* (Springer, 2014) 185–199, 186, doi.org/10.1007/978-3-319-01125-7_14.

5   Tony D'Alosio, 'Developments in the global regulatory system' (Speech, chairman, Australian Securities and Investments [ASIC], Financial Services Council Annual Conference, Melbourne, 12 August 2010) 8. Within Australia, the EMH was evident in the work of the Wallis Committee whose recommendations formed the basis of the *Corporations Act 2001* (Cth) (*Corporations Act*).

wisdom and underscored the need to reassess underlying assumptions in the existing theories.[6] In the process, academics such as Viñals et al ascribed greater importance to 'better supervision' for the stability of financial markets and argued that the lessons 'drawn from failures in supervision' during the global crisis could help prevent future crises.[7] Similarly, Jackson ascribed substantial importance to enforcement for markets by citing Coffee's article on formal enforcement in several jurisdictions, including the United Kingdom, Germany and Australia, which concluded that a 'high level of enforcement activity as in the United States explains the attraction of foreign issuers to US public capital markets'.[8]

The IOSCO Principles[9] underscore the academic view on the importance of supervision and enforcement in securities markets, particularly Principle 10, which mandates comprehensive inspection, investigation and surveillance powers for a securities regulator, and Principle 11, which requires the regulator to hold adequate enforcement powers.[10]

Thus, securities regulators must have a well-developed supervisory and enforcement framework and a fully functional array of powers to rely on to enforce the laws and policies within their jurisdictions and meet regulatory objectives.[11] The core requirements of IOSCO Principles 10 and 11 are discussed in the following sections.

---

6   Ibid 8–9. Chiefly, the GFC highlighted the following: markets do not self-correct; market participants do not always act rationally; disclosure is not adequate for tackling problems associated with information asymmetries and conflicts of interest; and, finally, over-reliance on gatekeepers could prove detrimental to the stability of markets.

7   Viñals et al (n 3).

8   See Howell E Jackson, 'The impact of enforcement: a reflection' (2007) 156 *University of Pennsylvania Law Review*; John C Coffee *Law and the Market: The Impact of Enforcement* (Columbia Law and Economics Working Paper No 304, March 7, 2007), doi.org/10.2139/ssrn.967482. Supervision and enforcement are among other important factors such as liquidity and reputation of the markets that influence foreign investments.

9   IOSCO has adopted three fundamental objectives of securities regulations (protecting investors, ensuring that markets are fair, efficient and transparent, and reducing systemic risk markets) and 38 Principles of securities regulation: see IOSCO, *Objectives and Principles of Securities Regulation* (2010).

10   Ibid.

11   Securities regulators are generally guided by a code of key objectives enshrined in the statutes or the preamble governing them. For a discussion on the key mandate and objectives of the Securities and Exchange Board of India (SEBI) and the Australian Securities and Investments Commission (ASIC), refer to the discussion in Chapter 3. See also s 11 of the *Securities and Exchange Board of India Act 1992* (*SEBI Act*). For ASIC's mandate, see ASIC, 'Our role', asic.gov.au/about-asic/what-we-do/our-role/.
IOSCO states that strong regulation that deters misconduct and makes entities liable for misconduct is central for the development of efficient markets: see IOSCO, *Credible Deterrence in the Enforcement of Securities Regulation* (June 2015) (FR09/2015) 6 [4].
In any financial contract, it is implicit that the legal system will be able to enforce the rights of the parties to the contract: see William A Reese Jr and Michael S Weisbach, 'Protection of minority

IOSCO Principles 10 and 11

Principle 10: The regulator should have comprehensive inspection, investigation and surveillance powers.

Principle 11: The regulator should have comprehensive enforcement powers.

For securities regulators, an effective enforcement and compliance regime is predicated on the availability of a comprehensive supervisory and enforcement toolkit. Therefore, this chapter determines the comprehensiveness of SEBI's and ASIC's supervisory and enforcement powers. IOSCO Principle 10 encapsulates the requirement of inspection, investigation and surveillance powers for regulators. A comprehensive set of these supervisory powers is critically important for regulators[12] to fulfil their regulatory goals.[13] Cihak and Tieman note that the quality of supervision in the securities sector is generally more aligned with international benchmarks compared with the banking or insurance sector.[14] This chapter examines the key features and adequacy of SEBI's and ASIC's supervisory frameworks for securities markets.

---

shareholder interests, cross-listings in the United States, and subsequent equity offerings' (2002) 66(1) *Journal of Financial Economics* 65–104, doi.org/10.1016/S0304-405X(02)00151-4. For another piece acknowledging the importance of a well-developed enforcement framework in the US, see Stephen M Cutler, 'Remarks at the F Hodge O'Neal Corporate and Securities Law Symposium' (Washington University School of Law, 2003).

In the context of Canadian securities markets regulation, Laureen Snider remarks that lenience could be problematic, as weak or ineffective enforcement could prove to be a threat to investor protection, leading to inefficiency, delays, duplication and added costs: see Laureen Snider, 'Accommodating power: the "common sense" of regulators' (2009) 18(2) *Social & Legal Studies* 179–197, doi.org/10.1177/0964663909103634, quoting *It's Time: Report of the Committee to Review the Structure of Securities Regulation in Canada* (Ottawa: Department of Finance, 2003). On views supporting a 'market approach' to securities regulation to make the enforcement of securities laws more effective, see generally Roberta Romano, 'Empowering investors: a market approach to securities regulation' (1998) 107(8) *Yale Law Journal* 2359–2430, doi.org/10.2307/797346.

12   The duty to develop a securities market regulatory framework and the supervision of registered and regulated entities is generally delegated to a public or statutory authority set up under a legislative Act: see Carvajal and Elliott, *Strengths and Weaknesses* (n 3). IOSCO has underscored the significance of rigorous and swift investigation and prosecution of misconduct: see IOSCO, *Credible Deterrence* (n 11).

13   Several authors have commented on the essentials of a good supervisory and regulatory regime: see for example Viñals et al (n 3); Cihák and Tieman (n 3). On how effective securities regulation relies upon the existence of a consistent, strong and effective framework that includes 'good contract and corporate law, a fair and timely judicial process, effective protection of property rights, good accounting and audit standards and sound taxation rules', see Carvajal and Elliott, *Strengths and Weaknesses* (n 3).

14   Cihák and Tieman (n 3).

As well as supervisory powers, IOSCO's Principle 11 requires regulators to have a comprehensive set of enforcement powers to initiate action for any violation of securities laws. 'Law enforcement' means 'the activity of making certain that the laws of an area are obeyed'.[15] In the context of regulation, the term 'enforcement' can refer to several dimensions. Hutter defines 'regulatory enforcement' as including two dimensions: 'enforcement strategy and enforcement styles'.[16] Discussing these dimensions, Bird et al explain 'enforcement strategy' as being 'the way in which the parameters for enforcement actions and daily practices are deliberately determined in accordance with the explicit goals of the particular regulatory project under analysis'.[17] They take Hutter's concept of 'enforcement style' to mean the 'choice between a broad, flexible and accommodative approach and a legalistic, sanctioning approach to enforcement'.[18]

In relation to the securities markets, enforcement can refer to the imposition of 'severe sanctions' that include criminal sanctions, such as those imposed on 'insiders for false or misleading disclosure', or alternative sanctions for other contraventions of securities laws.[19] Sanctions may be civil or criminal. Any deficiency in the ability of a regulator to effectively enforce compliance with the extant regulatory framework may result in a 'persistent weakness' for the entire regulatory system.[20] The requirements of Principle 11 are reiterated in IOSCO's 2015 report *Credible Deterrence in the Enforcement of Securities Regulation*, which emphasises the significance of a comprehensive set of enforcement powers to deter 'misconduct', particularly to boost 'public confidence, consumer protection and market integrity' within the financial system.[21]

---

15   *Cambridge Advanced Learner's Dictionary and Thesaurus* (Cambridge University Press, 2013) 'law enforcement'. Supervision and enforcement are essentially tools to implement the law and achieve compliance with the legal provisions: see Ana Carvajal and Jennifer Elliott, *The Challenge of Enforcement in Securities Markets: Mission Impossible?* (IMF Working Paper No 09/168, 2009) 4–5, doi.org/10.2139/ssrn.1457591. In the context of securities markets, enforcement is an ex post tool to hold accountable those who have committed contraventions and deter others from future wrongdoings, and may also have a remedial value if the regulator has powers such as disgorgement and return of ill-gotten gains.
16   Bridget M Hutter, *The Reasonable Arm of the Law? The Law Enforcement Procedures of Environmental Health Officers* (Clarendon Press, 1988) 131–132.
17   Helen Louise Bird et al, 'ASIC enforcement patterns' (2004) 71 *Public Law Research Paper* 8.
18   Ibid.
19   Bernard Black, 'The legal and institutional preconditions for strong stock markets: the nontriviality of securities law' in *Corporate Governance in Asia: A Comparative Perspective* (OECD, 2001) 55–84, 63.
20   Carvajal and Elliott, *The Challenge of Enforcement* (n 15) 5.
21   IOSCO, *Credible Deterrence* (n 11) 6.

Table 4.2: Snapshot of SEBI's and ASIC's mandate and key supervisory and enforcement powers for securities markets

Express mandate	Legislative objectives						
	Investor protection	Developing/promoting securities markets	Market regulation	Systemic risk regulation	Facilitating efficiency, flexibility, innovation	Promote fairness, honesty and professionalism in provision of financial services	Administer laws with minimum procedural requirements
SEBI	✓	✓	✓	✗	✗	✗	✗
ASIC	✓	✓	✓	✗	✓	✓	✓

Functions and powers	General						
	Investor protection	Promoting/developing securities markets	Market regulation	Consumer protection	Investor education	Extensive power to provide rules/regulations for market	Separate tribunal for securities appeals
SEBI	✓	✓	✓	✗	✓	✓	✓
ASIC	✓	✓	✓	✓	✓	✗	✗

Powers relating to prospectus	Powers relating to issue of prospectus/offer documents	
	Regulation of issue of prospectus/offer doc and soliciting money	Prohibition of issue of prospectus/offer doc and soliciting money
SEBI	✓	✓
ASIC	✓	✓

Licensing

Institutions and individuals	SROs	Stock exchanges	Auditors	CRAs	Research providers/analysts	Depositories	Clearing and settlement facilities	Stock brokers, underwriters, other intermediaries
SEBI	✓	✓	✗	✓	✓	✓	✓	✓
ASIC	✓	✓	✓	✓	✓		✓	✓

Inspection / **Market surveillance**

Powers	Stock exchanges	Mutual funds	Licensed intermediaries	SROs	Depositories	Clearing corporations	1st level market surveillance by stock exchanges	Independent market surveillance by regulator
SEBI	✓	✓	✓	✓	✓	✓	✗	✓
ASIC	✓	✓	✓	✓	✓	✓	✓	✓

Information gathering / **Investigation**

Powers	Call for information from any person	Inspect books or registers of listed companies	Powers to summon, enforce attendance and examine on oath	Telecom interception warrant
SEBI	✓	✓	✓	✗
ASIC	✓	✓	✓	✓

Investigation

Powers	Initiate formal investigation for securities law violation	Call for books, registers or documents during investigation	Powers to summon, enforce attendance and examine on oath	Punishment for failure to cooperate with investigation	Search and seizure in civil investigation	Search and seizure in criminal investigation
SEBI	✓	✓	✓	✓	✓	✓
ASIC	✓	✓	✓	✓	✓	✗

Enforcement

Civil and administrative powers	Suspend trading of a security	Restrain persons from accessing markets to buy/sell/deal in securities	Impound or retain proceeds/securities under investigation	Attach bank account with court orders on suspicion of violation	Direct persons associated with markets not to dispose/alienate assets under investigation	Disgorgement
SEBI	✓	✓	✓	✓	✓	✓
ASIC	✓	✓	✓	✓		

Monetary penalty, settlement, enforceable undertakings	Civil penalty action with court orders	Enforceable undertakings	Settlement of certain offences	Settlement of ongoing matters/appeals
SEBI	✗	✗	✓	✓
ASIC	✓	✓	✓	✗

Criminal	Prison term court ordered	Financial penalty court ordered
SEBI	✓	✓
ASIC	✓	✓

Cooperation with domestic and foreign authorities

Powers	Sign MoUs (domestic and foreign)	Share information	Commence investigation on behalf of foreign authority	Compel attendance for testimony	Auditor papers	Freeze assets or advise on how to freeze assets
SEBI	✓	✓	✗	✓	✓	✓
ASIC	✓	✓	✗	✓	✓	✓

Against this background, the next section presents an overview of SEBI's and ASIC's supervision and enforcement framework and powers. For an overarching comparative understanding, Table 4.2 provides a snapshot of the main powers of the two regulators. It focuses on the powers of the regulator, not actions that require court intervention such as freezing assets.

SEBI

SEBI's key supervisory and enforcement powers

This section describes and analyses SEBI's powers of inspection, surveillance, investigation, enforcement and settlement of securities laws violations.[22] This examination of SEBI's powers is necessary for evaluating SEBI's fulfillment of the core requirements of IOSCO Principles 10 and 11, as well as for informing the discussion in Chapter 5 on the use, implementation and effectiveness of SEBI's enforcement and compliance regime as required by IOSCO Principle 12.

SEBI's inspection framework

Comprehensive inspection powers are vital for ensuring the orderly functioning of intermediaries, participants and institutions operating in the securities markets. The *Securities and Exchange Board of India Act 1992* (*SEBI Act*) grants SEBI wide powers to call for information, undertake inspections, and conduct inquiries and audits of stock exchanges, mutual funds, other persons associated with securities markets, intermediaries and self-regulatory organisations.[23] SEBI is equipped to call for information from 'any person' that it regards as relevant to an ongoing investigation or inquiry in respect of a transaction in securities,[24] and is also able to call for information from and furnish information to other authorities, both within India or abroad if such sharing is connected to the 'prevention or detection of violations' in respect of securities laws.[25] Further, SEBI can

---

22   SEBI was constituted on 12 April 1988 as a non-statutory body through an administrative resolution of the government with the objective of dealing with development and regulation of the securities markets and investor protection; on 30 January 1992, SEBI acquired the status of a statutory body through an ordinance passed by the government that was replaced by the *SEBI Act* on 4 April 1992: see *Trade Execution Cost of Equity Shares in India* (Working Paper No 6, 2002).

23   See *SEBI Act* s 11(2)(i).

24   See ibid s 11(2)(ia). Prior to an amendment of s 11 in 2014, SEBI could call upon information only from such persons who were intermediaries or connected with the securities markets; however, post the 2014 amendment, SEBI can seek information from 'any' person: see *Securities Laws (Amendment) Act 2014*.

25   See *SEBI Act* s 11(2)(ib).

inspect any books, registers or other documents or records of a company where it has reason to believe that such entity has committed insider trading or fraudulent or unfair trade practices relating to a securities market.[26]

Apart from the *SEBI Act*, SEBI derives inspection powers from provisions in the *Companies Act 2013* and *Depositories Act 1996* as well as the *Securities and Contracts Regulations Act 1953*.[27] SEBI's inspection powers are also detailed across several regulations created by it for supervision and regulation of securities market intermediaries and other registered entities.[28] These regulations include powers to inspect or call for information from a variety of securities markets intermediaries and entities.[29]

SEBI's powers of inspection are exercised as a matter of routine or in the course of ensuring compliance with the securities laws or when SEBI receives a consumer complaint.[30] SEBI undertakes such inspections under an established procedure. First, one of SEBI's higher authorities, a whole time member (WTM),[31] appoints an inspection officer. Usually all routine inspections are conducted with prior notice.[32] During inspections, registered intermediaries as well as their employees are under a 'statutory obligation to co-operate' with the inspection process.[33] After completing an inspection, SEBI prepares a report based on its observations or allegations

---

26 See ibid s 11 2(A).

27 In the context of the *Companies Act 2013*, SEBI has been conferred powers under s 24 of that Act in respect of regulation of issue and transfer of securities that includes powers to inspect listed public companies and such public companies intending to have their securities listed. Under s 18 of the *Depositories Act 1996* SEBI can also call for information and make inquiries from any issuer, depository, depository participant or beneficial owner of securities that are held with a depository. Under reg 59 of the *SEBI (Depositories and Participants) Regulations 1996*, SEBI can inspect any issuer, depository, depository participant or beneficial owner, issuer or agent.

28 SEBI has as many as 45 regulations issued for various aspects of securities regulations: see SEBI, 'List of all SEBI regulations', www.sebi.gov.in/sebiweb/home/HomeAction.do?doListing=yes&sid=1&ssid=3&smid=0.

29 See for example regs 61–67 of the *SEBI (Mutual Funds) Regulations 1996* on inspection and audit of mutual funds.

30 Dharmishta Raval, *Improving the Legal Process in Enforcement at SEBI* (Indira Gandhi Institute of Development Research Working Paper No 2011-008, 2011) 15. Such inspections are usually authorised by the whole time member (WTM) on the board of SEBI who is in charge of intermediaries within SEBI. To illustrate, SEBI is empowered under the *SEBI (Stock-Broker and Sub-broker) Regulations 1992* to conduct an inspection of stock brokers and sub-brokers.

31 One WTM equals the rank of a full-time commissioner.

32 Raval (n 30). At times, where the situation so demands, prior notice for conducting an inspection may be waived by the inspecting officer: see for example reg 20(2) of the *SEBI (Stock Brokers and Sub-brokers) Regulations 1992*.

33 Raval (n 30) 15.

of irregularities and violations, which is shared with the intermediaries for their comments. Subsequently, the WTM decides whether further action is warranted.[34]

During these inspections, SEBI holds the same powers as are available to a civil court under the Indian Code of Civil Procedure.[35] To aid such regulatory inspections, requirements for 'record keeping' that are well aligned to international standards have been laid down for securities intermediaries and institutions, including the stock exchanges and depositories.[36] The stock exchanges are also required to furnish annual reports to SEBI.[37]

For transacting in securities, SEBI mandates intermediaries and other entities to obtain critical information from their clients, such as their identity through know your clients norms, and mandates adherence to anti-money laundering statutes.[38] Finally, where SEBI requires expertise and external guidance on aspects of inspections, it has the power to outsource inspections, such as by appointing an external auditor, with due respect to maintenance of confidentiality and prevention of any conflict of interest.[39]

---

34 Ibid 15.

35 SEBI's enforcement responsibilities are enumerated in s 11(3) of the *SEBI Act*. These powers include: 1) the discovery and production of books of account and other documents, at such place and such time as may be specified by the board; 2) summoning and enforcing the attendance of persons and examining them on oath; 3) inspection of any books, registers and other documents of any person referred to in s 12, at any place; 4) inspection of any book, or register, or other document or record of the company referred to in subsection (2A); 5) issuing commissions for the examination of witnesses or documents.

36 Rules 6 and 10 of the *Prevention of Money Laundering Rules* (PML Rules) require all intermediaries to maintain the record of identity of their clients for at least 10 years from the date of initial transactions as well as 'cessation' for the transactions between the client and the intermediary. Accordingly, SEBI has issued a Master Circular specifying that the PML Rules need to be followed in respect of securities markets (paras 8.2 and 8.1): see SEBI, 'Master Circular on anti money laundering standards/combating the financing of terrorism/obligations of securities market intermediaries under the Prevention of Money Laundering Act, 2002 and rules framed there under' (2010) ('Master Circular'). Complementing the PML Rules and SEBI Circular on anti-money laundering, rules 14 and 15 of the *Securities and Contracts (Regulation) Rules 1957* require stock exchanges and their members to maintain books of accounts for five years. Similarly, regs 38 and 49 of the *Securities and Exchange Board of India Depositories and Participants Regulations* require depositories and their participants to maintain records also.

37 See *Securities and Contracts (Regulation) Act 1956* s 7.

38 SEBI has specified the mandatory requirement of a Permanent Account Number for securities transactions: see SEBI, 'Permanent Account Number (PAN) to be the sole identification number for all transactions in the securities market' (SEBI Circular MRD/DoP/Cir- 05/2007, 2007). Additionally, SEBI has issued guidelines for identification of clients and maintenance of records: see SEBI, 'Master Circular' (n 36).

39 An example of this is reg 24 of the *SEBI (Stock Brokers and Sub-brokers) Regulations* that allows SEBI to appoint a qualitied auditor to assess the books of accounts and other records of a stock broker. Though available for other intermediaries too, such powers have not been frequently used by SEBI: see IMF, *India: Financial Sector Assessment Program—Detailed Assessments Report on IOSCO Objectives and Principles of Securities Regulation* (2013) (*India FSAP Report*) 42.

SEBI's investigation powers

Complementing SEBI's inspection framework, the *SEBI Act* empowers SEBI to initiate an investigation when it has reason to believe that 'transactions in securities' are being dealt with in a manner detrimental to investors or the markets, or if any person, including an intermediary, has acted in violation of the Acts or rules and regulations thereunder.[40] SEBI adopts a detailed and graded approach to its investigations. To conduct an investigation, SEBI appoints an 'investigating authority' and such authority is given wide-ranging powers to conduct the investigation.[41] During the course of such an investigation, SEBI can call for a variety of documents and information sets, including call data records and audit reports.[42] At the completion of an investigation, the investigating authority concludes with either an interim report or a final report that is presented before an internal committee of senior officials within SEBI for their review and recommendation.[43] Upon receiving the recommendation and report of the internal committee, the report is submitted before the WTM to make a decision on whether further action needs to be initiated.[44]

Surveillance

In addition to its inspection and investigation process, SEBI conducts in-house market surveillance activities through two main systems: SMARTS and the DWBIS.[45] This is separate from the surveillance carried out by

---

40   See *SEBI Act* s 11C(1).

41   Section 11C of the *SEBI Act* bestows a range of powers on the investigating authority (IA), such as calling for information, including books or registers or records for the purposes of investigation, and withholding records, books and other documents for six months for investigation. Upon failure or refusal by a person to cooperate with the IA, without reasonable cause, such person may be punished with a term that extends to one year imprisonment or a fine of a maximum of one crore rupees or both, and a further fine of five lakh for every day of such failure or refusal. Where circumstances enumerated by s 11C are present, the IA may seek an order from the magistrate or judge of the designated court to search and seize any person other than a listed company or a public one unless it is an insider trading or market manipulation matter: see ibid.

42   The Bombay High Court opined that SEBI has the power to call for call data records from telephone service providers: see *Indian Council of Investors vs Union of India & Ors* (2013). For SEBI's powers over auditors in fraud cases, see *Price Waterhouse & Co vs Securities and Exchange Board of India* (2010). See also Reena Zachariah, 'Bombay High Court says Sebi can seek call data, but must act with care', *The Economic Times* (6 May 2014), economictimes.indiatimes.com/markets/stocks/policy/bombay-high-court-says-sebi-can-seek-call-data-but-must-act-with-care/articleshow/34705827.cms.

43   Raval (n 30) 16. The process of submitting the investigating authority's report before the internal committee is not a statutory compulsion but rather a procedure adopted by SEBI as an additional internal measure.

44   Ibid 16.

45   World Bank–IMF, *Securities Regulation Technical Note* (Financial Sector Assessment Program Update India, 2017) 27.

the recognised stock exchanges (RSEs).[46] Prior to the introduction of the SMARTS surveillance system, SEBI relied on its in-house Integrated Market Surveillance System.[47] The two main RSEs, the National Stock Exchange and the Bombay Stock Exchange, monitor market activity on a real-time basis, and the data SEBI receives from these RSEs are 'delivered overnight and fed into a commercial system, SMARTS'.[48] The RSEs are regarded as the first-line regulator in the supervision and regulation of markets.[49] SEBI uses DWBIS for data mining and analytic work by its surveillance and investigations departments.[50] Further:

> In addition to trading data DWBIS stores a wide range of non-trading information, including news announcements and information linked to individual traders and entities. DWBIS can automatically generate consolidated analysis of trading data from both exchanges for a wide range of market misconduct, including front-running, wash sales, marking the close, and possible pump and dump schemes. It provides alerts whenever sales volume or price movements in a single stock exceed parameters dynamically adjusted. Trading in a given listed company can occur simultaneously on both exchanges. Because all Exchange trading identifies the specific buyer and seller, it is possible to identify trading patterns that occur on both exchanges and the historical trading patterns of persons previously investigated. DWBIS contains information on 78 million traders.[51]

---

46   As regards the operation of the RSEs, s 19 of the *Securities and Contracts Regulations Act 1956* (*SCRA*) prohibits the operation of a stock exchange, unless it has a prior recognition from SEBI while s 3 of the *SCRA* mandates that a stock exchange seeking recognition must file an application with SEBI for such recognition. According to s 4 of the *SCRA*, SEBI can impose conditions for recognition, such as qualifications for membership, manner in which contracts are entered into and enforced, and the maintenance of accounts by members, etc. Section 4A mandates that every stock exchange needs to be demutualised. Further, s 9 gives a range of powers to the RSEs to make rules, subject to the approval of SEBI, on a gamut of aspects, including hours of trade, clearinghouse, listing of securities, settlements of claims and disputes, levy and recovery of fees, fines and penalties, etc.

47   The IMSS surveillance system monitored market transactions in addition to the independent surveillance systems within each RSE. The IMSS generated alerts from any 'unusual market movements'. It also detected aberrations, analysed them and identified cases for investigation and further actions, when required. At times, the data from the surveillance systems were shared with the RSEs for them to take suitable action.

48   World Bank–IMF (n 45) 27.

49   On the role of stock exchanges as regulators, see 'Self-listing of exchanges pose conflict of interest risk: SEBI', *Business Standard* (13 March 2016) business-standard.com/article/markets/self-listing-of-exchanges-pose-conflict-of-interest-risk-sebi-116031300508_1.html.

50   See World Bank–IMF (n 45) 27.

51   Ibid 27.

Comprehensive enforcement powers

Broadly, in terms of its enforcement powers, SEBI can initiate both civil and criminal action, take administrative action, levy significant monetary penalties, block bank accounts for a period of one month, or direct an intermediary or any person associated with the securities markets who is being investigated to not dispose of or alienate an asset that forms part of any transaction, among other measures.[52]

For a breach of the securities legislation—namely, the *SEBI Act 1992*, *Depositories Act 1996* or *Securities Contracts (Regulation) Act 1956* or the regulations framed under these Acts—SEBI is empowered to impose a wide range of sanctions, including directions to a regulated intermediary or any person associated with the securities market,[53] stringent monetary penalties,[54] cease and desist orders,[55] and suspension and cancellation of certificates of licence/certificates of registration by initiating inquiry proceedings against intermediaries.[56] Orders passed by SEBI are appealable before the Securities Appellate Tribunal.[57] Another significant power available to SEBI is to require disgorgement of illicit gains.[58]

---

52   SEBI issues a range of directions in its powers under s 11(4) of the *SEBI Act*, including the power to suspend trading; restrain persons from accessing the securities markets, buying or selling or dealing in securities; suspend any office-bearer of an SRO or stock exchange; impound and retain the proceeds or securities in any transaction under investigation; attach for a period of one month one or more bank accounts of any person in violation of the provision of the Act. Under ss 11B, 11D and 12.3 of the *SEBI Act*, SEBI has the power to issue directions to a regulated entity or any other person, pass a cease-and-desist order and suspend or cancel a certificate of licence or registration by initiating inquiry proceedings against intermediaries. SEBI levies monetary penalties under s 15A that can be as high as Rs25 crore or US$5.23 million or three times the benefit obtained.

53   Ibid s 11B.

54   See ibid ch VIA.

55   Ibid s 11D.

56   SEBI can pass a variety of orders. A civil order against an intermediary taking action is different from an order imposing monetary penalties that is issued by the adjudicating officer. An adjudicating officer is an officer of SEBI not below the rank of a division chief to whom section 15I bestows the power to summon and enforce attendance of any person or document: see IMF, *India FSAP Report* (n 39). All orders of SEBI are appealable before a Securities Appellate Tribunal (SAT) as provided under s 15T of the *SEBI Act*. SEBI can initiate criminal action in a court of law that may be punishable with imprisonment of up to 10 years with a fine of up to 25 crores or both. Even if a person fails to pay a penalty imposed by the adjudicating officer, they may be punished with imprisonment of 10 years or a fine of up to 12 crores or both. The *Companies Act 2013* also empowers SEBI to initiate criminal action for any offences committed thereunder.

57   Sections 15L and 15N of the *SEBI Act* provide that the SAT shall comprise a presiding officer and two members appointed by the central government for a period of five years and may be reappointed. Section 15 lays down the minimum qualifications for appointment of a SAT member while s 15U states that the SAT shall not be bound by the *Procedures of the Civil Code*.

58   Section 11B of the *SEBI Act* was amended in 2014 to expressly provide SEBI the power to direct any person, who made profit or averted loss by indulging in any transaction or activity in contravention of the provisions of the *SEBI Act*, to disgorge an amount equivalent to the wrongful gain made or loss averted by such contravention.

183

SEBI's supervisory and enforcement toolkit was significantly strengthened by the *Securities Law (Amendment) Act 2014*, which brought in key reforms to the securities laws framework.[59] Most prominently, the legislative amendment of 2014 enhanced SEBI's powers by enabling it to attach properties in instances where a person failed to pay the monetary penalty imposed by SEBI's adjudicating officer for a securities law violation.[60] Under this amendment, SEBI has the power to:

> recover money from persons who fail to: pay the penalty imposed by an adjudicating officer, or comply with any directions of the Board for refund of money, or comply with the direction of disgorgement order, or fails to pay any fees due to the Board.[61]

Settlement

Apart from the above supervisory and enforcement mechanisms, SEBI also utilises another tool, 'settlement', for achieving its regulatory objectives.[62] In SEBI's settlement process, the alleged individual or company is allowed to settle a proceeding initiated or going to be initiated by SEBI under the provisions of the *SEBI Act* by neither admitting to nor denying guilt. A 'settlement order' is issued by SEBI that absolves charges against the entity on the payment of a 'settlement amount' and/or 'non-monetary terms' as contained in the settlement order.[63]

The *Securities Law (Amendment) Act 2014* equipped SEBI with the power to settle administrative and civil proceedings on the condition that SEBI exercise such power in accordance with the specified regulations under the *SEBI Act*.[64] Subsequently, the *SEBI (Settlement of Civil and Administrative Proceedings) Regulations 2014* were passed, and later replaced by a more

---

59   The *Securities Laws (Amendment Act) 2014* was notified in August 2014, amending the *SEBI Act, Depositories Act 1996* and *SCRA 1956* and widening SEBI's powers by making clear provisions for disgorgement, search and seizure powers, power to call for information from any person and not only those related with securities markets, extending the ambit of SEBI to unregistered schemes having a corpus of more than 100 crore and deeming them to be collective investment schemes.

60   SEBI's powers to attach include attachment and sale of movable and immovable property, attachment of bank accounts, appointment of a receiver for the management of the movable and immovable properties: see *SEBI Act* s 11(4)(e).

61   See SEBI, *Annual Report 2018–19* (2019) 164; see *SEBI Act* s 28A.

62   See *SEBI (Settlement Proceedings) Regulations 2018*.

63   The terms of settlement are laid out in ibid ch IV. SEBI's settlement process is similar to the US settlement process. Non-monetary settlement terms may include suspension or cessation of business activities for a limited period, exit from management, disgorgement, lock-in of securities, implementation of enhanced policies and procedures, or enhanced audit and reporting requirements.

64   A new s 15JB was inserted into the *SEBI Act* by the *Securities Laws (Amendment) Act 2014*.

refined iteration, the *SEBI (Settlement Proceedings) Regulations 2018* (*Settlement Regulations*).[65] Under SEBI's revamped settlement process, the SEBI Board may refuse to settle a proceeding if the violation is likely to have a 'market wide impact', 'loss to investors' or 'affects the integrity of the market'; or if the matter concerns a 'wilful defaulter', 'a fugitive economic offender' or a person who defaults in the 'payment of any fee or penalty imposed under securities laws'.[66] To infuse a greater level of transparency and independence into the settlement process, SEBI's settlement orders are based on the recommendations of the High Powered Advisory Committee, comprising a retired judge of the High Court along with 'two other external experts'.[67] Further, all settlement amounts, excluding legal costs and disgorgement amounts, are credited into the Consolidated Fund of India.[68] SEBI's *Settlement Regulations* also provide for 'settlement with confidentiality' with a person who provides 'material assistance' in SEBI's 'fact-finding process' as specified under the said regulations.[69]

Analysis

SEBI's supervisory and enforcement powers are extensive and emanate from a discernible historical context. In 1991, as India undertook significant market-oriented reforms that led to the establishment of new regulatory institutions, wide powers were granted to these institutions, including SEBI, to cater to the growing requirements of specialised knowledge and to keep pace with changes ensuing from the 'evolution of fast-paced private industries'.[70] Since then, against the demands of a vast, complex and fast-evolving securities market, the parliament has continually empowered SEBI with a significantly broad set of regulatory powers that include an array

---

65   A High Level Committee under the chairmanship of Justice AR Dave (ret'd) was set up to review the settlement process and, after receiving the recommendations of the High Level Committee and the public comments, SEBI notified the *SEBI (Settlement Proceedings) Regulation 2018* that came into effect from 1 January 2019: see SEBI, *Annual Report 2018–19* (n 61).

66   Ibid. In relation to the settlement process, the SEBI Board is empowered to specify the procedure and terms of settlement for any class of persons that are involved in similar types of securities violations.

67   Umakanth Varottil, *The Protection of Minority Investors and the Compensation of Their Losses: A Case Study of India* (NUS Law Working Paper No 2014/001, 2014), doi.org/10.2139/ssrn.2421119. See also *SEBI (Settlement Proceedings) Regulations 2018*.

68   *SEBI (Settlement Proceedings) Regulations 2018* reg 9(3).

69   See ibid reg 19(1).

70   Shubho Roy et al, 'Building state capacity for regulation' in Devesh Kapur and Madhav Khosla (eds), *Regulation in India: Design, Capacity, Performance* (2019) 3. See also Shreekant Vattiikuti, 'Accelerating towards globalization: Indian securities regulation since 1992' (1997) 23 *North Carolina Journal of International Law and Commercial Regulation* 105.

of supervisory and enforcement powers,[71] to enable it to achieve its three-pronged regulatory objective of protecting investors and developing and regulating markets.[72]

As enumerated earlier in this chapter, in regard to supervision, SEBI is equipped with vast powers for its surveillance, inspection and investigation activities. SEBI's surveillance system, a combination of the SMARTS and the DWBIS systems, is capable of generating 'useful data' and alerts on a T+1 basis on any kind of trading misconduct on an RSE.[73] Even though surveillance of the securities market is conducted by the stock exchanges on a real-time basis, SEBI is deeply invested in its market surveillance role. This is evident in its continual adoption of state-of-the-art surveillance systems and technology,[74] and upgrading of its surveillance practices[75] to generate more efficient outcomes.

The *Securities Law (Amendment) Act 2014* bolstered SEBI's powers, first, by enabling SEBI to call for information from 'any person' during the course of its investigation pertaining to a violation of securities laws;[76] and, second, by expanding SEBI's supervision and enforcement toolkit through powers like 'search and seizure, recording of statements under oath and calling for information and records, such as call data records'.[77] The actual use and effectiveness of SEBI's supervisory powers is analysed in Chapter 5.

Similarly, in terms of its enforcement toolkit, SEBI can exercise a variety of powers and impose severe sanctions to deal with securities law violations. These enforcement powers range from being preventive and protective in

---

71   Roy et al (n 70).
72   See *SEBI Act* s 11.
73   World Bank–IMF (n 45) 30.
74   In 2013, SEBI upgraded its IMSS to make it more effective: see 'Sebi to kick off new surveillance system today', *Business Standard* (14 June 2013), business-standard.com/article/markets/sebi-to-kick-off-new-surveillance-system-today-106120101080_1.html. At the time, SEBI was one of only five regulators to have such a sophisticated surveillance system in place, in addition to 12 stock exchanges, including London and Australia. SEBI's IMSS has 39 in-built typographs—as opposed to most other regulators/exchanges, which have only eight to nine typographs in place. See 'SEBI to strengthen surveillance system', *MoneyLife* (14 January 2013), moneylife.in/article/sebi-to-strengthen-surveillance-system/30732.html. SEBI keeps upgrading and reviewing its surveillance system to improve its effectiveness. In 2008, SEBI constituted a committee under the membership of Bimal Jalan, former governor of the RBI to examine issues arising from ownership, governance and listing of stock exchanges: see IMF, *India FSAP Report* (n 39).
75   See Pavan Burugula, 'SEBI plans platform for real-time surveillance', *The Economic Times* (5 March 2020), economictimes.indiatimes.com/markets/stocks/news/sebi-plans-platform-for-real-time-surveillance/articleshow/74485211.cms.
76   *SEBI Act* s 11(2)(ia).
77   Varottil, *The Protection* (n 67) 14.

nature, with a focus on curbing or removing the securities law offenders from participating in the securities markets,[78] to penal and punitive so as to punish such offenders for their wrongdoing.[79] Specifically in regards to the scope of SEBI's preventive and protective powers stemming from the *SEBI Act*, the apex judicial authority in India, the Supreme Court, in the matter of *SEBI v Pan Asia Advisors Limited and Others*,[80] noted that the statute provides SEBI with the necessary powers 'whenever it finds any fraud or other such misdeeds committed by any person which worked against the interests of Indian investors in securities'.[81] This position was reiterated by the same court in *Sahara India Real Estate Corporation Limited and others v SEBI*,[82] which reaffirmed SEBI's ability to take all necessary steps to fulfil its obligations, stating that the measures set out by the statute 'are couched in open terms and have no prearranged limits'.[83]

In addition to the above wide-ranging powers, it is meaningful to note other significant enforcement powers available to SEBI that may generally not be available in other securities markets globally. First is SEBI's capacity to levy remarkably high monetary penalties for securities markets offences under its internal adjudication process[84] without the need to approach a court of law for levying civil penalties.[85] Second, SEBI can, without going to the court, start recovery proceedings against securities market offenders to recover money for a failure to comply with its directions to refund money to investors or its disgorgement order through several means, including attachment of bank accounts, movable and immovable property, or even

---

78   SEBI's preventive measures range from suspending trading of a security on a stock exchange to restraining individuals from accessing securities markets and dealing in securities.

79   SEBI's penal measures include the ability to initiate criminal prosecution of securities law offenders and impose monetary penalties: see Varottil, *The Protection* (n 67) 15.

80   *SEBI v Pan Asia Advisors Limited and Others* [2015] 14 SCC 77.

81   CAM Markets Team, 'Securities law enforcement: calibrating the discipline of penalty imposition', *Cyril Amarchand Mangaldas Blogs* (24 September 2019) corporate.cyrilamarchandblogs.com/2019/09/securities-law-enforcement-calibrating-the-discipline-of-penalty-imposition/.

82   *Sahara India Real Estate Corporation Limited and Others v SEBI* [2013] 1 SCC 1.

83   CAM Markets Team (n 81).

84   For instance, SEBI's adjudication order can impose a penalty for fraudulent and unfair trade practices of up to 'twenty-five crore rupees or three times the amounts of profits made out of such failure, whichever is higher': see *Securities Laws (Amendment) Act 2014* s 15HA.

85   The penalties imposed by adjudication authorities under the *SEBI Act* are liabilities for breach of civil obligations that arise from the *SEBI Act* and regulations; these cannot be equated with a fine under a criminal proceeding and, therefore, do not require the establishment of mens rea before imposition of such penalty by SEBI: see *Securities and Exchange Board of India v Cabot International Capital Corporation* (2004) 51 SCL 307.

arrest.[86] The objective of SEBI's far-reaching powers is to enable it to levy high regulatory penalties that are of a civil and not criminal character,[87] and empower SEBI to recover dues efficiently.[88]

Similarly, SEBI's power of 'disgorgement of profits' that was formally included into the *SEBI Act* by the *Securities Laws (Amendment) Act 2014* deserves elaboration, as it is a rarer power and available to only some securities regulators.[89] For several years prior to its formal insertion into the statute, SEBI's disgorgement power was derived from necessary implication and was judicially contentious,[90] with diverging views on whether such power was based on a theory of compensation or unjust enrichment.[91] Initially, appellate authorities hearing appeals over SEBI's orders refused to grant orders of disgorgement of profits if these orders were found to be 'compensatory'[92] or 'penal'[93] in nature.[94] Subsequently, SEBI's disgorgement powers were upheld by courts on the ground that they were neither compensatory nor penal, but aimed to deprive the wrongdoers of their ill-gotten gains and prevent them from 'unjust enrichment'.[95] Finally, the *Securities Laws (Amendment) Act 2014* settled the position on SEBI's disgorgement power, first, by explicitly recognising the availability of this power to SEBI, and, second, by unequivocally conferring the power of disgorgement of 'an amount equivalent to the wrongful gain made or loss averted by such contravention'.[96] The amendment also made it clear that the disgorged amount collected by SEBI from wrongdoers was to be deposited into the Investor Education and Protection Fund (IEPF).[97] The funds

---

86   *SEBI Act* s 28A. This power has been subject to criticism for being too wide: see Aditya Shukla, Shil Kanuga and Vyapak Desai, 'In a first, SEBI imposes criminal sanction exercising new-found statutory powers', *Mondaq* (9 January 2015), mondaq.com/india/securities/365406/in-a-first-sebi-imposes-criminal-sanction-exercising-new-found-statutory-powers.

87   See generally *Securities and Exchange Board of India v Cabot International Capital Corporation* (2004) 51 SCL 307.

88   Shukla, Kanuga and Desai (n 86).

89   See *Securities Laws (Amendment) Act 2014* s 4. The provision was drafted in a clarificatory manner to state that, even prior to the amendment, the power of disgorgement had been available to SEBI. US SEC is among the few regulators that enjoys this power.

90   Varottil, *The Protection* (n 67).

91   See S Agrawal and RJ Baby, *Agrawal and Baby on SEBI Act* (Taxmann, 2011) 207.

92   *Hindustan Lever v SEBI* [1998] 18 SCL 311.

93   *Rakesh Agarwal v SEBI* [2004] 49 SCL 351.

94   Varottil, *The Protection* (n 67) 13.

95   *Karvy Stock Broking Ltd v SEBI* [2008] 84 SCL. For a deeper discussion of other cases, see Agrawal and Baby (n 91) 208–211.

96   See Varottil, *The Protection* (n 67) 13. See also *Securities Laws (Amendment) Act 2014* s 4.

97   Varottil, *The Protection* (n 67) 14.

in SEBI's IEPF are to be utilised in accordance with the *SEBI (Investor Protection and Education Fund) Regulation 2009*,[98] and one of the objectives for which the funds may be utilised is 'compensation of losses to investors'.[99]

Complementing these enforcement tools, SEBI's settlement process is another significant option available to SEBI to deal with securities violations as it is sufficiently broad and allows SEBI to settle many securities violations, though these are generally restricted to minor violations that are of a technical nature and that 'do not substantially affect investor rights'.[100]

In evaluating SEBI's supervisory and enforcement powers, it is necessary to point out that SEBI's powers granted under the legislative framework are to be exercised by SEBI under established procedure that is published and available in the public domain.[101] This requirement, among others, is vital for keeping a check on SEBI's powers as a regulator and preventing arbitrary action.

In conclusion, SEBI has comprehensive supervisory and enforcement powers that emanate from clear and 'substantive laws' that have been progressively upgraded by the parliament to enable SEBI to perform its regulatory duties efficiently.[102] Discussion of the adequacy of SEBI's supervisory and enforcement toolkit is predominantly centred around the dangers of excessive power available to SEBI and not the lack of such powers.[103]

In relation to SEBI's supervisory and enforcement toolkit, the detailed assessment of the Indian financial sector conducted in 2013 graded SEBI with a 'fully implemented' score in respect of IOSCO Principles 8 and 9 (corresponding to current IOSCO Principles 10–11) for comprehensiveness of SEBI's inspection, investigation, surveillance and enforcement powers.[104] More recently, in October 2017, the World Bank's *Securities Regulation*

---

98 *SEBI (Investor Protection and Education Fund) Regulations 2009* reg 4 (1)(h).

99 Varottil, *The Protection* (n 67). Despite this understanding, there is a continuing ambiguity around SEBI's powers to compensate investors, as such compensation is typically considered to be a function of an adjudicatory body, for instance, a civil court and not a function of the regulator: see Agrawal and Baby (n 91) 216.

100 Varottil, *The Protection* (n 67) 16. SEBI's settlement process has attracted criticism in the past on account of it being operated in an ad hoc manner and lacking transparency: see Umakanth Varottil, 'SEBI tightens consent order norms' (Blog Post, 27 May 2012), indiacorplaw.in/2012/05/sebi-tightens-consent-order-norms.html.

101 See generally Raval (n 30).

102 Varottil, *The Protection* (n 67).

103 See generally Roy et al (n 70).

104 See IMF, *India FSAP Report* (n 39).

Technical Note on India issued under the *Financial Sector Assessment Program Update* once again recognised the comprehensiveness of SEBI's powers of inspection, investigation, surveillance and enforcement while highlighting some recent upgrades to SEBI's power by the *Securities Laws (Amendment) Act 2014*, such as SEBI's power to 'access telephone records' for its investigations.[105] Notwithstanding this positive recognition, SEBI has been criticised for its 'lack of effective enforcement of these laws' and use of its enforcement powers,[106] as the analysis in Chapter 5 shows.

Conclusion

Driven by the necessities of a diverse and complex securities regime that caters to millions of investors—many of whom are unsophisticated—the legislation equips SEBI with a strong and compelling array of inspection, investigation, surveillance and enforcement powers to attain its regulatory objectives. These comprehensive powers, which are progressively upgraded by the parliament, fully enable SEBI to work towards its statutory responsibilities.

For these reasons, SEBI's degree of alignment with the core requirements of IOSCO Principles 10 and 11 is determined as being 'high', particularly considering some of SEBI's rarer powers, such as disgorgement. Even though such powers are not intrinsically regarded as indispensable for a regulator's enforcement toolkit, they do count as noteworthy for dealing with significant securities violations. Further, SEBI's supervision and enforcement powers operate with sufficient reliability and under an established procedure that is published and available in the public domain. This supports the assessment of the stage of development of SEBI's supervisory and enforcement toolkit as sufficiently 'mature'. Finally, continuous legislative upgrades carried out to equip SEBI with more powers suggests that the extent of change in recent years in this area has been 'substantial'.

ASIC

ASIC's key supervisory and enforcement powers

This section analyses ASIC's key supervisory and enforcement powers under the *Corporations Act 2001* (Cth) (*Corporations Act*) and the *Australian Securities and Investments Commission Act 2001* (Cth) (*ASIC Act*). The analysis

---

105 World Bank–IMF (n 45) 26.
106 Umakanth Varottil, 'Securities Laws Amendment Ordinance: an overview', *IndiaCorpLaw* (22 July 2013), indiacorplaw.in/2013/07/securities-laws-amendment-ordinance.html.

informs the conclusions in this chapter on the alignment of ASIC's powers with the core requirements of IOSCO Principles 10 and 11,[107] leading into the next chapter, which examines the use and effectiveness of ASIC's enforcement powers and compliance regime, and the alignment of the latter with IOSCO Principle 12.[108]

Investigation and information-gathering powers

IOSCO Principle 10 requires surveillance, inspection and investigation powers to be available to the regulator. ASIC is responsible for enforcing financial and company law in Australia.[109] It is empowered to take a variety of measures to investigate possible contraventions and to 'punish wrongdoing or to secure compliance'.[110]

ASIC's investigation and information-gathering powers are found in pt 3 of the *ASIC Act*.[111] ASIC's Information Sheet 145 on compulsory information-gathering powers categorises them into two categories: 1) surveillance and 2) investigations into any violation of financial laws.[112] According to ASIC, surveillance refers to 'activities that involve gathering and analysing information on a particular entity or entities to test and ensure compliance with the law'.[113] An investigation is carried out by ASIC's enforcement team when there is a suspicion of misconduct or violation of the law.[114]

For the purposes of surveillance or investigation, ASIC uses its compulsory information-gathering powers. The most commonly used are powers to require the production of documents, including 'books of a company,

---

107 Principles 10 and 11 require a regulator to possess a comprehensive set of surveillance, inspection, investigation and enforcement powers: see IOSCO, *Objectives and Principles of Securities Regulation* (n 9).
108 Principle 12 requires the regulator to use its range of powers to establish a robust, deterrent compliance regime: see ibid.
109 ASIC is an independent Commonwealth government body established as a body corporate with continued existence under the *Australian Securities and Investment Commission Act 2001* (Cth) (*ASIC Act*): see s 8 of the Act. ASIC's enforcement activities are mostly centred around the violations of the *Corporations Act* although ASIC is also responsible for overseeing the provision of the *ASIC Act*, and other Acts that regulate other financial aspects such as insurance, superannuation and managed funds: see Bird et al (n 17).
110 Bird et al, 'ASIC enforcement patterns' (n 17). The financial law violations include minor and significant breaches that attract civil or criminal action.
111 See *ASIC Act* pt 3. Part 3 explicates the investigations and information-gathering powers available to ASIC under divs 1, 2 and 3.
112 ASIC, 'ASIC's compulsory information gathering powers' (Information Sheet 145, 2020).
113 See ibid. Surveillance is conducted for companies, individuals, licensed or unlicensed individuals on a 'reactive basis' as a response to a complaint or incident or 'proactively' to examine a particular concern in the financial markets.
114 When a formal investigation process is started, ASIC utilises compulsory information-gathering powers to collect information: see ASIC, 'Credit rating agencies—guidance on certain AFS licence conditions' (Information Sheet 143, 2015).

managed investment schemes or an auditor'.[115] The second is the power to conduct on- and offsite inspections,[116] including of accounts.[117] The power to require the production of documents is generally used by issuing a 'notice' in writing,[118] whereas the power of inspection can be exercised without issuing a written notice.[119] The third information-gathering tool is ASIC's power to require 'disclosure of information' in relation to financial products or services.[120] ASIC may give written notice to a vast category of persons, dealing in a financial product or supplying a financial service, to produce specified books relating to such a product or service.[121]

In addition to these data-gathering powers, ASIC has significant powers to require a person to attend an examination and answer questions on oath or affirmation, such as by compelling a person to give testimony in regard to an ongoing investigation or prosecution.[122] ASIC can apply to a court for a warrant to search premises for 'books and records'.[123] ASIC

115 See *ASIC Act* ss 31–33. Division 3 of the Act relates to provisions on inspection of books and audit information-gathering powers. See also *National Consumer Credit Protection Act 2009* (Cth) ss 266, 267; *Retirement Savings Account Act 1997* (Cth) (s 100); *Superannuation Industry (Supervision) Act 1993* (Cth) s 269; Diana Nestorovska, 'Assessing the effectiveness of ASIC's accountability framework' (2016) 34(3) *Company and Securities Law Journal* 197; ASIC, 'ASIC's compulsory information gathering powers' (n 112).
116 IMF, *Australia: IOSCO Objectives and Principles of Securities Regulation—Detailed Assessment of Implementation* (Country Report No 12/314, 2012) (*Australia Country Report*) 63.
117 Nestorovska (n 115) 197. See *ASIC Act* s 29; *National Consumer Credit Protection Act 2009* s 264; *Retirement Savings Account Act 1997* s 99; *Superannuation Industry (Supervision) Act 1993* s 268.
118 ASIC may request electronic data and files and, in some cases, can request that documents be immediately provided by the person to whom such a notice is issued: see ASIC, 'ASIC's compulsory information gathering powers' (n 112).
119 ASIC, 'ASIC's compulsory information gathering powers' (n 112).
120 *ASIC Act* ss 31, 32A.
121 Ibid.
122 See ASIC, 'ASIC's compulsory information gathering powers' (n 112). See also *ASIC Act* ss 19, 51, 58; *National Consumer Credit Protection Act 2009* (Cth) ss 253, 277, 284; *Retirement Savings Account Act 1997* (Cth) s 101; *Superannuation Industry (Supervision) Act 1993* (Cth) s 270. This power of compelling testimony is extensive. A witness before ASIC cannot remain silent or use any immunity, such as citing self-incrimination or legal professional privilege, for refusing to answer questions: see *ASIC Act* ss 68 and 69. For literature on compelled testimony and self-incrimination, see Neal Modi, 'Toward an international right against self-incrimination: expanding the Fifth Amendment's "compelled" to foreign compulsion' (2017) 103(5) *Virginia Law Review* 966; Thomas Middleton, 'The privilege against self-incrimination, the penalty privilege and legal professional privilege under the laws governing ASIC, APRA, the ACCC and the ATO-suggested reforms' (2008) 30 *Australian Bar Review* 282–317. The power to compulsorily examine a person on oath can only be used by ASIC in a 'formal investigation': see IMF, *Australia Country Report* (n 116) 65.
123 ASIC, 'ASIC's compulsory information gathering powers' (n 112). ASIC has the power to obtain search warrants under s 3E of the *Crimes Act 1914* (Cth) (*Crimes Act*). See also s 225 of the *Proceeds of Crime Act 2002* (Cth). See further *National Consumer Credit Protection Act 2009* (Cth) ss 269 and 270; *Retirement Savings Account Act 1997* (Cth) ss 95, 103; *Superannuation Industry (Supervision) Act 1993* (Cth) ss 271, 272. For a more elaborate account of these powers, see generally Tom Middleton, 'ASIC's

also has the power to seek a warrant to obtain 'telecommunications data from service providers'.[124] Further, through its reformed breach reporting obligations,[125] ASIC has recently implemented key recommendations[126] of the Royal Commission into Misconduct in the Banking, Superannuation and Financial Services Industry (Hayne Royal Commission), which are set out in sch 11 of the *Financial Sector Reform (Hayne Royal Commission Response) Act 2020* (Cth).[127]

It is worth noting that ASIC's powers to obtain books and records for surveillance and investigation are 'supported by extensive record keeping and record retention requirements' for companies and financial services licence holders.[128] Any person failing to comply with the information-gathering process of ASIC may be subject to court action. The court may require the person to comply with ASIC and any further failure to comply may attract a contempt of court charge, with punishment including imprisonment of up to two years.[129]

Enforcement powers

IOSCO Principle 11 requires a legal framework to give the regulator significant civil and criminal enforcement powers.[130] Alongside its information-gathering and other investigative tools, ASIC has enforcement powers that prima facie meet the requirements of a 'comprehensive'

---

regulatory powers—interception and search warrants, credit and financial services licences and banning orders, financial advisers and superannuation: problems and suggested reforms' (2013) 31(4) *Company and Securities Law Journal* 208.

124 ASIC, 'ASIC's compulsory information gathering powers' (n 112). It is important to note that ASIC does not have the power to seek a warrant to 'intercept telecommunications'; however, the Australian Federal Police (AFP) can apply for a warrant to intercept telecommunications for an 'investigation into suspected insider trading and market manipulation offences'.

125 ASIC's new reporting obligations strengthen and clarify existing reporting obligations for Australian financial services licence (AFSL) holders and create new obligations for credit licensees: see, ASIC, 'ASIC publishes guidance on breach reporting' (Media Release, 7 September 2021), asic.gov.au/about-asic/news-centre/find-a-media-release/2021-releases/21-235mr-asic-publishes-guidance-on-breach-reporting/. Breach reporting obliges ASIC licensees to take certain actions to notify affected customers of a breach of the law, and also obliges them to investigate such a breach and remediate affected customers.

126 *Royal Commission into Misconduct in the Banking, Superannuation and Financial Services Industry* (Final Report, September 2018) (Hayne Report) vol 1, recommendations 1.6, 2.8, 2.9 and 7.2.

127 *Financial Sector Reform (Hayne Royal Commission Response) Act 2020* (Cth).

128 IMF, *Australia Country Report* (n 116). For example, an AFSL holder is obliged to keep financial records of the financial position of the business and a failure to comply may result in imprisonment of up to five years or a fine of $22,000 or both.

129 Ibid.

130 See IOSCO, *Objectives and Principles of Securities Regulation* (n 9). IOSCO Principle 11 requires regulators to have comprehensive enforcement powers.

enforcement toolkit necessitated by IOSCO Principle 11.[131] Whenever ASIC suspects a violation, it can initiate a formal investigation that can result in enforcement actions.[132] ASIC's enforcement powers emanate fundamentally from the *ASIC Act* and ch 7 of the *Corporations Act*, which establishes a detailed set of 'consequences provisions' for individuals and corporations,[133] including criminal and civil penalties and administrative and civil actions.[134] ASIC's Information Sheet 151 gives a detailed account of ASIC's 'enforcement tools'.[135] Essentially, these are powers to:

- investigate suspected breaches of law
- issue infringement notices
- seek civil penalties
- ban individual activity
- prosecute offenders.[136]

ASIC classifies these powers and enforcement action as:

- punitive
- protective
- preservative
- corrective
- compensatory
- negotiated resolution.[137]

---

131 Part 3 div 5 of the *ASIC Act* pertains to proceedings after an investigation, s 49 deals with where ASIC may initiate prosecution and s 50 deals with instances where ASIC may file civil proceedings.

132 'The salient Parts of Ch 7 of the *Corporations Act* and Div 2 of Part 2 of the *ASIC Act*' layout the consequences for any person that fails to comply with the law: see Pamela Hanrahan, 'Fairness and financial services: revisiting the enforcement framework' (2017) 35(7) *Company and Securities Law Journal* 421.

133 Ibid.

134 See ASIC, 'Senate inquiry into penalties for white-collar crime' (Australian Securities nd Investments Commission Submission No 49, April 2016) aph.gov.au/DocumentStore.ashx?id=1f36e671-95ee-4ed4-bf52-aa6c711af554&subId=412479. See also *Treasury Laws Amendment (Strengthening Corporate and Financial Sector Penalties) Act 2019* (Cth), which significantly strengthened and introduced new penalties. See also ASIC Enforcement Review, *Strengthening Penalties for Corporate and Financial Sector Misconduct* (Position Paper 7, 2017); ALRC, *Principled Regulation: Federal Civil and Administrative Penalties in Australia* (Report No 95, ALRC, 2002), ch 2.

135 ASIC, 'ASIC's approach to enforcement' (Information Sheet 151, 2013). Information Sheet 151 categorises enforcement actions under the following heads: Punitive, Protective, Preservative, Corrective, Compensatory, Negotiated Resolution and Infringement Notices.

136 See ASIC, 'Our role: powers', asic.gov.au/about-asic/what-we-do/our-role/powers/.

137 ASIC, 'ASIC's approach to enforcement' (n 135).

The main features of ASIC's powers in each of these categories are described below.

ASIC's punitive action powers

For a range of market misconduct cases,[138] ASIC may choose to use punitive options against a person or entity. ASIC's punitive actions comprise its ability to initiate criminal action and seek criminal financial penalties and civil penalties.

Criminal action and criminal financial penalties

ASIC may pursue punitive action in serious cases of misconduct where it envisages 'a widespread negative impact on investors or creditors', or where the conduct was 'dishonest, intentional or highly reckless'.[139] There are criminal consequences for several offences found in pt 7 of the *Corporations Act* and sch 3 of the Act lists the penalty for many such offences.[140] ASIC can prosecute without reference to the Commonwealth Director of Public Prosecutions (CDPP) in a limited number of cases 'for certain low-level contraventions'.[141] In a majority of criminal cases, ASIC refers the matter to the CDPP,[142] which considers each case on the basis of available evidence, seriousness and public interest.[143]

Under the recent *Treasury Laws Amendment (Strengthening Corporate and Financial Sector Penalties) Act 2019* (Cth), the existing penalty regime has been significantly strengthened.[144] Prison penalties for most serious violations under the *Corporations Act* and *ASIC Act*, such as 'breaches of director's duties, false or misleading disclosure and dishonest conduct', may

---

138 Ibid 5. Such market misconduct can be for minor regulatory violations, such as the failure to file a form, or for more serious violations of fraud or dishonesty, resulting in losses for investors.

139 Ibid.

140 Hanrahan (n 132) 424: see the discussion on criminal consequences. See also *Corporations Act* sch 3.

141 See Hanrahan (n 132) 425.

142 Ibid. The CDPP and ASIC entered into a memorandum of understanding on 1 March 2006: see CDPP, *Public Submission by the CDPP to the Senate Economic Reference Committee Inquiry into the Performance of ASIC* (13 December 2014). The CDPP decides whether a prosecution is to be pursued by it in terms of its Prosecution Policy, as published on its website: see CDPP, 'Prosecution Policy' (19 July 2021), cdpp.gov.au/prosecution-policy.

143 Hanrahan (n 132); IMF, *Australia Country Report* (n 116) 67–68.

144 *Treasury Laws Amendment (Strengthening Corporate and Financial Sector Penalties) Act.* For literature examining the strengthened penalty regime, see Christopher Symes, 'Ratcheting up corporate law penalties and the "bystander" impact on insolvency' (2020) 20(4) *Insolvency Law Bulletin* 77–79. On how the strengthened penalty regime is expected to augment the efficiency of the financial services regime, see also Paul Latimer, 'Providing financial services "efficiently, honestly and fairly": Part 2' (2020) 37(6) *Companies and Securities Law Journal* 382, doi.org/10.2139/ssrn.3751834.

now be punishable with up to 15 years of imprisonment.[145] Similarly, ASIC approaches the court to levy criminal fines for severe criminal or market offences 'that disrupt the smooth functioning of the regulatory regime'.[146] Criminal penalties for serious offences have also increased, with individuals now attracting 'greater of 4500 penalty units[147] ($945,000)' or 'three times the benefit derived from or detriment avoided by the violation', and body corporates attracting greater of 45,000 penalty units ($9.45 million) or three times the benefit from the violation or 10 per cent of the annual turnover.[148]

Civil penalties

In addition to criminal financial penalties, ASIC may pursue civil penalties in court.[149] Civil penalty provisions are contained both under the *Corporations Act*[150] and the *ASIC Act*.[151] Prior to the *Treasury Laws Amendment (Strengthening Corporate and Financial Sector Penalties) Act 2019* (Cth),[152] the maximum civil financial penalty that a court could impose on an individual was $200,000 and on a corporation $1 million.[153] The new

---

145 ASIC, 'About ASIC: fines and penalties', asic.gov.au/about-asic/asic-investigations-and-enforcement/fines-and-penalties/#Increased. Prior to the amendment, a small number of offences attracted a maximum penalty of 10 years' imprisonment, including offences such as dishonest conduct related to financial services in the *Corporations Act* (s 1041G), with most offences attracting only five years: see Rachel Nicolson, 'Major new corporate and financial sector penalties—what they mean for you', *Allens Insights & News* (22 February 2019), allens.com.au/insights-news/insights/2019/02/major-new-corporate-and-financial-sector-penalties---what/#Criminal%20penalties. For a detailed account of the updated penalties, see Revised Explanatory Memorandum, Treasury Laws Amendment (Strengthening Corporate and Financial Sector Penalties) Bill 2018, 13–19.
146 ASIC, 'ASIC's approach to enforcement' (n 135).
147 The value of each penalty unit is currently $222: see *Crimes Act*.
148 Nicolson (n 145). Previously, such individuals would have attracted a maximum of 2,000 penalty units ($420,000).
149 IMF, *Australia Country Report* (n 116) 66. See also Michelle Welsh, 'Civil penalties and responsive regulation: the gap between theory and practice' (2009) 33 *Melbourne University Law Review* 908. On how criminal penalties differ from civil, see *ASIC v Westpac Banking Corporation* [2018] No 3 1701, para 48. Judge Beach differentiates the two by observing that criminal penalties 'import notions of retribution and rehabilitation' while civil penalties are mainly 'protective in promoting the public interest in compliance' and aim at achieving both 'specific and general deterrence'. He further observes that pecuniary penalties must deter repetition by the violator and also deter others who may be tempted to violate the law and must certainly not be 'regarded as an acceptable cost of doing business'. For more on civil and criminal penalties, see Vicky Comino, 'Civil or criminal penalties for corporate misconduct—which way ahead?' (2006) 34(6) *Australian Business Law Review* 428–446.
150 See *Corporations Act* pt 9.4B.
151 See *ASIC Act* s 12GBA. For literature discussing core issues, see Vicky Comino, '"Australia's company law watchdog": the Australian Securities and Investments Commission and the civil penalties regime' (2014) 3 *Journal of Business Law* 228–251. See also Vicky Comino, 'James Hardie and the problems of the Australian civil penalties regime' (2014) 37 *UNSW Law Journal* 195.
152 *Treasury Laws Amendment (Strengthening Corporate and Financial Sector Penalties) Act.*
153 See *Corporations Act* repealed ss 1317G. An exception to this was a violation of s 962P or s 962S(1), for which a maximum lower penalty was $50,000 for individuals or $250,000 for corporations: see Hanrahan (n 132) fn 42.

penalty regime imposed by the aforementioned amendment extended the maximum civil penalty for contraventions by individuals to the greater of 5,000 penalty units ($1.11 million) or three times the benefit obtained or detriment avoided.[154]

Civil penalties are sometimes accompanied by other orders made by the court, such as an order for payment of compensation,[155] or for disqualification of an offender from managing a corporation.[156]

ASIC's protective or administrative action powers

Sometimes referred to as 'administrative action', ASIC's protective remedies are designed to 'protect investors' rather than 'punish' wrongdoers and include a variety of actions.[157] Depending on the nature and severity of a violation, ASIC may initiate administrative action especially where there is a 'risk of ongoing non-compliance with elements of the financial services law'.[158] In such circumstances, ASIC may issue a public 'warning' notice to a person who commits a violation of the financial laws;[159] vary, suspend or cancel a licence issued to an Australian financial service licence (AFSL) holder;[160] or ban a person from operating in the market.[161]

In contrast to criminal and civil action and penalties, ASIC has the authority to take administrative action without applying to the courts.[162] An appeal of an administrative action by ASIC goes to the Administrative Appeals Tribunal and further to the Federal Court.[163]

---

154 ASIC, 'Fines and penalties' (n 145). See also amended s 1317G of the *Treasury Laws Amendment (Strengthening Corporate and Financial Sector Penalties) Act* on pecuniary penalty orders.
155 *Corporations Act* s 1317HA.
156 Ibid s 206C.
157 ASIC, 'ASIC's approach to enforcement' (n 135) 5. In particular, ASIC refers to: 1) 'disqualification from managing a corporation' or banning the provision of financial services or engagement in credit activities, 2) revoking, suspending or varying conditions of licence, and 3) issuing public warning notices. For literature outlining ASIC's protective actions, see for example Thomas Middleton, 'ASIC's investigation and enforcement powers—current issues and suggested reforms' (2004) 22 *Company and Securities Law Journal* 503–530; Marina Nehme, 'Latest changes to the banning order regime: were the amendments really needed?' (2013).
158 Hanrahan (n 132) 426.
159 See *ASIC Act* s 12GLC.
160 See *Corporations Act* ss 914A, 915B and 915C.
161 See ibid s 920A. Hedges, Gilligan and Ramsay argue that banning orders by ASIC are the 'dominant mode of corporate law enforcement' in Australia: see Jasper Hedges, George Gilligan and Ian Ramsay, 'Banning orders: an empirical analysis of the dominant mode of corporate law enforcement in Australia' (2017) 39 *Sydney Law Review* 501.
162 ASIC, 'ASIC's approach to enforcement' (n 135) 6. ASIC may also seek a disqualification order from a court as part of court action that it initiates.
163 Ibid.

Regulatory Guide 98 on ASIC's powers to suspend, cancel and vary Australian financial services (AFS) licences and make banning orders describes its administrative powers as well as the instances in which it may choose to use such powers.[164] Banning orders and issuing of infringement notices are among ASIC's widely used protective enforcement options, and are discussed in greater detail below.

Banning and disqualification

ASIC derives its banning powers from the *Corporations Act*,[165] described in ASIC's Regulatory Guide 98 as follows:

> a written order by us that prohibits the banned person from providing financial services, whether as an AFS licensee or as a representative of such a licensee. We can make an order that either prevents a person from providing all financial services, or from providing specified financial services, in specified circumstances. A banning order may be permanent or for a specified period.[166]

Banning orders are an important tool used by ASIC to demonstrate zero tolerance for certain violations, to prevent illegal phoenix activity,[167] or to ensure financial offenders do not move around to another position within an institution or to another organisation.[168] Among other effects, banning orders are regarded as an effective tool due to their high and 'serious reputational consequences'.[169] Alongside its banning powers, ASIC can also disqualify a person from managing a corporation for up to five years

---

164 ASIC, *ASIC's Powers to Suspend, Cancel and Vary AFS Licences and Make Banning Orders* (Regulatory Guide 98, 2018). Similarly, Regulatory Guide 218 on administrative action against persons engaging in credit activities discusses the manner in which ASIC administers its responsibilities under the *National Consumer Credit Protection Act 2009* (Cth): see ASIC, *Licensing: Administrative Action against Persons Engaging in Credit Activities* (Regulatory Guide 2018, 2018). The national credit regime ensures that consumers can feel confident when dealing with persons licensed to engage in credit activities by making such licensees subject to legal obligations. This book focuses on ASIC's powers and responsibilities in relation to the securities markets only and not on ASIC's regulation of the credit regime.

165 *Corporations Act* s 290A.

166 ASIC, *ASIC's Powers to Suspend, Cancel and Vary AFS Licences and Make Banning Orders* (n 164) 9.

167 The term 'illegal phoenix activity' is used to describe the act of setting up a new company to continue the business of an existing company that is 'deliberately liquidated' with the intention to avoid paying existing debts, including taxes, creditors and employee entitlements: see ASIC, 'Illegal phoenix activity', asic.gov.au/for-business/small-business/closing-a-small-business/illegal-phoenix-activity/.

168 Senate Economic References Committee, 'Chapter 5—Banning orders and infringement notices' in *'Lifting the Fear and Suppressing the Greed': Penalties for White-Collar Crime and Corporate and Financial Misconduct in Australia* (2017) [5.7].

169 Ibid [5.9].

under the provisions of the *Corporations Act*.[170] ASIC maintains a register of banned and disqualified persons and organisations on its website, which publishes details of such errant individuals.[171] For instance, in its 2019 *ASIC Enforcement Update*,[172] ASIC stated that it had passed banning outcomes for 103 individuals who had been either 'removed' or 'restricted' from providing financial services or credit, while 29 persons had been disqualified or removed from directing companies.[173]

Infringement notices

ASIC's Regulatory Guide 216 on the Markets Disciplinary Panel (MDP) elaborates on the administrative remedies that are available to ASIC for breaches of its market integrity rules[174] and the associated 'disciplinary framework'.[175] Among other tools, ASIC has the power to issue infringement notices that are administrative actions that it can use on its own, or can authorise the MDP to issue.[176] Infringement notices are usually issued by ASIC for minor contraventions of the *ASIC Act*,[177] *Corporations Act*[178] and *National Consumer Credit Protection Act 2009* (Cth), and for violation

---

170 See *Corporations Act* s 206F. Under s 206C, a court may disqualify, on ASIC's application, any person from managing corporations for a period of time, if a person is convicted of specific offences or is an 'undischarged bankrupt' or in other situations specified under s 206B of the Act.

171 ASIC, 'Banned and disqualified', asic.gov.au/online-services/search-asics-registers/banned-and-disqualified/#whatinformation. The banned and disqualified register contains information about persons who are disqualified from involvement in the management of a corporation, disqualified from auditing self-managed superannuation funds and banned from practising in the Australian financial services or credit industry.

172 ASIC publishes reports on enforcement outcomes every six months that highlight the 'categories of gatekeeper' against whom ASIC has initiated enforcement action. See ASIC, 'ASIC enforcement outcomes: past periodic reports', asic.gov.au/about-asic/asic-investigations-and-enforcement/asic-enforcement-outcomes/.

173 ASIC, *ASIC Enforcement Update: January to June 2019* (Report 625, 2019) 5.

174 See *ASIC Market Integrity Rules (Securities Markets) 2017*; ASIC, *ASIC Market Integrity Rules (Securities Markets–Capital) 2017*.

175 ASIC, *Markets Disciplinary Panel* (Regulatory Guide 216, 2019).

176 ASIC, 'ASIC's approach to enforcement' (n 135) 7. See also ASIC, *Markets Disciplinary Panel* (n 175).

177 For breaches such as unconscionable conduct or of consumer protection provisions, see ASIC, 'ASIC's approach to enforcement' (n 135) 7. These notices aim at facilitating payment of small financial penalties that are levied by ASIC on account of minor violations.

178 ASIC has the power to issue an infringement notice under pt 9.4AA of the *Corporations Act* on reasonable grounds that a 'disclosing entity has breached s 674(2) (for listed disclosing entities) or s 675(2) (for unlisted disclosing entities): see Aakash Desai and Ian Ramsay, 'The use of infringement notices by ASIC for alleged continuous disclosure contraventions: trends and analysis' (2011) 547 *University of Melbourne Legal Studies Research Paper* 6, doi.org/10.2139/ssrn.1855891. ASIC's infringement notice regime operates within ss 1317DAA–DAJ of the *Corporations Act*. For more on the introduction of the infringement notice regime, see Explanatory Memorandum, Corporate Law Economic Reform Program (Audit Reform and Corporate Disclosure) Bill 2003 [5.454]–[5.465].

of ASIC's market integrity rules.[179] An infringement notice may also be served on an entity that has allegedly contravened certain provisions of the *Corporations Act* containing a 'voluntary financial penalty'.[180] In the case of greater market misconduct, an infringement notice can, after an opportunity of being heard is presented to the recipient of such a notice, impose 'higher financial penalties' or compliance and conduct directions.[181] If someone refuses to pay the penalty imposed by the infringement notice, ASIC can commence civil penalty proceedings.[182]

ASIC's preservative, corrective and compensation action powers

At times, ASIC may decide to pursue preservative or preventive action, such as preventing assets from being moved or used, or seeking an injunction from the court to compel a person to do or not do a particular thing.[183] ASIC may initiate corrective measures[184] or actions to compensate any person who has suffered a loss.[185] ASIC can initiate a range of such actions that are usually referred to as 'civil actions', which are 'court-based actions undertaken by ASIC primarily with a restitutionary aim'.[186]

Some of the most frequent civil or court-based actions include applications to the court by ASIC under the *Corporations Act* for restraining the payment or transfer of money or property;[187] to pass an order for an injunction;[188] for

---

179 ASIC, 'ASIC's approach to enforcement' (n 135) 7.

180 Desai and Ramsay (n 178).

181 ASIC, 'ASIC's approach to enforcement' (n 135).

182 IMF, *Australia Country Report* (n 116) 66. See ASIC, 'ASIC's approach to enforcement' (n 135).

183 ASIC, 'ASIC's approach to enforcement' (n 135) 6.

184 Such as correcting a misleading or deceptive advertising or other disclosure: see ibid.

185 See *ASIC Act* s 50. ASIC can initiate action to recover damages or property on a person's behalf if this is in the public interest thus going beyond the interest of the consumers who have been affected directly. Simultaneously, ASIC encourages investors to take up alternative options to recover damages or property from wrongdoers such as through private legal action or the Financial Ombudsman Service: see ASIC, 'ASIC's approach to enforcement' (n 135). It is useful to remember that ASIC's enforcement actions do not obstruct or impede the private rights to action for any misconduct under the *Corporations Act* or the *ASIC Act* such as action against company directors, and that it is also possible to initiate class actions in Australia: see IMF, *Australia Country Report* (n 116).

186 Bird et al, 'ASIC enforcement patterns' (n 17).

187 *Corporations Act* s 1323.

188 See *ASIC Act* s 12GD and *Corporations Act* s 1324. Such injunctions can be issued by ASIC to protect the public from any risk of wrongdoing when a person is likely to violate any financial laws: for example see *Australian Securities and Investments Commission v Mauer-Swisse Securities Ltd* [2002] 42 ACSR 605 [11].

a winding-up under s 461 of the *Corporations Act*;[189] or to pass an order for compensation for any violation that takes place in respect of pt 7.7A div 2[190] or pt 7.10 of the *Corporations Act*.[191]

ASIC may also file an application to the court to declare that a term of a consumer contract is an unfair term;[192] seek a disqualification order for a person from managing a corporation or providing financial services;[193] seek a variety of consumer protection orders under the provisions of the *ASIC Act*;[194] or any other order that the court deems fit for a violation of ch 7 of the *Corporations Act* or any other financial service provision.[195]

Finally, ASIC may also initiate 'representative proceedings' under the *ASIC Act*[196] or 'intervene in other proceedings arising under the *Corporations Act* or the *ASIC Act*'.[197]

ASIC's other enforcement powers

Negotiated settlement and enforceable undertakings

ASIC can choose to enter into a 'formal negotiated settlement' with a financial service provider who is suspected of a financial law violation instead of pursuing a 'civil penalty, [or] civil or administrative action'.[198] An 'enforceable undertaking' is a quintessential example of such a negotiated

---

189 *Corporations Act* s 461. In addition to its winding-up powers, ASIC also has the power to seek asset freezing, receivership and related remedies, and restitution orders: see IMF, *Australia Country Report* (n 116).
190 See *Corporations Act* s 961M pertaining to civil action for loss or damage.
191 See ibid s 1325 (2), which empowers the court to pass an order to compensate the person who has suffered loss or damage.
192 See *ASIC Act* s 12GND.
193 Ibid s 12GLD and *Corporations Act* ss 206E and 921A.
194 ASIC may apply to the court to issue a range of non-punitive orders under s 12GLA of the *ASIC Act*. ASIC may also apply under s 12GLB for a punitive order that requires adverse publicity for a person who has been ordered to pay a pecuniary penalty under s 12GBA or is guilty of an offence under s 12GB. Finally, the court may also pass an order to redress loss or damage suffered by non-party consumers in terms of its powers under s 12GNB.
195 See *Corporations Act* s 1101B.
196 Ibid s 50.
197 Hanrahan (n 132) 426. See also A Johnson, 'Public interest litigation under section 50 of the *ASIC Act*: the case for amendment' (2015)(33) *Company and Securities Law Journal* 528; *Corporations Act* s 1330; *ASIC Act* s 12GO; ASIC, 'ASIC's approach to involvement in private court proceedings' (Information Sheet 180, 2013), asic.gov.au/about-asic/asic-investigations-and-enforcement/asic-s-approach-to-involvement-in-private-court-proceedings/.
198 Hanrahan (n 132) 426.

settlement and is essentially a 'promise enforceable in court'.[199] ASIC's power to issue enforceable undertakings stems mainly from the *ASIC Act*[200] and from the *National Consumer Credit Protection Act 2009* (Cth).[201]

ASIC may accept enforceable undertakings in cases where such action would bring a better or quicker regulatory outcome for investors;[202] however, ASIC does not use enforceable undertakings as an alternative to criminal proceedings.[203] If a person who gave such an undertaking breaches the terms, ASIC can apply to the court for a range of orders.[204] ASIC's policy on enforceable undertakings, published in its Regulatory Guide 100, clarifies its approach and the considerations on which it accepts such undertaking.[205]

Analysis

Repeated calls for increased penalties and wider supervisory and enforcement powers for ASIC have been voiced within Australia's corporate academic and policy-making circles.[206] A stronger penalty regime is claimed to enhance deterrence of serious corporate offences and improve compliance

---

199 *ASIC Act* ss 93AA and 93A; see also Marina Nehme, 'Enforceable undertaking: a restorative sanction' (2010) 36 *Monash University Law Review* 108. Enforceable undertaking is a type of settlement where the negotiation between the alleged offender (the promisor) and the regulator (ASIC) can be referred to as a form of an alternative dispute resolution: see Christine Parker, 'Restorative justice in business regulation? The Australian Competition and Consumer Commission's use of enforceable undertakings' (2004) 67(2) *The Modern Law Review* 209–246, 213, doi.org/10.1111/j.1468-2230.2004.00484.x.

200 *ASIC Act* s 93AA or 93A.

201 See ASIC, 'About the enforceable undertakings register' (Information Sheet No 28, July 2022), asic. gov.au/about-asic/asic-investigations-and-enforcement/about-the-enforceable-undertakings-register/.

202 'Enforceable undertakings do not involve a court making a finding against a person, but they may include other beneficial regulatory outcomes, such as providing compensation or outlining a process to monitor a person's continuing compliance with the law': see ASIC, 'ASIC's approach to enforcement' (n 135) 6–7. For more on enforceable undertakings, see Helen Louise Bird, George Gilligan and Ian Ramsay, 'The who, why and what of enforceable undertakings accepted by the Australian Securities and Investments Commission' (2016) 34(7) *Company and Securities Law Journal* 491–517; Nehme, 'Enforceable undertaking' (n 199); Helen Louise Bird et al, *An Empirical Analysis of the Use of Enforceable Undertakings by the Australian Securities and Investments Commission Between 1 July 1998 and 31 December 2015* (CIFR Paper 106, 2016).

203 See Hanrahan (n 132) 426.

204 Such orders include an order by the court to make the person comply with the terms of the enforceable undertaking, or an order to pay the Commonwealth an amount up to the amount of financial benefit that was obtained by the person due to such violation of the law, any other order that the court deems fit to direct the person to compensate another person who has suffered loss or damage: see *ASIC Act* s 93AA(4).

205 See ASIC, 'About the enforceable undertakings register' (n 201). See also ASIC, *Court Enforceable Undertakings* (Regulatory Guide 100, 2021).

206 Brendon O'Neil, 'Corporate crime and regulatory discretion: rethinking the use of criminal, civil and administrative penalties' (2018) 42(5) *Criminal Law Journal* 322. See also Thomas Middleton, 'ASIC's regulatory powers—search warrants, telecommunications interception warrants, financial services licensing decisions and banning orders—suggested reforms' (2021) 38 *Company and Securities Law Journal* 179–196. Specifically on empirical studies of ASIC's enforcement regimes, see George Gilligan et al, 'Penalties

with corporate laws.[207] Accordingly, ASIC's supervisory and enforcement powers toolkit has been keenly scrutinised by academics,[208] frequently evaluated by government agencies and commissions,[209] and significantly strengthened by parliament over the past decades.[210] Complementing this, the general corporate penalties regime has also been extensively analysed[211] and progressively bolstered.[212]

The first impression that the description of ASIC's key powers (in the previous section) imparts is that ASIC is equipped with a wide-ranging palette of supervisory and enforcement powers that cater to its inspection, surveillance, investigation and enforcement duties for the corporate and securities markets. Under its surveillance and inspection framework, ASIC exercises all routine powers that are generally expected to be available to securities regulators, including the power to seek information, inspect books and documents, conduct both onsite and offsite inspections, and conduct market surveillance.[213] Additionally, for conducting investigations of

---

regimes to counter corporate and financial wrongdoing in Australia—views of governance professionals' (2017) 11(1) *Law and Financial Markets Review* 4–12, doi.org/10.1080/17521440.2017.1309162. See also Bird, Gilligan and Ramsay (n 202); Bird et al, *An Empirical Analysis* (n 202).

207 Parliament of Australia, Economics References Committee, *Performance of the Australian Securities and Investments Commission* (2014) 264–265.

208 See for example Vicky G Comino, 'The adequacy of ASIC's "tool-kit" to meet its obligations under corporations and financial services legislation' (2016) 34(5) *Company and Securities Law Journal* 360–386. See generally Middleton, 'ASIC's regulatory powers—search warrants' (n 206). See also Kate Hilder and Mark Standen, 'Stronger powers for ASIC?' *MinterEllison* (17 September 2019), www.minterellison.com/articles/summary-consultation-on-draft-legislation-to-strengthen-asic-enforcement-and-supervision-powers; 'Additional powers (and funding) for ASIC rather than a narrower remit and/or a separate regulator?', *MinterEllison* (11 November 2018), www.minterellison.com/articles/asic-submission-on-royal-commission-interim-report.

209 See for example ASIC Enforcement Taskforce Review, *ASIC Enforcement Review Taskforce Report* (2017). See also *Fit for the Future: A Capability Review of the Australian Securities and Investments Commission* (2015); *Financial System Inquiry: Final Report* (2014); ASIC, *Royal Commission into Misconduct in the Banking, Superannuation and Financial Services Industry. Submissions of the Australian Securities and Investments Commission. Response to Interim Report* (2018).

210 See for example ASIC's design and distribution powers accorded by the *Treasury Laws Amendment (Design and Distribution Obligations and Product Intervention Powers) Act*.

211 See for example George Gilligan et al, 'An analysis of penalties under ASIC administered legislation: scoping the Issues' (CIFR Paper 071, 2015), doi.org/10.2139/ssrn.2649724; George Gilligan, Helen Bird and Ian Ramsay, 'Civil penalties and the enforcement of directors' duties' (1999) 22 *UNSW Law Journal* 417; Helen Bird and George Gilligan, 'Deterring corporate wrongdoing: penalties, financial services misconduct and the *Corporations Act 2001* (Cth)' (2016) 34(5) *Company and Securities Law Journal*; Gilligan et al, 'Penalties regimes to counter' (n 206); George Gilligan et al, 'Understanding penalties regimes for corporate wrongdoing in Australia and implications for the teaching of corporate law' (Conference Paper, Corporate Law Teachers Association Conference, February 2015).

212 Liam Cavell, 'Banking and corporate law: tougher laws and more resources signal a new era in ASIC enforcement' (2019)(55) *LSJ: Law Society of NSW Journal* 84–85. See also Louise Petschler, 'Advocacy: change is coming' (2019) 35(1) *Company Director* 16–17; *Treasury Laws Amendment (Strengthening Corporate and Financial Sector Penalties) Act*.

213 IMF, *Australia Country Report* (n 116) 62–64.

securities violations, ASIC is equipped with powers that are less commonly available to securities regulators globally,[214] which include the ability to obtain audit work papers,[215] freeze assets[216] and compel testimony.[217] Some of ASIC's powers are even exceptional. For instance, ASIC's power to compel testimony is unusual in that the common law right to silence that allows a person to remain silent before an investigating agency[218] is overridden by the *ASIC Act*.[219] Another significant detail about ASIC's strong information-gathering and investigative toolkit is that it has been gradually enhanced to extend 'beyond Australia's borders'.[220] ASIC was among the very first and few national regulators to sign IOSCO's Enhanced Multilateral Memorandum of Understanding, which highlights its capacity to assist foreign regulators in a host of scenarios relating to investigations.[221]

Amid these factors there are other indicators to suggest that enhancing the information-gathering and investigation powers toolkit relevant for detection, investigation and prosecution of corporate and securities offences has been high on the government agenda, particularly in the last decade. The first suitable example of this is the amendment introduced to s 5D of the *Telecommunications (Interception and Access) Act 1979* (Cth) in 2010 that included in the definition of 'serious offences' serious corporate and securities markets violations, such as market rigging and manipulation, false and

---

214 For example, IOSCO refers to a set of powers collectively known as the ACFIT powers under IOSCO's EMMoU: see IOSCO, *Enhanced Multilateral Memorandum of Understanding Concerning Consultation and Cooperation and the Exchange of Information (EMMoU): Frequently Asked Questions (FAQs)*, iosco.org/about/pdf/EMMoU-Frequently-Asked-Questions.pdf. ASIC is among the few signatories to the upgraded MMoU, called the EMMoU, which highlights ASIC's ability to share significant information with other regulators.

215 On ASIC's process of seeking audit reports and conducting audit surveillances and inspections, see ASIC, 'Information Sheet 224: ASIC audit inspections' (2019).

216 See *Corporations Act* s 1323. See also Parliament of Australia, Senate Standing Committees on Economics, 'Chapter 3: Overview of ASIC' in *The Performance of the Australian Securities and Investments Commission* (2014).

217 See *ASIC Act* s 19, which requires persons to appear and answer questions under oath: see also Parliament of Australia (n 216).

218 For the latest amendment to the penalties regime, see *Treasury Laws Amendment (Strengthening Corporate and Financial Sector Penalties) Act*.

219 See Tom Middleton, 'The role of lawyers in the context of ASIC's investigative and enforcement powers' (2010) 28 *Company and Securities Law Journal* 107–129.

220 ASIC, 'ASIC enhances its enforcement toolkit beyond Australia's borders' (Media Release, 22 June 2018), asic.gov.au/about-asic/news-centre/find-a-media-release/2018-releases/18-182mr-asic-enhances-its-enforcement-toolkit-beyond-australia-s-borders/.

221 Australia is a signatory to Appendix A.2, which denotes that the regulator can share the ACF powers out of the total ACFIT powers: see IOSCO, 'IOSCO EMMoU: Appendix A.2 Signatories—8', *Signatories to EMMoU*. Appendix A.1 signatories, which include US SEC, MAS Singapore and FMA New Zealand among a total of 11 signatories, can share the full set of ACFIT powers with other foreign regulators: see IOSCO, 'IOSCO EMMoU: Appendix A.1 Signatories—11' *Signatories to EMMoU*.

misleading statements about financial products and insider trading.[222] This amendment enabled interception agencies to apply for telecommunications interception warrants in the course of investigations into insider trading and market manipulation offences,[223] and signalled a clear legislative intent towards placing serious corporate and securities misconduct in the highest category of offences within Australia.

Similarly, more recently, with the introduction of the *Treasury Laws Amendment (Strengthening Corporate and Financial Sector Penalties) Act 2019* (Cth) (*TLA Act*),[224] parliament enhanced ASIC's investigation powers by expanding the scope of ASIC's search warrant powers through an amendment to the *ASIC Act*.[225] The amendment now authorises a larger set of officers from ASIC to apply for search warrants under the *Crimes Act* (Cth),[226] instead of ASIC having to 'convince the Australian Federal Police (AFP) to apply for the search warrant on ASIC's behalf'.[227] Formerly, ASIC was even required to request the AFP release the evidential material seized by the warrant.[228] By eliminating the necessity of having to approach the AFP, ASIC's powers have clearly been strengthened.

Notwithstanding the legislative commitment reflected in these amendments to deterring serious corporate offences and empowering ASIC, the commission continues to lack necessary information-gathering and investigation powers, particularly in relation to serious market misconduct.[229] Some academics maintain that ASIC's investigation and enforcement toolkit is inadequate and ineffective for dealing with alleged market manipulation[230] and insider trading.[231] An example of such limitation in ASIC's investigation powers

---

222 See *Telecommunications (Interception and Access) Act 1979* (Cth) s 5D. For an in-depth understanding of the legislative framework relating to telecommunication, see Parliament of Australia, Report on Senate Standing Committees on Legal and Constitutional Affairs, *Comprehensive Revision of the Telecommunications (Interception and Access) Act 1979* (2015).
223 Parliament of Australia, Senate Economics Legislation Committee, 'Chapter 3: Higher penalties and improved detection powers for insider trading and market misconduct offences' in *Corporations Amendment (No 1) Bill 2010 [Provisions]* (2010).
224 *Treasury Laws Amendment (Strengthening Corporate and Financial Sector Penalties) Act*.
225 See amended by *ASIC Act* s 39G.
226 ASIC's staff can apply for a search warrant under s 3E of the *Crimes Act*.
227 Middleton, 'ASIC's regulatory powers—search warrants' (n 206) 180.
228 Ibid. See the erstwhile s 3F(5) and current s 3ZQU of the *Crimes Act*.
229 See generally Middleton, 'ASIC's investigation and enforcement powers' (n 157); Middleton, 'ASIC's regulatory powers—search warrants' (n 206).
230 See for example Paul Constable, 'Ferocious beast or toothless tiger—the regulation of stock market manipulation in Australia' (2011) 8 *Macquarie Journal of Business Law*.
231 Lingxiao Hou, 'The difficulties of ASIC in enforcing insider trading laws and the probable solutions' (Seminar Paper, 4th International Seminar on Education Innovation and Economic Management, 2020).

in relation to the *TLA Act*: although the Act empowers ASIC to apply for a search warrant independently of the AFP, it narrows and diminishes the scope of ASIC's search warrant powers in other respects. The amended provision under the *Crimes Act* now authorises ASIC to use its search and seizure power only for suspected 'indictable offences',[232] as opposed to the earlier position,[233] in which ASIC could apply for a search warrant for suspected 'administrative (non-judicial), civil, civil penalty and/or criminal' violations of the financial statutes.[234] Consequently, ASIC may be unable to use its search warrant power where it is investigating suspected securities violations under the *Corporations Act* or the *ASIC Act* that possibly only attract administrative, civil and civil penalty action.[235] This impairment challenges the notion that ASIC is equipped to exercise its full breadth of powers to take effective action for market violations.

Another deficiency attributed to ASIC's investigative toolkit relates to its exclusion from the list of telecommunications 'interception' agencies.[236] Although the *Financial Sector Reform (Hayne Royal Commission Response— Stronger Regulators (2019 Measures)) Act 2020* (Cth) now authorises ASIC to access telecommunications interception warrant information obtained by an interception agency,[237] the commission still cannot independently apply for a telecommunications interception power under the *TIA Act*.[238] ASIC needs to first approach and convince the AFP to apply for a telecommunications interception warrant, and then make another request for release of the intercepted information to ASIC.[239] Further, Middleton argues that even where the AFP has intercepted information, it is uncertain whether ASIC is able to access such intercepted material, or if the material may need to

---

232 Indictable offences refer to offences that are considered against a Commonwealth law that generally attracts imprisonment of at least a period of 12 months: see *Crimes Act* s 4G.

233 Prior to the amendment, the use of ASIC's search warrant powers was tied to the purposes of s 28 of the *ASIC Act*: see Parliament of Australia, Senate Economics Legislation Committee (n 223) [3.19].

234 Middleton, 'ASIC's regulatory powers—search warrants' (n 206) 181.

235 Ibid.

236 An interception agency is defined under s 5(1) of the *Telecommunications (Interception and Access) Act 1979* (Cth) (TIA Act).

237 Explanatory Memorandum, Final Sector Reform (Hayne Royal Commission Response—Stronger Regulators (2019 Measures)) Bill 2019 (Cth) [3.1]–[3.4] (Explanatory Memorandum). ASIC is now a s 68 agency, known as an authorised recipient, and ASIC can now use information intercepted by other agencies: see *TIA Act* s 68.

238 ASIC is not included in the definition of 'interception agency' and needs to approach an interception agency such as the AFP to apply for an interception warrant. The AFP, the state police, the Australian Security Intelligence Organisation and anti-corruption bodies are some of the authorities that come within the definition of interception agency: see generally Explanatory Memorandum (n 237).

239 See Parliament of Australia, Senate Economics Legislation Committee (n 233) [3.29]. See also Middleton, 'ASIC's regulatory powers—search warrants' (n 206) 185.

be directly shared with the CDPP instead.[240] For these reasons, he argues that the current framework creates serious hurdles for ASIC in initiating speedy and effective action in cases of serious corporate misconduct.[241] Since interception warrants are only granted by the court upon satisfaction that they are justified, appropriate and necessarily evidential, and that procedural requirements will be followed,[242] there have been several calls for ASIC to be included in the definition of 'interception agency' so that it can independently apply for such warrants.[243]

As regards ASIC's enforcement powers toolkit described earlier, the commission is equipped to pursue a wide breadth of sanctions classified as punitive, protective, preservative, corrective, compensatory and negotiated settlements.[244] In regard to penal or punitive action, the recent legislative amendments that increased penalties for serious corporate offences[245] signal lower tolerance for serious corporate and financial offences. However, the mechanism for bringing penal action for corporate offences is not entirely straightforward and saddled with intrinsic challenges. The most obvious challenge is in ASIC's inability to pursue criminal action independently[246] and its consequent lack of ownership in prosecution matters, particularly serious market offences such as market manipulation and insider trading. Thus, even if the current arrangement is, theoretically, a workable enforcement strategy,[247] practically, the inability of the specialised, corporate

---

240 Since the CDPP is the authority for initiating criminal action, ASIC may not have any role in the matter: see Middleton, 'ASIC's regulatory powers—search warrants' (n 206) 212–213.

241 Ibid.

242 C Bowen, 'Greater powers to the corporate regulator to pursue market misconduct' (Media Release, 28 January 2010).

243 See Justin Brereton, 'ASIC's growing sphere of influence' (Victoria Law Institute Conference Paper, 9 February 2011) [62] and [65], listgbarristers.com.au/publications/commercial-law-update-asics-growing-sphere-of-influence. See also Middleton, 'ASIC's regulatory powers—search warrants' (n 206).

244 ASIC, 'ASIC's approach to enforcement' (n 135). See generally Vivien R Goldwasser, 'The enforcement dilemma in Australian securities regulation' (1999) 27(6) *Australian Business Law Review* 482.

245 See *Treasury Laws Amendment (Strengthening Corporate and Financial Sector Penalties) Act*. For a general discussion of ASIC's enforcement tools, see Goldwasser (n 244); Middleton, 'ASIC's investigation and enforcement powers' (n 157); Hanrahan (n 132).

246 ASIC has prosecution powers under s 49 of the *ASIC Act* and under s 1315 of the *Corporations Act* but the CDPP has a more superior prosecution power under s 9(3) and (5) of the *Director of Public Prosecutions Act 1983* (Cth). For elaboration on this view, see Middleton, 'ASIC's regulatory powers—search warrants' (n 206).

247 ASIC and the CDPP interact and collaborate under a formal memorandum of understanding dated 1 March 2006: see *Memorandum of Understanding: Australian Securities and Investments Commission and Commonwealth Director of Public Prosecutions* (signed 1 March 2006), download.asic.gov.au/media/3343247/asic-cdpp-mou-march-2006.pdf. For more information on the relationship between the two, see CDPP (n 142).

regulator to initiate and pursue criminal action independently before a court of law creates weaknesses in the overall scheme that diminishes the value and significance of this enforcement tool.

Other factors, too, hinder effective criminal action in matters of serious market misconduct, such as ASIC's exclusion from the definition of 'interception agency' under the *TIA Act*[248] that limits ASIC's ability to directly apply for a telecommunications interception warrant for investigation of serious offences.[249] Although ASIC is now an authorised recipient of the information intercepted by other agencies,[250] having to approach an interception agency, such as the AFP, to apply for an interception warrant, and then having to request the release of the information intercepted, is both time consuming and ineffective, and does not efficiently promote the regulatory objectives stated in s 1(2) of the *ASIC Act*.[251]

The next two significant enforcement categories that are available to ASIC are civil penalty[252] and civil consequences.[253] ASIC can choose to initiate, either individually or in combination, criminal or civil penalty proceedings for serious crimes, including insider trading.[254] Since the standard of proof for evidence for criminal prosecution is higher,[255] ASIC has often chosen to rely on the civil penalty tool,[256] and has received criticism in some matters,[257] as examined in the next chapter. In fact, it is often argued that the corporate regulatory framework is designed to enable ASIC to pursue civil penalties

---

248 *TIA Act* s 5(1).

249 Middleton, 'ASIC's regulatory powers—search warrants' (n 206) 186–187.

250 *TIA Act* s 68(p). See also Explanatory Memorandum (n 237).

251 Section 1(2) of the *ASIC Act* requires ASIC to strive for a number of goals, including timely action, efficiency and reduction in business costs.

252 See Robert Baxt, Ashley Black and Pamela F Hanrahan, *Securities and Financial Services Law* (LexisNexis Butterworths, 9th ed, 2017) [2.85]–[2.91].

253 Civil consequences means that ASIC can seek civil remedies in court, such as injunctions, compensation orders, declarations of unfair contract term, disqualification orders, or other orders the court deems fit: see Hanrahan (n 132) 425.

254 Middleton, 'ASIC's regulatory powers—search warrants' (n 206) 188.

255 The challenge lies in proving the mental or fault element especially in insider trading contraventions in accordance with the standard of proof that is required in criminal proceedings under the *Criminal Code Act 1995* (Cth) sch s 13.2. See also Middleton, 'ASIC's regulatory powers—search warrants' (n 206); ASIC, 'ASIC's approach to enforcement' (n 135).

256 ASIC chose to rely on civil penalty rather than criminal proceedings in a number of high-profile matters: see 'ASIC commences civil proceedings against Stephen Vizard' (Media Release, 4 July 2005). For the full judgement, see *Australian Securities and Investments Commission v Vizard* [2005] 145 FCR 57. For another example of ASIC's preference for civil penalty, see also *Australian Securities and Investments Commission v Petsas* [2005] 23 ACLC 269.

257 See for example *Australian Securities and Investments Commission v Vizard* (n 256). See also V Comino, 'The challenge of corporate law enforcement in Australia' (2009) 23 *Australian Journal of Corporate Law* 233, 235, 236.

instead of criminal proceedings. This leads to a greater use of civil evidential and procedural requirements,[258] considering that civil penalties can achieve both punitive and protective objectives by promoting personal and general deterrence.[259] Civil penalties are imposed by courts. As an alternative to bringing these proceedings under the *ASIC Act*,[260] ASIC may issue an infringement notice.[261]

In regards to civil penalties and proceedings, the *Treasury Laws Amendment (Strengthening Corporate and Financial Sector Penalties) Act 2019* (Cth) strengthened penalties in this area[262] and introduced new powers that enable the court to relinquish the benefit derived and detriment avoided from contravention of a civil penalty provision.[263] Collectively, these support the view that greater emphasis is being laid on tackling corporate offences.

To curb the risk of ongoing non-compliance, or as a preventive action, ASIC relies upon its protective or administrative powers, which range from suspending or cancelling licences and banning persons from operating in the market to issuing infringement notices.[264] In recent years, the government machinery has recognised a need to further empower ASIC.[265] An example of such expansion by parliament has been ASIC's product intervention powers that were introduced by the *Treasury Laws Amendment (Design and Distribution Obligations and Product Intervention Powers) Act 2019* (Cth).[266]

---

258 Middleton, 'ASIC's regulatory powers—search warrants' (n 206) 188.

259 *Australian Securities and Investments Commission v Rich* (2009) 236 FLR 1 [531]–[534].

260 *ASIC Act* s 12GBA.

261 Hanrahan (n 132) 425.

262 Sean Hughes, 'ASIC's approach to enforcement after the royal commission' (Speech, 36th Annual Conference of the Banking and Financial Services Law Association, Gold Coast, Australia, 30 August 2019), asic.gov.au/about-asic/news-centre/speeches/asic-s-approach-to-enforcement-after-the-royal-commission/.

263 *Treasury Laws Amendment (Strengthening Corporate and Financial Sector Penalties) Act* s 1317GAB.

264 Hanrahan (n 132).

265 See generally ASIC Enforcement Taskforce Review (n 209).

266 *Treasury Laws Amendment (Design and Distribution Obligations and Product Intervention Powers) Act 2019* (Cth). See also ASIC, 'ASIC welcomes approval of new laws to protect financial service consumers' (Media Release, 4 April 2019), asic.gov.au/about-asic/news-centre/find-a-media-release/2019-releases/19-079mr-asic-welcomes-approval-of-new-laws-to-protect-financial-service-consumers/. Traditionally, financial product design was not the subject matter of investor protection regulation. But, more recently, as regulation started to widen its ambit, from point-of-sale to now the entire product lifecycle, financial product design has received much more regulatory attention. With this turn of events, three terms have grown in importance: 'product governance', 'product intervention' and 'product regulation'. 'Product governance' means 'regulation that requires product issuers (and distributors) to perform oversight processes in relation to their products'; 'product intervention' stands for 'a regulator exercising its powers to prescribe requirements for a class of financial products'; and 'product regulation' means 'products governance and product intervention' collectively. See Rosie Thomas, 'Regulating financial product design in Australia: an analysis of the UK approach' (2017) 28(2) *Journal of Banking and Finance Law and Practice* 95.

These powers empower ASIC to intervene in the financial product 'design' and 'distribution' stage instead of the traditional 'point-of-sale' stage.[267] Some academics regard these as the 'most interventionist requirements that a regulator can prescribe for a class of products', as they allow regulators to ban products from being sold to certain consumers and regulate the terms and conditions of the products more directly.[268] By adding these powers to ASIC's investor and consumer protection toolkit, parliament has enabled ASIC to intervene in cases of considerable consumer detriment.

In addition to such new powers, ASIC's existing powers, particularly its banning powers, have been bolstered by the *Financial Sector Reform (Hayne Royal Commission Response—Stronger Regulators (2019 Measures)) Act 2020* (Cth),[269] through amendments to the *Corporations Act*.[270] These amendments replace the former 'good fame and character' test with the 'fit and proper person' test[271] 'in relation to ASIC's decisions about whether to grant, suspend or cancel an AFSL and whether to make a banning order'.[272] Prior to this reform, ASIC's banning order powers were limited, as the commission was not able to ban a person on the basis that they were not 'fit and proper', 'adequately trained' or 'competent' to provide financial services, perform functions as an officer in a financial services firm and control an entity that carried on a financial services business.[273] Moreover, earlier, ASIC's banning powers were limited to preventing individuals from actually 'providing' financial services; however, ASIC was unable to prevent banned individuals from 'managing' financial service businesses, and its powers did not cover some situations in which ASIC wanted to ban directors or senior managers.[274] However, in 2017, the ASIC Enforcement Review assessed this position and recommended stronger banning powers

---

267 See generally Thomas (n 266) 95.

268 See ibid.

269 See *Financial Sector Reform (Hayne Royal Commission Response—Stronger Regulators (2019 Measures)) Act 2020* (Cth).

270 *Corporations Act* ss 913B (1)(c), 913BA. 913BB, 915C(1)(b) and 920A(1)(d).

271 See ASIC, 'Information Sheet 240: AFS licence applications: providing information for fit and proper people and certain authorisations' (2021). See also *McDermott v Australian Securities and Investments Commission* [2020] 3362 [120].

272 For a detailed discussion on the fit and proper test: see Middleton, 'ASIC's regulatory powers— search warrants' (n 206) 189.

273 See Hilder and Standen (n 208). For ASIC's submission on the limitations of its banning powers prior to their reform, see ASIC, *ASIC Enforcement Review Position and Consultation Paper 6—ASIC's Power to Ban Senior Officials in the Financial Sector* (Submission by ASIC, 2017) 15.

274 See Australian Government, The Treasury, *ASIC Enforcement Review, Position and Consultation Paper 6: ASIC's Power to Ban Senior Officials in the Financial Sector* (2017) 11. Previously, although ASIC could ban a director or senior manager who knowingly contravened the financial services law, it could not ban a

for ASIC,[275] which were incorporated into the Financial Regulation Reform (No 1) Bill 2019: Banning Orders,[276] and finally incorporated under the 2020 amendments.[277]

Finally, ASIC has the option to enter into a formal negotiated settlement, such as by accepting an 'enforceable undertaking' under the *ASIC Act*.[278] Even though ASIC's policy states that it does not use enforceable undertakings as an alternative to criminal proceedings,[279] the commission has made considerable use of this power in the financial services area,[280] as the next chapter discusses.

In sum, ASIC's repertoire of supervision and enforcement powers is wide-ranging, dynamic and responsive to changing market conditions and requirements. ASIC, on its own account or through the court, exercises an array of powers to maintain the integrity of financial and securities markets. ASIC's information-gathering powers, together with civil and criminal consequences provisions, enable it to take action in cases of financial misconduct or breaches of financial law. This sets the context and perimeter for the analysis in the next chapter on the effective use of the powers and performance of ASIC in the post–Wallis Inquiry period, with a specific focus on the commission's enforcement activities.[281] The detailed IMF–World Bank assessment of the Australian securities sector conducted in 2012 graded ASIC as 'fully implemented' in respect of IOSCO Principles 10 and 11.[282]

---

director or senior manager who failed to ensure that the business was conducted in a lawful manner, or if they were responsible for developing an environment or business model that caused the contraventions to occur even though the specific contraventions were engaged in by others. See Hilder and Standen (n 208).

275 See ASIC Enforcement Taskforce Review (n 209) recommendations 30 and 31. For the government's response, see Australian Government, 'Australian Government response to the ASIC Enforcement Review Taskforce Report' (2018).

276 Financial Regulation Reform (No 1) Bill 2019: Banning Orders 2019 (Cth). Amendments were proposed to div 8 of pt 7.6 of the *Corporations Act*.

277 *Financial Sector Reform (Hayne Royal Commission Response—Stronger Regulators (2019 Measures)) Act 2020* (Cth).

278 *ASIC Act* s 93AA.

279 Hanrahan (n 132) 426. See also ASIC, *Court Enforceable Undertakings* (n 205), which explains ASIC's approach to its use of enforceable undertakings.

280 See for example Bird et al, *An Empirical Analysis* (n 202).

281 There are several other provisions, such as div 2 of pt 2 of the *ASIC Act*, covering unfair contract terms, unconscionable conduct, consumer protection, and conditions and warranties in consumer transactions for financial services; these are expected to guide ASIC's regulatory outlook: see Hanrahan (n 132). The analysis in this chapter is restricted to examining ASIC's information-gathering and enforcement powers.

282 IMF, *Australia Country Report* (n 116).

Conclusion

ASIC's supervisory and enforcement toolkit is generally well equipped and frequently upgraded through legislative reform. There are some limitations in ASIC's supervisory powers relating to detection and investigation of serious market offences, and in this area the legislative intent indicates hesitancy in strengthening ASIC's powers. In some areas such as search warrant powers, reforms follow a queer pattern of two steps forward and one back as they fail to address the overall deficiencies in ASIC's ability to detect, investigate and prosecute serious offences. Further, ASIC's inability to initiate criminal action on its own is a serious drawback.

Despite the limitations, ASIC's supervisory and enforcement toolkit is well resourced with all necessary powers. ASIC's degree of alignment with the core requirements of IOSCO Principles 10 and 11 is therefore assessed as 'high'. ASIC's supervision and enforcement powers operate with sufficient checks and balances from the judiciary and under an established procedure that is available in the public domain. Thus, the stage of development of ASIC's supervisory and enforcement toolkit is assessed as sufficiently 'mature'. Finally, frequent legislative reviews and upgrades of ASIC's powers suggests that the extent of change in recent years in this area has been 'substantial'.

Synthesis and conclusion

This chapter's examination of the key features of SEBI's and ASIC's powers indicates that, broadly, both regulators are equipped with comprehensive powers and tools for their supervisory and enforcement responsibilities insofar as they relate to the core requirements of IOSCO Principles 10 and 11. The supervisory and enforcement powers of both regulators emerge from a deeper, historical context of their economies and the individual evolutionary journey of their financial and securities markets. SEBI's expansive powers, derived from India's historical background of liberalisation, have been progressively strengthened by the parliament taking into account India's complex socio-economic milieu, the diversity and complexity of its markets and participants, and the evident paramountcy of investor protection in SEBI's principal statute. As a regulator of a fast-growing and evolving economy with obvious limitations, SEBI's powers within the securities sector are sprawling and far-reaching in every sense. The main challenge is in ensuring a continued strengthening of the accountability mechanisms around the use of SEBI's powers, and maintaining effective checks and balances on SEBI as a regulator.

In comparison, ASIC's supervisory and enforcement powers, although also vast and comprehensive in many ways, are more restrained than SEBI's. ASIC's ability to exercise its powers, in many situations, is conditional or dependent on other variables and institutions. Further, there is apparent caution on the part of parliament in fully empowering ASIC with all possible investigative and enforcement tools and power. This reluctance could, perhaps, be attributed to the light-touch regulation model that Australia identifies with and that has caused parliament to be uneasy about granting abundant powers to regulators. Arguably, while this approach is sensible, the global shift away from the efficient market hypobook is indicative of a parallel reality in which financial and securities markets require more powers for supervision, governance and even intervention to effectively address instances of serious market misconduct, instil trust and confidence in markets, and enable the market to achieve optimal capacity in supporting the overall growth of the economy. To this end, the scales are tilted in favour of granting abundant powers to corporate and securities regulators, with sufficient checks and balances on their use of such powers.

In light of the discussion in this chapter, the degree of comparability of the two regimes is assessed as 'high' for Principles 10 and 11, as both regimes are sufficiently equipped with supervisory and enforcement powers. Further, the process and overall landscape for equipping the regulators with necessary powers, when required, is mature and reliable. The relevance for cooperation in this area is 'moderate', as both regulators already possess a sufficient and comparable set of powers and cooperation in regard to Principles 10 and 11 will be directed only towards minor upgrades and refinements. Cooperation in regard to supervision and enforcement powers is more relevant in the actual use of such powers to deliver effective compliance of securities rules and regulations, which Chapter 5 explores in detail.

5

Enforcement and compliance regimes of SEBI and ASIC: IOSCO Principle 12

Introduction

Credible and appropriate enforcement mechanisms play a critical role in protecting investors.[1] Considering the characteristics of an ideal regulatory regime, Jones states that:

> a primary objective of any securities regime must be to maintain justifiable public confidence in the integrity of the securities markets by ensuring the flow of reliable information to investors. To accomplish this goal, a securities regime must provide investors adequate remedies for fraud and deter wrongdoing by promising public enforcement efforts to detect and punish fraud.[2]

---

1 See generally Howell E Jackson and Mark J Roe, 'Public and private enforcement of securities laws: resource-based evidence' (2009) 93(2) *Journal of Financial Economics* 207–238, doi.org/10.1016/j.jfineco.2008.08.006. On the importance and significance of an effective securities market regulatory regime, see generally Rafael La Porta et al, 'Investor protection and corporate governance' (2000) 58(1–2) *Journal of Financial Economics* 3–27, doi.org/10.1016/S0304-405X(00)00065-9.
2 See Renee M Jones, 'Dynamic federalism: competition, cooperation and securities enforcement' (2004) 11 *Connecticut Insurance Law Journal* 107.

Table 5.1: Snapshot of the analysis in Chapter 5 relating to SEBI's and ASIC's enforcement and effective compliance

IOSCO Principles of Securities Regulation	SEBI's degree of alignment, stage of development and extent of reform in recent years	ASIC's degree of alignment, stage of development and extent of reform in recent years	Degree of comparability	Relevance for cooperation
Enforcement and compliance regimes (IOSCO Principle 12)				
Principle 12: Regulatory system should ensure effective and credible use of inspection, investigation, surveillance and enforcement powers and implementation of effective compliance program	**Moderate** Evolving Substantial	**High** Mature Substantial	**Moderate**	**High**
SEBI's FSAP 2013* rating: 'partly implemented' (Principle 12 corresponds to Principle 10 under the pre-GFC IOSCO document) ASIC's FSAP 2012** ratings: 'broadly implemented'				

Note: *FSAP 2013 refers to IMF, *India: Financial Sector Assessment Program – Detailed Assessments Report on IOSCO Objectives and Principles of Securities Regulation* (Country Report No 13/266, 2013). **FSAP 2012 refers to IMF, *Australia: IOSCO Objectives and Principles of Securities Regulation – Detailed Assessment of Implementation* (Country Report No 12/314, 2012).

Building on the analysis of the supervisory and enforcement powers of the Securities and Exchange Board of India (SEBI) and the Australian Securities and Investments Commission (ASIC) in Chapter 4, this chapter presents key empirical data on the use of these powers. It critically analyses the effectiveness of the compliance regimes in achieving their regulatory objectives, particularly to deter and punish wrongdoings, maintain integrity in the market and protect investors' interests.

An evaluation of SEBI's and ASIC's enforcement and compliance regimes: IOSCO Principles of Securities Regulation (Principle 12)

This chapter sets out the core requirements of IOSCO Principle 12 in relation to the implementation of an effective compliance regime. It presents empirical data on enforcement actions and analysis of SEBI's and ASIC's regimes. Each regulator's regime is evaluated separately for its alignment with Principle 12. This evaluation has three components:

1. empirical data on the use of enforcement powers

2. analysis of the empirical data to draw significant inferences and trends

3. critique of the effectiveness of the enforcement and compliance regime.

The chapter concludes with a brief synthesis of the discussion and relevant conclusions.

Principles for the enforcement of securities regulation

The IOSCO Principles of enforcement underscore the importance of effective enforcement of securities laws to 'foster investor confidence and maintain fair and efficient markets'.[3] Jackson and others emphasise the critical significance of a deterrent enforcement regime for securities markets.[4]

---

3   IOSCO, *Methodology for Assessing Implementation of the IOSCO Objectives and Principles of Securities Regulation* (2017) 63.
4   See Howell E Jackson, 'The impact of enforcement: a reflection' (2007) 156 *University of Pennsylvania Law Review* 402; Howell E Jackson, 'Variation in the intensity of financial regulation: preliminary evidence and potential implications' (2007) 24 *Yale Journal on Regulation* 253. See also Jackson and Roe (n 1).

Reasons include protecting investor interests—both foreign and domestic,[5] attracting foreign capital and investment,[6] and fostering a meaningful cross-border cooperation program, such as proposed by this book for India and Australia. The core requirements of a robust enforcement and compliance regime, encapsulated in IOSCO Principle 12, are detailed below.

IOSCO Principle 12

> Principle 12: The regulatory system should ensure an effective and credible use of inspection, investigation, surveillance and enforcement powers and implementation of an effective compliance program.

A strong enforcement regime is a critical precondition for a successful securities market.[7] IOSCO Principle 12 interprets 'enforcement' as taking place 'across a continuum' through an 'effective and credible use' of 'inspection, investigation, surveillance and enforcement powers' by the regulator and the 'implementation of an effective compliance programme'.[8] Principle 12 is closely linked with IOSCO Principles 10 and 11, discussed in Chapter 4, which require regulators to possess comprehensive supervisory and enforcement powers.

An analysis of the compliance regime of the regulator under Principle 12 is a useful marker of the effectiveness of a regulatory regime and the general regulatory environment within a jurisdiction.[9] An effective enforcement regime is also vital for any meaningful cross-border engagement or

---

5   From a legal standpoint, scholars such as David and Brierley argue that most existing commercial legal systems stem from either the English (common law), French or German systems: see R David and J Brierly, *Major Legal Systems in the World Today* (Stevens and Sons, London, 1985). Consequently, how legal systems protect their investors also differs, with the common law followers having the strongest protection for both outside investors (ie shareholders) and creditors: see La Porta et al, 'Investor protection' (n 1).

6   See John C Coffee, *Law and the Market: The Impact of Enforcement* (Columbia Law and Economics Working Paper No 304, March 7, 2007), doi.org/10.2139/ssrn.967482.

7   See Bernard S Black, 'The legal and institutional preconditions for strong securities markets' (2001) 48 *UCLA Law Review* 781, 798, doi.org/10.2139/ssrn.182169. Certain rules, such as those banning market manipulation of trading prices, need to be enforced by a specialised regulator.

8   See IOSCO (n 3) 63.

9   The term 'compliance' refers to 'voluntary or instinctive compliance or sanctioned non-compliance and [is] used to characterise part of a broader picture of the regulatory environment': see Helen Louise Bird et al, 'ASIC enforcement patterns' (2004)(71) *Public Law Research Paper* 8.

collaboration. Verdier asserts that it is imperative to address significant weaknesses in the area of enforcement, as these may jeopardise the ability of regulators to forge cooperation arrangements (ie recognition agreements).[10]

The quality and effectiveness of an enforcement and compliance regime is predicated upon several underlying variables. Becker and Stigler, as early as 1974, linked the quality of enforcement to the degree of honesty of the enforcers, the structure of incentives for honesty and the quantum of resources available for enforcement.[11] In their seminal article, 'Law and Finance', La Porta et al consider 'proxies for the quality of enforcement', which include five measures ranging from the efficiency of the judicial system and rule of law to more broad-based measures, such as corruption, 'risk of expropriation' and 'likelihood of contract repudiation' by the government.[12] La Porta et al, in 'What Works in Securities Laws', developed a public enforcement index with a narrower set of regulatory characteristics, such as the regulator's independence from the executive, the comprehensiveness of its investigation powers and, finally, the regulator's range of civil and criminal powers.[13] Coffee criticises the approaches adopted by La Porta et al to ascertaining the effectiveness and quality of enforcement,[14] instead embracing Jackson's more targeted approach to evaluating the impact and intensity of a regulatory regime.[15] Both Coffee and Jackson, thus, use two measures to evaluate an enforcement regime's effectiveness: first, the regime's 'regulatory inputs', such as 'staffing or budgets'; second, the 'regulatory outputs' that include 'enforcement actions or monetary sanctions.[16]

This variation in opinion among leading scholars on the precise factors responsible for an enforcement regime's effectiveness underscores the complexity of the issue. A practical way out of this conundrum is to embrace

---

10   Pierre-Hugues Verdier, 'Mutual recognition in international finance' (2011) 52 *Harvard International Law Journal*.

11   Gary S Becker and George J Stigler, 'Law enforcement, malfeasance, and compensation of enforcers' (1974) 3(1) *Journal of Legal Studies* 1, doi.org/10.1086/467507.

12   Rafael La Porta et al, 'Law and finance' (1998) 106(6) *Journal of Political Economy* 1113, 1140, doi.org/10.1086/250042.

13   Rafael La Porta, Florencio Lopez-de-Silanes and Andrei Shleifer, 'What works in securities laws?' (2006) 61(1) *Journal of Finance* 12, doi.org/10.1111/j.1540-6261.2006.00828.x.

14   Coffee (n 6) 249. Coffee's fundamental criticism concerns the generic nature of characteristics or variables proposed by La Porta et al that failed to incorporate the actual enforcement inputs and outputs that better represented the effectiveness of an enforcement regime.

15   See Jackson, 'The impact of enforcement' (n 4).

16   Coffee (n 6). See also Jackson, 'The impact of enforcement' (n 4). However, previously, Mark Roe and Jackson warned that each of the approaches had both advantages and disadvantages and was equally susceptible to a number of shortcomings, such as 'incompleteness, misdirection, and inadequate granularity'.

differing points of view to develop a more harmonious position that accepts that several variables—both generic and specific—are responsible for, and contribute in different degrees to, the effectiveness of an enforcement regime.

This chapter evaluates the strength and robustness of SEBI's and ASIC's enforcement regimes by focusing on one of the main factors of enforcement regime effectiveness: 'regulatory outputs', as referred to by Coffee and Jackson. Where appropriate, the analysis also examines the principles underpinning the enforcement regime of each regulator when this is necessary to determine the context of the use of its enforcement powers and approach. The critical evaluation of the enforcement regimes in this chapter is based on the empirical data of SEBI's and ASIC's enforcement actions, which include their range of civil, criminal, administrative and monetary sanctions, during a five-year period starting from FY 2014–15 to FY 2018–19 (the selected period).[17]

SEBI

As the analysis in Chapter 4 conveys, SEBI's legal and regulatory framework for enforcement and the associated powers are largely well aligned with international standards. Building on Chapter 4, this section evaluates the on-ground 'use' and 'implementation' of SEBI's powers and the enforcement provisions, to assess effectiveness. SEBI's main enforcement measures or outputs for the selected period are outlined first followed by an analysis.

Key empirical data on SEBI's enforcement actions

SEBI publishes its enforcement data in its annual reports. The data are mainly organised along the lines of 'nature of enforcement action' taken by SEBI and not along the lines of 'nature of violation'. The next section explains the main enforcement headings under which SEBI collates and publishes enforcement data. This is followed by a presentation of tables, figures and trends relating to SEBI's enforcement actions during the selected period.

---

17   In India, a financial year is the period between 1 April and 31 March. For Australia, it means the period between 1 July and 30 June.

SEBI's main enforcement mechanisms

As noted in its annual reports, SEBI actively utilises five main enforcement mechanisms spanning civil, administrative and criminal proceedings to address securities law violations.[18] SEBI's annual reports collect data under the following headings:

1. *Section 11/11B Proceedings*: presents data on SEBI's preventive, prohibitive or remedial directions and orders issued to safeguard investor interests and the securities market[19]

2. *Inquiry Proceedings*: presents data on inquiries undertaken against a licensed intermediary for a securities law violation[20]

3. *Adjudication Proceedings*: presents data on SEBI's adjudication action for imposing a monetary penalty under ch VIA of the *Securities and Exchange Board of India Act 1992 (SEBI Act)*[21]

4. *Prosecution Proceedings*: presents data on SEBI's criminal proceedings

5. *Summary Proceedings*: presents data on SEBI's summary inquiries or warning and deficiency letters issued against registered intermediaries for contraventions of *SEBI (Intermediaries) Regulations 2007.*[22]

In addition to these enforcement mechanisms, SEBI also relies on its 'settlement' mechanism.[23]

Tables, figures and trends on SEBI's enforcement actions

This subsection provides tables and figures on SEBI's enforcement data for the selected period. SEBI's main enforcement actions for this period are presented for the four of the five categories listed above. In addition to the enforcement statistics, some data and trends are presented on SEBI's

---

18   Securities and Exchange Board of India (SEBI), *Annual Report 2016–17* (2017) 149.

19   SEBI, 'Other functions: enforcement of regulations' in *Annual Report 2017–18* (2018) 137. These provisions confer vast powers on SEBI, including the power to 1) suspend trading of any security in a stock exchange, and restrain any person from accessing the securities market; 2) prohibit any person associated with the securities market from buying, selling or dealing in securities; and (3) pass directions against an intermediary or any person associated with the securities markets 'not to dispose of or alienate an asset forming part of any transaction which is under investigation'.

20   Ibid. SEBI has the power to suspend or cancel an intermediary's certificate of registration 'on the recommendation of the enquiry officer/designated authority for that purpose'.

21   SEBI appoints an adjudicating officer who conducts an inquiry and is empowered to impose monetary penalties after 'completing the investigations/inquiry' for violations of any securities laws.

22   *SEBI (Intermediaries) Regulations 2008* ch VA.

23   *SEBI (Settlement Proceedings) Regulations 2018*. SEBI may settle a matter in accordance with the mechanism established under these regulations.

'settlement' proceedings as well as on SEBI's investigations initiated and completed for market integrity violations, such as market manipulation, insider trading, issue-based manipulation and takeover violations for the selected period.

For the benefit of improved understanding and context, prior to the presentation of the data and trends, Tables 5.2 and 5.3 present key indicators and figures that are useful for assessing SEBI's enforcement regime. These tables specifically highlight the magnitude and scale and complexities of Indian securities markets.[24]

Table 5.2: Major indicators of Indian securities markets for the selected period

Indicators	2014–15	2015–16	2016–17	2017–18	2018–19
Indices					
S&P BSE Sensex (Avg)	26,557	26,322	27,338	32,397	35,972
Nifty 50 (Avg)	7,967	7,984	8,421	10,030	10,860
Annualised volatility (%)					
S&P BSE Sensex	13.5	17.0	12.1	10	12.1
Nifty 50	13.5	17.1	12.3	10	12.4
Total turnover (₹ crore)					
Equity cash segment	5,184,500	4,977,278	6,054,422	8,317,987	8,724,653
Equity derivatives segment	75,969,290	69,300,843	94,377,241	164,988,122	237,602,955
Currency derivatives segment	5,634,563	7,590,387	8,326,651	9,580,665	15,917,864
Interest rate derivatives segment	473,783	663,359	438,341	545,308	356,629
Commodity derivatives segment	-	-	6,499,637	6,022,530	7,377,945

---

24 For instance, the number of listed companies and intermediaries is directly relevant to evaluate and provide more context to the success, limitations and challenges of SEBI's enforcement and compliance actions.

Indicators	2014–15	2015–16	2016–17	2017–18	2018–19
Market capitalisation (₹ crore)					
BSE	10,149,290	9,475,328	12,154,525	14,224,997	15,108,711
NSE	9,930,122	9,310,471	11,978,421	14,044,152	14,934,227
MSEI	9,825,990	9,182,759	11,831,271	13,896,724	14,751,584
Number of listed companies					
BSE	5,624	5,911	5,834	5,619	5,262
NSE	1,733	1,808	1,817	1,931	1,931
MSEI	82	80	80	270	287
P/E ratio					
S&P BSE Sensex	19.1	19.3	22.6	22.7	28.0
Nifty 50	22.7	20.9	23.3	24.7	29.0

Table 6.2 collates key indicators of Indian securities markets from SEBI's annual reports for the selected period. This table conveys important parameters, such as the size and market capitalisation of the securities market, number of listed companies and performance of main indices, which is useful for contextualising and analysing SEBI's enforcement data and trends.

Table 5.3 provides recent data on recognised intermediaries in Indian securities markets, as available on SEBI's website. This list is indicative and not exhaustive in terms of the categories of intermediaries.[25]

Table 5.3: Categories and number of licensed or recognised intermediaries in Indian securities markets

Type of intermediary	Number of registered intermediaries
Registered alternative investment funds	1,482
Registered stockbrokers in equity segment	4,896
Registered stockbrokers in equity derivative segment	3,607
Registered stockbrokers in currency derivative segment	2,809
Registered stockbrokers in interest rate derivative segment	1,620
Registered stockbrokers in debt segment	705
Registered stockbrokers in commodity derivative segment	1,976

---

25   Figures current as of 22 January 2025. See SEBI, 'Recognised intermediaries', sebi.gov.in/sebiweb/other/OtherAction.do?doRecognised=yes.

Type of intermediary	Number of registered intermediaries
Banker to an issue	58
Credit rating agency	7
Registered custodians of securities	17
Debenture trustee	25
Designated depository participants	17
Qualified depository participants	62
Registered depository participants-CDSL	621
Registered depository participants-NSDL	301
FPIs/ deemed FPI/s (erstwhile FIIs/QFIs)	11,941
Registered foreign venture capital investors	287
Investment adviser	943
Registered infrastructure investment trusts	26
KYC registration agency registered with SEBI	5
Merchant bankers	230
Registered mutual funds	49
Registered portfolio managers	455
Registrars to an issue and share transfer agents	77
Research analyst	1,470
Self-certified syndicate banks under the syndicate ASBA facility (equity issuances)	54
Self-certified syndicate banks under the direct ASBA facility (equity issuances)	54
Underwriters	2
Registered venture capital funds	166
Self-certified syndicate banks eligible as issuer banks for UPI	54
Self-certified syndicate banks eligible as sponsor banks for UPI	7
Real estate investment trust	6
List of mobile applications for using UPI in public issues	35
Self-certified syndicate banks under the direct ASBA facility	38
Self-certified syndicate banks under the syndicate ASBA facility	44

SEBI's section 11/11B proceedings

Table 5.4: SEBI's regulatory/enforcement actions taken during the selected period

Indicators	2014–15	2015–16	2016–17	2017–18	2018–19	Total
Suspension	1	2	7	1	2	13
Warning issued	47	496	103	43	3	692
Prohibitive directions issued under s 11, *SEBI Act*	1,620	1,726	563	1,136	672	5,717
Cancellation	0	8	0	2	5	15
Administrative warning/ warning letter issued	274	454	239	524	481	1,972
Deficiency observations issued	94	9	24	116	100	343
Advice letter issued	139	32	17	22	54	264
Total	**2,175**	**2,727**	**953**	**1,844**	**1,317**	**9,016**

Table 5.4 presents data on the enforcement actions taken by SEBI under ss 11 and 11B of the *SEBI Act*. As seen, SEBI took a total of 9,016 actions under s 11/11B of the *SEBI Act* during the period selected for the analysis in this book. Of these 9,016 actions, SEBI relied upon two main actions and issued:

- 5,717 prohibitive directions under s 11 of the *SEBI Act*
- 1,972 administrative warnings and warning letters.

Under prohibitive directions, SEBI can take various measures, either pending investigation or on completion of such investigation, such as suspending trading of any security, restraining persons from accessing the markets or prohibiting any person from buying, selling or dealing in securities. The least or rarely used forms of s 11/11B directions are 'suspensions' or 'cancellation' of a certificate of registration by SEBI with only 13 suspensions and 15 cancellations in the selected period.

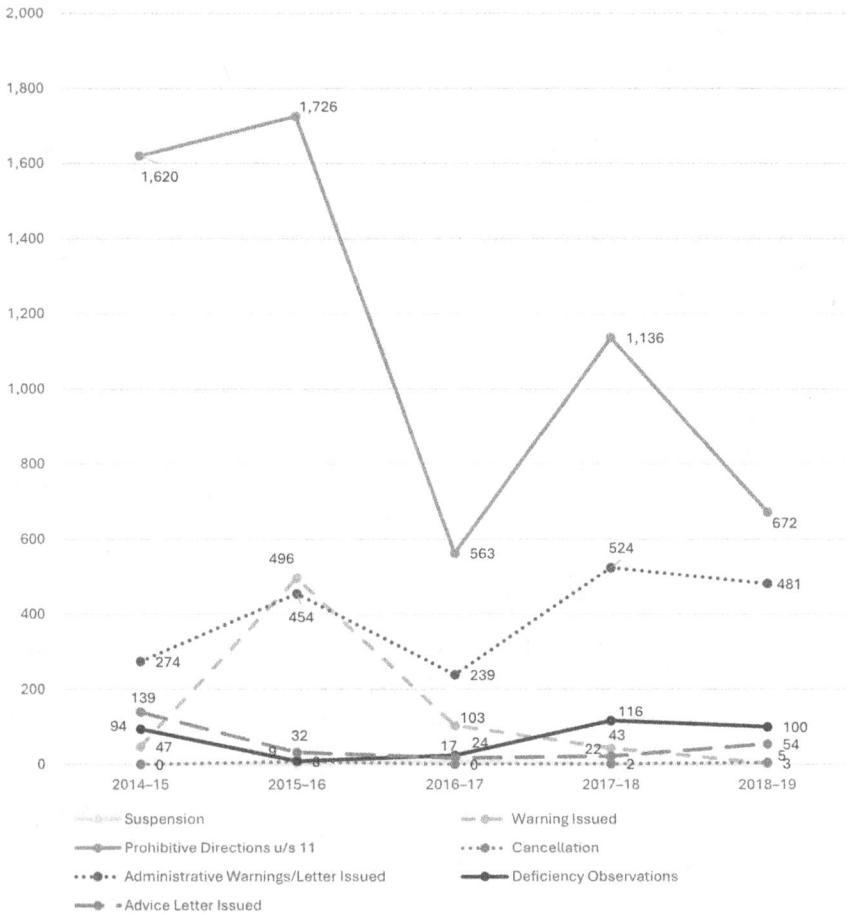

Figure 5.1: SEBI's enforcement trends for action under ss 11 and 11B of the *SEBI Act* in the selected period

Source: Author's research.

Figure 5.1 plots the five-year trend in SEBI's use of its enforcement powers under ss 11 and 11B of the *SEBI Act*. As evident, SEBI's prohibitive directions under s 11 of the *SEBI Act* saw a downward trend, with 1,620 prohibitive directions issued in FY 2014–15, 1,726 directions in FY 2015–16 and 672 prohibitive directions in FY 2018–19. In comparison, administrative warnings and warning letters issued in the selected period followed an upward trend, with 274 administrative warnings issued in FY 2014–15 and 481 issued in FY 2018–19.

SEBI's inquiry proceedings

Table 5.5: SEBI's inquiry proceedings in the selected period

	2014–15	2015–16	2016–17	2017–18	2018–19	Total
Inquiry proceedings disposed	11	11	7	23	103*	155
Inquiry proceedings initiated	23	17	19	16	309**	384

Note: *This figure reflects the number of inquiry proceedings conducted not completed. **This figure reflects the number of inquiry proceedings initiated.

SEBI initiates inquiry proceedings against licensed intermediaries. Table 5.5 relays the data on the number of such proceedings taken by SEBI, both proceedings initiated and disposed, for each financial year of the selected period. For FY 2018–19, the data are unclear regarding whether the figure 309 denotes the total 'number of cases' or the 'number of entities' against whom inquiry proceedings were initiated. Further, the starred figure 103 for FY 2018–19 reflects the inquiry proceedings 'conducted' and not 'completed'. This needs to be borne in mind when looking at the final figures on the total number of inquiry proceedings 'disposed' (155) and 'initiated' (384) in the selected period.

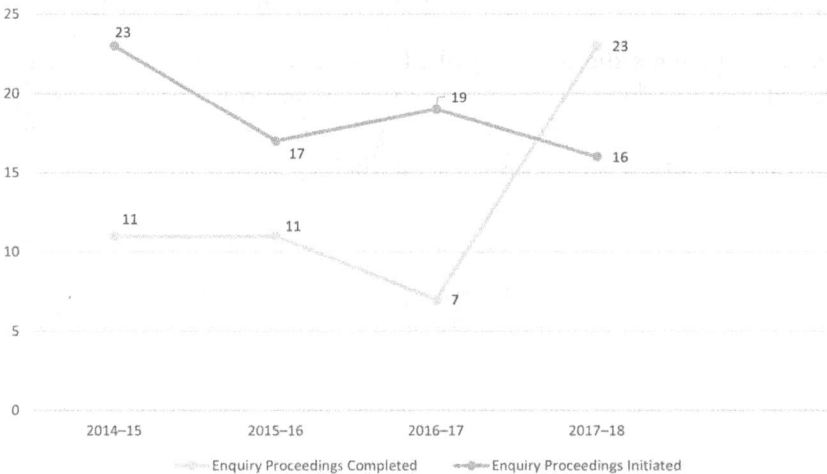

Figure 5.2: Trends in SEBI's inquiry proceedings during the selected period
Source: Author's research.

Figure 5.2 shows the trends for SEBI's inquiry proceedings for four of the five years of the selected period. While there was no dramatic difference in the inquiry proceedings numbers, both for initiated and completed proceedings, in the four-year period, the last year reflects a steep escalation in SEBI's completed inquiry proceedings. The data for FY 2018–19 is not included in the figure due to non-availability of the number of 'completed' inquiry proceedings in SEBI's annual report.

Adjudication proceedings

Table 5.6: SEBI's adjudication in the selected period

	2014–15	2015–16	2016–17	2017–18	2018–19	Total
Adjudication cases disposed	1,211	425	83[26]	888	811	3,418
Adjudication proceedings initiated	1,951	249	278	594	822	3,894

Table 5.6 presents data on SEBI's adjudication proceedings initiated and disposed in the selected period. Adjudication is SEBI's enforcement mechanism to levy significantly high monetary regulatory penalty for securities laws violations. As Table 5.6 shows, adjudication as an enforcement measure is frequently used by SEBI, with a total of 3,418 adjudication cases disposed and 3,894 proceedings initiated by SEBI in the selected period.

Figure 5.3 presents the trends in SEBI's adjudication proceedings for the selected period and shows that, after a sharp decline in FY 2015–16, SEBI's adjudication mechanism followed a rising trend, supporting the view that this enforcement mechanism is greatly utilised by SEBI.

---

26 'The disposal of Adjudication Proceedings in 2016–17 declined substantially pursuant to the judgement of the Hon'ble Supreme Court in the matter of Roofit Industries (Civil Appeal 1364–1365 of 2005) where it was held that the Adjudicating Officer has no discretion to decide the quantum of monetary penalty. This was differed by another bench in the matter of Siddharth Chaturvedi (Civil Appeal 14730 of 2015) and referred for a larger bench. The issue was ultimately resolved by the Finance Act, 2017, by amending the securities laws, which came into effect from 26th April, 2017': see SEBI, *Annual Report 2016–17* (n 18) 150.

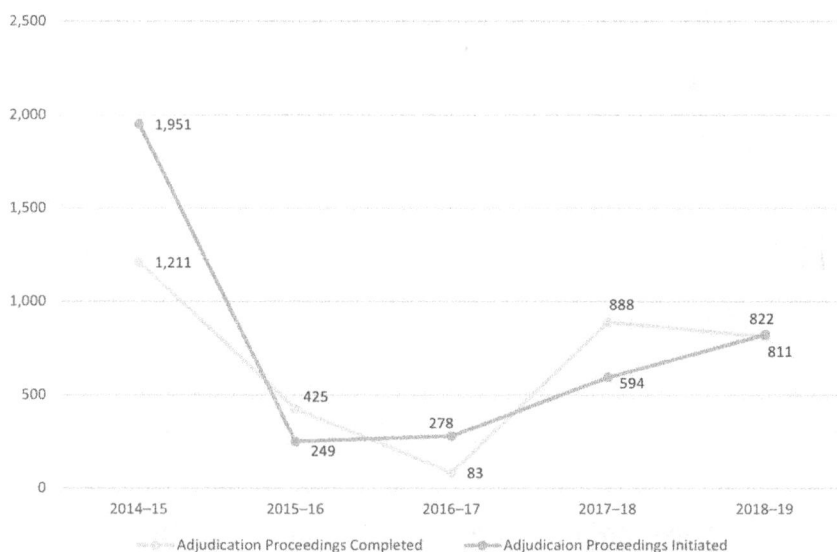

Figure 5.3: Trends in SEBI's adjudication proceedings during the selected period
Source: Author's research.

Inquiry and adjudication proceedings[27]

Table 5.7: SEBI's inquiry and adjudication proceedings against intermediaries in the period between FY 2014–15 and FY 2017–18

	2014–15	2015–16	2016–17	2017–18	2018–19	Total
Inquiries and adjudication cases disposed	1,232	436	90	867	-	2,625
Inquiries and adjudication proceedings initiated (issue of show cause notice)	1,351	562	235	782	-	2,930

Table 5.7 relays data about the inquiry and adjudication proceedings initiated and disposed by SEBI for the period between FY 2014–15 and FY 2017–18. As seen, a total of 2,625 inquiries and adjudication matters were disposed by SEBI and 2,930 matters were initiated by SEBI in the period between FY 2014–15 and FY 2017–18. Data for initiated and disposed cases was not available in the annual report for FY 2018–19.

---

27   If a registered intermediary contravenes any provisions of the securities law, SEBI may initiate an inquiry for suspension or cancellation of certificate as well as initiate adjudication proceedings to levy a regulatory penalty against such intermediary.

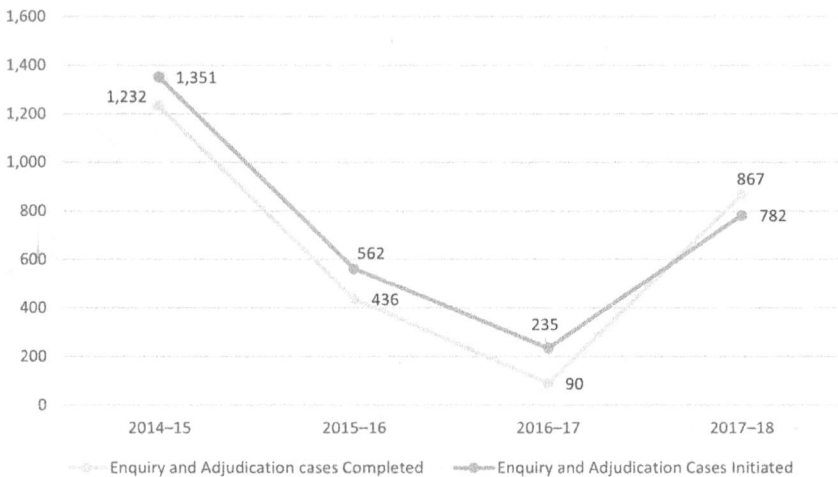

Figure 5.4: Trends in SEBI's inquiry and adjudication proceedings against registered intermediaries for the selected period

Source: Author's research.

Figure 5.4 presents the four-year trends in SEBI's inquiry and adjudication proceedings against SEBI's registered intermediaries for the selected period. As seen, the trends show a descending trend from FY 2014–15 to FY 2016–17 and then an ascending trend from FY 2016–17. Data in the figure reflect that SEBI makes strong use of its inquiry and adjudication enforcement mechanism against registered intermediaries.

Table 5.8: SEBI's inquiry and adjudication proceedings against specific intermediaries in the period between FY 2014–15 and FY 2018–19

	2014–15		2015–16		2016–17		2017–18		2018–19		Total	
	Adj.	Inq.	Adj.	Inq.	Adj.	Inq.	Adj.	Inq.	Adj.	Inq.	Adj.	Inq.
Registrar to an issue and share transfer agents	1	0	1	0	1	0	1	4	1	5	5	9
Merchant banker	6	2	1	2	0	0	3	0	2	3	12	7
Depository participants	1	0	2	0	0	0	2	1	4	0	9	1
CRAs	0	0	1	0	0	0	2	0	1	0	4	0
Debenture trustees	1	0	2	0	0	0	0	0	2	0	5	0
Brokers	-	-	-	-	-	-	-	-	66	92	66	92
Sub-brokers	-	-	-	-	-	-	-	-	13	0	13	0
Mutual fund	-	-	-	-	-	-	-	-	4	0	4	0

	2014–15		2015–16		2016–17		2017–18		2018–19		Total	
	Adj.	Inq.	Adj.	Inq.	Adj.	Inq.	Adj.	Inq.	Adj.	Inq.	Adj.	Inq.
Investment adviser	-	-	-	-	-	-	-	-	1	0	1	0
FPI/sub-account	-	-	-	-	-	-	-	-	2	0	2	0
Total	9	2	7	2	1	0	8	5	96	100	-	-

Table 5.8 on SEBI's inquiry and adjudication proceedings relays data regarding SEBI's adjudication (monetary penalty) proceedings initiated for registered intermediaries. For FY 2014–15 to FY 2017–18, the annual reports present data for the following intermediaries: registrars to an issue and share transfer agents, merchant bankers, depository participants, CRAs and debenture trustees. In the 2018–19 Annual Report, data are also presented for SEBI's adjudication and inquiry actions taken against brokers, sub-brokers, mutual funds, investment advisers and FPI/sub-account. Since the data for these categories were unavailable for the period between FY 2014–15 and FY 2017–19, only specific and limited trends can be drawn, as Figures 5.5 and 5.6 show.

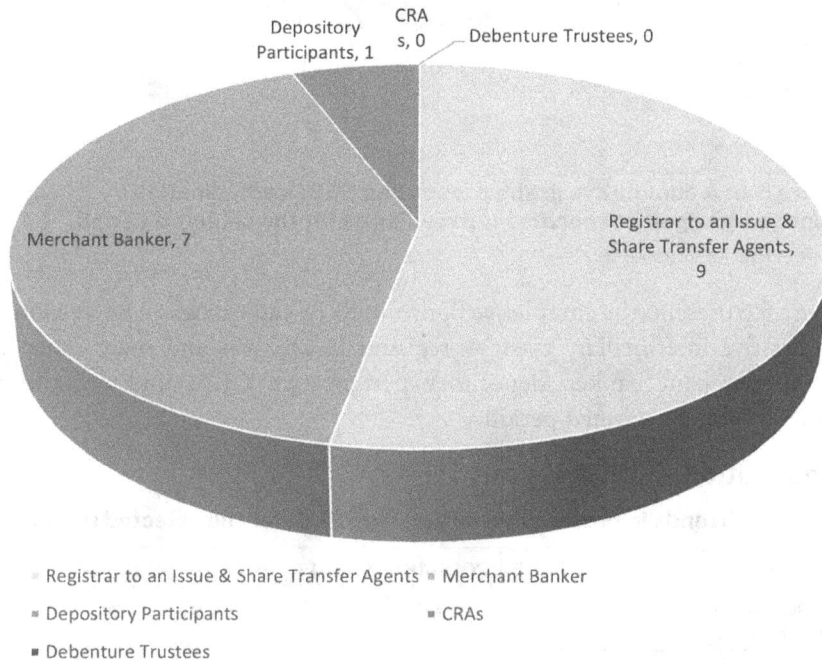

Figure 5.5: A cumulative graph presenting SEBI's inquiry proceedings against specific intermediaries for the selected period
Source: Author's research.

Figure 5.5 presents the cumulative figures of SEBI's inquiry proceedings against five intermediary categories—registrar to an issue and share transfer agent, merchant banker, depository participants, CRAs and debenture trustees—for the selected period.

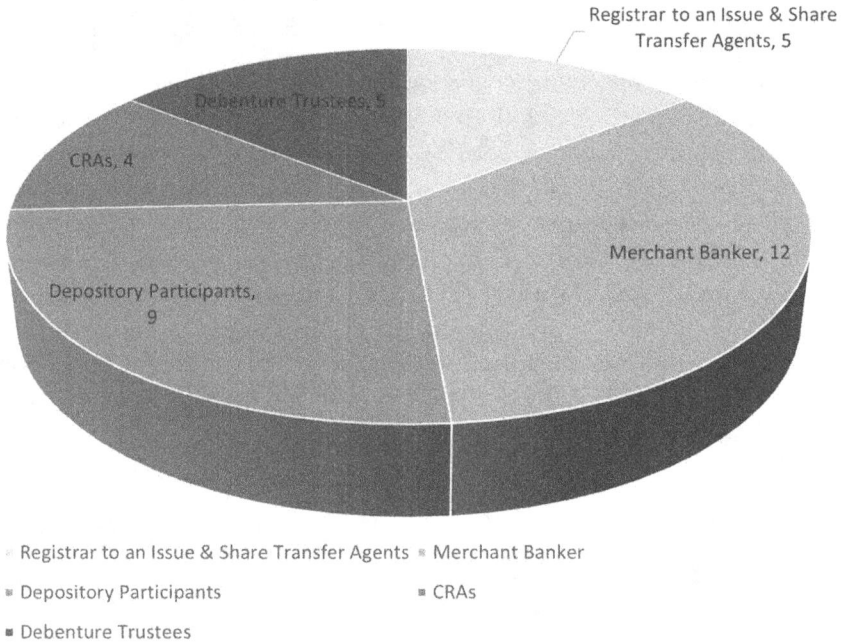

- Registrar to an Issue & Share Transfer Agents, 5
- Merchant Banker, 12
- Depository Participants, 9
- CRAs, 4
- Debenture Trustees, 5

- Registrar to an Issue & Share Transfer Agents
- Merchant Banker
- Depository Participants
- CRAs
- Debenture Trustees

Figure 5.6: A cumulative graph presenting SEBI's adjudication proceedings against specific intermediaries for the selected period
Source: Author's research.

Figure 5.6 presents the cumulative figures of SEBI's adjudication proceedings against five intermediary classes—registrar to an issue and share transfer agent, merchant banker, depository participants, CRAs and debenture trustees—for the selected period.

Prosecution

Table 5.9: Trends in prosecution initiated by SEBI for the selected period

	2014–15	2015–16	2016–17	2017–18	2018–19	Total
Prosecution cases launched	67	46	33	56	65	267
Entities against whom prosecution proceedings filed	157	268	237	407	399	1,468

Table 5.9 shows data on SEBI's prosecution cases initiated in the selected period. As evident, SEBI initiated fewer prosecutions each year when compared with other enforcement mechanisms, such as adjudication (monetary penalties). For the selected period, the total number of prosecutions initiated by SEBI was 267; however, seen from an 'entity' perspective, SEBI initiated criminal proceedings against 1,468 entities.

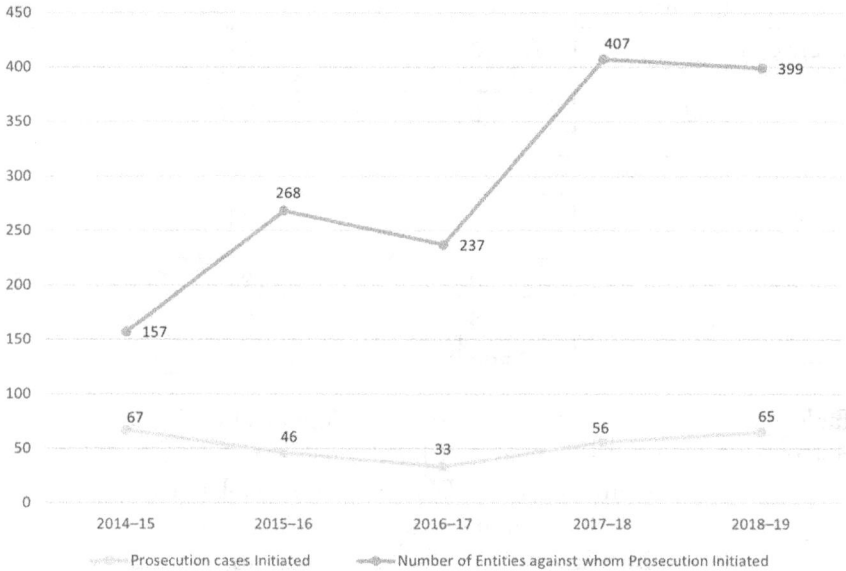

Figure 5.7: Trends in prosecution initiated by SEBI for the selected period
Source: Author's research.

Figure 5.7 shows that the prosecution cases initiated by SEBI during the selected period followed a stable trend, although the curve depicting the number of entities followed a rising trend. Further, in its FY 2018–19 Annual Report,[28] SEBI presented data regarding its prosecutions for a longer period—from FY 2003–04 to FY 2018–19. According to this, SEBI initiated criminal prosecution in 1,786 matters and against 7,822 over this 15-year period.

---

28 See SEBI, *Annual Report 2018–19* (2019) 161, Table 3.56.

Table 5.10: Nature of prosecution initiated by SEBI in the selected period

	Cases at 31 March 2015	Cases at 31 March 2016	Cases at 31 March 2017	Cases at 31 March 2018	Cases at 31 March 2019
SEBI Act	1,366	1,405	1,415	1,465	1,483
SEBI Act and SCRA	94	97	97	97	97
SEBI Act, SCRA and Companies Act 2013	2	2	2	2	2
SEBI Act and Companies Act	3	4	25	28	74
SEBI Act and Indian Penal Code	5	5	5	5	5
Companies Act	72	75	77	80	81
Securities Contracts (Regulation) Act 1956	7	7	7	7	7
Depositories Act 1996	29	29	29	29	29
Indian Penal Code	8	8	8	8	8
Total	**1,586**	**1,632**	**1,665**	**1,721**	**1,786**

Table 5.10 conveys the 'nature of prosecution' initiated by SEBI for securities violations based on the Act violated for the selected period. It shows that most prosecutions initiated by SEBI were against violations of the *SEBI Act*. The figures depict the 'number of entities' and not the 'number of matters' initiated by SEBI. While these data do try to reveal details about the nature of violations, this is not expressed in terms of 'themes', such as insider trading, market manipulation, mis-selling of financial products and the like. This makes it difficult to analyse the data against the prosecution data of other jurisdictions such as that regulated by ASIC.

Table 5.11 shows data regarding court cases for the selected period categorised according to 'nature of outcome'. The total number of court outcomes for securities laws violations was 2,070. According to the data, there were 896 court convictions in the five-year period, 764 cases were compounded and 324 cases were dismissed or discharged. The table also shows that court outcomes followed a rising trend, with FY 2014–15 recording 283 disposed cases, FY 2016–17 recording 400 cases and FY 2018–19 recording 578 disposed cases.

Table 5.11: Nature of outcomes in respect of court-based action in the selected period

Type of decision by courts	2014–15	2015–16	2016–17	2017–18	2018–19	Total
Convictions by courts	163	164	170	194	205	**896**
Compounded	62	84	154	207	257	**764**
Abated	4	10	12	14	18	**58**
Dismissed/discharged	50	50	59	75	90	**324**
Withdrawn	4	5	5	5	5	**24**
Adjourned sine die/ filed for the present	-	-	-	1	3	**4**
Cases disposed by courts	**283**	**313**	**400**	**496**	**578**	**2,070**

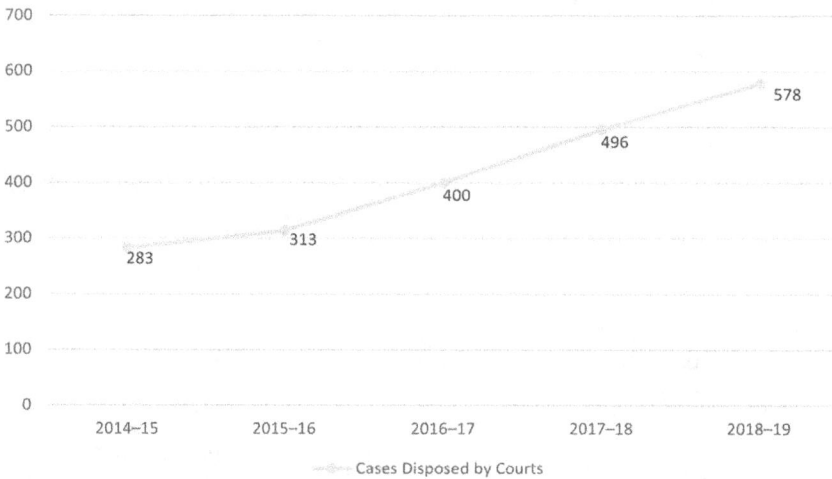

Figure 5.8: Five-year prosecution trends in the securities markets: Cases disposed by courts
Source: Author's research.

Figure 5.8 delineates a rising trend in prosecution cases disposed by courts for the selected period.

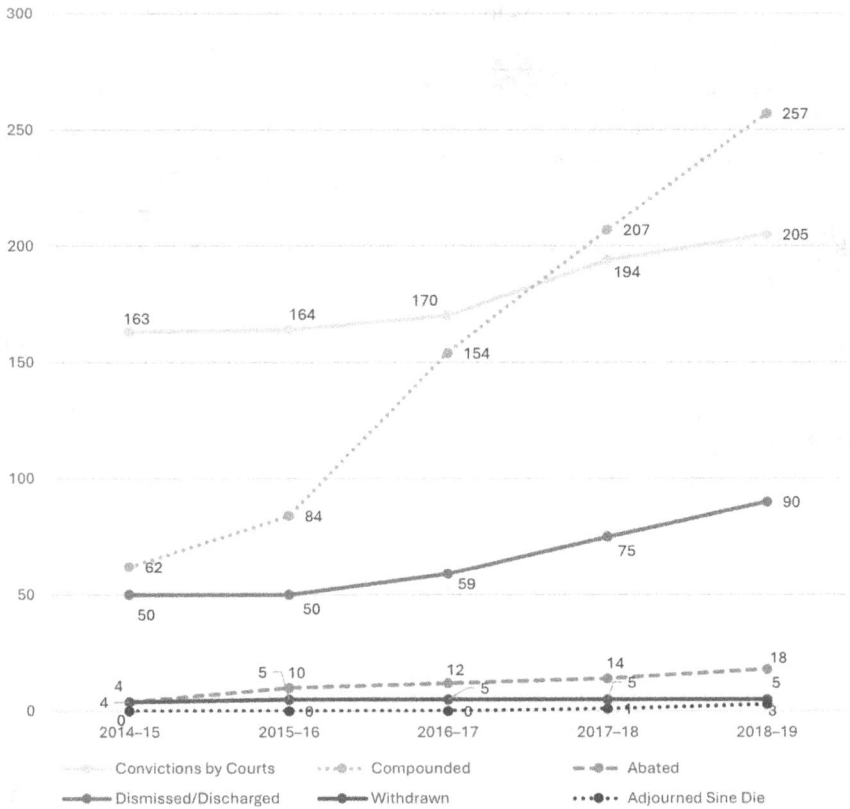

Figure 5.9: Trends in prosecution in securities markets in the selected period based on type of decisions by courts

Source: Author's research.

Figure 5.9 shows the trends in prosecution based on the type of decisions taken by courts in the selected period. It demonstrates a rising trend for cases 'compounded' and disposed by courts. Simultaneously, there is a rising trend in the overall number of 'convictions' by the courts in the selected five-year period. Although significant, the rise in the number of convictions on a yearly basis has been remarkably low: between FY 2014–15 and FY 2015–16, the number rose by 11 convictions, between FY 2015–16 and 2016–17 by six convictions, and, finally, between FY 2017–18 and FY 2018–19, the number of convictions rose by 11.

Settlement[29] applications filed with SEBI

Table 5.12: 'Settlement' in the securities markets in the selected period

	2014–15	2015–16	2016–17	2017–18	2018–19	Total
Pending at the beginning of the period	112	120	187	232	1,051	1,702
Settlement applications received	108	177	171	241	822	1,519
Applications disposed by passing of an order[30]	41	34	103	200	2,099	2,477
Applications rejected	59	82	23	79	1,064	1,307
Settlement amounts[31]	35,795,389 crore	44,226,748 crore	135,083,822 crore	308,670,956 crore	461,130,881 crore	

Table 5.12 presents data for the selected period on SEBI's settlement figures. SEBI disposed of 2,477 settlement matters in the selected period and rejected 1,307 matters. The table also shows the increase in the settlement amount collected by SEBI in the selected period.

Figure 5.10 depicts the trend for SEBI's settlement proceedings for the selected period. As seen, there was a sharp rise post FY 2017–18 in the settlement figures across all three categories: applications received, rejected and disposed by SEBI. This rise may be attributed to the revamped *SEBI (Settlement Proceedings) Regulations 2018.*

---

29   Settlement mechanism refers to the settlement of securities laws violations in terms of the *SEBI (Settlement Proceedings) Regulations 2018* that replaced the *SEBI (Settlement of Administrative and Civil Proceedings) Regulations 2014*; the 2018 regulations came into effect on 1 January 2019.

30   Under the *SEBI (Settlement of Administrative and Civil Proceedings) Regulations 2014* that were repealed and replaced by the *SEBI (Settlement Proceedings) Regulations 2018*, the process is now known as settlement instead of consent. The number of applications may include disposal of applications filed during previous financial years.

31   Settlement amount refers to the cumulative amount collected by SEBI towards 'settlement/legal/ administrative/disgorgement charges': see SEBI, *Annual Report 2017–18* (n 19) 143. 'Out of total amount of 46,11,30,881/-, 92,18,727/- was received towards disgorgement, 45,10,04,929/- towards settlement and 9,07,225/- towards legal expenses': see SEBI, *Annual Report 2018–19* (n 28).

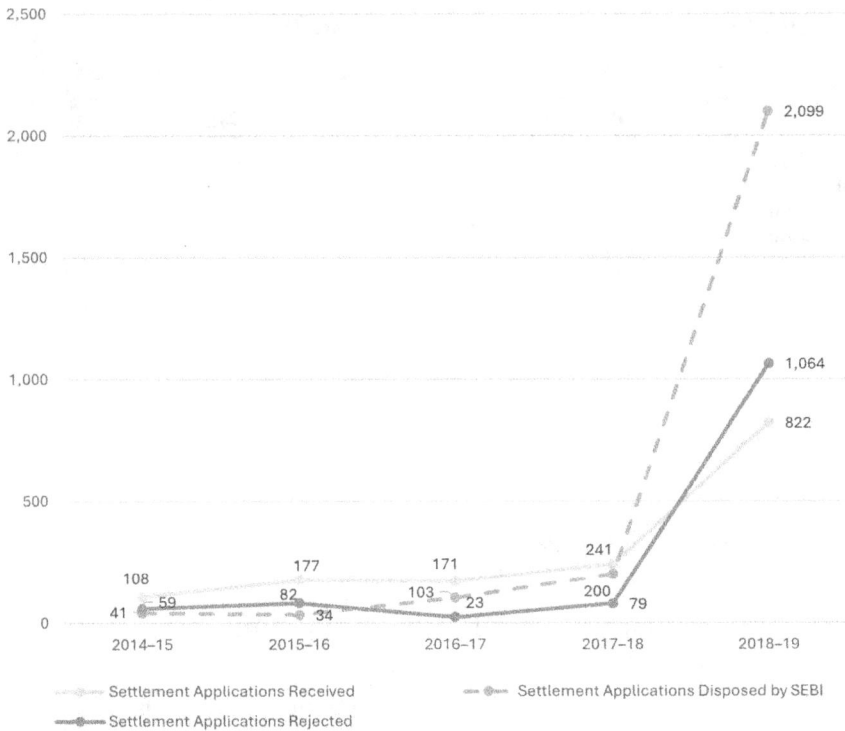

Figure 5.10: Trends in settlement in securities markets in the selected period for SEBI

Source: Author's research.

SEBI's investigations

Table 5.13: Area-wise investigations completed for securities violations in the selected period for SEBI

Nature of violation	2014–15	2015–16	2016–17	2017–18	2018–19	Total
PFUTP violations[32]	86	60	118	120	60	444
'Issue'-related manipulation	3	20	5	9	1	38
Insider trading	15	20	15	6	19	75
Takeover	3	2	4	0	3	12
Miscellaneous	15	21	13	10	27	86
Total	**122**	**123**	**155**	**145**	**110**	**655**

---

32   PFUTP: prevention of fraudulent and unfair trade practices.

Previous figures (Figures 5.1–5.10) and tables (Tables 5.4–5.12) on enforcement generally reveal limited information relating to the 'nature of violation'. Contrastingly, the investigations section in SEBI's annual reports reveals data on specific 'areas' or 'violations' that SEBI has taken cognisance of and for which investigations have been completed. These data are organised in SEBI's annual reports under the following labels: PFUTP violations or market manipulation, issue-related manipulation, insider trading, takeover violations and miscellaneous.

These data show that SEBI undertook 655 investigations of securities violations in the selected period. Of these, 444 actions were taken under the *SEBI (PFUTP) Regulations 2003* relating to violations such as market manipulation and price rigging. SEBI undertook 75 investigations in the insider trading category, 38 investigations for 'issue'-related manipulation, 12 for takeover violations and 86 for other securities violations.

Table 5.14: Area-wise investigations initiated by SEBI in SEBI's selected period

Nature of violation	2014–15	2015–16	2016–17	2017–18	2018–19	Total
PFUTP	41	84	185	40	84	434
'Issue'-related manipulation	3	9	8	1	2	23
Insider trading	10	12	34	15	70	141
Takeovers	3	2	3	1	6	15
Miscellaneous	13	26	15	60	32	146
Total	**70**	**133**	**245**	**117**	**194**	**759**

Table 5.14 reveals data on investigations initiated by SEBI according to 'nature of violation'. In total, SEBI initiated 759 investigations for securities violations in the stated period. SEBI initiated 434 investigations for fraudulent and unfair trading practices, 23 investigations for issue-related manipulations, 141 for insider trading, 15 for takeover violations and 146 investigations in the miscellaneous category. While the majority of SEBI's investigations were initiated for market manipulation and other forms of unfair trade practices, the numbers for insider trading were also high.

Analysis

Building on the analysis in Chapter 4 on SEBI's key supervisory and enforcement powers, and the empirical data on SEBI's enforcement and investigations actions presented thus far, this section evaluates the use of SEBI's supervisory and enforcement powers to gauge the effectiveness of its compliance regime.

Principles guiding SEBI's regulatory and enforcement regime

Prior to evaluating SEBI's use of its supervisory and enforcement powers, it is both necessary and useful to briefly discuss the basic principles that underpin SEBI's enforcement and compliance regime. Raval describes these underlying principles as:

- transparency and fairness in regulatory functioning
- adoption of the principles of natural justice and due recognition of fundamental rights guaranteed by the Constitution of India
- judicial control of administrative action.[33]

Transparency and fairness

SEBI's regulatory and enforcement approach is based on principles of 'transparency' and 'fairness'.[34] Transparency, according to Raval, 'provides for a salient and democratic safeguard against uncertainty, suspicion, mistrust and apprehension in the minds of the market participants about the regulatory framework'.[35] Transparency is also critical to ensure that the regulatory framework is not *de hors*, or going 'beyond the provisions of the parent Act or violating the fundamental rights guaranteed under the Constitution of India'.[36]

An example of transparency in SEBI's functioning is the 'consultative process' that allows stakeholders to be more involved in decision-making,[37] while aiding SEBI in its process of formulating subordinate regulation.[38]

---

33 Dharmishta Raval, *Improving the Legal Process in Enforcement at SEBI* (Indira Gandhi Institute of Development Research Working Paper No 2011-008, 2011) 21.

34 See for example SEBI, *Annual Report 2018–19* (n 28) 49. A good example of SEBI's incorporation of these principles into its own functioning and working is its reliance on a 'consultative approach' for the development and regulation of securities markets.

35 Raval (n 33) 21.

36 Ibid.

37 Ibid.

38 The term 'subordinate regulation' refers to a 'regulatory framework' that is notified in terms of the provisions of an Act, and which is subordinate to the Act itself.

The emphasis on transparency in SEBI's regulatory approach is also driven by the need to ensure no misuse or abuse of SEBI's wide powers conferred by the parliament for the fulfillment of its regulatory mandate.[39] SEBI's continuous interface with the 'public domain', and the systematic interactions among market stakeholders, investors and the regulator, reduce the incidence of 'misuse of powers'.[40]

Among other regulatory bodies in India, SEBI has pioneered the use of transparent practices in regulation making.[41] Notwithstanding this, Varottil points out that there is 'room for improvement' in SEBI's public consultation process.[42]

Natural justice and due process of law

SEBI's regulatory and enforcement regime is based on established principles of natural justice and due process of law.[43] The principles of natural justice demand that:

> a person who is directly affected by an administrative action be given prior notice of what is proposed so as to enable him to make a proper representation to defend his cause.[44]

In essence, natural justice principles assume adherence to two critical requirements:

1. the principle of *audi alteram partem*, which requires that a person who is affected should be heard before the decision is taken

2. a fair hearing, free from bias, must be accorded to such a person.[45]

---

39 Section 11 of the *Securities and Exchange Board of India Act 1992* (*SEBI Act*) grants SEBI wide powers to fulfil its mandate of investor protection, regulation and development of the securities markets. The adoption of the principle of 'transparency' ensures that such wide powers are exercised under adequate checks.
40 Raval (n 33) 22.
41 Umakanth Varottil, 'Securities markets' in Devesh Kapur and Madhav Khosla (eds), *Regulation in India: Design, Capacity, Performance* (Hart Publishing, 2019) 12, doi.org/10.5040/9781509927753. ch-005.
42 Ibid 12, 13. Varottil points out that due to the absence of legislative compulsion, SEBI's public consultation lacks uniformity and is not sufficiently elaborate.
43 Raval (n 33).
44 Order of C Achuthan in *DA Gadgil v SEBI* (Securities Appellate Tribunal Mumbai, 11 August 2000).
45 A well-established exception to the rule of a pre-decisional hearing is a 'post-decisional hearing': see Raval (n 33).

In India, courts have repeatedly held that natural justice principles are not to be excluded in the interpretation of any statutory instrument unless the language of the instrument specifically excludes these principles, and, therefore, that the 'procedural fairness embodying natural justice is to be *implied* whenever action is taken affecting the rights of parties'.[46] These principles are firmly entrenched in areas that deal with administrative action.[47]

For securities markets, both the Securities Appellate Tribunal (SAT) operating under the provisions of the *SEBI Act*,[48] and SEBI's administrative and enforcement actions are guided by the principles of natural justice.[49] In addition, SEBI is bound to follow the due process of law for conducting investigations and inquiries for alleged violations of the securities laws, and one way to ensure this is by 'providing for a procedure specifying the manner, method and circumstances in which an investigation and inquiry can be conducted'.[50] SEBI has laid down procedures outlining the precise manner and process for initiating an investigation, including the need to seek prior approval from a senior officer and, thereafter, reporting to a senior officer. SEBI regards these as sine qua non for 'ensuring fair investigation and inquiry'.[51]

Judicial control of administrative action

SEBI's independence and autonomy are subject to checks and balances. In addition to parliamentary oversight,[52] its executive functions may be 'tested before a judicial authority' on the touchstones of 'arbitrariness',

---

46   *Liberty Oil Mills & Others v Union of India & Others* (1984) AIR 1271 (emphasis added).

47   In rare circumstances, the principles of natural justice may be waived: for example, in the case of *R v Secretary of State*, cited by the Bombay High Court, it was held that the 'requirement of natural justice that a party affected by an administrative action should have a reasonable opportunity of presenting his case would be waived where the action contemplated was merely the provisional suspension of a licence or permit in an emergency situation which might result in the loss of many lives if action was not taken': see *Anand Rathi and Ors vs Securities and Exchange Board of India* (2002) 2 BomCR 403 [29].

48   *SEBI Act* s 15U.

49   See generally Kaushik Dhar, *Securities Exchange Board of India (SEBI) Act, 1992: A Summary* (2012), doi.org/10.2139/ssrn.2014351. See also 'SEBI overhauls enforcement norms', *The Hindu Business Line* (17 June 2020) thehindubusinessline.com/markets/stock-markets/sebi-overhauls-enforcement-norms/article31853639.ece.

50   SEBI, in the pursuit of its objectives as a regulator, enjoys wide powers such as the 'right of search and seizure of documents, property, bank accounts, attachment of securities' and other such mighty powers that affect the right of privacy and confidentiality of an individual along with the right of property granted by the Constitution of India: see Raval (n 33) 22.

51   Ibid.

52   In recent times, there have been calls to further strengthen this parliamentary oversight over regulatory institutions instead of 'governmental oversight' that impinges on the autonomy of the regulator: see 'Sebi chief pitches for stronger Parl oversight for regulators', *Financial Express* (7 October 2016) financialexpress.com/market/sebi-chief-pitches-for-stronger-parl-oversight-for-regulators/-410201/.

'discrimination', 'unfair treatment' and 'violation of fundamental rights'.[53] SEBI's regulatory proceedings with penal repercussions, such as its adjudication levying a monetary penalty for securities violations, are also subject to judicial control through appeal.[54]

To ensure delivery of speedy and efficacious justice, the *SEBI Act* appoints special tribunals with expert members, such as SAT, for appeals to SEBI's orders. Further, an aggrieved person may approach the High Court.[55] Policy decisions by SEBI, which generally lie beyond the purview of judicial control, are subject to oversight by the central government.[56]

To sum up, SEBI's underlying principles are well established and provide a foundation for its general regulatory approach and enforcement actions.

SEBI's use and implementation of its supervisory and enforcement powers

The subsections below analyse the empirical data to extrapolate meaningful trends and conclusions about the on-ground implementation of SEBI's supervisory and enforcement regime. However, it is imperative to first set out some limitations.

Limitations to the empirical analysis

SEBI's annual reports contain significant data with a variety of variables, enabling academics and practitioners to develop a better understanding of Indian securities markets, and particularly SEBI's regulatory and enforcement regime. However, there are several limitations to and discrepancies in these data, as the following discussion summarises. (It is relevant to note that the Ministry of Finance, too, recently made recommendations for improved data representation in SEBI's annual reports to better reflect SEBI's work as a regulator.[57])

First, SEBI's enforcement data, as presented in its annual reports, are sufficiently detailed to show that its supervisory and enforcement regime is active, engaged and present; however, such data are categorically inadequate for developing a comprehensive opinion on SEBI's enforcement

---

53 Raval (n 33) 25.
54 Ibid.
55 Ibid 25.
56 Ibid.
57 Shrimi Choudhary, 'Finmin asks Sebi to make greater disclosure in the annual report', *Business Standard* (14 March 2021) business-standard.com/article/economy-policy/finmin-asks-sebi-to-make-greater-disclosure-in-the-annual-report-121031300702_1.html.

strengths and weaknesses across different areas of market misconduct and irregularities. This criticism is substantiated by the following explanation. The data on SEBI's enforcement actions contained within 'Chapter 13: Other Functions—Enforcement Functions' of SEBI's annual reports is mainly expressed in terms of the 'nature of enforcement action' taken, not the 'nature of violation'. Only one annual report in the selected period (FY 2018–19) attempted to disclose the 'nature of violation' for SEBI's s 11/11B orders (SEBI's prohibitive/preventive actions).[58] Interestingly, to some extent, other chapters in the annual reports reveal limited data on SEBI's enforcement actions based on the 'nature of violation', but this only leads to critical data on the 'nature of violations' being scattered across different chapters and sections in a confusing manner instead of being available in the main chapter on enforcement. This issue is illustrated through the following example. In the report for FY 2018–19, the data on SEBI's enforcement actions against 'unauthorised/unregistered collective investment schemes' is not found in the enforcement data chapter—namely, 'Chapter 13: Other Functions—Enforcement Functions'—but, instead, in 'Chapter 3: Registration and Regulation of the Working of Collective Investment Schemes Including Mutual Funds'. In this latter chapter, Table 3.19 sets out the data concerning regulatory action taken by SEBI against 'unauthorised/unregistered collective investment schemes' (CISs) but the enforcement chapter does not reflect any such information on unauthorised/unregistered CISs. Thus, for obtaining such data on the 'nature of violation', a researcher would either need to peruse the annual report extensively or use numerous search words. Even upon doing so, there is no certainty that the information on the 'nature of violation' is recorded in a consistent format in the different chapters of the annual report each year.

Second, and closely related to the first limitation, the current layout of the enforcement data in SEBI's annual reports do not efficiently support establishing systematic trends across enforcement areas or developing a thematic understanding of SEBI's enforcement efforts in their entirety. For instance, if the research demands an understanding of SEBI's effectiveness in addressing corporate governance violations, such as breached directors' duties, the current enforcement data do not provide any relevant information.

---

58   See SEBI, *Annual Report 2018–19* (n 28) Table 3.51, 159.

Third, the enforcement data in SEBI's reports, in some places, are inconsistent and discrepant. This precludes the drawing of concrete and accurate conclusions regarding SEBI's enforcement actions. For instance, Table 3.20 of Chapter 3 of SEBI's 2018–19 Annual Report[59] reveals data on orders passed by SEBI in the case of deemed public issues against entities 'who raised money from investors by issuing non-convertible debentures/ non-convertible preference shares without complying with statutory/ regulatory provisions governing a public issue'. In this table, the number of final orders passed in FY 2018–19 for cases on deemed public issues is stated as '23', whereas in Table 3.51 of Chapter 13 on enforcement in the same annual report, the total number of cases in respect of such deemed public issues is stated to be '26'.

Fourth, keeping aside the limitations and discrepancies in data, the enforcement section of the annual report does not critically evaluate any of the enforcement outcomes achieved by SEBI. The annual reports would significantly benefit from a deeper, qualitative elaboration and analysis that complements the quantitative figures provided in a tabular format in the enforcement chapter.

Fifth, annual reports ought to use consistent terminology and data labels to enable drawing of trends over a selected period. For example, at times, the annual reports use the term 'regulatory action' and at times 'enforcement action' without clarifying whether the terms are exactly interchangeable or refer to different actions (eg whether 'regulatory action' refers to a wider set of action and 'enforcement action' is a subset of 'regulatory action'). Similarly, at times, the data are revealed on the basis of 'number of entities' against whom action is initiated, and, at other times, on 'number of cases' in which enforcement action was completed.

In sum, SEBI's annual reports are a repository of critically relevant data. With limited quality academic analysis on Indian securities markets, SEBI's annual reports are a fundamental tool for researchers, practitioners and investors from all over the world who are closely tracking the growth of, and opportunities in, Indian securities markets. Fortunately, the limitations noted above are easy to address, and removing these would lend further clarity and reliability to SEBI's publications.

---

59   See ibid Table 3.20, 115.

Context of the empirical analysis

Before analysing SEBI's use of its supervisory and enforcement powers, it is useful and necessary to briefly contextualise the data and trends against the scale, magnitude and depth of the securities markets, key institutions and intermediaries in India.

The securities markets in India are high-volume markets, with market capitalisation of the Bombay Stock Exchange (BSE) for FY 2018–19 at 15,108,711 (crore rupees) and of the National Stock Exchange (NSE) at 14,934,227 (crore rupees).[60] In FY 2018–19, the number of companies listed on BSE was 5,262 and on NSE 1931.[61] All segments of the stock exchange, such as the equity cash segment, equity derivatives segment and currency derivatives segments, have a strong turnover of several million crores rupees.[62] Similarly, as Table 5.3 shows, there are approximately 31,399 intermediaries and institutions operating under various licences in the securities markets.

With these broad statistics in mind, SEBI's use of its supervision, surveillance, investigation, enforcement and settlement powers is examined in the following sections.

SEBI's supervision in the securities markets

SEBI's annual reports indicate that it carries out ongoing supervision of securities markets entities regularly as part of its regulatory responsibilities.[63] SEBI has established oversight mechanisms that include periodic inspection, periodic compliance analysis and annual system audits in respect of important market infrastructure institutions (MIIs), such as stock exchanges, clearing corporations and depositories.[64] The objective of these inspections is to determine whether MIIs are operating and functioning in an orderly manner. For example, stock exchanges are inspected to broadly determine whether they are providing a 'fair, equitable, transparent and growing market to investors'; the organisational systems and practices are conforming with the requirements under the *Securities Contracts (Regulation) Act 1956* and the rules thereunder; and the exchanges have 'implemented the directions,

---

60 See Table 5.2 in this chapter.
61 Ibid.
62 In FY 2018–19, Equity Cash Segment had a total turnover of 8,724,653 crore rupees while the Equity Derivatives Segment had a turnover of 237,602,955 crore rupees: see Table 5.2 in this chapter.
63 See generally SEBI, *Annual Report 2018–19* (n 28) 139.
64 See ibid 138–139. As well as periodic inspections, SEBI also conducts special purpose inspections of these institutions whenever the need arises.

guidelines and instructions issued by SEBI/Government of India' and are complying with any condition imposed by SEBI at the time of renewal or grant of its recognition.[65]

In addition to checks of MIIs, SEBI conducts periodic assessments of registered intermediaries.[66] Table 5.3 of this chapter shows that SEBI has licensed 31,399 intermediaries across 36 different categories, of which 15,767 are registered stockbrokers and 1,313 investment advisers, among other intermediaries.[67] In relation to such intermediaries, until as recently as 2013, SEBI relied on 'institution-based' supervision, with a varying approach to supervision for each intermediary.[68] However, since 2016, SEBI has moved to 'risk-based supervision' and developed a more targeted and enhanced supervisory approach, particularly for stockbrokers and depository participants.[69] Similarly, SEBI has taken measures to enhance its supervision of other intermediaries by shifting from an entity-based supervisory approach to a risk-based approach.[70]

In supervising MIIs and intermediaries, SEBI relies on two main methods: offsite and onsite supervision. Under offsite supervision, SEBI employs three mechanisms to supervise regulated entities: offsite reporting by

---

65   Ibid 139. Similarly, oversight of clearing corporations and depositories is conducted to ascertain their compliance with the regulatory framework. Stock exchange licences are renewed and granted under s 4 of the *Securities and Contracts (Regulation) Act 1956*.

66   See SEBI, 'Recognised intermediaries' (n 25).

67   See Table 5.3 on recognised intermediaries.

68   Until recently, for brokers operating in the securities markets, SEBI has positioned recognised stock exchanges (RSEs) as 'front-line' supervisors, while SEBI directly supervises other intermediaries such as mutual funds, portfolio managers, asset management companies, etc: see International Monetary Fund (IMF), *India: Financial Sector Assessment Program—Detailed Assessments Report on IOSCO Objectives and Principles of Securities Regulation* (2013) (*India FSAP Report*).

69   SEBI constituted a committee for the 'enhanced supervision of stock brokers' whose recommendations were implemented in 2016. They cover areas such as 1) adoption of uniform nomenclature by stockbrokers when referring to demat accounts and banks; 2) monitoring of client funds lying with the stockbroker by the stock exchanges through sophisticated alerting and reconciliation mechanisms to detect any mis-utilisation of client funds; 3) changes in the internal audit for stockbrokers/depository participants through appointment, rotation of internal auditors, formulation of objective sample criteria, monitoring the quality of internal audit reports, timeline for submissions of internal audit reports, etc.; 4) monitoring the financial health and detection of problems through an early warning system to take pre-emptive and remedial measures; and 5) imposition of uniform penal action on brokers in case of defaults: see SEBI Circular, 'Enhanced supervision of all recognised stock exchanges and depositories' (2016).

70   In the past few years, SEBI has taken measures towards a risk-based supervisory regime. For instance, it has adopted a risk-based inspection policy for the inspection of mutual funds where inspections are carried out on the basis of various factors, such as assets under management and the number of complaints received against a fund. In 2016–17, 23 mutual funds were inspected and inspections of two registrars were initiated: see SEBI, *Annual Report 2016–17* (n 18). Similarly, the 2018–19 *Annual Report* notes that such risk assessments were carried out for other intermediaries: see SEBI, *Annual Report 2018–19* (n 28) 140.

intermediaries, use of third-party/independent experts as 'gatekeepers' and a grievance redressal system.[71] Under the onsite supervision mechanism, SEBI conducts inspections of supervised entities, and stockbrokers in particular are subject to detailed inspections through recognised stock exchanges (RSEs) annually, in addition to SEBI's own 'purpose-driven' inspections of such brokers.[72]

SEBI provides data on its inspections carried out each year in respect of market intermediaries. SEBI's Annual Report 2018–19 shows the main areas in which it directed its attention and resources for the purposes of conducting inspections.[73] It shows that SEBI conducted 159 inspections of stockbrokers and none for sub-brokers, three inspections of portfolio managers, seven of investment advisers and five of research analysts, among some others. In addition, stock exchanges conducted inspections of stockbrokers, with BSE conducting 527 and NSE conducting 552 such inspections.

Complementing its supervision of MIIs and intermediaries, SEBI adopts a risk-based inspection policy towards mutual funds.[74] In FY 2018–19, 'comprehensive inspections' of 22 mutual funds were initiated while thematic inspections were initiated in respect of six mutual funds.[75] Further, SEBI's annual report mentioned that it was migrating to automation of inspections and surveillance of mutual funds.[76]

---

71 See IMF, *India FSAP Report* (n 68). As an example of offsite reporting, SEBI requires intermediaries to submit an 'annual audited financial statement' and 'semi-annual unaudited financial statement'. Since 2009, brokers and portfolio managers have been mandated to undergo a 'semiannual audit on their operations' that is to be undertaken with an 'accountant paneled with the RBI'. Similarly, regarding mutual funds, trustees are regarded as the front line supervisors of compliance who are required to submit an annual report to SEBI about such activities of the MF. Brokers and MFs must also have their IT systems certified by experts. Intermediaries are required to have systems that address investors' complaints and any complaint pending for over 30 days is required to be reported to SEBI: see 'Investors can soon submit grievances directly to companies: SEBI' (29 March 2018) *The Economic Times*, economictimes.indiatimes.com/markets/stocks/news/investors-can-soon-submit-grievances-directly-to-companies-sebi/articleshow/63532174.cms.

72 RSEs conduct their inspections based on criteria developed by them. Previously, before 2006, SEBI had outsourced onsite inspections to the Reserve Bank of India (RBI). When SEBI inspects RSEs, it also reviews samples of inspections conducted by the RSEs: see IMF, *India FSAP Report* (n 68).

73 SEBI, *Annual Report 2018–19* (n 28) 141–142.

74 Ibid 142. This approach has been developed with 'risk parameters' (ie 'liquidity risk, credit risk, financial risk, market risk, technological risk, operation risk') and 'impact parameters' in mind.

75 Ibid 142.

76 Ibid. SEBI's *Annual Report 2018–19* states that an ongoing project is attempting to 'ingest MF-related data in SEBI's database' as well as 'develop algorithms in order to generate instances of breaches of regulator guidelines by MFs along-with alerts on possible non-compliance' [sic]: see SEBI, *Annual Report 2018–19* (n 28).

A conjoint reading of the data and SEBI's supervisory mechanisms indicates that SEBI undertakes regular supervision, using both onsite and offsite techniques, and has also adopted enhanced, risk-based and thematic supervision. Notwithstanding these measures, there are areas open to further improvement relating to the frequency and, possibly, quality of SEBI's inspection and oversight routines. As regards frequency, the number of inspections conducted by SEBI when compared with the number of intermediaries registered with SEBI appears to be significantly low. This shortfall is, possibly, linked to limitations of human and financial resources discussed in Chapter 3 (this volume) that SEBI is trying to overcome. In respect to quality, despite SEBI's shift to risk-based supervision, the qualitative content and tangible measures adopted during inspections and other supervisory activities are unknown. However, supervision of market and intermediaries appears to be a potential area for deeper collaboration between SEBI and ASIC.

SEBI's surveillance measures

Similar to its supervisory and inspection approach, surveillance of markets is another of SEBI's key regulatory responsibilities to ensure market integrity and enhance investor confidence.[77] SEBI and the stock exchanges have a well-developed market surveillance system.[78] While the stock exchanges are responsible for frontline, real-time surveillance of the various market segments through their individual surveillance infrastructures, SEBI too has its 'in-house' surveillance system through which markets are monitored across segments and exchanges for 'unfair trade practices like market manipulation, front running and insider trading'.[79]

SEBI's annual reports highlight the use of surveillance powers within the regulatory system. For instance, SEBI's FY 2018–19 Annual Report outlines the surveillance activities for the financial year.[80] This information includes surveillance conducted by the two premier stock exchanges, BSE and NSE, that monitored scrips traded on their exchanges. Based on the

---

77 Ibid 149.
78 RSEs perform their surveillance on a real-time basis while SEBI does its surveillance through its IMSS on a t+1 basis: see IMF, *India FSAP Report* (n 68); Ashley Coutinho, 'Vendors highlight chinks in Sebi's surveillance system', *Business Standard* (29 October 2015). See also SEBI, *Annual Report 2016–17* (n 18) 143.
79 SEBI, *Annual Report 2018–19* (n 28).
80 Ibid: see ch 11 of the report.

alerts generated and the analysis of trading, both institutions took actions such as 'suspension of trading in the scrips' and 'debarment of the suspected entities'.[81]

Complementing the surveillance and resultant actions by stock exchanges, SEBI's annual reports highlight its general and special or incremental surveillance measures for ensuring fair trading, information symmetry and investor protection in the markets. For example, in FY 2018–19, SEBI introduced a set of 'Additional Surveillance Measures in cash segment' as preventive measures to caution investors from investing in stock that has witnessed unusual price movements.[82] Similarly, SEBI reviewed its 'Graded Surveillance Measures' through which it checks for abnormal price increases in scrips, especially of companies with poor fundamentals.[83] Finally, SEBI and the stock exchanges took measures to strengthen confidentiality requirements relating to unpublished price-sensitive information and to 'prevent incidents of leakage' of such information by requiring all listed companies to disseminate any 'material information/event as soon as it becomes credible and concrete' and 'clarify' any 'rumours' in the media.[84]

SEBI's annual reports, in addition to highlighting the active use of SEBI's surveillance powers, also highlight the upgrades to SEBI's surveillance capabilities, particularly its surveillance infrastructure, technical and other capacity. A suitable example is the external, professional and project-oriented guidance SEBI seeks from experts, practitioners and academics to improve its existing IT software for surveillance.[85]

Based on publicly available information on SEBI's surveillance regime, SEBI is active in independently surveying the stock markets and its measures are supported by a reliable surveillance infrastructure. It is equally clear that SEBI relies heavily on the stock exchanges for market surveillance just as it relies on the exchanges for supervision and oversight of stockbrokers and listed companies. The extensive role played by stock exchanges in market

---

81   Ibid.

82   SEBI's Additional Surveillance Measures are also directed towards reducing manipulation and excessive speculation by restricting the movement of price and 'increasing delivery based trades': see ibid 150.

83   SEBI made available to the public the 'entry/exit parameters for GSM [Graded Surveillance Measures] along with thresholds': see ibid 151.

84   Ibid 152.

85   See for example the IT Projects Advisory Committee that has been established by SEBI with a number of reference terms including aiding SEBI in the empanelment of service providers for implementing the technology solutions in a number of areas such as process designing for automation and data analytics: see SEBI, 'IT Projects Advisory Committee (IT-PAC)', www.sebi.gov.in/sebiweb/about/AboutAction.do?doMember=yes&committeesId=50.

surveillance necessitates a separate and deeper analysis to ascertain whether this reliance is beneficial or detrimental to the larger interest of the market, given that it potentially creates some conflicts of interest in the era of demutualised stock exchanges.[86] That said, SEBI has taken several measures to reduce such conflict by imposing conditions on RSEs.[87] Finally, much like oversight and supervision of the markets, issues and opportunities around market surveillance are another potential area for cooperation and experience sharing between SEBI and ASIC, particularly in consideration of the amendments introduced in 2010 in Australia that shifted market surveillance from the Australian Securities Exchange (ASX) to exclusively under ASIC.[88]

SEBI's investigation measures

As detailed in Chapter 4, SEBI may initiate a formal investigation to gather evidence and identify persons responsible for violating securities laws based on a reference received from its surveillance or other departments within SEBI, or a reference from 'external government agencies'.[89] SEBI's annual reports provide the data on SEBI's initiated and completed investigations.[90] They also provide useful information on the broad categories under which SEBI completed its investigations in a financial year, such as market manipulation and price rigging, issue-related manipulation, insider trading and takeovers.[91]

SEBI's investigation figures in its annual reports indicate that it is active in initiating and disposing investigation matters.[92] The investigation data analysed in Tables 5.13 and 5.14 of this chapter show that SEBI cumulatively initiated 759 investigations and completed 655 investigations during the

---

86 This issue is discussed at length in Chapter 6 of this book under Principle 9 on use of self-regulatory organisations.

87 See s 4 of the *Securities and Contracts (Regulation) Act 1956 (SCRA)* relating to conflicts of interest. The international experience in this regard suggests that regulators try to ensure the independence of SROs by 'ring fencing' their regulatory functions from their business operations. SEBI's FSAP Report of 2013 also suggested a long-term measure of 'spinning off' the SRO function in a body separate from the RSEs: see IMF, *India FSAP Report* (n 68).

88 See the analysis in Chapter 6 of this book under Principle 9.

89 The process of investigation involves a series of actions that are aimed at analysing the data, such as 'order and trade log, transaction statements, KYC documents obtained from brokers, depository participants, bank records, financial results, events around major corporate developments, Call Data Records, etc': see SEBI, *Annual Report 2018–19* (n 28) 156.

90 See for example ch 12 on investigations in ibid.

91 Ibid.

92 During 2016–17, SEBI took up 245 new cases for investigation and completed 155 investigations; in the previous year, 133 new cases were taken up and 123 completed: see SEBI, *Annual Report 2016–17* (n 18) 146.

selected five-year period. Most completed investigations in this selected period (ie 444 investigations, Table 5.13), related to market manipulation and price rigging, followed by 75 insider trading investigations (Table 5.13). While these figures reflect continuous use of SEBI's vast investigation toolkit, it is debatable whether the number of investigations initiated each year by SEBI, for instance 84 investigations initiated in FY 2018–19 (Table 5.14), is adequate given the large number of intermediaries and the size of the Indian securities market.

SEBI's enforcement actions

As discussed in Chapter 4, SEBI is equipped with a plethora of powers, available under its governing statutes,[93] to pursue civil, criminal and administrative action or to settle matters for violations of securities laws. SEBI uses its enforcement mechanisms to ensure 'integrity, transparency and fairness' in the securities market.[94] The empirical data presented earlier in this chapter demonstrate SEBI's use of a variety of enforcement mechanisms, enabling the following inferences to be made about SEBI's enforcement and compliance regime.

Table 5.4 shows that SEBI uses its enforcement powers for suspending and cancelling licences, issuing warning letters and prohibitive directions, deficiency observation letters and advice letters to market participants and intermediaries for market irregularities and violations of securities laws.[95] However, apart from this overarching observation about SEBI's use of these powers, the current format of the data in SEBI's annual report inhibits drawing further conclusions for the following reasons. First, as pointed out earlier, the categories of actions do not define or explain the 'nature of violation' for which these actions were taken. For instance, Table 5.4 shows that a 'suspension' action of certificate of registration was taken by SEBI but the data do not state for which violation such action was taken. Second, some categories of actions, such as 'warnings issued', 'administrative warning/warning issued', 'deficiency observations issued' and 'advice letter issues', are not sufficiently explained in the report, and even appear to be repetitive, overlapping and confusing. Third, Table 5.4 shows that SEBI issued a large number of prohibitive directions in the selected period, but the data do not adequately convey the exact kind of prohibitive action

---

93   SEBI's main governing statutes include the *SEBI Act, SCRA* and *Depositories Act 1996*.
94   SEBI, *Annual Report 2017–18* (n 19) 137.
95   See SEBI's powers under ss 11 and 11 B of the *SEBI Act*.

that was taken by SEBI.[96] Fourth, other action categories in Table 5.4 also require more detailed explanation to impart a better understanding of the action taken. For instance, for the headings 'deficiency observations issued' and 'advice letter issued', more information and specific examples of the nature of 'deficiency' observed or kind of 'advice' letter issued could lend further clarity and bring context and transparency in relation to SEBI's use of these powers.

In the case of registered intermediaries, the enforcement mechanism that SEBI actively uses to address violations of securities laws or non-adherence to the rules of registration are SEBI's inquiry proceedings. Inquiry proceedings are initiated under s 11/11B of the *SEBI Act* and may result in suspension or cancellation of a certificate of registration. The data in Table 5.5 reveal the number of inquiry proceedings disposed of in the selected period as 155 (this figure includes data for FY 2018–19 that are stated in respect of the inquiry proceedings 'conducted' and not 'completed'). Notwithstanding these figures, the precise type of action that emerged at the 'disposal' of the inquiry proceedings remains unclear from the annual report data: we do not know whether the disposal resulted in suspension of registration, cancellation, warnings, any type of prohibitive order, and so forth. In sum, the data presented in Table 5.5 hinder a comprehensive understanding of SEBI's actions and of the strengths or effectiveness of SEBI's inquiry regime.

Next, SEBI's adjudication mechanism enables it to impose high monetary penalties for violations of securities laws, and, as evident from Table 5.6, SEBI utilises this enforcement tool frequently, with a total of 3,418 monetary penalty cases disposed in the selected period. Once again, there are considerable limitations to these data. For instance, the term 'disposed' does not clarify whether any monetary penalty was, in fact, levied in an adjudication matter. The data do not support further conclusions other than the detail that SEBI has actively relied on this enforcement tool in the past years.

For significant violations of securities laws, SEBI may initiate multiple proceedings simultaneously. The enforcement tool that SEBI often uses is a combination of inquiry and adjudication proceedings. Thus, SEBI may use a multi-pronged enforcement approach to initiate action against a registered

---

96 Under s11, SEBI can take a variety of prohibitive measures, either pending investigation or on completion of such investigation. These measures include suspending trading of any security, restraining persons from accessing the markets or prohibiting any person from buying, selling or dealing in securities.

intermediary for a contravention of securities laws, such as by initiating simultaneous inquiry proceedings for suspension or cancellation of registration and adjudication proceedings, to levy high monetary penalties. Table 5.7 and Figure 5.4 record the data and trends for such proceedings and reveal an upward trend since FY 2016–17. Further, Table 5.8 and Figures 5.5 and 5.6 reveal the category-wise data and trends for inquiry and adjudication proceedings initiated against intermediaries for the selected period.[97] Overall these figures show a relatively high number of proceedings initiated (2,930) and disposed (2,625) by SEBI in the selected period, supporting the conclusion that SEBI uses this multi-pronged enforcement measure against intermediaries.

Under the criminal prosecution enforcement option, SEBI may approach a court for a securities law violation. This enforcement tool is distinct from SEBI's other enforcement tools that authorise it to take action against a securities law offender independently,[98] without having to approach a court of law. As evident from Table 5.9, the number of criminal prosecution cases initiated by SEBI in the selected period is only 267, which is relatively low when compared with other enforcement actions taken by SEBI.[99] Figure 5.7 reveals that, for each year of the selected period, SEBI initiated 30–70 criminal prosecution cases. Importantly, what the figure does not reveal is the precise violation or reason a criminal prosecution was started—that is, whether the prosecution was for original offences under s 24(1) of the *SEBI Act* or for non-compliance with SEBI orders or investigations under s 24(2) or 24(3) of the Act.[100]

Table 5.10 attempts to provide a break-up of the nature of prosecution cases initiated by categorising the total number of prosecution actions in terms of the violation under the specific Act, such as the *SEBI Act, Companies Act 2013*, the *Depositories Act 1996*, the *Indian Penal Code*, and so on. However,

---

97 These categories include merchant bankers, depository participants, CRAs and debenture trustees.
98 SEBI's independent enforcement actions include imposing monetary penalties through its adjudication process; suspending, cancelling and revoking licences through its inquiry proceedings; and debarring an entity from accessing the markets.
99 Criminal prosecution may be started under s 24(1) of the *SEBI Act* for original offences such as market manipulation and insider trading, or under s 24(2) for non-compliance with the adjudicating officer's order levying a monetary penalty or a whole time member's orders, or under s 24(3) for non-compliance with summons at the stage of investigation in any matter. Further, as observed in most common law jurisdictions, the standard of proof for criminal proceedings is higher than other proceedings, which generally requires the prosecution to prove the case beyond reasonable doubt. This, among other factors, is responsible for the under-utilisation of this enforcement tool by SEBI.
100 Ibid.

the structure and format of the information hinders the drawing of concrete conclusions about the exact nature of the violation for which prosecution proceedings were initiated by SEBI.

Finally, Table 5.11 conveys some data on the 'nature of outcomes' by courts, though it still lacks data on the 'nature of violation' for which court action was initiated by SEBI. As seen from these data, out of the 2,070 cases disposed in the selected period, 896 were convictions by courts, 764 matters were compounded, 324 were dismissed or discharged, 58 were matters where the punishment was abated and four matters were adjourned sine die. Further, Figure 5.8 denotes an upward trend in the 'disposal' of cases by courts over the examined period. Though the numbers indicate a fairly low conviction rate for a sizeable market such as India's, the upward trend in convictions over the examined period indicates two possibilities. The first is that there has been an emphasis in recent years to dispose of older prosecution matters; the second, which is more unlikely, is that SEBI is pursuing more criminal actions. Figure 5.9 reveals that 'compounding' cases rose sharply in the selected five-year period,[101] while the number of 'convictions by courts' and 'dismissal/discharge' cases rose more gently.[102] These figures are especially important given that, in the past, the overall state of the justice delivery system in India suffered from excessive delays. However, as Table 5.11 reveals, the 283 cases disposed in FY 2014–15 nearly doubled in FY 2018–19 to 578 cases. Similarly, Figure 5.8 demonstrates the year-on-year ascending trend in the disposal of cases by the courts for the examined five-year period. This ascending trend in the disposal of cases can possibly be attributed to the Special Courts that were set up by the amendment in 2014 to the *SEBI Act* for securities laws violations.[103]

Settlement of matters

Driven by exigencies of time and resources, SEBI is empowered to settle matters and, as explained in Chapter 4, it mainly accepts settlement for violations that are more procedural than substantive.[104] Table 5.12 presents SEBI's settlement numbers for the selected period. During this period, SEBI

---

101 As stated, there is not much clarity on the nature of the violations; however, going by the high figures of 'compounding', we can presume that most of the cases were prosecuted under s 24(2) or 24(3).
102 The number of cases dismissed or discharged by the courts is significant from the point of view of ascertaining the strength of SEBI's 'investigation'.
103 Sections 26A–26E inserted by the *Securities Laws (Amendment) Act 2014* provide for the establishment of Special Courts for all offences committed under the *SEBI Act*.
104 SEBI has laid out criteria for the type of violations that may not be settled: see *SEBI (Settlement Proceedings) Regulations 2018*. For a detailed understanding of this power, see the discussion in Chapter 4.

received 1,519 applications for settlement, rejected 1,307 applications and disposed of 2,477 applications. Figure 5.10 shows a sudden surge in the settlement of matters by SEBI, as well as a surge in the applications received and rejected by SEBI in the period between FY 2017–18 and FY 2018–19. This sudden increase likely corresponds with the revised settlement process under the newly framed *SEBI (Settlement Proceedings) Regulations 2018*.

To sum up, it is fundamentally clear that SEBI is an active regulator that makes full use of its supervisory and enforcement powers toolkit. However, the current variables and headings that SEBI's annual reports use render it difficult, if not impossible, to make any meaningful conclusions or develop a thorough understanding of SEBI's precise actions against securities violations, even where it is evident that SEBI vigorously pursues enforcement action for violations. The current format also inhibits the drawing of systematic thematic trends for an effective comparison with other jurisdictions, including with Australia, as attempted in this book.

Effectiveness of SEBI's enforcement and compliance regime: A critique

If the effectiveness of an enforcement and compliance regime is premised upon the combined strength of several factors, such as the broader financial framework, underlying regulatory principles and practices, and the enforcement outcomes of the regulator, SEBI's regime is a mixed bag of hits and misses.

The analysis in this chapter of SEBI's underlying principles and enforcement data shows that SEBI's regime has definite strengths. First, the regime is founded on strong underlying principles of transparency, fairness, natural justice, due process of the law, and judicial control of regulatory and administrative action. SEBI is bound to give 'speaking orders' or 'reasoned orders' when proceeding against an entity for a securities law violation,[105] and adopts a consultative process before designing its policy.[106] SEBI's actions are subject to judicial control and are challenged before the SAT and

---

105 Varottil (n 41) 12, 13.
106 SEBI has recently issued a notice inviting comments on the recommendations made by the High Level Committee under the chairmanship of Justice AR Dave for suggesting improvements to its enforcement process: see 'SEBI invites comment on Report on Measures for Strengthening Enforcement Mechanism' (16 June 2020), taxguru.in/sebi/sebi-invites-comment-report-measures-strengthening-enforcement-mechanism.html.

other courts.[107] Notwithstanding some weaknesses in its public consultation process,[108] it is reasonable to conclude that SEBI adheres to principles of fairness and transparency in a meaningful way, and is guided by reason and rationality to the extent possible, considering the size and complexity of India's securities market and SEBI's own resource and capacity limitations.

Complementing this substratum, SEBI's enforcement outcomes, discussed earlier in the chapter, highlight its actual use of its expansive powers of supervision, surveillance, investigation and enforcement, thus supporting the conclusion that SEBI is actively engaged in supervising and enforcing securities laws. That said, the data on SEBI's actions have several limitations that inhibit extraction of comprehensive trends and inferences. Among the limited inferences that may be drawn from the available data, SEBI's enforcement approach indicates a preference for using administrative measures over criminal.[109] Among administrative measures, SEBI relies most on:

1. taking prohibitive or remedial measures under s 11/11B of the *SEBI Act*, which includes restraining a person from accessing or dealing in securities markets, and suspension and cancellation of licences[110]

2. imposing regulatory penalties (adjudication), symbolising punitive action.[111]

Finally, SEBI's enforcement actions, when viewed against other significant indicators of the securities market, such as the size and number of market intermediaries, appear to be significantly low, possibly due to SEBI's own resource and capacity restraints, as described in Chapter 3.

Notwithstanding these constraints, it is important to point out that SEBI demonstrates expertise in several areas of enforcement and a strong commitment towards its regulatory objectives. Despite having a very

---

107 The SAT was set under the *SEBI Act* to hear appeals from SEBI's orders. In 2014, SAT's jurisdiction was increased to hear appeals from PFRDA and IRDA: see Securities Appellate Tribunal, 'About us', satweb.sat.gov.in/.

108 See the analysis in Chapter 3 of this book.

109 See the figures in Table 5.9 indicating SEBI's criminal prosecution cases as compared to SEBI's administrative actions under ss 11 and 11B of the *SEBI Act* as well as SEBI's adjudication measures during the selected period.

110 See Kanwardeep Singh Kapany, 'Dissecting SEBI's powers under section 11B of the SEBI Act, 1992: Part 1', *IndiaCorpLaw* (1 June 2015), indiacorplaw.in/2015/06/dissecting-sebis-powers-under-section_3.html.

111 See Table 5.4 indicating a total of 9,016 actions taken by SEBI under ss 11 and 11B in the selected period and Table 5.6 on adjudication proceedings indicating 3,894 actions initiated by SEBI.

small enforcement team,[112] SEBI has successfully investigated and pursued enforcement actions in prominent matters, particularly against Ponzi schemes and other collective investment scams. In the matter of *PACL Ltd*, SEBI charged the entity, PACL, of wrongfully raising approximately 49,000 crore rupees from various collective schemes without following SEBI's regulations and ordered a return of the amount collected by PACL to the investors.[113] The promoters and directors of PACL appealed to both the SAT and the Supreme Court, but lost both cases, with the Supreme Court upholding SEBI's order for the sale of PACL properties and return of the amount to PACL's investors.[114]

The PACL matter is worth highlighting, as it successfully tested SEBI's 'recovery' processes and attachment powers within India and, more importantly, its capabilities in effectively pursuing cases outside India— including before the Federal Court of Australia (FCA), Queensland.[115] As SEBI's annual report noted, the FCA pronounced its judgment in 2018[116] and lauded SEBI for handling the matter with 'commendable efficiency'. Subsequently, in its order in *Securities and Exchange Board of India and MII Resorts Group 1 Pty Ltd and Another* in 2018, the FCA ruled in favour of SEBI, and appointed a receiver for sale of the PACL properties and deposit of the proceeds to a trust account for ultimately being distributed to investors in India.[117] With the sale of these properties, an amount of A\$72.24 million was made available (after deductions of levies, council rates, stamp duty, taxation and other such expenses) and held in trust for distribution to the

112 SEBI's annual report for 2018–19 includes a section on human resources, but, again, the data collected under many important variables are either absent or significantly limited. For instance, the report states that the number of officers is 699, including 86 secretarial staff. But these data preclude any department-wise classification of officers. Even if these 600 or so officers were equally divided across SEBI's various departments, it would still indicate a very low number for SEBI's enforcement team.
113 SEBI, 'Frequently asked questions (FAQs) on auction of PACL properties', www.sebi.gov.in/17dec2015/pacl_eoi_faq.pdf. Also see SEBI's order dated 22 August 2014 against PACL Ltd.
114 See 'Recovery actions' in SEBI, *Annual Report 2016–17* (n 18).
115 In the PACL Ltd. matter, as PACL failed to wind up its existing schemes and refund an amount of 49,100 crore to the investors, as directed by SEBI's order dated 22 August 2014, SEBI initiated recovery proceedings against PACL's promoters and directors. SEBI filed a petition before the Federal Court of Australia claiming the assets that were acquired out of the money mobilised by PACL and diverted to Australia (Hotel Sheraton Mirage situated on the Gold Coast and two properties at Sanctuary Cove, Australia): see SEBI, 'Box 3.1: Extraterritorial recovery through Federal Court of Australia in the matter of PACL' in SEBI, *Annual Report 2018–19* (n 28).
116 SEBI, *Annual Report 2018–19* (n 28) 165.
117 Order of Justice Lee in *Securities and Exchange Board of India v MIIResorts Group 1 Pty Ltd* (Federal Court of Australia, QUD147/2017, 23 July 2018).

PACL investors.[118] In fact, SEBI has, time and again, pursued enforcement action against high-profile entities such as it did recently *In the Matter of Reliance Petroleum Limited (Now Known as Reliance Industries Limited)* by an order dated 1 January 2021 for manipulative trading in shares.[119] Earlier, in 2017, SEBI passed another order against Reliance Industries Ltd and other entities that was upheld by the SAT, with SEBI ordering a disgorgement of a substantial amount, thereby demonstrating the use of its disgorgement powers.[120] Similarly, SEBI's order *In the Case of NSE Colocation* against the NSE is noteworthy, as it demonstrates SEBI's efforts to pressure infrastructure institutions in the market to maintain high standards.[121] Such examples have contributed to SEBI's reputation as a purpose-driven and result-oriented regulator.

Putting aside these stellar enforcement outcomes, several shortcomings in SEBI's enforcement regime need to be highlighted. Raval observes that the effectiveness of SEBI's enforcement regime is thwarted by a number of factors, such as the provision for multiplicity of proceedings under the *SEBI Act*, which allows SEBI to initiate multiple actions simultaneously. This effectively allows SEBI's adjudicating officer (appointed in an adjudication or monetary penalty proceedings) and the whole time member (in an inquiry proceeding for action under s 11/11B of the *SEBI Act*) to arrive at different conclusions in respect of the same offence.[122] Further, traditionally,

---

118 During the course of the matter, the SEBI authorities became aware of another property and the FCA allowed SEBI to procure sufficient evidence to establish the fund trails: see SEBI, *Annual Report 2018–19* (n 28).

119 See *In the Matter of Reliance Petroleum Limited (now known as Reliance Industries Limited)* (Adjudication Order No Order/BD/AA/2020-21/10063-10066, 1 January 2021). See also 'RPL case: SEBI fines Reliance Industries, Mukesh Ambani, two other entities', *The Times of India* (1 January 2021), timesofindia.indiatimes.com/business/india-business/rpl-case-sebi-fines-reliance-industries-mukesh-ambani-two-other-entities/articleshow/80062975.cms.

120 By its order dated 24 March 2017, SEBI ordered RIL to disgorge Rs 447 crore: see 'RPL case' (n 119).

121 Against NSE, SEBI imposed a penalty of Rs 1 crore on NSE and 25 lakh each on former CEOs Narain and Ramakrishna in a co-location matter: see Ashish Rukhaiyar, 'Explained: the SEBI order against NSE, Ravi Narain and Chitra Ramakrishna', *Money Control* (11 February 2021), moneycontrol.com/news/business/companies/explained-the-sebi-order-against-nse-ravi-narain-and-chitra-ramakrishna-6491891.html.

122 Raval (n 33). To an extent, this issue has been addressed through subsequent amendments to the *SEBI Act* that allow SEBI's whole time members to levy monetary penalties, thus removing the necessity of pursuing separate adjudication proceedings for the same securities law offence. However, in theory, SEBI has the ability to initiate separate proceedings for the same offence.

SEBI was not empowered to review its own orders, [123] which placed added strain on SEBI when the SAT disagreed with SEBI's order and instead of asking SEBI to review it, set it aside.

A further limitation pointed out in respect of the *SEBI Act* is that it does not provide for private action in securities markets, but envisages SEBI to function as the sole custodian of investor interests. [124] However, the Financial Sector Assessment Program (FSAP) in 2013 noted that, though private action by a person was not explicitly provided for, it was not expressly barred by the *SEBI Act*. As a corollary, a person may in principle approach the Consumer Forum for remedies for 'deficiency of services' in respect of a securities markets intermediary, or against a broker before the arbitration panel under the by-laws of the stock exchanges, or seek a private action, civil as well as criminal, in respect of the offences covered by the *Companies Act 2013*. [125] Yet, as was recommended by the International Monetary Fund's (IMF's) FSAP Report of 2013, it would be beneficial to have an express recognition of private rights of action in the statute itself. [126]

In addition to these limitations, SEBI's enforcement and compliance regime is impacted by many issues prevalent in the larger financial laws framework in India as highlighted in the report by the High Level Committee on Financial Sector Reforms (Raghuram Rajan Committee) in 2008, including fragmentation, regulatory gaps, overlaps, arbitrage and balkanisation and capture by regulators. [127] Such fragmentation and regulatory gaps have manifested in scams, financial frauds and other nefarious financial activities, such as money laundering, [128] and are continuously challenging

---

123 Ibid 32. This issue has been partly addressed through subsequent amendments to the *SEBI Act* that allow SEBI's adjudication orders levying monetary penalties to be sent back for review.

124 Sections 20A and 15Y of the *SEBI Act* authorise only SEBI to take action for any violation of the statutes and the regulations framed thereunder. Moreover, the jurisdiction of civil courts is barred from taking any matters of securities laws that fall within the ambit of the adjudicating officer, the SAT or SEBI. Jackson and Roe discuss the advantages and disadvantages of 'public' and 'private' enforcement of securities law: see Jackson and Roe (n 1).

125 See IMF, *India FSAP Report* (n 68) 44. Under the *Companies Act*, Indian citizens may file civil suits before NCLT seeking remedies against companies in respect of issues arising under the *Companies Act*.

126 Ibid 20.

127 The report also notes this as a potentially dangerous situation where no regulatory entity bears the full responsibility for the problems in the sector: see Government of India Planning Commission, *A Hundred Small Steps* (Report of the Committee on Financial Sector Reforms, 2008) 124–129. Refer to Chapter 2 on SEBI's financial framework and architecture.

128 In the context of collective investment schemes, chit funds and deposit-taking activities, the Raghuram Rajan Committee's Report remarks on the RBI's reluctance to assume full responsibility in certain cases such as for 'supervising cooperative banks' and the state governments' unwillingness to give up the responsibility: see ibid. Financial frauds and scams have been on the rise. A recent scam was the Punjab National Bank

SEBI's enforcement and compliance regime. The Raghuram Rajan Report further noted that the corrective measures and reforms that followed incidents of fraud and failures were rushed in a reactive manner, and the knee-jerk reaction to legislation left the financial sector in a haphazard and complex state, once again paving the way for more gaps and regulatory arbitrage.[129] The two collective investment scams of recent years, Sahara[130] and Saradha,[131] bear testimony to the problems of a fragmented approach to financial and securities regulation in India. This problem is unlikely to be addressed without a systematic overhaul of the financial sector architecture,

---

fraud, which the RBI described as 'a case of operational risk' arising from 'delinquent behavior by the bank's employees'. See Navmi Krishna, 'All you need to know about Nirav Modi and the $1.77 billion PNB fraud', *The Hindu* (14 February 2018); Tamal Bandyopadhyay, 'The anatomy of the PNB fraud', *Live Mint* (19 February 2018), livemint.com/Opinion/oiMKS98wBunYNviWCVq6hJ/The-anatomy-of-the-PNB-fraud.html; Nigam Prusty, 'Before mega scam, PNB lost $431 million to fraud last fiscal year', *Reuters* (9 March 2018), www.reuters.com/article/business/before-mega-scam-india-s-pnb-lost-431-million-to-fraud-last-fiscal-year-idUSKCN1GL1CO/; Satwik Gade and Radhika Merwin, 'Deconstructing the PNB scam: a graphic story', *The Hindu* (28 February 2018), thehindu.com/news/national/deconstructing-the-pnb-scam-a-graphic-story/article22874585.ece; Meetu Jain, 'On Nirav Modi fraud, PNB's damning report: last RBI audit in 2009, accounting software unlinked for years', *India Today* (27 February 2018), indiatoday.in/india/story/last-audit-by-rbi-was-done-in-2009-pnb-tells-govt-in-its-report-on-nirav-modi-fraud-1178522-2018-02-27.

129 Financial and securities market scams are representative of a wide spectrum of issues prevailing in the Indian financial regulatory framework that range from 'low tolerance for innovation and excessive micro-management', to 'regulatory gaps and overlaps', to 'balkanization and capture': see Government of India Planning Commission (n 127).

130 Similarly, in the Sahara scandal, two companies—Sahara India Real Estate Corporation and Sahara Housing and Investment Corporation—issued optionally fully convertible debentures and raised money through private placements, which it contended did not fall within the ambit of SEBI: see Raghuvir Srinivasan, 'The man who nailed Sahara', *The Hindu* (23 May 2016), thehindu.com/business/Industry/the-man-who-nailed-sahara/article5754009.ece. However, SEBI contended that the offering did fall within its regulatory purview on the grounds that it was made to 50 or more persons. 'SIREC alone showed about 6.6 million investors in its scheme' and when SEBI conducted 'a random test of four addresses in Mumbai', the fraudulent nature of Sahara's claim that there were genuine investors in the scheme stood exposed. SEBI's order against Sahara, upheld by the Supreme Court, inter alia stated that there was use of 'fictitious investors' for money laundering: see '"Money did not fall from heaven": Tell us how you raised Rs 25,000 crore in cash, SC asks Sahara', *The Times of India* (2 September 2016), timesofindia.indiatimes.com/india/Money-did-not-fall-from-heaven-Tell-us-how-you-raised-Rs-25000-crore-in-cash-SC-asks-Sahara/articleshow/53982317.cms; Priti Verma, 'Strategic integration of genuine CSR, spiritualism, ethics and communication: farsighted foundation of emerging economy' (2016) 6(4) *Effective Communication, Management and Organisational Growth* 129. On 4 March 2014, Subrata Roy, the Sahara Group's chief, was imprisoned: see Dr Ukey and L Krishnarao, 'The swindlers of corporate world: anatomy of NSEL scam and an overview of other corporate scams in India and abroad' (2014) 3(2) *International Journal of Entrepreneurship and Business Environment Perspectives* 881–888; Vaishali Khandelwal, 'Sahara India's downturn: a study on awareness and customer's perspectives' (2017) 3(3) *Imperial Journal of Interdisciplinary Research*.

131 The Saradha scam, a Ponzi scheme, adversely affected over 1.7 million investors, and collected US$4–6 billion before its collapse in April 2013: see 'RBI, Sebi come together to prevent Saradha like scam: launch website to prevent scams', *The Economic Times* (5 August 2016) economictimes.indiatimes.com/markets/stocks/policy/rbi-sebi-come-together-to-prevent-saradha-like-scam-launch-website-to-prevent-scams/articleshow/53550036.cms.

as recommended by the Financial Sector Legislative Regulatory Reforms Commission (FSLRC),[132] but that is yet to be fully implemented (as discussed in Chapter 2 of this book).

While securities market scandals in the early part of this century, particularly the Ketan Parekh[133] and the Satyam[134] scams, underscored some problems associated with fragmentation and gaps in the financial sector, other examples have highlighted further shortcomings across the financial sector, including the non-deterrent effects of the regulatory regime, and inadequacies in the risk evaluation, management and enforcement abilities of the regulatory authorities.[135]

The implementation of accounting and auditing standards, which falls outside SEBI's remit, is another area of widespread concern. The misuse of powers by auditors and their under-regulation were underscored in two significant financial market failures: the Satyam[136] and the Punjab National Bank scams.[137] These scams exposed other inadequacies, too, in technological

132 The 2013 FSLRC report recommended improving the regulatory architecture with more streamlined micro and macro prudential structures to tackle the problems of 'regulatory gaps, overlaps, inconsistencies and arbitrage': see *Report of the Financial Sector Legislative Reforms Commission* (22 March 2013).

133 The Ketan Parekh scam involved the rampant misuse of d-mat accounts. See Ana Carvajal and Jennifer Elliott, *The Challenge of Enforcement in Securities Markets: Mission Impossible?* (IMF Working Paper No 09/168, 2009), doi.org/10.2139/ssrn.1457591. See also Lalit Wadhwa and Virender Pal, 'Forensic accounting and fraud examination in India' (2012) 7(11) *International Journal of Applied Engineering Research* 10.

134 The Satyam scam displayed a complex matrix of political and financial connections, illegal transactions, accounting scams, poor internal controls and weak corporate governance: see Sandeep Gopalan, 'Punjab National Bank scam is an opportunity to reform India's public sector banks', *Faculty of Law, University of Oxford* (Blog Post, 1 March 2018), law.ox.ac.uk/business-law-blog/blog/2018/03/punjab-national-bank-scam-opportunity-reform-indias-public-sector; Gurbandini Kaur and Richa Mishra, 'Corporate governance failure in India: a study of academicians'' perception' (2010) 9(1/2) *IUP Journal of Corporate Governance*. See also Shradhanjali Panda and Anita Mishra, 'Corporate governance: journey of "Satyam" to "Mahindra Satyam": the way ahead' (2011) 1(1) *Kushagra International Management Review* 32.

135 See Madan Lal Bhasin, 'Menace of frauds in the Indian banking industry: an empirical study' (2015) 4(12) *Australian Journal of Business and Management Research* 1–13, doi.org/10.52283/NSWRCA.AJBMR.20150412A02; Richa Bhatia, 'PNB scam—can data and analytics clean up the mess?', *Analytics India Magazine* (19 February 2018); Eswar S Prasad, *Financial Sector Regulation and Reforms in Emerging Markets: An Overview* (National Bureau of Economic Research Working Paper No 16428, 2010), doi.org/10.3386/w16428.

136 See (n 134).

137 See Gopalan (n 134). For a clear understanding of the PNB scam, see Navmi Krishna, 'All you need to know about Nirav Modi and the $1.77-billion PNB fraud', *The Hindu* (14 February 2018), thehindu.com/business/Industry/all-you-need-to-know-about-nirav-modi-and-the-177-billion-pnb-fraud/article22753973.ece; Bandyopadhyay (n 128); 'PNB fraud: In a first, RBI officials examined by CBI', *Financial Express* (6 April 2018), financialexpress.com/industry/banking-finance/pnb-fraud-in-a-first-rbi-officials-examined-by-cbi/1123452/.

infrastructure, practices and supervision, and poor auditing regulations across the financial markets in India, and eventually led to the setting up of a new body, the National Financial Reporting Authority for auditing oversight.[138] This challenge is not limited to the securities markets, but extends across the financial markets in India. A report published by Deloitte in 2014, the *Indian Banking Fraud Survey Edition II*, highlighted challenges relating to a 'lack of oversight by line managers or senior management, business pressures to meet unrealistic targets, lack of tools to identify frauds, software and staff collusion' within companies and organisations in the financial sector.[139] Many of these issues extended to public sector organisations and even regulatory bodies, including the Reserve Bank of India and SEBI, particularly in relation to their 'supervisory capacity to conduct forensic audits', which needed to be 'strengthened with human as well as technological resources'.[140]

However, despite these shortcomings, SEBI's enforcement regime is fundamentally driven by an openness to reform. SEBI's proclivity towards continuous improvement is clearly evidenced by its regular appointment of internal committees, as well as high-level external committees, that recommend measures to further strength the existing regime. A fine example of this is the high-level committee under the chairmanship of Justice AR

---

138 TCA Sharad Raghavan, 'What is National Financial Reporting Authority', *The Hindu* (17 March 2018), www.thehindu.com/business/Economy/what-is-national-financial-reporting-authority/article2 3280972.ece. On the lack of supervision in auditing, see Richa Roy, Krishnamurthy Subramanian and Shamika Ravi, 'How to solve issue of rising non-performing assets in Indian public sector banks', *Brookings* (Blog Post, 1 March 2018), brookings.edu/blog/up-front/2018/03/01/how-to-solve-issue-of-rising-non-performing-assets-in-indian-public-sector-banks/; Palak Shah, 'PNB-Nirav Modi fraud: a replay of the Ketan Parekh scam of 2001', *Business Line* (14 February 2018), thehindubusinessline.com/money-and-banking/pnb-niravmodi-fraud-a-replay-of-the-ketan-parekh-scam-of-2001/article22754605.ece.
139 The survey highlights the ineffectiveness of post facto mechanisms in fraud detection, noting that frauds are discovered primarily by customer-complaints, whistleblowers or anonymous tips: see Deloitte, *India Banking Fraud Survey Edition II* (2015). See also Srikanth Srinivas, 'PNB Fraud: banks will have to be equipped with better risk management tools as NPAs pile-up', *Firstpost* (16 February 2018), firstpost. com/business/pnb-fraud-banks-will-have-to-be-equipped-with-better-risk-management-tools-as-npas-pile-up-4354027.html.
140 Roy, Subramanian and Ravi (n 138) 62; Venkatesan R, 'SEBI launches prosecution in 568 CIS cases, 1,100 others', *Business Line* (29 December 2016), thehindubusinessline.com/markets/sebi-launches-prosecution-in-568-cis-cases-1100-others/article9449534.ece. The regulators' lack of capabilities led to questions—such as 'Who's afraid of the RBI'—that displayed an absence of fear of the regulatory as well as the enforcement regime that failed to spot, let alone take severe action, in respect of a fraud: see Saubhik Chakrabarti, 'View: RBI needs to make an example out of guilty banks'; *The Economic Times* (20 February 2018) economictimes.indiatimes.com/industry/banking/finance/banking/rbi-needs-to-make-an-example-out-of-banks-guilty-banks/articleshow/62988814.cms.

Dave, retired judge, Supreme Court of India, that submitted the *Report on the Measures for Strengthening the Enforcement Mechanism of the Board and Incidental Issues* to SEBI.[141]

This shows that, broadly, SEBI's regime is built on a progressive outlook, with SEBI striving to adopt best practices and engage in a collaborative manner that is beneficial to all stakeholders. To this end, SEBI has prioritised the use of technology in its supervisory and enforcement functions. Leveraging India's information technology (IT) prowess, SEBI has introduced several reforms, upgrades and automation in processes. An ongoing example is the project for automation of inspection and surveillance of mutual funds.[142] Such technological developments aim to smooth issues and strengthen SEBI's oversight and supervisory regime.

The IMF–World Bank's FSAP Report in 2013 gave SEBI a 'partly implemented' grade in respect of IOSCO Principle 10 (corresponding to current IOSCO Principle 12) on credible and effective use of its inspection, investigation, surveillance and enforcement powers and the effectiveness of its compliance regime.[143]

Conclusion

The analysis of SEBI's supervision and enforcement statistics and underlying principles reveals some of SEBI's strengths and weaknesses as a regulator. SEBI is an active and engaged regulator that uses its wide powers unhesitatingly but with due regard to principles of transparency and natural justice. SEBI's enforcement actions demonstrate that it is a purpose-driven regulator fully invested in enforcement matters, and that it pursues these vigorously to fulfil its regulatory objectives, especially for investor protection. However, SEBI's compliance regime is significantly challenged by external problems emerging from a large, complex and fragmented financial sector, and dragged down by severe internal constraints around human resources and capacity, something of general concern for regulators in India.[144]

---

141 *Measures for Strengthening the Enforcement Mechanism of the Board and Incidental Issues, High Level Committee* (Report of High Level Committee under the chairmanship of Justice (Ret'd) Anil R Dave, 16 June 2020).

142 SEBI, *Annual Report 2018–19* (n 28) 142.

143 See IMF, *India FSAP Report* (n 68) 15.

144 Shubho Roy et al, 'Building state capacity for regulation' in Kapur and Khosla (eds) (n 41).

Despite impressive reforms in its supervisory approach and some remarkable enforcement outcomes, SEBI's supervisory and enforcement regime has more distance to cover before it attains its full potential. SEBI's degree of alignment with the core requirements of IOSCO Principle 12 is currently determined as 'moderate'. SEBI's use of its supervision and enforcement powers is predicated upon sound underlying principles of natural justice and transparency that, in practice, require further fine-tuning and strengthening. Thus, the stage of evolution of SEBI's supervisory and enforcement toolkit is assessed as 'evolving'. Finally, frequent reviews and reform by SEBI to improve its supervisory and enforcement capacity and performance indicate that the extent of change in recent years in this area has been 'substantial'.

ASIC

Building on the assessment of the adequacy of ASIC's powers in Chapter 4, this section evaluates the 'use' and 'implementation' of ASIC's powers and the enforcement provisions on the ground, and assesses the overall effectiveness of ASIC's enforcement and compliance regime. To this end, ASIC's enforcement outputs for the period between FY 2014–15 and December 2019 (ASIC's selected period) are outlined below, followed by an analysis.

Key empirical data on ASIC's enforcement actions

Since July 2011, ASIC has published six-monthly reports or updates on its enforcement actions, called 'ASIC Enforcement Outcome Reports'.[145] These reports aim at increasing the level of transparency with respect to ASIC's enforcement actions,[146] and the data in these reports are presented within ASIC's four strategic work areas: 'market integrity', 'corporate governance', 'financial services' and 'small business compliance and deterrence'.[147]

The main enforcement tools in relation to which ASIC's data are collated and published are outlined below, followed by a presentation of tables, figures and trends relating to ASIC's enforcement actions for its selected period.

---

145 Until the end of June 2019, ASIC has published 16 enforcement outcome reports: see ASIC, 'ASIC enforcement outcomes: past periodic reports' asic.gov.au/about-asic/asic-investigations-and-enforcement/asic-enforcement-outcomes/.
146 ASIC, *ASIC Enforcement Outcomes: July to December 2011* (Report 281, 2011) 5.
147 See ASIC, *ASIC Enforcement Update: January to June 2019* (Report 625, 2019) 2.

ASIC's main enforcement mechanisms

As explained in Chapter 4, ASIC utilises five main enforcement tools and publishes six-monthly data on the use of these tools:

- *Criminal proceedings*: refers to ASIC's punitive actions and represent data on criminal action and criminal financial penalties.
- *Civil proceedings*: refers to ASIC's punitive or corrective or compensatory action in respect of market offences and include civil penalties and any other court-based civil action such as an injunction or a winding-up order.
- *Administrative outcomes*: refers to the protective remedies that ASIC uses independently and includes issue of warning or infringement notices and power to cancel or vary a licence or ban entities from the market.
- *Enforceable undertakings or negotiated or remediation outcomes*: refers to ASIC's settlement powers under which it can negotiate or settle certain matters.
- *Warning notices*: refers to ASIC's administrative powers to issue a warning notice for certain offences.

Tables, figures and trends on ASIC's enforcement actions

This subsection provides tables and figures on ASIC's enforcement data for its selected period. Table 5.15 presents a detailed picture of ASIC's enforcement outcomes as published in its six-monthly updates for the period between FY2014–15 and December 2019 (ASIC's selected period). ASIC's enforcement actions are presented within the five most used categories of enforcement outcomes: 'criminal', 'civil', 'administrative', 'enforceable undertakings/negotiated/remediation outcomes' and 'warning notices'. Further, these enforcement outcomes represent the following strategic work categories. Within market integrity, the enforcement outcomes are divided into five subcategories: 'insider trading', 'market manipulation', 'continuous disclosure', 'market integrity rules' and 'other market misconduct'. Corporate governance is subcategorised as 'action against directors', 'misconduct related to insolvency', 'action against auditors', 'action against liquidators' and 'other corporate governance misconduct'. Similarly, financial services is divided into 'unlicensed conduct', 'dishonest conduct/misleading statements', 'misappropriation/theft/fraud', 'misconduct related to fraud', 'misconduct related to credit' and 'other financial services misconduct'. Finally, small business compliance and deterrence includes 'action against persons or companies' and action for 'misconduct related to registration and licensing'. While ASIC's enforcement data for small business compliance are included in Table 5.15, they are not analysed for the purposes of this chapter, as the main focus is on ascertaining the enforcement and compliance regime relating to securities violations.

Table 5.15 does not just detail the aggregate number of actions in each category for ASIC's selected period, but also presents more granular data, such as the exact six-monthly number of enforcement outcomes for each category. For instance, the first row of data for market integrity provides information about ASIC's aggregate enforcement outcomes across the five 'outcome categories'. Thus, it is clear that ASIC took 38 criminal actions and 20 civil actions; completed 82 administrative outcomes and 18 enforceable undertakings/negotiated/remediated outcomes; and, finally, issued zero warning notices in the selected period. Further, in each cell of the table, six-monthly data can be viewed under the aggregate number of actions. For example, within the market integrity row, the first cell shows the aggregate number of criminal actions as '38' as well as the six-monthly data that are recorded in chronological order within brackets as '(3+2+3+3+1+1+0+0+1+2+0)' from 11 of ASIC's enforcement updates published for ASIC's selected period. Thus, the first value '3' corresponds to the number of criminal actions undertaken by ASIC in the six-month period between 1 July 2014 and 31 December 2014 for market integrity offences; the value '2' relates to 1 January 2015 – 30 June 2015 and so forth; and the last value within the brackets above '0' stands for zero criminal actions taken by ASIC in the market integrity category between 1 July 2019 and 31 December 2019.

Finally, along with the six-monthly data, Table 5.15 presents the aggregate enforcement action figures for each category and subcategory of misconduct through ASIC's selected period that are used to extrapolate varying trends and developments in ASIC's enforcement regime. The data from Table 5.15 are extracted into graphs (figures) and trends to present the significant enforcement trends for ASIC's selected period.

Table 5.15: Aggregate of ASIC's enforcement actions from FY 2014–15 to 31 Dec 2019

Area/type of misconduct	Criminal	Civil	Administrative outcomes	Enforceable undertakings/ negotiated/ remediation outcomes	Warning notice	Total actions
Market integrity	38 (8+4+7+6+2+ 4+1+1+3+1)	20 (0+0+1+0+6+ 1+3+2+2+1+4)	82 (9+5+10+8+6+ 12+16+2+5+7+2)	18 (3+0+2+1+2+2+ 5+1+2+0+0)	0 (0+0+0+0+0+ 0+0+0+0+0)	158
Insider trading	16 (3+2+3+3+1+ 1+0+0+1+2+0)	2 (0+0+1+0+1+0+ 0+0+0+0+0)	1 (0+0+0+0+0+0+ 1+0+0+0+0)	2 (0+0+2+0+0+0+ 0+0+0+0)	0 (0+0+0+0+0+0+ 0+0+0+0)	21
Market manipulation	8 (2+2+2+0+0+0+ 0+1+0+0+1)	1 (0+0+0+0+0+0+ 0+0+1+0+0)	4 (0+1+0+0+0+0+ 2+0+0+1+0)	0 (0+0+0+0+0+0+ 0+0+0+0)	0 (0+0+0+0+0+0+ 0+0+0+0)	13
Continuous disclosure	2 (0+0+0+1+0+1+ 0+0+0+0+0)	5 (0+0+0+0+3+0+ 1+0+0+0+1)	17 (1+2+4+3+1+0+ 4+0+1+0+1)	2 (1+0+0+1+0+0+ 0+0+0+0)	0 (0+0+0+0+0+0+ 0+0+0+0)	26
Market integrity rules	0 (0+0+0+0+0+0+ 0+0+0+0)	1 (0+0+0+0+0+0+ 0+0+1+0+0)	40 (8+2+5+4+3+9+ 6+1+1+0+1)	2 (0+0+0+0+0+0+ 2+0+0+0)	0 (0+0+0+0+0+0+ 0+0+0+0)	43
Other market misconduct	12 (3+0+2+2+1+2+ 1+0+0+1+0)	11 (0+0+0+0+2+1+ 2+2+0+1+3)	20 (0+0+1+1+2+3+ 3+1+3+5+1)	12 (2+0+0+2+2+ 3+1+2+0+0)	0 (0+0+0+0+0+0+ 0+0+0+0)	55
Corporate governance	38 (7+4+4+8+4+3+ 2+1+2+2+1)	56 (5+3+5+4+3+2+ 13+1+18+1+1)	152 (21+19+19+15+19+3+ 5+8+9+11+23)	36 (1+3+7+7+6+2+ 5+4+1+0)	0 (0+0+0+0+0+0+ 0+0+0+0)	282
Action against directors	33 (7+4+3+7+3+2+ 2+1+2+1+1)	14 (4+2+4+0+2+1+ 0+0+0+0+1)	21 (0+5+4+4+1+1+ 1+0+3+0+2)	3 (0+0+0+0+0+0+ 0+3+0+0)	0 (0+0+0+0+0+0+ 0+0+0+0)	71

Area/type of misconduct	Criminal	Civil	Administrative outcomes	Enforceable undertakings/ negotiated/ remediation outcomes	Warning notice	Total actions
Misconduct related to insolvency	2 (0+0+1+0+1+0+ 0+0+0+0+0)	3 (0+0+0+0+0+1+ 2+0+0+0+0)	14 (0+12+0+0+0+0+ 0+0+0+2+0)	0 (0+0+0+0+0+0+ 0+0+0+0+0)	0 (0+0+0+0+0+0+ 0+0+0+0+0)	19
Action against auditors	0 (0+0+0+0+0+0+ 0+0+0+0+0)	0 (0+0+0+0+0+0+ 0+0+0+0+0)	54 (1+0+5+0+2+1+ 4+7+6+8+20)	5 (1+1+0+1+0+0+ 1+1+0+0+0)	0 (0+0+0+0+0+0+ 0+0+0+0+0)	59
Action against liquidators	3 (0+0+0+1+0+1+ 0+0+0+1+0)	5 (1+1+0+0+0+0+ 0+1+1+1+0)	7 (1+1+0+0+2+0+ 0+1+0+1+1)	25 (0+2+6+5+6+2+ 3+0+1+0+0)	0 (0+0+0+0+0+0+ 0+0+0+0+0)	40
Other corporate governance misconduct	0 (0+0+0+0+0+0+ 0+0+0+0+0)	34 (0+0+1+4+1+0+ 11+0+17+0+0)	56 (19+1+10+11+14+1+ 0+0+0+0+0)	3 (0+0+1+1+0+0+ 1+0+0+0+0)	0 (0+0+0+0+0+0+C+ 0+0+0+0+0)	93
Financial services	57 (7+5+3+8+5+3+ 8+2+6+3+7)	139 (14+8+12+7+14+14+ 26+16+9+12+7)	604 (50+50+67+48+77+118+ 48+49+32+28+37)	197 (18+15+32+27+34+10+ 23+17+9+8+4)	4 (1+3+0+0+0+0+ 0+0+0+0+0)	1001
Unlicensed conduct	2 (1+0+0+0+0+0+ 0+1+0+0+0)	2 (0+0+0+0+0+0+ 0+0+2+0+0)	2 (0+0+0+1+0+ 0+0+1+0+0)	23 (0+0+2+0+21+0+ 0+0+0+0+0)	2 (0+2+0+0+0+0+ 0+0+0+0+C)	31
Dishonest conduct, misleading statements	21 (1+2+0+3+2+1+ 4+1+2+2+3)	73 (8+6+9+6+7+2+ 23+2+3+3+4)	114 (9+9+18+10+22+8+ 8+12+7+7+4)	13 (2+0+2+2+1+1+ 4+0+1+0+0)	0 (0+0+0+0+0+0+ 0+0+0+0+0)	221
Misappropriation, theft, fraud	8 (1+0+0+2+1+0+ 0+0+1+1+2)	9 (0+0+0+0+0+0+ 0+2+2+3+2)	24 (2+4+2+2+4+ 0+4+1+2+1)	0 (0+0+0+0+0+0+ 0+0+0+0+0)	0 (0+0+0+0+0+0- 0+0+0+0+0I)	41

Area/type of misconduct	Criminal	Civil	Administrative outcomes	Enforceable undertakings/ negotiated/ remediation outcomes	Warning notice	Total actions
Misconduct related to credit	19 (2+2+3+2+2+2+ 2+0+3+0+1)	15 (1+1+2+0+2+3+ 0+6+0+0+0)	262 (12+21+31+26+34+80+ 23+16+11+0+8)	45 (7+4+4+8+3+1+ 9+5+3+0+1)	0 (0+0+0+0+0+0+ 0+0+0+0+0)	341
Other financial services misconduct	7 (2+1+0+1+0+0+ 2+0+0+0+1)	40 (5+1+1+5+9+ 3+6+4+4+1)	202 (27+16+16+10+18+26+ 17+17+12+19+24)	116 (9+11+24+17+9+8+ 10+12+5+8+3)	2 (1+1+0+0+0+0+ 0+0+0+0+0)	367
Subtotal of three areas	**133**	**215**	**838**	**251**	**4**	**1,441**
Small business compliance and deterrence	2,211 (182+192+222+202+ 244+203*+241+183+ 185+197+160)	0 (0+0+0+0+0+0+ 0+0+0+0+0)	291 (21+12+14+16+12+18+ 27+17+43+81+30)	0 (0+0+0+0+0+0+ 0+0+0+0+0)	1 (1+0+0+0+0+0+ 0+0+0+0+0)	2,503
Action against directors/ persons/ companies	2,083 (172+182+194+190+ 227+191+232+176+ 168+196+155)	0 (0+0+0+0+0+0+ 0+0+0+0+0)	291 (21+12+14+16+12+18+ 27+17+43+81+30)	0 (0+0+0+0+0+0+ 0+0+0+0+0)	0 (1+0+0+0+0+0+ 0+0+0+0+0)	2,374
Efficient registration and licensing	128 (10+10+28+12+ 17+12+9+7+ 17+1+5)	0 (0+0+0+0+0+0+ 0+0+0+0+0)	0 (0+0+0+0+0+0+ 0+0+0+0+0)	0 (0+0+0+0+0+0+ 0+0+0+0+0)	0 (0+0+0+0+0+0+ 0+0+0+0+0)	128
Total of all enforcement actions	**2344**	**215**	**1129**	**251**	**5**	**3944**

Note: * Incorrectly stated as 213: data on p 22 of the *ASIC Enforcement Outcomes: January to June 2017* (Report 536, 2017).

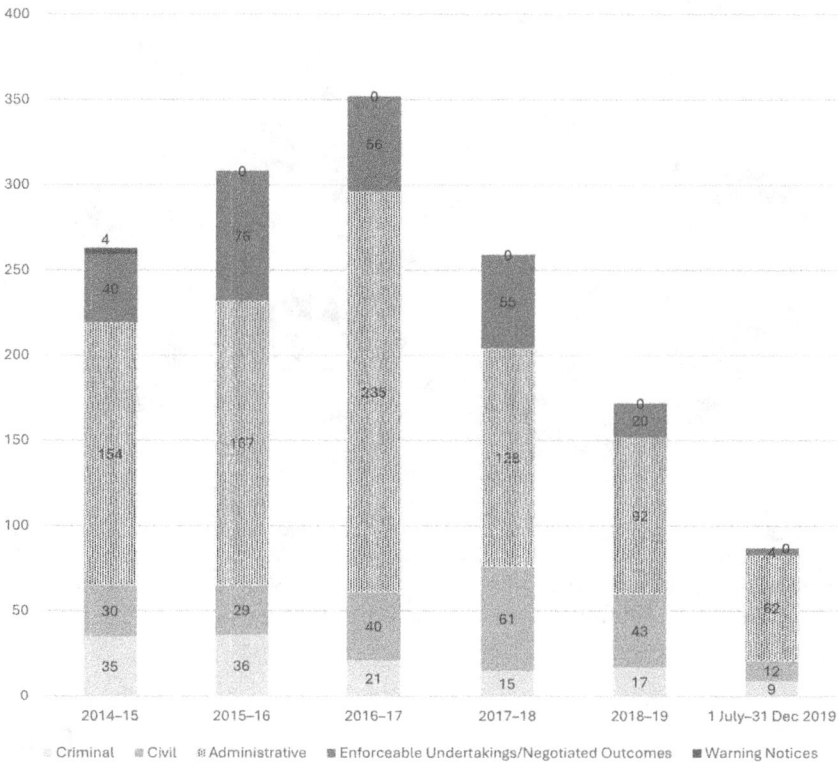

Figure 5.11: ASIC's Annual Enforcement Outcomes data (excluding actions against small businesses)
Source: Author's research.

Figure 5.11 illustrates the data on ASIC's completed enforcement outcomes for the selected period. The data reveal ASIC's year-wise number of enforcement actions across three main categories: market integrity, corporate governance and financial services.[148] 'Administrative outcomes' were, consistently, the leading form of action adopted by ASIC. 'Enforceable undertakings/negotiated outcomes' and 'civil action' form the next category of ASIC's most used enforcement tools, while 'criminal remedies' were, relatively, the least used form of action in the selected period. There were only four warning notices issued in FY 2014–15. Pertinently, while ASIC's enforcement actions observed an ascending trend from FY 2014–15 to FY 2016–17, there is a noticeable decline across all enforcement categories from FY 2017–18.

---

148 The figure excludes enforcement data for the 'small business' category.

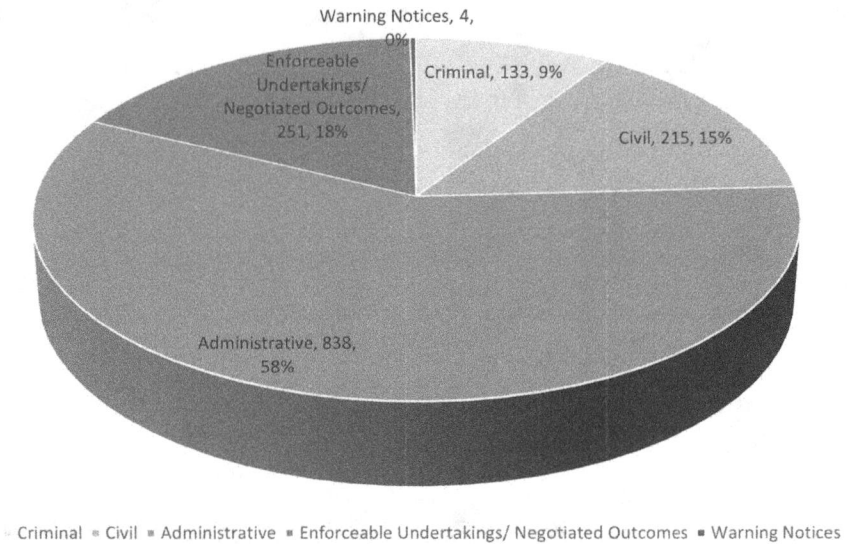

Criminal ■ Civil ■ Administrative ■ Enforceable Undertakings/ Negotiated Outcomes ■ Warning Notices

Figure 5.12: ASIC's aggregate enforcement (completed) outcomes for market integrity, financial services and corporate governance
Source: Author's research.

Figure 5.12 delineates the aggregate number and precise percentage of enforcement actions adopted during ASIC's selected period. In the administrative category, ASIC completed 838 enforcement actions that amount to 58 per cent of its total enforcement actions; 251 outcomes, or 18 per cent of ASIC's total enforcement outcomes, were in the enforceable undertakings/negotiated outcomes category for the stated time period. In the civil actions category, ASIC completed 215 cases, amounting to 15 per cent, while in the criminal category it undertook 133 enforcement actions, which was 10 per cent of its total enforcement outcomes. A negligible number of cases are evident in the public warning category for this period.

Figure 5.13 demonstrates the pattern of ASIC's completed enforcement outcomes (excluding the figures for small businesses) across the categories of market integrity, corporate governance and financial services. The graph also presents six-monthly figures for enforcement actions. It clearly shows a descending trend for enforcement actions in the financial services category, while the actions in market integrity and corporate governance follow a stable trend.

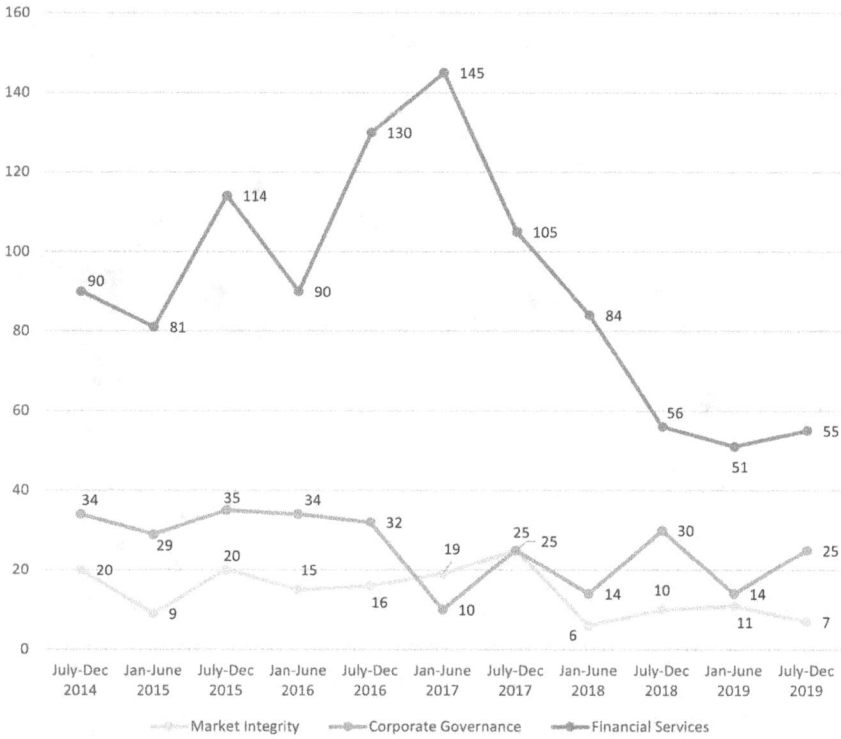

Figure 5.13: ASIC's enforcement outcome pattern for market integrity, financial services and corporate governance
Source: Author's research.

Figure 5.14 illustrates the use of various enforcement tools by ASIC across the categories of market integrity, financial services and corporate governance. The data exclude enforcement outcomes in the small business category. The figure shows that administrative outcomes, the most used form of enforcement action, peaked in FY 2016–17 before dropping over the next two years. Enforceable undertakings and civil actions were, largely, on a stable trend, though far less used than the administrative actions. Criminal outcomes, among the least used enforcement options, showed a slight declining trend across the five-year period.

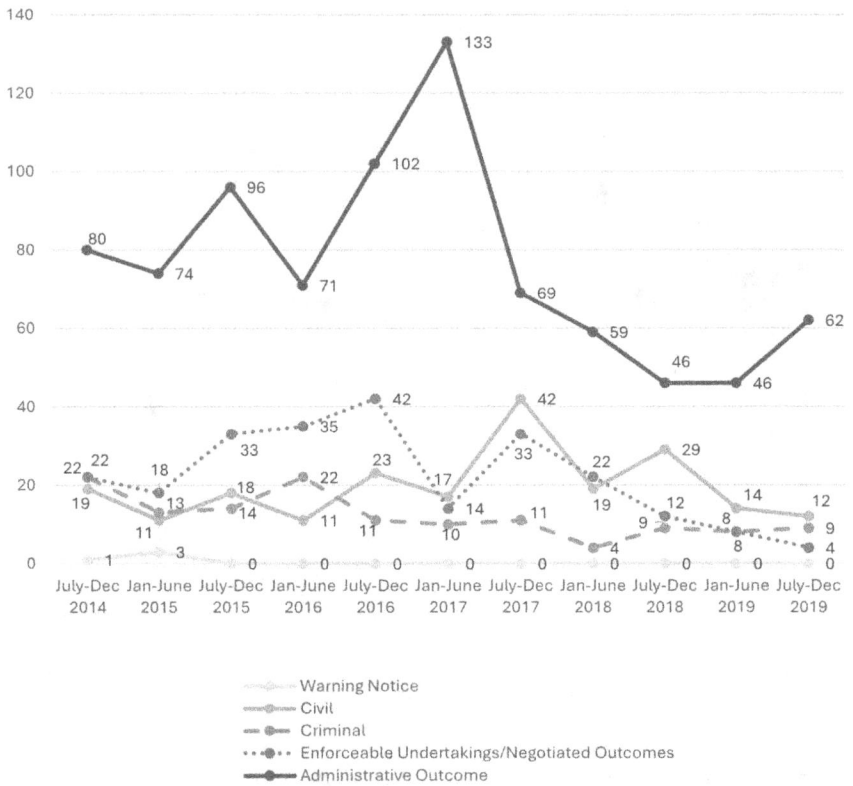

Figure 5.14: Pattern in the use of the enforcement methods by ASIC: civil, criminal, enforceable undertakings/negotiated outcomes, administrative outcomes and warning notices

Source: Author's research.

Figure 5.15 reveals significant facts about ASIC's overall enforcement outcomes over the FY 2014–15 to December 2019 period. First, 2,503 actions, the highest among ASIC's total enforcement actions, occurred in the small business compliance and deterrence category. This is followed by the financial services category, which observed 1,001 outcomes, followed by the corporate governance category at 282 actions. The 'market integrity' category witnessed the least number of outcomes at 159.

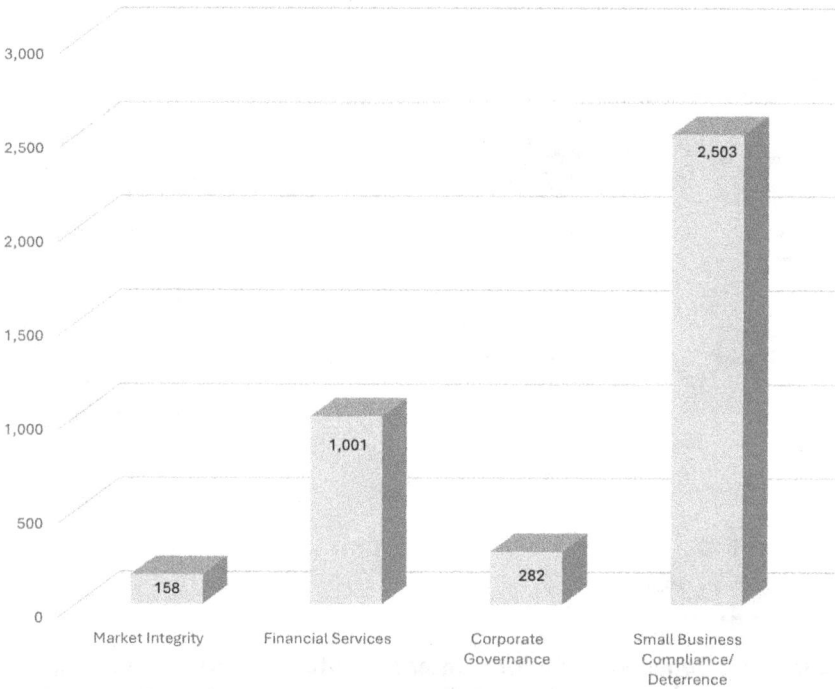

Figure 5.15: Aggregate enforcement outcomes by regulatory area: market integrity, financial services, corporate governance and small business compliance/deterrence

Source: Author's research.

Figure 5.16 demonstrates the data and patterns of the enforcement outcomes within the market integrity category. ASIC's enforcement data are provided for insider trading, market manipulation, continuous disclosure, market integrity rules and other market misconduct. As seen above, the total number of enforcement outcomes in the market integrity category was 158 for the period between FY 2014–15 and December 2019. Of these, the total number of outcomes for insider trading was 21, for market manipulation 13, continuous disclosure 26, for breach of market integrity rules 43 and other market misconduct 55.

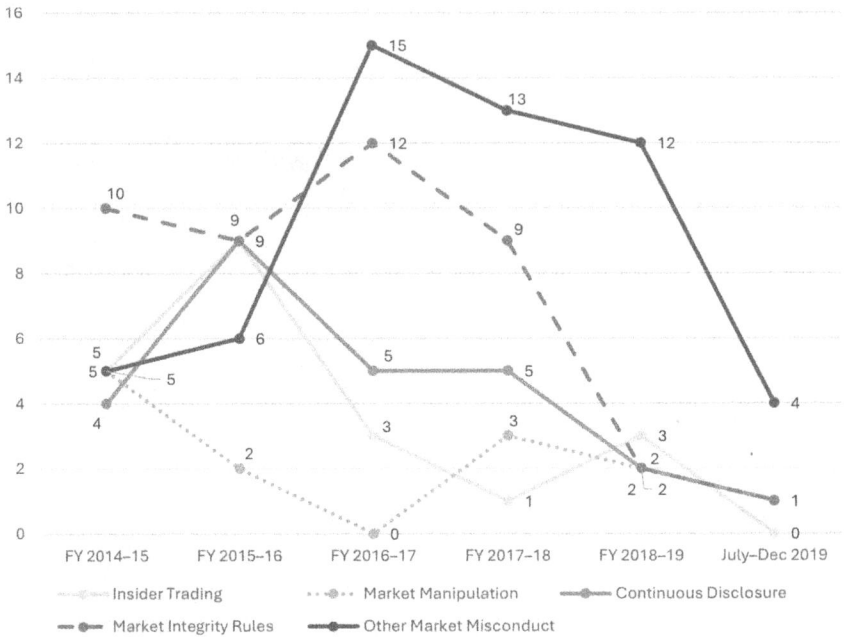

Figure 5.16: Consolidated market integrity outcomes: Insider trading, market manipulation, continuous disclosure, breach of market integrity rules and other market misconduct

Source: Author's research.

Figure 5.17 illustrates that ASIC's most used form of enforcement action for preserving market integrity over the FY 2014–15 to December 2019 period was administrative, with 82 outcomes for the entire period, amounting to 52 per cent of the total market integrity outcomes. There were 38 criminal outcomes in the category, amounting to 24 per cent, and 20 civil actions, amounting to 13 per cent. Enforcement outcomes in the enforceable undertakings and negotiated outcomes category were 18 (or 12 per cent), and nil warning notices were issued.

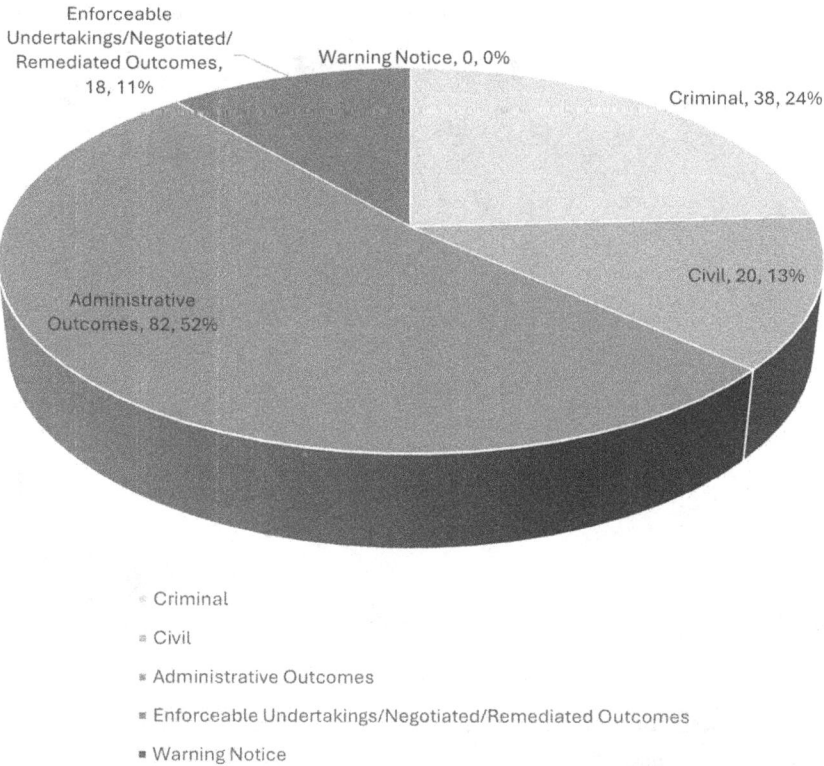

- Criminal
- Civil
- Administrative Outcomes
- Enforceable Undertakings/Negotiated/Remediated Outcomes
- Warning Notice

Figure 5.17: ASIC's aggregated outcomes for the market integrity category reflecting the most adopted form of enforcement
Source: Author's research.

Figure 5.18 sets out the enforcement trend for insider trading, a subcategory of market integrity. It shows that insider trading enforcement outcomes recorded a declining trend over the stated period. The total number of actions was 21 for the said period, with the maximum outcomes being nine for FY 2014–15, while FY 2017–18 recorded just one outcome in the administrative category. Of the total number of 21 outcomes, criminal outcomes totalled 16 for the stated period, followed by two civil actions, one administrative outcome and two outcomes in the enforceable undertakings/ negotiated category.

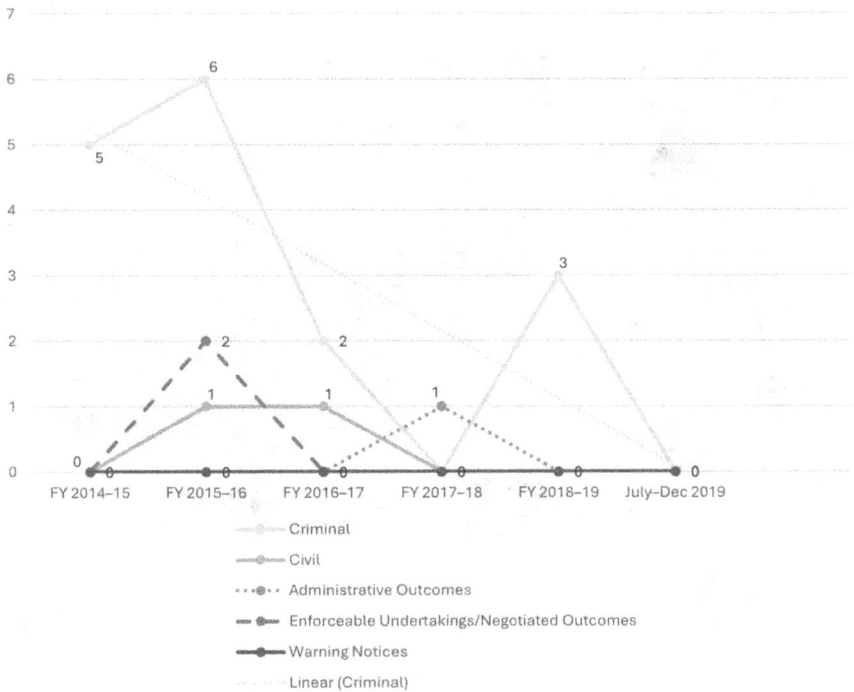

Figure 5.18: Enforcement trends for insider trading
Source: Author's research.

Figure 5.19 illustrates the enforcement trend for market manipulation, another subcategory of market integrity. It shows that market manipulation also recorded a declining trend over the stated period. The total number of actions was 13, with five occurring in FY 2014–15; FY 2016–17 recorded no outcomes in the market manipulation category. Of the total number of enforcement outcomes, criminal outcomes totalled eight for the stated period, followed by one civil action, four administrative outcome and no outcomes in the enforceable undertakings/negotiated category.

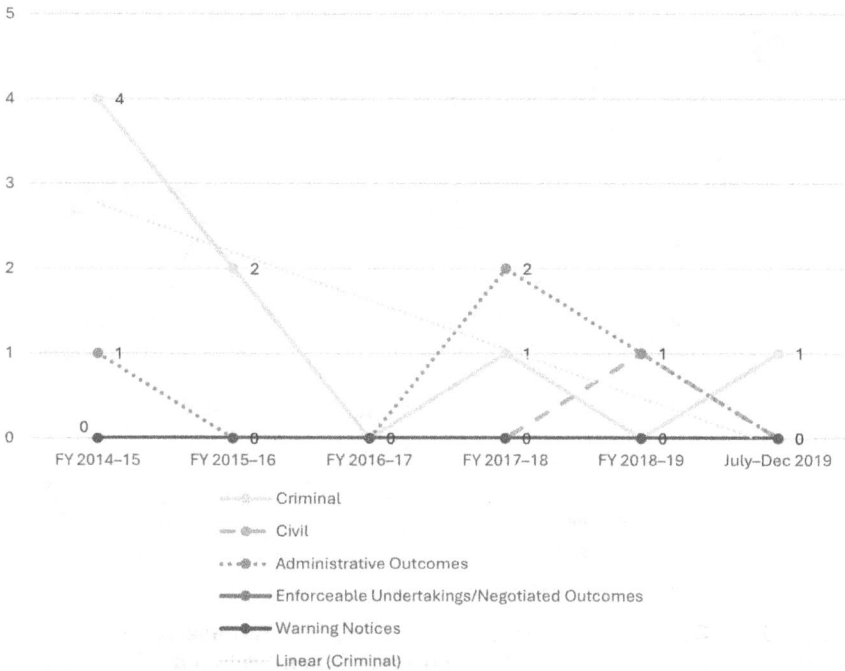

Figure 5.19: Enforcement trends for market manipulation
Source: Author's research.

Figure 5.20 represents the data and patterns of enforcement outcomes within the corporate governance category. ASIC's enforcement data are provided in respect of actions taken against directors, auditors and liquidators, and for misconduct related to insolvency as well as for other corporate governance misconduct. In the period FY 2014–14 to December 2019, ASIC accomplished 282 corporate governance outcomes. Among this total, there were 71 actions taken against directors, 59 against auditors and 40 against liquidators. Nineteen outcomes were for misconduct related to insolvency and 93 for other corporate governance misconduct.

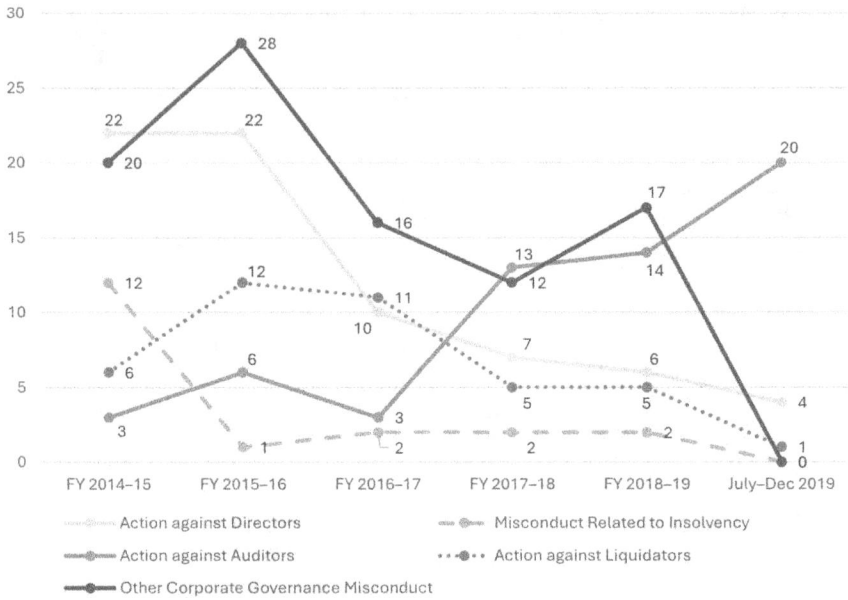

Figure 5.20: Consolidated corporate governance outcomes: Action against directors, misconduct related to insolvency, action against auditors, action against liquidators and other corporate governance misconduct

Source: Author's research.

Figure 5.21 represents ASIC's most used form of enforcement action for upholding corporate governance requirements over the FY 2014–15 to December 2019 period. In this period, ASIC achieved 152 administrative outcomes, amounting to 51 per cent of its total corporate governance outcomes. Criminal outcomes in the category were 38, amounting to 13 per cent, while 56 outcomes were in the civil category, amounting to 20 per cent. Thirty-six enforcement outcomes fell in the enforceable undertakings and negotiated outcomes category, amounting to 13 per cent, and a negligible amount of warning notices were issued.

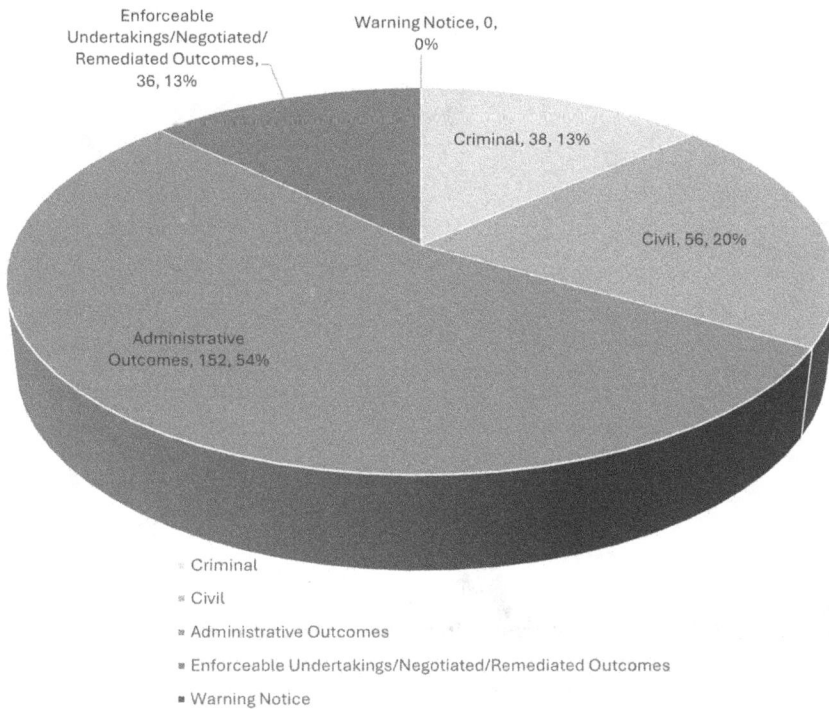

Figure 5.21: ASIC's aggregated outcomes for the corporate governance category, reflecting ASIC's preferred enforcement action
Source: Author's research.

Figure 5.22 illustrates the enforcement trend for actions taken against directors within ASIC's enforcement actions on corporate governance category for the period FY 2014–15 to December 2019. It shows that actions taken in respect of directors generally recorded a declining trend. The total number of actions was 71, with FY 2014–15 and FY 2015–16 recording 22 actions each in this category, while FY 2018–19 recorded just six outcomes. Of the total number of 71 outcomes, the most preferred form of enforcement adopted by ASIC for failure of directors' duties was 'criminal', totalling 33 outcomes for the stated period. Fourteen civil, 21 administrative and only three enforceable undertakings/negotiated settlements resulted for this category. No warning notices were issued for failure of directors' duties.

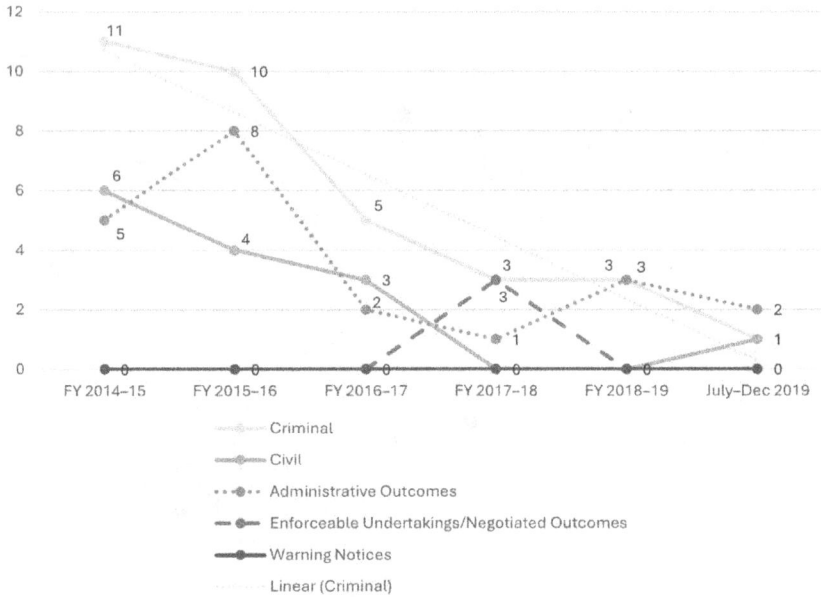

Figure 5.22: Enforcement trends in respect of directors

Source: Author's research.

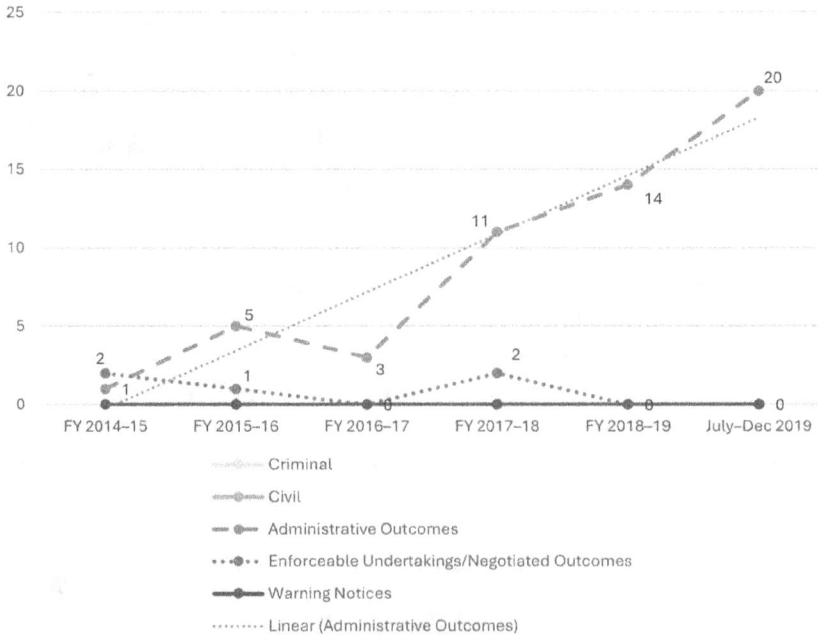

Figure 5.23: Enforcement trends in respect of auditors

Source: Author's research.

Figure 5.23 illustrates an upward enforcement trend for the period between FY 2014–15 and December 2019 for actions taken by ASIC against auditors within the category of corporate governance. A total of 59 enforcement outcomes were recorded against auditors, with the period between 1 July and 31 December 2019 observing the highest number of enforcement outcomes at 20, followed by FY 2018–19, which recorded 14 actions against auditors. The most used form of enforcement by ASIC was administrative, with outcomes totalling 54, followed by five enforceable undertakings and negotiated settlements. There were no 'criminal' or 'civil' outcomes against auditors nor were any warning notices issued in the category.

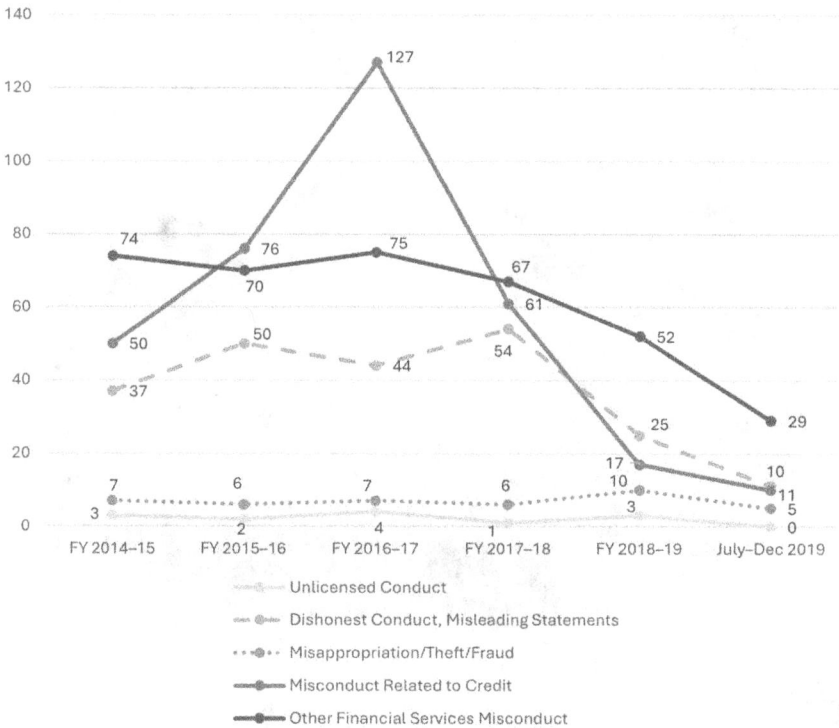

Figure 5.24: Consolidated enforcement outcomes for financial services: For unlicensed conduct, dishonest conduct and misleading statements, action against misappropriation/theft/fraud, misconduct related to credit and action taken in respect of other financial services

Source: Author's research.

Figure 5.24 represents the data and patterns of enforcement outcomes within the financial services category. ASIC's enforcement data are provided in respect of actions taken against unlicensed conduct, dishonest conduct and misleading statements; actions against misappropriation, theft and fraud; misconduct related to credit; and action taken in respect of other financial services misconduct. In the period FY 2014–14 to December 2019, ASIC accomplished a total of 1,001 enforcement outcomes in the financial services category, of which 31 actions were taken in respect of unlicensed conduct and 221 in respect of dishonest conduct and misleading statements. There were 41 outcomes for misappropriation, theft and fraud, 341 outcomes for misconduct related to credit and 367 outcomes for other financial services misconduct.

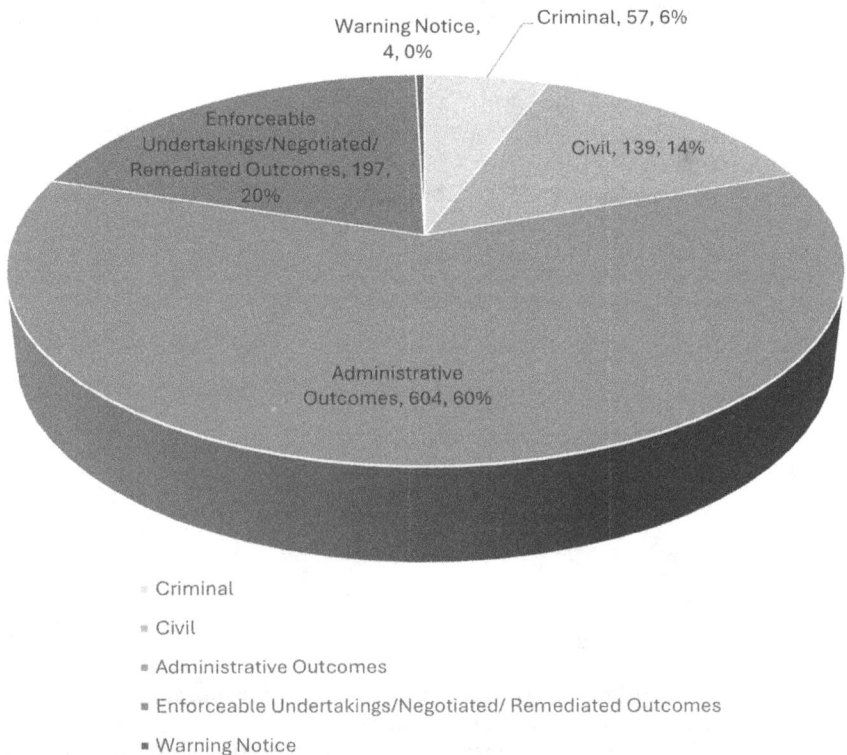

Criminal

Civil

Administrative Outcomes

Enforceable Undertakings/Negotiated/ Remediated Outcomes

Warning Notice

Figure 5.25: ASIC's aggregated outcomes for the financial services category reflecting the most adopted form of enforcement

Source: Author's research.

Figure 5.25 sets out ASIC's most used form of enforcement action for misconduct detected in the financial services area between FY 2014–15 and December 2019. In this period, from a total of 1,001 outcomes, ASIC achieved 589 administrative outcomes, amounting to 60 per cent of the total; 57 criminal outcomes, amounting to 6 per cent; and 139 civil outcomes, amounting to 14 per cent. There were 188 enforcement outcomes in the enforceable undertakings and negotiated outcomes category, amounting to 19 per cent; and four warning notices, amounting to 1 per cent.

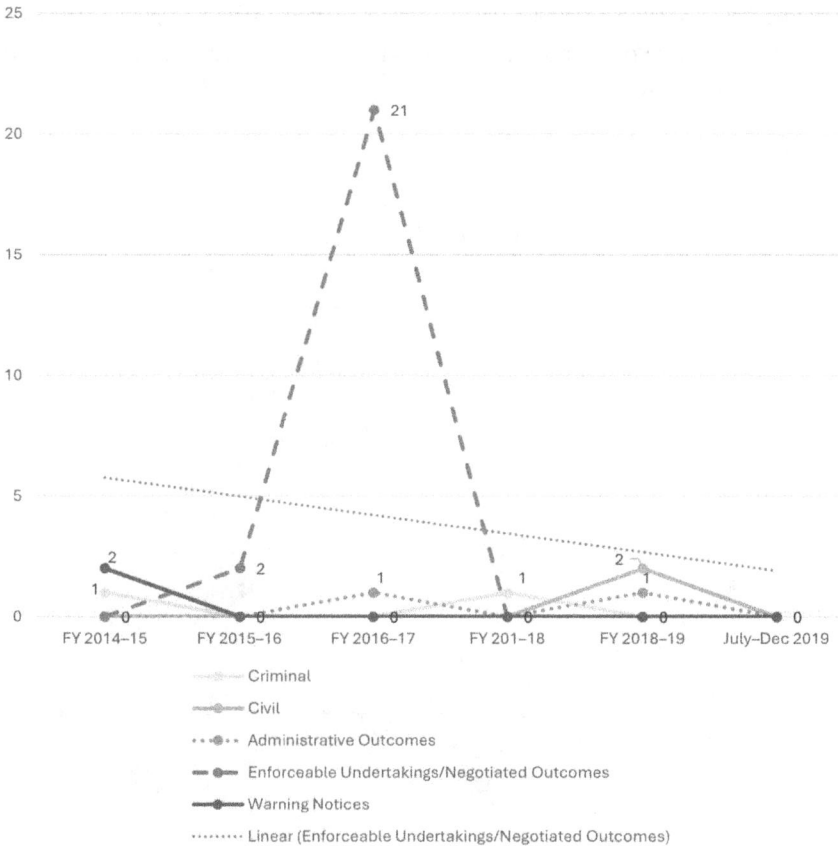

Figure 5.26: Enforcement trends for unlicensed conduct (within financial services)

Source: Author's research.

Figure 5.26 illustrates the enforcement trend for actions taken in respect of unlicensed conduct by ASIC within the category of financial services between FY 2014–15 and December 2019. As shown, actions taken in respect of unlicensed conduct recorded a generally declining trend over the stated period. The total number of actions against unlicensed conduct was 31. Most of these (22 enforcement outcomes) were taken in FY 2016–17. Of the total number of 31 outcomes, the most used form of enforcement adopted by ASIC for unlicensed conduct was enforceable undertakings/negotiated settlement, which saw a total of 23 outcomes in the stated period. There were two criminal outcomes, two civil outcomes, two administrative outcomes and two warning notices issued in this period for unlicensed conduct.

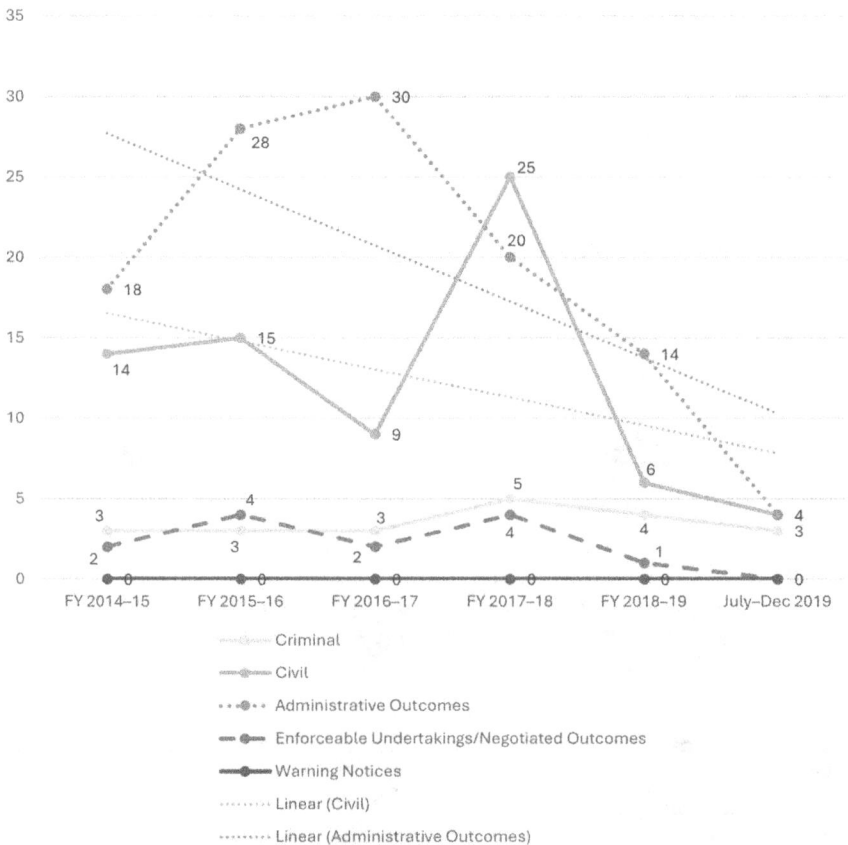

Figure 5.27: Enforcement trends for outcomes in relation to dishonest conduct and misleading statements (within financial services)

Source: Author's research.

Figure 5.27 illustrates ASIC's enforcement trends in respect of dishonest conduct and misleading statements within the category of financial services between FY2014–15 and December 2019. As shown, the actions taken in respect of dishonest conduct and misleading statements generally recorded a declining trend. A total of 221 enforcement outcomes were recorded for dishonest conduct and misleading statements, with FY 2017–18 recording the highest number at 54, while FY 2018–19 recorded 25 actions. Of the total number of enforcement outcomes in the category, the most used form of enforcement adopted by ASIC against dishonest conduct and misleading statements was 'administrative', totalling 114 outcomes, followed by civil outcomes, totalling 73, while 21 criminal outcomes and 13 enforceable undertakings and negotiated settlements were recorded. No warning notices were issued in the category.

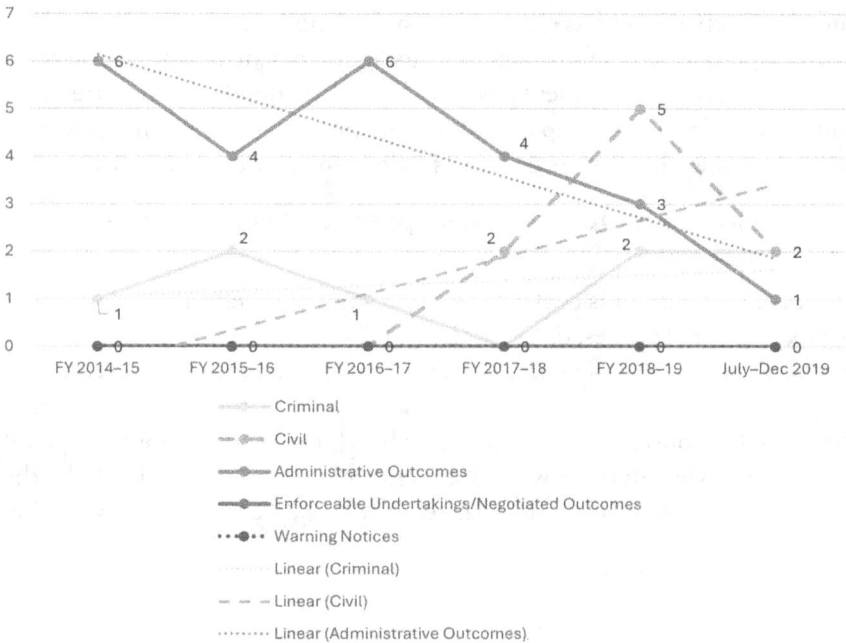

Figure 5.28: Enforcement trends for outcomes in relation to misappropriation, theft and fraud

Source: Author's research.

Figure 5.28 demonstrates a generally declining enforcement trend between FY 2014–15 and December 2019 for actions taken by ASIC in respect of misappropriation, theft and fraud within the category of financial services. A total of 41 enforcement outcomes resulted for misappropriation, theft and fraud during the period. The most used form of enforcement adopted by ASIC against misappropriation, theft and fraud was administrative action, totalling 24, followed by nine civil outcomes and eight criminal outcomes; no outcomes were recorded in the category of enforceable undertakings or warning notices.

Analysis

Building on the discussion of ASIC's supervisory and enforcement framework and powers in Chapter 4 and the empirical data on ASIC's enforcement outcomes above, this section analyses ASIC's use of its enforcement powers and the effectiveness of its enforcement and compliance regime. It examines ASIC's approach to enforcement and its 'enforcement pyramid', considers the use of ASIC's enforcement powers, extrapolates trends and draws relevant conclusions from the empirical enforcement data. Finally, it presents a critique of the effectiveness of ASIC's enforcement and compliance regime.

Responsive regulation: ASIC's approach to enforcement and compliance

The act of regulation is challenging for it requires an effective balancing of competing and, at times, divergent interests. On the one hand, the regulator needs to cater to specific needs of the financial industry and may even face allegations and complaints about regulatory actions stifling or obstructing the growth of business.[149] On the other hand, the general public may hold the contrary view that the wrongful conduct is treated too leniently by the regulator.[150] This paradox summarises ASIC's key challenge in balancing

---

149 See for example the accusation levelled by Jamie Dimon, chief executive of JP Morgan Chase, in early 2015: 'Banks are under assault … In the old days, you dealt with one regulator when you had an issue. Now it's five or six. You should all ask the question about how American that is, how fair that is': see N Popper, 'JP Morgan Chase chief says "banks are under assault"', *New York Times Deal Book* (14 January 2015) dealbook.nytimes.com/2015/01/14/jpmorgan-chase-profit-declines-7-percent/.

150 George Gilligan et al, 'Understanding penalties regimes for corporate wrongdoing in Australia and implications for the teaching of corporate law' (Paper, Corporate Law Teachers Association Conference 2015) 9. A taskforce was formed in October 2016 and reported in December of 2017 with 50 recommendations on how to increase the penalties for corporate crime and empower ASIC further: see Justice Francois Kunc, 'Penalties for corporate misconduct' (2018) 92 *Australian Law Journal* 403.

over-regulation that stifles innovation with regulation that is stringent enough to disincentivise corporate wrongdoing and effectively punish the wrongdoer.[151]

Bearing such unique challenges in mind, ASIC's *Penalties for Corporate Wrongdoing* notes that its regulatory approach is premised on achieving enforcement outcomes that 'act as a genuine deterrent to misconduct' through a credible and deterrent enforcement strategy and effective use of penalties.[152] To achieve effective enforcement outcomes, ASIC adopts a 'responsive regulation' approach to regulation[153] that the Senate Economic References Committee explained as follows:

> Responsive regulation 'recognises that it is not possible for any regulatory agency to detect and enforce every contravention of the law it administers and provides insights into how regulatory compliance can be achieved effectively'. It is essentially a convergence of the 'deterrence' and 'accommodative' models of regulation; responsive regulation focuses not on 'whether to punish or persuade, but when to punish and when to persuade' ... [To] achieve maximum regulatory compliance the theory promotes 'responsive' or 'strategic' supervision by regulators. Methods for promoting voluntary compliance, such as persuasion and education, are made more effective as a result of the credible sanctions of escalating severity available to the regulator that it can threaten to utilise or pursue. This structure of sanctions is generally referred to as the 'enforcement pyramid' or 'compliance pyramid'; the shape is intended to reflect the theoretical less frequent use of the most severe sanctions, which form the apex of the pyramid, compared to the persuasion-focused methods of resolution that form the pyramid's base.[154]

---

151 See for example Jane Searle, 'Regulation overload', *Financial Review* (6 July 2006).
152 ASIC, *Penalties for Corporate Wrongdoing* (Report 387, 2014) 4. The report recognises 'the damage that corporate wrongdoing' does to 'corporate, financial market and financial services sectors'.
153 For more on the regulation model, see Sonia Khosa, 'A game-changer or a routine drill? Cooperation in the Indo-Pacific Securities Markets' (2019) 47 *Australian Business Law Review* 182–199. See generally John Braithwaite, 'The essence of responsive regulation' (2011) 44 *UBCL Review* 475.
154 Commonwealth of Australia, Economics References Committee, *Performance of the Australian Securities and Investments Commission* (2014) 28 [4.10].

ASIC's adoption of the responsive regulation theory to its enforcement approach is expressed in terms of the enforcement pyramid shown in Figure 5.29.[155] The base of the pyramid promotes the use of preventive, persuasive and educative measures that are least coercive.[156] As the wrongdoing becomes more serious, or where persuasion and education fail in achieving the required results, ASIC resorts to administrative action that includes the issuing of warning or infringement notices, graduating to more stringent civil action if needed.[157] Finally, criminal penalties and action are resorted to in most serious corporate wrongdoing matters.[158]

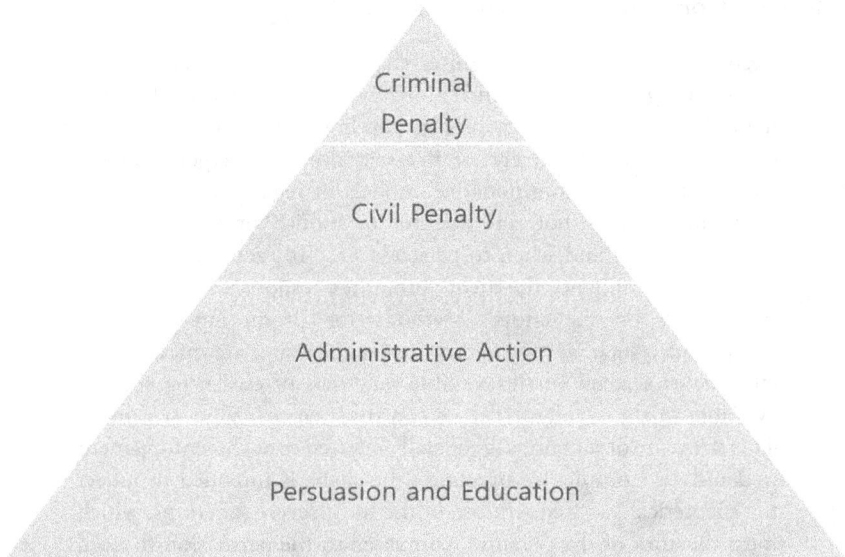

Figure 5.29: Adapted version Ayres and Braithwaite's enforcement pyramid[159]

Source: Author's research.

---

155 Ian Ayres and John Braithwaite, *Responsive Regulation: Transcending the Deregulation Debate* (Oxford University Press, 1992), doi.org/10.1093/oso/9780195070705.001.0001.

156 Brendon O'Neil, 'Corporate crime and regulatory discretion: rethinking the use of criminal, civil and administrative penalties' (2018) 42(5) *Criminal Law Journal* 322.

157 Ibid 323.

158 Australian Law Reform Commission (ALRC), *Principled Regulation: Federal Civil and Administrative Penalties in Australia* (Report No 95, 2002) 95. Criminal punishments are most effective in deterring corporate misconduct due to the possibility of imprisonment and stigma of a criminal conviction: see Vicky Comino, '"Australia's company law watchdog": the Australian Securities and Investments Commission and the civil penalties regime' (2014) 3 *Journal of Business Law* 228–251.

159 Since 1992, several illustrations of the enforcement pyramid have been developed ranging across different regulatory domains. This version was adapted from the original pyramid in Ayres and Braithwaite: see O'Neil (n 156).

In Australia, responsive regulation has generally been regarded as both influential and durable.[160] However, ASIC's responsive approach to enforcement has attracted significant criticism, especially in relation to 'financial services regulation'.[161] Hanrahan discusses the 'two practical points of friction' in adopting the responsive regulation approach to financial regulation. The problem arises from an inherent distinction between a 'regulatory' crime and a 'real crime'. As opposed to a regulatory violation, in a real crime, a person 'deliberately' defrauds another or obtains 'an unjust advantage by intentionally distorting or manipulating a market'. In such a scenario, the appropriate regulatory response would be to directly apply criminal prosecution and not wait for exhaustion of the 'regulatory strategies lower down the pyramid'.[162] It is here, Hanrahan emphasises, that 'friction' arises in deciding which strategy to implement to address a breach of a financial law.[163]

Friction also arises in relation to 'corporate defendants' for whom any use of the 'apex' part of the enforcement pyramid exhibits severe limitations.[164] Hanrahan asserts that this is because, first, for corporate crimes, a threat to 'impose a criminal rather than a civil penalty may not make much difference, except perhaps that criminal charges are harder to negotiate away'; second,

---

160 Khosa (n 153); Peter Mascini, 'Why was the enforcement pyramid so influential? And what price was paid?' (2013) 7(1) *Regulation & Governance* 48–60, doi.org/10.1111/rego.12003; Christine Parker, 'Twenty years of responsive regulation: An appreciation and appraisal' (2013) 7(1) *Regulation & Governance* 2–13, doi.org/10.1111/rego.12006; Jonathan Kolieb, 'When to punish, when to persuade and when to reward: strengthening responsive regulation with the regulatory diamond' (2015) 41 *Monash University Law Review* 136.

161 Dimity Kingsford Smith, 'A harder nut to crack—responsive regulation in the financial services sector' (2011) 44 *UBCL Review* 695. For example, one of the criticisms of the responsive or strategic regulation theory has been that it has remained 'trapped in the compliance/deterrence dialectic of regulation theory': see Helen Bird et al, 'Strategic regulation and ASIC enforcement patterns: results of an empirical study' (2005) 5(1) *Journal of Corporate Law Studies* 201, doi.org/10.1080/14735970.2005.11419934.

162 Pamela Hanrahan, 'Fairness and financial services: revisiting the enforcement framework' (2017) 35(7) *Company and Securities Law Journal* 420.

163 'Responsive regulation is a rich theory; sometimes its subtle and dynamic nature is poorly understood': see ibid 428, fn 74. In recent years, John Braithwaite has acknowledged that 'it may now be time to redirect evaluation research attention onto how to improve the quality of strategy selection when we do restorative justice or responsive regulation. That goes less to whether one single strategy is better than another more to which particular combination of multiple strategies together secure outcomes like reducing crime or increasing environmental compliance'. See John Bradford Braithwaite, *Restorative Justice and Responsive Regulation: The Question of Evidence* (RegNet Research Paper 51, 2016), doi.org/10.2139/ssrn.2839086. See also Julia Black, 'Paradoxes and failures: "new governance" techniques and the financial crisis' (2012) 75(6) *Modern Law Review* 1037, doi.org/10.1111/j.1468-2230.2012.00936.x.

164 At the apex, the enforcement pyramid envisages meting out the highest form of punishment for a corporate crime—that is, criminal penalties and, eventually, 'corporate capital punishment—permanently revoking the company's license to operate': see Hanrahan, 'Fairness and financial services' (n 162) 429.

'a corporation cannot be imprisoned or feel the shame or consequences of a criminal record'; and, finally, 'suspending or cancelling an AFS license that is held by a systemically important business or one that has many clients may be undesirable for a number of reasons'.[165] These problems render the 'top of the regulatory pyramid' ineffective or 'blunt'.[166]

Putting aside such theoretical criticisms, practically, the most substantial criticism of the application of this regulatory theory by ASIC has been that it is not adequately reflected in ASIC's enforcement strategies or actions.[167] Besides academia, policy circles have also recognised this shortcoming. For example, in 2014, the Senate Economic References Committee specifically noted that the pyramid was not applied to all the regulated parties, and that ASIC was reluctant to undertake criminal prosecutions and impose penalties in matters where the wrongdoing involved large, well-resourced corporations, blunting the apex of the pyramid.[168]

What emerges from this discussion is that, for a successful application of the responsive regulation theory and for 'enforcement action to be most effective', an equally effective 'framework of proportionate enforcement' is required.[169] Thus, it becomes pertinent to also understand ASIC's stated approach to enforcement.

In respect of enforcement, ASIC acknowledges that achieving enforcement outcomes is critical for effective regulation.[170] To ASIC's credit, it has published a well-defined strategy towards enforcement, a pictorial representation of which is reproduced from ASIC's website in Figure 5.30.[171]

---

165 See ibid 429.
166 Ibid.
167 Commonwealth of Australia, Economics References Committee (n 154) 264–265.
168 O'Neil (n 156) 324; Commonwealth of Australia, Economics References Committee (n 154) 264.
169 See O'Neil (n 156); see also ALRC, *Principled Regulation* (n 158).
170 ASIC, *Penalties for Corporate Wrongdoing* (n 152) 4.
171 ASIC, 'ASIC's approach to enforcement' (Information Sheet 151, 2013).

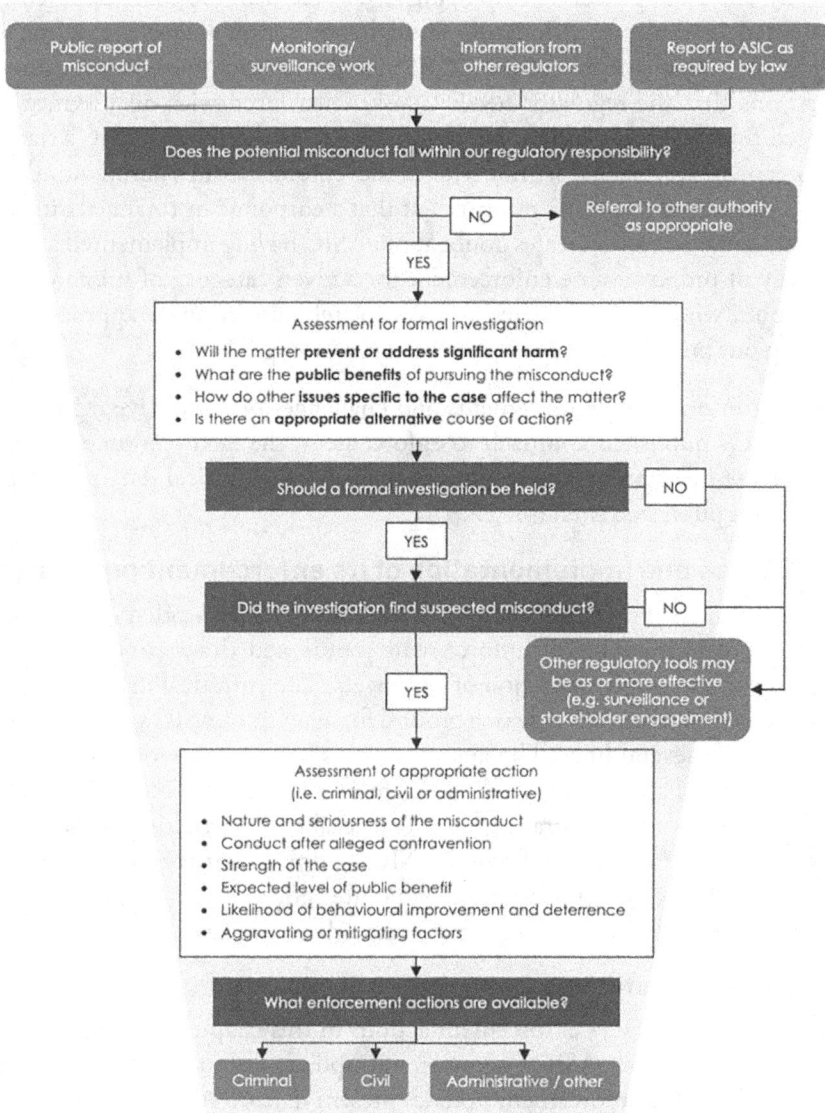

Figure 5.30: ASIC's approach to enforcement

Source: ASIC, *ASIC's approach to enforcement* (November 2021), download.asic.gov.au/ media/wrdetvvx/attachment-to-info151-published-22-november-2021.pdf.

Clearly, ASIC's approach to employing its enforcement tools is transparently presented in the public domain. Though not comprehensive, this stated approach raises some simple and straightforward—yet significant—questions that the regulator needs to ask when faced with an instance of alleged financial misconduct. However, despite its usefulness, ASIC's stated enforcement approach does not refer to the 'enforcement pyramid' nor does ASIC describe any specific punishment that a corporate or financial offence is likely to attract. This creates doubt about ASIC having implemented a clear strategy of proportionate enforcement for a given category of misconduct, and about whether ASIC relies on a completely discretionary approach for meting out punishments for corporate wrongdoing.[172]

Keeping in mind the requirements and challenges of responsive regulation and ASIC's published approach to enforcement, the next section examines ASIC's use of its enforcement powers against the empirical data presented above and published literature.

ASIC's use and implementation of its enforcement powers

This section analyses ASIC's empirical data and relevant academic literature to extrapolate meaningful enforcement trends and draw conclusions on ASIC's use and implementation of its powers. The empirical data in ASIC's enforcement updates provide rich ground for analysis of ASIC's enforcement trends along several lines. The analysis in this section is conducted on two main fronts. First, ASIC's use of its four main enforcement powers—criminal, civil, administrative and enforceable undertakings/negotiated settlement—are examined. Second, ASIC's enforcement regime for market integrity, financial services and corporate governance is thematically analysed. Some limitations are set out immediately below.

Caveats and limitations to the empirical analysis

The analysis of ASIC's enforcement actions in this chapter is based on data procured solely from ASIC's enforcement updates and not from its annual reports.[173] ASIC's enforcement updates present data on ASIC's enforcement outcomes in a clear and concise manner and have been relied upon by leading academics such as Ramsay and Webster for their analysis of ASIC's

---

172 Klettner argues that if ASIC places reliance on 'discretion' over 'enforcement strategy', 'its choices must be closely monitored: see Alice Klettner, 'Challenges for regulatory reform in the finance sector: learnings from the last decade' (2019) *Journal of Banking and Finance: Law and Practice* 151.

173 ASIC, 'ASIC annual reports', asic.gov.au/about-asic/corporate-publications/asic-annual-reports/.

enforcement regime.[174] Even though commentators have noted some inconsistencies in ASIC's published enforcement data,[175] for the purposes of the analysis in this chapter, accuracy is assumed without delving into the absolute correctness of the reported numbers.

Another limitation is that ASIC's enforcement updates cover aspects relating to the entire financial industry and not only to the securities markets as understood and used by the International Organization of Securities Commissions (IOSCO).[176] For instance, ASIC's data on enforcement outcomes related to corporate governance include the enforcement actions taken by ASIC against 'misconduct related to insolvency' and 'action against liquidators' and are, thus, broader in scope than corporate governance, which may otherwise be understood in relation to only the securities market. Similarly, the data for financial services outcomes include data on 'misconduct related to credit', which extends beyond securities markets. While the scope of this book is limited to securities markets, it is not practicable to extract data for securities markets enforcement actions from ASIC's overall financial enforcement outcomes. Hence, ASIC's entire enforcement data are reflected in the tables and figures presented above, but the following analysis of these data revolves around securities markets.

ASIC's enforcement: Use of powers
Criminal

Criminal sanctions, the apex of the enforcement pyramid, are the harshest form of penalty for securities offences in Australia. Publicly, ASIC recognises that criminal sanctions are the most effective measure against white-collar crime, as acknowledged by a previous ASIC chair, Greg Medcraft, in his statements on countering white-collar crime in Australia:

> The thing that scares white-collar criminals is going to jail and that's what scares them everywhere in the world. The penalties, particularly civil penalties, in Australia for white-collar offences are basically not

---

174 See Ian Ramsay and Miranda Webster, 'ASIC enforcement outcomes: trends and analysis' (2017) 35(5) *Company and Securities Law Journal* 289–321, 291.
175 Ibid 294.
176 The Foreword and Executive Summary of *IOSCO's Objectives and Principles of Securities Regulation* explains the meaning of the term 'securities markets' in the footnotes on p (i). It states that 'the words 'securities markets' are used, where the context permits, to refer compendiously to the various market sectors. In particular, where the context permits, they should be understood to include reference to the derivatives markets': see 'Foreword' and 'Executive Summary' in IOSCO, *Objectives and Principles of Securities Regulation* (2010).

strong enough, not tough enough. All you're doing is giving them a slap on the wrist [and] that is not deterring people. You have to lift the fear and suppress the greed.[177]

Interestingly, ASIC's enforcement outcomes between FY 2014–15 and December 2019 (ASIC's selected period) in areas of misconduct other than ASIC's small business category paint a contrasting picture regarding its actual use of its criminal powers, at least from the perspective of Medcraft's statements.

To start with, Table 5.15 reveals ASIC's aggregate enforcement actions in the selected period was 3,944, spanning four categories: small business compliance and deterrence, market integrity, financial services and corporate governance. Among these, ASIC's total number of criminal outcomes was 2,344 for the selected period. However, just 133 lay in the categories of market integrity, financial services and corporate governance, while the vast majority—2,211 criminal actions—lay in the small business compliance and deterrence segment. This statistic points to a significant conclusion—namely, that most of ASIC's resources, human and financial, have been dedicated to its criminal enforcement actions in the small business category.

Second, Table 5.15 shows that among ASIC's 133 criminal outcomes, 57 were for financial services misconduct, 38 for corporate governance misconduct and 38 for market integrity misconduct.

Third, the six-monthly data on ASIC's enforcement actions provided in Table 5.15 reveals other granular observations. For example, ASIC initiated between 160 and 244 criminal actions every six months for violations in the small business category. In a sharp contrast, ASIC initiated between one and eight criminal actions every six months for market integrity and corporate governance violations, and between two and eight criminal actions for financial services.

177 S Mitchell, 'Australia "paradise" for white-collar criminals, says ASIC Chairman Greg Medcraft' *Sunday Morning Herald* (21 October 2014), smh.com.au/business/australia-paradise-for-whitecollar-criminals-says-asic-chairman-greg-medcraft-20141021-119d99.html. When Finance Minister Senator Mathias Cormann stepped in, Medcraft clarified his earlier comment: see Georgia Wilkins, 'ASIC backflips on criminals' paradise comments' *Sunday Morning Herald* (23 October 2014), smh.com.au/business/asic-backflips-on-criminals-paradise-comments-20141022-119v22.html.

Fourth, another telling statistic that Table 5.15 and Figure 5.12 convey is that the use of criminal sanctions was the lowest (133) in the combined categories of market integrity, financial services and corporate governance, as compared with ASIC's cumulative civil actions (215), administrative outcomes (838) and enforceable undertakings/negotiated outcomes (251).

Fifth, Table 5.15 reveals that within the corporate governance and market integrity categories, ASIC preferred criminal enforcement to address directors' duties breaches (33 actions), insider trading (16 actions) and market manipulation (eight actions). However, within financial services misconduct, criminal action was not ASIC's preferred enforcement tool for any subcategory, and, even though ASIC pursued 21 criminal actions for dishonest conduct and misleading statements, ASIC's first choice for this subcategory was administrative enforcement (114 actions).

Sixth and finally, Figure 5.11 reveals a declining trend in ASIC's use of criminal enforcement actions during the selected period.

These observations on ASIC's use of its criminal powers reinforce the conclusion in earlier studies[178] about ASIC's limited use of criminal sanctions for corporate wrongdoings, other than in the small business category. The academic literature also points to other issues with ASIC's use of its criminal powers, such as its reluctance to utilise 'criminal sanctions in cases of serious corporate wrongdoing that involved high-profile individuals'.[179] A good example of this was ASIC's decision to launch civil

---

178 See generally Ramsay and Webster (n 174) 289. Ramsay and Webster conducted an analysis of ASIC's enforcement outcomes for the period between 1 July 2011 and 30 June 2016, which revealed a similar position.

179 Tom Middleton, 'ASIC's regulatory powers: interception and search warrants, credit and financial services licences and banning orders, financial advisers and superannuation: problems and suggested reforms' (2013) 31 *Company and Securities Law Journal* 208, 213. Middleton argues that individuals with 'deep pockets' exploit weaknesses for tactical purposes, such as achieving delay. According to Braithwaite, when laws are uncertain and unclear, the wealthy find the situation advantageous and 'deploy legal entrepreneurship' to exploit the uncertainty to serve their own interest: see John Braithwaite, *Markets in Vice Markets in Virtue* (Oxford University Press, 2005), doi.org/10.1093/oso/9780195222005.001.0001. See generally John Braithwaite, *Restorative Justice and Responsive Regulation* (Oxford University Press, 2002) 239–240, doi.org/10.1093/oso/9780195136395.003.0008. In relation to the infamous insider trading case of Stephen Vizard, see J Sexton, 'Vizard was "too well connected" for jail' *The Australian* (6 July 2005) 1–2. See also Roman Tomasic, 'Corporate crime and corporate culture in financial institutions: an Australian perspective' in Nic Ryder (ed) *White Collar Crime and Risk: Financial Crime, Corruption and the Financial Crisis* (Palgrave Macmillan, 2017) 283, doi.org/10.1057/978-1-137-47384-4_11.

penalty proceedings, and not criminal proceedings, in the high-profile matter against Stephen Vizard, who ASIC alleged breached his duties as director of Telstra Corporation Ltd.[180]

In conclusion, while ASIC acknowledges the importance, and the deterrent value, of its criminal sanctions, for a variety of reasons, it demonstrated a limited use of its criminal enforcement powers for financial and securities misconduct in the selected period. Undesirably, this signals a lack of intention on ASIC's part to use the top of the enforcement pyramid. However, with the recent reforms in ASIC's investigation and enforcement toolkit,[181] the upgrading of penalties,[182] and ASIC's new approach to pursue higher court-based action (even though modified),[183] ASIC's use of criminal penalties is likely to intensify.[184]

Civil

In relation to ASIC's statistics on the use of its civil powers, these are the main conclusions. First, Table 5.15 shows that ASIC achieved 215 civil outcomes across the three categories of market integrity, financial services and corporate governance during the selected period. Interestingly, there were no civil outcomes in the small business category.

Second, Figure 5.12 reveals that ASIC's 215 civil enforcement outcomes constituted only 15 per cent of its total actions for the three categories excluding small businesses categories. While this is low compared with ASIC's 838 administrative outcomes (constituting 58 per cent) and 251

---

180 See *Australian Securities and Investments Commission v Vizard* [2005] FCA 1037. On 4 July 2005, ASIC launched a civil penalty proceeding against Stephen Vizard, who the *Australian Financial Review* referred to as 'celebrity businessman, impresario, lawyer and one-time television presenter': see A Cornell, E Johnston and D Hughes, 'Steve Vizard quits over share-trading offences', *Australian Financial Review* (5 July 2005) 1. Vizard was charged with breaching his director duties as he used secret boardroom information to trade shares in three listed companies in which Telstra had an interest—Sausage Software Ltd, Computershare Ltd and Keycorp Ltd—and thus made unfair gains for himself and others: see ASIC, 'ASIC commences civil proceedings against Stephen Vizard' (Media Release, 4 July 2005).
181 See the discussion in Chapter 4.
182 See generally *Treasury Laws Amendment (Strengthening Corporate and Financial Sector Penalties) Act 2019* (Cth).
183 See generally Michael Legg and Stephen Speirs, 'Litigation: why not litigate?—the royal commission, ASIC and the future of the enforcement pyramid' (2019)(47) *Australian Business Law Review* 244.
184 See for example Clifford Chance, *ASIC's 'Why Not Litigate?' Strategy Alive and Well, with Multiple New Proceedings Commenced Against Major Organisations* (Regulatory Investigations and Financial Crime Insights, 10 March 2021). ASIC announced criminal charges against Alliance and AWP for violations against the *Corporations Act 2001* (Cth) (*Corporations Act 2001*).

enforceable undertakings/negotiated outcomes (constituting 18 per cent), it is only marginally higher than ASIC's criminal outcomes of 133 (constituting 9 per cent).

Third, ASIC achieved only 20 civil outcomes in the market integrity category, 56 outcomes in corporate governance and 139 outcomes in the financial services category during the entire period of examination.

Fourth, the six-monthly data on ASIC's enforcement actions within Table 5.15 reveal that, for every six months of the selected period of investigation, ASIC initiated between 0 and 6 civil actions for market integrity violations, between 1 and 18 civil actions for corporate governance violations, and between 7 and 26 criminal actions for financial services misconduct.

Fifth, Table 5.15 does not clearly reveal any particular category or subcategory of violation for which ASIC favoured civil action as a preferred tool of enforcement. The statistics do, however, indicate that ASIC generally pursued more civil than criminal enforcement: for violations in the 'continuous disclosure' subcategory within market integrity; for corporate governance contraventions; and for financial services misconduct, particularly in the 'dishonest conduct and misleading statements' subcategory.

Sixth, Figure 5.11 reveals a slight upward or more stable yearly trend in ASIC's use of civil enforcement actions during the selected period.[185]

Collectively, these statistics show that ASIC uses its civil enforcement powers across all categories, but, much like criminal enforcement, the use of civil enforcement has been limited. Further, civil enforcement was not ASIC's preferred tool of enforcement for any specific category of misconduct.

Apart from the conclusions drawn from ASIC's enforcement statistics, the literature points to other issues with ASIC's civil enforcement mechanism. Even where ASIC opted to pursue civil enforcement, its civil penalty approach was criticised,[186] as ASIC was able to secure only low penalties against corporate offenders in many matters, such as in the matter of Hardie

---

185 Excluding the last six months, as the graph reveals information for half of FY 2019–20.
186 George Gilligan et al, 'Penalties regimes to counter corporate and financial wrongdoing in Australia —views of governance professionals' (2017) 11(1) *Law and Financial Markets Review* 4–12, doi.org/ 10.1080/17521440.2017.1309162.

and AWB.[187] The Hardie case also illustrated classic problems of courts applying several protections in the civil penalty proceeding that took away the deterrent effect of the punishment.[188] Further, ASIC's civil enforcement was criticised for its lengthy nature,[189] and, in some cases, the time taken by ASIC to resolve civil penalty proceedings was noted as 'extreme and … unfortunate from a regulatory perspective'.[190] This claim against ASIC was illustrated by two cases, the first being the *Australian and Investments Commission v Rich*,[191] in which both ASIC and the defendants were criticised for delaying ASIC's civil penalty proceedings. The second case was *Forrest v Australian Securities and Investments Commission*, in which the judges noted that 'ASIC's pleaded case, and the way it was presented forensically, was lengthy and complex'.[192]

In addition to these issues, the Financial System Inquiry in 2014 highlighted the problem of insubstantial penalties, in response to which the ASIC Enforcement Review Taskforce was appointed by the government to review the adequacy of civil and criminal penalties for serious contraventions such as corporate fraud.[193] In the *ASIC Enforcement Review Proposal Paper 7*, the Enforcement Review Taskforce identified three problems with the penalties regime[194] that persisted during the period under review in this chapter.

---

187 In the Hardie case, Chief Financial Officer Morley received a penalty of only $20,000: see *Morley v Australian Securities and Investments Commission (No 2)* (2011) 83 ACSR 620. In AWB, the penalty imposed on Ingleby, the former CFO, by the Supreme Court of Victoria was only $10,000. This was increased by the Court of Appeal to $40,000: see *Australian Securities and Investments Commission v Ingleby* (2013) 39 ACSR 544. Other research on the use of civil penalties had come to similar conclusions about courts imposing low penalties on offenders in the financial sector: see George Gilligan, Helen Bird and Ian Ramsay, 'Civil penalties and the enforcement of directors' duties' (1999) 22 *UNSW Law Journal* 417, 458–461.

188 Vicky G Comino, 'The adequacy of ASIC's "tool-kit" to meet its obligations under corporations and financial services legislation' (2016) 34(5) *Company and Securities Law Journal* 372. See also Vicky Comino, 'James Hardie and the problems of the Australian civil penalties regime' (2014) 37 *UNSW Law Journal* 195, 198.

189 See Middleton (n 179) 209.

190 See G Golding and L Steinke, 'Directors in the regulatory enforcement pyramid—recent developments' (Paper, Directors' Duties Seminar, University of New South Wales, 20 March 2012) cited in Middleton (n 179) 209.

191 *Australian Securities and Investments Commission v Rich* (2009) 236 FLR 1 [56]. Austin J noted that ASIC ought to have been proactive in the matter.

192 *Forrest v Australian Securities and Investments Commission* (2012) 86 ALJR 1183 [79].

193 See ASIC Enforcement Review, *Strengthening Penalties for Corporate and Financial Sector Misconduct* (Position Paper 7, 2017).

194 Ibid.

In recent years, substantial reforms to ASIC's civil enforcement regime have been introduced to overhaul the mechanism. For example, the issue of low, inadequate and inconsistent penalties has been addressed through upgrades under *Treasury Laws Amendment (Strengthening Corporate and Financial Sector Penalties) Act 2019* (Cth).[195] Further, ASIC itself has undertaken to substitute its current enforcement approach with a more litigious approach and its recent measures show commitment to this decision.[196] And, finally, it is also worth mentioning the Hayne Royal Commission's suggestion for a 'new independent federal civil enforcement agency if the recommended structural separation of enforcement staff inside ASIC does not produce the desired results'.[197]

In conclusion, even though ASIC's civil enforcement regime appears tepid for ASIC's selected period, new and continuous reforms and keener scrutiny over ASIC's enforcement performance are likely to reboot ASIC's civil enforcement approach.

Administrative

Table 5.15 and Figure 5.11 reveal administrative action as ASIC's highest used form of enforcement across the three enforcement categories (excluding small businesses).[198] From a total of 1,441 enforcement actions that ASIC pursued in the three categories during the selected period, 838 were administrative.

From among 838 administrative actions, 604 lay in the financial services category, followed by 152 in corporate governance and 82 in the market integrity category. Figure 5.12 reinforces the high use of administrative actions by ASIC, which stood at 58 per cent of ASIC's aggregate actions for the three categories.

These deductions reveal that ASIC has relied heavily on this enforcement tool for market misconduct. The frequent and substantial use of administrative powers has been discussed repeatedly in recent years, particularly ASIC's

---

195 *Treasury Laws Amendment (Strengthening Corporate and Financial Sector Penalties) Act 2019* (Cth). Also refer to the discussion on powers in Chapter 4 of this book.

196 Chance (n 184). ASIC has initiated civil proceedings against the National Australia Bank (NAB), Commonwealth Securities Ltd and Australian Investment Exchange Ltd, and against the superannuation trustee Retail Employees Superannuation Pty Ltd.

197 Jason Harris, 'Corporate law lessons from the Banking Royal Commission' (2019) 93 *Australian Law Journal* 364. See also *Royal Commission into Misconduct in the Banking, Superannuation and Financial Services Industry* (Final Report, 2019) (Hayne Report) vol 1, 431.

198 The three enforcement categories are market integrity, corporate governance and financial services.

use of its infringement notice powers.[199] As explained in Chapter 4, an infringement notice is an allegation of a violation of the law, 'payment of which causes the regulator to not pursue the alleged contravention any further'.[200] Despite its many advantages, which the *ASIC Enforcement Review Proposal Paper 7* recounts,[201] the use of infringement notices as an enforcement tool has received criticism from several quarters, including the Australian Law Reform Commission,[202] as well as the Law Council of Australia, which called it 'lazy regulation'.[203] More recently, Commissioner Hayne in the final report of the royal commission recognised that:

> infringement notices should principally be used in respect of administrative failings by entities, will rarely be appropriate for provisions that require an evaluative judgment and, beyond purely administrative failings, will rarely be an appropriate enforcement tool where the infringing party is a large corporation.[204]

In conclusion, the empirical data show a most definite use of administrative action by ASIC. However, as noted by the Hayne Royal Commission, administrative powers ought to be used for 'administrative failings' only and not for 'substantive' violations of corporations law.[205]

Enforceable undertakings and negotiated resolutions

Table 5.15 reveals that ASIC pursued 251 enforceable undertakings/negotiated outcomes out of a total 1,441 outcomes for the period under review (FY 2014–15 to December 2019) across the three categories excluding small businesses. Figure 5.12 illustrates ASIC's use of this enforcement tool in percentage terms as 18 per cent of ASIC's total enforcement actions.

---

199 The infringement notice, as an area of study, has received considerable attention from academics and regulators, and its many advantages have been recognised: see for example M Welsh, 'Enforcing contraventions of the continuous disclosure provisions: civil or administrative penalties' (2007) 25 *Company and Securities Law Journal* 315; M Nehme, M Hyland and M Adams, 'Enforcement of continuous disclosure: the use of infringement notice and alternative sanctions' (2007) 21 *Australian Journal of Corporate Law* 118; RG Morison and I Ramsay, 'Enforcement of ASIC's market integrity rules: an empirical study' (2015) 30 *Australian Journal of Corporate Law* 32.
200 ASIC Enforcement Review (n 193).
201 Ibid 74.
202 Ibid.
203 Commonwealth of Australia, Economics Reference Committee, *Lifting the Fear and Suppressing the Greed: Penalties for White-Collar Crime and Corporate and Financial Misconduct in Australia* (2017) 71.
204 Hayne Report (n 197) 37. See also Sean Hughes, 'ASIC's approach to enforcement after the royal commission' (Speech, 36th Annual Conference of the Banking and Financial Services Law Association, Gold Coast, Australia, 30 August 2019), asic.gov.au/about-asic/news-centre/speeches/asic-s-approach-to-enforcement-after-the-royal-commission/.
205 See Harris, 'Corporate law lessons' (n 197) 365.

Table 5.15 reveals that ASIC's use of this enforcement tool lay mostly in the financial services category. Out of ASIC's 251 outcomes, 197 actions were for financial services, 36 for corporate governance and 18 for the market integrity category.

Within the financial services category, 23 outcomes lay in the subcategory of 'unlicensed conduct', 13 for 'dishonest conduct and misleading statements', 45 for misconduct related to 'credit' and 116 for miscellaneous financial services misconduct. For cases of misappropriation, theft and fraud, ASIC completely refrained from using this enforcement tool.

Finally, Figure 5.11 illustrates a declining trend in ASIC's use of this enforcement tool since FY 2016–17.

Enforceable undertaking are ASIC's most frequently utilised forms of negotiated resolution.[206] Much like the use of infringement notices under ASIC's administrative powers, ASIC's use of enforceable undertakings and negotiated outcomes has been a subject of intense discussion.[207] As Chapter 4 explained in detail, the *Australian Securities and Investments Commission Act 2001* (Cth) (*ASIC Act*) stipulates conditions when enforceable undertakings may be accepted by ASIC,[208] and ASIC's Regulatory Guide 100 elaborates on ASIC's approach to accepting such undertakings.[209] In an environment of financial budget pressures and time constraints, ASIC relies on 'negotiated resolution' as an enforcement tool for 'improved compliance program or a better (eg quicker) outcome for investors'.[210]

---

206 An enforceable undertaking is a type of negotiated settlement that is used by ASIC as an alternative to court action, infringement notice or other administrative action: see ASIC, 'ASIC's approach to enforcement' (n 171).

207 For further discussion of ASIC's use of powers of civil settlements and enforceable undertakings, see Comino, 'James Hardie and the problems' (n 188). See also Helen Louise Bird, George Gilligan and Ian Ramsay, 'The who, why and what of enforceable undertakings accepted by the Australian Securities and Investments Commission' (2016) 34(7) *Company and Securities Law Journal* 491–517; Christine Parker, 'Restorative justice in business regulation? The Australian Competition and Consumer Commission's use of enforceable undertakings' (2004) 67(2) *Modern Law Review* 209–246, doi.org/10.1111/j.1468-2230.2004.00484.x; Marina Nehme, 'Monitoring compliance with enforceable undertakings' (*2009*) 23 *Australian Journal of Corporate Law* 76–102.

208 *ASIC Act* ss 93A and 93AA.

209 ASIC, *Regulatory Guide 100: Enforceable Undertakings* (2021).

210 See 'ASIC's approach to enforcement' (n 171) 6. See generally Nehme, 'Monitoring compliance' (n 207); Joe Longo, 'Enforceable undertakings: quicker and more flexible regulatory responses' (2000) 16(5) *Company Director* 28.

The academic literature on ASIC's use of enforceable undertakings is extensive and detailed,[211] and offers insights into numerous aspects, including the characteristics of the parties offering such undertakings; the misconduct for which such undertakings may be accepted; and the various kinds of undertakings, such as 'cease and desist', 'training and supervision', and 'rectification, refund and compensation'.[212] Many advantages are credited to enforceable undertakings: for example, 'influencing behaviour and encouraging a culture of compliance',[213] providing a quick and cheap alternative to costly and lengthy court process,[214] and contributing 'to the goals of rehabilitation and restorative justice'.[215] At the same time, these undertakings have been the subject of much concern and criticism for several reasons. For example, Bird et al argue that 'the most common area of legal misconduct in enforceable undertakings accepted by ASIC was non-compliance with financial service laws' where a 'third of enforceable undertakings involved issues of non-compliance over a range of different areas of regulation', specifically 'misleading and deceptive conduct'.[216]

---

211 See Marina Nehme, 'Enforceable undertaking: a restorative sanction' (2010) 36 *Monash University Law Review* 108; Richard Johnstone and Christine Parker, 'Enforceable undertakings in action: report of a roundtable discussion with Australian regulators' (2010), doi.org/10.2139/ssrn.1551627; Bird, Gilligan and Ramsay (n 207). See also Marina Nehme, 'Enforceable undertakings: a new form of settlement to resolve alleged breaches of the law' (2007) 11(1) *University of Western Sydney Law Review* 104; Marina Nehme and Michael Adams, 'The active use of enforceable undertakings by ASIC: Part 1' (2007) 59(5) *Keeping Good Companies* 326; Marina Nehme and Michael Adams, 'The active use of enforceable undertakings by ASIC: Part 2' (2007) 59(6) *Keeping Good Companies* 326; Marina Nehme, 'Enforceable undertakings in Australia and beyond' (2005) 18 *Australian Journal of Corporate Law* 68; Helen Louise Bird et al, *An Empirical Analysis of the Use of Enforceable Undertakings by the Australian Securities and Investments Commission between 1 July 1998 and 31 December 2015* (CIFR Paper, 2016); D Nehme et al, *The General Deterrence Effects of Enforceable Undertakings on Financial Services and Credit Providers* (2018). See generally Jasper Hedges, George Gilligan and Ian Ramsay, 'Banning orders: an empirical analysis of the dominant mode of corporate law enforcement in Australia' (2017) 39 *Sydney Law Review* 501.
212 Bird, Gilligan and Ramsay (n 207).
213 See ASIC, 'ASIC releases policy on cooperation and third enforcement report' (Media release, 9 April 2013), asic.gov.au/about-asic/news-centre/find-a-media-release/2013-releases/13-073mr-asic-releases-policy-on-cooperation-and-third-enforcement-report/.
214 Misa Han, James Eyers and Edmund Tadros, 'ASIC's "why not litigate" strategy kills enforceable undertakings', *Financial Review* (16 May 2019), afr.com/companies/financial-services/asic-s-why-not-litigate-strategy-kills-enforceable-undertakings-20190516-p51o14.
215 Johnstone and Parker (n 211).
216 Bird et al, *An Empirical Analysis* (n 211) 86. Bird et al conducted an empirical study to examine the nature and characteristics of each enforceable undertaking accepted by ASIC between 1 July 1998 and 31 December 2015. They noted that undertakings offered in financial service misconduct involved three common activities— 'promotion, marketing, advertising and sale of financial services; the provision of specific financial advice or product recommendations; and the governance of financial services firms'. See also Bird, Gilligan and Ramsay (n 207). For more literature on misleading and deceptive conduct, see Gill North, 'Companies take heed: the misleading or deceptive conduct provisions are gaining prominence' (2012) 30 *Company and Securities Law Journal* 342.

The use of enforceable undertakings by ASIC was seriously questioned in the wake of a series of financial misconduct cases.[217] The Hayne Royal Commission 'disapproved of ASIC's negotiated outcome approach to enforcement and indicated that ASIC "must" consider whether legal proceedings should be initiated'.[218] ASIC responded to these criticisms by adopting a mantra of 'Why not litigate?' in 2019, signalling its decision to reduce its use of enforceable undertakings as a tool of enforcement and pursue court-based action.[219]

However, while both the interim and final reports of the Hayne Royal Commission criticised ASIC's 'negotiated outcome approach', they also 'accepted that negotiation and persuasion were important regulatory tools' that played a significant role in the enforcement pyramid.[220] This leads to the conclusion that reliance on negotiated settlements is not bad in itself: an enforceable undertaking can be effective if it is accompanied by 'more penetrating terms'[221] or if the matter is 'escalated up the pyramid'.[222] The problem with ASIC's approach, as the Hayne Commission's final report noted, was that it 'failed to utilise the peak of the pyramid effectively',[223] specifically 'against large well-resourced corporations'.[224]

In conclusion, ASIC appears to have used enforceable undertakings/negotiated outcomes liberally and thereby attracted criticism. While this regulatory tool is admittedly important, the challenge before ASIC is to use it sparingly or only for minor violations that do not signal a definite or systematic abuse of the regulatory requirements.

---

217 *Royal Commission into Misconduct in the Banking, Superannuation and Financial Services Industry* (Interim Report, September 2018) vol 1, 277.

218 Legg and Speirs (n 183). See also James Frost and James Thomson, 'Banking royal commission interim report: Hayne skewers greedy banks, lazy regulators', *Financial Review* (28 September 2018), www.afr.com/companies/financial-services/banking-royal-commission-interim-report-hayne-skewers-greedy-banks-lazy-regulators-20180928-h15zoc.

219 Hughes (n 204) 202. See also Hayne Report (n 197) 427. Since the changes in 2021, ASIC has arguably dialled back from this approach.

220 Legg and Speirs (n 183) 71.

221 Clinton Free, Dimity Kingsford Smith and Hannah Harris, 'In defence of ASIC: there's more to regulation than prosecution' (15 November 2018) *The Conversation*, theconversation.com/in-defence-of-asic-theres-more-to-regulation-than-prosecution-106239.

222 Legg and Speirs (n 183) 71. Smith argues that the quality of discretion used by ASIC contributed to a 'mixed' track record, as softer enforcement actions such as low civil penalties and enforceable undertakings were utilised against big corporations and criminal prosecution and disproportionate penalties were taken up against smaller players: see Smith (n 161).

223 Legg and Speirs (n 183).

224 O'Neil (n 156) 329.

ASIC's enforcement: A thematic review

Building on the analysis of ASIC's use of its criminal, civil, administrative and negotiated settlement powers, the analysis now turns to the area-wise use of ASIC's enforcement powers, spanning market integrity, corporate governance and financial services.

Market integrity

Upholding and protecting the 'integrity' or' 'fairness' of the markets is one of the main reasons for having securities regulation and regulatory frameworks in place.[225] Despite their significance, the terms 'fairness' and 'integrity' are difficult to define; a useful definition is 'informal norms of behaviour, reflective perhaps of one's own individual assessment of what is honest and moral'.[226] Thus, more often than not, the term 'market integrity' simply translates as ensuring that markets are 'unimpaired', 'unbroken' and 'sound',[227] while 'fairness' stands for 'impartial' and 'equitable' behaviour in the market.[228]

The normative character of the terms has been criticised as 'vague' and 'devoid of principled content'.[229] Notwithstanding this challenge, the concept of market integrity has been adopted by securities regulators and international organisations such as the G-20 and IOSCO.[230] In IOSCO's framework, 'ensuring that markets are fair, efficient and transparent' is a key objective set out for securities regulation.[231] In Australia, the *ASIC Act* requires ASIC to exercise power to, inter alia:

---

225 Janet Austin, 'What exactly is market integrity? An analysis of one of the core objectives of securities regulation' (2016) 8(2) *William and Mary Business Law Review* 218, doi.org/10.2139/ssrn.2814986.
226 Ibid 219.
227 Werner Erhard and Michael C Jensen, *Putting Integrity into Finance: A Purely Positive Approach* (National Bureau of Economic Research Working Paper No 19986, 2014) 3, doi.org/10.3386/w19986.
228 Austin (n 225). Fairness along with honesty and efficiency are deeply imbedded within the Australian financial services regime: see Joshua Anderson, 'Duties of efficiency, honesty and fairness post-Westpac: a new beginning for financial services licensees and the courts?' (2020) 37 *Company and Securities Law Journal* 450. For other significant literature on this theme, see Paul Latimer, 'Providing financial services "efficiently, honestly and fairly"' (2006) 24 *Company and Securities Law Journal* 362; Paul Latimer, 'Providing financial services "efficiently, honestly and fairly": Part 2' (2020) 37 *Company and Securities Law Journal* 382, doi.org/10.2139/ssrn.3751834. For insights on and criticism of the financial services framework insofar as it supports fairness, see Hanrahan, 'Fairness and financial services' (n 162).
229 Austin (n 225). For criticism of 'market fairness' see generally Ian B Lee, 'Fairness and insider trading' (2002) *Columbia Business Law Review* 119.
230 Market integrity features as a principal objective in the securities framework of many advanced countries including the SEC (US), ASIC (Australia) and BaFin (Germany): see Austin (n 225) 218. The G-20 called on the international standard-setting body, IOSCO, to make recommendations to promote markets' integrity and efficiency to reduce risks to the financial system: see G20 Research Group, 'The G20 Seoul Summit Leaders' Declaration' *University of Toronto Library* (12 November 2010), g20. utoronto.ca/2010/g20seoul.html.
231 IOSCO, *Objectives and Principles of Securities Regulation* (n 176).

(a) maintain, facilitate and improve the performance of the financial system and the entities within that system in the interests of commercial certainty, reducing business costs, and the efficiency and development of the economy; and

(b) promote the confident and informed participation of investors and consumers in the financial system.[232]

ASIC interprets the emphasis on market confidence to mean 'promoting investor and financial consumer trust and confidence'[233] and sets forth ASIC's vision for 'a fair, strong and efficient financial system' as its vision and mission.[234] Thus, the function of monitoring and promoting market integrity in relation to the Australian financial system is well entrenched in ASIC's regulatory regime.[235]

The statutory emphasis on maintaining and promoting market integrity was reflected in ASIC's enforcement actions to the following extent. First, Table 5.15 reveals that ASIC completed 158 enforcement outcomes in the market integrity category for the selected period.

Second, of the aggregate 158 actions taken towards market integrity during the selected period, 21 actions related to insider trading, 13 to market manipulation, 26 to continuous disclosure, 43 to market integrity rules and 55 to other market misconduct.

Third, and notably, Figure 5.17 indicates that ASIC's preferred enforcement tool for dealing with market integrity misconduct was 'administrative' action (82 outcomes aggregating 52 per cent), followed by criminal (38 outcomes aggregating 24 per cent), civil (20 outcomes aggregating 13 per cent) and, finally, enforceable undertakings/negotiated/remediation action (18 outcomes aggregating 11 per cent).

---

232 See *ASIC Act* s 1(2).

233 ASIC, 'Our role', asic.gov.au/about-asic/what-we-do/our-role/.

234 ASIC states on its website that its vision is 'to act against misconduct to maintain trust and integrity in the financial system': see ASIC, 'Our vision and strategic priorities', asic.gov.au/about-asic/what-we-do/our-role/asic-vision-and-mission/.

235 ASIC, *Senate Inquiry into Consumer Protection in the Banking, Insurance and Financial Services Sector: Submission by the Australian Securities and Investments Commission* (2017).

Fourth, deviating from its general preference for 'administrative action', ASIC preferred criminal sanctions for two subcategories within market integrity: 1) insider trading, with 16 criminal actions and one administrative action; and 2) market manipulation, with eight criminal actions and four administrative outcomes, as detailed below.

Insider trading

Insider trading is widely acknowledged to be a significant threat to market integrity and is prohibited the world over.[236] Insider trading cases receive significant attention from academics and regulators,[237] as both view actions against insider trading misconduct as an important measure to gauge the proactiveness and resilience of a regulatory regime. Despite its notorious character, the rigorous enforcement and prosecution of insider trading offences remains elusive. Detecting the offence is challenging,[238] as it requires the establishment of 'knowledge' and 'intent' on the part of the offender.[239]

---

236 See for example, ASIC, *Consultation Paper 68: Competition for Market Services—Trading in Listed Securities and Related Data* (2007); Utpal Bhattacharya and Hazem Daouk, 'The world price of insider trading' (2002) 57(1) *Journal of Finance* 75–108, doi.org/10.1111/1540-6261.00416; Laura N Beny, 'Insider trading laws and stock markets around the world: an empirical contribution to the theoretical law and economics debate' (2007) 32 *Journal of Corporation Law*. US SEC claims insider trading to be a priority: see Lev Bromberg, George Gilligan and Ian Ramsay, 'Insider trading and market manipulation: the SEC's enforcement outcomes' (2017) 45(2) *Securities Regulation Law Journal* 109–125. On comparative aspects of the US and Australian regime, see Xiaoyan Chen, Allan Hodgson and Martina K Linnenluecke, 'Transferring and trading on insider information in the United States and Australia: just a case of happy hour drinks?' (2018) 58(S1) *Accounting and Finance* 83–95, doi.org/10.1111/acfi.12321.

237 Victor Lei and Ian Ramsay, 'Insider trading enforcement in Australia' (2014) 8(3) *Law and Financial Markets Review* 214–226, doi.org/10.5235/17521440.8.3.214.

238 Juliette Overland, *ASIC Enforcement Review Taskforce Submission on Positions and Consultation Paper: ASIC's Access to Telecommunications Intercept Material* (2017). Although the surveillance and real-time monitoring of securities markets has significantly improved in recent decades, detecting and obtaining evidence for establishing an act of insider trading is very challenging: see Roman Tomasic and Brendan Pentony, 'The prosecution of insider trading: obstacles to enforcement' (1989) 22(2) *Australian and New Zealand Journal of Criminology* 65, doi.org/10.1177/000486588902200201.

239 To be proven, insider trading offences require two things: that the offender knew or ought reasonably to have known that the information was inside information, and that the information was likely to have a 'material' impact on the price or value of securities: see *Corporations Act* s 1043(1)(b). For more on insider trading, see Explanatory Memorandum, Financial Services Bill [2.78]–[2.79]. See also Roman Tomasic and Brendan Pentony, *Casino Capitalism? Insider Trading in Australia* (Australian Institute of Criminology Canberra, 1991) 115–26; Simon Rubenstein, 'The regulation and prosecution of insider trading in Australia: towards civil penalty sanctions for insider trading' (2002) 20(2) *Company and Securities Law Journal* 89–113; Gregory Lyon and Jean Jacques Du Plessis, *The Law of Insider Trading in Australia* (Federation Press, 2005).

In Australia, the *Corporations Act* prohibits insider trading,[240] which refers to trading by a person on the basis of material, non-public information in a manner that provides them with an unfair advantage over those trading without access to such information.[241] The Australian courts can impose both criminal and civil penalties for insider trading offences.[242]

ASIC's data give useful insights into its insider trading enforcement. Table 5.15 shows an aggregate of 21 insider trading enforcement outcomes for the selected period. ASIC's preferred form of enforcement action for insider trading misconduct during this period was 'criminal', with 16 completed actions, followed by two civil, one administrative and two enforceable undertakings/negotiated outcomes. Figure 5.18 indicates a declining trend in the enforcement of insider trading laws.[243]

These statistics correspond well with Hanrahan's argument that criminal prosecution is the preferred enforcement option for insider trading offences,[244] although Hanrahan posits that civil penalty proceedings may be a 'more effective deterrent of unlawful conduct by individual wrongdoers motivated by corporate success, or by corporations'.[245] Given the significance of insider trading, academic interest in this area has been high for several decades, with some noteworthy studies examining ASIC's insider trading enforcement patterns. For example, in the context of the Australian regime, Lei and Ramsay in 2014 conducted an empirical study of enforcement cases of insider trading in Australia between 1973 and 2013.[246] They concluded

---

240 *Corporations Act* s 1043A.

241 See generally Overland (n 238). For more on the law of insider trading, see Lyon and Du Plessis (n 239).

242 Arie Freiberg, 'Researching white-collar crime: an Australian perspective' in *The Handbook of White-Collar Crime*, 422. For more on insider trading, see Juliette Overland, 'Liability for insider trading: learning lessons from Australia' (28 July 2008), doi.org/10.2139/ssrn.1184332; Juliette Overland, *Corporate Liability for Insider Trading* (Routledge, 2019), doi.org/10.4324/9781315098210; Pamela F Hanrahan, 'Deterring white-collar crime: insights from Australia's insider trading penalties regime' (2017) 11(2–3) *Law and Financial Markets Review* 61–74, doi.org/10.1080/17521440.2017.1373440.

243 The period of investigation of ASIC's enforcement outcomes in this chapter was from FY 2014–15 to 31 December 2019; hence, only six months of data for the last FY is included.

244 Hanrahan, 'Deterring white-collar crime' (n 242).

245 See ibid.

246 Lei and Ramsay (n 237). The study found 79 cases in this 20-year period of which 92 per cent were criminally prosecuted. Among the many aspects that the study considered, chief were aspects of the alleged profit made by the offenders, background of the offender, the company, the case initiated by the regulator and the time taken to complete the case: see Freiberg (n 242).

that, each year, ASIC initiated more cases in response to allegations of insider trading, with a better rate of success and also a reduction in the time to complete such cases.[247]

Similarly, Bromberg et al conducted a rich, comparative study of insider trading enforcement cases by examining the outcomes of insider trading cases in several jurisdictions, including Australia, Canada, Hong Kong, Singapore, the UK and the United States between 2009 and 2015.[248] The study found that there were only 30 actions initiated against offenders in Australia, 20 in Hong Kong, 24 in Ontario, 20 in Singapore, 53 in the UK, and 682 in the US.[249] It concluded that, even though the jurisdictions had similar insider trading laws, the actions initiated by the regulator reflected different enforcement priorities, budgets, strategies, and prosecution policies and practices.[250]

In conclusion, it is clear that insider trading is an area of priority for ASIC,[251] and that ASIC has demonstrated determination in prosecuting insider trading through cases such as the Oliver Curtis prosecution.[252] More recently, the maximum penalty for insider trading was increased to 15 years imprisonment, signalling tougher sanctions for this offence.[253]

Recent studies of ASIC's approach to insider trading show that ASIC has been getting better at proving the offence in a time-efficient manner.[254] Yet, ASIC's empirical data, particularly in Figures 5.16 and 5.18, indicate a declining trend in insider trading cases in the period between FY 2014–15 and December 2019. Nevertheless, the enforcement data and the literature indicate that insider trading offences are treated as serious offences by ASIC and generally pursued with 'criminal prosecution to maximise the deterrent

---

247 See Lei and Ramsay (n 237).

248 Freiberg (n 242) 422. The study looked into several aspects, including the nature of sanctions given to the offenders: see Lev Bromberg, George Gilligan and Ian Ramsay, 'The extent and intensity of insider trading enforcement—an international comparison' (2017) 17(1) *Journal of Corporate Law Studies* 73–110, doi.org/10.1080/14735970.2016.1223952.

249 Freiberg (n 242).

250 Ibid.

251 Chairman Tony D'Alosio, ASIC, 'Insider trading and market manipulation' (Speech, Supreme Court of Victoria Law Conference, Melbourne, Australia, 13 August 2010), asic.gov.au/about-asic/news-centre/speeches/insider-trading-and-market-manipulation/.

252 Greg Medcraft, 'Opinion piece—insider trading' (2016), asic.gov.au/about-asic/news-centre/articles/opinion-piece-insider-trading/. Oliver Curtis was found guilty of insider trading on 2 June 2016 and sentenced to two years' imprisonment.

253 *Treasury Laws Amendment (Strengthening Corporate and Financial Sector Penalties) Act 2019* (Cth).

254 Lei and Ramsay (n 237).

effect'.[255] This, in itself, is arguably a point of strength for ASIC's enforcement regime, which seeks to use criminal sanctions, such as imprisonment, for insider trading offences by individuals. Of course, the true success of ASIC's enforcement approach to insider trading remains significantly tied to other factors such as availability of financial and other resources within ASIC.

Market manipulation

Market manipulation is another significant threat to the 'reputation, integrity and fairness of financial markets'.[256] Constable explains 'market manipulation' as market malpractices that affect the price of securities, and primarily include 'information-based' manipulation that uses fictitious information, such as rumours or other misleading information to affect prices, and 'trade based' manipulation, in which manipulation occurs by trading alone, 'without the accompanying rumours and false or misleading information'.[257] Goldwasser argues that price manipulation in the trading of financial products[258] 'strikes at the heart of the pricing system on which all investors' rely'.[259]

In Australia, the *Corporations Act* contains provisions on 'market manipulation'.[260] Further, the *Telecommunications (Interception and Access) Act 1979* (Cth) classifies the offence of market manipulation as a 'serious offence'.[261] Due to the seriousness of market manipulation, ASIC, as well as other securities regulators the world over, prefers the use of criminal

---

255 Ramsay and Webster (n 174) 23; see also D'Alosio (n 251).

256 Paul Constable, 'Ferocious beast or toothless tiger—the regulation of stock market manipulation in Australia' (2011) 8 *Macquarie Journal of Business Law* 54. Market abuse has existed for over 300 years. Its origins are traced to share trading in coffee shops in London: see Joe Coffey and Jonathan Overett Somnier, 'Market abuse' (2003) 3(4) *Journal of Asset Management* 323–331, doi.org/10.1057/palgrave. jam.2240086. Market manipulation is as old a practice as stock markets themselves: see Louis Loss, *Fundamentals of Securities Regulation* (Aspen Publishers Online, 1983).

257 Constable (n 256) 55.

258 The term 'financial products' is defined in div 3 of pt 7.1 of the *Corporations Act*.

259 Vivien R Goldwasser, 'Regulating manipulation in securities markets: historical perspectives and policy rationales' (1999) 5 *Australasian Journal of Legal History* 149.

260 See *Corporations Act* ss 1311(1) and 1041A. Under these provisions, the aim is to 'ensure that the market reflects the forces of genuine supply and demand': see *North v Marra Developments Ltd* (1981) 148 CLR 42, [59].

261 See *Telecommunications (Interception and Access) Act 1979* (Cth) (*TIA Act*) s 5D(5C). The *TIA Act* allows designated 'interception agencies' to seek warrants for interception of telecommunications during an ongoing investigation of serious offences defined under s 5D of the *TIA Act*: see ASIC Enforcement Taskforce Review, *ASIC Enforcement Review Taskforce Report* (2017) 26. Such agencies include those bodies who are in the exclusive area of operation in law enforcement. ASIC is not considered as an interception agency under the *TIA Act*. The Australian Federal Police (AFP) has the power to obtain a telecommunications interception warrant for ongoing investigations of suspected offences: see Middleton (n 179) 211.

enforcement for dealing with offenders.[262] ASIC's enforcement data for FY 2014–15 to December 2019 substantiates this viewpoint. Figure 5.16 reveals that of ASIC's 13 market manipulation outcomes, eight were criminal, followed by one civil and four administrative outcomes. ASIC pursued no enforceable undertaking/negotiated action in this entire period for market manipulation offences. Conversely, Table 5.15 reveals that in market integrity subcategories other than market manipulation and insider trading, ASIC pursued mainly administrative outcomes for violations.[263]

While the above statistics confirm ASIC's intent of pursing serious offences with criminal sanctions, the aggregate enforcement outcomes, 13, for market manipulation through ASIC's entire period of investigation is abysmally low and translated to ASIC pursuing zero to two criminal actions for each six-month period during the period of investigation. As with insider trading, the overall trend of ASIC's actions against market manipulation offences witnessed a declining trend during the period of investigation.[264] These conclusions and trends are particularly unsatisfactory alongside claims that 'anecdotal evidence, reported cases, academic research and the experience of [ASX's] Surveillance Division suggest that market manipulation is a continuing problem in Australia'.[265]

Consequently, despite statutory attention and ASIC's enforcement action to deter market manipulation, ASIC clearly needs to strengthen enforcement in this area through continued pursuit of strong enforcement outcomes.[266] Notwithstanding that pursing criminal instead of civil penalty proceedings for market manipulation offences results in a longer preparation time for cases (because criminal proceedings require a higher standard of proof),[267]

---

262 See for example *Australian Securities and Investments Commission v Westpac Banking Corporation (No 3)* [2018] FCA 1701. ASIC pursued court action against Westpac for a range of contraventions including market manipulation.

263 ASIC pursued 26 enforcement actions for violations of continuous disclosure norms, 43 enforcement actions for violations of market integrity rules and 55 enforcement actions for other kinds of market misconduct: see Table 5.15, this book.

264 See Figure 5.16, this chapter.

265 Constable (n 256) 55.

266 Beach J noted some of ASIC's allegations against Westpac were not specific or strong enough: see *Australian Securities and Investments Commission v Westpac Banking Corporation (No 3)* [2018] FCA 1701. The Court concluded that Westpac engaged in unconscionable conduct (s 12 of the *ASIC Act*) on four occasions in 2010 while trading prime bank bills in the bill market with the fundamental objective of influencing yields.

267 See Ramsay and Webster (n 174) 23.

it is imperative for ASIC to continue using more criminal enforcement, as it has been, to ensure integrity and uphold the confidence of investors and consumers in the larger financial and securities markets.

To maintain market integrity, especially for insider trading and market manipulation offences, ASIC has demonstrated its use of strong criminal enforcement actions. However, ASIC's total number of enforcement actions across all subcategories within market integrity is 158 for the entire investigation period, which suggests that there is considerable scope for strengthening enforcement outcomes in this area of market misconduct.

Corporate governance

In the HIH Royal Commission, Justice Owen explained 'corporate governance' as:

> the framework of rules, relationships, systems and processes within and by which authority is exercised and controlled within corporations. It encompasses the mechanisms by which companies, and those in control, are held to account.[268]

ASIC regards corporate governance as a key 'driver of the operations and performance of a company',[269] and strives to maintain high corporate governance standards within Australia and periodically reviews existing corporate governance and accountability mechanisms within the financial system.[270]

In terms of the enforcement outcomes for ASIC's selected period, the main conclusions are as follows. First, ASIC's second-highest enforcement actions lay in the corporate governance category, after financial services misconduct. Table 5.15 reveals that ASIC pursued an aggregate of 282 enforcement outcomes for corporate governance violations, ahead of its 158 market integrity outcomes but well beyond its 1,001 financial services outcomes.

---

268 Justice Owen in HIH Royal Commission, *The Failure of HIH Insurance: A Corporate Collapse and Its Lessons* (2003) vol 1, xxxiv. For recent literature on corporate governance, see Jean Jacques Du Plessis, Anil Hargovan and Jason Harris, *Principles of Contemporary Corporate Governance* (Cambridge University Press, 2018), doi.org/10.1017/9781108329453.

269 See ASIC, 'Corporate governance', asic.gov.au/regulatory-resources/corporate-governance/.

270 James Shipton, 'Chartered secretary: what is non-financial risk and why does it matter to ASIC?' (2019) 71(10) *Governance Directions* 535. A Corporate Governance Taskforce was set up in 2018 with the objective of reviewing corporate governance and accountability mechanisms in the Australian financial system.

Second, ASIC pursued mostly administrative outcomes for corporate governance violations. Out of ASIC's aggregate 282 outcomes, 152 were administrative, 56 civil, 38 criminal and 36 enforceable undertakings and negotiated settlements. Figure 5.21 delineates this in percentage terms, revealing that 54 per cent of the corporate governance violations ASIC pursued were administrative, 20 per cent civil, 13 per cent criminal and 13 per cent enforceable undertakings/negotiated settlements.

Third, ASIC pursued the highest number of actions in the directors' subcategory (excluding the miscellaneous misconduct subcategory). Table 5.15 shows ASIC's aggregate actions against directors as 71, well ahead of its actions in other subcategories of corporate governance misconduct.

Fourth, ASIC preferred criminal action against directors during the selected period. Table 5.15 and Figure 5.22 convey that criminal enforcement against directors accounted for nearly half of ASIC's total enforcement actions against directors. Thus, out of an aggregate 71 enforcement actions against directors, 33 were criminal actions.

Fifth, ASIC's strong use of criminal enforcement action against directors was marginally subdued against a declining trend during the selected period. As Table 5.15 and Figure 5.22 illustrate, ASIC's criminal enforcement against directors followed a descending trend for the period of investigation.

Sixth, sharply contrasting with ASIC's enforcement approach against directors' violations, ASIC used mainly administrative action and some enforceable undertakings/negotiated outcomes against auditors. Table 5.15 reveals that the auditors subcategory recorded zero criminal and zero civil actions, but 54 administrative outcomes and five enforceable undertakings/negotiated settlement outcomes. Further, Figure 5.23 recorded an ascending trend of ASIC's enforcement actions against auditors for the selected period.

It is useful to evaluate these enforcement data and trends in the context of the broader corporate governance landscape in Australia. Globally, Australia is known for the strength of its corporate governance practices.[271] Despite

---

271 The 2018 Corporate Governance Watch Report showed that Australia led the way in corporate governance among the other Asian markets: see Asian Corporate Governance Association and CLSA Ltd, *Hard Decisions: Asia Faces Tough Choices in CG Reform* (Corporate Governance Watch, 2018). Among the 12 countries examined in the report, Australia led the tally with an overall corporate governance score of 71 per cent, followed by Hong Kong at 60 per cent, Singapore at 59 per cent, Malaysia at 58 per cent, Taiwan at 56 per cent, Thailand at 55 per cent, India and Japan at 54 per cent each, Korea at 46 per cent, China at 41 per cent, the Philippines at 37 per cent and Indonesia at 34 per cent. These rankings were aggregated from scores in a variety of categories.

the robustness of Australia's corporate governance regime,[272] failures such as the flagrant flouting of principles and practices of corporate governance by Commonwealth Financial Planning Ltd (CFPL),[273] part of the Commonwealth Bank of Australia (CBA) Group, have impacted the overall effectiveness of Australia's corporate governance regime. Consequently, the 2018 Corporate Governance Watch Report noted that Australia's corporate governance regime, 'while still ahead of Asian markets', had fallen to 71 per cent in its overall score from an earlier score of 78 per cent in 2016.[274] The report attributed this fall mainly to revelations made at the Hayne Royal Commission, noting that Australia's strong corporate governance performance was 'tarnished by bank scandals that have gone from bad to worse and political infighting in the federal government'.[275] Additionally, the report flagged issues, such as the lack of an independent, federal anti-corruption commission (instead of the current state-based anti-corruption system) and the need for an overhaul of 'bank governance', for corporate governance reforms in Australia.[276]

While evaluating the failures of corporate governance in Australia, Pearson, through the CFPL case study, aptly summarises the problems with Australia's corporate governance structure:

> There was a wide gap between governance and reporting structures and actual practices. There needs to be further excavation of the gap between the structures of compliance, risk management and governance, and the practices of those individuals and groups responsible … for compliance, risk management and governance. Who knew about the illegal conduct and compliance failures? Why were the requirements of the regulator so easily dismissed? How far were these matters reported, and why did they not go to a board committee? The theories of compliance and corporate governance

---

272 See for example OECD, 'The corporate and market landscape' in *OECD Corporate Governance Factbook 2019* (2019).

273 See 'Commonwealth Financial Planning Limited: what went wrong at CFPL and why?' in Commonwealth of Australia, Economics References Committee (n 154) ch 8. See also Gail Pearson, 'Failure in corporate governance: financial planning and greed' in Christine A Mallin (ed), *Handbook on Corporate Governance in Financial Institutions* (Edward Elgar Publishing, 2016), doi.org/10.4337/9781 784711795.00016.

274 Australian Institute of Company Directors, 'How well does Australia's corporate governance perform?' (1 March 2019), aicd.companydirectors.com.au/membership/company-director-magazine/2019-back-editions/march/update-corporate-governance.

275 The report blamed individual and institutional greed for the financial misconduct, noting that the quest for profits was regarded as a priority instead of the interest of consumers and compliance with the law: see Hayne Report (n 197) 138, 395.

276 Asian Corporate Governance Association and CLSA Ltd (n 271) 13, 93.

had little purchase on reality within the firm. It may be that the global financial crisis triggered in 2008 is a partial explanation for the focus on profits and bonuses at the expense of clients. Part of the problem was the regulator's failure to make CFPL law-breaking public early enough. But this does not answer the failure of corporate governance.[277]

Recently, the Hayne Royal Commission highlighted deficiencies in corporate governance, with a specific focus on directors,[278] who are expected to 'exercise their powers and discharge their duties in good faith, in the best interests of the corporation, and for a proper purpose'.[279] In the past, flagrant breaches of directors' duties, such as in the matters of One. Tel,[280] James Hardie[281] and ABC Learnings Centres,[282] garnered academic discussion and criticism of ASIC's tepid action. However, in recent years ASIC has pursued a higher number of criminal actions for breaches of directors' duties, as the analysis in the chapter shows. ASIC pursued and relied on administrative action for most other subcategories of corporate governance misconduct, a trend that was called out by the Hayne Royal Commission and needs to be reassessed if ASIC is determined to send a stronger and more resolute message about punishing corporate governance violations.

---

277 Pearson (n 273).

278 According to Harris, the overarching theme of the report was 'accountability': see Harris, 'Corporate law lessons' (n 197).

279 Andrew Lumsden, 'The wider implications of the Hayne Report for corporate Australia' (27 February 2019), doi.org/10.2139/ssrn.3342855.

280 ASIC's enforcement case against the directors of One.Tel alleged breaches of directors' duties: see Comino, 'The adequacy of ASIC's "tool-kit"' (n 188). ASIC suffered a 'humiliating defeat' in its One. Tel matter against one of the directors, John David (Jodee) Rich. For a detailed discussion of the One. Tel proceedings, see VG Comino, 'High Court relegates strategic regulation and pyramidal enforcement to insignificance' (2005) 18(1) *Australian Journal of Corporate Law* 48–67. For more literature analysing the One.Tel case, see Will Heath, 'One.Tel Wipe-Out—ASIC v Rich' (2009) 61(11) *Keeping Good Companies* 665; Reza Monem, 'The One.Tel collapse: lessons for corporate governance' (2011) 21(4) *Australian Accounting Review* 340–351, doi.org/10.1111/j.1835-2561.2011.00151.x; Matthew Hooper, 'The business judgment rule: ASIC v Rich and the reasonable-rational divide' (2011) 1(1) *Corporate Governance eJournal* 6919, doi.org/10.53300/001c.6919.

281 In the James Hardie case, although ASIC won the proceedings against the directors, some of the penalties laid by ASIC were reduced: see Comino, 'The adequacy of ASIC's "tool-kit"' (n 188) 360–361, fn 3. For more on the James Hardie case, see Comino, 'James Hardie and the problems' (n 188); Anil Hargovan, 'Australian Securities and Investments Commission v Macdonald [No 11]: corporate governance lessons from James Hardie' (2009) 33 *Melbourne University Law Review* 984; Anil Hargovan, 'Corporate law: honesty is no excuse for liability of James Hardie Officers' (2011) 63(6) *Keeping Good Companies* 354; Vicky Comino, 'The enforcement record of ASIC since the introduction of the civil penalty regime' (2007) 20(2) *Australian Journal of Corporate Law* 183–213.

282 In the ABC Learning Centre case, ASIC pursued the case against the CEO, Edmund (Eddie) Groves, but later dropped the charges against Groves: see Comino, 'James Hardie and the problems' (n 281) 361, fn 3. See also Adele Ferguson, Ben Butler and Ruth Williams, 'Scrutinising ASIC: is it a watchdog or a dog with no teeth?' *The Age* (23 November 2013).

In conclusion, ASIC's enforcement data and the literature clearly show ASIC's use of a variety of enforcement actions to address corporate governance violations, in particular, its preference for administrative and enforceable undertakings/negotiated settlement tools for all subcategories other than directors' duties. Given the systemic nature of corporate governance lapses that the CFPL case study indicates, ASIC's enforcement approach appears mild rather than vigorous. To maintain Australia's competitive edge and global reputation for high corporate governance standards, most areas of corporate governance need a rejuvenated, harder enforcement approach that not only encourages but compels institutions and individuals to adhere to the highest standards and practices.

Financial services

The *Corporations Act* provides for 'fairness, honesty and professionalism by those who provide financial services' as key objects of the statute.[283] This objective is supported by extensive provisions for financial services in ch 7 of the Act that 'mark out the perimeter of the regulatory field', 'create a licensing regime for financial services providers' and provide 'conduct and disclosure obligations on licensees and their representatives'.[284] Financial services provisions apply to, but are not limited to, securities. For violations of these provisions, the *Corporations Act* and div 2 of pt 2 of the *ASIC Act* set out detailed 'consequence provisions' that include administrative, civil, civil penalty and criminal consequences.[285]

Several trends from the analysis of ASIC's enforcement data for the selected period emerge. First, ASIC pursued its highest number of enforcement actions for financial services misconduct, excluding the small businesses category. Table 5.15 illustrates that ASIC completed an aggregate 1,001 enforcement outcomes,[286] as compared to 282 actions for corporate governance and 158 actions for market integrity violations.

---

283 See *Corporations Act* s 760A(b).
284 Hanrahan, 'Deterring white-collar crime' (n 242). The provisions are contained in the *Corporations Regulations 2001* (Cth) and in ASIC's other legislative instruments made under the *Corporations Act 2001* contained in ss 926A, 951B and 992B that grant ASIC powers to give exemptions from, or modify, pts 7.6, 7.7 and 7.8 in many cases. These provisions co-exist and apply along with pt 2 div 2 of the *ASIC Act* dealing with 'unconscionable conduct and consumer protection in relation to financial services' and specifically exclude provisions of the Australian Consumer Law. For a detailed discussion on this, see Robert Baxt, Ashley Black and Pamela F Hanrahan, *Securities and Financial Services Law* (LexisNexis Butterworths, 9th ed, 2017) [8.14].
285 See generally ALRC, *Principled Regulation* (n 158). See also Hanrahan, 'Deterring white-collar crime' (n 242) 421.
286 The total number of actions in the financial services category is 1,001, compared with the total number of enforcement outcomes for the market integrity category, 158, and for corporate governance category, 282: see Table 5.15, this chapter.

Second, within financial services, ASIC pursued the highest enforcement outcomes in respect of 'dishonest conduct and misleading statements'. Table 5.15 shows that, out of ASIC's aggregate 1,001 enforcement outcomes, 221 actions related to 'dishonest conduct and misleading statements', 31 to 'unlicensed conduct', 41 to 'misappropriation, theft and fraud', 341 to 'credit'[287] and 367 to 'other financial services misconduct'.

Third, the enforcement outcomes indicate ASIC's preference for administrative actions over other enforcement tools for financial services misconduct. Table 5.15 shows that out of ASIC's 1,001 actions for financial services, 604 were administrative, followed by 197 enforceable undertakings/negotiated outcomes and 139 civil and 57 criminal actions. In comparison, whereas ASIC pursued 82 administrative outcomes and 18 enforceable undertakings/negotiated outcomes for violations across the market integrity category, it pursued 152 administrative outcomes and 36 enforceable undertakings/negotiated outcomes for corporate governance violations. Figure 5.25 illustrates ASIC's enforcement figures for financial services misconduct in percentage terms as follows: administrative actions constituted 60 per cent, enforceable undertakings/negotiated outcomes 20 per cent, criminal outcomes 6 per cent and civil actions 14 per cent.

Fourth, Figure 5.13 denotes a rising trend in ASIC taking enforcement actions against financial services misconduct between FY 2014–15 and FY 2016–17, and thereafter a steady decline in enforcement actions in this category (mainly administrative and enforceable undertakings and other negotiated outcomes).

Fifth, ASIC pursued a number of criminal and civil enforcement outcomes for the 'dishonest conduct and misleading statements' subcategory. Table 5.15 shows that ASIC secured 21 criminal outcomes, 73 civil, 114 administrative and 13 enforceable undertakings/negotiated outcomes in respect of this subcategory.

Sixth, there were no enforceable undertakings/negotiated outcomes for misappropriation, theft and fraud. Table 5.15 shows that ASIC pursued 25 administrative, eight criminal and nine civil outcomes for this subcategory.

---

287 Credit-related misconduct is beyond the scope of this book.

Seventh, Figures 5.24–5.28 illustrate other trends for ASIC's actions in the financial services category. Figure 5.24 shows a stable enforcement trend for 'unlicensed conduct' and 'misappropriation theft and fraud' across ASIC's selected period. Figure 5.26 shows a heavy use of enforceable undertakings/ negotiated settlements for 'unlicensed conduct' along with a slight decline in the trend for ASIC's enforcement actions for this subcategory. Figure 5.27 illustrates a downward trend for enforcement actions for the 'dishonest conduct and misleading statements' subcategory, while Figure 5.28 illustrates an ascending trend overall in ASIC's enforcement relating to misappropriation, theft and fraud subcategory.

At a first glance, ASIC's high number of enforcement actions for financial services suggest ASIC's commitment to address misconduct in this area. However, on closer analysis, the choice or nature of enforcement outcomes pursued by ASIC—mainly comprising administrative and enforceable undertakings/negotiated settlements—diminishes the overall intensity of ASIC's enforcement action against financial services misconduct, and contributes to the laundry list of problems associated with the financial services regime. First, at the framework level, despite 'extensive, prescriptive and detailed' requirements imposed by ch 7 of the *Corporations Act* on providers of financial services,[288] specifically in respect of 'retail clients',[289] Hanrahan argues that the financial services regime has not been 'effective' or 'fit-for-purpose'. Financial service providers are not seen to 'comply with most substantive provisions most of the time' and the community does not have 'confidence that the financial services it acquires will mostly be provided with fairness, honesty and professionalism'.[290] Hanrahan further states that the ineffectiveness of the financial services regime is shown in the level of rampant non-compliance with the most 'basic regulatory requirements' by even the 'largest and the best-resourced providers in core service areas' as exposed in ASIC's surveillance over the past years.[291] Viewed in this context,

---

288 'Financial services' is referred to in this chapter and book as defined in ch 7 of the *Corporations Act 2001* and not as understood in pt 2 div 2 of the *ASIC Act*.

289 The term 'retail client' is defined in ss 761G and 761A of the *Corporations Act*; see also Baxt, Black and Hanrahan (n 284) [13.30]–[13.33].

290 Hanrahan, 'Deterring white-collar crime' (n 242) 421.

291 Ibid 421. For example, ASIC stated that: 'In general, our review identified a high degree of non-compliance across nearly all AFS licensees reviewed. Many of the compliance concerns were detected related to contraventions of well-established regulatory requirements or non-compliance with fundamental AFS licensing obligations': see ASIC, *Compliance Review of the Retail OTC Derivatives Sector* (Report 482, 2016) [34]. See also ASIC, *Financial Advice: Review of How Large Institutions Oversee Their Advisers* (Report 515, 2017); ASIC, *Financial Advice: Fees for No Service* (Report 499, 2016); ASIC, *Culture, Conduct and Conflicts of Interest in Vertically Integrated Businesses in the Funds-Management*

ASIC's enforcement approach using mainly administrative and enforceable undertakings can hardly be said to have evoked confidence or a sense of justice against repeated misconduct in this area.

Financial advice scandals have underscored shortcomings both within the larger Australian financial framework and in relation to ASIC's enforcement responses, contributing to the dissatisfaction about ASIC's handling of financial services misconduct.[292] In particular, financial products advice and mis-selling have been a prominent source of disquiet and criticism;[293] hence, it is relevant to explore this area, and the adequacy of ASIC's response to such misconduct, in more detail.

Financial advice and mis-selling

Financial advice is central to Australia's financial system for several reasons, including limited financial literacy, complexity of financial investment decisions and biases affecting such decisions.[294] Despite its centrality, Batten and Pearson show that such advice is often 'given without a reasonable basis', suffers on account of 'conflicted remuneration' and has led to parliamentary inquiries.[295] Gilligan et al have pointed to concerns around corporate wrongdoing in the financial advice area and the inadequacy of penalties that such wrongdoings have attracted.[296] Similarly, Comino discusses scrutiny of ASIC in the wake of several high-profile financial advice scandals involving

---

Industry (Report 474, 2016); ASIC, *Review of Retail Life Insurance Advice* (Report 413, 2014); ASIC, *Review of Advice on Retail Structured Products* (Report 377, 2013); ASIC, *SMSFs: Improving the Quality of Advice Given to Investors* (Report 337, 2013).

292 See generally Hayne Report (n 197).

293 See for example ASIC, *Financial Advice: Review of How Large Institutions Oversee Their Advisers* (n 291). It is significant that the *Financial Services Reform Act 2001* (Cth) differentiates between 'general' and 'personal' advice: see RP Austin and Michael Vrisakis, 'Personal financial product advice under the Corporations Act' (2017) 35(8) *Company and Securities Law Journal* 503–532. The *Corporations Act*, s 766B(3), states that 'personal advice' refers to the advice that is given to a person by a financial advice provider regarding the person's financial situation, requirements and goals.

294 Australian Government, Productivity Commission, *Default Superannuation Funds in Modern Awards* (Productivity Commission Inquiry Report, 2012) 4.

295 Richard Batten and Gail Pearson, 'Financial advice in Australia: principles to proscription; managing to banning' (2013) 87(2–3) *St John's Law Review* 511. See generally Commonwealth of Australia, Parliamentary Joint Committee on Corporations and Financial Services, *Inquiry into Financial Products and Services in Australia* (2009). For more on financial advice, see Gill North, 'Financial advice in Australia: important issues for further debate' in Shelley Griffiths and Sheelagh McCracken (eds), *Making Banking and Finance Law: A Snapshot* (Ross Parsons Centre, 2015).

296 George Gilligan et al, *An Analysis of Penalties under ASIC Administered Legislation: Scoping the Issues* (CIFR Paper No 71, 2015) 8, doi.org/10.2139/ssrn.2649724.

premier banking institutions such as the CBA,[297] National Australia Bank[298] and Macquarie Private Wealth.[299] In all these cases, ASIC was criticised for failing to respond 'promptly on early warning signs'.[300]

The Hayne Royal Commission, too, noted that ASIC had failed to respond effectively in this area of corporate wrongdoing. The final report of the commission highlighted two aspects: 1) poor behaviour of the financial sector—banks and institutions—as they were motivated by 'greed' and pursued business 'at the expense of basic standards of honesty';[301] and 2) when such misconduct was revealed to the regulator, 'it was insufficiently punished or not punished at all'.[302]

In regards to the commission's first observation, Jenkins and Braithwaite highlighted the profit motive or greed as a recurrent theme responsible for corporate crime in the early 1990s.[303] The second observation against the 'company law watchdog',[304] ASIC, although serious, did not come as a

---

297 In the CBA scandal, Commonwealth Financial Planning (CFPL), a CBA subsidiary, was accused of placing clients' money in high risk investments without permission, forging documents and earning large commissions: see Pat McGrath and Michael Janda, 'Senate inquiry demands royal commission into Commonwealth Bank, ASIC', *ABC News* (25 June 2014). The Senate inquiry reviewed ASIC's performance and 'showed ASIC as a timid, hesitant regulator, too ready and willing to accept uncritically the assurances of a large institution that there were no grounds for ASIC's concerns or intervention': see ASIC, 'Corporate governance' (n 269).

298 In the NAB case, ASIC commenced civil proceedings against NAB alleging 'fee for no service' conduct: see Kate Hilder and Mark Standen, 'ASIC has commenced proceedings against NAB' (17 December 2019) *MinterEllison*, www.minterellison.com/articles/asic-ffns-proceedings-against-nab-december-2019.

299 See Comino (n 188).

300 Ibid.

301 Hayne Report (n 197) xix. The interim report noted a shocking example of charging deceased persons for an advice to substantiate its claim that financial advice, bank and loan intermediaries had acted from greed: see *Royal Commission into Misconduct in the Banking, Superannuation and Financial Services Industry* (n 217).

302 Josh Frydenberg, 'Banking royal commission: ASIC failed to enforce the law', *The Australian* (29 September 2018). See also Justin O'Brien, '"Because they could": trust, integrity, and purpose in the regulation of corporate governance in the aftermath of the *Royal Commission into Misconduct in the Banking, Superannuation and Financial Services Industry*' (2019) 13(2–3) *Law and Financial Markets Review* 141–156, doi.org/10.1080/17521440.2019.1612616.

303 Anne Jenkins and John Braithwaite, 'Profits, pressure and corporate lawbreaking' (1993) 20(3) *Crime, Law and Social Change* 221–232, 222, doi.org/10.1007/BF01308451. See also Harold C Barnett, 'Corporate capitalism, corporate crime' (1981) 27(1) *Crime & Delinquency* 4–23, doi.org/10.1177/00111 2878102700102.

304 See Comino, 'Australia's company law watchdog' (n 158); Vicky Comino, *Company Law Watchdog: ASIC and Corporate Regulation* (Thomson Reuters, 2015). ASIC refers to itself as the corporate watchdog: see Greg Medraft, 'ASIC explained: who is the corporate watchdog, what does it do and why should Australians care?' (Speech, National Press Club of Australia, 3 December 2014), download.asic.gov.au/media/2311430/speech-to-the-national-press-club-published-3-december-2014.pdf.

surprise to many.[305] Collectively, these observations led to the inference that the problems highlighted by the Hayne Royal Commission in respect of financial advice misconduct and mis-selling within the Australian financial system have been ongoing for several years. Two prominent corporate failures, from the post-Wallis era, are discussed below to illustrate some key issues.

The first significant case is that of the Westpoint Collapse of 2005, which saw the failure of the Westpoint Corporation, a well-established property developer. The Westpoint business involved 'raising finance for its development projects primarily through issuing unsecured promissory notes to retail investors in amount of $50,000 or greater, offering returns of 12 per cent per annum'.[306] When the Westpoint group collapsed, investigations revealed several illegalities and areas of misconduct that resulted in severe losses for retail investors,[307] and brought to the fore malpractices by financial advisers who were charging as high as 10 per cent commissions per client.[308] It is pertinent to note that the Wallis Report had considered the issue of such commissions and had highlighted the need for their disclosure to clients, but had made no recommendations to cap such fees or regulate them.[309]

Similarly, the Storm Financial collapse in 2008, which resulted in colossal losses of approximately $830 million for its 14,000 clients, nearly a third of whom 'were invested in leveraged investments', exposed the weaknesses and excesses in the financial advice industry.[310] For its financial advice, Storm Financial charged 7 per cent per transaction, and thus benefitted

---

305 See generally Ferguson, Butler and Williams (n 282).

306 Mathew Peckham, 'From the Wallis Report to the Murray Report: a critical analysis of the financial services regime between two financial system inquiries' (2015) 33 *Company and Securities Law Journal* 481.

307 Ibid. When the Westpoint group collapsed, it owed 4,300 investors a sum that was nearly $388 million in total.

308 Ibid. See *Statutory Oversight of the Australian Securities and Investments Commission (Westpoint Report)* (2006) [2.3]–[2.5]. Commissions were the main type of remuneration being charged for financial advice and the existing law did not prohibit or regulate commissions if they were declared to the client by the adviser: see Joint Committee on Corporations and Financial Services, *Inquiry into Financial Products* (n 295).

309 See Commonwealth of Australia, Financial System Inquiry, *Final Report* (1997) (Wallis Report).

310 Peckham (n 306) 481. Many clients were advised by Storm Financial to borrow money against the equity in their homes, invest in the share market and borrow more money through margin loans to expand their financial portfolio. According to ASIC, the estimated losses, which increased due to the simultaneous share market fall of 2008, were approximately $830 million: see ASIC, 'ASIC and CBA Storm financial settlement' (8 March 2013), download.asic.gov.au/media/1310959/ASIC-and-CBA-Storm-financial-settlement-8-March-2013.pdf.

when it advised clients to borrow more and increase their investments.[311] A parliamentary inquiry in 2009 revealed rampant misconduct: for example, clients of Storm Financial were advised to borrow on a leveraged investment model without care to individual financial capacity and capability.[312] In sum, this scandal re-emphasised the unjust and dangerous nexus between 'remuneration structures' and 'financial advice' provided by financial advisers that incentivised such advisers to pursue their own interests over the interests of their clients.[313]

These financial collapses and frauds highlight the vulnerabilities that exist even within an advanced financial system such as Australia's. They also show the limitations of the regulatory framework, such as the challenges of information exchange and coordination between Australian regulators,[314] and, to some extent, the insufficiency of active and effective regulatory oversight and supervision of financial market participants. While financial and corporate frauds cannot be completely eliminated in even the most robust regulatory systems, the effective use of enforcement powers can certainly generate more deterrence and restore trust in the financial system and its players—areas in which ASIC has faced severe criticism.[315]

To conclude the analysis of ASIC's enforcement of financial services misconduct, ASIC's own statistics and the academic literature suggest that this, perhaps, is ASIC's Achilles' heel. The Hayne Royal Commission, too, in discussing recent advice scandals in its final report,[316] severely criticised ASIC for its heavy reliance on administrative action and its use of enforceable undertakings and negotiated settlement, strategies that failed in curbing misconduct in financial services and the mis-selling of financial products.

---

311 Joint Committee on Corporations and Financial Services, *Inquiry into Financial Products* (n 295) [3.12]–[3.16].

312 Ibid.

313 Peckham (n 306) 482.

314 See Andrew Godwin and Ian Ramsay, *Twin Peaks—The Legal and Regulatory Anatomy of Australia's System of Financial Regulation* (CIFR Paper No 074/2015; University of Melbourne Legal Studies Research Paper No 725, 2015), doi.org/10.2139/ssrn.2657355. The Parliamentary Joint Committee on Corporations and Financial Services found that communication 'between ASIC and APRA was lacking'. Among other recommendations, it asked ASIC and APRA to continue 'sharing information, even when a request for … information [had] not been received': see Parliament of Australia Joint Committee on Corporations and Financial Services, *Inquiry into the Collapse of Trio Capital* (2012) 77, 84.

315 The Senate inquiry in 2014 into the performance of ASIC held that there was excessive reliance on disclosure as a method to protect retail investors and that the same had failed: see Commonwealth of Australia, Economics References Committee (n 154) 28 [4.10].

316 The royal commission highlighted advice scandals involving the Big 4 banks and entities like the AMP, which were found to be charging a 'fee for no service': see Hayne Report (n 197) 136.

While ASIC responded quickly to these criticisms with a renewed strategy and focus on 'litigation' and 'court action',[317] the new approach appears to have been somewhat dampened in recent times.[318]

With this understanding of ASIC's use of its enforcement powers, the next section critiques the effectiveness of ASIC's enforcement and compliance regime in its entirety.

Effectiveness of ASIC's enforcement and compliance regime: A critique

Deterring corporate wrongdoing and realising high compliance levels have been consistent discussion themes in Australia and across the world.[319] The ongoing Australian Law Reform Commission Review (ALRC Review) of the legislative framework for corporations and financial services regulation is a fine example of Australia's many efforts to further strengthen its financial marks and enhance levels of compliance.[320] As well as an array of specific legislative changes, the ALRC Review is the Australian government's direct response to the Hayne Royal Commission,[321] marking an entry into the

317 Legg and Speirs (n 183). See also George Gilligan and Ian Ramsay, 'Is there underenforcement of corporate criminal law? An analysis of prosecutions under the ASIC Act and Corporations Act: 2009–2018' (2021) 38(6) *Company and Securities Law Journal* 435–458.

318 See Ronald Mizen, 'ASIC dumps "why not litigate" policy as Frydenberg resets path', *Financial Review* (26 August 2021), afr.com/politics/federal/asic-dumps-why-not-litigate-as-frydenberg-resets-path-20210825-p58lyx.

319 Helen Bird and George Gilligan, 'Deterring corporate wrongdoing: penalties, financial services misconduct and the Corporations Act 2001 (Cth)' (2016) 34(5) *Company and Securities Law Journal*. This concern is stated in the final report of the Economics References Committee: see Commonwealth of Australia, Economics References Committee (n 154). On self-regulation as a strategy to overcome corporate crime, see John Braithwaite and Brent Fisse, 'Self-regulation and the control of corporate crime' (1987) 21 *Private Policing* 221; John Braithwaite, 'Enforced self-regulation: a new strategy for corporate crime control' (1982) 80(7) *Michigan Law Review* 1466–1507, doi.org/10.2307/1288556. See also John Braithwaite and Gilbert Geis, 'On theory and action for corporate crime control' (1982) 28(2) *Crime & Delinquency* 292–314, doi.org/10.1177/001112878202800207; Gilligan et al, *An Analysis of Penalties* (n 296); O'Neil (n 156).

320 ALRC, 'Terms of reference', *Review of the Legislative Framework for Corporations and Financial Services Regulation* (2020). See also ALRC, *Australian Law Reform Commission: Interim Report a Financial Services Legislation* (2021).

321 In Australia, royal commissions are the highest form of independent inquiry ordered into matters of public importance: see Australian Government, 'About royal commissions', www.royalcommission.gov.au/about-royal-commissions. The Royal Commission into Misconduct in the Banking, Superannuation and Financial Services Industry (also known as the Hayne Commission) was established on 14 December 2017: see Superannuation and Financial Services Industry Royal Commission into Misconduct in the Banking, 'Home', www.royalcommission.gov.au. The final report by the Hayne Commission was presented on 1 February 2019: see Hayne Report (n 197).

long list of reviews and inquiries into Australia's financial system.[322] Many of these reviews and inquiries focus on ASICs powers and performance[323] and have been conducted by both domestic and international bodies.[324]

Domestically, ASIC's functioning is continuously monitored and overseen through parliamentary mechanisms such as the Joint Parliamentary Committee on Corporations and Financial Services.[325] Reviews and inquiries are commissioned periodically to critically assess ASICs powers and effectiveness.[326] A significant example was the Senate Economics Reference Committee's report published in June 2014 entitled *Performance of the Australian Securities and Investments Commission*.[327]

Several important assessments of ASIC's use of investigative and enforcement powers have been carried out under the direction of the Department of Treasury, including the *ASIC Enforcement Review Task Force Report* of

322 The Australian financial system is subject to periodic reviews. An important review was conducted by the Campbell Committee in 1981: see *Australian Financial System: Final Report of the Committee of Inquiry* (1981). A second watershed moment was the review chaired by Stan Wallis in 1997: see Wallis Report (n 309). This report restructured the regulatory architecture of the Australian financial system from sectoral to functional. A third significant inquiry occurred under the chairmanship of David Murray in 2014: see Financial System Inquiry, *Final Report* (2014) (Murray Report).

323 The Murray Report recommended the provision of stronger regulatory tools to ASIC, particularly product intervention power: see Murray Report (n 322) 236.

324 In terms of domestic reviews, financial system inquiries, royal commissions and parliamentary committees assess the working of the financial system with specific focus on the regulators and their performance in implementing financial policies and laws. On the international front, the Australian financial system, and ASIC specifically, is subject to periodic assessments by bodies such as the IMF and the Financial Stability Board: see Council of Financial Regulators, 'International assessments', cfr.gov. au/financial-stability/resources/international-assessments.html.

325 This committee is established under s 243 of the *ASIC Act* to inquire into the activities of ASIC and report to both houses of parliament. See Parliament of Australia, *Parliamentary Joint Committee on Corporations and Financial Services*, aph.gov.au/Parliamentary_Business/Committees/Joint/ Corporations_and_Financial_Services. See also Parliament of Australia, 'Oversight of ASIC: reports tabled between 1997–2019' aph.gov.au/Parliamentary_Business/Committees/Joint/Corporations_and_ Financial_Services/Membership/asic.

326 Several parliamentary committees monitor, review and inquire into matters pertaining to corporations and financial services and the performance of ASIC: see Parliament of Australia, 'Committees', aph.gov.au/Parliamentary_Business/Committees.

327 For example, in 2014, a Senate Economics References Committee Inquiry into the Performance of ASIC was established by the federal government: see Commonwealth of Australia, Economics References Committee (n 154). See also Parliament of Australia, 'Senate Standing Committees on Economics', aph.gov.au/Parliamentary_Business/Committees/Senate/Economics. For the federal government's response to the Murray Report, see Australian Government, The Treasury, *Government Response to the Financial System Inquiry* (20 October 2015), treasury.gov.au/publication/government-response-to-the-financial-system-inquiry.

2017[328] and the ASIC Capability Review of 2016.[329] Moreover, a review of ASIC's funding model was carried out in 2015,[330] and, in response to the Hayne Royal Commission, the government announced additional funds for ASIC's budget to support 'an accelerated enforcement strategy'.[331]

Internationally, the IMF[332] and the Financial Stability Board (FSB)[333] have published reviews of Australia's financial system. The IMF's *Financial System Stability Assessment Report 2019* states that 'Australia benefits from a robust regulatory framework' that is 'generally in conformity with international best practices'.[334] The FSB's country-wise reviews have assessed individual sectors of the Australian financial system in great detail, namely banking,[335] insurance[336] and securities markets.[337]

---

328 Australian Government, *ASIC Enforcement Review Taskforce Report* (2017).

329 One of the recommendations of the Murray Inquiry was to ensure regular reviews of the capability of financial regulators. The ASIC Capability Review was established by the Australian government in December 2015: see Australian Government, The Treasury, *Fit for the Future: A Capability Review of the Australian Securities and Investments Commission* (2015). The review aimed to ensure that ASIC had the skills and culture to perform the 'enhanced role which the FSI has laid out for ASIC in its report': see ASIC, 'ASIC capability review', asic.gov.au/about-asic/what-we-do/how-we-operate/performance-and-review/asic-capability-review/. See also ASIC's self-assessments against the Australian government's regulator performance framework: ASIC, *Regulator Performance Framework: ASIC Self-Assessment 2019–20* (Report 691, 2021).

330 The Australian government released a consultation paper on 28 August 2015: see Australian Government, The Treasury, *Proposed Industry Funding Model for the Australian Securities and Investments Commission* (2015).

331 An additional A$400 million was granted to ASIC: see Josh Frydenberg, 'Record funding and resources for ASIC and APRA to help restore trust in Australia's financial sector' (Media Release, 22 March 2019).

332 So far, the FSAP findings for Australia have been published in the Financial System Stability Assessments on three occasions: February 2019, November 2012 and October 2006. See Council of Financial Regulators, 'International assessments' (n 324).

333 The FSB monitors the implementation of the G-20's FSB recommendations on international financial reforms and periodically reviews the progress of each country, with Australia's reviews having occurred in August 2016 and September 2011: see ibid.

334 IMF, *Australia: Financial System Stability Assessment* (IMF Staff Country Report No 19/54, 2019) 6, doi.org/10.5089/9781484398999.002.

335 On Australia's detailed review of its banking regime conducted by the IMF, see generally IMF, *Australia: Basel Core Principles for Effective Banking Supervision—Detailed Assessment of Observance* (IMF Staff Country Report No 12/313, 2012), doi.org/10.5089/9781475540093.002. For a recent review, see generally IMF, *Australia: Financial Sector Assessment Program—Detailed Assessment of Observance—Basel Core Principles for Effective Banking Supervision* (Financial Sector Assessment Program, 2019).

336 For a detailed review of Australia's insurance sector, see generally IMF, *Australia: Financial Sector Assessment Program, Technical Note—Insurance Sector: Regulation and Supervision* (Financial Sector Assessment Program, 2019).

337 For a detailed review of Australia's securities sector, see IMF, *Australia: IOSCO Objectives and Principles of Securities Regulation—Detailed Assessment of Implementation* (IMF Staff Country Report No 12/314, 2012) (*Australia Country Report*), doi.org/10.5089/9781475563412.002.

These examples highlight the focused and intense attention on ASIC's performance as regulator, particularly on its enforcement and compliance mechanisms, which are continually appraised to ensure their effectiveness against corporate wrongdoing and misconduct. Corporate wrongdoing is a worldwide phenomenon[338] that has sparked many debates globally on the best ways to punish wrongdoers.[339] Several studies conducted in different parts of the world show the larger community or the 'general public' to be 'growing intolerant of certain types of white-collar crime'.[340] Kristy et al associate the term 'white-collar crime' with Edwin Sutherland who, in the 1940s, analysed 'crime in the upper, or white-collar class'.[341] Despite this, 'definitional clarity' of the term 'corporate wrongdoing' still eludes

---

338 Corporate wrongdoing extends beyond borders, such as in Ireland and US: see Joe McGrath, *Corporate and White-Collar Crime in Ireland: A New Architecture of Regulatory Reinforcement* (Manchester University Press, 2015), doi.org/10.7228/manchester/9780719090660.001.0001; Charles WL Hill et al, 'An empirical examination of the causes of corporate wrongdoing in the United States' (1992) 45(10) *Human Relations* 1055–1076, doi.org/10.1177/001872679204501003.

339 See for example Gilligan et al, *An Analysis of Penalties* (n 296); Bird and Gilligan (n 319). Some academics believe that white-collar crime is not as serious as other 'real crimes', such as murder. Comino refers to the distinction between 'regulatory and real-crimes' drawn in the academic literature, where serious crimes like murder and robbery are treated differently from other offences. Those who favour this distinction do not place regulatory violations in the same basket as 'traditional crimes' and therefore consider the 'criminalisation' of the former 'inconsistent with public morality': see Vicky Comino, 'Civil or criminal penalties for corporate misconduct—which way ahead?' (2006) 34(6) *Australian Business Law Review* 428–446.

Other academics believe white-collar crimes to be more serious. For example, Seumus Miller argues that the 'problem of a corrupt or incompetent corporate leader is of an entirely different order of magnitude from that of a crooked or inept corner store grocer': see Seumus Miller, 'The current simplification process and questions of corporate ethics' (Paper, National Corporate Law Teachers Conference, 6–7 February). For a better understanding of the legal debate on the utilisation of criminal sanctions as a regulatory tool and a sociological perspective on white-collar crime, see Bridget M Hutter, *The Reasonable Arm of the Law?: The Law Enforcement Procedures of Environmental Health Officers* (Clarendon Press, 1988) 30–34.

340 See Kristy Holtfreter et al, 'Public perceptions of white-collar crime and punishment' (2008) 36(1) *Journal of Criminal Justice* 50–60, doi.org/10.1016/j.jcrimjus.2007.12.006. According to Holtfreter et al, a substantial proportion of the American population would prefer while-collar criminals to be punished as harshly, or more harshly, than violent criminals, and many believe that government should allocate more or equal resources to the control of while-collar crime. For similar data collected in the UK, see Michael Levi and Sandra Jones, 'Public and police perceptions of crime seriousness in England and Wales' (1985) 25(3) *The British Journal of Criminology* 234–250, doi.org/10.1093/oxfordjournals.bjc.a047529. See also Robert C Holland, 'Public perceptions of white collar crime seriousness: a survey of an Australian sample' (1995) 19(1) *International Journal of Comparative and Applied Criminal Justice* 91–105, 91, doi.org/10.1080/01924036.1995.9678540.

341 Gilligan et al, *An Analysis of Penalties* (n 296) 10. See LK Schuessler and Edwin H Sutherland, 'On analysing crime' (University of Chicago Press, 1973) xix.

researchers.[342] In Australia, corporate wrongdoing is understood quite broadly.[343] ASIC's Report 387 on penalties for corporate wrongdoing refers to it as:

> misconduct that occurs in the corporate, financial market or financial services sectors. This type of misconduct generally breaches corporate, financial market or financial services laws. It may involve the misuse of a professional position or information obtained in a professional capacity.[344]

Against this objective of deterring corporate wrongdoing, the following discussion reflects on ASIC's enforcement approach and the empirical data analysis conducted earlier in this chapter, as well the academic literature and other reviews, to evaluate whether ASIC's use of its enforcement powers was optimal or effective during the period under review.

The first factor relevant for assessing the effectiveness of ASIC's enforcement and compliance regime is ASIC's successful application of the responsive regulation approach and its enforcement pyramid. The contribution of responsive regulation theory to corporate law in Australia is acknowledged;[345] however, as discussed above, its application has been lacking.[346] Despite ASIC's continuous use of its enforcement powers, the literature shows that ASIC's effectiveness in penalising corporate wrongdoers has been wanting.[347] This is attributed to ASIC's vague, hesitant and weak application of (especially) the apex of the enforcement pyramid. This, consequently, has diminished the overall effectiveness of ASIC's enforcement regime during the selected period.

The second indicator of effectiveness of ASIC's regime is the actual number of enforcement outcomes achieved. The analysis above shows that ASIC's enforcement actions in the financial and services markets have been

---

342 HC Finney and HR Lesieur, 'A contingency theory of organizational crime, in SB Bacharach (ed) *Research in the Sociology of Organisations* (1982) 263.

343 For the purposes of this book, the term 'corporate wrongdoing' is used interchangeably with 'corporate malfeasance', 'corporate misconduct' and 'corporate crime'. The book does not use the term in its narrow technical sense nor does it differentiate between 'corporate crime' and 'illegal corporate behaviour'. On this aspect, see Melissa S Baucus and Terry Morehead Dworkin, 'What is corporate crime? It is not illegal corporate behavior' (1991) 13(3) *Law & Policy* 231, doi.org/10.1111/j.1467-9930.1991.tb00068.x.

344 Extensive harm is attributed by ASIC to the all-encompassing category of corporate wrongdoing: see ASIC, *Penalties for Corporate Wrongdoing* (n 152).

345 See 'Regulatory theories and their application to ASIC' in Commonwealth of Australia, Economics References Committee (n 154) ch 4.

346 For example, ASIC was criticised for not taking 'on the big end of town'; see ibid ch 17.

347 See for example Constable (n 256); Ferguson, Butler and Williams (n 282).

consistently on the lower rather than higher side. ASIC's enforcement outcomes across all categories totalled 3,944 for the selected period; out of these, 2,503 actions belonged to the small business category and 1,441 to offences within financial and securities markets. Of these 1,441 actions, the number for securities markets is even smaller, although, as explained earlier, ASIC's current data do not enable the segregation of securities markets enforcement figures from the rest of its enforcement data. Even so, the statistic of 1,441 actions for financial markets misconduct out of 3,944 implies that a large majority of ASIC's enforcement resources and efforts were directed towards small business deterrence and compliance matters during the selected period.

Further, in regard to some categories within the financial and securities markets, such as market manipulation, ASIC's enforcement actions are extremely low. ASIC's enforcement data revealed a total of 13 actions pursued by ASIC for market manipulation, averaging one enforcement action every six months of ASIC's selected period. This statistic is shocking. It not only detracts from ASIC's effectiveness, but also begets a larger question: does ASIC have too much on its regulatory plate?[348]

The third marker of effectiveness, linked to the first point on the weak application of ASIC's enforcement pyramid, is ASIC's choice of enforcement actions and/or the nature of these. ASIC's discretion, judgment or 'choice of enforcement options' has been questioned by scholars in recent years.[349] As ASIC's empirical data show, the majority of its enforcement actions for misconduct in all areas of financial misconduct (other than in the small business category) were administrative or enforceable undertaking/ negotiated settlements. ASIC's substantial use of these powers, and significantly low use of criminal and civil powers, indicated a 'soft' approach towards wrongdoings in financial services and corporate governance areas,[350] leading the Hayne Royal Commission to note ASIC's failure in addressing

---

348 For instance, in the Bank Bill Swap Rate case, ASIC was criticised for failing to make its case adequately against Westpac: see *ASIC v Westpac Banking Corporation* [2018] No 3 1701.

349 See Comino, 'The adequacy of ASIC's "tool-kit"' (n 188) 370. See also Jason Harris, 'Is ASIC the watchdog that no one fears?' *University of Sydney* (Opinion, 22 February 2019), sydney.edu.au/news-opinion/news/2019/02/22/is-asic-the-watchdog-that-no-one-fears-.html.

350 Refer to the comments of the Commonwealth of Australia, Economics References Committee (n 154).

corporate misconduct in financial services.[351] In particular, the commission uncovered shortcomings in retail markets and suggested improvement to ASIC's enforcement regime.[352]

Further, Comino argues that the principles of 'rule of law' and 'equality before the law' have been undermined in ASIC's enforcement regime, which has only sought to prosecute smaller players in the financial industry while giving a long rope to more serious but 'well-sourced' offenders, such as big organisations and companies.[353]

Collectively, these criticisms highlight issues with ASIC's internal decision-making processes relating to enforcement, necessarily affecting the standing of ASIC's enforcement regime.

Limitations in ASIC's powers have, possibly, contributed to ASIC's reluctance to pursue stronger enforcement actions against wrongdoers,[354] in turn, negatively affecting the effectiveness of ASIC's enforcement regime. It is fair to state that limitations in ASIC's investigative and enforcement powers toolkit, discussed in Chapter 4 of this book, may have impacted ASIC's decisions about which enforcement actions to pursue. However, the Hayne Royal Commission was reluctant to grant much latitude to ASIC on this point, attributing the lack of strong enforcement measures to ASIC's culture rather than to a dearth of powers.[355] In any case, the recent reforms introduced to increase ASIC's powers and the penalties for corporate wrongdoing (discussed in Chapter 4) are a step in the right

---

351 The royal commission made lengthy observations on many aspects of the financial services industry, such as misconduct in banking, financial advice, superannuation, insurance, role of the regulator, culture and governance: see Hayne Report (n 197) 37. The royal commission, in its interim report, was very critical of ASIC's efforts to address a range of misconduct issues: see *Royal Commission into Misconduct in the Banking, Superannuation and Financial Services Industry* (n 217). See also George Gilligan, 'The Hayne Royal Commission—just another piece of official discourse?' (2019) 13(2–3) *Law and Financial Markets Review* 114–123, doi.org/10.1080/17521440.2019.1612991.

352 The royal commission found 'serious misconduct within ASIC's remit', and criticised ASIC for its 'overall enforcement actions against financial services entities' as well as its tendency to rely heavily on negotiated outcomes and administrative sanctions rather than court actions and criminal sanctions: see Harris, 'Corporate law lessons' (n 197).

353 See V Comino, 'The challenge of corporate law enforcement in Australia' (2009) 23 *Australian Journal of Corporate Law* 252–253. See also Smith (n 161).

354 See for example Thomas Middleton, 'ASIC's regulatory powers—search warrants, telecommunications interception warrants, financial services licensing decisions and banning orders—suggested reforms' (2021) 38 *Company and Securities Law Journal* 179–196.

355 See for example Hughes (n 204) 202.

direction, as they show the federal government's commitment to removing hurdles relating to powers and penalties, thereby enabling ASIC to pursue enforcement matters more effectively.

Financial constraints have also, arguably, influenced ASIC's choice of enforcement, in turn impacting the effectiveness of ASIC's enforcement and compliance actions. In the past, IMF–World Bank FSAP reviews have commented on the financial constraints affecting ASIC's ability to carry out adequate inspection and surveillance programs.[356] Budgetary cuts are a perpetual source of worry, as they directly limit the surveillance measures adopted by ASIC.[357]

In this context, it is relevant to highlight the Wallis Committee's recommendations: both ASIC and the Australian Prudential Regulation Authority (APRA) were envisaged to have 'operational autonomy' to fulfil their regulatory mandates in a manner that was 'efficient' and 'cost-effective'.[358] For this purpose, the Wallis Committee proposed that ASIC and APRA finance their 'operational costs through levies upon the institutions they supervise'—a suggestion that, until recently, had been endorsed by the Australian government only in respect of APRA,[359] but has now has been extended to ASIC through an industry-funding model.[360] Prior to the introduction of this model, and during most of the period under review (2014–19), ASIC was largely dependent on government funding. Voicing its concerns about this funding model, ASIC stated:

> ASIC is largely funded by government appropriation. Variance in funding from year to year exacerbates the uncertainty inherent in the budget process and results in inefficiencies in the allocation of

---

356 See generally IMF, *Australia Country Report* (n 337).

357 For instance, in 2014, ASIC's budget was reduced by 12 per cent, impacting several aspects of the organisation. ASIC Chair Medcraft made it clear that ASIC would need to rely on whistleblowers to uncover corporate wrongdoing as its budget would be insufficient to undertake surveillance. 'We will not undertake the same level of proactive surveillance that we did previously and will have to be more careful in selecting those matters we pursue. At the end of the day … where people see white-collar crime occurring, it becomes more important for people to report that': see G Wilkins, 'You're on your own: watchdog ASIC's warning after budgetary cuts', *Sydney Morning Herald* (4 June 2014), smh.com.au/business/youre-on-your-own-watchdog-asics-warning-after-budget-cuts-20140604-39i4s.html.

358 Andrew Godwin, Steve Kourabas and Ian Ramsay, 'Twin Peaks and financial regulation: the challenges of increasing regulatory overlap and expanding responsibilities' (2016) 49(3) *The International Lawyer* 279. See also Wallis Report (n 309) 531–532.

359 See Godwin, Kourabas and Ramsay (n 358) 279. See also *Australian Prudential Regulation Authority Act 1998* (Cth) pt 5 div 1 on APRA's funding arrangements.

360 Chapter 3 discusses ASIC's new industry funding model, but also highlights reasons why it may not be sufficient.

> ASIC's resources to achieve regulatory outcomes ... ASIC's current funding model was criticised by the Financial Stability Board (FSB) and the International Monetary Fund (IMF) in November 2012. The IMF expressed concerns about the government-funded models of Australia, the United States, Japan and Argentina. They were concerned about a lack of stable funding, an inability to commit resources to longer term projects and weaknesses in proactive supervision.[361]

In addition to these issues, other problems that reduced the effectiveness of ASIC's enforcement and compliance regime have been identified. For example, in the wake of the Hayne Royal Commission, fears of 'regulatory capture' were voiced.[362] Questions about ASIC's integrity and anti-corruption arrangements, along with regulatory capture risks, were also raised by the 2019 Parliamentary Joint Committee on Corporations and Financial Services.[363]

In conclusion, while ASIC has most certainly used its enforcement powers, it has demonstrated effective and deterrent use of these powers only in a minority of areas of misconduct (other than small business), such as breach of directors' duties and insider trading. In the majority of areas, ASIC's enforcement options have been mild and not deterrent enough to curb specific systemic problems within Australia's larger financial system, specifically in financial advice and mis-selling. In 2012, the World Bank–IMF Country Report on Australia noted ASIC as 'an enforcement focused regulator', but granted ASIC's regime a 'broadly implemented' rating in respect of IOSCO Principle 12.[364] In 2019, the IMF highlighted several shortcomings and gaps in ASIC's performance, including in enforcement and compliance, signifying a decline in its regime.[365]

---

361 ASIC, *Financial System Inquiry: Submission by the Australian Securities and Investments Commission* (2014) 52–55. See also Godwin, Kourabas and Ramsay (n 358), 279.

362 See Rod Maddock, 'It's not lack of resources: Hayne report shows regulator ASIC has been captured', *Financial Review* (30 September 2018), afr.com/opinion/its-not-lack-of-resources-hayne-report-shows-regulator-asic-has-been-captured-20180930-h161sk. See also Harris, 'Corporate law lessons' (n 197) 366.

363 Parliament of Australia, *Parliamentary Joint Committee* (n 325) 25.

364 IMF, *Australia Country Report* (n 337) 5. A 'broadly implemented' rating is better than 'partly implemented' rating though not as good as a 'fully implemented' rating.

365 Some of the gaps that have been identified in the report relate to the 'lack of independence and resourcing of the regulatory agencies', weakness in 'enforcement powers' and their 'use' and inability in preventing 'misconduct': see IMF, *Australia: Financial System Stability Assessment* (n 334), 6–7.

That said, there is also a bigger picture to consider in scrutinising ASIC's enforcement effectiveness—namely, the fact that the number of participants and retail investors in the financial market surged in the post-Wallis era, putting the entire financial regime to a severe test.[366] As a result, and in spite of a well-constructed and resilient financial regulatory framework comprising the twin-peaks model, the growing financial system has periodically witnessed corporate failures that have resulted in financial losses to investors and exposed regulatory gaps, overlaps and inaction in the regulatory structure.[367] In the face of these challenges and other limitations in ASIC's enforcement regime, ASIC acknowledges the 'increasing community and public expectation' towards punishing those who are responsible for corporate wrongdoing.[368] ASIC is aware of the large community expectation—over and above the political, professional, academic, media and other formal means of scrutiny—to deliver credible and deterrent enforcement of corporate wrongdoing. This expectation is fuelled by societal intolerance of corporate misconduct, stemming both from its 'financial costs' to the general society[369] as well as from its ability to 'undermine faith in social institutions'.[370] Consequently, alongside repeated calls for strengthening the regulatory powers of ASIC and improving the 'levels of corporate compliance',[371] there is now immense pressure on ASIC to deliver on this requirement.[372]

---

366 Peckham (n 306).

367 For example, the failure of the HIH Insurance Group led to the setting up of the royal commission in 2001. Other corporate failures since the Wallis Report include the Westpoint, ABC Learnings Centre and Storm Financial collapses, and the Trio Capital fraud: see generally Peckham (n 306).

368 ASIC, *Penalties for Corporate Wrongdoing* (n 152). ASIC's report notes that recent domestic and international corporate scandals have emphasised this expectation and refers to comments made by Chief Justice Warren of the Supreme Court of Victoria: see M Dunckley, 'Top judge warns of harsher sentences for corporate crimes', *Australian Financial Review* (7 January 2014).

369 For more on the financial costs of such corporate wrongdoing, see generally James C Helmkamp, Kitty J Townsend and Jenny A Sundra, 'How much does white collar crime cost?' *National White Collar Crime Center*, ojp.gov/ncjrs/virtual-library/abstracts/how-much-does-white-collar-crime-cost; Cedric Michel, John K Cochran and Kathleen M Heide, 'Public knowledge about white-collar crime: an exploratory study' (2016) 65(1–2) *Crime, Law and Social Change* 67–91, doi.org/10.1007/s10611-015-9598-y.

370 Comino, 'Civil or criminal penalties for corporate misconduct' (n 339) 429. See also JH Farrar, 'The ASC and the criminal process' (1993) 67 *Law Institute Journal* 603.

371 O'Neil (n 156) 322.

372 See generally John Price, 'Emerging lessons from the Financial Services Royal Commission for the regulation of health practitioners' (AHPRA, National Registration and Accreditation Scheme Combined Meeting, Melbourne, Australia, 28 February 2019), asic.gov.au/about-asic/news-centre/speeches/emerging-lessons-from-the-financial-services-royal-commission-for-the-regulation-of-health-practitioners/.

Conclusion

From an international perspective, ASIC's compliance regime, buttressed by twin peaks, a sound responsive regulation approach, high-quality academic and industry feedback loops, and strong accountability mechanisms, undoubtedly sits among the top percentile of the world's financial regulatory regimes. However, from a domestic viewpoint, ASIC's enforcement and compliance response to flagrant and systemic corporate wrongdoings, especially in the area of financial advice and mis-selling, can, at best, be termed tepid. When compared to other significant Australian regulators such as the ACCC, it may even be termed ineffective and poor. By relying mainly on its administrative and negotiated settlement toolkit, ASIC has played it safe and, consequently, has punched well below its weight and capability. ASIC's enforcement response to corporate misconduct has been unanimously criticised by Australia's highest independent accountability body, reputed academics and the wider community.

The effectiveness of ASIC's enforcement and compliance regime is somewhat dampened by the shortcomings highlighted in this chapter. Accordingly, ASIC's degree of alignment with the core requirements of IOSCO Principle 12 is currently determined as 'moderate'. Given the strength of ASIC's underlying enforcement approach, and high-quality accountability and feedback mechanisms, the stage of evolution of its enforcement and compliance regime is assessed as 'mature'. Finally, frequent reviews and reforms to improve ASIC's enforcement performance indicate that the extent of change in recent years in this area has been 'substantial'.

Synthesis and conclusion

This chapter separately analysed SEBI's and ASIC's use of their enforcement powers and the effectiveness of their enforcement and compliance regimes to ascertain their degree of alignment with IOSCO's Principle 12. The analysis—based on empirical enforcement data for ASIC and SEBI for their respective selected periods along with the available literature—facilitates a broad understanding of SEBI's and ASIC's use of their enforcement powers and the implementation of a credible and deterrent enforcement regime. It provides a useful foundation for future, deeper comparative research on SEBI and ASIC's regimes. However, the current available data inhibit the making of accurate comparative assessments of the two regimes for two reasons. First, the terminology and variables used by both regimes are vastly different, with SEBI's data presenting further limitations as discussed above. Second, while SEBI's enforcement data strictly relate to securities markets, ASIC's mandate as the financial conduct regulator is much wider, and, hence, its enforcement data represent actions for the entire financial market.

Broadly, the analysis reveals that SEBI's enforcement regime is advancing in the desirable direction to enhance core market fundamentals, such as integrity, transparency, fairness, resilience and investor protection. SEBI's enforcement action demonstrates determination and expertise in pursuing matters vigorously in some areas of regulation. Despite resource and capacity limitations, SEBI outperformed expectations in a host of important enforcement matters. Even so, SEBI is constrained by a multitude of external and internal factors. Further, the conspicuous scarcity of quality academic literature on securities markets in India renders SEBI's own publications, such as its annual report, the main source of understanding its enforcement and compliance regime. However, the data in these publications do not present SEBI's enforcement activities in an optimal manner, but rather appear confusing and underdeveloped. In particular, the format adopted for SEBI's annual report lacks consistent, quantitative variables, as well as critical and qualitative analysis, which prevents an in-depth understanding of SEBI's approach to enforcement, its strengths and weaknesses.

In contrast, details of ASIC's enforcement approach and enforcement data are readily available and well presented, along with an ample and rich literature that analyses ASIC's enforcement regime. These enable a more detailed examination of ASIC's enforcement and compliance regime. The analysis of ASIC's regime in this chapter leads to several conclusions. First, most of ASIC's enforcement resources and efforts were directed towards the small business compliance and deterrence category as compared to the market integrity, financial services and corporate governance categories. Second, in the smaller number of enforcement actions initiated by ASIC for categories other than small businesses, ASIC's enforcement strategy was mainly 'persuasive' rather than 'deterrent'. To achieve credible deterrence and regain investors' trust and confidence in the markets, ASIC must bite hard at systemised corporate wrongdoing and practices—occurring across the financial sector in financial advice, mis-selling and insider trading among other areas—to prevent them from eroding, and potentially weakening, the core fundamentals of the financial market. To a large extent, the establishment of the Hayne Royal Commission, the decisive increase in both civil and criminal penalties for white-collar crimes, and ASIC's resolve to initiate more enforcement actions address the wider community sentiment to penalise corporate wrongdoings in a much stronger way than before. To this end, ASIC's new approach to pursue more court-based actions, with multiple proceedings (even though modified) is likely to send out a stronger message to corporations and other financial participants.

In conclusion, it is reasonable to assert that the challenge before a financial regulator is not to entirely eliminate financial misconduct or fraud, but to minimise it by the credible and effective use of its supervisory and enforcement powers. To this end, SEBI's enforcement, despite limitations, is clearly evolving to a higher level of effectiveness, while ASIC's enforcement, though mature, is on a path to reinvent its approach to address corporate wrongdoing more strongly. In light of this discussion, broadly, the degree of comparability on the use of SEBI's and ASIC's supervisory and enforcement powers is assessed as 'moderate'. This reflects the wider and more fundamental challenges before SEBI as compared to ASIC, which faces a specific and narrower set of challenges to deliver an effective enforcement and compliance regime. The relevance of cooperation is assessed as 'high', as engagement in this area entails deeper discussions around enforcement strategies and approaches to augment compliance with securities regulations. Such cooperation will offer a wider perspective on the challenges faced by SEBI and ASIC, and a chance for them to creatively collaborate towards effective solutions.

6

Self-regulation and gatekeepers: IOSCO Principles 9 and 19–23

Introduction

This chapter analyses the securities regulation regimes of the Securities and Exchange Board of India (SEBI) and the Australian Securities and Investments Commission (ASIC) in light of the International Organization of Securities Commissions' *Objectives and Principles of Securities Regulation* (IOSCO Principles) 9 and 19–23 concerning self-regulation and select gatekeepers. Principle 9 lays down the requirements for self-regulatory organisations (SROs) within a securities regulation regime while Principles 19–23 relate to the role, responsibilities and requirements for gatekeepers of the securities markets, namely the auditors, credit rating agencies (CRAs), and evaluative and analytical research service providers (referred to as 'market analysts' in this book).

A robust regime for SROs and gatekeepers is essential for the maintenance of effective first-level supervision of listed companies. It supports the integrity of the market and investor confidence and protection. Coffee argues that 'corporate governance depends upon "gatekeepers" to protect the interests of investors and shareholders by monitoring the behaviour of corporate "insiders" and by reporting the financial results of corporate performance' accurately and unbiasedly to allow for an 'objective valuation of the firm'.[1] Tuch specifically considers the role of CRAs as gatekeepers,[2] and discusses the different meanings ascribed to the term 'gatekeepers' by Kraakman[3] and Coffee.[4] Kraakman defines gatekeepers as 'private actors who are able to prevent wrongdoing', while Coffee defines them as agents who act as 'a reputational intermediary to assure investors as to the quality of the "signal" sent by the corporate issuer'.[5] With this significance of SROs and gatekeepers in mind, this chapter begins with an evaluation of SEBI's and ASIC's regimes.

An evaluation of the Indian and Australian securities regulation regimes: IOSCO Principles 9 and 19–23

The comparative analysis for each IOSCO Principle examined in this chapter is presented along the lines set out in Chapter 3, with the regimes' key features and implementation separately analysed against key requirements of the IOSCO Principle(s). Accordingly, each regime is assessed in terms of the degree of alignment, stage of development and extent of change. The final part of chapter synthesises the analysis and draws conclusions on the degree of comparability and relevance for cooperation between the two regimes.

---

1   John C Coffee, *The Acquiescent Gatekeeper: Reputational Intermediaries, Auditor Independence and the Governance of Accounting* (Columbia Law and Economics Working Paper No 191, 2001) 1.

2   Andrew F Tuch, 'Multiple gatekeepers' (2010) *Virginia Law Review* 1664.

3   Reinier H Kraakman, 'Gatekeepers: the anatomy of a third-party enforcement strategy' (1986) 2(1) *Journal of Law, Economics, & Organization,* 53.

4   John C Coffee, *Gatekeepers: The Professions and Corporate Governance* (Oxford University Press, 2006), doi.org/10.1093/oso/9780199288090.001.0001.

5   Cited in Tuch, 'Multiple gatekeepers' (n 2) 1664.

Table 6.1: Snapshot of the analysis in this chapter relating to SROs and select gatekeepers

IOSCO Principles of Securities Regulation	SEBI's degree of alignment, stage of development and extent of reform in recent years	ASIC's degree of alignment, stage of development and extent of reform in recent years	Degree of comparability	Relevance for cooperation
Principle for self-regulatory organisations				
Principle 9: Self-Regulatory Organisations (SROs) should be subject to oversight of regulators, and observe high standards of fairness and confidentiality	**Moderate** Evolving Substantial	**High** Mature Minor	**High**	**High**
SEBI's FSAP 2013* rating: 'not assessed' and 'broadly implemented' (P9 corresponds to P6 and P7 under the pre-GFC IOSCO document**) ASIC's FSAP 2012*** ratings: 'fully implemented'				
Principles for auditors, credit ratings agencies and other information service providers				
Principle 19: Auditors should be subject to adequate levels of oversight	**Moderate** Evolving Substantial	**High** Mature Minor	**Low/Moderate**	**High**
SEBI's FSAP 2013 rating: 'not assessed' (P19 was included post-GFC as a new principle) ASIC's FSAP 2012 ratings: 'fully implemented'				
Principle 20: Auditors should be independent of the issuing entity that they audit	**Moderate** Evolving Substantial	**High** Mature Minor	**Low/Moderate**	**High**
SEBI's FSAP 2013 rating: 'not assessed' (P20 was included post-GFC as a new principle) ASIC's FSAP 2012 ratings: 'fully implemented'				
Principle 21: Audit standards should be of a high and internationally acceptable quality	**Moderate** Evolving Substantial	**High** Mature Minor	**Low/Moderate**	**High**
SEBI's FSAP 2013 rating: 'partly implemented' (P21 corresponds to P16 under the pre-GFC IOSCO document) ASIC's FSAP 2012 ratings: 'fully implemented'				

IOSCO Principles of Securities Regulation	SEBI's degree of alignment, stage of development and extent of reform in recent years	ASIC's degree of alignment, stage of development and extent of reform in recent years	Degree of comparability	Relevance for cooperation
Principle 22: Credit rating agencies should be subject to adequate levels of oversight; should be registered with the regulator and subject to ongoing supervision	**Moderate** Evolving Substantial	**High** Mature Substantial	**Moderate**	**High**
SEBI's FSAP 2013 rating: 'not assessed' (P22 was included post-GFC as a new principle) ASIC's FSAP 2012 ratings: 'fully implemented'				
Principle 23: Entities offering investors analytical and evaluative services should be subject to oversight and regulation appropriate to their impact on the market or the degree to which the regulatory system relies on them	**Moderate** Evolving Substantial	**High** Mature Substantial	**Moderate**	**High**
SEBI's FSAP 2013 rating: 'not assessed' (P23 was included post-GFC as a new principle) ASIC's FSAP 2012 ratings: 'fully implemented'				

Note: *FSAP 2013 refers to IMF, *India: Financial Sector Assessment Program — Detailed Assessments Report on IOSCO Objectives and Principles of Securities Regulation* (Country Report No 13/266, 2013). **pre-GFC IOSCO document refers to IOSCO, *Objectives and Principles of Securities Regulation* (May 2003); ***FSAP 2012 refers to IMF, *Australia: IOSCO Objectives and Principles of Securities Regulation — Detailed Assessment of Implementation* (Country Report No 12/314, 2012).

Principles for self-regulation

Regulatory regimes sometimes rely on SROs, such as stock exchanges, to achieve their objectives.[6] IOSCO defines an organisation as an SRO if 'it has been given the power or responsibility to regulate and its rules are subject to meaningful sanctions regarding any part of the securities market or industry'.[7] It regards SROs as valuable to a regulator in the process of securities regulation and highlights benefits to business conduct, production of information, flexibility and technology from such self-regulation.[8] It addresses inadequate oversight of SROs by referring to the 'appropriate use'[9] and 'inappropriate use'[10] of SROs. Principle 9 enunciates the core requirements for SROs.

Principle 9: Where the regulatory system makes use of Self-Regulatory Organisations that exercise some direct oversight responsibility for their respective areas of competence, such SROs should be subject to the oversight of the regulator and should observe standards of fairness and confidentiality when exercising powers and delegated responsibilities.

---

6   IOSCO, *Methodology for Assessing Implementation of the IOSCO Objectives and Principles of Securities Regulation* (2017).

7   There are some quintessential features of self-regulated organisation (SROs). For example, such entities make rules that are relevant for a certain industry (ie eligibility norms for individuals and firms), specify conduct or qualifications for staff members and make disciplinary rules in case of violations: ibid 53. In common parlance, 'SRO' refers to a non-governmental entity with powers to create and enforce industry and professional rules and standards: see *Investopedia*, 'Self-regulatory organization (SRO): definition and examples', investopedia.com/terms/s/sro.asp.

8   IOSCO notes four main benefits of an SRO: a) SROs are useful as they often require 'observance of ethical and business conduct standards which go beyond government regulations'; b) SROs are often more capable of compelling 'production of information' than government regulators; c) SROs have more depth and expertise in understanding market operations and, thus, respond faster to market conditions and are more flexible than regulators; d) SROs 'build and maintain technology infrastructures' that allow them to carry out their own regulatory functions: see IOSCO (n 6).

9   Appropriate use of SROs are gauged by: a) 'SRO's capacity to carry out the purposes of relevant governing laws, regulations, including the development and implementation of SRO rules'; b) if the SRO is subject to adequate regulatory oversight; c) enhancement of a regulator's resources if SRO's expertise is used; and d) if there are appropriate standards of corporate governance to ensure that conflicts of interest that are inherent in self-regulation are managed effectively: see ibid.

10   Inappropriate use of SROs refers to: a) if SRO activities are carried out without authorisation; or b) without any or insufficient oversight from the regulator; or c) if SRO functions are being carried out by regulatory institutions that are incapable of meeting appropriate standards of authorisation; or d) if SROs abuse or misuse the quasi-governmental powers: see ibid.

Principle 9

Historically, stock exchanges across the world were owned and operated by brokers[11] and performed a self-regulatory role, 'essentially regulating themselves'.[12] Given this history, IOSCO Principle 9 enumerates two core requirements:

1. oversight and supervision of SROs by the regulator
2. adoption of appropriate standards by SROs that essentially provide for:
   a. prohibition of fraudulent and unfair or manipulative practices that cause harm to market integrity and to investors
   b. organisation and capacity to monitor compliance
   c. an effective disciplinary mechanism to enforce rules including powers to expel, suspend, fine and censure a member.[13]

This section discusses the manner and the extent to which IOSCO's SRO requirements are reflected within SEBI's and ASIC's regimes.

SEBI

Key features of the SRO framework

Section 11(2)(d) of *Securities and Exchanges Board of India Act 1992* empowers SEBI to promote and regulate SROs. However, presently, there are no organisations officially designated as SROs in the Indian securities markets, though recognised stock exchanges (RSEs) act like SROs, as they perform a range of supervisory and regulatory functions.[14] SEBI oversees the functioning of these RSEs through the legal and regulatory framework that includes the *Securities Contracts (Regulation) Act 1956* (*SCR Act*) and *Securities Contracts (Regulation) (Stock Exchanges and Clearing Corporations) Regulations 2018* (*SCR Regulations*), as well as circulars and guidelines that it issues periodically.

---

11 For more on the self-regulation role of SROs, see Janet Austin, 'Governments to the rescue: ASIC takes the reins of the stock markets' (2010) 28 *Company and Securities Law Journal* 446. For example, in India, the Bombay Stock Exchange, Asia's oldest stock exchange (established 1875) has traditionally performed many self-regulation functions.

12 J Board, C Sutcliffe and S Wells, *Transparency and Fragmentation: Financial Market Regulation in a Dynamic Environment* (Palgrave MacMillan, 2002) 8.

13 IOSCO (n 6).

14 There are now seven recognised stock exchanges (RSEs) in India of which four have been granted permanent recognition: see SEBI, 'Details of stock exchanges: list of stock exchanges', www.sebi.gov.in/stock-exchanges.html. To understand the role of self-regulatory organisations in the Indian securities markets: see also World Bank, *India: Role of Self-Regulatory Organizations in Securities Market Regulation* (2007).

In their SRO-like capacity, RSEs perform functions of 'front line regulators and supervisors for brokers' and play a 'role in market surveillance'.[15] Stock brokers registered with SEBI are mandatorily required to be members of an RSE, which ensures their front line supervision.[16] Further, through an intricate grid of rules, by-laws and regulations,[17] RSEs establish standards for dealing in securities,[18] create norms for fair trading and market integrity,[19] provide for matters relating to the day-to-day functioning and operations of the exchange,[20] and establish elaborate and effective disciplinary and grievance mechanisms.[21]

Just as RSEs self-regulate stock brokers, depositories perform self-regulatory functions vis-a-vis depository participants that are registered with them.[22] Other organisations, such as the Association of National Exchanges Members of India, Association of Mutual Funds of India, Association of Merchant Bankers of India and the Financial Planning Standards Boards of India also operate in the securities markets, but their functions are akin to industry associations and not self-regulation.[23] However, in recent years, SEBI has explored the establishment of SROs in different sectors of the securities markets and sought public comments through consultative papers,[24] such as for distributors of mutual fund products[25] and investment advisers.

Analysis

As the above description shows, RSEs perform SRO-like functions for the Indian securities markets. SEBI relies on RSEs for three main roles: listing of securities, regulation and oversight of brokers, and surveillance of markets.[26] To ensure their proper functioning, the *SCR Act* and *SCR Regulations*

---

15 IMF, *India: Financial Sector Assessment Program—Detailed Assessments Report on IOSCO Objectives and Principles of Securities Regulation* (2013) (*India FSAP Report*).

16 See *SEBI (Stock Brokers and Sub-brokers) Regulations 1992* reg 6A(1)(a).

17 See for example National Stock Exchange, 'NSE regulations', nseindia.com/regulations/exchange-market-regulations-rules-byelaws-nseil.

18 See *National Stock Exchange of India Limited—Bye Laws*, ch IV, 'Dealing in securities', archives.nseindia.com/global/content/regulations/NSEbyelaws.pdf.

19 See ibid ch XIV, 'Miscellaneous'.

20 See ibid ch III, 'Regulations'.

21 See ibid ch XI, 'Arbitration', and ch XII, 'Default'.

22 See generally *Depositories Act 1996*.

23 See IMF, *India FSAP Report* (n 15).

24 SEBI floated a consultation paper on forming an SRO for mutual fund distributors and investment advisers: see 'SEBI floats consultation paper on SRO for distributors and RIAs', *Morningstar* (1 April 2019), morningstar.in/posts/51879/sebi-floats-consultation-paper-sro-distributors-rias.aspx.

25 SEBI, 'Applications invited for being recognized as SRO for distributors of mutual fund products', www.sebi.gov.in/sebi_data/attachdocs/1372333934152.pdf.

26 See generally SEBI, *Annual Report 2018–19* (2019).

establish a concrete foundation and framework for matters relating to oversight and governance of RSEs. For example, the *SCR Act* requires the central government and SEBI to oversee their functioning through a grant of recognition to them and by approving their by-laws for regulation and control of contracts.[27] Further, while granting such recognition to RSEs, the framework allows SEBI to impose a range of conditions, such as for avoidance and management of conflicts of interest,[28] while also mandating appointment of independent members on the RSEs' boards.[29] The *SCR Regulations* impose further obligations in relation to the recognition of stock exchanges,[30] net worth requirements,[31] and ownership requirements for stock exchanges to ensure institutional strength and robustness.[32] Similarly, the RSEs carry out their SRO-like functions through a vast framework of internal documents, namely their by-laws, rules and regulations that stipulate core requirements for fair and equitable trading and functioning of trading members and platforms. Overall, this framework reflects the core requirements of IOSCO Principle 9 to a great degree.

The implementation of this oversight and supervisory framework—over both RSEs and brokers—poses some challenges. First, although SEBI carries out comprehensive inspections of RSEs,[33] the frequency of such inspections is relatively low and needs strengthening and greater resources.[34] One suggestion is to create a separate regulatory arm of the stock exchanges to self-monitor their regulatory functions.[35] In order to avoid conflicts of interest, such a regulatory arm could be solely 'answerable to the market regulator' and not to the Board of the RSE.[36]

---

27 See *Securities and Contracts (Regulation) Act 1956* ss 4 and 9.

28 IOSCO notes that 'effectiveness of an SRO may be compromised by conflicts of interest': see IOSCO (n 6) 56.

29 IMF, *India FSAP Report* (n 15).

30 See *Securities Contracts (Regulation) (Stock Exchanges and Clearing Corporations) Regulations 2018* ch II.

31 Ibid ch III.

32 Ibid ch IV.

33 See 'Oversight of stock exchanges' in SEBI, *Annual Report 2018–19* (n 26) 139.

34 While SEBI's *Annual Report 2018–19* reveals several instances of surveillance activities and inspections carried out in respect of market intermediaries, inspections carried out in respect of RSEs are comparatively rare: ibid 155. Further, it is unclear how many human, monetary or other resources are allocated for supervision and inspection of exchanges.

35 Shikha Rawal, 'Stock exchanges: conflicts in governance upon listing' (2017), ssrn.com/abstract =3079351.

36 Ibid.

Second, more resources need to be devoted by RSEs to oversight of their trading members. Statistics published in SEBI's 2018–19 Annual Report reveal that SEBI conducted 159 inspections of brokers.[37] RSEs carried out the majority of broker inspections, namely 1,396.[38] This number is insufficient given the sheer number of registered brokers in the market.[39]

The detailed FSAP Review of 2013 of the Indian securities sector gave SEBI's regime a 'broadly implemented' grade in respect of the principle corresponding with IOSCO Principle 9.[40] However, as revealed in the FSAP Review of 2017 (the most recent), enhancing oversight of 'financial market infrastructures' (ie stock exchanges) remains a recurrent area of further development for SEBI.[41]

Conclusion

While the legal and regulatory framework for oversight and supervision of RSEs by SEBI, and of trading members by RSEs is comprehensive, there is scope for strengthening their implementation, particularly the supervision of RSEs by SEBI. The general degree of alignment of the SRO regime with IOSCO Principle 9 is, thus, assessed as 'moderate' in this book. Over the past decade, particularly after the FSAP Review of 2013, SEBI's initiatives in the area of oversight and supervision of RSEs surged; therefore, the extent of change in recent years is assessed as 'substantial', with a perceptible shift to risk-based supervision in respect of RSEs and enhancement of measures, such as conflicts of interest requirements for RSEs. The promising developments in this area suggest that the overall landscape for oversight and supervision of RSEs is 'evolving' rapidly.

---

37 NSE conducted 552 inspections; BSE, 527; and MCX, 317: see SEBI, *Annual Report 2018–19* (n 26). The inspections, according to SEBI, were focused on the themes that included compliance by stock brokers of norms related to 'Investor Redressal Mechanism, [h]andling of funds and securities clients, [s]ettlement of accounts of clients on timely basis, [s]egregation of clients and propriety funds/ securities, [p]ledging of securities by the broker, KYC norms'.

38 Ibid 141. These inspections were carried out by the RSEs after consultation with SEBI.

39 For the current list of intermediaries recognised and registered with SEBI: see SEBI, 'Recognised intermediaries', sebi.gov.in/sebiweb/other/OtherAction.do?doRecognised=yes. See Chapter 5 of this book for more detail.

40 The extant Principle 9 corresponds to the earlier Principles 6 and 7 under the erstwhile 30 IOSCO Principles of Securities Regulations. The FSAP Review of 2013 did not give a rating for Principle 6 and gave a 'broadly implemented' rating for Principle 7: see IMF, *India FSAP Report* (n 15).

41 IMF, *India: Financial System Stability Assessment—Press Release and Statement by the Executive Director for India* (IMF Country Report No 17/30, 2017).

ASIC
Key features of the SRO framework

Similar to India, no institution is formally endowed with an SRO status in the Australian securities markets.[42] However, some institutions, such as stock exchanges, perform functions that are similar to SROs. These are examined in detail below.[43]

The Australian Securities Exchange[44] (ASX), formally the Australian Stock Exchange,[45] is the dominant stock exchange operating in Australia.[46] As part of its licence requirements,[47] it performs a number of self-regulatory functions in the securities markets.[48] Pursuant to these requirements, ASX is required to 'do all things necessary to ensure the market is fair, orderly and transparent'. It is also required to have in place adequate arrangements for operating the market, handling conflicts of interest, and monitoring and enforcing compliance with market's operating rules.[49] Further, the ASX is required to provide 'reasonable assistance to ASIC' in performance of its functions,[50] and to notify ASIC about any 'significant contravention' of the *Corporations Act 2001* (Cth) (*Corporations Act*).[51] The ASX clearing

---

42 IMF, *Australia: IOSCO Objectives and Principles of Securities Regulation—Detailed Assessment of Implementation* (IMF Staff Country Report No 12/314, 2012) (*Australia Country Report*) 59, doi.org/10.5089/9781475563412.002.

43 This analysis focuses on the SRO-like functions performed by the Australian market licence holders. There are other bodies within the securities and financial markets that establish rules in codes of conduct that market actors must abide by, such as the Australian Financial Complaints Authority: see Australian Financial Complaints Authority, 'Investments and financial advice complaints', afca.org.au/make-a-complaint/investments-and-financial-advice.

44 The ASX was formed in 1987: see Janet Austin, 'A rapid response to questionable trading—moving towards better enforcement of Australia's securities laws' (2009) 27 *Companies and Securities Law Journal* 203, doi.org/10.2139/ssrn.1338374. The ASX is the most significant of Australia's exchanges with the highest 'listing of securities' and level of activity: see IMF, *Australia Country Report* (n 42).

45 The Australian Stock Exchange merged with the Sydney Futures Exchange in 2006 to become Australian Securities Exchange, known as ASX Ltd: see ASX, 'ASX story', asx.com.au/about/asx-story.

46 See generally ch 11 in Robert Baxt, Ashley Black and Pamela F Hanrahan, *Securities and Financial Services Law* (LexisNexis Butterworths, 2016) 415. The other significant, relatively new exchange is Chi-X. It began its operations in 2011 with only eight tradeable stocks and now has over 2,100 ASX listed companies. There are some other market licence operators; however, the analysis relating to SROs in this book is restricted to the ASX.

47 The ASX is licensed to operate the Australian Securities Exchange under s 795B of *Corporations Act 2001* (Cth) (*Corporations Act*). For a deeper understanding of the regulatory framework and the Australian market license regime: see Australian Government, The Treasury, *Australia's Financial Market Licensing Regime: Addressing Market Evolution* (Options Paper, 2012) 5.

48 See Austin, 'A rapid response' (n 44).

49 The *Corporations Act* sets out 'General Obligations' for a market licensee: see s 792A.

50 Obligation to assist the Australian Securities and Investments Commission (ASIC) is set out in ibid s 792D.

51 Obligation to notify ASIC of certain matters is set out in ibid s 792B.

and settlement entities must have a clearing and settlement facility licence (CSFL) and also perform self-regulation functions in relation to their participants.[52]

In addition to the statutory requirements prescribing the ASX's self-regulation responsibilities, the ASX maintains operating rules to deal with matters that are prescribed in regulations,[53] which mainly ensure 'execution of orders' as well as 'disclosure of transactions'.[54] Self-regulation is also evident in how the ASX takes certain enforcement decisions against market, clearing and settlement participants, which may be brought before the ASX Appeal Tribunal.[55] ASIC's Regulatory Guide 172.126 reiterates the requirement of appropriate organisational structures to ensure fair, orderly and transparent operation of markets without conflicts between the market licence holders compliance and supervision duties and commercial functions.[56] In fact, market licence holders, such as the ASX, as well as CFSL holders, must observe the same confidentiality, procedural fairness and conflicts of interest standards as apply to ASIC.[57] The ASX and other listing markets also hold the primary responsibility for the listing rules, which include enforcing continuous disclosure by listed companies.[58]

The statutory provisions and ASIC's regulatory documents thus make it clear that the ASX and CSFL holders are required to regulate participants that use their markets and facilities.[59]

---

52   An application for CSFL is granted under ibid s 824A(2). A CS facility licensee must have adequate arrangements to handle conflicts of interest and enforce compliance with operating rules: see ibid s 821A. Relevant entities include ASX Clear, ASX Settlement and ASX Clearing Corporation.

53   Ibid s 793A.

54   The operating rules generally provide for matters that include requirements of directors or the supervisory structure of a company whose shares are listed, business integrity requirements, organisational competency requirements, technical or human resource requirements, and insurance requirements, among others: see IMF, *Australia Country Report* (n 42) 142.

55   The ASX Appeal Tribunal is an independent body that has the duty to determine, through a peer review process, appeals that are made before it by market participants or clearing and settlement members against orders passed by the ASX: see Australian Stock Exchange, 'ASX Appeal Tribunal', asx.com.au/about/regulation/asx-compliance/participants-compliance/asx-appeal-tribunal.

56   ASIC's Regulatory Guide 172 on financial markets applies to domestic and overseas operators; it explains the obligations of market operators under pts 7.2 and 7.2A of the *Corporations Act*: see ASIC, *Financial Markets: Domestic and Overseas Operators* (Regulatory Guide 172, 2018).

57   See IMF, *Australia Country Report* (n 42).

58   ASX, 'ASX listing rules', asx.com.au/regulation/rules/asx-listing-rules.htm. Corporate governance norms are discussed later in this chapter under Principle 17.

59   Australian market licence holders are required to meet extensive obligations including ensuring fair, orderly and transparent markets; monitoring participant conduct and compliance with operating rules; complying with licence conditions; having adequate conflict management arrangements in place;

Analysis

As foreshadowed, the legal and regulatory provisions envision SRO-like functions to be carried out by several entities within the Australian securities markets. Arguably, the ASX, in its capacity as a market licence holder, performs the most evident and prominent self-regulatory function. The ASX's SRO responsibilities have been subject to continuous change and transformation spanning decades. At the start of the 1990s,[60] Australia followed what Goldwasser described as the US model of 'co-regulation' of securities markets,[61] in which ASIC[62] carried out licensing duties for markets and the ASX regulated markets and participants by enforcing its rules.[63] With the demutualisation of stock exchanges in the late 1990s,[64] exchanges began playing the role of both market operator and regulator, leading to concerns and problems including around conflicts of interest.[65] Since the ASX, the 'dominant exchange' in Australia, also controlled clearing and settlement facilities, there was a risk that it could potentially use these to 'engage in anti-competitive behaviour against new entrants'.[66] An attempt to resolve these issues was made in 2006, when the ASX hived off its regulatory functions to a separate subsidiary,[67] although this proved unsatisfactory.[68]

---

having sufficient resources; having adequate compensation arrangements in place to cover client losses; providing assistance to ASIC; reporting on compliance and notifying people about clearing and settlement arrangements: see Australian Government, The Treasury, *Australia's Financial Market* (n 47) 5–6, 128.

60   Austin, 'Governments to the rescue' (n 11). Australia adopted a model similar to the US almost 50 years later. In the US, the *Securities Exchange Act 1934* started the practice of self-regulation by the stock exchanges.

61   Vivien Goldwasser, *Stock Market Manipulation and Short Selling* (Centre for Corporate Law and Securities Regulation, 1999) 39.

62   ASIC was referred to as the Australian Securities Commission until the passing of the new Act in 2001.

63   The rules were referred to as 'operating rules' and consisted of business rules, listing rules, clearing and settlement rules: see Goldwasser (n 61). See also *Corporations Act* pt 7.2.

64   Demutualisation refers to the shift in the ownership structure of stock exchanges: see generally JW Carson, *Conflicts of Interest in Self-Regulation: Can Demutualized Exchanges Successfully Manage Them?* (World Bank Policy Research Working Paper No 3183, 2003), doi.org/10.1596/1813-9450-3183.

65   Ibid 6–17. See also Roberta S Karmel, 'Turning seats into shares: causes and implications of demutualization of stock and futures exchanges' (2002) 53 *Hastings Law Journal* 367; Caroline Bradley, 'Demutualization of financial exchanges: business as usual?' (2001) *Northwestern Journal of International Law and Business* 657. For deliberation on the conflicts of interest, see Explanatory Memorandum to the Corporations Amendment (Financial Market Supervision) Bill 2010 (Cth) 18.

66   Austin, 'Governments to the rescue' (n 11) 447. Self-regulation was anticipated to also lead to other issues around reduction in resources allocated by exchanges towards their regulatory functions: see Carson (n 64).

67   The ASX moved its surveillance and regulatory functions into a separate subsidiary, the ASX Markets Supervision Pty Ltd: see Austin, 'Governments to the rescue' (n 11) 448.

68   Ibid. The hiving-off of regulatory functions was unsatisfactory because the subsidiary still remained under the control of, and was funded by, the public listed company. There were several other factors, such as the introduction of competition, problems of conflicts of interest, and difficulty in detecting market manipulation and insider trading, that eventually caused problems for the ASX's self-regulatory model.

Eventually, in 2010, the ASX transferred supervision responsibilities for trading of securities to ASIC.[69] According to Baxt et al, the amendment introduced on 1 August 2010 to the *Corporations Act* by the *Corporations Amendment (Financial Market Supervision) Act 2010* (Cth)[70] changed:

> the administrative and legal arrangements for the regulation of securities markets in Australia, by switching much of the responsibility previously held by the Australian Securities Exchange in dealing with these matters to the Australian Securities and Investments Commission.[71]

In particular, the amendment curtailed some of the ASX's important SRO functions relating to the supervision and surveillance of its securities markets and market participants,[72] specifically regarding the trading of securities.[73]

It is noteworthy that the ASX's erstwhile larger supervisory and self-regulatory role in the trading of securities in Australia throughout the 1990s was supported and justified despite several problems during the period, including 'the lack of adequate and imaginative enforcement of existing laws, drafting laws and appropriate funding for the regulatory machinery'.[74]

However, by 2009, against mounting concerns and criticism of the self-regulation or co-regulation framework,[75] the Australian government consciously moved to a 'whole-of-market' supervision model,[76] which it

---

69   ASX, 'ASX story' (n 45).
70   Explanatory Memorandum to the Corporations Amendment (Financial Market Supervision) Bill 2010 (Cth).
71   Baxt, Black and Hanrahan (n 46).
72   Austin, 'Governments to the rescue' (n 11). See also ASIC, 'ASIC welcomes government's announcement' (n 69).
73   The introduction of the amendment meant that the ASX was 'no longer the sole market operator regulating the trading of securities': see Baxt, Black and Hanrahan (n 46) 414.
74   Barrie Dunstan, 'Regulation is more than black letter law' (*Financial Review*, 6 March 1992), afr.com/politics/regulation-is-more-than-black-letter-law-19920306-jl0g0.
75   See generally Andy Lie, 'Securities market competition regulation—issues in ASIC's Takeover of ASX's Market Integrity Rules' (2012), doi.org/10.2139/ssrn.2017260. Several concerns, such as conflict of interest, were discussed by the Australian government: see Explanatory Memorandum, *Corporations Amendment (Financial Market Supervision) Act 2010* (Cth). For criticism of the co-regulation model in relation to the disclosure regime, see Gill North, 'The corporate disclosure co-regulatory model: dysfunctional and rules in limbo' (2009) 37 *Australian Business Law Review* 75, doi.org/10.2139/ssrn.2379304.
76   Explanatory Memorandum to the *Corporations Amendment (Financial Market Supervision) Act 2010* (Cth) [3.28].

adopted after considering many moves in other comparable jurisdictions towards 'centralised or independent regulation or, in some cases, government regulation of markets and / or market participants'.[77]

This consolidation of regulation of market trading in ASIC was justified by the Australian government as necessary for 'eliminating the real or perceived conflict issues' existing in the prevailing 'model of market self-regulation', improving the integrity and stability of the Australian markets through ASIC's whole-of-market supervision.[78]

However, concerns have been raised over the reduced remit of the ASX's self-regulation, as it has increased pressure on ASIC, bringing it to the 'front and centre of market regulation', with sole responsibility for 'detection of market offences and the enforcement of breaches' that are detected.[79] A recent study on the impact of self-regulation on stock market liquidity and corporate transparency associated centralised, independent or government models for trading supervision with lower liquidity and transparency.[80] It found strongly self-regulated exchanges to be more transparent in enforcing insider trading and disclosure rules.[81]

Notwithstanding the above discussion and divergent viewpoints on the role played by SROs, in particular the ASX, in the supervision of financial markets, 'it is fair to say that the regulatory regime that is in operation [in Australia] is a dual regulatory regime'.[82] The ASX exercises significant ongoing compliance requirements,[83] is empowered to sanction and discipline participants, and also suspend or terminate market participants.[84] In IOSCO's view, cited in the Explanatory Memorandum

---

77 Ibid [3.15]. The memorandum noted that Canada had 'introduced independent, non-government supervision of trading activity in all of its equity security markets'; that the US had 'separated participant supervision from market supervision and established a non-government, industry supervisor for market participants'; and that the UK had set up the Financial Services Authority, a non-governmental authority to regulate company listings.
78 Ibid [3.30].
79 Austin, 'Governments to the rescue' (n 11) 459.
80 Jeong-Bon Kim, Mark Shuai Ma and Wenjia Yan, *The Efficiency of Stock Exchange Self-Regulation: Evidence from Stock Market Liquidity and Transparency* (2020). The study compared 46 world-leading stock exchanges from 2001 to 2015, and found that the ASX displayed 'lower liquidity and transparency' after its shift in 2010 from a 'strong self-regulation model' to a more centralised version of supervision with ASIC.
81 Ibid.
82 Baxt, Black and Hanrahan (n 46) 454.
83 Section 5 of the ASX Operating Rules lays down the conditions that market participants are required to comply with on a continuing basis: see ASX, 'ASX operating rules', asx.com.au/about/regulation/rules-guidance-notes-and-waivers/asx-operating-rules-guidance-notes-and-waivers.
84 For an elaborate description, see Baxt, Black and Hanrahan (n 46) 457–459.

to the Corporations Amendment (Financial Market Supervision) Bill 2010 (Cth), 'there is no universal right regulatory path to follow' and there is no 'definitive blueprint' that must be used by all securities authorities.[85] Bearing this in mind, it is appropriate to conclude that the ASX plays a significant self-regulatory role, as set out under IOSCO Principle 9, cooperates with ASIC, and observes 'standards of fairness and confidentiality' in relation to its self-regulatory responsibilities as envisaged by the *Corporations Act*.[86] A formal memorandum of understanding[87] clarifies the ASIC–ASX relationship, sets out the coordination expectations, and contains clauses on how to promote 'efficiency' and address 'duplication'.[88] ASIC oversees the conduct of Australian market licence and CFSL holders in discharging their regulatory obligations through a number of checks, including periodic assessments.[89] Moreover, as explained by ASIC in its Regulatory Guide 172.87, the market licence holders' commercial activities are separate from their supervisory role, which appears to be a wise measure.

In sum, a detailed examination of the on-ground effects of the transfer of supervisory functions from the ASX to ASIC (while retaining other features of the SRO model) may provide interesting insights into the impact on market integrity and stability, and will be useful beyond Australia for other jurisdictions. The detailed FSAP Review of 2012 accorded a 'fully implemented' rating to ASIC for Principle 9, as the oversight by ASIC of the Australian market licence and CFSL holders was found to be robust and effective.

Conclusion

Though the ASX's surveillance remit was curtailed, with ASIC assuming direct responsibility of surveillance and supervision of securities markets and its participants in 2009–10, ASIC's regime still relies on operators of exchanges and clearing and settlement facilities to carry out certain SRO-like functions, such as the supervision of their members in a fair and transparent manner. On the whole, ASIC's regime for monitoring

---

85 Explanatory Memorandum to the *Corporations Amendment (Financial Market Supervision) Act 2010* (Cth) [3.15].

86 IMF, *Australia Country Report* (n 42) 18.

87 *Memorandum of Understanding between Australian Securities and Investments Commission and ASX Limited* (signed 28 October 2011), download.asic.gov.au/media/1311115/ASIC-ASX-mou.pdf.

88 Ibid cl 8 and 10.

89 ASIC has the power to assess any AML or CFSL holder with respect to its compliance of the legal obligations. It is also required by the *Corporations Act* to make assessments of AML holders and CFSL holders with respect to their obligations under the Act: see Explanatory Memorandum to the Corporations and Financial Sector Legislation Amendment Bill 2013 (Cth).

and oversight of institutions that perform duties similar to SROs appears sophisticated. Hence, the degree of alignment with core requirements of IOSCO Principle 9 is assessed as 'high' in this book. The extent of reform in the recent past is assessed as 'minor', while the overall landscape is assessed as sufficiently 'mature'.

Principles for auditors, credit ratings agencies and other information service providers

There is an extensive literature examining the role of 'gatekeepers' in securities markets.[90] Much of this examines 'gatekeeper liability'[91] and considers the liability rules that would encourage gatekeepers to take optimal precautions to deter client wrongs.[92] In recent years, the literature has suggested alternatives to conventional gatekeeper liability strategy through models such as the 'collaborative gatekeeper',[93] which proposes that gatekeepers adopt a collaborative approach with regulators by reporting to them any wrongful conduct committed by their clients.

IOSCO Principles 19–23 relate to such entities and most prominently cover auditors, CRAs and other information service providers such as 'sell-side research analysts' (market analysts).[94]

---

90   See for example Tuch, 'Multiple gatekeepers' (n 2).

91   See Andrew F Tuch, 'The limits of gatekeeper liability' (2017) 73 *Washington & Lee Law Review Online* 619, doi.org/10.2139/ssrn.2945739. Gatekeeper liability is conventionally understood as an approach to impose liability on gatekeepers, such as investment bankers, accountants and lawyers, when their corporate clients engage in wrongdoing, with the aim of making gatekeepers more liable and accountable and encouraging them to influence the conduct of their corporate clients and deter wrongdoing.

92   Tuch, 'Multiple gatekeepers' (n 2). For literature examining the liability rules for gatekeepers: see John C Coffee, 'Gatekeeper failure and reform: the challenge of fashioning relevant reforms' (2004) 84 *Boston University Law Review* 301. See also Frank Partnoy, 'Strict liability for gatekeepers: a reply to Professor Coffee' (2004), ssrn.com/abstract=620841. See further John C Coffee, 'Partnoy's complaint: a response' (2004) 84 *Boston University Law Review* 377.

93   Stavros Gadinis and Colby Mangels, 'Collaborative gatekeepers' (2016) 73 *Washington and Lee Law Review* 797. See also Tuch, 'The limits of gatekeeper liability' (n 91) 622. Collaborative gatekeepers are meant to work with regulators, reporting any conduct on the part of corporate clients that involves wrongdoing.

94   IOSCO (n 6).

Principles 19, 20, and 21

Principle 19: Auditors should be subject to adequate levels of oversight.

Principle 20: Auditors should be independent of the issuing entity that they audit.

Principle 21: Audit standards should be of a high and internationally acceptable quality.

IOSCO Principles 19, 20 and 21 highlight the importance of high and internationally acceptable audit standards and the unique role of auditors in securities markets. Teck-Heang and Ali describe audits as the mechanism that seeks to 'monitor conduct and performance' and to 'secure or enforce accountability'.[95] An auditor plays a critical role in the financial system by delivering an independent and expert assessment of a financial report that is prepared by a corporation.[96] According to Coffee, auditors serve as the most 'paradigmatic' example of 'gatekeepers' who are 'independent professionals … interposed between investors and managers in order to play a watchdog role that reduces the agency costs of corporate governance'.[97]

The roles and responsibilities of auditors, and their independence, oversight and regulation have drawn heightened public concern and attention particularly since the 'high-profile collapses of corporate entities' such as Enron and WorldCom in the US in the 2000s and Carillon in the UK in 2018.[98] The key features of the audit landscape for securities markets relating to India and Australia are examined below.

---

95   LEE Teck-Heang and Azham Md Ali, 'The evolution of auditing: an analysis of the historical development' (2008) 4(12) *Journal of Modern Accounting and Auditing* 1, 1.

96   Roman Tomasic, Stephen Bottomley and Rob McQueen, *Corporations Law in Australia* (Federation Press, 2002) 148.

97   Coffee, 'The acquiescent gatekeeper' (n 1).

98   Australian Government, The Treasury, *Parliamentary Joint Committee on Corporations and Financial Services: Regulation of Auditing in Australia* (Interim Report, 2020) 7–8. 'Auditors are required to be independent from and unbiased by their clients' interests': see Don A Moore et al, 'Conflicts of interest and the case of auditor independence: moral seduction and strategic issue cycling' (2006) 31(1) *Academy of Management Review* 10–29, 12, doi.org/10.5465/amr.2006.19379621; Blue Ribbon Committee on Improving the Effectiveness of Corporate Audit Committees, 'Report and recommendations of the Blue Ribbon Committee on improving the effectiveness of corporate audit committees' (1999) *The Business Lawyer* 1067–1095. See also Sugata Roychowdhury and Suraj Srinivasan, 'The role of gatekeepers in capital markets' (2019) 57(2) *Journal of Accounting Research* 295–322, doi.org/10.1111/1475-679X.12266.

SEBI/India
Key features of the auditor's framework

In terms of the legislative framework, the *Companies Act 2013 (Companies Act)* and the *SEBI (Listing Obligations and Disclosure Requirements) Regulations 2015* set out a number of requirements for listed companies to ensure and enhance the quality of disclosure, financial statements and audit.[99] Chapter X of the *Companies Act* contains provisions for auditing and auditors.[100] Every company must appoint an individual or a firm as an auditor.[101] There is a procedure for the removal and the resignation of auditors.[102] Auditors are subject to supervision through eligibility, qualifications and disqualifications requirements.[103]

The *Companies Act* also sets out the powers and duties of auditors and auditing standards.[104] Auditors have powers to access books of account and vouchers of companies.[105] Auditors must make 'a report to the members of the company on the accounts' and financial statements.[106] To ensure that auditors are effective and independent, auditors are prohibited from rendering certain services, particularly accounting and book-keeping services, internal audits, actuarial services, investment advisory services and investment banking services.[107]

In India, a statutory financial auditor must be a chartered accountant.[108] Traditionally, the independence of these statutory auditors was ensured through several bodies, including the Ministry of Corporate Affairs of the central government, SEBI and the Institute of Chartered Accountants of India.[109] More recently, the regulatory framework for auditors has been

---

99 See *Companies Act 2013 (Companies Act)* ch X. See also *SEBI (Listing Obligations and Disclosure Requirements) Regulations 2015*.

100 See *Companies Act* ch X.

101 Ibid s 139.

102 See ibid s 140.

103 See ibid s 141.

104 See ibid s 143.

105 See ibid s 143(1).

106 See ibid s 143(2).

107 See ibid s 144.

108 Mitrendu Narayan Roy and Siddhartha Sankar Saha, 'Statutory auditors' independence in India: an empirical analysis from the stakeholders' interest perspective' (2016) 41(1) *Vikalpa* 29, doi.org/10.1177/0256090915626791.

109 Auditors are guided by a Code of Ethics for Professional Accountants, Standards on Auditing, Standards on Quality Control, the provisions of the *Companies Act* and the SEBI Listing Requirements, among other documents: see ibid. On auditors' independence, see also S Ghosh, 'Independence of statutory auditors of companies: a myth or reality?' (1999) 18(2) *Research Bulletin* 76.

reformed with the establishment of the National Financial Reporting Authority (NFRA).[110] The NFRA is the responsible authority for matters pertaining to auditing standards, including monitoring and enforcing compliance with auditing standards and overseeing the 'quality of service of the professions associated with ensuring compliance with such standards'.[111]

Analysis

Bhasin vociferously attributes the legislative and regulatory reforms of the past decade to financial frauds and manipulations, particularly the infamous Satyam Computers Ltd scandal that unfolded in 2009.[112] Prior to these reforms, the auditing landscape in India, both from a legislative and governance perspective, was disorganised and in a state of confusion, eventually manifesting in corporate failures like Satyam. This position was reflected in the FSAP Assessment of 2013, which granted the Indian audit regime a 'partly implemented' grade in relation to IOSCO Principles 19–21.

Much like India's accounting landscape,[113] the past decade has witnessed a rapid overhaul in two areas of auditing activity: 1) the legislative framework has been revamped through the enactment of the *Companies Act* and 2) the governance framework for auditors in India has been strengthened with the establishment of the NFRA. Even though these arrangements are still evolving, they have given rise to sincere expectations that the recent reforms will strengthen the audit regime, curb malpractices and, most importantly, give a fillip to the existing corporate governance architecture in India.

---

110 National Financial Reporting Authority, 'About the organization', nfra.gov.in/about-department/introduction/.

111 See *Companies Act* s 132 (2).

112 The Satyam Computers scam unfolded in 2009 with a letter by its chairman, Ramalinga Raju, confessing that he had been manipulating the company's accounting numbers for several years by inter alia using 'a number of different techniques to perpetuate the fraud', along with the 'company's global head of internal audit': see Madan Lal Bhasin, 'Debacle of Satyam Computers Limited: a case study of India's Enron' (2016) 23(3) *Wulfenia Journal* 136. See also Madan Lal Bhasin, 'Creative accounting practices at Satyam Computers Limited: a case study of India's Enron' (2016) 6(6) *International Journal of Business and Social Research* 24–48, doi.org/10.18533/ijbsr.v6i6.948; Madan Lal Bhasin, 'Fraudulent financial reporting practices: case study of Satyam Computer Limited' (2016) 4(3) *Journal of Economics, Marketing and Management* 12–24; Madan Lal Bhasin, 'Creative accounting scam at Satyam computer limited: how the fraud story unfolded?' (2016) 5(04) *Open Journal of Accounting* 57, doi.org/10.4236/ojacct.2016.54007; Shradhanjali Panda and Anita Mishra, 'Corporate governance: journey of "Satyam" to "Mahindra Satyam"—the way ahead' (2011) 1(1) *Kushagra International Management Review* 32.

113 Refer to the analysis of the accounting landscape in Chapter 7 of this book.

Conclusion

The requirements of IOSCO Principles 19, 20 and 21 relating to the oversight and independence of auditors and audit quality are, arguably, reflected to a great degree in the reformed audit landscape, though it remains to be seen how successful these changes will be. Therefore, the degree of alignment of the securities markets audit regime with these principles is collectively assessed as 'moderate'. The overall landscape is evolving rapidly, with 'substantial' reform undertaken in the past decade.

ASIC/Australia

Key features of the auditor's framework

Australia has a robust framework for auditors that reflects the requirements of IOSCO Principles 19–21. The legislative and regulatory framework for auditing is governed by 'legislation, standards, regulatory and professional bodies, and disciplinary boards'.[114] Chapter 2M of the *Corporations Act* provides comprehensive requirements for financial reporting and auditing, and mandates public companies and large propriety companies to file audited annual financial reports to ASIC.[115] Besides laying down the legislative framework for financial reporting and auditing, it also emphasises the necessity for auditors to give a true and fair analysis of the financial condition of the company.[116]

Requirements under IOSCO Principle 19 are reflected in the Australian framework—for instance, auditors of public limited companies must be registered with ASIC and meet stringent eligibility criteria under the law.[117]

---

114 See 'Legislative and regulatory framework' in Australian Government, The Treasury, *Parliamentary Joint Committee* (n 98) ch 2.

115 *Corporations Act* s 301. Section 45A(3) of this Act provides threshold limits for companies and defines them as large if they meet at least two of the following thresholds in a given financial year: $50 million or more in consolidated revenue; $25 million or more in consolidated gross assets; and 100 or more employees: see also Australian Government, The Treasury, *Parliamentary Joint Committee* (n 98).

116 See *Corporations Act* (ch 2M). See also Australian Government, The Treasury, *Parliamentary Joint Committee on Corporations and Financial Services: Inquiry into the Regulation of Auditing in Australia* (Submission, 11 October 2019) 7.

117 An individual must meet the requirements in s 1280 while a company may be registered as an authorised audit company if such entity is eligible to be registered under s 1299B of the *Corporations Act*. Auditors must meet extensive conditions that relate to their education, experience, competency and integrity to be registered with ASIC and maintain such registration: see Australian Government, The Treasury, *Parliamentary Joint Committee* (n 98) 13. For a detailed explanation of the registration criteria and requirements of auditors, see ASIC, *Auditor Registration* (Regulatory Guide 180, 2016). Auditors are required to be suitably qualified; they are supposed to satisfy the requirements of auditing competency standards approved by ASIC; ASIC needs to be assured that the auditor can perform all duties and is a fit and proper person to be registered in the capacity of the auditor: see IMF, *Australia Country Report* (n 42).

Similarly, IOSCO's requirements on auditors' independence (Principle 20) and high and international quality of auditing (Principle 21) are reflected in the Australian system through two levels: first, in detailed provisions of the *Corporations Act*;[118] and, second, in the standards and codes provided by relevant statutory bodies that include the Australian Auditing and Assurance Standards Board (AUASB),[119] the Australian Accounting Standards Board (AASB)[120] and other professional bodies that set professional and ethical standards for auditors.[121]

For greater visual clarity of Australia's financial reporting framework, see the flow chart in Figure 6.1.[122]

ASIC is responsible for the governance of auditors under the *Corporations Act*, including compliance with the requirements for auditors' independence and audit quality.[123] To fulfil its compliance role in relation to auditors, ASIC has powers of surveillance, investigation, inspection and information gathering and can initiate regulatory action.[124] Its powers include:

1. suspension or cancellation of registration by making an application before the Companies Auditors Disciplinary Board (CADB)[125]
2. accepting an enforceable undertaking from the auditor
3. initiation of prosecution or civil action against the defaulting auditor
4. revoking, adding or varying the terms of conditions on auditors.[126]

---

118 The *Corporations Act* sets out general and specific requirements relating to auditor independence and aims to address conflicts of interest in regard to the audited entity: see *Corporations Act* pt 2M.4 div 3. The Act further mandates that financial reports and audits comply with accounting and auditing standards: see ibid ss 296 and 307A.

119 Ibid s 336.

120 Ibid s 334.

121 For example, apart from the standards developed by the AASB and AUASB, the Accounting Professional and Ethical Standards Board sets the Code of Ethics for auditors; see Australian Government, The Treasury, *Parliamentary Joint Committee* (n 98) 14. Examples of relevant standards include Australian Auditing Standards (ASA) 102 and 220, Accounting Professional and Ethical Standards (APES) 110, ASQC 1 and APES 320.

122 Australian Government, The Treasury, *Parliamentary Joint Committee* (n 98) 14.

123 ASIC, 'Financial reporting and audit: auditors' (nd), asic.gov.au/regulatory-resources/financial-reporting-and-audit/auditors/.

124 ASIC's Financial Reporting and Audit Team carries out inspections and surveillance of auditors and is well qualified to identify possible anomalies: see IMF, *Australia Country Report* (n 42).

125 The CADB is an independent statutory body established under pt 11 of the *Australian Securities and Investments Commission Act 2001* (*ASIC Act*) and has powers and duties in pt 9.2 of the *Corporations Act* and pt 11 of the *ASIC Act*: see CADB, 'Overview' in *Annual Report for the Year Ended 30 June 2020* (2020).

126 See IMF, *Australia Country Report* (n 42).

Corporations Act 2001

Primary legislation outlining financial reporting and auditing framework

ASIC – Regulatory oversight of Corporations Act

ASIC Act 2001

Creates statutory bodies

Companies Auditor Disciplinary Board – Administrative Disciplinary Body for auditors. Cases are referred by ASIC

Financial Reporting Council – Advisory role to ASIC, and Government and Strategic guidance to AASB and AUASB

Accounting and Auditing Standards

Legislative Instruments outlining Australia's Accounting and Auditing standards

Include a requirement to comply with the APES code

Australian Accounting Standards Board (AASB) and Auditing and Assurance Standards Board (AUASB) – Standard setting bodies for accounting and auditing standards

Accounting Professional and Ethical Standards –

Code of Ethics for Professional Accountants

Accounting professional and Ethical Standards Board –

Set the Code of Ethics for auditors

Professional Bodies: Chartered Accountants Australian & New Zealand, CPA Australia, Institute of Public Accountants –

Set professional standards for their members

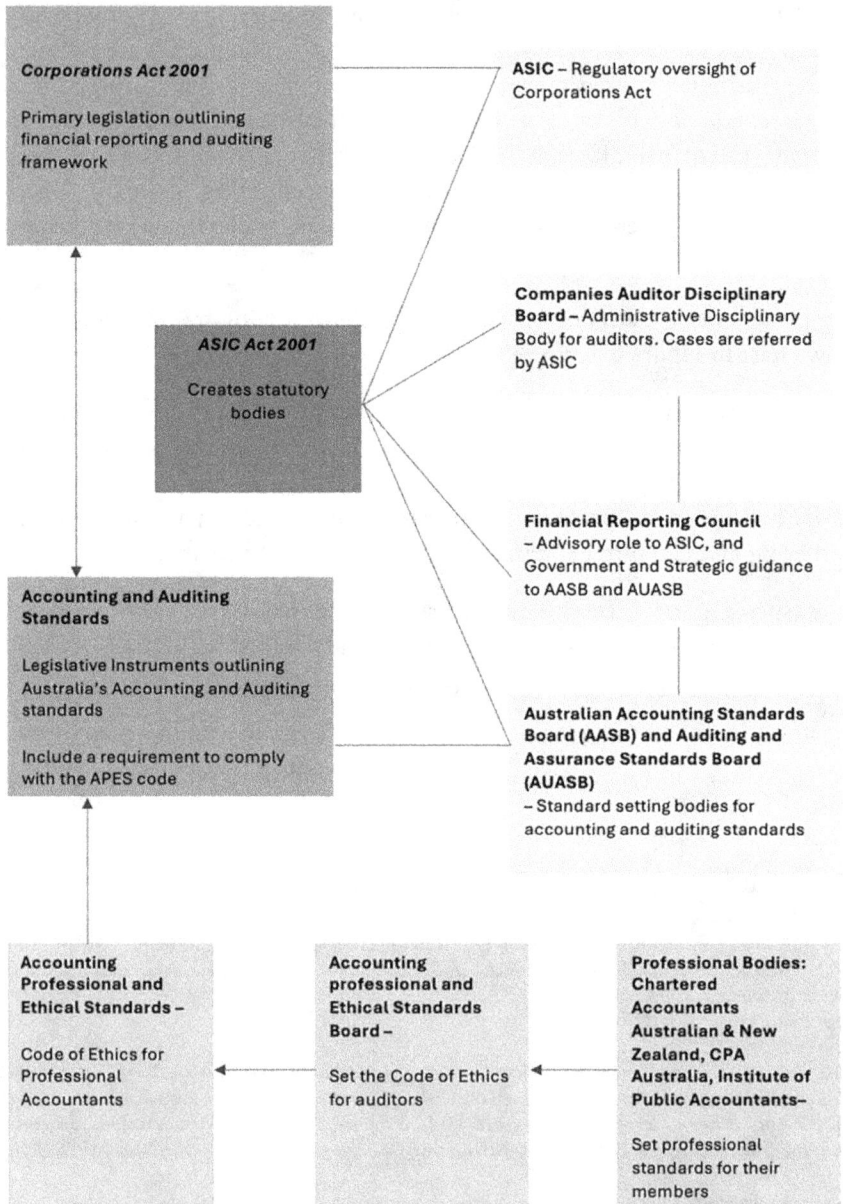

Figure 6.1: Overview of Australia's financial reporting framework

Source: Australian Government, The Treasury, *Parliamentary Joint Committee on Corporations and Financial Services* (2019) 15.

A violation of the *Corporations Act* by an auditor can also attract varying monetary penalties or imprisonment for up to six months, or both.[127] For instance, the penalty for 'engaging in audit activity despite unresolved conflict of interest' or 'failure to meet auditor rotation obligation' can be as high as 60 penalty units or six months' imprisonment, or both for an individual.[128]

Apart from ASIC, which is the main authority responsible for audit compliance, the Financial Reporting Council (FRC)[129] is responsible for maintaining the effectiveness of Australia's financial reporting framework.[130] While the FRC is unable to direct that accounting and auditing standards be set in a specific way, it is empowered to maintain oversight and set a broad strategic direction of the AASB and AUASB.[131] Additionally, audit standards within Australia are maintained through oversight by several other bodies including the AUASB,[132] the AASB,[133] the CADB,[134] and the Accounting and Professional Ethical Standards Board.[135]

---

127 See Australian Government, The Treasury, *Parliamentary Joint Committee* (n 98). See also IMF, *Australia Country Report* (n 42).

128 See Attachment A, 'Auditor related offences' in Australian Government, The Treasury, *Parliamentary Joint Committee* (n 98) 21. A penalty unit is prescribed by s 4AA of the *Crimes Act 1914* (Cth). The penalty rate is currently A$222 for offences committed after 1 July 2020.

129 See FRC, 'About the FCR: Financial Reporting Council', frc.gov.au/about-frc.

130 The FRC is responsible for overseeing the process of setting auditing standards and monitoring the independence requirements for auditors in Australia: see IMF, *Australia Country Report* (n 42).

131 The FRC also provides strategic advice to ASIC and the government: see Australian Government, The Treasury, *Parliamentary Joint Committee* (n 98) 15. It is worth noting that the FRC in the UK is responsible for regulation, standard setting and enforcement; however, in Australia, ASIC is responsible for regulatory oversight and enforcement, while standard setting and advisory bodies, including the FRC, exist separately from the legislative framework.

132 An independent authority, the AUASB sets Australian audit and assurance standards according to the International Auditing and Assurance Standards Board (IAASB): AUASB, 'Framework pronouncements', auasb.gov.au/standards-guidance/framework-pronouncements/.

133 The AASB is an independent accounting standard setter established under statute and charged with the task of developing a single set of high-quality, understandable accounting standards: see AASB, 'Home', aasb.gov.au/Home.

134 See CADB (n 125). Prior to 2017, the CADB was constituted as CALDB (Companies Auditors and Liquidators Disciplinary Board): see CALDB, *Companies Auditors and Liquidators Disciplinary Board: Annual Report for the Year Ending 30 June 2016*, (Commonwealth of Australia, 2016) download. asic.gov.au/media/4043426/caldb-annual-report-2016.pdf. The *Insolvency Law Reform Act 2016* (Cth) transferred the disciplinary functions of liquidators out from CALDB to ASIC and hence the body was reorganised as CADB.

135 The APESB was established in 2006 'to develop and issue, in the public interest, high quality professional and ethical standards': see Accounting Professional and Ethical Standards Board, 'Home', www.apesb.org.au/.

Analysis

A robust audit regime contributes significantly to the overall strength of corporate governance and investor protection within a strong securities and financial market.[136] As ASIC states, 'high-quality audits support the quality of financial reports and enable investors to rely on the auditor's independent assessment of financial reports'.[137] This is critical for ensuring listed companies meet their disclosure obligations and for upholding market integrity.

Generally, Australia's audit standards and corresponding regulatory regime are well developed, of high quality and meet international standards.[138] These auditing standards are extensive and well aligned with international standards, including the International Standards on Auditing,[139] the International Ethical Code and the International Quality Control Standard.[140] Moreover, as foreshadowed in the earlier section outlining the key features of Australia's audit landscape, the legislative and regulatory framework for auditors is well supported with significant powers of investigation, inspection and information gathering that are available to ASIC for any audit contravention,[141] although ASIC does not, under general circumstances, have the 'power to unilaterally cancel or suspend the registration of a company auditor for disciplinary reasons'.[142]

Notwithstanding these strengths, the role and independence of auditors[143] and the adequacy of regulatory oversight and enforcement have been the subject of debate and examination for several years in Australia.[144] Concerns

---

136 See generally Jere R Francis, Inder K Khurana and Raynolde Pereira, 'The role of accounting and auditing in corporate governance and the development of financial markets around the world' (2003) 10(1) *Asia-Pacific Journal of Accounting and Economics* 1–30, doi.org/10.1080/16081625.2003.10510613.

137 ASIC, 'Audit quality—the role of directors and audit committees' (Information Sheet 196, June 2017).

138 IMF, *Australia Country Report* (n 42) 6, 25.

139 See Dawn McGeachy and Christopher Arnold, 'Future implementation support for international standards on auditing', *International Federation of Accountants* (15 January 2019), ifac.org/knowledge-gateway/discussion/future-implementation-support-international-standards-auditing.

140 See International Auditing and Assurance Standards Board, 'Quality control', iaasb.org/projects/quality-control.

141 IMF, *Australia Country Report* (n 42).

142 Ian Ramsay and Miranda Webster, 'An analysis of ASIC enforcement against auditors and liquidators' (2021) 38(2) *Company and Securities Law Journal* 114, doi.org/10.2139/ssrn.3769734. ASIC is dependent upon CADB for such disciplinary proceedings.

143 Ladakis argues that, due to inherent limitations in auditing process, auditors will remain a poor gatekeeper for the investing public: see Emma Ladakis, 'The auditor as gatekeeper for the investing public: auditor independence and the CLERP reforms—a comparative analysis' (2005) 23(7) *Company and Securities Law Journal* 416. See also Chapter 3 'Audit quality in Australia' in Australian Government, The Treasury, *Parliamentary Joint Committee* (n 98). See also Michael De Martinis, 'Do directors, regulators, and auditors speak, hear, and see no evil? Evidence from the Enron, HIH, and One.Tel collapses' (2002) 15(1) *Australian Journal of Corporate Law* 66–79.

144 See for example Australian Government, The Treasury, *Parliamentary Joint Committee* (n 98). See also De Martinis (n 143).

have been raised around auditors meeting 'public expectations' and recognition of the 'expectation gap' in light of the 'disconnect' between the regulatory requirements for auditing and the general public's expectations.[145] In terms of supervision, enforcement and compliance, ASIC has a well-developed strategy, especially in relation to the 'Big Four' audit firms that cater to approximately 83 per cent of the listed companies on the exchanges; this is aligned with ASIC's overall risk-based supervision and strategy for the supervision and oversight of the markets.[146] However, in terms of ASIC's enforcement approach to auditors and audit contraventions, a recent analysis by Ramsay and Webster for the period between July 2011 and December 2019 shows that ASIC relies heavily on the use of its 'negotiated enforcement outcomes and administrative remedies rather than court based outcomes'.[147] Their analysis further reveals that ASIC has made 'limited use of the CADB/CALDB and disciplinary committees' and accepted enforceable undertakings instead.[148]

Nevertheless, the auditing landscape remains a high-priority area that attracts lengthy and comprehensive inquiries at the highest level of government.[149] Australia's high rank for its audit practices both globally[150] and regionally[151] supports the conclusion that Australia has a well-designed, sophisticated and clear regime for the oversight and regulation of auditors and audit quality.

The FSAP Assessment in 2012 in relation to Principle 19, which requires adequate oversight of auditors, rated ASIC's regime as 'fully implemented'. The rating was given in recognition of several strengths of the regime, including ASIC's significant oversight powers, such as inspection and information gathering in relation to auditors and audit practices, which

145 See the lengthy discussion in Chapter 5 'Meeting user expectations' and in Chapter 3 'Audit quality in Australia', in Australian Government, The Treasury, *Parliamentary Joint Committee* (n 98). See also Alison Lansley and Melissa Fogarty, 'Sleepers awake! Future directions for auditing in Australia' (2002) 25(2) *UNSW Law Journal* 408–433.
146 The Big Four audit firms are Price Waterhouse Coopers, KPMG, Ernst and Young and Deloitte: see Madison Marriage, 'Big four UK accountancy firms face radical shake-up', *Financial Review* (18 December 2018), afr.com/world/big-four-uk-accountancy-firms-face-radical-shakeup-20181218-h198gr. See also Australian Government, The Treasury, *Parliamentary Joint Committee* (n 98) 6. These firms had a combined revenue of $8.57 billion in 2019. The next largest audit firms in 2019 were BDO and Grant Thornton with revenues of $299 million and $266 million, respectively.
147 Ramsay and Webster (n 143) 137.
148 Ibid 137.
149 See Australian Government, The Treasury, *Parliamentary Joint Committee* (n 98) 2.
150 Klaus Schwab, *The Global Competitiveness Report 2019* (World Economic Forum, 2019) 67.
151 CLSA, *Hard Decisions: Asia Faces Tough Choices in CG Reform* (Corporate Governance Watch, 2018) 15.

ASIC uses in a 'coherent and consistent manner'.[152] Likewise, ASIC secured a 'fully implemented' rating from the International Monetary Fund (IMF) in respect of Principles 20 and 21, as the audit standards and auditor independence levels were recognised as being extensive and consistent with international standards.

Conclusion

In light of the strength of audit standards, continuous oversight and monitoring of the audit architecture, and ASIC's commitment to ensuring high-quality audited reports to support investor interests, the degree of alignment of ASIC's securities markets' audit regime with IOSCO Principles 19, 20 and 21 is collectively assessed as 'high'. The audit regime is assessed to be operating in a considerably 'mature' manner, with 'minor' reforms undertaken in the past years.

Principles 22 and 23

Principle 22: Credit rating agencies should be subject to adequate levels of oversight. The regulatory system should ensure that credit rating agencies whose ratings are used for regulatory purposes are subject to registration and ongoing supervision.

Principle 23: Other entities that offer investors analytical or evaluative services should be subject to oversight and regulation appropriate to the impact their activities have on the market or the degree to which the regulatory system relies on them.

CRAs rank credit risk and are thus a unique category of 'gatekeepers'.[153] Tuch effectively pinpoints their uniqueness, observing that they 'certify the credit risk of company debt'[154] and do not 'certify the accuracy of a corporations disclosures' like other traditional gatekeepers.[155] Notwithstanding their

---

152 See IMF, *Australia Country Report* (n 42).

153 See Coffee, *Gatekeepers* (n 4). See also Frank Partnoy, *How and Why Credit Rating Agencies Are Not Like Other Gatekeepers* (San Diego Legal Studies Paper No 07–46, 2006). According to Partnoy, prior to the GFC, credit rating agencies (CRAs), even while performing poorly, did not suffer some of the reputational consequences that other gatekeepers suffered. CRAs in the US benefit from an 'oligopoly market structure' that is 'reinforced by regulations that depend exclusively on credit ratings' issued by Nationally Recognised Statistical Rating Organizations (NRSROs) that are controlled by the US SEC. The 'regulatory licenses' create 'economic rents for NRSROs that persist even when they perform poorly and otherwise would lose reputational capital'.

154 Stephen Choi, 'Market lessons for gatekeepers' (1997) 92 *Northwestern University Law Review* 916, 934.

155 Tuch, 'Multiple gatekeepers' (n 2) 1666.

niche, CRAs play a significant role by influencing investor opinion on financial companies and their products.[156] Nociri argues that CRAs have considerable influence on markets, regulators and 'nation states' since their ratings are critical to obtaining finance and, thus, financial stability.[157] The global financial crisis (GFC) of 2007–08, in particular, raised serious questions about adequate and effective oversight and regulation of CRAs.[158]

The IOSCO Principles of Securities Regulation address the centrality of CRAs and market analysts. IOSCO Principle 22 creates norms for CRA registration, oversight and ongoing supervision. IOSCO Principle 23 requires regulators to oversee entities that offer analytical or evaluative services in the securities markets. In many regulatory regimes, investor opinion on financial products and securities is guided by the reports and papers published by such entities.[159] Investors rely upon a variety of documents when making investment decisions and the information they use is often prepared by market analysts that 'analyse, evaluate or provide assurance of information for investors about issuers, or their securities' and who are referred to as 'information service providers'.[160]

The sections below examine the broad landscape pertaining to CRAs and market analysts in India and Australia.

---

156 Credit rating agencies are in the business of providing 'credit ratings', which is understood as an opinion about the creditworthiness of an institution or the ability of an issuer of a financial product to meet its obligations under the financial product: see ASIC, *Licensing: Credit Rating Agencies* (Consultation Paper No 65, 2005), download.asic.gov.au/media/1336556/Credit_rating_agencies_CP.pdf.

157 Ahmed Naciri, *Credit Rating Governance: Global Credit Gatekeepers* (Routledge, 2015) xvi, doi. org/10.4324/9781315757834. Naciri supports his argument through several examples, such as the impact of the rating agencies reports on Greece and France and the unique power of CRAs in the downgrading of countries—'sending them to pasture for speculators and completely destabilizing to the breaking edge their economies'.

158 The GFC led to calls to 'revamp' the regulatory framework of credit rating agencies: see for example Frank Partnoy, *Rethinking Regulation of Credit Rating Agencies: An Institutional Investor Perspective* (San Diego Legal Studies Paper No 09–014, 2009). See also Sulette Lombard, 'Credit rating agencies as gatekeepers: what went wrong' (2008) 43(43) *Washington University Law Quarterly* 1–18. For literature on the role of the credit rating industry in the GFC, see Josh Wolfson and Corinne Crawford, 'Lessons from the current financial crisis: should credit rating agencies be re-structured?' (2010) 8(7) *Journal of Business & Economics Research (JBER)*, doi.org/10.19030/jber.v8i7.745. See also Efraim Benmelech and Jennifer Dlugosz, 'The credit rating crisis' (2009) 24(1) *NBER Macroeconomics Annual* 161–208, doi.org/10.1086/648293; Anno Stolper, 'Regulation of credit rating agencies' (2009) 33(7) *Journal of Banking & Finance* 1266–1273, doi.org/10.1016/j.jbankfin.2009.01.004; Lawrence J White, 'Credit-rating agencies and the financial crisis: less regulation of CRAs is a better response' (2010) 25(4) *Journal of International Banking Law* 170; Dieter Kerwer, 'Holding global regulators accountable: the case of credit rating agencies' (2005) 18(3) *Governance* 453–475, doi.org/10.1111/j.1468-0491.2005.00284.x.

159 IOSCO (n 6) 145.

160 Ibid 127.

SEBI

Key features of the framework relating to CRAs and market analysts

Currently, seven CRAs in India are registered under the *SEBI (Credit Rating Agency) Regulations 1999* (*CRA Regulations*).[161] The *CRA Regulations* are fairly wide and cover all important aspects relating to CRA regulation and governance, including clauses on their registration, obligations, restrictions on rating of securities issued by promoters, and their liability and procedures in case of breach of obligations.[162] SEBI requires CRAs to be audited on a half-yearly basis by independent chartered accountants, and conducts onsite inspections to ensure their effectiveness and proper functioning.[163] In addition, SEBI periodically issues circulars and guidelines to intensify and tighten norms on CRAs.[164]

In relation to IOSCO Principle 23, entities such as brokers, portfolio managers and investment advisers are all subject to an appropriate level of oversight and regulation.[165] In the detailed IMF–World Bank FSAP Report of 2013, the evaluation of this principle noted that SEBI did not have specific requirements for 'research analysts'.[166] Subsequently, in 2014, SEBI issued new regulations for research analysts, the *SEBI (Research Analysts) Regulations 2014*.[167] A registration obligation is imposed on the entity that employs individual research analysts.[168] SEBI does not require these research analysts to be registered or licensed, but does prescribe certain 'qualification'

---

161 These registered CRAs are Acuite Ratings & Research Ltd, Brickwork Ratings India Private Ltd, Care Ratings Ltd, Crisil Ratings Ltd, ICRA Ltd, India Ratings and Research Pvt Ltd, Informerics Valuation and Rating Pvt Ltd.

162 See *SEBI (Credit Rating Agencies) Regulations 1999*.

163 IMF, *India: Financial System* (n 41).

164 'SEBI tightens norms for credit rating agencies', *The Hindu BusinessLine* (13 November 2018), www.thehindubusinessline.com/markets/sebi-tightens-norms-for-credit-rating-agencies/article25487208.ece.

165 Brokers, portfolio managers and investment advisers provide investment advice and, therefore, can be said to be subject to this principle. Portfolio managers are regulated under the *SEBI (Portfolio Managers) Regulations 1993*. Brokers are governed by the *SEBI (Stock Brokers and Sub-brokers) Regulations 1992*. Investment advisers are regulated by the *SEBI (Investment Advisers) Regulations 2013*.

166 IMF, *India: Financial System* (n 41) 103.

167 See *SEBI (Research Analysts) Regulations 2014*.

168 SEBI, *Frequently Asked Questions (FAQs): SEBI (Research Analysts) Regulations 2014* (2014). At present, there are 693 research analysts registered with SEBI: see SEBI, 'Recognised intermediaries' (n 39).

and 'certification' requirements.[169] SEBI also requires CRAs to frame appropriate internal procedures and systems for monitoring trading of securities by its employees.[170]

Analysis

SEBI's regulations for CRAs are comprehensive. SEBI implements this regulatory framework through inspections and disclosure requirements,[171] and its annual reports show how it periodically monitors and upgrades the CRA infrastructure through enhanced disclosure and transparency norms.[172] Recent amendments to the *CRA Regulations* show that SEBI consciously enhances its existing framework to align with international norms.[173] In addition, SEBI takes enforcement actions, including levying a monetary penalty for violations by CRAs.[174]

An overview of the CRA regime indicates that SEBI has a detailed framework for CRAs under which CRAs are obliged to seek registration with SEBI and are closely supervised. Despite this, the monitoring and supervision of CRAs in India has recently evoked much discussion, particularly since 2018 when India's leading infrastructure finance giant IL&FS 'defaulted on payments' to lenders, 'triggering panic in the markets'[175] that led to a sharp downgrade of the company's debt ratings. Subsequently, the CRA regulatory framework was questioned, with debates around whether SEBI

---

169 See SEBI, *Frequently Asked Questions* (n 168).

170 *SEBI (Research Analysts) Regulations 2014* reg 17. SEBI has mandated this to avoid violations of its insider trading regulations as well as the market manipulation regulations.

171 SEBI's annual reports show how SEBI monitors and upgrades the CRA infrastructure: see SEBI, *Annual Report 2018–19* (n 26). SEBI periodically monitors and upgrades the CRA infrastructure through enhanced disclosure and transparency norms.

172 See for example ibid 36. SEBI enhanced the said disclosures and transparency norms through the issue of circulars dated 30 May 2018 and 13 November 2018: see SEBI, 'Enhanced Disclosure and Transparency Norms for Credit Rating Agencies' (Circular, 2018); SEBI, 'Guidelines for Enhanced Disclosures by Credit Rating Agencies (CRAs)' (Circular, 2018).

173 By the amendment notification of 30 May 2018, reg 4(d), a foreign CRA can come only from a jurisdiction that is a member of FATF: see *SEBI (Credit Rating Agencies) (Amendment) Regulations 2018*.

174 SEBI, *Annual Report 2018–19* (n 26) 161. See also *Brickwork Rating India Pvt Ltd* (Adjudication Order No EAD-6/PM-AB/23/2018-19, 2018). The adjudication order imposing a monetary penalty was passed against the CRA on 31 August 2018 against Brickwork Rating India Pvt Ltd after SEBI conducted an inspection and found breaches of SEBI's regulations and guidelines for CRAs.

175 'IL&FS: the crisis that has India in panic mode', *The Economic Times* (1 October 2018), economic times.indiatimes.com/industry/banking/finance/banking/everything-about-the-ilfs-crisis-that-has-india-in-panic-mode/articleshow/66026024.cms?from=mdr. See also Anant Kothari and Anindita Ghosh, 'The IL&FS Fiasco and the lessons learnt' (2020) *Asian Journal of Economics, Finance and Management* 35–48.

ought to prescribe a 'peer-review' of the ratings and a 'rotation' of CRAs.[176] Further, various academic studies have pointed to reduced investor trust and confidence in the CRA industry post the IL&FS debacle,[177] and suggested the need for the CRA regime to be strengthened.[178] In light of the scandal, SEBI has strengthened its framework of onsite inspections for CRAs over the past years although there is scope for even further regulatory action that would require increased resources and capacity.

SEBI has an elaborate framework for market analysts, referred to as 'research analysts' under SEBI's framework.[179] In terms of actual implementation of this framework, SEBI is seen to conduct annual inspections[180] and issue warning and deficiency letters[181] to providers, although these actions need further bolstering when juxtaposed with the number of registered providers.[182]

The detailed FSAP Assessment in 2013 did not rate SEBI's regime for these principles.

Conclusion

SEBI has a clear framework for CRAs and market analysts, which it continually adjusts and expands as necessary. However, as foreshadowed, there is scope for improvement in the implementation of the CRA framework, particularly in relation to monitoring and supervision. The degree of alignment for Principles 22 and 23 is therefore assessed as 'moderate' at this stage. The overall landscape is assessed as 'evolving' rapidly, with 'substantial' reform introduced in the past decade.

---

176 K Ram Kumar, 'SEBI may moot peer review mechanism for credit ratings', *The Hindu Business Line* (online, 23 July 2019), thehindubusinessline.com/companies/sebi-may-moot-peer-review-mechanism-for-credit-ratings/article28691796.ece#.

177 MVS Sudhakar and PS Viswanadh, 'Retail investors' perception towards credit rating agencies after IL&FS crisis—a study' (2021) 17(1) *SMART Journal of Business Management Studies* 42–51, doi.org/10.5958/2321-2012.2021.00005.1.

178 See Karry Lai, 'India's rating systems in urgent need of a facelift', *International Financial Law Review* (14 August 2019), iflr.com/article/b1lmxbbzxrh7s1/indias-rating-systems-in-urgent-need-of-a-facelift.

179 *SEBI (Research Analysts) Regulations 2014.*

180 For example, for FY 2018–19, three inspections were conducted for portfolio managers, seven for investment advisers and five for research analysts: see SEBI, *Annual Report 2018–19* (n 26) 142.

181 For FY 2018–19, two deficiency letters were issued to portfolio managers, three administrative warning letters were issued to investment advisers, and one deficiency letter and three warnings were issued to research analysts: see ibid.

182 For the year ending 31 March 2019, the number of registered portfolio managers was 321; investment advisers, 1,149; and research analysts, 625: see ibid 94.

ASIC

Key features of the framework relating to CRAs and market analysts

Since 2010, and following the GFC, CRAs in Australia are required to obtain a licence from ASIC.[183] Six CRAs are licensed by ASIC, all of whom are subject to ASIC's surveillance activities.[184] As Australian financial services (AFS) licence holders, CRAs are required to observe a range of general licensee obligations that include management of conflicts of interest and having appropriate risk management systems and adequate resources to carry out their business of providing credit rating services.[185] CRAs offering ratings for investment products that are offered to retail investors[186] are also required to have effective dispute resolution systems comprising an internal dispute resolution procedure and membership of an external dispute resolution scheme.[187]

In addition to general licence obligations, CRAs are required to adhere to several 'tailored conditions' as AFS licence holders,[188] which include compliance with the IOSCO Code of Conduct Fundamentals for Credit Rating Agencies,[189] reporting annually to ASIC on their compliance with

---

183 CRAs were required to seek an Australian financial services licence from ASIC from 1 January 2010: see ASIC, 'Credit rating agencies—guidance on certain AFS license conditions' (Information Sheet 143, 2015). For more on the regulation of CRAs and research houses, see *Review of Credit Rating Agencies and Research Houses: A Joint Report by the Treasury and the Australian Securities and Investments Commission* (2008).

184 ASIC, 'ASIC reports on credit rating agencies' (Media Release, 15 February 2018), asic.gov.au/about-asic/news-centre/find-a-media-release/2018-releases/18-042mr-asic-reports-on-credit-rating-agencies/.

185 ASIC, 'ASIC outlines improvements to regulation of credit rating agencies in Australia' (Media Release, 12 November 2009), asic.gov.au/about-asic/news-centre/find-a-media-release/2009-releases/09-224mr-asic-outlines-improvements-to-regulation-of-credit-rating-agencies-in-australia/.

186 Credit ratings are primarily used by wholesale clients as understood under s 761G of the *Corporations Act*, but some retail clients also use credit ratings: see *Review of Credit Rating Agencies and Research Houses* (n 183) 21.

187 *Corporations Act* s 912A(1)(g). See also *Review of Credit Rating Agencies and Research Houses* (n 183) 21. Under the AFS licensing regime, CRAs that provide services to retail clients are required to fulfil a number of conditions, including maintenance of appropriate compensation arrangements under s 912B of *Corporations Act*.

188 ASIC, 'ASIC outlines improvements' (n 185). For example, CRAs have to disclose procedures, methodologies and assumptions for ratings, and have training programs for credit analysts that are adequate and appropriate.

189 IMF, *Australia: IOSCO Objectives* (n 42). See also ASIC, 'ASIC reports on credit rating agencies' (n 184).

the 'IOSCO CRA Code and other licence conditions',[190] and having arrangements to review ratings affected by material changes to rating methodologies within six months of the change.[191]

To oversee the functioning of CRAs, ASIC uses a risk assessment approach based on risk mapping using probability of occurrence and impact of occurrence.[192] Any CRA seen to violate the quality or integrity of rating process, or who fails to 'adopt reasonable measures to ensure the quality of their ratings process', or for any other violation, can be subjected to sanctions by ASIC: for example, they may be penalised for 'misleading or deceptive conduct, making false or misleading statements, in relation to financial services and products'.[193] They may also be liable to investors.

Principle 23, which requires all market analysts to be regulated, is also reflected under the Australian financial services licence framework that applies to all persons providing advice or preparing analysis in the financial services markets.[194] With respect to the requirements of this principle, the provisions governing the operations and conduct of a 'research house' are relevant, and in the post-GFC era, notably revamped.[195] Further, ASIC's Regulatory Guide 79 explains how such research report providers are required to improve the quality of investment research.[196]

---

190 ASIC, *Surveillance of Credit Rating Agencies* (Report 566, 2018) 4.

191 ASIC, 'ASIC outlines improvements' (n 185).

192 In cases in which ASIC identifies a 'high' risk factor, it initiates immediate action: see IMF, *Australia: IOSCO Objectives* (n 42) 97–98.

193 *Review of Credit Rating Agencies and Research Houses* (n 183) 16. See also Aarushi Sahore, 'ABN Amro Bank NV v Bathurst Regional Council: Credit rating agencies and liability to investors' (2015) 37 *Sydney Law Review* 437. See also *ABN AMRO Bank NV v Bathurst Regional Council* (2014) FCAFC 65. For provisions relating to supplementary product disclosure statement and misleading or deceptive conduct: see *Corporations Act* ss 1014E and 1041H. See also *ASIC Act* ss 12DA-12DB.

194 See *Corporations Act* s 912A.

195 A research house has been broadly defined as 'firms that provide objective, independent ratings (except credit ratings), recommendations or opinions on financial products (eg managed funds, structured products, superannuation funds and insurance products), and are subject to the AFS licence regime: see *Review of Credit Rating Agencies and Research Houses* (n 183) 23, 26.

196 ASIC, *Research Report Providers: Improving the Quality of Investment Research* (Regulatory Guide 79, 2012).

Analysis

Concerns and questions raised globally in respect of CRAs in the post-GFC period,[197] particularly about the reliability of their rating,[198] resonated in Australia.[199] This led to the passing of a joint report by the Treasury and ASIC in 2008 that reviewed the existing regulatory requirements for CRAs and research houses.[200] Consequently, ASIC removed the prevailing general exemptions available to these entities,[201] and imposed new regulatory norms by bringing them under the AFSL regime.[202] The tightening of supervision and governance norms for CRAs was also a consequence of significant judicial decisions following the GFC that examined the liability of credit rating agencies, two chief examples of which are the *Wingecarribee Shire Council v Lehman Brothers Australia Ltd*[203] and *ABN AMRO Bank NV v Bathurst Regional Council.*[204]

These developments and judicial decisions have contributed significantly to the systematic expansion of norms applicable to CRAs over the past decade. For example, ASIC's Information Sheet 143 discusses the obligations on CRAs, such as 'separating advisory services from credit rating services', 'applying methodologies in a continuous manner', 'disclosure of actual and potential conflicts of interest' and 'periodic review of methodologies

---

197 See for example Siegfried Utzig, *The Financial Crisis and the Regulation of Credit Rating Agencies: A European Banking Perspective* (ADBI Working Paper, 2010). CRAs were in part responsible for the GFC and must be made more liable for their ratings. On the role played by CRAs in the GFC and civil liability imposed on CRAs in the US, see Nan S Ellis, Lisa M Fairchild and Frank D'Souza, 'Is imposing liability on credit rating agencies a good idea: credit rating agency reform in the aftermath of the global financial crisis' (2011) 17 *Stanford Journal of Law, Business and Finance* 175. See generally Timothy J Sinclair, 'Credit rating agencies and the global financial crisis' (2010) 12(1) *Economic Sociology: The European Electronic Newsletter* 4–9.

198 See for example Partnoy, *Rethinking Regulation of Credit Rating Agencies: An Institutional Investor Perspective* (n 158).

199 See Tin A Bunjevac, 'Credit rating agencies: a regulatory challenge for Australia' (2009) 33 *Melbourne University Law Review* 39, 51.

200 *Review of Credit Rating Agencies and Research Houses* (n 183).

201 Before 2010, ASIC had exempted CRAs from the requirement to hold AFSL: see ASIC, 'Credit Ratings Agencies' (Class Order No 03/1093, 2003). This was replaced by ASIC, 'Credit Ratings Agencies' (Class Order No 05/1230, 2005).

202 Harry New, 'ASIC cracks down on credit rating agencies', *Hall & Wilcox* (online, 18 December 2009).

203 See Harry Edwards, 'Liability for the rating and sale of structured credit products: Australian cases and their (much) wider implications' (2013) 7(2) *Law and Financial Markets Review* 88–96, doi.org/10.5235/17521440.7.2.88; *Wingecarribee Shire Council v Lehman Brothers Australia Ltd (in liq)* (2012) FCA 1028.

204 *ABN AMRO Bank NV v Bathurst Regional Council* (2014) FCAFC 65. The Federal Court of Australia imposed liability on Standard & Poor's for losses sustained due to its negligence and misleading credit ratings of complex structured financial products.

and models'.[205] Additionally, ASIC's Information Sheet 147 highlights matters to be presented by CRAs in their annual compliance report to ASIC, which include 'quality and integrity of the credit rating process', 'transparency and timelines of ratings disclosure', and rating decisions to be made in an independent manner without conflicts of interest and while observing confidentiality of information.[206]

Similarly, Regulatory Guide 79 on market analysts describes ASIC's strengthened focus on improving the overall quality of research, transparency and methodology used while preparing research reports through detailed requirements around the management of conflicts of interest, business models and organisational structure.[207] Following this, ASIC's Regulatory Guide 264 on 'sell-side research'[208] has extended its guidance on how an AFS licensee must manage conflicts of interest in the preparation and production of investor education reports during the different stages of a capital raising transaction.[209]

ASIC monitors the compliance of CRAs periodically through targeted surveillance that focuses particularly on the governance arrangements adopted by CRAs, such as their 'conflict of interest and corporate structure', transparency and disclosure.[210] Based on such surveillance, ASIC recommends changes relating to their governance. For instance, ASIC conducted surveillance in respect of six CRAs in the period between 1 January 2016 and 31 October 2017 and recommended several changes 'in the areas of board reporting, compliance testing, analytical evaluation of credit ratings, human resources, rating committee composition and annual compliance reporting'.[211]

In sum, ASIC's regime for CRAs and for market analysts is clear, comprehensive and focused on minimising conflicts of interest and maintaining confidentiality of 'inside' information to reduce the risk of

---

205 ASIC, 'Credit rating agencies—guidance on certain AFS license conditions' (n 183).

206 ASIC, 'Credit rating agencies—lodging compliance report with ASIC' (Information Sheet 147, 2015).

207 ASIC, *Managing Conflicts of Interest: An ASIC Guide for Research Report Providers* (Regulatory Guide 79, 2012).

208 ASIC describes sell-side research as 'general financial advice prepared and distributed by an AFC licensee to investors to help them make decisions about financial products': see ASIC, 'ASIC releases guidance on sell-side research' (Media Release, 21 December 2017), asic.gov.au/about-asic/news-centre/find-a-media-release/2017-releases/17-456mr-asic-releases-guidance-on-sell-side-research/.

209 See generally ASIC, *Sell-Side Research* (Regulatory Guide 264, 2017).

210 ASIC, *Surveillance of Credit Rating Agencies* (n 190) 6.

211 For further details on the recommendations made by ASIC for CRA, see ibid 6.

violation of any financial services law. In relation to both Principles 22 and 23, the detailed FSAP Review of 2012 assessed ASIC's regime to be 'fully implemented'.

Conclusion

As foreshadowed, after the GFC there has been a complete revamp of the regulatory requirements and framework relating to CRAs and other research service providers that has led to a more streamlined approach to overseeing their activities. They are now consistently monitored and regulated and ASIC periodically pushes the governance envelope through detailed guidance on effective management of conflicts of interest and confidentiality provisions. Accordingly, ASIC's degree of alignment in relation to Principles 22 and 23 is collectively assessed as 'high'. The overall landscape for CRAs and research providers is assessed as 'mature' and the extent of change in the past decade as 'significant' .

Synthesis and conclusion

Self-regulation by RSEs in the Indian securities markets is a fundamental aspect of the securities landscape. The RSEs are the first-line regulators, both for trading systems and for overseeing the members of the exchange. The analysis reveals a sufficiently detailed framework for these RSEs, but the implementation of this framework requires further strengthening, both from the viewpoint of SEBI's supervision of RSEs and RSEs' supervision of brokers. Comparatively, the ASX has a narrower SRO function, as its SRO role was significantly curtailed in 2010. The ASX also operates within a generally more mature ecosystem (ie listed companies with high corporate governance practices and market participants better aligned with legal and regulatory expectations). Thus, the degree of comparability between the two SRO regimes is assessed as 'moderate' and the relevance for cooperation is assessed as 'high'. In particular, Australia's experience of ASIC taking over the first-level regulation of trading from the ASX is as an area of interest and use for SEBI. Further, a good understanding of the roles played by stock exchanges in both jurisdictions, particularly in relation to the oversight and supervision of brokers, will be useful for deeper integration measures in the future, including any mutual recognition agreements between the two regimes.

The analysis also reveals that India's landscape for auditing and auditors, CRAs and market analysts is still evolving to a more effective form. Although the frameworks are being continuously strengthened, the implementation is marred by significant challenges and uncertainties. Notwithstanding these, significant expansion and reforms in the governance framework encompassing auditors, CRAs and market analysts show that efforts are underway to improve the landscape in these areas. In comparison, the Australian regime relating to auditors, CRAs and market analysts is significantly more mature and operates with reliability. Despite this, the analysis also indicates that constant refinements and adjustments are being carried out in respect of these regimes to further enhance their competitiveness and efficiency, which is a creditable feature of the Australian regulatory and governance approach. The degree of comparability is assessed as 'low' or 'moderate' for the principles relating to auditing, and 'moderate' for those relating to CRAs and market analysts. The relevance for cooperation is assessed as 'high' for all principles.

To sum up, though it is neither easy nor fair to engage in a simplistic comparison of the Indian and Australian securities markets given the wide chasm that exists between the two countries in terms of their diversity, complexity and size, the Australian market currently exhibits a greater alignment with the international standards, more maturity and reliability for the areas examined in this chapter. The Indian securities market reflects substantial reforms in the past decade that indicate a commitment towards more resilient and efficient securities regulation.

7

The regimes for issuers, collective investment schemes and hedge funds: IOSCO Principles 16–18 and 24–28

Introduction

This chapter analyses key features of the Indian and Australian securities regimes in relation to the core requirements of the International Organization of Securities Commissions (IOSCO) Principles 16–18 and 24–28. Principles 16–18 on issuers of securities focus on disclosure of information, fair and equitable treatment of holders of securities and the use of high-quality accounting standards for preparation of financial documents. Similarly, Principles 24–28 lay down the necessary conditions for the effective functioning and governance of collective investment schemes (CISs) and hedge funds within a securities market.

The analysis in this chapter of the regimes for issuers of securities, CISs and hedge funds informs the understanding of the overall level of maturity and safety of each of the securities markets. It also highlights the unique character of each market and its varying challenges and limitations. Developing such understanding is a necessary first step towards a deeper and meaningful collaboration between the securities regimes of India and Australia, as this book proposes.

An evaluation of the Indian and Australian securities regimes: IOSCO Principles of Securities Regulation (Principles 16–18 and 24–28)

This section evaluates the core requirements of IOSCO Principles 16–18 (including disclosure) and 24–28 (including governance) in relation to the Securities and Exchange Board of India (SEBI) and the Australian and Securities Commission (ASIC). The comparative analysis for each IOSCO Principle examined in this chapter is presented along the lines set out in Chapter 3, with each regime's key features and implementation analysed against key requirements of the IOSCO Principle(s). Based on the analysis, each regime is assessed in terms of degree of alignment, stage of development and extent of change. The concluding section of this chapter synthesises the degree of comparability and the relevance for cooperation relating to the discussed IOSCO Principles.

Table 7.1: Snapshot of the analysis in this chapter relating to issuers, collective investment schemes and hedge funds

IOSCO Principles of Securities Regulation	SEBI's degree of alignment, stage of development and extent of reform in recent years	ASIC's degree of alignment, stage of development and extent of reform in recent years	Degree of comparability	Relevance for cooperation
Regime for issuers				
Principle 16: There should be full, accurate and timely disclosure of financial results, risk and other information material to investors' decisions	**Moderate** Evolving Substantial	**High** Mature Minor	**Moderate**	**High**
SEBI's FSAP 2013* rating: 'partly implemented' (P16 corresponds to P14 under the pre-GFC IOSCO document**) ASIC's FSAP 2012*** ratings: 'fully implemented'				
Principle 17: Holders of securities in a company should be treated in a fair and equitable manner	**Moderate** Evolving Substantial	**High** Mature Minor	**Moderate**	**High**

IOSCO Principles of Securities Regulation	SEBI's degree of alignment, stage of development and extent of reform in recent years	ASIC's degree of alignment, stage of development and extent of reform in recent years	Degree of comparability	Relevance for cooperation
SEBI's FSAP 2013 rating: 'broadly implemented' (P17 corresponds to P15 under the pre-GFC IOSCO document) ASIC's FSAP 2012 ratings: 'fully implemented'				
Principle 18: Accounting standards used by issuers to prepare financial statements should be of high and internationally acceptable quality	**Moderate** Evolving Substantial	**High** Mature Minor	**Moderate**	**High**
SEBI's FSAP 2013 rating: 'partly implemented' (P17 corresponds to P15 under the pre-GFC IOSCO document) ASIC's FSAP 2012 ratings: 'fully implemented'				
Principles for collective investment schemes and hedge funds				
Principle 24: Regulatory system should establish standards for eligibility, governance, organisation and operational conduct of those who market or operate a collective investment scheme	**Moderate** Evolving Substantial	**Moderate** Mature Substantial	**Moderate**	**High**
SEBI's FSAP 2013 rating: 'broadly implemented' (P24 corresponds to P17 under the pre-GFC IOSCO document) ASIC's FSAP 2012 ratings: 'partly implemented'				
Principle 25: Regulatory system should establish rules governing the legal form and structure of collective investment schemes, segregation and protection of client assets	**High** Mature Minor	**High** Mature Minor	**High**	**Moderate**
SEBI's FSAP 2013 rating: 'fully implemented' (P25 corresponds to P18 under the pre-GFC IOSCO document) ASIC's FSAP 2012 ratings: 'broadly implemented'				

IOSCO Principles of Securities Regulation	SEBI's degree of alignment, stage of development and extent of reform in recent years	ASIC's degree of alignment, stage of development and extent of reform in recent years	Degree of comparability	Relevance for cooperation
Principle 26: Regulation should require sufficient disclosure to evaluate the suitability of a CIS for an investor	**High** Mature Minor	**High** Mature Minor	**High**	**High**
SEBI's FSAP 2013 rating: 'fully implemented' (P26 corresponds to P19 under the pre-GFC IOSCO document) ASIC's FSAP 2012 ratings: 'broadly implemented'				
Principle 27: Regulation should ensure for proper and disclosed basis for asset valuation and pricing and redemption of units in a CIS	**High** Mature Minor	**High** Mature Minor	**High**	**Moderate**
SEBI's FSAP 2013 rating: 'fully implemented' (P27 corresponds to P20 under the pre-GFC IOSCO document) ASIC's FSAP 2012 ratings: 'fully implemented'				
Principle 28: Regulation should ensure that hedge funds, their managers and advisers are subject to regulatory oversight	**High** Mature Substantial	**High** Mature Minor	**Moderate**	**High**
SEBI's FSAP 2013 rating: not assessed (P28 was adopted post-GFC as an IOSCO Principle) ASIC's FSAP 2012 ratings: 'broadly implemented'				

Note: *FSAP 2013 refers to IMF, *India: Financial Sector Assessment Program — Detailed Assessments Report on IOSCO Objectives and Principles of Securities Regulation* (Country Report No 13/266, 2013). **pre-GFC IOSCO document refers to IOSCO, *Objectives and Principles of Securities Regulation* (May 2003); ***FSAP 2012 refers to IMF, *Australia: IOSCO Objectives and Principles of Securities Regulation — Detailed Assessment of Implementation* (Country Report No 12/314, 2012).

Principles for issuers

IOSCO Principles 16, 17 and 18 relate to disclosure of information by issuers to investors 'when they invest in securities and on an ongoing basis'.[1] The collective objectives of these principles are to:

a. improve investor protection through provision of information about the issuer, the investment risk of its securities and information that enables 'better investment decisions'

b. enable the 'operation of fair, orderly, efficient and transparent markets' through accurate and relevant information to investors

c. reduce systemic risk by enhancing transparency in markets.[2]

The description and analysis relating to these principles in this book mainly focuses on equity securities, although IOSCO's methodology states that Principles 16 and 18 apply to equity, debt and other securities, and Principle 17 applies to only equity securities.[3]

The sections below discuss the key features of Indian and Australian securities regimes relating to these principles.

Principles 16 and 17

Principle 16: There should be full, accurate and timely disclosure of financial results, risk and other information which is material to investors' decision.

Principle 17: Holders of securities in a company should be treated in a fair and equitable manner.

Disclosure of full and accurate information in a timely manner is critical in securities markets, as it ensures protection for investors and minority shareholder.[4] Coffee, while analysing the attractiveness of the US securities

---

1 International Organization of Securities Commission (IOSCO), *Methodology for Assessing Implementation of the IOSCO Objectives and Principles of Securities Regulation* (2017) 100. Further, Principles 16 and 18 apply to issuers while Principle 17 applies to companies whose securities are listed or publicly traded.

2 Ibid 100.

3 Ibid 102.

4 See generally Gail Pearson, 'The role of disclosure in the distribution of financial products' in *Financial Services Law and Compliance in Australia* (Cambridge University Press, 2009) ch 5. See also King & Wood Mallesons, 'Fundraising and disclosure' in *Australian Finance Law* (Thomson Reuters, 7th ed, 2015) ch 5; Alastair Hudson, 'Securities regulation and raising capital' in *Understanding Company Law* (Routledge, 2nd ed, 2018) ch 11, 205–227, 205, doi.org/10.4324/9781315158099-13; Rafael La Porta

markets, emphasises the 'bonding hypothesis', which states that, 'by subjecting themselves to the Securities and Exchange Commission's higher disclosure standards and the greater prospect of enforcement in the United States, foreign firms reduce their agency costs'.[5] IOSCO Principle 16 encapsulates this significance of disclosure.

Principle 17 embodies the principle of fair and equitable treatment of holders of securities through a focus on disclosures that enhance 'investor protection and fair, efficient and transparent markets'.[6] In essence, it calls for protection of interests of holders of securities through provisions for 'rights of shareholders',[7] and disclosures that ensure fair and equitable treatment of shareholders in instances of a 'change of control'.[8] This principle addresses similar issues as covered by Principles I and II of the *G20/ OECD Principles of Corporate Governance* published by the Organisation for Economic Co-operation and Development (OECD).[9]

The essence of Principle 17 finds validation in the academic literature. Shareholder protection has been an important area of research across the world for several decades.[10] Rights of shareholders, including voting rights, are

---

et al, 'Investor protection and corporate governance' (2000) 58(1–2) *Journal of Financial Economics* 3–27, doi.org/10.1016/S0304-405X(00)00065-9. Principles 16 and 17 are closely interconnected: see IOSCO, *Methodology for Assessing Implementation* (n 1) 101–102.

5   See John C Coffee, *Law and the Market: the Impact of Enforcement* (Columbia Law and Economics Working Paper No 304, March 7, 2007), doi.org/10.2139/ssrn.967482. On use of the term 'bonding hypothesis', see John C Coffee, 'Future as history: the prospects for global convergence in corporate governance and its implications' (1998) 93 *Northwestern University Law Review* 641. See also John C Coffee, 'Racing towards the top? The impact of cross-listings and stock market competition on international corporate governance' (2002) 102(7) *Columbia Law Review* 1757–1831, doi.org/10.2307/1123661.

6   See IOSCO, *Methodology for Assessing Implementation* (n 1) 112.

7   The rights of shareholders include voting rights, equitable dividends and other distribution rights; rights to hold a company's management accountable for their actions; and rights to fair and equitable treatment in case of bankruptcy: see ibid 113.

8   Such measures include disclosure of changes in control and of substantial shareholdings above a certain threshold; information that is material for 'informed decision-making' in respect of takeover bids, tender offers or other procedures that may result in change of control; shareholding of directors and of the other senior management; and persons with substantial beneficial ownership interest in a company: see ibid 113–114.

9   See OECD, *G20/OECD Principles of Corporate Governance* (2015) 13–28. Principle I calls for ensuring the basis for an effective corporate governance framework while Principle II requires rights and equitable treatment of shareholders and key ownership functions.

10   See for example Katharina Pistor, 'Patterns of legal change: shareholder and creditor rights in transition economies' (2000) 1(1) *European Business Organization Law Review* 59–107, doi.org/10.1017/S1566752900000069. This article analyses the development of shareholder rights in transiting economies. See also Jonathan R Macey, 'The legality and utility of the shareholder rights bylaw' (1997) 26 *Hofstra Law Review* 835. Among other things, this article argues that shareholders rights should be protected to safeguard their interests in takeover actions. See generally Ralph K Winter, 'State law, shareholder protection, and the theory of the corporation' (1977) 6(2) *Journal of Legal Studies* 251, doi.org/10.1086/467572. This article discusses state–federal dynamics in the US and shareholder rights.

held to be 'fundamental features of a sound corporate governance system'.[11] Studies such as that conducted by Gompers et al have found firms with stronger shareholder rights to have 'higher firm value, higher profits, higher sales growth, lower capital expenditures' and to have made fewer corporate acquisitions.[12] Similarly, Black argues that a 'strong public securities market' depends upon two perquisites: first, publicly available information about the value of a company's business; and second, good checks and balances to minimise, if not eradicate, the occurrence of insider trading that wipes out investor investments and deters market confidence—and these can be fostered through 'good capital market rules' and an effective investor protection framework that most appropriately caters to the country's existing laws and needs.[13] Finally, Varotil argues that the 'level of investor protection conferred by law upon minority investors has a strong bearing on the quality and depth of the securities markets', and that the tools to ensure such protection to minority investors include disclosure and transparency rules, corporate governance norms and enforcement of shareholder rights.[14]

Given the significance of disclosure and fair and equitable treatment of holder of securities for sound and strong securities markets, the sections below discuss how ASIC and SEBI's regimes align with IOSCO Principles 16 and 17.

SEBI

Key features of the framework relating to issuers

The overarching framework relating to disclosure and rights of shareholders of listed securities is found in the *Companies Act 2013* (*Companies Act*),[15] supplemented by several SEBI regulations, such as the *SEBI (Issue of Capital*

---

11   Chris Mallin and Andrea Melis, 'Shareholder rights, shareholder voting, and corporate performance' (2012) 16(2) *Journal of Management and Governance* 171.
12   Paul Gompers, Joy Ishii and Andrew Metrick, 'Corporate governance and equity prices' (2003) 118(1) *The Quarterly Journal of Economics* 107–156, doi.org/10.1162/00335530360535162.
13   Bernard S Black, 'The legal and institutional preconditions for strong securities markets' (2000) 48 *UCLA Law Review* 781, 783, 848. To gain further insights on the essentials for strong and robust securities markets, see generally Coffee, 'Future as history' (n 5); Bernard S Black, 'Information asymmetry, the internet, and securities offerings' (1998) 2 *Journal of Small & Emerging Business Law* 91, doi.org/10.2139/ssrn.84489; Bernard Black and Reinier Kraakman, 'A self-enforcing model of corporate law' (1996) 109(8) *Harvard Law Review* 1911–1982, doi.org/10.2307/1342080.
14   Umakanth Varottil, 'Capital markets and the regulatory state in India' (2019) in Devesh Kapur and Madhav Khosla (eds), *Regulation in India: Design, Capacity, Performance* (Hart Publishing, 2019).
15   Corporate governance is a big aspect of disclosure regime. The *Companies Act 2013* (*Companies Act*) provides a 'formal structure for corporate governance' through extensive provisions on 'disclosures, reporting and transparency': see Deloitte, 'Governance 101: all you need to know on corporate governance practices in India'.

and *Disclosure Regulations) Regulations 2018 (SEBI (ICDR) Regulations)* and *SEBI (Listing Obligations and Disclosure Requirements) Regulations 2015 (SEBI (LODR) Regulations)*, even as several other laws, regulations, guidelines and codes apply.[16] Under s 24 of the *Companies Act*, SEBI has the power to regulate the issue and transfer of securities by listed or to-be-listed companies.[17] The *Securities and Exchange Board of India 1992 (SEBI Act)* also empowers SEBI to regulate public issuances and frame guidelines and regulations on issues of capital, listing requirements and other matters relating to a listed company or a company intending to be listed.

The *Companies Act* defines a 'prospectus' as a document that invites deposits from the public or invites offers for subscription or purchase of shares or debentures of a body corporate.[18] The Act also details matters that are required to be 'specified in the Prospectus' and makes any contravention punishable with a fine not less than 50,000 rupees that may be extended to 3 lakh rupees or imprisonment for a term that may be extended to three years, or both.[19] Sections 34 and 35 of this Act describe the civil and criminal liabilities for misrepresentation and misstatement in a prospectus.[20]

Additionally, SEBI has wide powers regarding disclosure for equity and convertible issues prescribed under the *SEBI (ICDR) Regulations*[21] and under the *Companies Act* that cover liability of directors, promoters and every person connected with any misstatements in the prospectus.[22] The framework incorporates periodic and continuous disclosure requirements that are sufficiently detailed and granular to allow shareholders to accurately understand the state of affairs of the company.[23] Finally, separate regulations

---

16   The *Companies Act, Competition Act 2002, Foreign Exchange Management Act 1999* and codes such as the *Desirable Corporate Governance Code* share the architecture relating to corporate governance in India: see Deloitte, 'Governance 101' (n 15).

17   *Companies Act* s 24.

18   Ibid s 2(70).

19   Ibid s 26.

20   Ibid ss 34 and 35. See also Sudipto Dey, 'Any misrepresentation in prospectus is treated as fraud', *Business Standard* (19 October 2014), business-standard.com/article/opinion/any-misrepresentation-in-prospectus-is-treated-as-fraud-114101900724_1.html.

21   The issue of capital and disclosure norms has been subject to repeated upgrade over the past two decades. Prior to the 2018 Regulations, the 2009 Regulations were the applicable code: see SEBI , *Securities and Exchange Board of India (Issue of Capital and Disclosure Requirements) Regulations 2009.*

22   Civil liability for misstatement in a prospectus is covered in s 35 of the *Companies Act.*

23   See generally *SEBI (Listing Obligations and Disclosure Requirements) Regulations.*

by SEBI for equity/convertible issues and for debt[24] enumerate the details and contents of disclosures that are required to be made, focusing generally on the 'need for [the] prospectus to be true, fair and accurate'.[25]

In relation to IOSCO Principle 17, the following features of the securities framework are noteworthy. The *Companies Act* empowers shareholders with voting rights to elect directors,[26] while the *Companies Act* and the *SEBI (LODR) Regulations* impose a detailed set of corporate governance requirements.[27] SEBI has also framed extensive regulations for takeovers and substantial acquisition of shares,[28] prohibition of insider trading[29] and several other such regulations in an attempt to ensure fair treatment for shareholders. In the case of major structural changes within a company, or where the control is changing, the process for such merger or amalgamation needs to first be approved by a majority of shareholders.[30]

Analysis

The importance of high disclosure and corporate governance standards to ensure fair and equitable treatment of shareholders is well established and reflected in the Indian landscape. The current landscape is a result of continuous legal and regulatory reform over three decades.[31] In the early 1990s, SEBI took a lead in strengthening and upgrading disclosure requirements for listed securities,[32] and continues the trend to date, a recent example being in the area of continuous disclosure.[33] For years, SEBI's disclosure requirements have been elaborate and extensive, going beyond financial information to 'issue-related communications such as

---

24   See for example *Simplified Listing Agreement for Debt Securities 2009*.
25   International Monetary Fund (IMF), *India: Financial Sector Assessment Program—Detailed Assessments Report on IOSCO Objectives and Principles of Securities Regulation*) (Country Report No 13/266, 2013) 54.
26   Section 149 of the *Companies Act* mandates the appointment of independent directors.
27   Hemang Parekh et al, 'Corporate governance and directors' duties in India: overview' (2020) *Practical Law*, uk.practicallaw.thomsonreuters.com/0-506-6482?transitionType=Default&contextData =(sc.Default)&firstPage=true.
28   *SEBI (Substantial Acquisition of Shares and Takeovers) Regulations 2011*.
29   See also *SEBI (Prohibition of Insider Trading) Regulations 2015*.
30   See *Companies Act* ch IX. See also IMF, *India FSAP Report* (n 25).
31   For a brief account of the major changes introduced in these areas since the early 1990s, see G Sabarinathan, 'SEBI's regulation of the Indian securities market: a critical review of the major developments' (2010) 35(4) *Vikalpa* 17–18, doi.org/10.1177/0256090920100402.
32   SEBI enhanced the disclosure requirements by building on the provisions of the *Companies Act 1956*: see ibid 17. SEBI based these on the recommendations of two committees led by Mr YH Malegam.
33   See SEBI, 'Strengthening the continuous disclosure requirements for listed entities' in *Annual Report 2015–16* (2016).

advertisements'.[34] Simultaneously, SEBI has also focused on adoption of technology to ease the burden of compliance, such as through the introduction of system-driven disclosures.[35]

Similarly, from the 1990s, SEBI has actively introduced reforms to enhance shareholder rights and 'corporate governance norms for Indian listed companies' based on 'recommendations of several committees appointed to examine the issue'.[36] These committees include the Kumar Mangalam Birla Committee on Corporate Governance (2000),[37] the SEBI Committee on Corporate Governance (2003), also known as the Narayana Murthy Committee,[38] and, finally, the committee established under the chairmanship of Uday Kotak to report on corporate governance (2017).[39] However, the biggest overhaul of the issuers' framework in recent years has been, arguably, the enhancement and consolidation of the disclosure regime through the introduction of the *SEBI LODR Regulations 2015*. These regulations effectively replaced the earlier listing norms and agreement,[40] and aligned SEBI's provisions more effectively with the *Companies Act*.[41] The conversion from 'contractual obligations' (under the erstwhile listing agreement) into the 'mandatory statutory requirements' of the *SEBI LODR Regulations* has been, to a large extent, lauded as a paradigm shift[42] that significantly improved the overall base for corporate governance in India.

The key features of and changes to the *Companies Act* and SEBI's regulations relating to issuers highlighted so far reflect a predominant emphasis on disclosure of material information, a corporate governance framework

---

34 Sabarinathan, 'SEBI's regulation' (n 31) 17.
35 SEBI eased the compliance burden on individuals and companies with the introduction of the *SEBI (Substantial Acquisition and Shares and Takeovers) Regulations 2011*.
36 See generally Varottil (n 14).
37 See SEBI, *Report of the Kumar Mangalam Birla Committee on Corporate Governance* (Committee Reports, 2000).
38 SEBI, *Report of Shri NR Narayana Murthy Committee on Corporate Governance* (Committee Reports, 2003).
39 SEBI, *Report of the Committee on Corporate Governance* (Committee Reports, 2017).
40 A listing agreement is 'essentially a contract that the listed entity enters into with any stock exchange where it lists its securities': see Anuradha Roy Chowdhury Ghosh, 'Corporate governance under the SEBI (Listing Obligations and Disclosure Requirements) Regulations 2015' (2018) *International Journal of Legal Studies and Research*. Corporate governance for listed companies was regulated by cl 49 of the listing agreement.
41 Varun Mansinghka and Kastubh Madhavan, 'Disclosure obligations of listed companies in India: the past, the present and the future' (2016) *International Business Law Journal* 323.
42 See Roy Chowdhury Ghosh (n 40) 119. The shift to the *LODR Regulations* increased the 'legal force behind provisions'. See also Jayshree P Upadhay, 'Farewell listing agreement, welcome new regulation', *Business Standard* (29 November 2015), business-standard.com/article/opinion/farewell-listing-agreement-welcome-new-regulation-115112900675_1.html.

and, generally, the fair and equitable treatment of shareholders, and is well aligned to the fundamental requirements of IOSCO Principles 16 and 17. SEBI's efforts in some of these areas are globally recognised and have been rewarded through a 'stellar fourth in the world' ranking for protection of minority investors in the 'Doing Business' rankings published by the World Bank:[43] the regime scored a 'perfect 10 in the index measuring shareholder rights and role in major corporate decisions'.[44] Similarly, the country evaluations in *The Global Competitiveness Report 2019* published by the World Economic Forum continued to record an upward trend for India on corporate governance, with an overall score of 74.2 and a world rank of 15.[45] Significantly, India's score for shareholder governance stood at 87, with a rank of second among 141 nations.[46]

Despite these positives, the actual implementation of the issuers' framework remains far from being simple and straightforward. Several reasons are cited for the weaknesses in implementation, from deficiencies in 'enforcement' of corporate governance norms and narrow disclosure practices of Indian companies that 'do not go beyond mandatory requirements',[47] to SEBI's traditional, heavy reliance on recognised stock exchanges for the oversight of listed companies, resulting in gaps between the framework and its effective implementation.[48] Due to such inadequacies in implementation, some recent studies have found corporate governance reforms in India to not have had any significant impact on financial performance of the companies.[49] Since good corporate governance performance is a useful tool for attracting foreign investors,[50] enhancing investor protection and ensuring the overall strength of the securities markets, it is evident that SEBI's regime is constantly being

---

43   See Varottil (n 14) 7.

44   See World Bank Group, 'Doing business report: with strong reform agenda, India is a top improver for 2nd consecutive year' (Press Release, 31 October 2018), worldbank.org/en/news/press-release/2018/10/31/doing-business-report-with-strong-reform-agenda-india-is-a-top-improver-for-2nd-consecutive-year.

45   See Klaus Schwab, *The Global Competitiveness Report 2019* (World Economic Forum, 2019). NZ scored the highest among 141 countries for corporate governance.

46   Ibid. Kazakhstan scored the highest among 141 countries for shareholder governance.

47   G Sabarinathan, *Securities and Exchange Board of India and the Regulation of the Indian Securities Market* (IIM Bangalore Research Paper No 309, 2010), doi.org/10.2139/ssrn.2145220.

48   IMF, *India FSAP Report* (n 25) 58–59. Although, in recent years, SEBI has codified corporate governance norms instead of them being a part of the listing agreement. Stock exchanges continue to play a major role in the implementation of these norms.

49   See Puneeta Goel, 'Implications of corporate governance on financial performance: an analytical review of governance and social reporting reforms in India' (2018) 3(1) *Asian Journal of Sustainability and Social Responsibility* 1–21, doi.org/10.1186/s41180-018-0020-4. Corporate governance performance is a useful tool to attract foreign investors.

50   Ibid.

revamped in terms of the framework. Similarly, SEBI's insider trading and takeover regimes, despite ongoing enhancement,[51] continue to experience implementation issues due to low enforcement rates.[52]

The detailed FSAP Assessment of 2013 graded SEBI's regime as 'partly implemented' for the requirements of Principle 16 (erstwhile Principle 14) and as 'broadly implemented' for the requirements of Principle 17 (erstwhile Principle 15). However, since then considerable reform has occurred within this area, both at the framework and implementation level.

Conclusion

The above analysis illustrates that reform of disclosure, shareholder rights and corporate governance norms has been high on the Indian central government's and SEBI's agenda. Notwithstanding the improvements in the disclosure and corporate governance frameworks, and the recent high rankings obtained for corporate governance in India, the degree of alignment of the securities regimes with Principles 16 and 17 is assessed as 'moderate' against the prevailing limitations in implementation at this stage. Given the fast-evolving landscape relating to these principles, the overall landscape is assessed as 'evolving' for both principles and the extent of change undertaken in the past decade in these areas is assessed as 'substantial'.

ASIC

Key features of the framework relating to issuers

Generally, disclosure requirements relating to IOSCO Principle 16 are contained in the *Corporations Act 2001* (Cth)[53] (*Corporations Act*) and the Australian Securities Exchange (ASX) Listing Rules,[54] and further elaborated

---

51   For example, the 2020 reforms to SEBI's takeover and insider trading regulations: see Khaitan & Co, 'SEBI approves amendments to regulations governing listed companies' (Blog Post, 2 July 2020) *Lexology*, lexology.com/library/detail.aspx?g=435ac169-01d7-4193-85df-89685c793f95.

52   See for example Roopanshi Sachar and Afzal Wani, 'Regulation of insider trading in India: dissecting the difficulties and solutions ahead' (2017) 2 *Journal on Contemporary Issues of Law (JCIL)* 1–20; Anil Kumar Manchikatla and Rajesh H Acharya, 'Insider trading in India—regulatory enforcement' (2017) 24(1) *Journal of Financial Crime* 48–55, doi.org/10.1108/JFC-12-2015-0075.

53   Ch 6D on fundraising applies to disclosure requirements for securities in general but does not cover crowd source funding offers.

54   See generally ASX, 'ASX listing rules', asx.com.au/regulation/rules/asx-listing-rules.htm. On the initial listing rules, see ASX, *ASX Listing Rules Guidance Note 1* (2019). On continuous disclosure, see *ASX Listing Rules Guidance Note 8* (2020). ASX listing obligations are published by the Australian Securities Exchange whose role is discussed in greater detail in Chapter 6 of this book.

on and explained in ASIC's regulatory guides.[55] In respect of securities,[56] s 706 of the *Corporations Act* states that an offer of securities for issue needs disclosure to investors unless exempt.[57] To ensure full, accurate and timely disclosure of financial results, risks and other material information by issuers, the Australian regime prescribes a detailed set of information to be presented by issuers of capital through prospectuses,[58] annual reports,[59] half-yearly reports[60] and continuous disclosure requirements.[61] The differences between the requirement for a prospectus and a product disclosure statement in the issue and sale context are complex and the subject of an inquiry by the Australian Law Reform Commission.[62]

As regards initial disclosure, in addition to the legislative provisions in the *Corporations Act*, ASIC's Regulatory Guide 228 provides comprehensive guidance for effective presentation and reporting of material information in a prospectus to enable retail investors to make informed decisions,[63] while Regulatory Guide 254 further explains the obligations for 'all parties involved in the process of preparing a disclosure document, lodging a disclosure document and offering securities for issue or sale under

---

55 See for example ASIC, *Effective Disclosure in an Operating and Financial Review* (Regulatory Guide 247, 2019).

56 For ch 6D of the *Corporations Act*, 'securities' has the meaning assigned to the term in s 700, which in turn means that securities includes shares, debentures, a legal or equitable right to interest shares or debentures, and an option to acquire shares or debentures.

57 Exemptions are stated in ibid s 708 or 708AA.

58 A prospectus is defined as an unabridged document containing the information necessary for investors and their professional advisers to make an informed assessment of an offer for securities: see ibid s 713.

59 Annual financial reports are required to be prepared in accordance with ch 2M of the *Corporations Act*, and all such reports are required to be audited and lodged with ASIC within four months of financial year end, see ASIC, 'Reporting obligations for public companies', asic.gov.au/regulatory-resources/financial-reporting-and-audit/preparers-of-financial-reports/reporting-obligations-for-public-companies/.

60 A disclosing entity's half-year financial report is lodged with ASIC using Form 7051: see ibid.

61 See for example *Corporations Act* s 674(2). This section accords statutory backing for listing rules and a continuous disclosure rule, such as under ASX Listing Rule 3.1. See also John Price, 'Continuous disclosure' (Speech, Chartered Secretaries Australia Annual Conference, 3 December 2012), asic.gov.au/about-asic/news-centre/speeches/continuous-disclosure/.

62 For an updated discussion of issues around disclosure, and a detailed comparison of the product disclosure statements and prospectus regime, see Australian Law Reform Commission, *Disclosure Preliminary Analysis of Legislative Framework for Product Disclosure Statements and Product Disclosure Statements* (2021), alrc.gov.au/inquiry/review-of-the-legislative-framework-for-corporations-and-financial-services-regulation/data-analysis/disclosure/.

63 See for example Regulatory Guide 228, which has information on how to present material information in documents in a clear and precise manner: see ASIC, *Prospectuses: Effective Disclosure for Retail Investors* Regulatory Guide 228, 2019). See also ASIC, *Disclosure: Product Disclosure Statements (and Other Disclosure Obligations)* (Regulatory Guide 168, 2011).

a disclosure document'.[64] Similarly, ASIC's Regulatory Guide 69 covers disclosure requirements for issuers of debentures, secured and unsecured notes and deposit notes.[65]

As regards continuous disclosure requirements, ASX Listing Rule 3.1 requires listed entities to promptly provide ASX with information that is likely to have a material effect on the price and value of its securities.[66] Continuous disclosure requirements are further clarified and explained through ASX's *Guidance Note 8 Continuous Disclosure: Listing Rules 3.1– 3.1B*.[67] Other sources, such as ASIC's Regulatory Guide 73, describe ASIC's approach to less serious breaches of continuous disclosure requirements placed on entities.[68]

In relation to cross-border offer of securities, such as when foreign companies offer securities in Australia, ASIC requires such companies to comply with the prospectus provisions prescribed by the *Corporations Act*, unless an exemption has been granted.[69] Where there is a mutual recognition agreement in force, such as the trans-Tasman mutual recognition scheme signed by Australia and New Zealand, the issuer is permitted to offer securities 'in both countries using one disclosure document prepared under the fundraising laws in its home country'.[70]

In addition to disclosure, and conforming with the requirements of IOSCO Principle 17, the Australian financial and securities framework prioritises and safeguards the interests of holders of securities through provisions on rights of shareholders,[71] and measures that ensure fair and equitable

---

64 ASIC, *Offering Securities under a Disclosure Document* (Regulatory Guide 254, 2020). This guide helps issuers and their advisers to understand ASIC's interpretation and administration of procedural aspects of ch 6D of the *Corporations Act*.

65 ASIC, *Debentures and Notes: Improving Disclosure for Retail Investors* (Regulatory Guide 69, 2012).

66 See Ian Ramsay, 'Enforcement of continuous disclosure laws by the Australian Securities and Investments Commission' (2015) 33(3) *Company and Securities Law Journal* 196.

67 *ASX Listing Rules Guidance Note 8* (n 54).

68 ASIC, *Continuous Disclosure Obligations: Infringement Notices* (Regulatory Guide 73, 2017). For a detailed discussion on the continuous disclosure laws and enforcement options available with ASIC, see generally R Austin and I Ramsay, *Ford's Principles of Corporations Law* (LexisNexis, 16th ed, 2014).

69 See IMF, *Australia: IOSCO Objectives and Principles of Securities Regulation—Detailed Assessment of Implementation* (Country Report No 12/314, 2012) 82.

70 See Regulatory Guide 190, which was developed jointly by New Zealand and Australian authorities for guiding issuers offering financial products or interest in managed or collective investment schemes in both countries: see ASIC and New Zealand Financial Markets Authority, *Offering Financial Products in New Zealand and Australia under Mutual Recognition* (Regulatory Guide 190, 2017).

71 See *Corporations Act* s 1.5.6 on shares and shareholders. Shareholders can participate in shareholder meetings and are entitled to voting rights.

treatment of shareholders through disclosure in the instance of a 'change of control'.[72] The *Australian Securities and Commission Act 2001* (Cth) (*ASIC Act*), *Corporations Act* and the stock exchange rules framed for listed companies support rights to security holders and adoption of stringent procedures to ensure no disadvantage accrues to a security holder when there is a change of control or a merger, acquisition or takeover in a listed company.[73] Further, the *Corporations Act* contains provisions for minority shareholder rights and remedies,[74] shareholder rights in case of bankruptcy proceedings and disclosure of directors' interests.[75]

In relation to corporate governance, the approach adopted by Australia is 'more non-prescriptive' and, thus, listed companies are required to comply with, or explain their divergence from, the principles set out in ASX's corporate governance guidelines.[76] However, unlike corporate governance, takeover provisions are provided in a more prescriptive format,[77] under chs 6–6C of the *Corporations Act*.[78] Further, ASIC's extensive collection of regulatory guides puts forth and elaborately discusses its interpretation on a variety of areas, including takeovers and exceptions,[79] schemes of arrangement,[80] and compulsory acquisitions and buy-outs.[81]

---

72   Section 912DA of the *Corporations Act* imposes an obligation on an entity to notify ASIC with any change in control.

73   A wide ambit of rights is available for holders of securities, such as the 'right to vote on changes that affect the terms of the securities they hold and on certain other fundamental changes': see IMF, *Australia Country Report* (n 69) 83.

74   See s 232 of the *Corporations Act* on conduct that is oppressive and unfairly prejudicial to a shareholder.

75   For a detailed analysis of this principle see IMF, *Australia Country Report* (n 69).

76   See Richard Mitchell et al, 'Shareholder protection in Australia: institutional configurations and regulatory evolution' (2014) 38 *Melbourne University Law Review* 71. See also ASX Corporate Governance Council, *Corporate Governance Principles and Recommendations* (4th ed, 2019).

77   OECD, *OECD Corporate Governance Factbook 2019* (2019) 101. Australia follows a system of mandated takeover bids.

78   For literature tracing evolution of takeover legislation, see Emma Armson, 'Evolution of Australian takeover legislation' (2014) 39(3) *Monash University Law Review* 654–701.

79   See ASIC, *Takeovers: Exceptions to the General Prohibition* (Regulatory Guide 6, 2020). This guide is for listed and unlisted entities that seek to rely on exceptions to the general prohibition in s 606 of the *Corporations Act* in connection with a transaction, acquisition or corporate action.

80   See ASIC, *Schemes of Arrangement* (Regulatory Guide 60, 2020).

81   See ASIC, *Compulsory Acquisitions and Buyouts* (Regulatory Guide 10, 2013). This guide discusses the compulsory acquisition provisions under ch 6A of the *Corporations Act* and how ASIC administers these and other buyout rights provisions.

Analysis

In the absence of the market providing requisite and sufficient incentives for 'adequate disclosure', many disclosures are 'mandated by law',[82] as is reflected in the key features of the disclosure framework discussed above. ASIC regards the framework for disclosure, particularly continuous disclosure, as a 'bedrock' of market integrity,[83] and also a key tenet for fair and efficient financial markets.[84] Thus, the disclosure landscape in Australia has been continuously updated since its introduction as a statutory obligation by the *Corporate Law Reform Act 1994* (Cth). The importance of continuous disclosure has been judicially upheld, most vociferously in the James Hardie decision.[85] Similarly, any contravention of statutory continuous disclosure obligations is liable enforcement action by ASIC, which can be:

> a criminal action; a civil action; an administrative action for an infringement notice; an enforceable undertaking; or a determination by ASIC under s 713(6) of the *Corporations Act* that a company cannot issue a prospectus with reduced content.[86]

Notwithstanding the emphasis on disclosure, and powers available to ASIC, ASIC's implementation of the disclosure regime, particularly its choice of action in case of breaches of continuous disclosure, has been criticised for its over-reliance on infringement notices as the mode for addressing breaches of continuous disclosure.[87]

---

82 Michael James Legg, 'Public and private enforcement of securities laws in Australia: an examination of the continuous disclosure regime' (PhD Thesis, Melbourne Law School, 2019) 20. See also Commonwealth of Australia, Financial System Inquiry, *Final Report* (1997) 177, 188; Corporate Law Economic Reform Program, *Corporate Disclosure: Strengthening the Financial Reporting Framework (Proposals for Reform: Paper No 9* (2002) 129.

83 Belinda Gibson and John Price, 'Continuous disclosure: ASX Guidance Note 8 rewrite' (Speech, ASX Forum, 29 April 2013) 2, asic.gov.au/about-asic/news-centre/speeches/continuous-disclosure-asx-guidance-note-8-rewrite. See also John Price, 'Continuous disclosure' (Speech, Chartered Secretaries Australia 2012 Annual Conference, 3 December 2012), asic.gov.au/about-asic/news-centre/speeches/continuous-disclosure/.

84 ASIC, 'ASIC welcomes consultation on continuous disclosure' (Media Release, 17 October 2012), asic.gov.au/about-asic/news-centre/find-a-media-release/2012-releases/12-253mr-asic-welcomes-consultation-on-continuous-disclosure/.

85 In *James Hardie Industries NV v ASIC* (NSW Court of Appeal, 2010) 332 [355]. The court described the role of continuous disclosure regime: 'to enhance the integrity and efficiency of Australian capital markets by ensuring that the market is fully informed'; to maintain and increase 'confidence of investors in Australian markets'; and to minimise 'incidences of insider trading and other market distortions'.

86 Ramsay (n 66) 197.

87 Ibid 201. See also the detailed analysis in Chapter 5, this book, on ASIC's enforcement actions in relation to continuous disclosure.

In relation to IOSCO Principle 17 on fair and equitable treatment of holders of securities, it is relevant to consider both the framework and its implementation for shareholder protection, takeovers and, more generally, corporate governance requirements. In terms of the framework, the regime is generally equipped with robust provisions to support fairness and equitable treatment for holders of securities, as discussed above. In particular, shareholder rights per se have been accorded high scholarly attention. Some studies have traced the regulatory evolution of shareholder protection in Australia,[88] while others have undertaken sophisticated longitudinal, leximetric analysis to reveal comparative trends in shareholder protection across the globe.[89] A number of common understandings emerge from these studies. The first is that 'Australia has a comparatively shareholder-centric system of corporate law' that operates at the 'high end of shareholder protection and power', especially in relation to corporate governance.[90] Second, that markets in Australia, along with the US, the UK and Canada, generally reveal characteristics of 'dispersed ownership' as compared to the vast majority of markets that have a concentrated or 'dominant' ownership system.[91] Third, that—although Anderson et al showed, through quantitative analysis, that shareholder protection in Australia was robust in 2012[92]—in recent years, as shown in *The Global Competitiveness Report 2019*, Australia has recorded downward trends on corporate governance, with a score of 67.1 and an overall rank of 39, and specifically a score of 60 for shareholder governance, with a world ranking of 64.[93] Similarly, while Australia retained its number one rank in the 2018

---

88 Mitchell et al (n 76).

89 Helen Anderson et al, 'The evolution of shareholder and creditor protection in Australia: an international comparison' (2012) 61(1) *International & Comparative Law Quarterly* 171, doi.org/10.1017/S0020589311000595. This research built on an earlier study by Lele and Siems: see Priya P Lele and Mathias M Siems, 'Shareholder protection: a leximetric approach' (2007) 7(1) *Journal of Corporate Law Studies* 17–50, doi.org/10.1080/14735970.2007.11421508.

90 Mitchell et al (n 76) 110.

91 OECD, 'The corporate and market landscape' in *OECD Corporate Governance Factbook 2019* (2019) 17. See also John C Coffee, 'The rise of dispersed ownership: the roles of law and the state in the separation of ownership and control' (2001) 111(1) *Yale Law Journal* 1, doi.org/10.2307/797515. According to Coffee, a 'dispersed ownership system' is 'characterised by strong securities markets, rigorous disclosure standards, and high market transparency'. It is one in which the 'market for corporate control constitutes the ultimate disciplinary mechanism'. By contrast, a 'concentrated ownership system' has features of 'controlling blockholders, weak securities markets, high private benefits of control', 'low disclosure and market transparency standards, with only a modest role played by the market for corporate control'.

92 Anderson et al (n 89). Both Australia and the UK were found to be stronger in shareholder protection as compared with the US.

93 Schwab (n 45).

Corporate Governance Watch Report,[94] and is slotted well ahead of other Asia-Pacific markets, the report commented that Australia's corporate governance structure had weakened in the face of significant decreases in the 'fair treatment of consumers and shareholders',[95] as the Hayne Royal Commission's 2019 report also revealed.[96] This general drop in Australia's corporate governance standing raises concerns and questions over the effectiveness of its non-prescriptive approach towards corporate governance requirements.[97] Given that other advanced markets, such as the US, have shifted to 'a legislative rules-based approach to corporate governance, with a higher level of mandatory governance standards' in response to repeated corporate failures,[98] it begets the question whether a more prescriptive approach to corporate governance is desirable for Australia also (in light of the failings uncovered by the Hayne Royal Commission).

Regarding takeovers, the requirements are generally mandated by law and contain the necessary aspects, as discussed above, to balance conflicting interests of the parties, such as shareholders and directors of the target company and the acquirers, that are involved in takeovers. Takeover panels are employed to balance such conflicting interests, which Armson argues operate, to a large extent, with the objectives of 'speed, flexibility and certainty'.[99]

The detailed FSAP Assessment in 2012 for IOSCO Principles 16 and 17 granted ASIC a 'fully implemented' status due to the strength of its disclosure regime for public offerings; policy of bringing court actions against companies, directors and advisers for violations of their obligations; and takeover regime.

---

94   See CLSA, *Hard Decisions: Asia Faces Tough Choices in CG Reform* (Corporate Governance Watch, 5 December 2018).

95   Even though the levels of transparency and accountability in Australian markets remained 'largely intact': see Australian Institute of Company Directors, 'How well does Australia's corporate governance perform?' (1 March 2019), aicd.companydirectors.com.au/membership/company-director-magazine/2019-back-editions/march/update-corporate-governance.

96   See generally *Royal Commission into Misconduct in the Banking, Superannuation and Financial Services Industry* (Final Report, September 2018) vol 1.

97   OECD, 'The corporate and market landscape' (n 91). Australia and the UK have a corporate governance code prescribed through listing rules while the US and India have a more prescriptive legal and regulatory requirement for corporate governance.

98   J Hill, 'Regulatory responses to corporate governance scandals' (2005) 23 *Wisconsin International Law Journal* 367.

99   Emma Armson, 'Assessing the performance of takeover panels: a comparative study' in Umakanth Varottil and Wai Yee Wan (eds), *Comparative Takeover Regulation: Global and Asian Perspectives* (Cambridge University Press, 2018) 134–62.

Conclusion

Despite certain weaknesses and a reduction in corporate governance standards in recent years, Australia's disclosure and corporate governance standards are remarkably high and effective in comparison to most jurisdictions. This leads to the conclusion that the degree of alignment of the Australian landscape with the core requirements of Principles 16 and 17 is 'high', even as certain weaknesses need to be addressed. The overall landscape relating to these principles is assessed as 'mature' against a generally high degree of stability and reliability regarding disclosure and corporate governance. However, developments in this area, in recent years, particularly with reference to stronger enforcement actions by ASIC, are assessed as 'minor'.

Principle 18

Principle 18: Accounting standards used by issuers to prepare financial statements should be of a high and internationally acceptable quality.

IOSCO Principle 18 encompasses the 'objectives of investor protection and fair, efficient and transparent markets' by requiring 'high-quality' financial statements to be prepared using internationally acceptable accounting standards.[100] Even though accounting standards are a key focus area in companies' regulation for several reasons,[101] IOSCO does not specify any particular set of accounting standards for preparation of financial statements.[102] Despite the need for the adoption of an agreed set of financial reporting standards, as voiced on several occasions by practitioners and academics,[103] debate on this topic continues. The sections below examine some key features of the Indian and Australian accounting regimes for securities markets.

---

100 IOSCO, *Methodology for Assessing Implementation* (n 1) 118.
101 For instance, the use of quality accounting standards ensures that the financial statements are 'comprehensive, consistent, relevant, reliable and comparable': see ibid 118.
102 IMF, *India FSAP Report* (n 25) 67.
103 Many academics have favoured the adoption of the International Financial Reporting Standards (IFRS): see Donald T Nicolaisen, 'A securities regulator looks at convergence' (2004) 25 *Northwestern Journal of International Law* 661.

SEBI/India
Key features of the accounting standards framework

Currently, India has not adopted the International Financial Reporting Standards (IFRS) issued by the International Accounting Standards Board,[104] but has committed to the adoption of the IFRS in a phased manner.[105] India follows the Indian Accounting Standards that converge with the IFRS.[106]

Companies issuing securities in India, both debt and equity, are required to submit annual audited financial statements.[107] Section 134 of the *Companies Act* mandates that financial statements shall be approved by a board of directors, be signed and sent to an auditor for a report, and that such a report and statement must together be placed before the general meeting of the company.[108]

The Institute of Chartered Accountants of India (ICAI) is a statutory body set up under the *Chartered Accountants Act of 1949*,[109] and is recognised as a standard-setter under s 133 of the *Companies Act*.[110] Alongside the ICAI, s 132 of the *Companies Act* provides for the constitution of the National Financial Reporting Authority (NFRA),[111] which is responsible for matters relating to accounting and auditing standards under the said Act.[112] The roles

---

104 IFRS, [Home], www.ifrs.org/.

105 IFRS, 'Who uses IFRS Accounting Standards?', ifrs.org/use-around-the-world/use-of-ifrs-standards-by-jurisdiction/.

106 India has not formally adopted the IFRS standards: see ibid. See also IMF, *India FSAP Report* (n 25). For a study reflecting on some of the underlying issues that have caused impediments in India's adoption of the IFRS, see Sharad Sharma, Mahesh Joshi and Monika Kansal, 'IFRS adoption challenges in developing economies: an Indian perspective' (2017) 32(4/5) *Managerial Auditing Journal* 406–426, doi.org/10.1108/MAJ-05-2016-1374. See also PR Parvathy, 'IFRS convergence: opportunities and challenges in India' (2017) 1(2) *Accounting and Financial Control* 13–18, doi.org/10.21511/afc.01(2).2017.02.

107 IMF, *India FSAP Report* (n 25) 62. Since the focus of this book is on SEBI's role as a regulator, the analysis is limited to listed companies, as unlisted companies fall under the purview of the Ministry of Corporate Affairs.

108 See *Companies Act* s 134.

109 Institute of Chartered Accountants of India (ICAI), 'Overview', icai.org/overview.shtml.

110 Under s 133 of the *Companies Act*, the central government is given the responsibility of prescribing the standards of accounting, as recommended by the ICAI, in consultation with, and after the examination of, recommendations made by the National Financial Reporting Authority (NFRA).

111 The NFRA was constituted on 1 October 2018 by the Government of India under s 132(1) of the *Companies Act*: see NFRA, 'About the organization', nfra.gov.in/about-department/introduction/. NFRA's stated objectives include improving the quality of corporate reporting in India, with specific focus on principles of objectivity, integrity, impartiality, independence, fairness and transparency. The establishment of the NFRA was an outcome of a number of major financial scams, including Enron and the Satyam scandal: see Janhavi Phadnis, 'NFRA or ICAI: who is the ultimate authority?', *FinancePost* (16 November 2018), financepost.in/nfra-or-icai-who-is-the-ultimate-authority/.

112 The NFRA is mandated to make recommendations to the central government on the formulation of accounting and auditing policies and standards for adoption by companies or classes of companies or their auditors: see *Companies Act* s 132(2).

of the ICAI and NFRA are designed to be separate in relation to standards setting, oversight and governance,[113] though certain problems of 'overlap' and 'turf-wars' surfaced soon after of the latter's establishment.[114]

Analysis

The accounting regime per se does not come under the regulatory purview of SEBI. As evident from the short description above, India has taken several steps in the past decade to upgrade and consolidate the accounting standards landscape. Several notorious accounting practices and scandals[115] led to the legal and regulatory overhaul of the accounting framework with significant changes to the *Companies Act*[116] and the establishment of the NFRA. Further, India's commitment towards adopting the IFRS in a phased manner has been clearly stated.

These changes indicate that India has embarked on a journey towards more sophisticated and improved accounting practices that, over time, are expected to yield positive results. It is also evident that governance of the accounting regime lies beyond the regulatory realm of SEBI and is, in fact, dispersed among several bodies under a regulatory arrangement that is essentially still in its nascent stages. However, the new governance structure has raised some concerns around overlapping responsibilities among different authorities

---

113 See 'No conflict between jurisdictions of NFRA, ICAI: Thakur', *Business Standard* (16 March 2020), business-standard.com/article/pti-stories/no-conflict-between-jurisdictions-of-nfra-icai-thakur-120031601055_1.html. The ICAI's primary role is to recommend accounting standards for India and also to exercise disciplinary control over accountants and auditors, which is not the role designed for the NFRA. The NFRA's main objective is to be an independent body for oversight of the 'quality of accounting and auditing services with respect to listed companies as well as unlisted companies above a prescribed threshold': see Injeti Srinivas, 'NFRA is a necessity, ICAI contentions are contrary to international standards; here's why', *Financial Express* (22 October 2018), financialexpress.com/opinion/nfra-is-a-necessity-icai-contentions-are-contrary-to-international-standards-heres-why/1356439/. The Quality Review Board (QRB) continues to perform quality audits in relation to private limited companies and public unlisted companies below a threshold limit as prescribed, and also for any company that is delegated to the QRB by the NFRA.

114 See Veena Mani, 'NFRA–ICAI turf war intensifies further; govt's intervention sought', *Business Standard* (3 June 2019), business-standard.com/article/economy-policy/nfra-icai-turf-war-intensifies-further-govt-s-intervention-sought-119060300029_1.html.

115 On the Satyam scandal, see Madan Lal Bhasin, 'Creative accounting scam at Satyam computer limited: how the fraud story unfolded?' (2016) 5(4) *Open Journal of Accounting* 57, doi.org/10.4236/ojacct.2016.54007; Madan Lal Bhasin, 'Creative accounting practices at Satyam Computers Limited: a case study of India's Enron' (2016) 6(6) *International Journal of Business and Social Research* 24–48, doi.org/10.18533/ijbsr.v6i6.948.

116 Yan Luo and Linying Zhou, 'Satyam scandal' in H Kent Baker, L Purda-Heeler and S Saadi (eds) *Corporate Fraud Exposed* (Emerald Publishing Ltd, 2020), doi.org/10.1108/978-1-78973-417-120201025.

and, in turn, around the efficacy of arrangements. Yet, other opinions assert that there are no contradictions or overlaps in the new regulatory structure for accounting[117] and that the regime is off to a reformed start.

Overall, while recent reforms reflect the fast-evolving nature of governance of accounting standards and financial reports in India, the reality remains that 'a range of factors, captured within a country's culture and its legal, financing and taxation systems, will affect the output of the financial reporting process'.[118] Finally, SEBI's lack of authority in the accounting sphere relating to listed companies must be reconsidered, as it does not appear ideal or sustainable from a long-term perspective.

At the time of the detailed FSAP Review of 2013, certain deficiencies relating to the accounting standards adopted by companies were observed in the Indian regime, leading to a grade of 'partly implemented' in respect of Principle 18 (erstwhile Principle 16).[119] However, since then, the accounting regime in India has, in some ways, embarked on a transformative and promising journey.

Conclusion

Adopting internationally recognised, high-quality accounting standards is critical for strong investor protection, and also for positioning India globally as an investment destination and for long-term, cross-border cooperation and integration measures, among other reasons. Considering recent measures towards consolidation and enhancement of the regulatory framework for accounting standards, the degree of alignment of India's accounting regime with the core requirements of Principle 18 is assessed as 'moderate'. With many new inclusions, such as the overhaul of the *Companies Act* and the establishment of the NFRA, the accounting regime is in a state of transition and the overall landscape is thus assessed as 'evolving', with 'substantial' changes and reform undertaken in the past decade.

---

117 Srinivas (n 113). The NFRA has the core responsibility under s 132 of the *Companies Act 2013* of recommending accounting and auditing policies and standards, undertaking investigations and imposing sanctions for violations by auditors through monetary penalties and/or debarment for up to 10 years. In comparison, the ICAI is required to conduct CA exams, register qualified CAs, issue certificates of practice, specify codes of conduct for members and regulate auditors of private companies.
118 Philip Brown, John Preiato and Ann Tarca, 'Measuring country differences in enforcement of accounting standards: an audit and enforcement proxy' (2014) 41(1–2) *Journal of Business Finance and Accounting* 5, doi.org/10.1111/jbfa.12066.
119 IMF, *India FSAP Report* (n 25) 17. This rating was given for several other reasons, including that the IFRS-equivalent standards were not adopted, and that the review of financial statements in respect of listed companies lay with the Ministry of Corporate Affairs and not with SEBI.

ASIC

Key features of the accounting standards framework

At the general level, s 710 of *Corporations Act* requires a prospectus to contain all material information needed by investors to make an informed decision.[120] Documents such as an audited financial statement, cash flow statement, statement of financial position or balance sheet, and statement of comprehensive income, among others, are required to be provided by the issuer of securities to ASIC or a listing body such as the ASX.[121] Particularly, ch 2M of the *Corporations Act* specifies the requirements for making and filing of financial reports and audit statements by companies. In addition to these statutory provisions under the *Corporations Act*, ASIC periodically issues comprehensive regulatory guides and information on various aspects, such as reporting requirements, financial reports, and directors and financial reporting.[122]

In conjunction with the requirements under the *Corporations Act*, pt 12 of the *ASIC Act* describes the financial reporting framework. Section 224 of the *ASIC Act* outlines the objects of the financial reporting system, which include:

> developing accounting standards that require the provision of information that is relevant, reliable, easy to understand, allows investors to make and evaluate financial decisions, and assists directors to fulfil their statutory financial reporting obligations.[123]

To this end, the *ASIC Act* establishes three agencies under pt 12 as 'administrative arms of the financial reporting system':[124] the Financial Reporting Council (FRC),[125] the Auditing and Assurance Standards Board[126] and the Australian Accounting Standards Board (AASB).[127] The AASB is responsible for 'developing, issuing and maintaining accounting standards'.[128]

---

120 See *Corporations Act* s 710.

121 IMF, *Australia Country Report* (n 69).

122 See ASIC, 'Regulatory resources: regulatory tracker', asic.gov.au/regulatory-resources/regulatory-index/financial-reporting/.

123 Parliament of Australia, 'Review of annual reports of bodies established under Part 12 of the *ASIC Act*', aph.gov.au/Parliamentary_Business/Committees/Joint/Corporations_and_Financial_Services/Membership/Annual_Reports/201011/c03.

124 Ibid.

125 The Financial Reporting Council (FCR) is primarily responsible for overseeing the effectiveness of the financial reporting framework in Australia: see FRC, 'About the FCR', frc.gov.au/about-frc.

126 The AUASB and the auditing regime are discussed in detail under the analysis of IOSCO Principles 19–21.

127 See *ASIC Act* pt 12.

128 AASB, 'Frequently asked questions', aasb.gov.au/research-resources/general-faqs/. The chairman of the AASB Board is appointed by the relevant minister while other board members of different backgrounds are appointed by the FRC.

The AASB reports to the relevant minister and to the FRC.[129] The *ASIC Act* gives the FRC information-gathering powers,[130] its main responsibilities being to oversee the effectiveness of the financial reporting framework in Australia through 'oversight of accounting and auditing standards'.[131] Meanwhile, the responsibility for surveillance, investigation, enforcement and compliance with financial reporting requirements for entities lies with ASIC.[132] To maximise the effectiveness of their powers, the FRC and ASIC have signed an agreement to cooperate and exchange information.[133]

In terms of accounting standards, Australia's standards have been fully aligned with the IFRS since 2005.[134] Section 9 of *Corporations Act* defines the term 'accounting standard' with reference to s 334 of the said Act,[135] which empowers the AASB to make the requisite standards.[136] The AASB Accounting Standards are high quality, comprehensive and equivalent with the IFRS.[137] The AASB regularly specifies and amends accounting standards for entities, including listed companies.[138] For example, AASB 101 on the presentation of financial statements ensures companies delineate an accurate picture of their financial position.[139]

The overall oversight as well as reporting of financial requirements rests with ASIC in terms of the *Corporations Act*, and ASIC may, for any contravention, impose a penalty of up to $220,000 or imprisonment for five years or both.[140]

---

129 AASB, 'About the AASB', aasb.gov.au/about-the-aasb/about-the-aasb/. The relevant minister appoints the chairman of the AASB.

130 See *ASIC Act* s 225A.

131 FRC (n 125).

132 See generally ASIC, 'Financial reporting and audit', asic.gov.au/regulatory-resources/financial-reporting-and-audit/.

133 *Memorandum of Understanding between The Australian Securities and Investment Commission and The Financial Reporting Council* (signed 1 May 2008).

134 See AASB, 'The standard-setting process', aasb.gov.au/media/egdnmbhb/aasb-standard-setting-process.pdf.

135 Section 9 defines 'accounting standard' as an instrument in force under s 334 of the *Corporations Act*.

136 Ibid s 334. The AASB is an independent agency of the Australian government with responsibility to make accounting standards under s 334 of the *Corporations Act*.

137 IFRS, 'Who uses IFRS Standards?' (n 105).

138 AASB, *Review of Adoption of International Reporting Standards in Australia* (Research Report No 4, 2017), www.aasb.gov.au/admin/file/content102/c3/aasb_review_of_ifrs_research_report_03-17.pdf.

139 See AASB, 'AASB 101—presentation of financial statements', legislation.gov.au/Details/F2009 C00140.

140 ASIC is empowered to initiate both civil and criminal proceedings for any violation of the financial reporting requirements under the *Corporations Act*.

Analysis

The governance of financial reporting in Australia occurs through a combination of statutes,[141] regulations, accounting standards, professional standards and other sources.[142] A number of regulatory and statutory institutions, as highlighted in the previous section, oversee and regulate this accounting landscape. Australian financial markets make use of high-quality accounting standards that are fully consistent with the IFRS standards,[143] the adoption of which has been linked to an 'increase in the quality of the published financial reports of entities'.[144] While all these have collectively contributed towards Australia's high rank for accounting globally,[145] and for corporate governance within the Asia-Pacific region,[146] the financial reporting regime has been described as 'complex', particularly considering the multiple codes that apply and the many bodies responsible for standard setting, oversight and enforcement of the accounting framework.[147] In some areas, the framework mitigates the complexity of accounting requirements for preparation of financial statements by creating a differential accounting framework as specified under AASB 1053 for certain entities.[148] Such a framework is available to entities based on 'user dependency', and employs the concept of a 'reporting entity' referred to under AASB 101,[149] which is defined and elaborated in SAC 1 *Definition of the Reporting Entity*.[150]

---

141 *ASIC Act* and *Corporations Act*.

142 Deloitte, *Australian Financial Reporting Guide* (9th ed, 2020) 2.

143 See also IFRS, 'Who uses IFRS Standards?' (n 105).

144 Thomas Mathew Alappatt, 'Impact of adoption of International Financial Reporting Standards and financial crisis on accounting quality of Australian listed companies' (Phd Thesis, Curtin University, 2020) 16. See also William J Ihlanfeldt, 'International accounting standards: why should you care?' (1997) 79(5) *Strategic Finance* 6.

145 Schwab (n 45) 67. Australia has a global rank of 14 for accounting and auditing standards.

146 CLSA (n 94) 111. Australia ranks first among 12 Asia-Pacific countries with a score of 84 per cent for its accounting and auditing standards.

147 See Deloitte, *Australian Financial Reporting Guide* (n 142).

148 Under the AASB standards, a tier-based accounting structure is incorporated to subject certain entities to IFRS standards, while allowing certain others to reduced disclosure requirements: see *AASB, Application of Tiers of Australian Accounting Standards* (AASB 1053, 2015).

149 See Deloitte, *Australian Financial Reporting Guide* (n 142).

150 Australian Accounting Research Foundation and Accounting Standards Review Board, *SAC1 8: Definition of the Reporting Entity* (Statement of Accounting Concepts, SAC 1 (8/90) nd).

For compliance with the financial reporting requirements of entities that are subject to the *Corporations Act*, such as listed companies, ASIC is the main authority.[151] In cases of a breach of these requirements, ASIC relies on its enforcement repertoire,[152] as it did in Gina Rinehart's case,[153] and against other 'companies for financial reporting non-compliance'.[154]

In recognition of the comprehensive accounting standards in place and ASIC's effective surveillance and sanctions regime, the FSAP Assessment of 2013 rated the Australian regime as 'fully implemented' on Principle 18.

Conclusion

Given the sophisticated accounting standards adopted by Australia, and the high global and regional rank of its accounting regime, the degree of alignment is assessed as 'high' for Principle 18. The overall landscape is assessed 'mature', while the extent of change relating to this area is assessed as 'minor' for recent years.

Principles for collective investment schemes and hedge funds

Principles 24–28

Principle 24: The regulatory system should set standards for the eligibility, governance, organisation and operational conduct of those who wish to market or operate a collective investment scheme.

Principle 25: The regulatory system should provide for rules governing the legal form and structure of collective investment schemes and the segregation and protection of client assets.

---

151 ASIC, 'Financial reporting and audit' (n 132).

152 ASIC has discretion to use civil penalties, including deregistering a company or cancelling an AFSL licence, or it may initiate court proceedings against the directors and officers for breach of their reporting obligations: see *Corporations Act* s 1311.

153 'Gina Rinehart's companies fined for failing to lodge financial reports on time', *ABC News* (19 August 2015), abc.net.au/news/2015-08-10/gina-rinehart-companies-fined-for-failing-to-lodge-reports/6685998. In 2015, Gina Rinehart's private company, Hancock Prospecting Pty Ltd, along with its two related entities, Hancock Minerals and Hope Downs, were convicted and fined $130,000 for failure to lodge annual financial reports on time. ASIC's investigations revealed that the companies had failed to lodge their annual reports for over five years since 2008.

154 See Ben Smits, 'Caught in the crosshairs: financial reporting obligations under the Corporations Act', *Norton Rose Fulbright* (October 2016), nortonrosefulbright.com/en-au/knowledge/publications/f182fa15/caught-in-the-crosshairs-financial-reporting-obligations-under-the-corporations-act.

Principle 26: Regulation should require disclosure, as set forth under the principles for issuers, which is necessary to evaluate the suitability of a collective investment scheme for a particular investor's interest in the scheme.

Principle 27: Regulation should ensure that there is a proper and disclosed basis for asset valuation and the pricing and the redemption of units in a collective investment scheme.

Principle 28: Regulation should ensure that hedge funds and/or hedge funds managers/advisers are subject to appropriate oversight.

IOSCO Principles 24–27 lay down the regulatory principles for CISs while Principle 28 relates to regulatory oversight of hedge funds, their managers and advisers. The governance of CISs, along with their operators, has been an area of keen focus for decades.[155] IOSCO's predecessor committee, the Technical Committee, in its report of July 1995, published detailed Principles for the Regulation of Collective Investment Schemes that defined a CIS as 'an open ended collective investment scheme that issues redeemable units and invests primarily in transferable securities or money market instruments'.[156] In 1997, the Technical Committee published another report outlining the key principles for supervising the conduct of the operators of CISs.[157]

Similarly, the oversight and regulation of hedge funds has been widely discussed, particularly in the aftermath of the global financial crisis (GFC) of 2007–08.[158] IOSCO refers to a hedge fund as an investment scheme that

---

155 IOSCO, representing the world's leading securities markets, has written at length about the significance of ensuring that collective investment schemes are strengthened against risks they face: see IOSCO, *Recommendations for Liquidity Risk Management for Collective Investment Schemes* (Final Report, 2018). For recent perspectives on the governance of collective investment schemes in the UK and Europe, see Jonathan Kirk, Thomas Samuels and Lee Finch, 'Collective investment schemes' in *Mis-Selling Financial Services* (Edward Elgar Publishing, 2019), doi.org/10.4337/9781788117678. The regulation of hedge funds received much support in the wake of the GFC as IOSCO published several reports on their oversight and regulation: see for example IOSCO, *Hedge Funds Oversight* (Final Report, Technical Committee of the IOSCO, June 2009), iosco.org/library/pubdocs/pdf/IOSCOPD293.pdf.

156 IOSCO, *Report on Investment Management: Principles for the Regulation of Collective Investment Schemes* (1994). Investopedia defines a 'Collective Investment Fund' as 'a group of pooled accounts held by a bank or trust company': see T Segal, 'Collective Investment Fund (CIF)' *Investopedia* (7 February 2025), investopedia.com/terms/c/collective-investment-fund.asp.

157 Technical Committee of the IOSCO, *Principles for the Supervision of Operators of Collective Investment Schemes* (1997).

158 The G-20 formally deliberated on the regulation of the hedge fund industry for the first time after the GFC: see Orfeo Fioretos, 'Capitalist diversity and the international regulation of hedge funds' (2010) 17(4) *Review of International Political Economy* 696–723, doi.org/10.1080/09692291003723789. See also Eric Helleiner and Stefano Pagliari, 'The end of self-regulation? Hedge funds and derivatives in global financial governance' in *Global Finance in Crisis: The Politics of International Regulatory Change* (Routledge, 2009).

generally involves high levels of leverage and high performance fees, and relies on more complex underlying products, including derivatives, that are significantly different from a typical CIS.[159]

During the GFC, the role of hedge funds in financial markets was highlighted amid concerns around systemic risks.[160] This concern led to the adoption of IOSCO Principle 28 on oversight of these funds, while also paving the way for six new high-level principles published in the IOSCO 2009 report *Hedge Funds Oversight*.[161]

The broad landscape for regulation of CIS and hedge funds, for India and Australia, is discussed below.

SEBI

Key features of the CIS and hedge funds framework

Broadly, securities laws in India recognise and lay separate regulatory frameworks for two types of CIS that are described by IOSCO: mutual funds (MFs) and CISs.[162] Additionally, SEBI introduced the *SEBI (Alternate Investment Funds) Regulations 2012 (AIF Regulations)*, which applies to a

---

159 IOSCO, *Hedge Funds Oversight* (n 155) 4. For US perspectives on hedge funds, see Henry Ordower, 'The regulation of private equity, hedge funds, and state funds' (2010) 58(suppl 1) *The American Journal of Comparative Law* 295–322, doi.org/10.5131/ajcl.2009.0035.

160 See for example Robert J Bianchi and Michael E Drew, 'Hedge fund regulation and systemic risk' (2010) 19(1) *Griffith Law Review* 6–29, doi.org/10.1080/10854666.2010.10854666. See also Wulfa Kaal and Timothy A Krause, 'Hedge funds and systemic risk' in *Hedge Funds: Structure, Strategies, and Performance* (2017) 305, doi.org/10.1093/oso/9780190607371.003.0017.

161 These high-level principles include mandatory registration of hedge funds, their managers and advisers; appropriate ongoing regulatory requirements relating to organisational and operational standards, conflict of interest and other conduct of business rules, disclosures to investors and prudential regulation; 'development, implementation and convergence' of 'industry good practices'; and co-operation and sharing of information between regulatory authorities to 'facilitate oversight of globally active managers/advisers and/or funds to help identify systemic risks, market integrity risks and other risks' with 'a view to mitigating such risks across borders': see IOSCO, *Hedge Funds Oversight* (n 155) 3.

162 Essentially, for the purposes of the Indian markets, 'a mutual fund is a mechanism for pooling money by issuing units to the investors and investing funds in securities in accordance with objectives as disclosed in offer document': see SEBI, *Investments in Mutual Funds—FAQs*, www.sebi.gov.in/sebi_data/attachdocs/1475063737177.pdf. On the other hand, 'a collective investment scheme', defined in s 11AA(2) of the *SEBI Act*, is understood as 'a scheme or arrangement made or offered by any company under which the contributions, or payments made by the investors, are pooled and utilised with a view to receive profits, income, produce or property, and is managed on behalf of the investors': see SEBI, *FAQs—Collective Investment Schemes*, www.sebi.gov.in/sebi_data/faqfiles/jan-2017/1485846814724.pdf. See also SEBI, 'List of all SEBI regulations', sebi.gov.in/sebiweb/home/HomeAction.do?doListing=yes&sid=1&ssid=3&smid=0. SEBI's mutual funds and collective investment schemes regimes are laid out in separate regulations: see *SEBI (Mutual Funds) Regulations 1996*; *Securities and Exchange Board of India (Collective Investment Scheme) Regulations 1999*.

variety of funds, including private equity funds, venture capital funds (VCFs)[163] and foreign venture capital funds (FVCFs),[164] as well as real estate funds, strategy funds and hedge funds.

The requirements of IOSCO Principles 24–27 are reflected in SEBI's framework for MFs under the *SEBI (Mutual Fund) Regulations 1996* (*MF Regulations*) and for CISs under the *SEBI (Collective Investment Scheme) Regulations 1999* (*CIS Regulations*). The requirements under these regulations are extensive, covering aspects from registration of MFs and CISs,[165] to their establishment as a trust through a registered trust deed, to eligibility criteria for those who desire to sponsor or manage an MF or CIS.[166] The *MF Regulations* include elaborate provisions for constitution and management of the fund, operation of trustees, constitution of the asset management company, provisions relating to the schemes of an MF and valuation.[167] Further, the regulations contain elaborate provisions on pricing and redemption of units of MFs, including clauses specifying the 'repurchase price' of such units.[168] The regulations also lay down express provisions on inspection, auditing and the procedure to be adopted in the case of a violation.[169]

Similarly, SEBI's framework for CISs specifies, among other things, the criteria for the appointment of trustees and their obligations;[170] the requirements for investment management companies on disclosure; the prohibitions on issuing misleading statements; and the guidelines on

---

163 Prior to the *AIF Regulations*, venture capital funds were governed by the *SEBI (Venture Capital Funds) Regulations 1996*.

164 Prior to the *AIF Regulations*, foreign venture capital funds were governed by the *SEBI (Foreign Venture Capital Investors) Regulations 2000*.

165 See *SEBI (Mutual Funds) Regulations* ch II (on registration of mutual funds) regs 3–13. See *SEBI (CIS) Regulations* ch II (on registration of collective investment management company) regs 3–12.

166 For the eligibility criteria of a mutual fund, see *SEBI (Mutual Funds) Regulations* reg 7. For the eligibility criteria of a collective investment scheme, *SEBI (CIS) Regulations* reg 9.

167 In the *SEBI (Mutual Funds) Regulations* ch III (on constitution and management of mutual fund and the operation of trustees); ch IV (on constitution and management of asset management company and custodian) regs 14–18; ch V (on schemes of mutual fund), regs 19–27; ch VI (on investment objectives and valuation policies) regs 28–42A.

168 Regulation 49 requires 'open-ended funds to publish the sale and redemption price of units at least once a week in a daily newspaper of all India circulation'; it also requires the repurchase price to not be less than 93 per cent of the net asset value and the sale price to not be higher than 107 per cent of the NAV: see ibid reg 49. Further, cl 6 of the Eight Schedule to the *SEBI (Mutual Funds) Regulations* sets the threshold of tolerance as 1 per cent in terms of the errors in pricing, requiring the asset management company (AMC) to pay the difference to the unit holder from its capital if the error exceeds such 1 per cent.

169 See ibid ch VIII containing regs 61–67 on inspection and audit, and ch IX containing regs 68–76 on procedure for action in case of default.

170 See *SEBI (CIS) Regulations* ch IV (on trustees and their obligations) regs 16–23.

keeping investors' money in separate accounts and for using such money, the segregation of funds and listing of CISs.[171] The *CIS Regulations* also provide guidelines for the inspection, audit and procedure to take against a CIS in case of any violation.[172]

The regulatory framework also enumerates the 'legal forms' that are permissible for constituting an MF or a CIS,[173] and several measures that ensure protection of investors' rights, such as through appointment of trustees for the protection of unit holders and by placing limitations on fees and expenses.[174] Further, the regulations contain sufficient guidelines on the separation of assets to ensure that investor's interests are not eroded, and clauses on the winding-up of schemes in certain circumstances.[175]

The framework for MFs and CISs also enumerates their disclosure obligations,[176] including annual and ongoing disclosures.[177] For instance, reg 29(1) of the *MF Regulations* mandates that the offer documents should have disclosures that can assist investors in making an 'informed investment decision'.[178] To protect investors' interests, SEBI is empowered to require a change to the offer document after reviewing such document.[179] The regulations also provide an advertisement code for marketing units of MFs that is specific and comprehensive.[180] The framework under both regulations specifies the basis for asset valuation, pricing and redemption of units.[181] In the case of MFs, SEBI has mandated the frequency of the

---

171 See ibid ch V (collective investment schemes of investment management company) regs 24–39.

172 See ibid ch VII (on inspection and audit) regs 52–57; ch VIII (on procedure for action in case of default) regs 58–67.

173 See for example reg 14 of the *SEBI (Mutual Funds) Regulations* states that a mutual fund shall be constituted in the form of a trust, and specifies other details pertaining to the trust deed.

174 See for example ibid reg 52 (on limitation on fees and expenses on issue of schemes).

175 For winding up of a mutual fund scheme, see regs 39–42.

176 See ibid reg 28. An AMC is required to file a copy of the offer document with SEBI in order to launch a scheme.

177 The AMC, for example, is required to submit an annual report and separate annual statements of accounts for the MF that it is managing: see ibid reg 54. Regulation 58 requires submission of the half-yearly unaudited accounts while reg 59 requires the publication of such accounts within a month from the close of each half year.

178 IMF, *India FSAP Report* (n 25). Another instance of disclosure mandated by the regulations is the requirement for filing an abridged form of offer document known as a 'Key Information Memorandum'.

179 See *SEBI (Mutual Funds) Regulations* reg 28.

180 See ibid reg 30.

181 In terms of reg 47 of the *SEBI (MF) Regulations*, each 'MF is required to compute and carry out valuation of investments in its portfolio in accordance with valuation norms specified in the Eighth Schedule and guidelines issued by SEBI': see IMF, *India FSAP Report* (n 25).

NAV calculation to be 'daily for both open and close end funds', more specifically, that it is to be published in at least two daily newspapers that have circulation all over India.[182]

Analysis

As foreshadowed, SEBI's overarching framework for the functioning and operation of disclosures, asset valuation and pricing requirements for CISs and MFs is extensive, granular and generally well aligned with the core requirements of IOSCO Principles 24–27. The framework for MSs and CISs is trust-based, with the trustees assuming fiduciary responsibility.[183] While shareholders are beneficial owners of units, trustees are registered with SEBI and are controlling owners of the assets of the fund.[184] The framework also contains provisions for inspection, oversight and supervision through a risk-based approach.

In terms of the implementation of the CIS and MF framework, SEBI is seen to effectively utilise not just its inspection and supervisory powers[185] but also enforcement actions for violations of the CIS and MF regulations.[186] Further, as seen for FY 2018–19, SEBI passes winding-up orders against existing CISs for carrying out unauthorised activity while requiring them to make repayments to investors,[187] and even passes orders in cases of 'deemed public issues' against entities that 'raise money from [the] public through non-convertible debentures/non-convertible preference shares' in breach of statutory and regulatory provisions governing public issues.[188] In this regard, SEBI's approach and record in following through with enforcement in relation to scams has been remarkable, for which SEBI has received recognition and accolades both from the apex court in India as well as from courts in Australia.[189]

---

182 See *SEBI (Mutual Funds) Regulations* reg 48(2) on computation of net asset value. See also G Sethu, 'Governance of mutual funds and the institution of trustee' (2006) *Economic and Political Weekly* 1413–1416.

183 Ibid 1414.

184 Ibid.

185 For instance, in FY 2018–19, 47 warning letters and 24 deficiency letters were issued to MFs/AMCs and two warning letters were issued to trustees of MFs for non-compliance with SEBI regulations/guidelines: see SEBI, *Annual Report 2018–19* (2019) 115. As at 31 March 2019, there are 45 mutual funds registered with SEBI.

186 For example, SEBI initiated adjudication proceedings against five AMCs, four trustee companies, and one CEO during 2018–19: see ibid 115.

187 SEBI passed 12 orders against entities that were carrying out unauthorised CISs: see ibid.

188 In FY 2018–19, SEBI passed 23 final orders for such violations: see ibid.

189 See the discussion in Chapter 5 of this book on the PACL matter in which the court applauded SEBI's tenacity in pursuing the matter outside of India in view of investors' interest.

Notwithstanding SEBI's broad framework and efforts towards supervision and enforcement, limitations are observed in the effective operation of the CIS regime. The most significant problem with the CIS landscape is that gaps and fragmentation have led to a number of Ponzi schemes in the past decade.[190] Curiously, as at 31 March 2019 only one entity was registered with SEBI as a CIS,[191] and several entities have been hauled up by SEBI for carrying out activities similar to CISs without a registration or licence (possibly to evade regulatory obligations and supervision). In response to such challenges, SEBI took the following initiatives:

- led a blitzkrieg of mass media campaigns and investor education drives to generate awareness among investors[192]
- was a party in a high number of cases (179) in FY 2018–19 before different courts in India in respect of alleged unauthorised CIS activity or violations of CIS laws by an entity[193]
- extended its regulatory perimeter by framing regulations to strengthen and smooth the procedure for refunds to investors in cases where unregistered CISs were liquidated.[194]

It is also evident that SEBI cooperates with other authorities across India and refers unauthorised money mobilisation to the concerned jurisdictional agencies.[195] The effectiveness of SEBI's proactive approach to improving the governance of CISs is dependent on a number of variables, including the allocation by SEBI of appropriate budget, time and resources to oversight and regulation, and factors beyond SEBI's jurisdiction. In addition to SEBI's efforts, other measures are continuously being taken to address issues in this area. Recently, the *Banning of Unregulated Deposit Scheme Act 2019*, which prohibits accepting and soliciting deposits

---

190 See the discussion on the Saradha and Sahara Ponzi schemes in Chapter 5 of this book.

191 M/s GIFT Collective Investment Management Company Ltd, registered as CIS with SEBI in 2008–9: see SEBI, *Annual Report 2018–19* (n 185) 115.

192 For instance, SEBI carried out a media campaign on the theme of 'unrealistic returns' and another advising 'Don't go by hearsay' in respect of CISs: see ibid 130.

193 Ibid 171.

194 *Securities and Exchange Board of India (Appointment of Administrator and Procedure for Refunding to the Investors) Regulations 2018.*

195 For example, in FY 2018–19, SEBI examined and referred 163 cases of unauthorised money mobilisation to agencies and regulators including state governments, the RBI, Ministry of Corporate Affairs and Ministry of Agriculture, where the matters lay beyond SEBI's purview: see SEBI, *Annual Report 2018–19* (n 185) 115.

to unregulated deposit schemes, has been enacted.[196] This Act aims to protect gullible investors and depositors from Ponzi schemes and is likely to intensify holistic efforts towards cleansing the financial sector of issues relating to unregulated CISs.[197]

To fulfil requirements of IOSCO Principal 28, as mentioned above, SEBI extended its regulatory perimeter from VCFs and FVCFs to alternative investment funds (AIFs). Within this perimeter, SEBI now regulates a variety of funds including hedge funds.[198] The provisions of the *AIF Regulations 2012* are detailed and prescriptive.[199] Complementing this framework, SEBI carries out routine inspections of books of accounts and other records to ensure their proper functioning,[200] and issues administrative warning or deficiency letters in case of discrepancies.[201] At a high level, these indicate that SEBI is active in this area of regulatory activity.

The FSAP Assessment of 2013 in respect of the requirements for CISs granted the following ratings to SEBI's regime: Principle 24 (erstwhile Principle 17) was rated as 'broadly implemented'; Principles 25, 26 and 27 (erstwhile Principles 18, 19 and 20) were rated as 'fully implemented'; Principle 28 was not rated.

Conclusion

India's framework for CISs and hedge funds is sufficiently detailed and SEBI's oversight and regulation in this area has been proactive and quite commendable in response to the vast challenges and complexities of markets in India. The degree of alignment for Principle 24 is assessed as 'moderate' given the on-ground challenges discussed for the CIS landscape

---

196 See *The Banning of Unregulated Deposit Scheme Act 2019*.

197 See also Nilesh Sharma, 'Summary: the banning of Unregulated Deposit Schemes Act, 2019' *LinkedIn* (31 August 2019), linkedin.com/pulse/summary-banning-unregulated-deposit-schemes-act-2019-nilesh-sharma/.

198 *SEBI (Alternative Investment Funds) Regulations 2021 (AIF Regulations)*. These regulations were introduced as an omnibus measure to consolidate the regulatory requirements applying to a variety of funds other than those specifically excluded from the scope of the regulation including mutual funds, collective investment schemes and some others.

199 The *AIF Regulations* cover registration, eligibility criteria, conditions and procedure for the grant of a certificate of registration, publication of investment strategy to be placed in the memorandum to investors, schemes, tenures and other similar provisions.

200 For example, for FY 2018–19, five AIFs were inspected by SEBI: see SEBI, *Annual Report 2018–19* (n 185) 141.

201 For FY 2018–19, no such administrative warning letters were issued: see ibid.

in India. The overall landscape is assessed as 'evolving' to greater degree of effectiveness through the streamlining of supervisory and governance aspects, with 'substantial' reform and measures undertaken in the past decade.

For Principles 25, 26 and 27, the degree of alignment is assessed as 'high' given SEBI's strong frameworks for MFs and CISs. The overall landscape is assessed to be sufficiently 'mature', with 'minor' enhancements introduced in recent years.

Finally, for Principle 28, the degree of alignment is assessed as 'high', with a reasonably 'mature' regime and 'substantial' changes introduced in the past decade to govern hedge funds.

ASIC
Key features of the CIS and hedge funds framework

In Australia, the term 'collective investment schemes' refers to managed investment schemes (MISs),[202] and the regulatory framework for their governance is set out in ch 5C of the *Corporations Act*.[203] Section 9 of *Corporations Act* defines an MIS as a scheme to which people contribute their money, and such investments are pooled without the members having any day-to-day control over the operation of the scheme.[204] Australia's mutual fund markets are very large in relation to its overall population.[205] A prominent feature of ASIC's regulatory regime is that it distinguishes between a 'retail client' and 'wholesale client'.[206] This distinction is based on the underlying assumption that the former requires more protection

---

202 See *Corporations Act* ch 5C. For a detailed discussion of the managed investments regime, including product disclosure statements, see Robert Baxt, Ashley Black and Pamela F Hanrahan, 'Offering managed investments, derivatives and other financial products' in *Securities and Financial Services Law* (LexisNexis Butterworths, 2016) ch 6. There are eight main kinds of managed investment schemes in Australia: see Pamela Hanrahan and Ian Ramsay in 'Regulation of mutual funds in Australia' in WA Birdthistle and J Morley (eds) *Research Handbook on the Regulation of Mutual Funds* (Edward Elgar Publishing, 2018), doi.org/10.4337/9781784715052.00026.

203 MISs, also referred to as 'managed funds', 'pooled investments' or 'collective investments', are schemes in which 'people are brought together to contribute money to get an interest in the scheme'; such 'money is pooled together with other investors or used in a common enterprise'; and 'investors do not have day to day control over the operation of the scheme': see ASIC, 'Managed funds', asic.gov.au/regulatory-resources/funds-management/. See also IMF, *Australia Country Report* (n 69) 100.

204 See John Flood and Adrian McCullagh, *The Technology, the Market, and the Regulation of ICOs* (Treasury Consultation Paper, 2019) 19.

205 Hanrahan and Ramsay (n 202).

206 In terms of the *Corporations Act*, a client is understood to be a 'retail client' unless they are specifically designated as a 'wholesale client': see *Corporations Act* s 761G. See ASIC, *Doing Financial Services Business in Australia* (Regulatory Guide 121, 2013). See also IMF, *Australia Country Report* (n 69) 100.

than the latter because of a lesser ability to assess risk in a financial transaction. The laws require the registration of a retail MIS that has more than 20 members or that is promoted by a professional promoter.[207] The scheme may be registered by a registered Australian public company or an Australian financial services licence (AFSL) holder specifically authorised as a responsible entity (RE) to operate the scheme.[208] The operator of the MIS, also known as the RE, is subject to a number of regulatory requirements laid out in ch 5C of the *Corporations Act,* including the obligation to be registered as an AFSL in dealing with and providing financial advice and services.[209] Thus, essentially, for an MIS, there is 'no mandated separation between the roles of trustee and manager' and both these roles are 'merged' into a single category of 'responsible entity' in Australia.[210] The RE owes fiduciary-like duties to investors. Another innovation is the requirement for a formal compliance monitoring committee.

A failure to comply with the registration requirements attracts punishment under s 1311 of the *Corporations Act.*[211] ASIC receives and reviews each application for registration of the retail MIS and may refuse to grant registration in certain circumstances, such as when the MIS's constitution does not conform with the conditions of ss 601GA and 601GB of the *Corporations Act.*[212] In certain cases, operators of foreign collective investment schemes may be exempt from holding an AFSL or registering under ch 5C.[213]

The distinction between retail and wholesale clients was first introduced into the *Corporations Act* by the *Financial Services Reform Act 2001* (Cth): see Revised Explanatory Memorandum, Financial Services Reform Bill 2001 (Cth).

207 See *Corporations Act* s 601ED.

208 ASIC, 'How to register a managed investment scheme', asic.gov.au/for-finance-professionals/fund-operators/establishing-and-registering-a-fund/how-to-register-a-managed-investment-scheme/#commentaries.

209 *Corporations Act* ch 5C. The responsible entity (RE) is subjected to a number of special conditions and additional financial requirements that are imposed over and above the requirements for AFSL holders. The RE is required to act in the best interests of the members and not to use the information for an 'improper advantage': see IMF, *Australia Country Report* (n 69) 101.

210 Hanrahan and Ramsay (n 202).

211 See *Corporations Act* s 1311.

212 See ibid.

213 This exemption may be made available if ASIC is convinced that the regulations by a foreign regulator are equivalent to the regulation by ASIC on the counts of 'investor protection, market integrity and systemic risk': see IMF, *Australia Country Report* (n 69).

MISs and REs are both subject to supervision and continuous monitoring by ASIC[214] as well as to several record-keeping requirements[215] and the maintenance of arrangements that identify and address any issues related to conflicts of interest.[216]

Collectively, the above provisions suitably reflect IOSCO's requirements under Principle 24 relating to eligibility, governance and conduct of operators of a CIS. In addition to these, other features and provisions of the MIS regulatory regime echo the requirements of IOSCO Principles 25, 26 and 27. For instance, Principle 25 requiring investment schemes to have a 'legal form' and 'structure' while ensuring the protection of client assets is reflected through the incorporation of MISs as trusts.[217] Similarly, as regards Principle 26, the regulatory framework requires disclosure to investors about the suitability of an investment scheme.[218] The requirements of Principle 27 on issues of pricing, asset valuation and related disclosures are also reflected, as the framework calls for proper asset valuation and pricing and redemption of units of an MIS.[219]

In relation to Principle 28, which outlines the requirement of hedge funds to be regulated, hedge funds in Australia are regulated under the managed funds industry.[220] Hedge funds are structured as unit trusts and are required to fulfil additional disclosure obligations that ASIC imposes on them, as explained in ASIC's Regulatory Guide 240.[221]

---

214 MISs and REs are monitored through yearly and half-yearly reports as well as through auditor's reports, and a significant requirement is to have 'risk management systems in place': see ASIC, 'Managed investment schemes', asic.gov.au/regulatory-resources/managed-funds/managed-investment-schemes/. ASIC's investment management and superannuation stakeholder department mainly relies on 'desk-based high intensity' methods of surveillance: see IMF, *Australia: IOSCO Objectives* (n 69) 102.

215 See ASIC, *ASIC Class Order* (CO 13/657) ss 601QA(1) and 1020F(1).

216 See IMF, *Australia Country Report* (n 69) 103.

217 An MIS is not mandated to be established in accordance with a specific legal structure; however, a registered MIS is usually incorporated as a trust: see Pamela Hanrahan, 'ASIC and managed investments' (2011) 29 *Company and Securities Law Journal* 287, 288.

218 Following the extensive reforms introduced through the Corporate Law Economic Reform Program (CLERP), specifically CLERP 6, the disclosure obligations in respect of MISs were enhanced and included the provision of a product disclosure statement that was applicable to unlisted and listed MISs: see ibid 303.

219 Section 601FC (1)(j) of the *Corporations Act* requires the responsible entity to value any property at regular intervals while s 601HA(1)(c) of the *Corporations Act* requires the managed investment scheme to develop a compliance plan that ensures the obligations under this requirement are met.

220 The Australian managed funds industry is valued at $3.9 trillion. See Australian Bureau of Statistics, 'Managed funds Australia' (1 March 2024), abs.gov.au/statistics/economy/finance/managed-funds-australia/latest-release.

221 See ASIC, *Hedge Funds: Improving Disclosure* (Regulatory Guide 240, 2013). This Regulatory Guide provides extensive requirements for disclosure.

Analysis

Perhaps due to the sheer size and significance of the Australian managed investments industry,[222] coupled with serious failures of the past,[223] the MIS sector has attracted high and constant government,[224] academic,[225] legal[226] and regulatory[227] attention within Australia.

In terms of adequacy of framework, as foreshadowed previously, the Australian MIS framework generally reflects the core requirements of IOSCO Principles 24–28 relating to CISs and hedge funds. This is evidenced by the extensive initial entry standards for operators of MISs that are controlled by ASIC,[228] as well as by the provision whereby 'ASIC receives regulatory filings and breach reports' to maintain a check on the industry.[229] ASIC's Regulatory Guide 240 provides guidance on improving disclosures for hedge funds,[230] and its Report 370 considers the risks posed

---

222 Around $3.6 trillion of assets are invested across the retail investment and wholesale funds category: see ASIC, 'Terms of reference' in *Funds Management Industry* (ASIC Market Study Consultancy, 2019). Australia's funds under management sector is substantial and exceeds Australia's GDP.

223 Hanrahan mentions three main areas of MIS that resulted in major loss and failures: 1) frozen funds, 2) agribusiness schemes and 3) complex schemes that failed and resulted in severe loss to investors: see Hanrahan (n 217) 308–311. Frozen funds comprised 'mortgage funds and (some) unlisted property funds', such as the MFS Premium Income Fund, while complex funds had complex financing terms or were exposed to GFC assets including collateralised debt obligations. In 2009, two of Australia's largest agribusiness MISs collapsed: Timbercorp and Great Southern. See Commonwealth of Australia, Senate Economic References Committee, *Agribusiness Managed Investment Schemes: Bitter Harvest* (2016) xvii.

224 Inquiries have been undertaken at the highest level by Senate standing committees: see for example Senate Economic References Committee (n 223).

225 See for example Hanrahan and Ramsay (n 202); Rosemary Teele Langford, 'Managed investment schemes: liability of directors of responsible entities where the responsible entity breaches the law' (2016) *Companies and Securities Law Journal* 599.

226 A number of legal judgments have emerged in the area of MISs that have reaffirmed and highlighted a range of duties towards investors in MISs, including acting in good faith, acting honestly, considering the interests of beneficiaries rather than just the interests of shareholders and avoiding conflict of interest: see Langford (n 225).

227 For example, a search on ASIC's website revealed 66 matches for the term 'managed investment schemes' within just the category of Regulatory Guides published by ASIC: sitesearch.asic.gov. au/s/search.html?f.By+document+type%7Ce=regulatory+guide&query=managed+investment +schemes&profile=asic&collection=asic. Further, ASIC appoints independent studies of the managed investments industry: see ASIC, 'Competition in the funds management sector', www.asic.gov.au/ regulatory-resources/managed-funds/competition-in-the-funds-management-sector/. See generally Christine Brown, Colm Trusler and Kevin Davis, 'Managed investment scheme regulation: lessons from the Great Southern failure' (2010)(2) *JASSA* 23–28. See also Michael Duffy, 'Barely managing? Troubles with agricultural managed investment schemes' (2012) 27(1) *Australian Journal of Corporate Law* 91.

228 Refer to the licensing and registration requirements discussed above.

229 Hanrahan (n 217) 311.

230 See generally ASIC, *Hedge Funds: Improving Disclosure* (n 221).

by hedge funds to the Australian economy.[231] Further, specific provisions of the *Corporations Act* allow ASIC to monitor compliance by the operator with MIS legal and regulatory requirements.[232]

While, generally, the Australian MIS framework imposes adequate requirements on the MIS and its operators,[233] against the backdrop of several failures within the managed funds industry some features of the extant framework for managed funds and their operators have been criticised and called out for reform.[234] For instance, the MIS framework has attracted severe criticism for 'the (lack of) an independent entity such as a trustee or depository or fund-specific board to oversee the operator's conduct of the fund'.[235] Hanrahan and Ramsay assert that the lack of an 'Independent Entity'—also recommended by IOSCO—has severely affected the ongoing monitoring' of the RE's management of the fund.[236]

Such issues have raised corresponding challenges for effective implementation of the MIS framework and led to criticism of ASIC's compliance regime.[237] ASIC ensures compliance with the MIS framework and addresses instances of non-compliance or violations with the legal and regulatory requirements through its 'enforcement pyramid'.[238] The commission uses a range of administrative powers or suspends licences of MIS operators or approaches the courts for appointment of a temporary responsible entity. In cases of serious contraventions or financial loss, ASIC is able to refer the offence to the Commonwealth Director of Public Prosecutions, initiate civil penalty proceedings in public interest or cancel licences altogether.

Notwithstanding this, as Hanrahan aptly summarises, questions remain about the effectiveness of the implementation of such a framework by ASIC. Reducing the 'expectation gap' between ASIC's role in administering the MIS landscape and the powers it holds in relation to MISs remains a continuing challenge for ASIC.[239] Millhouse points out that, even though

---

231 See generally ASIC, *The Australian Hedge Funds Sector and Systemic Risk* (Regulatory Guide 370, 2013).
232 *Corporations Act* ss 601FF and 912C.
233 The responsibilities imposed by the *Corporations Act* are 'onerous by global standards': see Hanrahan and Ramsay (n 202).
234 See generally Stewart Maiden, *Insolvent Investments* (LexisNexis Butterworths, 2015). See also Langford (n 225).
235 Hanrahan and Ramsay (n 202).
236 Ibid.
237 See for example ASIC's criticism in Senate Economic References Committee (n 223) 275.
238 Hanrahan (n 217) 311. The enforcement pyramid is discussed at length in Chapter 5 of this book.
239 Ibid 312.

the managed investments framework has facilitated exponential growth in the managed funds sector, deficiencies in implementation have caused large investor losses.[240] Other limitations of, and gaps in, ASIC's MIS supervisory regime, such as the 'reactive and desk-based activities' that are conducted instead of 'on-site inspections', were pointed out in the detailed FSAP Assessment of 2012.[241] In light of these, the FSAP Assessment rated ASIC's CIS regime as 'partly implemented' for Principle 24, 'broadly implemented' for Principles 25 and 26, and 'fully implemented' for Principle 27. ASIC's regime for hedge funds and their oversight was rated as 'broadly implemented'.

Conclusion

The current framework for MISs including hedge funds is both extensive and observant of the functioning of MISs and their operators. In light of the above, the degree of alignment for Principle 24 is assessed as 'moderate', especially given the scope for further improvement in the supervisory and governance regime pertaining to CISs. The overall landscape is assessed as 'mature'. This is because the CIS regime is sufficiently mature and reliable, requiring only refinements rather than structural reforms to overcome the existing issues and challenges. The extent of change is assessed as 'substantial' in this area in the past decade.

For Principles 25, 26 and 27, the degree of alignment is assessed as 'high' and the overall landscape is assessed as sufficiently 'mature', with 'minor' changes having been introduced in the past decade. Finally, for Principle 28 on hedge funds, the degree of alignment is assessed as 'high' for a 'mature' regime. Even though several changes to enhance disclosure have been introduced in the past decade, they are assessed as 'minor'.

Synthesis and conclusion

The analysis in this chapter shows that disclosure and corporate governance norms are areas of high focus and priority both in India and Australia. Corporate governance norms in India have been recently codified and are now prescribed through regulations while corporate governance in

---

240 David G Millhouse, 'Empirical analysis supports the Hayne long run reform book' (2019) 13(2–3) *Law and Financial Markets Review* 179. Millhouse argues that disclosure has been insufficient and that financial advice has been conflicted and lacking in discipline.

241 See IMF, *Australia Country Report* (n 69) 26.

Australia is mainly non-prescriptive, with the exception of takeover norms that are prescribed. While Australia's regime for shareholders and corporate governance has traditionally been an area of strength, SEBI's regime for shareholder rights and corporate governance reforms have also garnered global attention and recognition in recent years. Despite a strong framework and norms, the implementation of disclosure norms and shareholder rights remains challenging in India. The degree of comparability between SEBI's and ASIC's regimes for Principle 16 and 17 is thus assessed as 'moderate'. However, the relevance for cooperation is 'high', as this is a key focus area for both jurisdictions, with several common themes of interest. Australia's strength of corporate governance norms is well recognised, and India's landscape is fast evolving against a substantial legal and regulatory focus.

Accounting standards in India are not fully aligned with the internationally recognised IFRS for accounting, while Australian accounting standards are fully aligned with the IFSR. The framework for accounting standards has been reset in India in recent years and is mainly overseen and governed by authorities other than SEBI. Australia's standards, framework and oversight mechanisms for accounting are lucid, comprehensive and of high quality. SEBI lacks powers of oversight and the ability to initiate enforcement action for violations relating to accounting, while ASIC has strong powers in regard to financial and accounting surveillance, reporting and enforcement in this area. The degree of comparability for Principle 18 is thus assessed as 'moderate/low'. However, the relevance for cooperation is 'high'. Australia's experience especially in regard to the accounting governance framework can be both useful and relevant for India.

The norms for CISs, including MFs, in India and Australia are granular and comprehensive, covering all necessary requirements, including registration, eligibility criteria, disclosure obligations, legal form, separation and protection of client assets and norms for asset valuation, price and redemption. However, the Indian landscape has, in the past, suffered from several Ponzi schemes and unregulated CISs that, to a large extent, have been caused by gaps and inconsistencies within the larger financial regulatory framework (as also discussed in Chapters 2 and 5 of this book) rather than any deficiencies in SEBI's CIS and MF framework and its implementation. The Australian landscape for CISs has witnessed some implementation issues in regard to responsible entities for CISs and limitations in ASIC's compliance regime. Overall, given the strong regimes for CISs both in India and Australia, the degree of comparability for Principles 25–27 is assessed as 'high', and 'moderate' in respect of Principle 24 given the diversity of existing issues. The relevance for cooperation is also 'high', as collaboration in this area is likely to interest and benefit both jurisdictions, and future integration measures can also be explored.

Finally, the hedge funds regimes in India and Australia are subject to adequate oversight by authorities and are comprehensive in terms of the framework and requirements. The degree of comparability for Principle 28 is thus assessed as 'high' and the relevance for cooperation is also 'high' given that the regulation of hedge funds will be increasingly relevant in future. Cooperation in this area can be undertaken with a view to harmonising and strengthening hedge fund norms.

8

Secondary markets, market intermediaries and settlement systems: IOSCO Principles 8 and 29–38

Introduction

This chapter continues the analysis of the key features of the securities regimes of the Securities and Exchange Board of India (SEBI) and the Australian Securities and Investment Commission (ASIC), this time as they relate to IOSCO Principles 8 and 29–38. Broadly, these principles encompass the effective functioning of secondary markets, market intermediaries, conflicts of interest, and clearing and settlement systems. Capital markets are described in two main market categories: primary or initial issue markets and secondary markets that allow for trading in securities, price discovery for securities after their initial issue in the primary markets[1] and a number of other functions that chiefly aim at promoting transparency in the markets.[2] Market intermediaries play a critical role in advancing trades in the markets, promoting fair and orderly markets and maintaining investor

---

1   Robert Baxt, Ashley Black and Pamela Hanrahan, 'Market infrastructure providers' in *Securities and Financial Services Law* (LexisNexis Butterworths, 9th ed, 2017) ch 10, 382.

2   Secondary markets also perform the function of minimising the price impact of transactions and reducing transaction costs, and are associated with the clearing and settlement of trades and dissemination of information on trades to further transparency in the markets: see ibid.

confidence in the financial markets.[3] Trades in securities within secondary markets are effected through clearing and settlement facilities that enable a smooth and transparent transfer of such securities from the buyer to a seller.[4] Finally, effective management and mitigation of conflicts of interest are considered to be vitally important across all areas of the financial markets and intermediaries.

Collectively, the IOSCO Principles discussed in this chapter, relating to conflicts of interest, secondary markets, intermediaries and clearing and settlement facilities, underscore the importance of oversight and regulation of financial entities through licensing and other regulatory standards to promote fairness, integrity and transparency, deter market manipulation, minimise risk (particularly systemic risk) and losses to investors, and address market failure.

An evaluation of the Indian and Australian securities regimes: IOSCO Principles of Securities Regulation (Principles 8 and 29–38)

This chapter evaluates both SEBI's and ASIC's regimes for the core requirements of IOSCO Principles 8 and 29–38. The comparative analysis for each IOSCO Principle is presented along the lines set out in Chapter 3, with each regime's key features and implementation analysed against key requirements of the IOSCO Principle(s). Based on the analysis, each regime is assessed in terms of the degree of alignment, stage of development and extent of change. The final section synthesises and concludes on the degree of comparability and relevance for cooperation relating to the discussed IOSCO Principles.

---

3   Robert Baxt, Ashley Black and Pamela Hanrahan, 'Australian financial services licensing' in *Securities and Financial Services Law* (LexisNexis Butterworths, 9th ed, 2017) ch 13, 512.
4   Baxt, Black and Hanrahan, 'Market infrastructure providers' (n 1).

Table 8.1 Snapshot of the analysis in this chapter relating to secondary markets, market intermediaries and settlement systems (IOSCO Principles 8 and 29–38)

IOSCO Principles of Securities Regulation	SEBI's degree of alignment, stage of development and extent of reform in recent years	ASIC's degree of alignment, stage of development and extent of reform in recent years	Degree of comparability	Relevance for cooperation
Principles for secondary markets and other markets				
Principle 33: The establishment of trading systems including securities exchanges should be subject to regulatory oversight	**High** Mature Substantial	**High** Mature Minor	**High**	**Moderate**
SEBI's FSAP 2013* rating: 'fully implemented' (P33 corresponds to P25 under the pre-GFC IOSCO document**) ASIC's FSAP 2012*** ratings: 'fully implemented'				
Principle 34: There should be ongoing regulatory supervision of exchanges and of trading systems that ensure integrity of trading through fair and equitable rules	**Moderate** Evolving Substantial	**High** Mature Minor	**Moderate**	**High**
SEBI's FSAP 2013 rating: 'fully implemented' (P34 corresponds to P26 under the pre-GFC IOSCO document) ASIC's FSAP 2012 ratings: 'fully implemented'				
Principle 35: Regulation should promote transparency of trading	**High** Evolving Substantial	**High** Mature Minor	**Moderate**	**High**
SEBI's FSAP 2013 rating: 'fully implemented' (P35 corresponds to P27 under the pre-GFC IOSCO document) ASIC's FSAP 2012 ratings: 'fully implemented'				
Principle 36: Regulation should detect and deter manipulation and other unfair trading practices	**Moderate** Evolving Substantial	**High** Mature Minor	**Moderate**	**High**
SEBI's FSAP 2013 rating: 'fully implemented' (P36 corresponds to P28 under the pre-GFC IOSCO document) ASIC's FSAP 2012 ratings: 'fully implemented'				

IOSCO Principles of Securities Regulation	SEBI's degree of alignment, stage of development and extent of reform in recent years	ASIC's degree of alignment, stage of development and extent of reform in recent years	Degree of comparability	Relevance for cooperation
Principle 37: Regulation should aim to ensure the proper management of large exposures, default risk and market disruption	**High** Mature Substantial	**High** Mature Substantial	**High**	**High**
SEBI's FSAP 2013 rating: 'fully implemented' (P37 corresponds to P29 under the pre-GFC IOSCO document) ASIC's FSAP 2012 ratings: 'fully implemented'				
Principles for markets intermediaries				
Principle 29: Regulation should provide for minimum entry standards for market intermediaries	**Moderate** Evolving Substantial	**Moderate** Mature Minor	**Moderate**	**High**
SEBI's FSAP 2013 rating: 'partly implemented' (P29 corresponds to P21 under the pre-GFC IOSCO document) ASIC's FSAP 2012 ratings: 'broadly implemented'				
Principle 30: There should be initial and ongoing capital and other prudential requirements for market intermediaries reflecting the risks that such intermediaries take	**Moderate** Evolving Substantial	**Moderate** Mature Substantial	**Moderate**	**High**
SEBI's FSAP 2013 rating: 'partly implemented' (P30 corresponds to P22 under the pre-GFC IOSCO document) ASIC's FSAP 2012 ratings: 'partly implemented'				
Principle 31: Market intermediaries should be required to establish an internal function to deliver compliance with internal organisation and operational conduct, to protect the interests of clients and their assets and ensuring proper management of risk	**Moderate** Evolving Substantial	**Moderate** Evolving Substantial	**Moderate**	**High**
SEBI's FSAP 2013 rating: 'broadly implemented' (P31 corresponds to P23 under the pre-GFC IOSCO document) ASIC's FSAP 2012 ratings: 'broadly implemented'				

IOSCO Principles of Securities Regulation	SEBI's degree of alignment, stage of development and extent of reform in recent years	ASIC's degree of alignment, stage of development and extent of reform in recent years	Degree of comparability	Relevance for cooperation
Principle 32: There should be procedures for dealing with the failure of a market intermediary to minimise damage and loss to investors and contain systemic risk	**Moderate** Mature Substantial	**High** Mature Minor	**High**	**High**
SEBI's FSAP 2013 rating: 'broadly implemented' (P32 corresponds to P24 under the pre-GFC IOSCO document) ASIC's FSAP 2012 ratings: 'fully implemented'				
Principle 8: Regulator should seek to ensure that conflicts of interest and misalignment of incentives are avoided	**Moderate** Evolving Substantial	**High** Mature Minor	**High**	**High**
SEBI's FSAP 2013 rating: not rated (P8 was added post-GFC to the IOSCO document) ASIC's FSAP 2012 ratings: 'fully implemented'				
Principles relating to clearing and settlement				
Principle 38: Securities settlement systems, central securities depositories, trade repositories and central counterparties should be subject to regulatory and supervisory requirements that ensure fairness, effectiveness and efficiency and reduce systemic risk	**High** Evolving Substantial	**High** Mature Minor	**Moderate**	**High**
SEBI's FSAP 2013 rating: not assessed (P38 corresponds to P30 under the pre-GFC IOSCO document) ASIC's FSAP 2012 ratings: not assessed				

Note: *FSAP 2013 refers to IMF, *India: Financial Sector Assessment Program — Detailed Assessments Report on IOSCO Objectives and Principles of Securities Regulation* (Country Report No 13/266, 2013). **pre-GFC IOSCO document refers to IOSCO, *Objectives and Principles of Securities Regulation* (May 2003); ***FSAP 2012 refers to IMF, *Australia: IOSCO Objectives and Principles of Securities Regulation — Detailed Assessment of Implementation* (Country Report No 12/314, 2012).

Principles for secondary markets and other markets

Principle 33: The establishment of trading systems including securities exchanges should be subject to regulatory authorisation and oversight.

Principle 34: There should be ongoing regulatory supervision of exchanges and trading systems which should aim to ensure that the integrity of trading is maintained through fair and equitable rules that strike an appropriate balance between the demands of different market participants.

Principle 35: Regulation should promote transparency of trading.

Principle 36: Regulation should be designed to detect and deter manipulation and other unfair trading practices.

Principle 37: Regulation should aim to ensure the proper management of large exposures, default risk and market disruption.

Principles 33, 34, 35, 36 and 37

IOSCO Principles 33–37 promote the objectives of fair, efficient and transparent markets.[5] Secondary markets refer to that component of securities markets in which the securities issued in primary markets are traded or bought and sold by investors.[6] Since secondary markets are responsible for providing liquidity and assist in producing information, many believe that their regulation can improve the functioning of markets by disseminating key information among investors.[7] The IOSCO Principles stress maintaining market integrity through fairness; this is regarded by many academics as a 'key justification for having securities regulators and securities regulation'.[8] IOSCO Principles 33–37 deal with different facets of secondary markets regulation, some of the prominent features of which are discussed below in relation to SEBI's and ASIC's regimes.

---

5   IOSCO, *Methodology for Assessing Implementation of the IOSCO Objectives and Principles of Securities Regulation* (2017) 221. The term 'markets' is used more broadly by IOSCO. In addition to traditional organised exchanges, the term 'secondary and other markets' as used by IOSCO for these principles also refers to other markets, including alternative trading systems, multilateral trading facilities and organised trading facilities. However, for the purpose of this book, secondary markets and other markets refers only to traditional organised exchanges.

6   See Richard Sylla, *The Rise of Securities Markets: What Can Government Do?* (World Bank, 1999) 3.

7   Ibid 5. On the significance of markets and regulation to deter and address market abuse, see generally Emilios E Avgouleas, *The Mechanics and Regulation of Market Abuse: A Legal and Economic Analysis* (Oxford University Press, 2005), doi.org/10.1093/acprof:oso/9780199244522.001.0001.

8   Janet Austin, 'What exactly is market integrity: an analysis of one of the core objectives of securities regulation' (2016) 8(2) *William and Mary Business Law Review*, doi.org/10.2139/ssrn.2814986.

SEBI

Key features of the secondary markets regime

Stock exchanges and trading mechanisms in India are subject to extensive regulation that aligns with the core requirements of IOSCO Principle 33. The *Securities and Contracts (Regulation) Act 1956 (SCRA)* prohibits the operation of any stock exchange unless it has been recognised by SEBI.[9] Alongside the provisions of the *SCRA*, SEBI has introduced a comprehensive set of regulations for stock exchanges, the *Securities Contracts (Regulation) (Stock Exchanges and Clearing Corporations) Regulations 2018 (SCRR)*, which reiterates the obligation to seek recognition for stock exchanges.[10] Recognised stock exchanges (RSEs) are required to seek further approval from SEBI to establish new trading floors or segments.[11] While considering the application for recognition as a stock exchange, SEBI can impose conditions that are explicitly stated in s 4 of the *SCRA*.[12] Section 4A mandates demutualisation of stock exchanges, thereby separating ownership of the exchange from its management.[13] In addition to these measures, RSEs are required to seek approval from SEBI of their by-laws and regulations that establish operational details for the functioning of the stock exchange.[14]

IOSCO Principle 34 states that the regulatory framework for stock exchanges must be supported with 'ongoing regulatory supervision of exchanges and trading systems'.[15] To this end, the daily operations of, and trading in, RSEs are monitored by the RSEs themselves in the first

---

9   See *Securities and Contracts (Regulation) Act 1956 (SCRA)* s 9. The *SCRA* is an Act of the Parliament of India to prevent undesirable exchanges in securities and to provide a mechanism for the recognition and functioning of stock exchanges in India.

10   *Securities Contracts (Regulation) (Stock Exchanges and Clearing Corporations) Regulations 2018* reg 3.

11   See *SCRA* s 13A. Any exchange that wishes to start a derivate segment also requires approval from SEBI.

12   SEBI can impose a range of restrictions or conditions while granting recognition to a stock exchange that includes qualifications for membership, the manner in which contracts ought to be entered into and enforced, maintenance of accounts of members and their audit: see ibid s 4.

13   See ibid s 4A.

14   SEBI's by-laws contain clauses for the governance of stock exchanges and include provisions for the following areas: trading segments; executive committee; formulation of regulations; trading members; dealing in securities; transactions and settlements; rights and liabilities of members and constituents; arbitration; and investor protection: see *National Stock Exchange of India Limited: Bye Laws*, archives. nseindia.com/global/content/regulations/NSEbyelaws.pdf. Regulations pertain to the day-to-day operations and functioning of the exchange and deal with issues such as 'hours of trade; clearing house; number and class of contracts in which settlements will be made; terms and conditions of contracts including margin; listing of securities; settlement of claims or disputes; levy and recovery of fees, fines and penalties': see IMF, *India: Financial Sector Assessment Program—Detailed Assessments Report on IOSCO Objectives and Principles of Securities Regulation* (2013) (*India FSAP Report*) 88–90.

15   IOSCO, *Objectives and Principles of Securities Regulation* (2010).

instance, with the oversight of SEBI.[16] To ensure integrity of trading, RSEs use advanced technology to generate online alerts, in real time,[17] followed by an investigation by the RSE into any defaulting broker. As well as this first-instance supervision and monitoring by RSEs, there is in-house market surveillance conducted by SEBI through two effective systems: SMARTS,[18] and the Data Warehouse and Business Intelligence System (DWBIS) that Chapter 4 of this book discusses in relation to SEBI's surveillance powers and abilities. The DWBIS is capable of performing a number of significant and sophisticated data warehousing and data mining functions.[19]

As regards ongoing supervision of exchanges, in recent years SEBI has moved to risk-based supervision, which Chapter 5of this book discusses in detail. Further, the *SCRA* empowers SEBI to issue a range of directions, both to RSEs and clearing corporations, to ensure trading platforms are robust and maintain trading integrity, oversee compliance with the listing norms,[20] and conduct onsite inspections and supervision.[21] Likewise, the *SCRR* categorically provides SEBI with powers to call for information, undertake inspection, conduct inquiries and audit any RSE, and issue directions to an RSE.[22]

In addition to initial and ongoing supervision requirements, IOSCO Principles 35 and 36 require the regulatory system to promote 'transparency of trading' and 'detect and deter manipulation and other unfair trading practices'. To ensure transparency, Indian securities laws make several provisions for secondary markets transactions as well as for over-the-counter

---

16   IMF, *India FSAP Report* (n 14) 90–91.

17   Real-time alerts are 'based on certain present parameters like price and volume [and] variation in securities' or if trading members are seen to take 'unduly large positions not commensurate with their financial position or having large concentrated position in one or few securities': see ibid.

18   SMARTS is a globally used commercial surveillance system that receives data overnight from the stock exchange: see World Bank-IMF, 'Securities Regulation Technical Note' in *Financial Sector Assessment Program Update India* (2017) 27. Prior to SMARTS, SEBI relied on the Integrated Market Surveillance System (IMSS) to perform its surveillance across stock exchanges: see IMF, *India FSAP Report* (n 14).

19   The DWBIS has a predictive forecast capability: it performs scenario development and research and what-if analysis. See IMF, *India FSAP Report* (n 14).

20   A listing agreement was codified through SEBI regulations: see *SEBI (Listing Obligations and Disclosure Requirements) Regulations 2015*.

21   Under s 10 of the *SCRA*, SEBI has powers to make by-laws or amend them if necessary; under s 12A, it can issue directions to an exchange or clearing corporation or any company whose securities are listed; under s 11 it can supersede the governing body of an RSE; under s 5 it can withdraw recognition of an exchange.

22   See *Securities Contracts (Regulation) (Stock Exchanges and Clearing Corporations) Regulations 2018* regs 47, 48 and 49.

(OTC) trades.[23] For example, in the context of RSEs, it enables market participants to 'view best five bids' and offer securities 'on real-time basis'; and the information about executed transactions in securities can be viewed with the details of the last price.[24] In the case of bulk trades, more stringent disclosure requirements have been put in place.[25] Similarly, RSEs are allowed to make provisions for a 'separate window' that can facilitate the execution of 'block deals'.[26]

In an attempt to ensure transparency in OTC transactions, SEBI has put in place certain reporting obligations, for example in relation to corporate bonds.[27] Such obligations include the requirement that OTC trades need to be reported to the corporate bond platform of the RSE.[28] Similarly, in the equity cash segment of the exchange, SEBI has imposed requirements for reporting on all transactions that are completed on a spot basis on the same day.[29]

Along with transparency, the securities laws framework in India focuses on ensuring that markets operate without improper, fraudulent or deceptive conduct or market abuse or manipulation. The *SEBI Act* contains express provisions such as ss 11(2)(e) and 12A, which prohibit market manipulation or fraudulent or deceptive practices.[30] Additionally, SEBI has introduced detailed guidelines and regulations prohibiting market misconduct and insider trading, with stringent punishment of up to 10 years, and fines of

---

23   IMF, *India FSAP Report* (n 14) 92–93.

24   In addition, market participants can also view the last price at which transactions were executed: see ibid 92.

25   'Bulk' trade refers to a transaction in securities 'where the total quantity of shares bought/sold is more than 0.5 per cent of the number of equity shares of the company listed on the exchange': see SEBI, 'Guidelines for execution of block deals on the stock exchanges' (Circular, MRD/DoP/SE 19/05, 2 September 2005), www.sebi.gov.in/legal/circulars/sep-2005/guidelines-for-execution-of-block-deals-on-the-stock-exchanges_8382.html. Brokers are required to disclose to the RSE the name of the security; name of the client; and quantity of shares bought and sold, and the trading price. The RSE is responsible for disseminating such information on the same day after market hours to the general public: see IMF, *India FSAP Report* (n 14) 93.

26   Block deals are, essentially, large trades permitted to be executed through a single transaction with adequate measures taken to ensure efficiency and transparency. Block deals are different from bulk trades: see SEBI, 'Guidelines for execution of block deals' (n 25). For block deals, the trading window is required to be kept open for a limited period of 35 minutes from the beginning of the trading: see IMF, *India FSAP Report* (n 14).

27   Section 18 of the *SCRA* allows for OTC trades in corporate bonds.

28   SEBI, 'FAQs on secondary market', www.sebi.gov.in/sebi_data/faqfiles/jan-2017/1485843476566.pdf.

29   SEBI, 'Reporting of spot and off-the-floor transactions' (Circular, SMD/RCG/CIR/(BKG)/293/95, 14 March 1995).

30   See *Securities and Exchange Board of India Act 1992* (*SEBI Act*) ss 11 and 12Ae.

up to 25 crore rupees in case of a violation.[31] SEBI's and the RSE's effective market surveillance systems, discussed earlier under Principle 34, also aid SEBI in identifying unfair trade practices or market manipulation.[32]

Finally, IOSCO Principle 37, which garnered significant attention in the wake of the global financial crisis (GFC), requires the regulatory system to ensure proper management of large exposures, default risk and market disruption.[33] To this end, RSEs maintain 'robust' risk management systems designed to address a situation such as a market disruption or crises.[34] For maintenance of these systems by RSEs, SEBI has drafted a detailed set of model by-laws covering a gamut of provisions, such as capital adequacy requirements, margin requirements and special risk-containment measures.[35] Further, to cover large risks and curb volatility in stock markets, 'circuit breakers' have been put in place.[36] These circuit breakers are triggered when the BSE Sensex or NIFTY 50 breaches the thresholds of 10, 15 and 20 per cent of the previous quarter's index closing.[37] Another notable feature of SEBI's regime has been the shift to risk-based supervision in the past decade, further strengthening its management of large exposures.[38] Lastly, a 'crisis management contingency contact group' known as the Financial Stability and Development Council comprising the Government of India and Ministry of Finance officials, and regulators such as SEBI, the Reserve

31 See *SEBI (Prohibition of Insider Trading) Regulations 2015* (*SEBI (Prohibition of Insider Trading) Regulations*); *SEBI (Prohibition of Fraudulent and Unfair Trade Practices Relating to Securities Markets) Regulations 2003*.

32 IMF, *India FSAP Report* (n 14) 94–95.

33 See IOSCO, *Objectives and Principles of Securities Regulation* (n 15).

34 IMF, *India FSAP Report* (n 14) 95.

35 SEBI, 'Risk management' in *Model Bye-Laws*, www.sebi.gov.in/sebi_data/commondocs/ch10_p.pdf.

36 'Circuit breakers' are automatically triggered upon a 'runaway move in any security or index on either direction': see 'Definition of "circuit breakers"', *The Economic Times*, economictimes.indiatimes.com/definition/circuit-breakers. See also National Stock Exchange of India Ltd, 'Circuit breakers', www.nseindia.com/products-services/equity-market-circuit-breakers.

37 The BSE Sensex refers to 30 of the largest and most actively traded BSE stocks and, as such, provides an active gauge of the Indian economy: see Investopedia, 'What is Sensex?', investopedia.com/terms/s/sensex.asp. 'In India, the Nifty 50 is the index of 50 stocks that are diversified across 12 sectors of the nation's economy: financial services, energy, information technology, consumer goods, automobiles, metals, construction, pharmaceuticals, cement and cement products, telecommunications, fertilisers and pesticides, media and entertainment, and services': see National Stock Exchange of India Ltd, 'Nifty 50', niftyindices.com/indices/equity/broad-based-indices/NIFTY-50.

38 SEBI's Market Intermediaries Regulation and Supervision Department states that it has recently started to monitor intermediaries based on risk-based supervision: see SEBI, 'Market Intermediaries Regulation and Supervision Department', www.sebi.gov.in/department/market-intermediaries-regulation-and-supervision-department-14/overview.html.

Bank of India (RBI), the Insurance Regulatory and Development Authority and other stock exchanges has been set up to provide a quick and coordinated response in case of a financial crisis.[39]

Analysis

The rapid overhaul of secondary markets since the 1990s is, arguably, among the greatest accomplishments of the securities market in India.[40] This transformation is attributed to 'noteworthy institutional developments' and other reforms introduced by SEBI.[41] These institutional improvements and the myriad fast-paced technological reforms carried out within secondary markets,[42] in addition to the significant 'changes to the regulatory and governance framework', have directly contributed towards building investor confidence in India.[43]

Keeping this transformative journey in mind, the existing regulatory framework for secondary markets under the *SCRA*, along with SEBI's *SCRR* and the broader framework of the RSEs, scores well on counts of depth and detail, as it adequately covers all main requirements for secondary markets regulation under IOSCO Principles 33–36 relating to licensing, oversight, ongoing supervision, transparency and fairness in trading. While there is no dearth of powers available to SEBI to oversee and regulate secondary markets,[44] and despite SEBI's keen focus, continuous and effective implementation of these principles has been challenging for a large, complex market, especially in respect of maintaining integrity and transparency in trading, and deterring and detecting market manipulation.[45] SEBI's annual

---

39   For more detail on this body, Government of India, Ministry of Finance, 'Financial Stability and Development Council (FSDC)' (3 May 2013), pib.gov.in/newsite/PrintRelease.aspx?relid=95543.

40   BK Muhammed Juman and MK Irshad, 'An overview of India capital markets' (2015) 5(2) *Bonfring International Journal of Industrial Engineering and Management Science* 17. For a critical review of the pre-1990 and post-1990 Indian secondary markets, see Rajasekhara Mouly Potluri et al, 'A critical analysis on capital market developments in India: pre and post liberalization period' (2014) 12(10) *Journal of Distribution Science* 5–9, doi.org/10.15722/jds.12.10.201410.5.

41   G Sabarinathan, 'Securities and Exchange Board Of India and the regulation of the Indian securities market' (IIM Bangalore Research Paper No 309, 2010) 4, doi.org/10.2139/ssrn.2145220.

42   Some of the prominent changes included introduction of a fully automated screen-based trading system, 'dematerialisation of shares', introduction of rolling settlement and shortening of the trading cycle to T +2, among others: see Juman and Irshad (n 40) 22–23.

43   PB Rama Kumar and K Madhava Rao, 'Growth and performance of secondary markets: a review of emerging trends' (2015) 6(3) *International Journal of Research in Commerce & Management*.

44   The *SCRA* grants SEBI wide powers to approve an RSE's by-laws and suspend or revoke any licence granted to such RSE in case of unauthorised conduct.

45   See generally Harpreet Kaur, 'Securities market in India: regulation of undesirable practices by the Securities and Exchange Board of India' in Jing Bian and Kıymet Tunca Çalıyurt (eds), *Regulations and Applications of Ethics in Business Practice* (Springer, 2018) 273–293, doi.org/10.1007/978-981-10-8062-3_15.

reports indicate that it has enhanced its surveillance mechanisms, and is actively supervising and investigating market manipulation, price rigging, insider trading violations, and fraudulent, deceptive and unfair trade practices. Despite this, as the analysis in Chapter 5 shows, SEBI's overall supervision of the secondary markets and enforcement outcomes in these areas of market violations requires further strengthening.[46]

In respect of IOSCO Principle 37, the RSEs monitor exposures on a real-time basis,[47] and have well-designed measures such as 'settlement guarantee funds', 'margin requirements' and 'circuit breakers' that ensure management of large exposures, default risk and market disruption. Moreover, early warning mechanisms were introduced by SEBI in 2018 to ensure that clients' securities received as collateral were not diverted by brokers towards its margin obligations and/or settlement obligations.[48] Further, SEBI's risk-based supervisory approach allows it to examine information, such as the alerts generated from monthly/weekly submissions by stock brokers, in a more effective manner, further strengthening the regime's overall response towards large market exposures and risks.[49]

To a large extent, SEBI's regime for secondary markets supervision and regulation has been found to be comparable with international standards, as seen in SEBI's FSAP Review of 2013, which rated Principles 33–37 as 'fully implemented' for SEBI.[50]

Conclusion

The above discussion and preliminary analysis leads to the following conclusions. First, SEBI's framework for stock exchanges and secondary markets regulation is comprehensive and subject to continuous review and expansion. Second, keeping in view the analysis in Chapter 5 on supervision and enforcement, the implementation of the framework for secondary markets requires further strengthening given the size and complexity of the Indian markets. Hence, the overall degree of alignment with the core

---

46   On the recent measures taken by SEBI to curb securities malpractices as well as address insider trading, see generally SEBI, *Annual Report 2017–18* (2018). SEBI has strengthened surveillance mechanisms for detecting market manipulation and unfair trading practices, front running and insider trading. However, the enforcement outcomes in this category are relatively low when viewed against the number of intermediaries, listed companies and transactions within the Indian securities markets.

47   IMF, *India FSAP Report* (n 14) 19.

48   SEBI, *Annual Report 2018–19* (2019) 37.

49   Ibid.

50   See IMF, *India FSAP Report* (n 14) 19. Principles 33–37 correspond to the erstwhile Principles 25–29 under the earlier IOSCO Principles.

requirements of IOSCO Principles 33, 35 and 37 is assessed as 'high', while, for Principles 34 and 36, it is assessed as 'moderate', as supervision of exchanges and trading systems needs further enhancement and more deterrent enforcement outcomes are required against manipulation, insider trading and unfair trade practices.

The overall landscape is assessed as rapidly 'evolving' for Principles 34, 35 and 36 and sufficiently 'mature' for Principles 33 and 37. Finally, at a general level, this area pertaining to secondary markets has witnessed 'substantial' activity and several changes in the past decade that demonstrate SEBI's inclination to further strengthen the secondary markets regime.

ASIC
Key features of the secondary markets regime

IOSCO Principle 33, requiring authorisation and oversight of stock exchanges and trading systems, is appropriately reflected in the Australian financial markets framework. The framework requires licensing of a 'financial market' as defined under s 767A of the *Corporations Act 2001* (Cth) (*Corporations Act*).[51] The licence to operate as a domestic financial market in Australia[52] is accorded by the relevant minister and not ASIC, and currently 17 such licensed financial markets are in operation.[53] Upon the grant of a licence, the minister is empowered to disallow changes to the operating rules or suspend or cancel the licence altogether in case of a breach of the licensee's obligations.[54]

Part 7.2A of the *Corporations Act* pertains to supervision of financial markets where the primary responsibility of supervision is given to ASIC.[55] Section 798J empowers ASIC to give directions in the public interest,

---

51   A financial market is a facility through which: a) offers to acquire or dispose of financial products are regularly made or accepted; b) offers or invitations are regulatory made to acquire or dispose of financial products that are intended to result in either the making of offers to acquire or dispose of financial products or acceptance of such offers: see IMF, *Australia: IOSCO Objectives and Principles of Securities Regulation—Detailed Assessment of Implementation* (Country Report No 12/314, 2012) (*Australia Country Report*) 135.

52   The statutory regime mandates that the securities exchange can be operated only after obtaining a licence under s 791A of the *Corporations Act 2001* (Cth).

53   See ASIC, 'Licensed domestic financial markets operating in Australia', asic.gov.au/regulatory-resources/markets/market-structure/licensed-and-exempt-markets/licensed-domestic-financial-markets-operating-in-australia/.

54   IMF, *Australia Country Report* (n 51) 135.

55   Section 798F authorises ASIC to supervise financial markets. Section 798G authorises ASIC to make market integrity rules dealing with the conduct of licensed markets, all activities and persons in relation to such markets and in relation to the financial products traded on these licensed markets: see *Corporations Act* pt 7.

including a direction to suspend dealings in a financial product.[56] The details of the financial markets regime are specified by ASIC in Regulatory Guide 172.[57]

ASIC's financial market infrastructure department assesses applications for financial market licences by ensuring that the operating rules and procedures are adequate to ensure fair and transparent trading.[58]

Principle 34 requires ongoing supervision of exchanges and trading systems to ensure integrity of trading through fair and equitable rules. ASIC is in charge of 'the supervision of real-time trading on Australia's domestic licensed markets',[59] a responsibility that it assumed from the Australian Securities Exchange (ASX) on 1 August 2010 when it commenced market supervision and real-time surveillance.[60] Since 2010, ASIC has invested heavily in new technologies and systems as part of its 'monitoring and supervisory responsibilities' and a Market Analysis and Intelligence surveillance system in 2013 replaced ASIC's previous SMARTS surveillance system.[61]

Even though ASIC has the primary responsibility for surveillance, market operators such as the ASX also 'monitor trading information and unusual price and volume movements' to ensure compliance with operating rules.[62] In addition to this, ASIC, during the course of its annual assessment of an Australian market licence (AML) holder, examines the surveillance practices of an AML holder, in line with the published market integrity rules on securities markets.[63] The minister may intervene if an AML holder does not comply with directions.[64]

---

56   See ibid s 798J.
57   ASIC, *Financial Markets: Domestic and Overseas Operators* (Regulatory Guide 172, 2018) pt 1.
58   The department conducts surveillance based on a 'post-trade' and 'real-time' basis through the electronic data provided by ASX and Chi-X: see IMF, *Australia Country Report* (n 51) 137–138.
59   ASIC, 'Regulatory framework', asx.com.au/about/regulation.
60   See ASIC, *ASIC Supervision of Markets and Participants: August to December 2010* (Report 227, 2011) 4. ASIC's direct market surveillance led to a reduction in the time taken to commence investigations or actions against market misconduct.
61   Ibid. The previous 'SMARTS automated trade surveillance system had the ability to reconstruct trading activity instantaneously in listed instruments across markets, participants and clients': see IMF, *Australia Country Report* (n 51) 139.
62   IMF, *Australia Country Report* (n 51) 139.
63   *ASIC Market Integrity Rules (Securities Markets) 2017*. Before 2017, ASIC's 2011 market integrity rules on competition were enforced: see *ASIC Market Integrity Rules (Competition in Exchange Markets) 2011*.
64   IMF, *Australia Country Report* (n 51) 139.

Principle 35 requires the regulatory framework to promote transparency of trading. Chapter 6 of ASIC's market integrity rules on securities markets makes pre- and post-trade transparency a requirement for all orders in 'equity market products and CGS [government securities] depository interests'.[65] Rule 6.1.2 further requires the market operator to immediately make available pre-trade information to all persons that have an arrangement with the operator to access such information.[66] Any breach of this rule would result in a maximum penalty of $1 million.[67] Similarly, pt 6.3 of the rules applies to post-trade transparency.[68] Rule 8.3.1 of pt 8.3 further requires the operator to have transparent cancellation policies in place.[69]

Principle 36 requires regulation to detect and deter manipulation and other unfair trading practices. Part 7.10 of the *Corporations Act* prohibits market misconduct and other fraudulent and manipulative activities, such as market manipulation,[70] false trading and market rigging,[71] false or misleading statements,[72] and misleading or deceptive conduct[73] in relation to financial products. The Act imposes civil and criminal liability for all these violations except for misleading or deceptive conduct, which is punishable with only civil liability.[74]

Similarly, insider trading prohibitions are contained in div 3 of pt 7.10 of the *Corporations Act*.[75] Any violation of the insider trading provisions attracts both civil and criminal penalties.[76]

Finally, IOSCO Principle 37 lays down that regulation should aim to ensure proper management of large exposures of risk and market disruption. In this context, ASIC's endeavours are directed to manage the 'open positions and risks associated with exposure from open positions' to ensure that the

---

65 See *ASIC Market Integrity Rules (Securities Markets) 2017* r 6.1.1AA (1)(e).
66 Ibid. Rule 6.1.2(A) also requires the operator to keep records of such pre-trade information for a period of seven years.
67 See ibid r 6.1.2.
68 See ibid pt 6.2.
69 See ibid.
70 See *Corporations Act* s 1041A.
71 See ibid ss 1041B and 1041C.
72 See ibid s 1041E.
73 See ibid s 1041H.
74 Criminal penalties can be as high as A$950,000 or imprisonment for 10 years or both: see IMF, *Australia Country Report* (n 51) 145.
75 See *Corporations Act* pt 7.10 div 3.
76 Refer to the rich body of academic literature relating to insider trading that has been referenced in Chapter 5 of this book under the analysis of ASIC's enforcement and compliance regime.

market functions without any disruption.[77] To this end, the regulatory system imposes conditions on clearing and settlement facility licence (CSFL) holders,[78] specifies market integrity rules,[79] and governs markets and participants through prudential norms.[80] Similarly, as another measure to ensure that markets are safe and properly functioning without undue risk, the Australian system prohibits naked short selling and makes it an offence under s 1311(1).[81]

Analysis

Generally, the legal and regulatory framework for secondary markets comprises strong, ongoing and detail-oriented features for ensuring exchanges and trading systems operate in a fair, orderly and transparent manner.[82] As regards the effective implementation of this framework, the *Corporations Act* empowers ASIC with powers that ASIC uses to accomplish a range of functions in the secondary markets.[83] These aim at maintaining integrity of the markets, promoting transparency in trading, and detecting and deterring market manipulation and other unfair trading practices.[84] Further, after 2010, recognising the importance of market integrity, ASIC

---

77   See IMF, *Australia Country Report* (n 51) 148.

78   CSFL holders are governed under the provisions of the *Corporations Act* and certain obligations are imposed on them by the Reserve Bank of Australia under the Financial Stability Standards: see Reserve Bank of Australia, *Clearing and Settlement Facilities—Financial Stability Standards*, rba.gov.au/payments-and-infrastructure/financial-market-infrastructure/clearing-and-settlement-facilities/standards/.

79   See *ASIC Market Integrity Rules (Securities Markets) 2017*.

80   IMF, *Australia Country Report* (n 51) 148.

81   In Australia, a person may sell only such financial products that are within the description of s 1020B of the *Corporations Act*: see ASIC, *Short Selling* (Regulatory Guide 196, 2018). Section 1020B of the *Corporations Act* refers to securities, managed investment products and financial products referred to in s 764A(1)(j). 'Naked short selling' refers to a situation in which a seller does not have 'a presently exercisable and unconditional right to vest' financial products in the buyer at the time of the sale of such products: see IMF, *Australia Country Report* (n 51) 151.

82   For more on the secondary markets framework, see Baxt, Black and Hanrahan, 'Market infrastructure providers' (n 1) 381, 386. In addition to the *Corporations Act* framework, ASIC took measures to minimise market volatility and misconduct through the introduction of extreme price movement rules for the two main stock exchanges—the ASX and the Chi-X—in 2012. It introduced rules for reporting suspicious trading activity in January 2013, increased data reporting obligations in 2013 and enhanced rules for the automated order processing systems in 2014.

83   For a detailed overview of ASIC's functions, see Robert Baxt, Ashley Black and Pamela Hanrahan, 'Overview of regulation of the securities markets and the regulation participants' in *Securities and Financial Services Law* (LexisNexis Butterworths, 9th ed, 2017) ch 11, 417.

84   Chapters 4 and 5 of this book discuss the availability of powers and their use by ASIC to maintain integrity and fairness in markets.

assumed key responsibilities for supervision of trading from the ASX,[85] and continues to intensify supervision of the markets, such as it did in 2018 with the introduction of a 'risk-based, two-tiered market licensing regime'.[86]

Despite a strong legislative and regulatory framework, and supervision of markets, limitations in ASIC's successful enforcement of insider trading and market manipulation matters have been highlighted as an area of concern.[87] To some extent, ASIC's record of low enforcement in the areas of market manipulation and insider trading was attributed to a lack of powers and inadequacy of monetary penalties in non-criminal cases.[88] The recent legislative upgrades have addressed many of these issues relating to ASIC's powers and penalty regime.[89]

Finally, in respect of IOSCO Principle 37, the description of key features of the regime reveals that ASIC has been continuously improving its system pertaining to large exposures, default risk and market disruption by strengthening norms applicable to CSFL holders, as well as through a tightening of the market integrity rules.

ASIC's regime for secondary markets supervision and regulation has been recognised as being on par with international standards, as held in the detailed FSAP Assessment of 2012, which graded Principles 33, 34, 35 and 36 as 'fully implemented' for ASIC. In relation to Principle 37, a 'partly implemented' rating was given; however, ASIC has undertaken significant reform since then.

---

85   Baxt, Black and Hanrahan, 'Market infrastructure providers' (n 1). See also Chapter 7, this book.
86   ASIC, 'Licensed domestic financial markets operating in Australia' (n 53). An operator of a tier 1 market is subject to all regulatory obligations while tier 2 market operators are required to fulfil a customised and smaller set of obligations.
87   See generally Lev Bromberg, George Gilligan and Ian Ramsay, 'Insider trading and market manipulation: the SEC's enforcement outcomes' (2017) 45(2) *Securities Regulation Law Journal* 109–125; Ian Ramsay and Miranda Webster, 'ASIC enforcement outcomes: trends and analysis' (2017) 35(5) *Company and Securities Law Journal* 289–321. For discussion of why there have been no successful criminal prosecutions against corporations, see Juliette Overland, *Corporate Liability for Insider Trading* (Routledge, 2019), doi.org/10.4324/9781315098210.
88   See 'Monetary penalties and disgorgement' in ASIC, *'Lifting the Fear and Suppressing the Greed': Penalties for White-collar Crime and Corporate and Financial Misconduct in Australia* (2017) 73, aph.gov. au/Parliamentary_Business/Committees/Senate/Economics/WhiteCollarCrime45th/Report/footnotes #c06f42. ASIC highlighted that, for individuals, a maximum penalty of $200,000, and for body corporates, up to $1 million, are both inadequate and much lower than various other jurisdictions such as the UK, Canada and the US.
89   See *The Treasury Laws Amendment (Strengthening Corporate and Financial Sector Penalties) Act 2019.* For a deeper discussion, see Chapter 4 of this book.

Conclusion

In the light of the above, the degree of alignment of ASIC's regime with the requirements of IOSCO Principles 33, 34, 35, 36 and 37 is assessed as 'high' despite criticism of ASIC's enforcement of insider trading and market manipulation cases. The overall landscape for Principles 33–37 is measured as sufficiently 'mature', with 'minor' changes undertaken in most areas and 'substantial' steps taken in respect of Principle 37 in recent years.

Principles for market intermediaries

Principle 29: Regulation should provide for minimum entry standards for market intermediaries.

Principle 30: There should be initial and ongoing capital and other prudential requirements for market intermediaries that reflect the risks that intermediaries undertake.

Principle 31: Market intermediaries should be required to establish an internal function that delivers compliance with standards for internal organisation and operational conduct, with the aim of protecting the interests of clients and their assets and ensuring proper management of risk, through which management of the intermediary accepts primary responsibility for these matters.

Principle 32: There should be procedures for dealing with the failure of a market intermediary in order to minimise damage and loss to investors and to contain systemic risk.

Principles 29, 30, 31 and 32

Market intermediaries[90] play a vital role in securities markets and thus are subject to various forms of oversight and regulation.[91] Pearson asserts that licensing of intermediaries not only ensures that minimum standards are imposed on a provider of financial service but also safeguards the interests

---

90 The term 'market intermediaries' generally refers to persons who manage 'individual portfolios', execute orders and deal in or distribute securities, and includes entities that engage in 'receiving and transmitting orders'; 'propriety trading/dealing on own account'; 'providing advice' on the 'investing in, purchasing, or selling of securities' or the 'value of securities'; and 'securities underwriting': see IOSCO, *Methodology for Assessing* (n 5).

91 See generally Stephen J Choi, 'A framework for the regulation of securities market intermediaries' (2004) 1 *Berkeley Business Law Journal* 45.

of investors in the market.[92] Similarly, a specified code of conduct for intermediaries ensures 'a consonance between regulatory objectives and the industry bodies'.[93]

IOSCO Principles 29–32 require proper oversight, supervision and regulation of market intermediaries through a framework that provides for suitable 'entry criteria, capital and prudential requirements, conduct of business, ongoing supervision, and discipline of market intermediaries, and the consequences of default and financial failure'.[94] Given the significant role played by these intermediaries, IOSCO has formed a separate and dedicated committee, Committee 3 on Regulation of Market Intermediaries, to strengthen oversight and supervision of market intermediaries and promote investor protection and market efficiency through its recommendations on issues related to market intermediaries.[95]

In relation to market intermediaries, Principles 29–32 are deeply interconnected and, therefore, these principles are discussed collectively in this book and 'assessed in conjunction with each other',[96] as opposed to being elaborated on separately. The following sections discuss key features of the Indian and Australian regimes for securities markets intermediaries in relation to Principles 29–32.

SEBI
Key features of the intermediaries regulatory framework

As required by IOSCO Principle 29, SEBI's regime provides for licensing of securities markets intermediaries and lays down entry standards for them. Section 12 of the *SEBI Act* makes it mandatory for a market intermediary associated with the securities market to buy, sell or deal in securities to obtain a certificate of registration from the SEBI Board.[97] SEBI's registered intermediaries are broadly categorised as follows:

---

92   Gail Pearson, 'Licensing financial services providers' in *Financial Services Law and Compliance in Australia* (Cambridge University Press, 2009) 104, doi.org/10.1017/CBO9781139113816.005. See also Cindy Davies, Samuel Walpole and Gail Pearson, 'Australia's licensing regimes for financial services, credit and superannuation: three tracks toward the twin peaks' (2021) 38(5) *Company and Securities Law Journal* 332–354, doi.org/10.2139/ssrn.3895447.
93   Gail Pearson, 'The place of codes of conduct in regulating financial services' (2006) 15(2) *Griffith Law Review* 333, doi.org/10.1080/10383441.2006.10854577.
94   IOSCO, *Methodology for Assessing* (n 5).
95   See IOSCO, 'Committee on Regulation of Market Intermediaries (Committee 3)', iosco.org/about/?subsection=display_committee&cmtid=14.
96   IOSCO, *Methodology for Assessing* (n 5).
97   See *SEBI Act* s 12.

1. stock brokers and sub-brokers

2. merchant bankers

3. portfolio managers

4. underwriters

5. investment advisers.[98]

Complementing the provisions of the *SEBI Act*, SEBI has issued the *SEBI (Intermediaries) Regulations 2008* (*SEBI Intermediaries Regulations*), which provide a general framework for the registration of intermediaries and set forth their obligations.[99] Importantly, the *SEBI Intermediaries Regulations* provide for a fit and proper framework for each registered intermediary, including requirements around 'integrity, reputation and character', competence and financial solvency.[100] When an intermediary applies for registration, it is required to include prescribed information to allow SEBI to properly assess the application for registration.[101] SEBI also holds powers to accept, impose conditions or reject applications subject to the observance of natural justice principles.[102]

In addition to the *SEBI Act* and the *SEBI Intermediaries Regulations*, SEBI has created separate regulations for each intermediary, such as the *SEBI (Stock Brokers and Sub-broker) Regulations 1992*,[103] *SEBI (Merchant Bankers) Regulations 1992*,[104] *SEBI (Underwriters) Regulations 1993*,[105] *SEBI (Portfolio Managers) Regulations 1992*[106] and *SEBI (Investment Advisers) Regulations 2013*.[107] These regulations contain detailed and separate provisions for each

---

98   In terms of reg 8 (2) of the *SEBI (Intermediaries) Regulations 2008*, a person who needs to register with SEBI in more than one category is required to obtain separate certificates of registration from SEBI.
99   See also *SEBI (Intermediaries) Regulations 2008*.
100 For the complete 'fit and proper' framework, see ibid sch II.
101 See IMF, *India FSAP Report* (n 14) 76–80. Such information may include complete details of the applicant, its affiliates and key management personnel; details of any arbitration or litigation matters pending; information about persons in control; management details of directors, partners, trustees and promoters and financial information such as audited financial statements of past years and net worth details.
102 See reg 8 of the *SEBI (Intermediaries) Regulations 2008* on when SEBI may reject the application. Further, under reg 9, SEBI can impose conditions for registration. Section 11(3) of the *SEBI Act 1992* also empowers SEBI to suspend or cancel registration of any intermediary where there has been a contravention of the securities laws.
103 *SEBI (Stock Brokers and Sub-brokers) Regulations 1992* (*SEBI (Stock Brokers and Sub-brokers) Regulations*).
104 *SEBI (Merchant Bankers) Regulations 1992* (*SEBI (Merchant Bankers) Regulations*).
105 *SEBI (Underwriters) Regulations 1993* (*SEBI (Underwriters) Regulations*).
106 *SEBI (Portfolio Managers) Regulations 1993* (*SEBI (Portfolio Managers) Regulations*).
107 *SEBI (Investment Advisers) Regulations 2013* (*SEBI (Investment Advisers) Regulations*).

type of SEBI-registered intermediary. The provisions for brokers and sub-brokers include registration requirements with the RSEs that are responsible for overseeing their operations.[108] Brokers are subject to continuous supervision and monitoring by 'off-site reporting' to, and 'on-site inspections' by, the RSEs.[109] For intermediaries other than brokers, such as portfolio managers, merchant bankers, investment advisers and underwriters, the governing regulations cover areas of registration, offsite reporting and onsite inspections, record-keeping requirements and eligibility criteria for individuals, including the requirement of certification programs.[110]

With respect to the initial and ongoing capital and other prudential requirements for market intermediaries under IOSCO Principle 30, SEBI's regulations for each type of intermediary specify the minimum capital (net worth) that is to be maintained.[111] SEBI directly oversees compliance with the capital adequacy requirements by all intermediaries except brokers, which come under the supervision of the RSEs.[112]

In relation to IOSCO Principle 31, which requires all intermediaries to comply with standards for internal organisation and operational conduct that protects the interests of clients and minimises risk, the *SEBI Intermediaries Regulations* make it mandatory for intermediaries to abide by an extensive code of conduct.[113] This code requires the establishment of good corporate policies, corporate governance practices and internal control procedures to protect clients and investors from facing theft, fraud or dishonest acts.[114] The code of conduct also requires intermediaries to segregate each client's funds and securities separately from their own[115] and contains clauses on

---

108 In addition to the SEBI Acts and regulations, brokers are governed by the by-laws of the recognised stock exchange that they are registered with: see IMF, *India FSAP Report* (n 14).

109 As an example of off-site reporting by brokers to the RSEs, brokers submit annual audited financial statements, semi-annual unaudited financial statements and an audit report that explains their compliance with the *SEBI Act* and the effectiveness of their systems for redressing investors' grievances: see ibid. Since 2009, RSEs have been directed by SEBI to conduct on-site inspections of active brokers, which complements SEBI's own on-site supervision of such brokers: see ibid.

110 See ibid 79. All intermediaries are required to maintain records for a period of 10 years. The certification examinations and programs are conducted by the National Institute of Securities Markets (NISM): see NISM, 'Welcome to NISM', nism.ac.in/about-nism/.

111 For example, reg 7 of the *SEBI (Underwriters) Regulations* specifies the net worth for underwriters. Similarly, reg 7 specifies the net worth for merchant bankers: see *SEBI (Merchant Bankers) Regulations*. For portfolio managers also, the net worth is provided by reg 7: see *SEBI (Portfolio Managers) Regulations*.

112 IMF, *India FSAP Report* (n 14).

113 On the Code of Conduct see *SEBI (Intermediaries) Regulations 2008* reg 16.

114 In addition, intermediaries are required to provide suitable infrastructure and operating procedures and systems that are backed by operation manuals: see IMF, *India FSAP Report* (n 14).

115 For examples, in the case of portfolio managers, see reg 15 of the *SEBI (Portfolio Managers) Regulations*.

avoidance and management of any conflicts of interest. Intermediaries are also required to appoint compliance officers for ensuring compliance of all legal and regulatory requirements.[116] Additionally, SEBI's insider trading norms, the *SEBI (Insider Trading) Regulations 2015*, necessitate all intermediaries to lay down procedures that ensure confidentiality of information, segregation of funds and a Chinese wall system to prevent any misuse of price-sensitive information.[117] Finally, SEBI's regulations together with the by-laws framed by the RSEs have elaborate provisions on the process and mechanisms for 'redress of investor grievances', including arbitration and mediation mechanisms that have served as an efficient means of investor response in the Indian securities markets.[118]

IOSCO Principle 32 on market intermediaries requires regulators to provide sufficient procedures to address the failure of a market intermediary, minimise loss and damage and contain systemic risk. As a first step, securities market intermediaries are required to observe strict segregation of clients' money from that of brokers' or portfolio managers' accounts, and, in case of any default, SEBI, along with the RBI, RSEs and the clearing banks, coordinates efforts towards crisis management.[119] SEBI's regulatory regime for brokers prepares for dealing with all kinds of broker defaults.[120] In addition, SEBI has early warning mechanisms in place, and the RSEs, too, have established systems of alerts to manage the exposures taken by brokers.[121]

Analysis

Securities market intermediaries play an essential role in India as they provide greater depth to the markets by 'matching preferences of risk, liquidity and maturity characteristics of both suppliers and buyers of securities'.[122] Agarwal reveals the strong correlation between the value

---

116 Regulation 18A of the *SEBI (Stock Brokers and Sub-brokers) Regulations*. See also reg 23A of the *SEBI (Portfolio Managers) Regulations*, s 28A of the *SEBI (Merchant Bankers) Regulations* and s 17A of the *SEBI (Underwriters) Regulations*.

117 *SEBI (Prohibition of Insider Trading) Regulations*.

118 IMF, *India FSAP Report* (n 14) 87.

119 In the case of financial conglomerates, the RBI and SEBI have established committees to address areas of common concerns: see ibid.

120 See generally *SEBI (Stock Brokers and Sub-brokers) Regulations*.

121 IMF, *India FSAP Report* (n 14) 88.

122 Manjari Agarwal, 'Contribution of market intermediaries to the growth of securities market in India: assessing the relationship and impact' (2017) 23(4) *IUP Journal of Applied Finance* 18.

added by market intermediaries in India and share prices.[123] The regulatory framework applying to intermediaries[124] reflects the importance of securities markets intermediaries through a detailed and comprehensive set of norms: 'eligibility conditions, registration requirements, continuous compliance requirements, code of conduct, renewal of registrations, investigations, inquiry, maintenance of records, inspection, disciplinary proceedings, adjudication, appeal powers, enforcement orders'.[125] Further, SEBI is empowered with adequate powers to inspect, investigate, and pass orders and directions against intermediaries.[126] Thus, SEBI's market intermediaries framework fulfils, to a large degree, the core requirements laid down by IOSCO Principles 29–32.

Notwithstanding this achievement, the overall implementation of the regulatory framework for intermediaries is still a work in progress, for several reasons. First, the effectiveness and robustness of the supervisory and enforcement mechanisms for intermediaries continues to be an ongoing challenge for SEBI, considering the number of market intermediaries on the one hand[127] and the low number of human resources on the other.[128] Second, the *SEBI (Intermediaries) Regulations* have been criticised for containing a 'lengthy' investigation and inquiry process that involves duplication of inquiry proceedings for intermediaries in case of alleged violations.[129] To a certain extent, the FSAP Review of 2013 reflected the limitations in implementation of the intermediaries framework, as SEBI garnered only a 'partly implemented' rating for compliance with the requirements of IOSCO Principles 29 and 30 (erstwhile Principles 21 and 22), and a 'broadly implemented' grade for compliance with the requirements of IOSCO Principles 31 and 32 (erstwhile Principles 31 and 32).[130]

---

123 There exists a long-term relationship between the value added by market intermediaries, referred to as market capitalisation per market intermediary, and the price of shares: see ibid.

124 SEBI's market intermediaries' regulatory framework includes a review of the *SEBI Act*, the *SEBI (Intermediaries) Regulations 2008* as well as the respective regulations for intermediaries, such as stock brokers, share transfer agents and portfolio managers.

125 Ekta M Chotaliya and Pankaj Trivedi, 'Financial intermediaries in securities market: an Indian perspective' (2014) 29 *International Journal of Advance Research in Computer Science and Management Studies* 2(10) 24.

126 For an exposition of these powers, see Dharmishta Raval, *Improving the Legal Process in Enforcement at SEBI* (Indira Gandhi Institute of Development Research Working Paper No 2011-008, 2011).

127 See Table 5.3 in Chapter 5 of this book, which indicates that 31,399 intermediaries were licensed by SEBI at the end of FY 2018–19.

128 Refer to the discussion on SEBI's limitations around human resources in Chapter 3 of this book.

129 Pallavi Mishra, 'A need to revisit the SEBI (Intermediaries) Regulations, 2008', *IndiaCorpLaw* (Blog Post, 7 January 2021), indiacorplaw.in/2021/01/a-need-to-revisit-the-sebi-intermediaries-regulations-2008.html.

130 IMF, *India FSAP Report* (n 14).

Despite the challenges posed by a large, complex market, SEBI's efforts in the administration of securities intermediaries, relative to its human resource capacity, have been commendable, and several fast-paced reforms and upgrades to the regulatory requirements have been undertaken in recent years. For instance, SEBI expanded its regulatory ambit to new categories of intermediaries such as investment advisers,[131] and continues to strengthen the existing norms for intermediaries.[132]

Conclusion

The current regulatory regime for securities market intermediaries in India is evolving rapidly. SEBI's framework for intermediaries is broad, fairly extensive and detailed but its implementation requires further bolstering, specifically in the area of inspections, continuous oversight, supervision and enforcement. Faster, better mechanisms and approaches need to be employed for effective oversight and supervision of intermediaries and their conduct. For these reasons, the degree of alignment of SEBI's regime with the core requirements of IOSCO Principles 29–32 is assessed as 'moderate' and the overall landscape for these principles as 'evolving' to a greater level of maturity. 'Substantial' changes have been introduced in this area of regulatory activity in the past decade, which supports the view that SEBI is strengthening this area of practice.

ASIC

Key features of the intermediaries regulatory framework

Chapter 7 of the *Corporations Act* deals with financial services and markets. As regards minimum entry standards, licensing and other initial and ongoing capital and prudential requirements for intermediaries (IOSCO Principles 29 and 30), pt 7.2 of the *Corporations Act* deals with licensing of financial markets and makes it mandatory for a person to procure an

---

131 See generally *SEBI (Investment Advisers) Regulations*.

132 See SEBI, *Guidelines on Outsourcing of Activities by Intermediaries* (Circular, CIR/MIRSD/24/2011, 15 December 2011), www.sebi.gov.in/legal/circulars/dec-2011/guidelines-on-outsourcing-of-activities-by-intermediaries_21752.html. On norms introduced by SEBI for more effective record keeping by intermediaries, see SEBI, *Amendments to Prevention of Money-Laundering (Maintenance of Records) Rules, 2005* (Circular, SEBI/HO/MIRSD/DOSR1/CIR/P/2018/93, 6 June 2018), www.sebi.gov.in/legal/circulars/jun-2018/amendments-to-prevention-of-money-laundering-maintenance-of-records-rules-2005_39207.html. See generally Ayush Verma, 'Everything you need to know about SEBI intermediaries and how are they regulated', *iPleaders* (Blog Post, 25 October 2020), blog.ipleaders.in/everything-need-know-sebi-intermediaries-regulated/.

Australian market licence that authorises them to operate the markets.[133] Part 7.6 deals with the licensing of providers of financial services and s 911A lays down the need for an AFSL.[134]

AFSLs are granted for an array of financial services, such as for providing financial product advice to clients, dealing in a financial product, making 'a market for a financial product' or operating a registered managed investment scheme.[135] Sections 916A and 916B allow for persons to act as authorised representatives of licensed market intermediaries without procuring an AFSL. Similarly, if a person is engaged in providing 'discretionary portfolio management services', the framework clarifies that such person needs to be licensed, while ASIC provides further requirements for such persons in its Regulatory Guide 179.[136]

The *Corporations Act* stipulates a number of minimum standards or entry requirements that need to be fulfilled for the grant of an AFSL licence.[137] The licensing procedure for an AFSL is set out in ASIC's licensing kit, consisting of Regulatory Guides 1, 2 and 3, which provide detailed and transparent guidelines for gaining the licence.[138] The licensing guidelines cover aspects specified under IOSCO Principles 30 and 31 for 'initial capital requirements', assessments of 'internal organisation and risk management systems of the applicant' as well as its dispute resolution systems.[139] In certain cases, where the AFSL holder is subject to prudential regulation, ASIC is

---

133 See *Corporations Act* s 791A.
134 See ibid s 911A. For more on the various facets of the AFSL regime, see Baxt, Black and Hanrahan, 'Australian financial services licensing' (n 3) 511. See generally Davies, Walpole and Pearson (n 92).
135 ASIC, 'What is an AFS licence?', asic.gov.au/for-finance-professionals/afs-licensees/do-you-need-an-afs-licence/what-is-an-afs-licence/. See also Royal Commission into Misconduct in the Banking, Superannuation and Financial Services Industry, *Financial Products Available to Retail Investors* (Background Paper 6 (Part C) 2018. A financial product is a facility that involves: i) making a financial investment (where an investor gives money to another person to generate financial return that will benefit the investor) (s 763B); ii) managing a financial risk (s 763C) , and/or iii) making non-cash payments (s 763D), see ibid.
136 See ASIC, *Managed Discretionary Accounts* (Regulatory Guide 179, 2016).
137 Section 913A of the *Corporations Act* requires the application for grant of needs to contain all necessary information and must be submitted along with the necessary documents. Further, s 912A of the *Corporations Act* requires the AFSL holder to provide financial services 'efficiently, honestly and fairly'; to have a mechanism in place to manage any 'conflict of interest' and risk; and to have adequate resources, such as 'financial, human and technological', to provide its financial services. In addition, ASIC must also be assured that the applicant is of good character and has provided ASIC with any information sought by the former and agrees to meet any conditions imposed by the regulator in connection with its licence application.
138 See ASIC, 'AFS licensing kit', asic.gov.au/for-finance-professionals/afs-licensees/applying-for-and-managing-an-afs-licence/afs-licensing-kit/.
139 See IMF, *Australia Country Report* (n 51) 116. See ASIC, 'AFS licensee obligations', asic.gov.au/for-finance-professionals/afs-licensees/your-ongoing-afs-licence-obligations/your-afs-licence-obligations-explained/.

required to consult with the prudential regulator, APRA, before 'imposing, revoking or varying any AFSL conditions or suspending or cancelling an AFSL'.[140] The *Corporations Act* also imposes 'ongoing requirements' on AFSL holders, such as through s 914A(8).[141] Some of the requirements for AFSL holders include compliance with ongoing capital[142] and reporting requirements,[143] monitoring of risk[144] and auditing of the financial standing of the licence holders.[145]

ASIC's general obligations, as set forth in Regulatory Guide 104, cover aspects of appropriate management and organisational structures.[146] The *Corporations Act* requires AFSL holders to ensure that financial services are provided in an efficient, honest and fair manner.[147] Regulatory Guide 104 recommends that AFSL holders conduct an external review of their compliance measures, processes and procedures to ensure they are effective.[148] ASIC also assesses an intermediary's compliance function when they apply for an AFSL licence.[149] Further, there are specific provisions for the protection of client money that apply to all AFSL holders as well as to the holding of client assets by the AFSL holder.[150]

As regards effective ongoing monitoring and regulation of market intermediaries, the recently introduced *Treasury Laws Amendment (Design and Distribution Obligations and Product Intervention Powers) Act 2019* (Cth) confers powers of product intervention to ASIC to address instances of consumer detriment or where, despite disclosures, consumers fail to

---

140 IMF, *Australia Country Report* (n 51). In certain cases, ASIC can suspend or cancel an AFSL without adhering to natural justice principles, such as when a licence holder is rendered insolvent or convicted of a serious offence: see *Corporations Act* s 915B.

141 AFSL holders are required to report material changes to their financial position or if there is any change in control to ASIC: see reg 7.6.04 of the *Corporations Regulations 2001* (Cth) (*Corporations Regulations*).

142 Regulation Guide 166 sets forth the capital requirements or financial resources that an AFSL holder is expected to hold to create a 'financial buffer' that minimises the chance of 'disorderly or non-compliant wind-up if the business fails': see IMF, *Australia Country Report* (n 51) 119.

143 Several reporting requirements are imposed on market participants and AFSL holders, ranging from weekly to monthly reports to annual reports that are submitted to either ASX Clear, ASX Clear (Futures) or ASIC: see ibid.

144 In certain cases, AFSL holders may be subject to APRA's supervision (s 912A(1)(d)CA). In these cases, APRA applies the 'risk-based Basel' capital requirements and monitors the risk: see ibid 121.

145 The Australian securities regime requires the reports of market participants and other AFSL holders to be audited and reviewed by an independent auditor: see ibid 124.

146 See ASIC, *AFS Licensing: Meeting the General Obligations* (Regulatory Guide 104, 2020).

147 *Corporations Act* s 912A(1)(a).

148 See ASIC, *AFS Licensing: Meeting the General Obligations* (n 146).

149 IMF, *Australia Country Report* (n 51) 126.

150 See *Corporations Act* pt 7.8 div 2; see also IMF, *Australia Country Report* (n 51) 127.

understand the risk/return trade-off involved in a product.[151] To bolster the reforms termed 'Future of Financial Advice' (FOFA) and introduced in 2012 to ban conflicted remuneration and establish a statutory best interests duty,[152] further reforms were introduced through the *Corporations Amendment (Professional Standards of Financial Advisers) Act 2017* (Cth) to enhance the standards for education, training and ethics applicable to financial advisers.[153] At the same time, a code of ethics and compliance for financial advisers[154] was developed by the Financial Adviser Standards and Ethics Authority.[155]

Another form of ongoing obligation imposed on market intermediaries is the 'know your customer' requirements set forth in the *Anti-Money Laundering and Counter-Terrorism Financing Act 2006* (Cth). Internal organisational requirements also include record-keeping and an obligation to provide information to clients through the Financial Services Guide[156] and work in their best interests.[157] Further, 'investment advisers' are also subject to the same requirements of licensing, capital, conflict of mechanism and organisational obligations as other AFSL holders.[158]

ASIC monitors the conduct and supervises the operation of market participants through its Market and Participant Supervision stakeholder team.[159] The commission conducts risk-based surveillance of market participants and uses a unique risk measurement strategy—the Risk

151 See ASIC, *Product Intervention Power* (Consultation Paper 313, 2019).

152 See ASIC, 'Future of Financial Advice (FOFA) reforms', asic.gov.au/regulatory-resources/financial-services/regulatory-reforms/future-of-financial-advice-fofa-reforms/. See also Richard Batten and Gail Pearson, 'Financial advice in Australia: principles to proscription: managing to banning' (2013) 87 *John's Law Review* 511.

153 *Corporations Amendment (Professional Standards of Financial Advisers) Act 2017* (Cth). For a brief overview of these standards, see ASIC, 'Financial services: professional standards', asic.gov.au/for-finance-professionals/afs-licensees/professional-standards-for-financial-advisers/.

154 The Financial Adviser Standards and Ethics Authority Ltd (FASEA) is the standards body under pt 7.6 of the *Corporations Act*: see Australian Government Transparency Portal, 'Our purpose' (FASEA Annual Report 2020–21), transparency.gov.au/publications/treasury/financial-adviser-standards-and-ethics-authority-ltd/financial-adviser-standards-and-ethics-authority-ltd-annual-report-2020-21/our-purpose. FASEA was established through the Corporations Amendment Act in 2017 to set standards for financial advisers.

155 See *Financial Planners and Advisers Code of Ethics 2019*. However, the manner in which the code of ethics was developed sparked a controversy: see Mike Taylor, 'ASIC went direct to academics to commission controversial submission', *Money Management* (16 February 2021), moneymanagement.com.au/news/financial-planning/asic-went-direct-academics-commission-controversial-submission.

156 *Corporations Act* (s 941A). See also IMF, *Australia Country Report* (n 51) 128.

157 See *Corporations Act* s 912A.

158 IMF, *Australia Country Report* (n 51).

159 In 2012, ASIC had the responsibility of supervising about 137 market participants and had about 54 MPS staff members, of whom 19 were responsible for surveillance: see ibid 130.

Assessment Detection and Response—to assess the risk rating of each financial intermediary.[160] In addition, ASIC publishes its priorities for supervision of market intermediaries on an annual basis, consistently enhances supervision of 'the most high-risk and complex entities' and tailors its 'proactive and reactive supervision approach' in respect of intermediaries with medium and low risk.[161]

Finally, in the context of IOSCO Principle 32, which requires market intermediaries to have a system in place to check any failure that may lead to systemic risk or damage or loss to investors, the regime has several provisions, such as early warning systems, that focus on mitigation and management of any market failure.[162] In the case of a threat to the markets or investors, ASIC may invoke a range of powers, including freezing of accounts, removing the licence of any AFSL holder, deciding to wind up or according compensation.[163]

Analysis

The regulatory framework for financial market intermediaries in Australia is, on the one hand, characterised by its simplicity and lucidity,[164] and, on the other, 'descends into complexity and technicality on application'.[165] As the previous section exemplifies,[166] on the whole, the requirements pertaining to AFSL holders under the Australian financial markets framework are sufficiently broad and largely fulfil the core requirements of IOSCO Principles 29–31. To that extent, the framework for financial services, encapsulated primarily in the *Corporations Act* and secondarily in ASIC's regulatory documents, has been described as 'extensive, prescriptive and detailed', particularly in relation to 'retail clients'.[167] However, concerns

---

160 See ASIC, 'Strategic Priority 1: Technology, risk and resilience' in *ASIC's Market Supervision Strategic Priorities 2017–18* (2017).

161 ASIC, 'Enhanced supervision for market intermediaries' in *ASIC's Priorities for Supervision of Market Intermediaries in 2019–20* (2019).

162 See IMF, *Australia Country Report* (n 51) 132.

163 See ibid 132–134.

164 All financial market intermediaries are regulated by ASIC and are required to hold an AFSL licence that allows them to engage in a specific intermediary activity: see ASIC, 'AFS licensees', asic.gov.au/for-finance-professionals/afs-licensees/.

165 Helen Bird and George Gilligan, 'Deterring corporate wrongdoing: penalties, financial services misconduct and the Corporations Act 2001 (Cth)' (2016) 34(5) *Company and Securities Law Journal* 337.

166 The descriptive analysis shows that the AFSL holders' framework comprises licensing and other minimum entry standards, initial and ongoing capital and prudential requirements, reporting requirements, guidelines for internal organisation and conduct, and risk management mechanisms, while being subject to ASIC's risk-based surveillance.

167 Pamela Hanrahan, 'Fairness and financial services: revisiting the enforcement framework' (2017) 35(7) *Company and Securities Law Journal* 421.

have been raised in recent years about the successful implementation of the AFSL regime, with many questioning whether the framework has indeed been 'effective and fit-for-purpose'.[168] This scepticism is primarily due to the numerous instances of financial services misconduct,[169] particularly 'inappropriate financial advice, unlicensed (financial market or service) conduct, and fraud or misleading representations' that have come to the fore in recent years,[170] and that have prompted inquiries at the highest level.[171] Thus, within domestic circles in Australia, the AFSL regime/framework,[172] and implementation from a regulatory perspective[173] (ie ASIC's overall approach in terms of its monitoring, supervision and enforcement mechanisms adopted towards for misconduct in financial services), has been criticised as being ineffective and has been found wanting in several ways.[174] Chapter 5 of this book elaborates on this aspect. However, to overcome these industry reservations and strengthen ASIC's regime for financial service providers, enforcement has been largely refreshed[175] and invigorated through enhanced budgetary and other resources to 'deliver effectively on its mandate' as a regulator.[176]

In relation to Principle 32, in general, Australia's regulatory framework for systemic financial stability has been found to be effective and robust,[177] even as there are recommendations to improve the existing systemic stability

---

168 Ibid.

169 For a detailed discussion on failure in financial advice see Chapter 5 of this book.

170 Bird and Gilligan (n 165) 337. Pearson draws a distinction between advice, information and selling: see Gail Pearson, 'Selling financial products and other conduct' in *Financial Services Law and Compliance in Australia* (Cambridge University Press, 2012) ch 6, 199.

171 *Royal Commission into Misconduct in the Banking, Superannuation and Financial Services Industry* (Final Report, September 2018) vol 1.

172 The Financial System Inquiry of 2014 stated: 'In terms of fair treatment for consumers, the current framework is not sufficient. The GFC brought to light significant numbers of Australian consumers holding financial products that did not suit their needs and circumstances—in some cases resulting in severe financial loss. The most significant problems related to shortcomings in disclosure and financial advice, and over-reliance on financial literacy'. See GFC Financial System Inquiry, *Financial System Inquiry: Final Report* (2014) (FSI Final Report).

173 ASIC's handling of corporate misconduct, especially its penalties regimes, has been criticised severely: see generally George Gilligan et al, 'Penalties regimes to counter corporate and financial wrongdoing in Australia— views of governance professionals' (2017) 11(1) *Law and Financial Markets Review* 4–12, doi.org/10.1080/17521440.2017.1309162.

174 See generally FSI Final Report (n 172). ASIC was advised to consider a host of aspects while granting a licence and imposing effective 'conditions requiring licensees to address concerns about serious or systemic non-compliance with licence obligations'.

175 See for example Michael Legg and Stephen Speirs, 'Litigation: why not litigate?—the royal commission, ASIC and the future of the enforcement pyramid' (2019)(47) *Australian Business Law Review*.

176 FSI Final Report (n 172).

177 Ibid ch 5.

mechanisms.[178] ASIC's procedures for dealing with any failure of a market intermediary are sufficiently elaborate and have been successful in ensuring that such failure does not lead to losses for investors or any systemic risk.

The detailed FSAP Review of 2012 rated ASIC's regime for these IOSCO Principles as follows: Principle 29 was 'broadly implemented', Principle 30 was 'partly implemented', Principle 31 was 'broadly implemented' and Principle 32 was 'fully implemented'.

Conclusion

In light of the limitations in the implementation of the intermediaries framework, ASIC's degree of alignment with IOSCO Principles 29–31 is assessed as 'moderate'. However, the overall landscape for market intermediaries is assessed as 'mature', as the nature of reforms required are akin to adjustments or refinements rather than structural or fundamental reforms. 'Substantial' changes have been adopted in the past decade to overcome the problems associated with this area of financial activity, and better mechanisms are being adopted to improve both conduct and supervision of market intermediaries, which highlights the importance being accorded to this area of regulation. For IOSCO Principle 32 dealing with systemic risk, the degree of alignment of the Australian regime is assessed as 'high' and the overall landscape 'mature', with continuous refinement being adopted through 'minor' changes in the past years.

Principle 8

> Principle 8: The regulator should seek to ensure that conflicts of interest and misalignment of incentives are avoided, eliminated, disclosed or otherwise managed.

The years prior to the GFC witnessed several examples of misalignment of incentives, leading to the adoption of IOSCO Principle 8 on managing and mitigating risks associated with conflicts of interest and misalignment of incentives.[179]

A conflict of interest refers to a situation in which 'an entity or individual becomes unreliable because of a clash between personal (self-serving) interests and professional duties or responsibilities'; when this occurs, 'the party

---

178 See for example Steve Kourabas, *Improving Australia's Regulatory Framework for Systemic Financial Stability* (2018).

179 IOSCO, *Methodology for Assessing* (n 5) 48.

is usually asked to remove themselves', which is 'often legally required of them'.[180] Such conflicts relate to what is described as 'agency problems',[181] and is a focus area for securities regulators because it damages investor protection, undermines 'fair, efficient and transparent operation of markets' and creates systemic risk.[182] Similarly, misalignment of incentives refers to a situation 'where the incentives and interests of those engaged in bringing financial products to market are not aligned with the interest of investors', causing such persons to not act in the best 'interests of the end consumer or investor'.[183]

The following sections discuss how, and to what extent, SEBI's and ASIC's regimes reflect the core requirements of IOSCO Principle 8, specifically in the context of SEBI-registered intermediaries and the AFSL holders.

SEBI

Key features of the framework on conflicts of interest and misalignment of incentives

At a broad level, the securities legal framework addresses conflicts of interest for securities market intermediaries either through provisions in the SEBI regulations[184] or in the code of conduct applicable to such intermediaries.[185] Over the past decade, SEBI has increased its focus on managing such conflicts for intermediaries, for its own functioning[186] as well as for other market participants. In 2013, SEBI issued a circular specifying norms for various participants in the securities markets.[187]

---

180 T Segal, 'What is a conflict of interest?' *Investopedia* (22 April 2025), investopedia.com/terms/c/conflict-of-interest.asp.
181 Agency problems refer to the condition where market participants who are entrusted to act in the interest of their clients or investors use their 'powers, position or information to advance their own interest instead': see IOSCO, *Methodology for Assessing* (n 5) 48.
182 Ibid. Conflicts of interest are reflected across many other IOSCO Principles, such as in the requirements of Principles 5, 9, 22, 23, 24, 28, 29 and 31.
183 A specific example of such 'misalignment of incentives' is in the case of complex financial products or asset backed securities 'where different firms are responsible for design, manufacture and distribution of a financial product' but where such firms do not owe any duty of care to the end consumer or investor and therefore their actions may not be aligned with the best interest of the end users of their products: see ibid.
184 For example *Securities and Exchange Board of India (Portfolio Managers) Regulations 2020* (*Securities and Exchange Board of India (Portfolio Managers) Regulations*) reg 22. Refer also to SEBI's description in the detailed FSAP Review of 2013 on this Principle: see IMF, *India FSAP Report* (n 14) 100.
185 For example, cl 3 of the Code of Conduct (Portfolio Manager): see *Securities and Exchange Board of India (Portfolio Managers) Regulations*.
186 See for example SEBI, 'Code on conflict of interests for members of board', www.sebi.gov.in/conf.html. SEBI addresses conflicts of interest through its supervision and on-site supervision program: see IMF, *India FSAP Report* (n 14) 100.
187 SEBI, *General Guidelines for Dealing with Conflicts of Interest of Intermediaries, Recognised Stock Exchanges, Recognised Clearing Corporations, Depositories and Their Associated Persons in Securities Market*

Analysis

On a perusal of the conflicts of interest norms across SEBI regulations, circulars and guidelines, it is evident that SEBI is consciously enhancing the framework for addressing such conflicts through a variety of measures. These include avoidance or management of such conflicts by 'active involvement of senior management' of the market participants, imposing suitable requirements for 'disclosure', introducing 'information barriers' and 'incentive structures', and specifying appropriate restrictions on transactions in securities.[188] However, the onus for implementation of the framework addressing conflicts of interest is placed on the board members of the market participants along with other senior management, and the literature in this area does not reveal the extent to which such arrangements are effective. It is also clear that conflicts of interest provisions are not mandated or mentioned in the legislative Acts governing securities markets. Nevertheless, a notable takeaway from the above-mentioned SEBI conflicts of interest circular of 2013 is that it mentions that it is 'on the lines of' the requirements of Principle 8, which exhibits SEBI's commitment and sensitivity to transposing international best standards to the domestic realm.[189] On the whole, despite strengthened norms for governance of such conflicts being ushered in by SEBI, the implementation of these norms is still in an evolving stage, with substantial room for further streamlining in future.

The detailed FSAP Review of 2013, while noting that SEBI was enhancing norms for the handling of such conflicts, did not officially assess SEBI's regime for this newly incorporated IOSCO Principle.[190]

Conclusion

Provisions on conflicts of interest are not specified in the securities legislation, but instead within the regulatory framework established by SEBI for securities markets and participants. This framework is being upgraded and enhanced in line with the requirements of IOSCO Principle 8; however, the framework and its effective implementation, particularly considering human resource constraints faced by SEBI, suggest that the regime for conflicts of interest is evolving. Thus, at this stage, the degree of alignment

---

(2013).

188 See ibid.

189 Ibid.

190 The report also recommended that conflicts of interest provisions be strengthened for the stock exchanges in relation to their conflicting self-regulatory functions. See IMF, *India FSAP Report* (n 14) 21, 100. SEBI's regime was not assessed for the newly incorporated principles in the IMF detailed assessment of 2013.

of SEBI's regime with this Principle 8 is assessed as 'moderate'. Given the recent past, particularly since the detailed FSAP Review of SEBI in 2013, the extent of reform or changes introduced relating to Principle 8 is assessed as 'substantial', while the overall landscape is determined as 'evolving'.

ASIC

Key features of the framework on conflicts of interest and misalignment of incentives

The *Corporations Act* requires AFSL holders to have adequate arrangements in place to manage conflicts of interest.[191] ASIC's Regulatory Guide 181 sets out the policy and approach that AFSL holders need to adopt to manage such conflicts.[192] ASIC's conflicts of interest policy is set out in wide terms and applies to different circumstances;[193] it obliges all licensees, including vertically integrated businesses, to establish 'adequate conflicts management arrangements' as well as to evaluate their adequacy.[194] Regulator Guide 181 expressly states that 'merely having a conflict management policy is not sufficient' and that such a policy needs to be 'implemented and maintained'.[195] Further, for a responsible entity of a managed investment scheme,[196] s 601FC(1)(c) of the *Corporations Act* requires such entities to 'act in the best interests of investors' and, in case of a conflict of interest between such an entity and its clients or members, 'give priority to the member's interests'.[197] In addition, conflicts of interest for financial advisers are addressed through the provisions on conflicted remuneration.[198] ASIC's Regulatory Guide 79 on research report providers deals with management of conflicts of interest for research providers, financial advisory firms and other industry parties.[199]

---

191 See *Corporations Act* s 912A (1)(aa). This section obliges an AFSL holder to 'have in place adequate arrangements for the management of conflicts of interest that may arise wholly, or partially, in relation to activities undertaken by the licensee or a representative of the licensee in the provision of financial services as part of the financial services business of the licensee or the representative'.

192 ASIC, *Licensing: Managing Conflicts of Interest* (Regulatory Guide 181, 2004).

193 Regulatory Guide 181 defines conflicts of interest in wide terms: see ibid 15.

194 ASIC, *Culture, Conduct and Conflicts of Interest in Vertically Integrated Businesses in the Funds-Management Industry* (Report No 474, 2016) 6.

195 Ibid.

196 A responsible entity of a registered scheme is the company that is named in ASIC's record: see *Corporations Act* s 9. For a better understanding of a responsible entity's role, see ASIC, 'AFS licensees' (n 164).

197 See ASIC, *Culture, Conduct and Conflicts of Interest* (n 194) 7. For a detailed discussion of 'best interest', see Han-Wei Liu et al, 'In whose best interests? Regulating financial advisers, the royal commission and the dilemma of reform' (2020) 42(1) *Sydney Law Review* 37.

198 Conflicted remuneration is defined in *Corporations Act* s 963A.

199 ASIC, *Research Report Providers: Improving the Quality of Investment Research* (Regulatory Guide 79, 2012).

Analysis

The above discussion highlights key provisions on conflicts of interest in the Australian financial law framework. It shows that avoidance of such conflicts is prioritised across the entire Australian financial system through clear and consistent provisions contained not only in ASIC's documents but also at the statutory level (ie, in the *Corporations Act* itself).

ASIC monitors requirements relating to conflicts of interest through a risk-based surveillance approach, and particularly focuses on 'disclosures' to clients when such situations arise.[200] A recent example of ASIC's intervention in this area is manifest through its *Report 562 Financial Advice: Vertically Integrated Institutions and Conflicts of Interest*, which reviews the manner in which 'financial advice arms of Australia's largest financial institutions manage conflicts of interest in providing financial advice'.[201] Through this report, ASIC identified areas for improvement in compliance, advice quality and public reporting practices in vertically integrated firms.[202]

Despite the sound framework and ASIC's supervision in this area, there have been widespread concerns in the past about conflicts of interest in some areas, such as executive remuneration[203] and financial advice.[204] Such issues around conflicts of interest and misalignment of incentives have led to significant academic deliberations in recent decades in Australia,[205] and have even caused high-level inquiries.[206]

---

200 IMF, *India FSAP Report* (n 14).

201 MinterEllison, 'ASIC reports on how large financial institutions manage conflicts of interest in financial advice' (2018).

202 ASIC, *Financial Advice: Vertically Integrated Institutions and Conflicts of Interest* (Report No 562, 2018).

203 For literature relating to issues in executive remuneration, see Jennifer G Hill and Charles M Yablon, 'Corporate governance and executive remuneration: rediscovering managerial positional conflict' (2002) 25(2) *UNSW Law Journal* 294.

204 Paul Chen and Martin Richardson, 'Conflict of interest, disclosure and vertical relationships: an experimental analysis' (2019) 38(3) *Economic Papers: A Journal of Applied Economics and Policy* 167–181, doi.org/10.1111/1759-3441.12245.

205 See for example Adam Steen, Dianne McGrath and Alfred Wong, 'Market failure, regulation and education of financial advisors' (2016) 10(1) *Australasian Accounting, Business and Finance Journal* 3–17, doi.org/10.14453/aabfj.v10i1.2; Julie-Anne Tarr, Jeanette Van Akkeren and Rania Shibl, 'Financial advisers—new remuneration constraints and competency requirements addressing perverse incentives and poor advice' (2017) 35(8) *Company and Securities Journal* 561–571.

206 See for example Parliament of Australia, 'Parliamentary Joint Committee on Corporations and Financial Services', aph.gov.au/Parliamentary_Business/Committees/Joint/Corporations_and_Financial_Services.

Academics, such as Pearson, discuss persisting problems around conflicts of interests, particularly the 'commission culture' in the sale of financial products, arguing that this culture is deeply embedded in Australia's financial system and is considered 'necessary to sell socially desirable products and critical for retaining market share', although it often creates 'conflicts of interest between firm and consumers and within the firm'.[207] The FOFA reforms[208] that were mandated in Australia to, among other things, address problems of 'conflicted remuneration' did not resolve this issue.[209]

The necessity of reforms was reinforced by a number of financial scandals, such as the Macquarie Private Wealth[210] and the Commonwealth Financial Planning Ltd scandals,[211] that caused severe damage to the overall trust and confidence in the financial system.[212] Likewise, the NAB financial scandal revealed extensive manipulations by financial planners and advisers and significant breaches due to conflicts of interest.[213]

Despite these issues, on balance, the legislative framework and ASIC's regulatory framework deal with issues pertaining to conflicts of interest in an extensive manner, as evident from the FSAP Review of 2012 that rated ASIC's regime as 'fully implemented' in relation to Principle 8.[214] However, despite this rating, further refinements and reforms have been continuously adopted to enhance the conflicts of interest regime.

---

207 Gail Pearson, 'Commission culture: a critical analysis of commission regulation in financial services' (2017) 36 *University of Queensland Law Journal* 155.

208 See ASIC, 'Future of Financial Advice (FOFA) reforms' (n 152).

209 Chen and Richardson (n 204). Conflicted remuneration refers to financial advisers receiving incentives when they sell certain financial instruments.

210 To gain an understanding of the Macquarie scandal, see ASIC, 'ASIC accepts enforceable undertaking from Macquarie Equities Ltd' (Media Release, 2013).

211 For an in-depth account of the CFPL case, see Senate Standing Committees on Economics, 'Commonwealth Financial Planning Limited: what went wrong at CFPL and why?' in *Performance of the Australian Securities and Investments Commission* (2014) ch 8. For more on corporate governance, see Gail Pearson, 'Failure in corporate governance: financial planning and greed' in Christine A Mallin (ed), *Handbook on Corporate Governance in Financial Institutions* (Edward Elgar Publishing, 2016), doi.org/10.4337/9781784711795.00016.

212 See generally ASIC, 'ASIC permanently bans former Commonwealth Financial Planning adviser' (Media Release (30 April 2012).

213 Ashley Matthews, 'The financial services industry: whistleblowing and calls for a royal commission' (2016)(136) *Precedent* 35. See also A Ferguson and R Williams, 'Whistleblower's NAB leak reveals persistent bad behaviour in financial planning, fuels royal commission calls', *Sydney Morning Herald* (21 February), smh.com.au/business/banking-andfinance/whistleblowers-nab-leak-reveals-persistent-bad-behaviour-in-financialplanning-fuels-royal-commission-calls-20150217-13hv1f.html#ixzz3jGGLHzBk.

214 IMF, *India FSAP Report* (n 14).

Conclusion

The above discussion in respect of IOSCO Principle 8 shows that the Australian financial legal and regulatory framework places high importance on eradicating conflicts of interest. Despite issues in implementation, particularly in financial advice, the framework and requirements imposed by ASIC are of a high standard. Given the strength of the framework for avoidance of conflicts of interest, and the close scrutiny to and measures for strengthening the implementation of this principle, it is concluded that ASIC's regime generally demonstrates a 'high' degree of alignment with IOSCO Principle 8. 'Minor' refinements have been introduced in this area of activity in recent years, but the overall landscape is sufficiently 'mature'—considering the detailed incorporation of provisions on conflicts of interest and misalignment of incentives within all areas of the financial markets, the reliability of these norms and constant scrutiny in this area.

Principle relating to clearing and settlement

Principle 38: Securities settlement systems and central counterparties should be subject to regulatory and supervisory requirements that are designed to ensure that they are fair, effective and efficient and that they reduce systemic risk.

Principle 38

Financial market infrastructures (FMIs) 'facilitate the clearing, settlement, and recording of money and other financial transactions', and play 'a critical role in fostering financial stability' within the financial system.[215] Securities settlement systems (SSSs) and central counterparties (CCPs)—the FMIs that operate within the securities markets—serve as vital components of a financial system.[216] In recent times, policymakers have noted the importance of CCPs and have introduced greater measures to promote their soundness

---

215 See Committee on Payment and Settlement Systems and Technical Committee of the International Organization of Securities Commissions, *Principles for Financial Market Infrastructures* (2012). If FMIs are not managed appropriately, they 'can pose significant risks to the financial system and be a potential source of contagion, particularly in the periods of market stress'.

216 European Central Bank, 'Payments and markets: securities settlement systems and central counterparties', ecb.europa.eu/paym/pol/activ/clearing/html/index.en.html. CCPs are 'financial market infrastructures that can reduce and mutualise—that is, share between their members—counterparty credit risk in the markets in which they operate': see Randall S Kroszner, 'Central counterparty clearing: history, innovation, and regulation' (2006) 30(4) *Economic Perspectives*.

and stability through enhanced regulation and oversight.[217] Although FMIs are being subject to greater governmental or regulatory scrutiny, academics caution that such enhanced measures ought not be confused or mistaken with any 'promise of government financial support in the event of a risk-management failure'.[218]

Given the critical importance of FMIs in facilitating the role of clearing and settlement of financial transactions, the Committee on Payment and Settlement Systems (CPSS) and IOSCO, in 2012, adopted and published separate, detailed principles for their governance entitled *Principles for Financial Market Infrastructures*: a set of 24 standards or principles for the effective working, oversight and regulation of these FMIs.[219]

By and large, both the Australian and Indian securities regimes have well-developed settlement systems and CCPs with adequate measures for their regulation, and this aspect is discussed in detail below.

SEBI

Key features of the securities clearing and settlement framework

The securities clearing and settlement systems in India cater to different financial products including 'government securities, money market instruments, forex instruments and derivatives, and Indian Rupee derivatives'; corporate securities and financial derivatives; and, finally, commodity derivatives.[220] In the context of the securities and financial derivatives that are traded on the stock exchanges, such as the Bombay Stock Exchange (BSE), National Stock Exchange (NSE) or the Metropolitan Stock Exchange of India Ltd (MSEI), a number of entities perform clearing and settlement functions.[221] The Indian Clearing Corporation Ltd, a wholly owned subsidiary of BSE, carries out the functions of clearing, settlement, collateral management and risk management

---

217 If not managed properly, CCPs could present significant risks that would impact the entire financial system: see Amandeep Rehlon and Dan Nixon, 'Central counterparties: what are they, why do they matter, and how does the Bank supervise them?' (2013) *Bank of England Quarterly Bulletin* Q2.

218 See Kroszner (n 216).

219 Committee on Payment and Settlement Systems and Technical Committee of the International Organization of Securities Commissions (n 215).

220 See Financial Sector Assessment Program, *India—CPMI IOSCO Principles for Financial Market Infrastructures—Detailed Assessment of Observance of Clearing Corporation of India Limited (CCIL) Central Counterparty (CCP) and Trade Repository (TR)* (2017).

221 See ibid 11–12.

transactions for BSE.[222] NSE Clearing Ltd (NSE Clearing), a wholly owned subsidiary of NSE, is responsible for clearing and settlement of all trades on the NSE,[223] while the Metropolitan Clearing Corporation of India Ltd clears the transactions executed on the MSEI.[224] Similarly, commodity derivatives that are traded on a number of commodity exchanges in India use similar platforms for clearing and settlement of their trades, and are also supervised and regulated by SEBI.[225]

SEBI is the chief regulator for clearing and settlement activities in the securities markets and, in this capacity, introduced the *Securities Contracts (Regulation) (Stock Exchanges and Clearing Corporations) Regulations 2012*, which were recently replaced by the *Securities Contracts (Regulation) (Stock Exchanges and Clearing Corporations) Regulations 2018*. These regulations provide an extensive framework for the oversight and supervision of clearing corporations, including provisions that mandate their licensing and set them up as separate legal entities from RSEs.[226] From time to time, SEBI issues circulars and guidelines to amend the wide range of requirements that apply to these clearing corporations, a recent example being SEBI's move to introduce and promote interoperability among them.[227]

Analysis

The clearing and settlement systems architecture lies at the heart of a securities transaction and is of critical importance to a securities system, and, thus, as described in the previous section, detailed regulations have

---

222 See Indian Clearing Corporation Ltd, 'Company profile', icclindia.com/Static/about/company profile.aspx. IICL 'undertakes to act as the central counterparty to all the trades it provides clearing and settlement services for'.

223 NSE Clearing was formerly known as National Securities Clearing Corporation Ltd; it is responsible for clearing and settlement of trades executed on NSE: see NSE Clearing, 'About NSE clearing', nscclindia.com/.

224 MCCIL was jointly promoted by the Metropolitan Stock Exchange of India Ltd, Multi-Commodity Exchange of India Ltd and the Financial Technologies India Ltd as a clearing corporation for a number of asset classes: see Metropolitan Clearing Corporation of India Ltd, 'About MCCIL', www.mclear.in/.

225 There are four main national commodity exchanges: see Financial Sector Assessment Program (n 220) 12, 196.

226 Section 2(d) defines a 'clearing corporation' as 'an entity that is established to undertake the activity of clearing and settlement of trades in securities or other instruments or products that are dealt with or traded on a recognised stock exchange and includes a clearing house': see *Securities Contracts (Regulation) (Stock Exchanges and Clearing Corporations) Regulations 2012*.

227 See Rajalakhshmi Nirmal, 'All you wanted to know about interoperability', *The Hindu Business Line* (10 June 2019), thehindubusinessline.com/opinion/columns/slate/all-you-wanted-to-know-about-interoperability/article27765847.ece. For SEBI's proposal on interoperability, see SEBI, 'Interoperability among clearing corporations—amendments to *Securities Contracts (Regulation) (Stock Exchanges and Clearing Corporations) Regulations, 2012*', www.sebi.gov.in/sebi_data/meetingfiles/oct-2018/153958190 5488_1.pdf.

been framed by SEBI for these institutions. During the World Bank–IMF FSAP Review of 2017, a detailed assessment report prepared on India's compliance with the CPMI-IOSCO *Principles for Financial Market Infrastructures* revealed India's overall high compliance with the stated principles.[228] In the past also, the World Bank and IMF's joint reports assessing the implementation of the CPSS–IOSCO Recommendations for SSSs and CCPs in India noted that the overall risk management framework for securities and derivatives clearing and settlement systems in India was 'prudent', 'the operational reliability [was] high', and the supervision and regulation of these were 'effective'.[229]

Further, through several ongoing measures to enhance the functioning of the clearing corporations and settlement mechanisms in securities markets, SEBI is working towards harmonisation and convergence of standards in this area.[230] As acknowledged in the IMF–World Bank reports, SEBI has taken significant steps towards adoption and implementation of the *Principles for Financial Market Infrastructures* in respect of the market infrastructure institutions. This Principle 38 was not assessed in FSAP Assessment of 2013 for SEBI.[231]

Conclusion

SEBI's framework for clearing and settlement systems is widely acknowledged as reliable and comprehensive and, thus, the degree of alignment of SEBI's regime with the core requirements of IOSCO Principle 38 is assessed as 'high'. Further, 'substantial' changes in the past decade have been introduced to enhance the efficacy of the clearing and settlement systems, streamline their operations and improve the process of monitoring and supervision of these facilities. The overall landscape is thus assessed as 'evolving' for this principle.

---

228 Financial Sector Assessment Program (n 220). The assessment was conducted in relation to securities and derivatives clearing and settlement systems for the following financial products: government securities, money market instruments, forex instruments and Rupee derivatives that come primarily within the purview of the RBI. It was not conducted in relation to corporate securities and financial derivatives or the commodity derivatives that come within the purview of SEBI and are relevant for this book.

229 FINSEC Law Advisors, 'Recent development in clearing and settlement systems in India', finseclaw.com/service/recent-development-in-clearing-and-settlement-systems-in-india/ (page discontinued).

230 SEBI, 'Qualified central counterparties in securities markets' (Press Release No 1/2014 , 3 January 2014), www.sebi.gov.in/media/press-releases/jan-2014/qualified-central-counterparties-in-securities-market_25998.html. See also SEBI, 'Principles of Financial Market Infrastructures (PFMIs)' (SEBI Circular, 2013).

231 IMF, *India FSAP Report* (n 14) 87. As per standard practice, the principle was not assessed under this assessment as there exists a separate, detailed set of IOSCO standards/principles under which FMIs are assessed.

ASIC

Key features of the Australia clearing and settlement facility

In Australia, a clearing and settlement facility (CS facility) is defined in s 768A of the *Corporations Act*,[232] and several entities have been licensed by the relevant minister to perform the clearing and settlement functions as permitted under ch 7 of the *Corporations Act*.[233]

Complementing the *Corporations Act* provisions, ASIC's website and guidelines elaborate on ASIC's approach and regime for a CS facility.[234] ASIC's Regulatory Guide 211 details all significant aspects relating to the oversight and regulation of these facilities, their licensing and operating, and the continuing obligations imposed on them as well as ASIC's approach to assessment of such facilities required under s 823 of the *Corporations Act*.[235] Thus, to a large extent, ASIC oversees and specifies details pertaining to the CS facilities, including receiving applications for obtaining a CS facility licence that is required to be lodged with ASIC with all necessary documents accompanying such application.[236] Simultaneously, the Reserve Bank of Australia (RBA) also plays a key role in determining financial stability standards in respect of the CS facility, aiming to promote overall stability in the Australian financial system.[237]

Finally, the international standards and principles relating to clearing and settlement are given due regard within the Australian framework. ASIC's Information Sheet 166 details how the *CPSS–IOSCO Principles for Financial Market Infrastructures* apply in Australia to central counterparties and securities settlement facilities, payment systems and trade repositories.[238]

---

232 A 'clearing and settlement facility is a facility that provides a regular mechanism for the parties to transactions relating to financial products to meet obligations to each other': see *Corporations Act* s 768A.
233 ASIC, 'Licensed and exempt clearing and settlement facilities', asic.gov.au/regulatory-resources/markets/market-structure/licensed-and-exempt-clearing-and-settlement-facilities/. For a detailed account, see Baxt, Black and Hanrahan, 'Market infrastructure providers' (n 1) 396.
234 See for example ASIC, 'Licensed and exempt clearing and settlement facilities' (n 233); ASIC, *Clearing and Settlement Facilities: Australian and Overseas Operators* (Regulatory Guide 211, 2012).
235 See ASIC, *Clearing and Settlement Facilities* (n 234) 3, 4, 10, 11, 59.
236 *Corporations Act* s 824A(1). See also Baxt, Black and Hanrahan, 'Market infrastructure providers' (n 1).
237 *Corporations Act* s 827D.
238 ASIC, 'Implementing the CPSS IOSCO Principles for financial market infrastructures in Australia' (Information Sheet No 166, 2013).

Analysis

The Australian financial markets framework for clearing and settlement facilities has been recognised to 'operate reliably',[239] and operates under continuous supervision from ASIC. The detailed FSAP Report of 2012 in respect of the 38 IOSCO Principles did not rate this principle for Australia.[240] However, the *Technical Note—Supervision, Oversight, and Resolution Planning of FMIs* provided as part of the 2019 FSAP Report on Australia noted that Australia has a well-developed and advanced framework monitoring the functioning of clearing and settlement facilities in the financial system.[241]

Moreover, the Executive Summary of FSAP's 2019 report on Australia found the FMIs in Australia reliable and the overall landscape considerably 'competitive', with new entrants emerging.[242] The report gave Australia 'the highest ratings in all categories', noting that Australia was adopting its 'final implementation measures' for all FMIs.[243] The report also commended the supervision of, and oversight mechanisms for, FMIs but highlighted some gaps and limitations in the enforcement powers and mechanisms operating between the RBA and ASIC.[244] Overall, the comprehensive obligations placed on FMIs,[245] requiring them to operate in a fair and effective manner while reducing systemic risk,[246] and the supervisory arrangements over them,[247] collectively indicate that the clearing and settlement regime is detailed and effective.

---

239 IMF, *Australia: Financial Sector Assessment Program: Technical Note—Supervision, Oversight, and Resolution Planning of Financial Market Infrastructures* (February 2019) (*FSAP Technical Note*).

240 Principle 38 was not assessed in this report due to the existence of separate principles for securities settlement systems and central counterparties: see IMF, *Australia Country Report* (n 51) 7.

241 IMF, *FSAP Technical Note* (n 239).

242 The report notes that, since 2011, the ASX Ltd group that operates an integrated infrastructure of trading platforms, central counterparties and securities settlement systems has 'faced competition from foreign infrastructures in some markets': see 'Insurance sector: regulation and supervision' in IMF, *FSAP Technical Note* (n 239) 5.

243 IMF, *FSAP Technical Note* (n 239).

244 In Australia, the clearing and settlement systems are monitored and overseen by ASIC and the RBA.

245 See *Corporations Act* s 821A. Besides licensing, certain other obligations are placed on FMIs: see Baxt, Black and Hanrahan, 'Market infrastructure providers' (n 1) 399.

246 *Corporations Act* s 821A(aa) and (a).

247 Baxt, Black and Hanrahan, 'Market infrastructure providers' (n 1) 400.

Conclusion

The reliability and strong supervisory regime for FMIs indicates that the degree of alignment of the Australian regime with the core requirements of IOSCO Principle 38 is 'high'. The overall landscape for FMIs in Australia is 'mature' and continuous 'minor' refinements and changes to the FMIs regime are being ushered in by ASIC.

Synthesis and conclusion

For secondary markets, the analysis of SEBI's and ASIC's regimes reveals that the organised exchanges and trading systems in both jurisdictions are governed under well-developed and comprehensive legal and regulatory frameworks that are predominantly aligned with the core requirements of the IOSCO standards. There are comprehensive norms for licensing and initial authorisation of exchanges in both jurisdictions. The degree of comparability for Principle 33 is thus assessed as 'high'. However, the relevance for cooperation is 'moderate' given the already high standards of initial authorisation requirements in both regions.

As regards requirements for ongoing regulatory supervision of exchanges and trading systems, both regulators have copious powers to conduct ongoing supervision of markets and are seen to use and invest heavily in technology for surveillance of markets.[248] In the Indian context, there is further scope for enhancing the process and mechanisms for supervision including onsite supervision and inspection. SEBI's and ASIC's surveillance regimes differ in that securities markets trading in India is mainly monitored at the first level on a real-time basis by RSEs, while in Australia, since 2010, trading is monitored by ASIC on a real-time basis. The difference in surveillance approaches offers an opportunity to conduct a detailed analysis into the benefits and limitations of each approach. The degree of comparability for Principle 34 is assessed as 'moderate' but the relevance for cooperation is 'high'. Both regimes may find it useful to cooperate through onsite field visits, sharing risk-based approaches and developing strategies towards effective risk-based supervision.

---

248 As the analysis shows, SEBI upgraded its surveillance technology from the previous IMSS to the SMARTS system, while ASIC's analysis shows that ASIC upgraded from SMARTS to a more advanced market analysis and intelligence surveillance system in 2013.

The analysis also reveals that the legislative and regulatory frameworks in both jurisdictions promote transparency in trading, which is reflected to a high degree in both markets through pre- and post-trade transparency norms, but, generally, the maturity and reliability of transparency norms are evolving in the Indian context. This assessment takes into account the fundamental complexities of size, volume and number of listed companies and other dependencies,[249] as opposed to Australia's more compact and mature landscape. Similarly, the analysis reveals that both regimes have well-articulated legislative frameworks and norms for deterring and detecting market misconduct, with an aim to promote fairness and transparency, but enforcement outcomes need further strengthening in both jurisdictions, although more in the case of India than Australia.[250] The degree of comparability for Principles 35 and 36 is thus assessed as 'moderate'. However, the relevance for cooperation is 'high'.

Finally, both Australia's and India's secondary markets regimes are well equipped to handle large exposures, default risks and market disruptions. Both regimes are supported by robust risk management systems, capital adequacy norms and risk-containment measures. The degree of comparability for principle 37 is assessed as 'high' and so is the relevance for cooperation. For integration measures in the future, including mutual recognition agreements between the two jurisdictions, collaboration in this area will be useful for both regimes.

The analysis of the intermediaries framework and its implementation reveals that there are strict licensing norms for securities intermediaries in both jurisdictions that make relevant an intermediary's competence, character, reputation and solvency. Both jurisdictions also impose sufficient initial and ongoing capital and prudential requirements. However, despite strong norms in India, the intermediaries landscape is evolving given the level of maturity of market intermediaries, skills and their capacity, and there is further scope to strengthen SEBI's supervision and oversight mechanisms and capacity relating to these intermediaries. The conflicts of interest norms are particularly evolving for the Indian context, as compared to a significantly mature landscape in Australia. For such reasons, the degree of comparability for Principles 8 and 29–32 is generally assessed as 'moderate'.

---

249 Dependencies include resource and capacity limitations.
250 Refer also to the enforcement analysis in Chapter 5 of this book.

However, the relevance for cooperation is 'high'. Cooperation to create a stronger and more effective intermediaries regime in both jurisdictions will likely be very beneficial in the long term.

Lastly, both jurisdictions have a strong legal and regulatory framework for clearing and settlement systems. However, a generic limitation remains in relation to the strength and effectiveness of SEBI's oversight mechanisms. The degree of comparability for Principle 38 is assessed as 'moderate' and the relevance for cooperation is 'high', from the perspective of future cross-border integration measures.

9

Conclusion—and a proposal

Conclusion

With increasing globalisation and convergence in securities markets, regulatory cooperation is increasingly relevant.[1] Cross-border cooperation, when explored optimally, can be instrumental in solving many of the challenges faced by the securities sectors.[2] Despite the contribution and growing influence of transnational regulatory networks,[3] particularly in

---

1   See for example Jennifer G Hill, 'Regulatory cooperation in securities market regulation: perspectives from Australia' (2020) 17(1) *European Company and Financial Law Review* 11–34, doi.org/10.1515/ecfr-2020-0003. Globalization, mutual recognition and substituted compliance cast upward pressure on establishing a credible regulatory regime: see John C Coffee, 'Racing towards the top? The impact of cross-listings and stock market competition on international corporate governance' (2002) 102(7) *Columbia Law Review* 1757–1831, doi.org/10.2307/1123661. On how globalization benefits national securities markets by stimulating better governance that in turn lowers the cost of capital, see René M Stulz, 'Globalization, corporate finance, and the cost of capital' (1999) 12(3) *Journal of Applied Corporate Finance* 8–25, doi.org/10.1111/j.1745-6622.1999.tb00027.x. For literature on why regulatory 'cooperation' and not 'competition' is a far better approach to convergence and harmonisation of securities laws, see generally Tafara Ethiopis and Robert J Peterson, 'A blueprint for cross-border access to US investors: a new international framework' (2007) 48 *Harvard International Law Journal* 1, 36. Countries have been exploring cross-border cooperation in securities markets from several decades: see for example Robert Bordeaux-Groult, 'Problems of enforcement and cooperation in the multinational securities market: a French perspective' (1987) 9 *University of Pennsylvania Journal of International Business Law* 453.
2   See generally Sonia Khosa, 'A game-changer or a routine drill? Cooperation in the Indo-Pacific securities markets' (2019) 47 *Australian Business Law Review* 182.
3   See Pierre-Hugues Verdier, 'Transnational regulatory networks and their limits' (2009) 34 *Yale Journal of International Law* 113. See also M-L Djelic and K Sahlin-Andersson (eds), *Transnational Governance: Institutional Dynamics of Regulation* (Cambridge University Press, 2006), doi.org/10.1017/CBO9780511488665; Geoffrey RD Underhill, 'Keeping governments out of politics: transnational securities markets, regulatory cooperation, and political legitimacy' (1995) 21(3) *Review of International Studies* 251–278, doi.org/10.1017/S0260210500117681.

the aftermath of the global financial crisis,[4] Ethiopis and Peterson argue that the 'traditional methods' used by regulators, such as the US SEC and its foreign counterparts, 'to oversee cross-border market activity have lost some of their historical efficacy'.[5] More recent forms of collaboration in the securities markets,[6] too, have either failed or had limited success or on-ground benefits.[7] Collectively, these limitations suggest a critical need to recreate and reinvent cooperation techniques within securities markets to unlock greater benefits.

The Indo-Pacific region is poised for high financial activity, bolstered by strong factors underpinning its growth.[8] The Indo-Pacific securities markets reveal several deficiencies in key areas of market development, integration and regulation, and cross-border collaboration can be harnessed as an effective tool to overcome some of the existing challenges.[9] To this end, this book proposes a deeper, strategic collaboration program that would facilitate a fast-growing or emerging market and an advanced market to cooperate strategically on a wider set of issues that advance the objectives of market development, integration and regulation, as highlighted in Chapter 1 of this book. Unlike existing techniques and models of cooperation,[10] the proposed strategic cross-border collaboration model is broad-based, and encompasses multidimensional cooperation initiatives among:

---

4   See Hill (n 1) 9. Transnational regulatory networks were criticised for their failure to prevent the global financial crisis: see Pierre-Hugues Verdier, 'Mutual recognition in international finance' (2011) 52 *Harvard International Law Journal* 55, 56.

5   Ethiopis and Peterson (n 1). For criticism of the transnational regulatory network (TRN) in securities markets, see Cally Jordan, 'The new internationalism? IOSCO, international standards and capital markets regulation' (2018), doi.org/10.2139/ssrn.3257800. In the context of Indo-Pacific emerging markets and their specific needs, despite the rich contribution of the main TRNs such as IOSCO's Asia-Pacific Regional Committee and Asia Pacific Economic Cooperation, there are several limitations that create room for new techniques for cooperation: see Khosa (n 2) 193–194.

6   In recent years, three main techniques or tools of cross-border securities collaboration have emerged, namely, national treatment, recognition and passporting: see generally IOSCO, *IOSCO Task Force on Cross-Border Regulation* (Consultation Report 9, 2014).

7   See Hill (n 1) 16. See also *Mutual Recognition Arrangement between the United States Securities and Exchange Commission and the Australian Securities and Investments Commission, together with the Australian Minister for Superannuation and Corporate Law* (signed 25 August 2008), download.asic.gov.au/media/1346672/SEC_framework_arrangement_aug_08.pdf.

8   See pre-COVID-19 projections in International Monetary Fund (IMF), *Regional Economic Outlook Asia Pacific—Good Times, Uncertain Times: A Time to Prepare* (World Economic and Financial Surveys, 2018) 29.

9   See Khosa (n 2) 186–191. See also IMF, *Asia's Stock Markets: Are There Crouching Tigers and Hidden Dragons?* (IMF Working Paper No 14/37, 2014), doi.org/10.5089/9781484320143.001.

10   The existing models of collaboration have limited impact because they mainly envisage a regulator-to-regulator engagement, usually involving limited interaction among select members or high-level officials of a regulator only.

1. regulators and government authorities

2. markets and participants

3. academia.

This book proposes such a strategic collaboration between India and Australia in the securities markets[11] as a first step towards more ambitious cross-border measures such as mutual recognition agreements.[12]

The analysis conducted in this book reveals that, notwithstanding the divergent structures and approach to financial sector regulation in India[13] and Australia,[14] there are several complementarities and reasons that support the proposal for deeper collaboration between these two Indo-Pacific countries.[15] First, India, is the fastest growing economy, consistently

---

11 See for example Ethiopis and Peterson (n 1), stating that 'not so long ago a major financial firm' employed a ton of 'telephones to conduct just a single cross-border transaction' whereas today an entire stock exchange, without consideration to its location, can be easily accessed through 'trading screens' located in the offices of brokers, citing Howell E Jackson, Andreas M Fleckner and Mark Gurevich, 'Foreign trading screens in the United States' (2006) 1(1) *Capital Markets Law Journal* 54–76, doi.org/10.1093/cmlj/kml003.

12 In recognition agreements, a host regulator 'recognises' a foreign regulatory regime, or parts thereof, following an assessment of the foreign regulatory regime by the host regulator. These agreements may be mutual or unilateral depending on whether the recognition has been granted by both regulators or only by one: see IOSCO, *IOSCO Task Force on Cross-Border Regulation* (Final Report No 23, 2015). Regulatory compatibility is best gauged using the IOSCO Principles, see *IOSCO: Facilitating Mutual Recognition and Substituted Compliance* (Paper by the Transatlantic Coalition on Financial Regulation, 2012). For more on recognition agreements, see Verdier, 'Mutual recognition' (n 4); Kalypso Nicolaidis and Gregory Shaffer, 'Transnational mutual recognition regimes: governance without global government' (2005) 68(3/4) *Law and Contemporary Problems* 263–317, doi.org/10.2139/ssrn.723150; Lucy McKinstry, 'Regulating a global market: the extraterritorial challenge of Dodd-Frank's margin requirements for uncleared OTC derivatives and a mutual recognition solution' (2012) 51 *Columbia Journal of International Law* 776. Recognition agreements have found tremendous purchase in the context of the European Union: see E Waide Warner, '"Mutual recognition" and cross-border financial services in the European Community' (1992) 55(4) *Law and Contemporary Problems* 7–28, doi.org/10.2307/1192103. To know the different forms of cooperation available, see Eddy Wymeersch, 'Global and regional financial regulation: the viewpoint of a European securities regulator' (2010) 1(2) *Global Policy* 201–208, 202, doi.org/10.1111/j.1758-5899.2010.00031.x. For the role of IOSCO in the development of cross-border regulation and equivalence, see Jean-Paul Servais, 'The International Organization of Securities Commissions (IOSCO) and the new international financial architecture: what role for IOSCO in the development and implementation of cross-border regulation and equivalence?' (2020) 17(1) *European Company and Financial Law Review* 3–10, doi.org/10.1515/ecfr-2020-0001.

13 India's financial sector regulation takes a sectoral-, institution- and rule-based form that is markedly different from Australia's approach. For a detailed discussion, see Chapter 2 in this book.

14 Australia's financial system regulation is characterised by the twin-peaks approach, which is neutral and principles-based in nature.

15 In recent years, India and Australia's cooperation has taken a significant bilateral focus under several governmental-level initiatives, particularly in the economic and commercial realm, leading to more engagement and cooperation between the two countries. See for example Peter Varghese, *An India Economic Strategy to 2035* (2018); High Commission of India, *India–Australia Economic and Commercial Relations* (September 2017), hcicanberra.gov.in/docs/1528097501eco-commercial-relations-may-2012.

projected by the International Monetary Fund to grow well above other global markets,[16] with a promising, and steadily improving, financial and business environment.[17] Australia's advanced economy is forecast to grow more rapidly than the other advanced economies, namely the G-7 countries,[18] and is characterised by strong institutions and high credentials.[19] Second, India's financial sector evolution and recent developments in the sector suggest that India is continuing to adopt liberalisation and reform for this sector[20] 'in a phased manner and calibrated to local conditions', essentially due to its 'complex and diverse socio-political and economic conditions'.[21] Australia's financial system is stable, sophisticated and resilient, offering multiple areas of strength.[22] Finally, there are substantial commonalities between the political and legal systems of these countries to support a strategic collaboration.[23]

---

pdf; Barry Bosworth and Susan M Collins, 'Accounting for growth: comparing China and India' (2008) 22(1) *Journal of Economic Perspectives* 45–66, doi.org/10.1257/jep.22.1.45. For ongoing bilateral and multilateral engagements and dialogues, see Australian Government, Department of Foreign Affairs and Trade, 'Australia–India Comprehensive Economic Cooperation Agreement', dfat.gov.au/trade/agreements/negotiations/aifta/australia-india-comprehensive-economic-cooperation-agreement; Australian Government, Department of Foreign Affairs and Trade, 'Regional Comprehensive Economic Partnership', dfat.gov.au/trade/agreements/negotiations/rcep/Pages/regional-comprehensive-economic-partnership.aspx.

16   India's growth is projected at 9.5 per cent for 2021 and 8.5 per cent for 2022: IMF, *Fault Lines Widen in the Global Recovery* (World Economic Outlook Update, July 2021). India's data and forecast are presented on a fiscal year basis (ie 1 April – 31 March). The global growth average projection is 4.9 per cent for 2022: see generally ibid. Prior to the COVID-19 pandemic, India was a forerunner with growth prospects at '7.4–7.8 per cent for the year 2018–19 as opposed to the global growth average of 3.9 per cent and the emerging and developing Asian countries' average of 6.5 per cent: IMF, *World Economic Outlook Update: Brighter Prospects, Optimistic Markets, Challenges Ahead* (January 2018). For pre-COVID statistics that show India's growth on a continuous trajectory, see Government of India, Ministry of Finance, *State of the Economy: An Analytical Overview and Outlook for Policy* (Economic Survey 2017–2018, 2018) 1.7.

17   As an important indicator of India's positive investment environment, in the pre-COVID world, India received the highest ever inflow of equity in the form of foreign direct investments worth US$43.4 billion in 2016–2017, which rose to US$59.64 billion between 2020 and 2021, had a foreign exchange reserve of US$404.92 billion at the end of December 2017 and even made steady strides towards a more open global structured economy embracing liberalisation. India produced 28 unicorns in 2021 on the back of reforms. Additionally, India's thriving start-up sector is expected to grow from 4,750 technology start-ups in 2016 to a 100,000 start-ups by 2025, thereby creating employment for over 3.25 million people, valued at US$500 million: see Department of Commerce, India Brand Equity Foundation, 'About Indian economy growth rate & statistics', ibef.org/economy/indian-economy-overview.

18   See generally Australian Government, Australian Trade and Investment Commission, *Why Australia Benchmark Report 2021* (2021).

19   Australia's areas of strength include its creative, resourceful and enterprising outlook and people, strong foundations for business and good governance. It ranks 14th in ease of doing business compared with 63rd for India: see ibid.

20   See Chapter 2, this book, for a detailed analysis of India's changing financial sector landscape.

21   Reserve Bank of India, 'India: financial system stability assessment' (Press Release, 2012–2013/1194, 16 January 2013), rbi.org.in/scripts/BS_PressReleaseDisplay.aspx?prid=27964.

22   See generally Varghese (n 15).

23   These commonalities include a democratic system, federal form of government, common law foundations and language (English is an official language in India).

This book proposes a deeper, strategic collaboration between India and Australia in regard to the securities sector and supports this proposal with a high-level analysis of the securities regimes of the Indian securities regulator, the Securities and Exchange Board of India (SEBI), and the Australian market regulator, the Australian Securities and Investment Commission (ASIC), applying the 38 IOSCO Principles of Securities Regulation as the basis for the comparative analysis. The analysis across Chapters 3–8 of this book provides an academic overview of the core requirements of each IOSCO Principle and evaluates SEBI's and ASIC's legal and regulatory securities framework and implementation relating to each principle, highlighting areas of weakness and strength. Based on this examination, the book offers conclusions on the degree of alignment of both securities regimes with each of the 38 IOSCO Principles,[24] the degree of comparability to each other and the relevance for cooperation in relation to each IOSCO Principle.[25] Table 9.1 presents a consolidated picture of the analysis in this book.

Table 9.1: Summary of the analysis of SEBI's and ASIC's securities regimes

IOSCO Principles of Securities Regulation	SEBI's degree of alignment, stage of development and extent of reform in recent years	ASIC's degree of alignment, stage of development and extent of reform in recent years	Degree of comparability	Relevance for cooperation
The role and responsibilities of the regulator and its cooperation regime (IOSCO Principles 1–8 and 13–15)				
Principle 1: Regulator's responsibilities should be clearly stated	**High** Evolving Substantial	**High** Mature Substantial	**Moderate**	**High**
Principle 2: Regulator should be independent and accountable	**Moderate** Evolving Minor	**Moderate** Evolving Substantial	**High**	**Low**

---

24   The analysis determines not only the degree of alignment with each of the 38 IOSCO Principles, but also comments on the overall stage of development for each principle in terms of it being 'evolving' or 'mature', and also discusses the extent of reform in recent years in terms of it being 'minor' or 'substantial'.
25   'Compatibility', 'comparable standards' and 'equivalence' are key attributes of a recognition agreement: see Verdier, 'Mutual recognition' (n 4). See also Nicolaidis and Shaffer (n 12); J Morrall, *Determining Compatible Regulatory Regimes between the US and the EU* (The George Washington University Regulatory Studies Center Working Paper, 2011) 43.

IOSCO Principles of Securities Regulation	SEBI's degree of alignment, stage of development and extent of reform in recent years	ASIC's degree of alignment, stage of development and extent of reform in recent years	Degree of comparability	Relevance for cooperation
Principle 3: Regulator should have adequate power, resources and capacity to perform its duties	**Moderate** Evolving Minor	**Moderate** Mature Substantial	**Moderate**	**High**
Principle 4: Regulator should adopt clear and consistent processes	**Moderate** Evolving Minor	**High** Mature Minor	**Moderate**	**High**
Principle 5: Regulator's staff should observe the highest professional standards	**High** Evolving Minor	**High** Mature Minor	**Moderate**	**Low**
Principle 6: Regulator should have, or contribute to, a process to monitor, mitigate and manage systemic risk	**High** Evolving Substantial	**High** Mature Substantial	**Moderate**	**High**
Principle 7: Regulator should have or contribute to a process to review the perimeter of regulation	**High** Mature Substantial	**High** Mature Minor	**High**	**High**
Principle 13: Regulator should have power to share public and non-public information with domestic and foreign counterparts	**High** Mature Substantial	**High** Mature Minor	**High**	**High**
Principle 14: Regulator should establish information-sharing mechanisms that state when and how information will be shared with domestic and foreign counterparts	**High** Mature Substantial	**High** Mature Minor	**High**	**High**

IOSCO Principles of Securities Regulation	SEBI's degree of alignment, stage of development and extent of reform in recent years	ASIC's degree of alignment, stage of development and extent of reform in recent years	Degree of comparability	Relevance for cooperation
Principle 15: Regulatory system should allow for assistance to foreign regulators in their discharge of regulatory responsibilities	**High** Mature Substantial	**High** Mature Minor	High	Moderate
Supervision and enforcement powers and regimes (IOSCO Principles 10 and 11)				
Principle 10: Regulator should have comprehensive inspection, investigation and surveillance powers	**High** Mature Substantial	**High** Mature Minor	High	Moderate
Principle 11: Regulator should have comprehensive enforcement powers	**High** Mature Substantial	**High** Mature Minor	High	Moderate
Enforcement and compliance regimes (IOSCO Principle 12)				
Principle 12: Regulatory system should ensure effective and credible use of inspection, investigation, surveillance and enforcement powers and implementation of effective compliance program	**Moderate** Evolving Substantial	**High** Mature Substantial	Moderate	High
Self-regulation and gatekeepers (IOSCO Principles 9, 19–23)				
Principle 9: Self-regulatory organisations should be subject to oversight of regulators, and observe high standards of fairness and confidentiality	**Moderate** Evolving Substantial	**High** Mature Minor	High	High

IOSCO Principles of Securities Regulation	SEBI's degree of alignment, stage of development and extent of reform in recent years	ASIC's degree of alignment, stage of development and extent of reform in recent years	Degree of comparability	Relevance for cooperation
Principle 19: Auditors should be subject to adequate levels of oversight	**Moderate** Evolving Substantial	**High** Mature Minor	**Low/ Moderate**	**High**
Principle 20: Auditors should be independent of the issuing entity that they audit	**Moderate** Evolving Substantial	**High** Mature Minor	**Low/ Moderate**	**High**
Principle 21: Audit standards should be of a high and internationally acceptable quality	**Moderate** Evolving Substantial	**High** Mature Minor	**Low/ Moderate**	**High**
Principle 22: Credit rating agencies should be subject to adequate levels of oversight; should be registered with the regulator and subject to ongoing supervision	**Moderate** Evolving Substantial	**High** Mature Substantial	**Moderate**	**High**
Principle 23: Entities offering investors analytical and evaluative services should be subject to oversight and regulation appropriate to their impact on the market or the degree to which the regulatory system relies on them	**Moderate** Evolving Substantial	**High** Mature Substantial	**Moderate**	**High**
Regimes for issuers, collective investment schemes and hedge funds (IOSCO Principles 16–18 and 24–28)				
Principle 16: There should be full, accurate and timely disclosure of financial results, risk and other information material to investors' decisions	**Moderate** Evolving Substantial	**High** Mature Minor	**Moderate**	**High**

IOSCO Principles of Securities Regulation	SEBI's degree of alignment, stage of development and extent of reform in recent years	ASIC's degree of alignment, stage of development and extent of reform in recent years	Degree of comparability	Relevance for cooperation
Principle 17: Holders of securities in a company should be treated in a fair and equitable manner	**Moderate** Evolving Substantial	**High** Mature Minor	**Moderate**	**High**
Principle 18: Accounting standards used by issuers to prepare financial statements should be of high and internationally acceptable quality	**Moderate** Evolving Substantial	**High** Mature Minor	**Moderate**	**High**
Principle 24: Regulatory system should establish standards for eligibility, governance, organisation and operational conduct of those who market or operate a collective investment scheme	**Moderate** Evolving Substantial	**Moderate** Evolving Substantial	**Moderate**	**High**
Principle 25: Regulatory system should establish rules governing the legal form and structure of collective investment schemes, segregation and protection of client assets	**High** Mature Minor	**High** Mature Minor	**High**	**Moderate**
Principle 26: Regulation should require sufficient disclosure to evaluate the suitability of a CIS for an investor	**High** Mature Minor	**High** Mature Minor	**High**	**High**

IOSCO Principles of Securities Regulation	SEBI's degree of alignment, stage of development and extent of reform in recent years	ASIC's degree of alignment, stage of development and extent of reform in recent years	Degree of comparability	Relevance for cooperation
Principle 27: Regulation should ensure for proper and disclosed basis for asset valuation and pricing and redemption of units in a CIS	**High** Mature Minor	**High** Mature Minor	**High**	**Moderate**
Principle 28: Regulation should ensure that hedge funds, their managers and advisers are subject to regulatory oversight	**High** Mature Substantial	**High** Mature Minor	**Moderate**	**High**
Secondary markets, market intermediaries and settlement systems (IOSCO Principles 29–38)				
Principle 33: The establishment of trading systems including securities exchanges should be subject to regulatory oversight	**Moderate** Mature Substantial	**High** Mature Minor	**High**	**Moderate**
Principle 34: There should be ongoing regulatory supervision of exchanges and of trading systems that ensure integrity of trading through fair and equitable rules	**Moderate** Evolving Substantial	**High** Mature Minor	**Moderate**	**High**
Principle 35: Regulation should promote transparency of trading	**Moderate** Evolving Substantial	**High** Mature Minor	**Moderate**	**High**
Principle 36: Regulation should detect and deter manipulation and other unfair trading practices	**Moderate** Evolving Substantial	**High** Mature Minor	**Moderate**	**High**

IOSCO Principles of Securities Regulation	SEBI's degree of alignment, stage of development and extent of reform in recent years	ASIC's degree of alignment, stage of development and extent of reform in recent years	Degree of comparability	Relevance for cooperation
Principle 37: Regulation should aim to ensure the proper management of large exposures, default rick and market disruption	**High** Mature Minor	**High** Mature Substantial	**High**	**High**
Principle 29: Regulation should provide for minimum entry standards for market intermediaries	**Moderate** Evolving Substantial	**Moderate** Mature Minor	**Moderate**	**High**
Principle 30: There should be initial and ongoing capital and other prudential requirements for market intermediaries reflecting the risks that such intermediaries take	**Moderate** Evolving Substantial	**Moderate** Mature Substantial	**Moderate**	**High**
Principle 31: Market intermediaries should be required to establish an internal function to deliver compliance with internal organisation and operational conduct, to protect the interests of clients and their assets and ensuring proper management of risk	**Moderate** Mature Substantial	**Moderate** Mature Substantial	**Moderate**	**High**

IOSCO Principles of Securities Regulation	SEBI's degree of alignment, stage of development and extent of reform in recent years	ASIC's degree of alignment, stage of development and extent of reform in recent years	Degree of comparability	Relevance for cooperation
Principle 32: There should be procedures for dealing with the failure of a market intermediary to minimise damage and loss to investors and contain systemic risk	**Moderate** Mature Substantial	**High** Mature Minor	**High**	**High**
Principle 8: Regulator should seek to ensure that conflicts of interest and misalignment of incentives are avoided	**Moderate** Evolving Substantial	**High** Mature Minor	**Moderate**	**High**
Principle 38: Securities settlement systems, central securities depositories, trade repositories and central counterparties should be subject to regulatory and supervisory requirements that ensure fairness, effectiveness and efficiency and reduce systemic risk	**High** Evolving Substantial	**High** Mature Minor	**Moderate**	**High**

The analysis of SEBI's securities regime reveals that, for the majority of the IOSCO Principles, the existing securities framework and implementation in India is, at least, 'moderately' aligned with the international standard,[26] with some areas even showing a 'high' degree of alignment,[27] and no areas where the alignment to the international standard is low. The analysis

---

26   The degree of alignment with the core requirements of the IOSCO Principles is assessed as 'moderate' with an 'evolving' landscape in respect of 23 principles.

27   In respect of 15 IOSCO Principles, the analysis indicates a 'high' alignment but, of these, four are assessed to have an 'evolving' landscape; a mature landscape is assessed for the remaining 11 principles.

further reveals that, in relation to at least 27 of the 38 IOSCO Principles, the securities regime is in an 'evolving' rather than a 'mature' phase. Importantly, the analysis demonstrates that the extent of reform in recent years in relation to at least 30 principles has been 'substantial'. Collectively, these findings establish SEBI's regime as predominantly characterised by a developing environment, with a strong propensity for extensive reform, a progressive mindset and a commitment to enhancing the overall quality and status of the Indian securities markets and regulation. However, as the analysis reveals at several places, there is an intrinsic and overdue need for a strategic and ambitious vision for capacity building, securities research and publication, supervision and enforcement, among other areas, to enable SEBI's regime and the Indian securities markets to fully ascend to their optimal level. Shortcomings in these areas are likely to overshadow, impact and even diminish the positive attributes of SEBI's securities framework, weakening its implementation and impairing strategic vision and decision-making in the securities markets, thus creating a repetitive and reinforcing cycle.

The analysis of Australia's securities regime reveals that the degree of alignment of the framework and its implementation relating to most IOSCO Principles is 'high',[28] and the overall landscape for most principles is 'mature'.[29] Despite this, the extent of reform in recent years has been 'substantial' in several areas.[30] According to these findings, the Australian securities framework and its implementation are typified by an advanced and mature environment, one that is supported by effective and efficient policy and governance, with industry and academic networks that cater to fundamental areas of concern within the securities system. As an advanced market, with all intrinsic and fundamental requirements addressed, Australia's securities regime through ASIC is progressively adopting more refinements and these are likely to unlock even greater benefits for the entire financial system and, resultantly, the economy.

---

28 ASIC's degree of alignment is 'high' for 32 principles and 'moderate' for the remaining six.
29 For almost all principles, the overall landscape is 'mature'.
30 In respect of at least 11 principles, the extent of reform in recent years has been 'substantial'.

On the whole, the analysis of SEBI's and ASIC's regimes reveals a 'moderate' degree of comparability,[31] but a 'high' relevance for cooperation in as many as 30 of the 38 IOSCO Principles.[32] Bilateral cooperation within the securities regimes will potentially accrue long-term benefits for both regimes through creative initiatives that strengthen market development, integration and regulation in both regions.

In conclusion, the deeper, strategic collaboration proposed in this book is a long-term, output-driven proposal to create multiple linkages and share and transfer knowledge and expertise between two strategically aligned securities jurisdictions. Such collaboration will potentially establish closer working relationships between the two jurisdictions and connect and strengthen the existing securities ecosystems to support efficiency and transparency within their securities markets. This novel collaboration, between a fast-emerging and an advanced economy, is a critical step towards more ambitious future initiatives, including a mutual recognition agreement,[33] a passport regime and other integration measures. Further, a successful pilot of India–Australia collaboration in their securities sectors can later also be extended to the other areas of the financial systems of these two jurisdictions, such as banking, insurance and pensions (where Australia also has considerable and demonstrable strengths), or even across other areas of the economy. Finally, the India–Australia collaboration can later be converted into a multilateral strategic collaboration program in the securities or financial markets within the Indo-Pacific region, or outside the region.[34]

---

31 The degree of comparability of SEBI's and ASIC's regimes is 'high' in respect of 15 principles, 'moderate' for 20 and 'low/moderate' for three.

32 The analysis suggests that the relevance for cooperation is 'high' for 32 principles, which is most areas of securities regulation. The relevance of cooperation is 'moderate' or 'low' for six principles mainly as these are areas that are beyond ASIC's or SEBI's jurisdiction.

33 For a complete understanding of mutual recognition agreements as conceived by the majority of the securities commissions, see IOSCO, *IOSCO Task Force on Cross-Border Regulation* (n 12). In ascertaining the possibility of two or more countries entering such agreements, IOSCO acknowledged that a 'process of analysis will have to go beyond the Principles, particularly in the area of supervision and enforcement': see *IOSCO: Facilitating Mutual Recognition and Substituted Compliance* (n 12). Further, the literature in this area supports the view that the functioning of such mutual recognition agreements, apart from the convergence of laws and objectives, relies on comparable levels of supervision and enforcement capabilities: see Verdier, 'Mutual recognition' (n 4). On the suitability of 'selective substitute compliance' in securities markets, see Howell E Jackson, 'A system of selective substitute compliance' (2007) 48 *Harvard International Law Journal* 105. See also Ethiopis and Peterson (n 1) 33.

34 For instance, such bilateral cooperation can later be extended to strategic partners within the Indo-Pacific, such as Singapore or Japan, or may be extended to strategic partners outside the Indo-Pacific, such as the US.

Deeper, strategic collaboration between India and Australia in their securities sectors: A proposal

This book proposes a novel, strategic bilateral cooperation technique for targeted, speedy and specific benefits to securities jurisdictions in the Indo-Pacific region in three specific areas: market development, regulation and integration. Bilateral collaboration between India and Australia would strengthen and connect the securities ecosystems in the two jurisdictions, bringing mutual benefits. As illustrated below, a program for this strategic bilateral cooperation has two main elements:

1. Cube Vision
2. strategic action plan (SAP).

Cube vision (2025–35)

The Cube Vision is a long-term vision for securities cooperation between India and Australia with three components: core values for the cooperation, a strategy for cooperation and measurable outcomes.

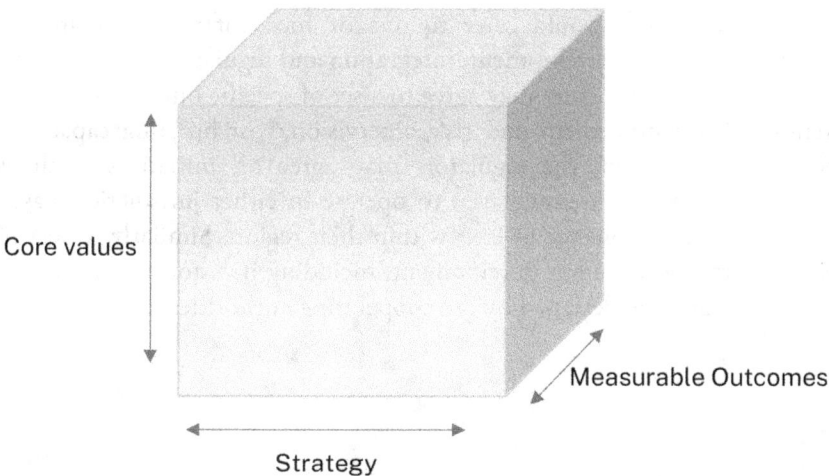

Figure 9.1: Cube Vision for deeper, strategic collaboration between India and Australia in their securities sectors
Source: Author's research.

Core values

The Cube Vision for deeper, strategic bilateral collaboration would be guided by a set of core values mutually agreed by the securities regulators of India and Australia. These values could include innovation, efficiency and competency. On the basis of such values, a strategy for strategic collaboration would be evolved to achieve pre-agreed measurable outcomes and specific goals within the three areas of market development, integration and regulation.

Strategy

To advance the core values and attain specific outcomes, the strategy for bilateral collaboration would involve:

a. enhanced and closer SEBI–ASIC initiatives

b. cross-border initiatives for cooperation between key securities market infrastructure companies,[35] formal and informal self-regulatory organisations (SROs) and market participants

c. ambitious academic, research and education partnerships.

Measurable outcomes

The measurable outcomes under the India–Australia strategic securities sector collaboration would cater to one or more of these overarching objectives of market development, integration and regulation. For example, the cooperating authorities may agree to a set of specific outcomes, such as strengthening enforcement and risk supervision,[36] or building capacity.[37] To boost integration, the regulators may agree on initiatives, such as recognising specific intermediaries to operate in either jurisdiction based on substituted compliance of laws within their region. Similarly, a host of initiatives to boost market development, including investor education and awareness, could be designed by the cooperating authorities.

---

35 These include stock exchanges, depositories and clearing corporations.
36 For example, through joint or collaborative short-term supervision exercises between the two regulators.
37 For example, capacity building exercises directly between the regulator and academic institutions in Australia.

Strategic action plan (2025–35)

The Cube Vision for securities collaboration between India and Australia would be effected through a SAP. This plan could be developed with short-, medium- and/or long-term goals.

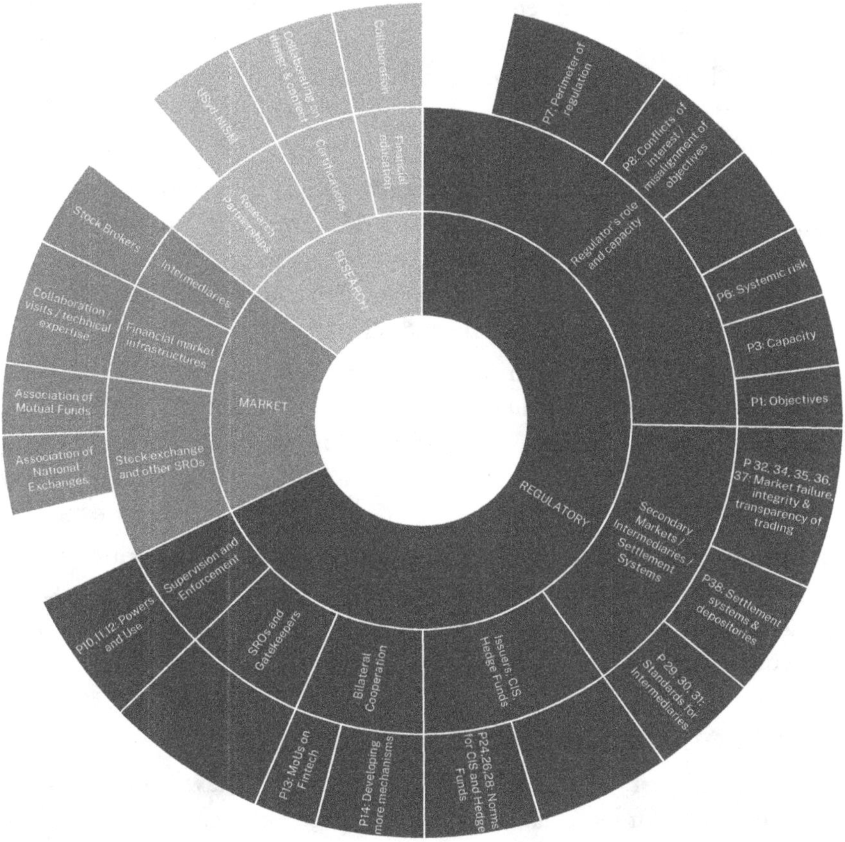

Figure 9.2: Proposed strategic action plan for bilateral collaboration
Source: Author's research.

Regulatory SEBI–ASIC

SEBI–ASIC strategic collaboration could have a transformational impact on market development, integration and regulation of the securities markets within the two countries, and, going forward, within the Indo-Pacific.

Current position

- Currently, there is limited understanding of the Indian financial sector and SEBI's regulatory regime in Australia. Similarly, there is little understanding in India of the twin-peaks model, neutrality and other features of the Australian financial regime.

- There is limited bilateral engagement between SEBI and ASIC, outside of multilateral forums. There are no bilateral memoranda of understanding (MoUs) between these two regulatory authorities.

Proposal

- The analysis in this book shows a 'high' relevance for cooperation in 32 areas of securities regulation. SEBI and ASIC may consider collaborating on issues relating to these areas, keeping in mind the core values of innovation, efficiency and competency and the outcomes of strengthening market development, integration and regulation in both regions.

- Key areas of collaboration include joint supervision and enforcement exercises in securities regulation, short-term secondment and exchange programs, and academic visits and training to strengthen and expand securities-related knowledge, both of jurisprudence and new regulatory areas.

- Among other strategic cooperation initiatives in the securities sector, SEBI and ASIC may consider formal MoUs in a number of areas, including technical assistance, capacity building and new areas of securities regulation, such as cryptocurrencies and Fintech.[38]

Market and participants

India–Australia strategic collaboration in securities law and regulation envisages cross-border collaboration among stock exchanges, formal or informal SROs, depositories, clearing corporations, and their participants, brokers, investment bankers and other market participants. Strategic collaboration may include multiple initiatives in the funds sector, where Australia's funds have a dominant share valued at A\$2.95 trillion.[39] The proposed collaboration will potentially strengthen institutional linkages between the two regions, provide on-ground information about existing

---

38   Varghese (n 15) recommendation 59.
39   Australian High Commission, 'Australian investment funds look to India' (PA/05/20, 8 October 2020), india.highcommission.gov.au/ndli/pa0520.html.

market operations, securities systems and processes in both countries, and predominantly focus on proposed outcomes in the areas of market development and integration.

Current position

- Australia–India two-way investment flow has doubled in the past five years reaching A$30.7 billion in 2019.[40] Yet, there is limited understanding and interaction among market institutions and participants of both regions. While some funds—like Australian Super and Australia's sovereign wealth fund, the Future Fund—are already,[41] or are looking to, invest in India, there is a need to increase bilateral dialogue and discussion to extract the full potential, particularly in the financial and securities market.

Proposal

- Cross-border visits and exchanges (virtual or otherwise) to be facilitated between the stock exchanges, clearing corporations, SROs and other relevant market stakeholders to enhance an understanding of the functioning of these entities in both jurisdictions.
- ASX, NSE and BSE to collaborate on application of the blockchain distributed ledger technology for clearing and settlement systems; other spheres of the market to be considered.[42]
- Building on the virtual meeting between Indian and Australian delegations in 2020,[43] more streamlined dialogues to be facilitated between the Australian funds and SEBI, NSE and BSE.
- Explore future cross and dual listing of securities.

Academia

India–Australia strategic research and academic collaboration will be directed to achieve several outcomes to strengthen market development, integration and regulation in the two countries across a 10-year period with short-, medium- and long-term goals.

---

40   Ibid.
41   Ibid.
42   Varghese (n 15) recommendation 60.3.
43   Australian High Commission (n 39).

Current position

- Currently, there is a lack of quality literature comparing the Indian securities markets with other securities jurisdictions, such as Australia. Similarly, there is little literature in Australia analysing the Indian securities markets, although there is a great amount of literature comparing the Australian securities regime with other global destinations, including the US, Hong Kong, Singapore and the UK. The lack of literature on India in Australia, and vice versa, translates into limited knowledge of India's tremendous potential as a high-yield investment destination to Australians and Australia's credentials as a high-quality investment destination to Indians.

- Further, as Chapter 5 of this book discusses, there are particular and widespread limitations in the area of securities research and publication in India, including the scarcity of quality literature with effective narratives, robust analysis and a theme-based understanding of issues.[44]

Proposal

- India–Australia partnerships in academia and research to establish multiple cross-border institutional ties and research partnerships and deepen the understanding of the two securities jurisdictions, among several other benefits.

- High-quality research and publication in top-tiered, peer-reviewed international journals as an effective source of new perspectives and feedback on regulatory policy and enforcement, thereby improving the quality of financial education.

- Research collaboration between high-ranking Australian universities and key securities institutions in India, such as the National Institute of Securities Markets, Mumbai, the Indian Institutes of Technology, the Indian Institutes of Management, Delhi University, Mumbai University and other universities with academic interest and capabilities in securities law and regulation.

---

44   As noted in Chapter 5, current securities market data and variables are not optimal, and thus restrict the drawing of effective trends and patterns on enforcement.

- India–Australia collaboration to develop and expand the content of certifications and modules available and mandated for securities markets professionals in both regions. This will enable market professionals to develop a wider and comparative understanding of the securities markets of both countries.

- Cross-border collaboration in financial education initiatives across both countries. In India, such collaboration will import financial education ideas and processes from a developed and advanced nation; in Australia, such collaboration will improve understanding of a large, complex and diverse emerging market full of possibilities and challenges.

Annexures

Table A1.1: APRA-regulated institutions

	Number of entities [1,8]			Assets ($ billion) [2]		
	30 Jun 20	30 Jun 21	% change	30 Jun 20	30 Jun 21	% change
ADIs [3,4]	146	143	-2.1%	5,466	5,355	-2.0%
Banks	98	97	-1.0%	5,403	5,290	-2.1%
Credit Unions & building societies	40	37	-7.5%	58	58	0.7%
Other ADIs	7	8	14.3%	6	7	26.8%
Restricted ADIs	1	1	0	0	0	0
Representative offices of foreign banks [5]	14	15	7.1%	0	0	0
General insurers	95	93	-2.1%	135	150	10.6%
Life insurers	28	27	-3.6%	129	133	2.8%
Friendly societies	12	11	-8.3%	8	9	12.8%
Licensed trustees	107	95	-11.2%	0	0	0
Superannuation entities [6,7]	1,671	1,674	0.2%	1,930	2,263	17.2%
Public offer funds	113	111	-1.8%	1,653	1,982	19.9%
Non-public offer funds	38	36	-5.3%	272	278	2.2%
Small APRA funds	1,479	1,486	0.5%	2	2	-5.3%
Approved deposit funds	10	10	0	0	0	0
Eligible rollover funds [9]	7	7	0	3	2	-53.1%
Pooled superannuation trusts	24	24	0	150	188	25.1%

	Number of entities [18]			Assets ($ billion) [2]		
	30 Jun 20	30 Jun 21	% change	30 Jun 20	30 Jun 21	% change
Private health insurers	37	35	−5.4%	17	18	7.2%
Non-operating holding companies	30	31	3.3%	0	0	0
Total	**2,126**	**2,109**	**−0.8%**	**7,685**	**7,927**	**3.1%**

Notes:

[1] Number of entities for end-June 2020 has been revised to reflect wind up of entities finalised during FY 2020/21.

[2] Asset figures for end-June 2021 are based on the most recently submitted returns. Asset figures for end-June 2020 have been revised slightly from APRA's 2020 Annual Report in line with audited returns received during the year.

[3] The ADI classification does not include representative offices of foreign banks.

[4] Asset figures for ADIs for June 2020 and June 2021 have been sourced from the Economic and Financial Statistics (EFS) domestic books data collection, which has a new treatment of certain assets, including all securitisation of assets.

[5] Number of representative offices of foreign banks has not been included in the total number of entities, as APRA does not regulate them.

[6] This data excludes superannuation entities that APRA does not regulate, that is, exempt public sector superannuation schemes and Australian Tax Office-regulated self-managed superannuation funds.

[7] Pooled superannuation trust assets are not included in totals as these assets are already recorded in other superannuation categories.

[8] The 'number of entities' includes entities that are currently in the process of winding up but have not formally been wound-up or had their licence revoked as yet.

[9] The movement in total assets for eligible rollover funds is due to transfers out during FY 2020/21, including from funds which are currently in the process of winding up.

Source: APRA, *APRA Annual Report 2020–21* (2021).

The Global Competitiveness Index in detail

Australia

Index Component	Rank/137	Value	Trend
1st pillar: Institutions	18	5.4	
1.01 Property rights	18	5.8	
1.02 Intellectual property protection	17	5.8	
1.03 Diversion of public funds	14	5.7	
1.04 Public trust in politicians	22	4.6	
1.05 Irregular payments and bribes	12	6.2	
1.06 Judicial independence	8	6.3	
1.07 Favoritism in decisions of government officials	21	4.5	
1.08 Efficiency of government spending	47	3.6	
1.09 Burden of government regulation	80	3.3	
1.10 Efficiency of legal framework in settling disputes	25	4.7	
1.11 Efficiency of legal framework in challenging regulations	34	4.0	
1.12 Transparency of government policymaking	21	5.2	
1.13 Business costs of terrorism	47	5.5	
1.14 Business costs of crime and violence	43	5.1	
1.15 Organized crime	30	5.5	
1.16 Reliability of police services	14	6.2	
1.17 Ethical behavior of firms	11	5.7	
1.18 Strength of auditing and reporting standards	10	6.1	
1.19 Efficacy of corporate boards	8	6.1	
1.20 Protection of minority shareholders' interests	21	5.1	
1.21 Strength of investor protection 0-10 (best)	61	5.8	
2nd pillar: Infrastructure	28	5.3	
2.01 Quality of overall infrastructure	39	4.7	
2.02 Quality of roads	35	4.8	
2.03 Quality of railroad infrastructure	35	4.1	
2.04 Quality of port infrastructure	35	4.9	
2.05 Quality of air transport infrastructure	36	5.2	
2.06 Available airline seat kilometers millions/week	7	5,007.4	
2.07 Quality of electricity supply	44	5.7	
2.08 Mobile-cellular telephone subscriptions /100 pop	86	109.6	
2.09 Fixed-telephone lines /100 pop	31	33.8	
3rd pillar: Macroeconomic environment	27	5.7	
3.01 Government budget balance % GDP	66	-2.7	
3.02 Gross national savings % GDP	62	21.9	
3.03 Inflation annual % change	1	1.3	
3.04 Government debt % GDP	51	41.1	
3.05 Country credit rating 0-100 (best)	11	90.0	
4th pillar: Health and primary education	12	6.5	
4.01 Malaria incidence cases/100,000 pop	n/a	n.l.	
4.02 Business impact of malaria	n/a	6.7	
4.03 Tuberculosis incidence cases/100,000 pop	12	6.0	
4.04 Business impact of tuberculosis	12	6.8	
4.05 HIV prevalence % adult pop	1	0.1	
4.06 Business impact of HIV/AIDS	9	6.6	
4.07 Infant mortality deaths/1,000 live births	17	3.0	
4.08 Life expectancy years	10	82.5	
4.09 Quality of primary education	18	5.4	
4.10 Primary education enrollment rate net %	52	97.0	
5th pillar: Higher education and training	9	5.9	
5.01 Secondary education enrollment rate gross %	4	137.6	
5.02 Tertiary education enrollment rate gross %	5	90.3	
5.03 Quality of the education system	16	5.1	
5.04 Quality of math and science education	30	4.8	
5.05 Quality of management schools	17	5.4	
5.06 Internet access in schools	5	6.0	
5.07 Local availability of specialized training services	15	5.7	
5.08 Extent of staff training	22	4.9	

Index Component	Rank/137	Value	Trend
6th pillar: Goods market efficiency	28	4.9	
6.01 Intensity of local competition	8	5.9	
6.02 Extent of market dominance	47	4.0	
6.03 Effectiveness of anti-monopoly policy	26	4.5	
6.04 Effect of taxation on incentives to invest	94	3.3	
6.05 Total tax rate % profits	102	47.6	
6.06 No. of procedures to start a business	7	3	
6.07 Time to start a business days	4	2.5	
6.08 Agricultural policy costs	12	4.9	
6.09 Prevalence of non-tariff barriers	28	4.9	
6.10 Trade tariffs % duty	38	2.2	
6.11 Prevalence of foreign ownership	15	5.5	
6.12 Business impact of rules on FDI	60	4.7	
6.13 Burden of customs procedures	31	5.0	
6.14 Imports % GDP	123	20.0	
6.15 Degree of customer orientation	23	5.5	
6.16 Buyer sophistication	32	4.0	
7th pillar: Labor market efficiency	28	4.7	
7.01 Cooperation in labor-employer relations	72	4.3	
7.02 Flexibility of wage determination	109	4.4	
7.03 Hiring and firing practices	110	3.2	
7.04 Redundancy costs weeks of salary	46	12.0	
7.05 Effect of taxation on incentives to work	102	3.4	
7.06 Pay and productivity	31	4.5	
7.07 Reliance on professional management	6	6.1	
7.08 Country capacity to retain talent	23	4.6	
7.09 Country capacity to attract talent	17	4.7	
7.10 Female participation in the labor force ratio to men	55	0.86	
8th pillar: Financial market development	6	5.5	
8.01 Availability of financial services	26	5.1	
8.02 Affordability of financial services	38	4.3	
8.03 Financing through local equity market	14	5.2	
8.04 Ease of access to loans	15	5.0	
8.05 Venture capital availability	40	3.4	
8.06 Soundness of banks	4	6.5	
8.07 Regulation of securities exchanges	7	6.0	
8.08 Legal rights index 0-10 (best)	4	11	
9th pillar: Technological readiness	27	5.7	
9.01 Availability of latest technologies	27	5.7	
9.02 Firm-level technology absorption	24	5.3	
9.03 FDI and technology transfer	27	5.0	
9.04 Internet users % pop	17	88.2	
9.05 Fixed-broadband Internet subscriptions /100 pop	24	30.4	
9.06 Internet bandwidth kb/s/user	48	88.3	
9.07 Mobile-broadband subscriptions /100 pop	6	130.2	
10th pillar: Market size	22	5.1	
10.01 Domestic market size index	20	5.1	
10.02 Foreign market size index	34	5.3	
10.03 GDP (PPP) PPP $ billions	19	1,187.3	
10.04 Exports % GDP	107	19.3	
11th pillar: Business sophistication	28	4.9	
11.01 Local supplier quantity	79	4.4	
11.02 Local supplier quality	22	5.3	
11.03 State of cluster development	51	4.0	
11.04 Nature of competitive advantage	24	4.7	
11.05 Value chain breadth	48	4.2	
11.06 Control of international distribution	27	4.5	
11.07 Production process sophistication	26	5.2	
11.08 Extent of marketing	19	5.2	
11.09 Willingness to delegate authority	9	5.7	
12th pillar: Innovation	27	4.5	
12.01 Capacity for innovation	24	5.1	
12.02 Quality of scientific research institutions	10	5.7	
12.03 Company spending on R&D	25	4.4	
12.04 University-industry collaboration in R&D	33	4.3	
12.05 Gov't procurement of advanced technology products	71	3.3	
12.06 Availability of scientists and engineers	16	4.9	
12.07 PCT patents applications/million pop	22	77.7	

Figure A1.1: The Global Competitiveness Index in detail

Source: Klaus Schwab, *The Global Competitiveness Report 2017–2018* (World Economic Forum Insight Report, 2017), www3.weforum.org/docs/GCR2017-2018/05FullReport/TheGlobalCompetitivenessReport2017–2018.pdf.

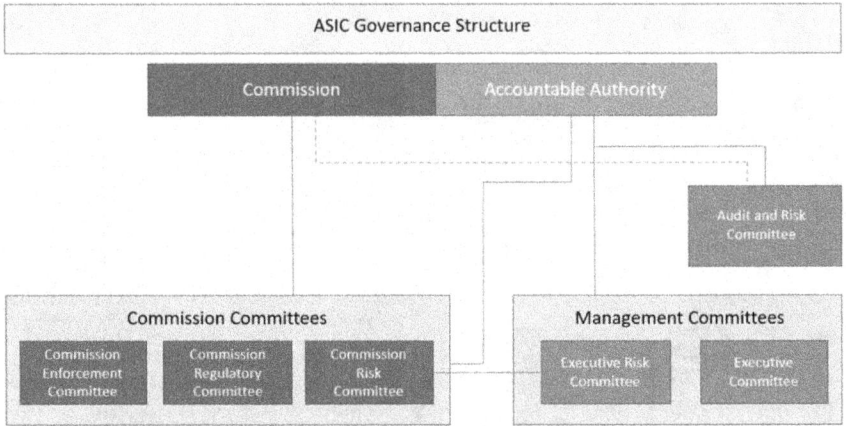

Figure A1.2: ASIC governance structure

Source: ASIC, 'ASIC's governance and accountability framework', asic.gov.au/about-asic/what-we-do/how-we-operate/asic-s-governance-and-accountability/#framework.

www.ingramcontent.com/pod-product-compliance
Lightning Source LLC
Chambersburg PA
CBHW072000260326
41914CB00004B/869